UNIVERSITY OF WOLVERHAMPTON

American Cultural Studies

A Reader

Edited by

John Hartley
and
Roberta E. Pearson

with Eva Vieth

OXFORD
UNIVERSITY PRESS

OXFORD

UNIVERSITY PRESS

Great Clarendon Street, Oxford OX2 6DP

Oxford University Press is a department of the University of Oxford.
It furthers the University's objective of excellence in research, scholarship,
and education by publishing worldwide in

Oxford New York

Athens Auckland Bangkok Bogotá Buenos Aires Calcutta
Cape Town Chennai Dar es Salaam Delhi Florence Hong Kong Istanbul
Karachi Kuala Lumpur Madrid Melbourne Mexico City Mumbai
Nairobi Paris São Paulo Singapore Taipei Tokyo Toronto Warsaw

with associated companies in Berlin Ibadan

Oxford is a registered trade mark of Oxford University Press
in the UK and in certain other countries

Published in the United States
by Oxford University Press Inc., New York

Introduction and editorial arrangement © John Hartley and Roberta E. Pearson 2000

British Library Cataloguing in Publication Data

Data available

Library of Congress Cataloging in Publication Data

Data available

ISBN 0–19–874254–1

1 3 5 7 9 10 8 6 4 2

Typeset by RefineCatch Limited, Bungay, Suffolk
Printed in Great Britain by
The Bath Press
Bath

Contents

Part One The Intellectual Context

Section I. The New Journalism and Its Legacy

Section II. European Cultural Theory and its Legacy

Section VI. Practices

Section VII. Media

List of Illustrations

Section I: The New Journalism
"Muhammad Ali's fist (actual size)", *Esquire*, October 1974.
Photo: Pierre Houles.

Section II: European Cultural Theory
John Downing, "The King Is Dead", *Daily Express*, 1977. Reproduced by permission
of Express Newspapers.

Section III: American Social Science
Roy Lichtenstein, *Whaam!*, © Estate of Roy Lichtenstein/DACS 2000. Photo © Tate
Gallery, London 1999.

Section IV: History and Literature
Robert Mapplethorpe, "Dolphina Neil-Jones, 1987", © The Estate of Robert
Mapplethorpe. Used with permission.

Section V: Identities
Hulleah Tsinhnahjinnie, "Damn! There goes the Neighborhood!" © 1998 Hulleah J.
Tsinhnahjinnie.

Section VI: Practices
Sally Mann, "Jessie Bites, 1985", © Sally Mann. Courtesy: Edwynn Houk Gallery,
New York.

Section VII: Media
Tom Wolfe, Sketch of Marshall McLuhan, from "What if He is Right?", in *The Pump
House Gang*, by Tom Wolfe. Copyright © 1968, renewed 1996 by Tom Wolfe. Reprinted
by permission of Farrar, Straus and Giroux LLC.

Notes on Contributors

Arjun Appadurai is Samuel N. Harper Professor of Anthropology and of South Asian Languages and Civilizations and Director of the Globalization Project at the University of Chicago. His books include *Worship and Conflict Under Colonial Rule: A South Indian Case* (1981) and *Modernity at Large: Cultural Dimensions of Globalization* (1996).

Houston A. Baker, Jr. is Director of the Center for Study of Black Literature and Culture, Professor of English, and Albert M. Greenfield Professor at the University of Pennsylvania. His books include *Afro-American Poetics: Revisions of Harlem and the Black Aesthetic* (1988) and *Black Studies, Rap, and the Academy* (1993).

James W. Carey was long-term Dean of the College of Communications at the University of Illinois and is now Professor of Journalism at Columbia University. He is the author of *Television and the Press* (1988), *Communication as Culture* (1989), and *James Carey: A Critical Reader* (1997).

Stokely Carmichael was an African-American leader who was a founding member and then chair of the Student Nonviolent Coordinating Committee (SNCC) during the height of the civil rights struggle in the 1960s. He is best known for coining the phrase "black power" and for his advocacy of black separatism.

Manuel Castells is Professor of Sociology and of Planning at the University of California, Berkeley. He is author of the trilogy *The Information Age: Economy, Society and Culture*, Vol. 1 *The Rise of the Network Society* (1996); Vol. 2 *The Power of Identity* (1997); Vol. 3 *End of Millennium* (1997).

Ward Churchill is an Associate Professor of American Indian Studies and Communications at the University of Colorado/Boulder and co-director of the American Indian Movement of Colorado. Among his books are *A Little Matter of Genocide* (1997) and *Struggle for the Land* (1993).

Vine Deloria, Jr. is an Indian rights activist and former Executive Director of the National Congress of American Indians. He is author or editor of several popular books including *Custer Died for Your Sins: An Indian Manifesto* (1969, 1988), *American Indian Policy in the 20th Century* (ed., 1985), and *Behind the Trail of Broken Treaties: An Indian Declaration of Independence* (1985).

Umberto Eco is President of the Scuola Superiore di Studi Umanistici, University of Bologna, and a renowned semiotician, novelist, and journalist. His most influential English language publications include *A Theory of Semiotics* (1976) and *The Role of the Reader* (1981). He is also the author of the international best-selling novel, *The Name of the Rose* (1983).

Rita Felski is Professor of English at the University of Virginia. She is the author of *Doing Time: Feminist Theory and Postmodern Culture* (2000), *The Gender of Modernity* (1995), and *Beyond Feminist Aesthetics: Feminist Literature and Social Change* (1989).

John Fiske is Professor of Communication Arts at the University of Wisconsin-Madison He is the author of several books including *Power Plays, Power Works* (1993), *Understanding Popular Culture* (1989), and *Television Culture* (1989).

Jean Franco is Professor of Spanish at Columbia University. She founded the magazine *Tabloid: A Review of Mass Culture and Everyday Life* in the 1980s and is the author of nine books, including *Plotting Women: Gender and Representation in Mexico* (1989).

Betty Friedan is a feminist leader and author. Her 1963 book *The Feminine Mystique* became the bible of the second-wave American feminist movement. In 1966 Friedan founded the National Organization of Women and served as its first president until 1970.

Marjorie Garber is Professor of English and Director of the Center for Literary and Cultural Studies at Harvard University. She is the author of *Cross-Dressing and Cultural Anxiety* (1991) and *Vice-Versa: Bisexuality and the Eroticism of Everyday Life* (1995).

George Gerbner is Bell Atlantic Professor of Telecommunications at Temple University and Dean Emeritus of the Annenberg School for Communication at the University of Pennsylvania. He is Director of the Cultural Indicators Project, which has monitored and analyzed prime-time network television program content since the 1967–68 season. He is the author and co-author of numerous articles stemming from the Cultural Indicators Project in such journals as *Public Opinion Quarterly, Political Communication,* and *The Journal of Communication.*

Herman Gray is Associate Professor of Sociology at the University of California, Santa Cruz, and is the author of several articles on the representation of African-Americans in American television.

Lawrence Grossberg is Morris Davis Professor of Communication Studies, University of North Carolina at Chapel Hill. He is the editor of *Cultural Studies.* His publications include *We Gotta Get Out Of This Place: Popular Conservatism and Postmodern Culture, Dancing in Spite of Myself: Essays in Cultural Studies,* and *'It's a Sin' and other essays on Popular Culture and Postmodernity.*

John Hartley is Dean of Arts, Queensland University of Technology, Australia. His publications include *Uses of Television* (1999), *Popular Reality: Journalism, Modernity, Popular culture* (1996), *The Politics of Pictures: the Creation of the Public in the Age of Popular Media* (1992), *Tele-ology: Studies in Television* (1992) and *Understanding News* (1982).

Paul M. Hirsch is the James Allen Distinguished Professor of Strategy and Organization at Northwestern University's Kellogg Graduate School of Management. His publications include *Pack your own Parachute: How to Survive Mergers, Takeovers, and Other Corporate Disasters* (1987).

James Holston is an Associate Professor of Anthropology at the University of California, San Diego. He is the author of *The Modernist City: An Anthropological Critique of Brasilia* (1989).

Henry Jenkins is Professor of Literature and Film & Media Studies at the Massachusetts Institute of Technology (MIT) and Director of the Comparative Media Studies Program. He is the author of *Textual Poachers: Television Fans and Participatory Culture* (1992), editor of *The Children's Culture Reader* (1998) and co-editor of *From Barbie to Mortal Kombat: Gender and Computer Games* (1998).

Elihu Katz is Trustee Professor at the Annenberg School of the University of Pennsylvania, and Emeritus Professor of Sociology and Communication at the Hebrew University of Jerusalem. Among his publications are *The Export of Meaning: Cross-Cultural Readings of 'Dallas'* (1990) and *Media Events: The Live Broadcasting of History* (1992).

George Lipsitz is Professor of Ethnic Studies at the University of California, San Diego, and the author of *Possessive Investment In Whiteness: How White People Profit From Identity Politics* (1998) and *Time Passages: Collective Memory and American Popular Culture* (1989).

Marshall McLuhan, who was Professor of English at the University of Toronto, was one of the key mass media theorists of the twentieth century. His concepts of 'the global village' and 'the medium is the message' have been profoundly influential. His works include *The Gutenberg Galaxy* (1963), *Understanding Media* (1964), and *The Mechanical Bride: Folklore of Industrial Man* (1951).

Toby Miller is Associate Professor of Cinema Studies at New York University. He is the author of *The Well-Tempered Self: Citizenship, Culture and the Postmodern Subject* (1993), *The Avengers* (1997), and *Technologies of Truth: Cultural Citizenship and the Popular Media* (1997).

Horace Newcomb is F. J. Heyne Centennial Professor of Communication at the University of Texas-Austin. Author of numerous articles he is also the editor of *The Encylopedia of Television* (1996) and *Television: the Critical View* (1994).

Cindy Patton is the author of *Last Served? Gendering the HIV Pandemic* (1994) and *Inventing Aids* (1990).

Roberta E. Pearson is Senior Lecturer in the School of Journalism, Media and Cultural Studies at Cardiff University. Her publications include *The Critical Dictionary of Film and Television Theory* (2000), *Back in the Saddle Again: New Writings on the Western* (1998), *Reframing Culture: The Case of the Vitagraph Quality Films* (1993), and *The Many Lives of the Batman* (1991).

Marge Piercy is a prolific poet, essayist, and novelist whose work frequently expresses her feminist convictions. Among her best known novels are *Woman On The Edge of Time* (1976), *Gone To Soldiers* (1987), *He, She and It* (1991) and *City of Darkness, City of Light* (1996).

Mark Poster teaches in Film Studies and in History at the University of California, Irvine. About to appear are *The Information Subject* and *What's the Matter with the Internet*. His recent books include *Cultural History and Postmodernity* (1997), *The Second Media Age* (1995), and *The Mode of Information* (1990).

Janice Radway is Frances Hill Fox Professor in Humanities and Professor of Literature at Duke University. Her publications include *Reading the Romance* (1984) and *A Feeling for Books: The Book-of-the-Month Club, Literary Taste and Middle Class Desire* (1998).

Andrew Ross is Professor of Comparative Literature and Director of the American Studies program at New York University. A writer for *Artforum, The Nation, The Village Voice,* and many other publications, he is the author or editor of eleven books, including *Real Love* (1998), *The Chicago Gangster Theory of Life* (1994), *Strange Weather* (1991), and *No Respect* (1989).

Marshall Sahlins is Charles F. Grey Distinguished Service Professor Emeritus of Anthropology and of Social Sciences at the University of Chicago. His books include *How 'Natives' Think: About Captain Cook, For Example* (1995), *Culture and Practical Reason* (1977), and *Stone Age Economics* (1974).

Michael Schudson is Professor of Communication at the University of California, San Diego. His books include *The Good Citizen: A History of American Civic Life* (1998), *Watergate in American Memory* (1992), and *Advertising the Uneasy Persuasion* (1984).

Carroll Smith-Rosenberg is Professor of History at the University of Michigan. Her best known work is *Disorderly Conduct: Visions of Gender in Victorian America* (1985).

Susan Sontag established herself as one of America's public intellectuals in the 1960s with her essays in *The New York Review of Books, Commentary,* and *Partisan Review.* Among her books are *Against Interpretation, and Other Essays* (1966), *AIDS and Its Metaphors* (1989), *Illness as Metaphor* (1978), and *On Photography* (1977).

Lynn Spigel is Professor in the School of Cinema and Television at the University of Southern California. Her publications include *The Revolution wasn't Televised: Sixties Television and Social Conflict* (1997), *Feminist Television Criticism: A Reader* (1997) and *Make Room for TV: Television and the Family Ideal in Postwar America* (1992).

Robert Stam is Professor of Cinema Studies at New York University. His publications include *Subversive Pleasures: Bakhtin, Cultural Criticism and Film* (1989), *New Vocabularies in Film Semiotics: Structuralism, Post-Structuralism and Beyond* (1993) *Unthinking Eurocentrism: Multiculturalism and the Media* (1994).

Hunter S. Thompson is a journalist and essayist whose articles in *Rolling Stone* contributed to the emergence of the new journalism. His first book, *Hell's Angels* (1966), was a non-fiction novel in the style of Truman Capote's *In Cold Blood.* Other works include *Fear and Loathing in Las Vegas: A Savage Journey to the Heart of the American Dream* (1971) and several collections of his essays.

Paula A. Treichler teaches in the College of Medicine, Institute of Communications Research, and Women's Studies Program at the University of Illinois, UC. Among her books are *How to Have Theory in an Epidemic: Cultural Chronicles of AIDS* (1999) and *The Visible Woman: Imaging Technologies, Gender, and Science* (1998).

Eva Vieth is completing her doctorate in the School of Journalism, Media and Cultural Studies at Cardiff University and has lectured at Utrecht University.

Susan Willis is an Associate Professor of English at Duke University. Among her publications are *Specifying: Black Women Writing the American Experience* (1987) and *Inside the Mouse: Work and Play at Walt Disney World* (1995).

Tom Wolfe. One of the key figures of the new journalism of the 1960s and holder of a PhD in American Studies from Yale University, Tom Wolfe is an essayist, novelist, and cultural critic. His books include *The Kandy-Kolored Tangerine-Flake Streamline Baby* (1965), *The Pump House Gang, The Electric Kool-Aid Acid Test* (1968), and *The Bonfire of the Vanities* (1987).

Acknowledgements

We thank all the contributors to this volume; without their inspiring, argumentative, funny, strange, compelling, and insightful work, it would not have been worth doing. We have enjoyed reading an immense amount of material in the course of compiling the *Reader*, and sincerely wish that it could have been at least twice as big (indeed it was at one point), because of the wealth of absolutely first-rate, important, and brilliantly written work that can be collected under the heading of "American cultural studies." We hope that the book will assist new readers to explore this rich terrain, and equally that it will remind those who are already familiar with the field just how interesting it is.

We are grateful to the many readers, referees, advisors, consultants, and friends who have commented on, criticized, and encouraged this project during its rather prolonged gestation. They include some known to us and some not; thanks especially to Oxford's formidable panel of anonymous referees. We are equally grateful to a series of different but uniformly helpful editors at OUP: Andrew Lockett for listening to the original pitch, Sophie Goldsworthy for keeping it going during a period of rapid change at the Press, and Angela Griffin for bringing it safely to a conclusion.

Our most substantial debt of gratitude goes to Eva Vieth, who was at the time the Tom Hopkinson Scholar in the Tom Hopkinson Centre for Media Research at Cardiff University. She has acted as our research assistant and editorial assistant at different stages of the project, and she wrote the epilogue. Without her dedicated, careful, and intellectually sophisticated input we could not have completed the book. Her name on the title-page signals the extent of her contribution. Thanks too to Christian Schneider for his generous assistance in the final stages.

J. H. and R. E. P.

Introduction: "Cultural Exceptionalism"
Freedom, Imperialism, Power, America

John Hartley

Provincializing America

American cultural studies: a reader marks a new point of departure in the growing field of cultural studies, the implications of which may be controversial despite the apparently technical nature of the task the book sets itself. In fact there are several consequences that follow from choosing the title *American Cultural Studies*:

1. The "provincialization" or regionalization of *cultural studies*. This move itself has two consequences. First, it introduces to the object of study "culture" a very proper structure of differences based on regional location. Second, it serves to limit the universalism of cultural studies as a disciplinary discourse.

2. American culture is not only a province of cultural studies, but also of *American studies*. Some dialogue, differentiation, and debate between these two interdisciplinary fields is necessary (and has of course taken place—see Janice Radway herein).

3. The formula "American cultural studies" raises the question of what is meant by *America* —specifically, the inclusion or exclusion from the term of American places outside the United States.

Our configuration of the field of cultural studies is based on region. Such an organization of the material has the effect of making American cultural studies one species among others, such as British (Turner 1990), Australian (Frow and Morris 1993), African (Tomaselli 1998), Asian (Chen 1998, see also Palumbo-Liu 1999), or even Kenyan-Appalachian-Danish (Wright 1998). This is controversial in the sense that America has hitherto tended in this context, as in many others, to be presumed as an *ex-nominated* category or one that *does not want to be named* (Barthes 1973: 138–41). "America" has occurred naturally, as it were, as the universal subject of the disciplinary discourse, while other regions, where they were considered at all, appeared as departures, sub-categories or derivatives.

A provincialized American cultural studies can be seen as part of a historical process of import and export, of dialogue, translation, and exchange between different regions in a larger "cultural universe" or "semiosphere" (Lotman 1990). Such exchange of meanings has applied not only to the sphere of culture itself (the object of study), but also to the realm of ideas and disciplinary knowledge (the means of study).

Naming what is done in this context as *American* cultural studies, and not by default claiming it to be cultural studies as such, imposes a modesty of ambition on the explanatory power of the studies concerned. Here *American Cultural Studies: A Reader* differs from numerous edited collections in the field (see for instance Grossberg, Nelson, and Treichler 1992; During 1999; Jenkins, Shattuc, and McPherson 2000). They have sought to encapsulate cultural studies as a whole. This anthology seeks not only to limit the reach of the field's claims over other regions, but also to introduce that sense of limit to cultural studies' own disciplinary gaze.

It is some time since Graeme Turner (1990) helpfully distinguished a school of study as *British* cultural studies when many of the practitioners within that tradition had neglected to identify their perspective in such a way. The "Birmingham" approach seemed to count as cultural studies *tout court* for its first decade of expansion, but after Turner it could be seen much more clearly as a very specific element of a British (in fact very *English*, see Rojek 1998: 55–59) intellectual and political project. But since then a concomitant regionalization has not taken place in the place where its expansion has been most notable, in the USA. This book seeks to identify such expansive developments as American in the same way that others are seen as African or Asian cultural studies.

American Cultural Studies: A Reader is not only an intervention in cultural studies, but also has a potentially controversial bearing on developments in what has historically been an entirely different discipline: American studies.

American studies grew out of the expansion of American*ism* after the Second World War. After Hiroshima, American economic and military strength led international developments in politics, commerce, and culture. People were interested in America as never before—and United States policy itself promoted the study of its history, politics, arts, and culture. People in postwar Europe and the Pacific region were encouraged to learn about "the American way" as part of their individual preparation for emigration and assimilation to the USA. They were also encouraged to apply American principles of democratic government and economic liberalism to their own war-torn political systems. America meant modernization. Out of this context arose the best-known theory designed to explain and export American success, the conceptual rock upon which American studies was built as an academic discipline: the notion of American "exceptionalism."

This was a nationalist doctrine inherited from the nineteenth century, but over time the United States' "manifest destiny" to occupy the continent from coast to coast exceeded geographical boundaries and began to apply to populations. Many US apologists argued for a new kind of manifest destiny—the implementation of modernity throughout the world, starting with America's own Indigenous nations and immigrants from the Old World, and proceeding to that world itself after the Second World War. Here of course modernization meant free enterprise capitalism—not the socialist "democratic centralism" of the USSR, for instance.

Unlike the empires of the nineteenth century, American supremacy in the postwar era was not usually expressed by direct control of territory, nor by coercive subjugation of peoples and nations. If there was an American empire, it found its fullest expression in control of international flows of communication, capital, and commodities, including knowledge, information, "intelligence," and ideas (see Richards 1993: 1–8). American studies, as an *instance* of such knowledge, could not remain an indifferent bystander, observing American culture from the sidelines, but was an integral part of and player in a new form of political activism—the "politics of culture."

The doctrine of exceptionalism originated in the founding optimism of 1776 and in that context applied to the difference between the new American polity and the regimes of the Old World. However, by the mid-twentieth century, partly because of the growth of US economic and military power, the notion of exceptionalism became a tool of national advancement both at home and abroad. It was a weapon in the new politics where ideologies contended rather than armies. It was, in short, a participant in the Cold War, using the weapon of the "American Dream" to extend American supremacy beyond its own hemisphere.

"Cultural Exceptionalism"

Cultural studies, for its part, was a product of a later period. Indeed part of its own pre-history, certainly in Britain, was *anti*-Americanism in reaction to the developments noted above. British cultural studies was a product of the postwar baby boom generation, who inherited American exceptionalism in the most literal way, being born into the wave of optimism and demographic expansion that followed from the establishment of the *pax americana*. While the often-cited founding parents of cultural studies were not themselves baby-boomers, their most influential students were, and it was the expansion and internationalization of this group that secured the eventual institutional ascendancy of cultural studies (see Hebdige 1988).

Cultural studies was a political as well as an intellectual enterprise from the start, an active participant in European leftist reactions to the Cold War, to intensified class antagonisms of the "boom and bust" period of economic expansion, and to problems of modernization in the Old World. Such problems were pretty intractable in places like Britain, with its nineteenth-century economy, eighteenth-century political infrastructure, seventeenth-century pattern of (aristocratic) land ownership, and its medieval constitution. The work that eventually became cultural studies was one attempt to provide a theoretical and intellectual framework within which such "peculiarities of the English" might be understood, in order for remedial action to be taken (Thompson 1978).

This was not *American* exceptionalism but what we may identify as "*cultural* exceptionalism." That is, culture became the chosen sphere for political action designed to produce radical social, political, and economic change. Radical activism directed to the traditional sites, i.e. the factory gate (the economy) and political institutions themselves, had failed. Extensions of the franchise, and democratization of the political system to represent the interests of the industrial workforce, had not produced the desired changes. Observers of the national and international scene in the 1950s and 1960s were struck by how the benefits of modernization had managed to miss so many people, inflict such damage on so many economies, and produce so many unwanted side effects, from environmental pollution to boring uniformity or disaffection in everyday life. Since activism in the workplace (industrial action) and on the streets (political action) had failed to provoke the radical rupture that would, it was hoped, lead to systemic change, attention increasingly moved to the realms of consciousness, culture, and communication. If these things could be the means and locus of structural (i.e. revolutionary) change, perhaps the other problems would be soluble thereafter. *Culture* became a focus for intellectual work on *politics* designed to restructure the *economy*. That was the essence of the Birmingham project in cultural studies.

The place where this "cultural exceptionalism" began to interact with American exceptionalism was the USA (see Brantlinger 1990). We shall discuss the encounter below. But first, it is appropriate at this point to suggest that "*American Cultural Studies*" as a term belongs primarily to the *United States* of America, from Polynesia to Puerto Rico, not to the north American continent (i.e. to Canada and Mexico), much less to the Americas as a whole, from Cuba to Tierra del Fuego. Here is another potential source of controversy in relation to the title of this book. We have retained the commonsense application of "American" to the USA, precisely because of the problems of "ex-nomination" referred to above. There already exist identifiable corpuses of *Canadian* and *Latin-American* cultural studies. There is important and distinct work in *Indigenous* or Native American cultural studies. In each case these have identified themselves partly by differentiation from the big sibling.

American cultural studies *needs* to refer primarily to the USA, not only to produce a provincialized version of the enterprise of cultural studies in that country, but also to avoid subsuming distinct traditions of cultural studies in the different intellectual semiospheres of Hispanic and Indigenous America and Commonwealth Canada.

It *need not* be presumed that Canadian, Mexican, Latin American, Native, or other American contributions to cultural studies are derivative of US cultural studies—somewhat the reverse, in fact. One of the most influential early theorists in the field was an Argentinian, Ernesto Laclau. His work became known in the field partly via the writing of Stuart Hall, whose own "Englishness" (Rojek 1998) was adopted, since he was born continentally American, coming from Jamaica to Britain in the 1950s as a Rhodes Scholar. Another pivotal figure in the development of cultural studies, Marshall McLuhan (represented herein), was a Canadian. And some of the most cogent critiques of the attempt to apply Western knowledge in general to inappropriate contexts have been made by Indigenous writers (see Vine Deloria and Churchill Ward, herein).

Thus American cultural studies includes all such work. But the deployment of it in the United States, including its institutionalization in the US academic system, means that American cultural studies nevertheless refers importantly to what is done *with* all these international and regional voices in the specifically US context. It is that articulation of global and regional cultural studies to the US instance that we wish to sample in this collection.

Liberty is Imperialism?

The Scottish Americanist George McKay points to "two poles" in the analysis of culture, both of which have sought to explain the global phenomenon of Americanization since the Second World War (McKay 1997: 20). The fact that both of these apparently mutually exclusive poles can be argued with equal conviction suggests that both need to be held in mind in any consideration of American culture.

One pole saw Americanization as imperialism—the imposition of global mass culture on a previously highly differentiated patchwork of indigenous cultures, in the service of the commercial and military expansionism of the US military-industrial complex. The other pole saw Americanization as liberation—the way that the products of American popular culture in particular were taken up by communities from the French to the hippies to express resistance to their local hegemonic or dominant cultures. A telling example was the suppression of "American"—meaning African-American—influences via jazz in Nazi Germany, and the concomitant expression of resistance to Nazism among those Germans who continued to attend jazz clubs and listen to American jazz recordings (see Hans Peter Bleuel 1973).

Both poles applied not only to the object of study but also to the means—American cultural studies: there was a disciplinary aspect to the issue. As McKay points out, the cultural imperialism thesis belonged to "mass cultural analysis" with its origins in social critique, political economy, and social science methods, whereas the liberatory discourse belonged to "popular cultural analysis," which tended to take root in disciplines associated with the arts and humanities.

Perhaps for these disciplinary reasons, insistence on American imperialism in the cultural field focused on the macro level of production, in social structures and ideologies, and in large-scale commercial trading patterns. The characteristic methods of analysis were derived from the social sciences. Meanwhile, a focus on American culture's liberating potential was directed at the micro level of consumerism, at individual subjectivity and identity, and at the circulation not of goods but of meanings. A characteristic (though by no means exclusive) methodological technique at this level was textual analysis.

Of course both the macro and micro levels required analysis to understand what America might mean in a given context. There was, and remains, a need for *synthesis* of analytical perspectives as well as for interdisciplinarity. While interdisciplinary work, between the social sciences and humanities in particular, offered the possibility of a meeting of minds, methods, and mutual understanding it was equally prone to displays of mutual incomprehension, misunderstanding, and sometimes willful blindness to what observers at the opposite disciplinary pole were trying to explain.

Did the interdisciplinary discipline of American studies supply that synthesis? American Studies within the USA itself may have offered too celebratory an account of American nationalism and exceptionalism. It presumed that Americanization was a process that migrants would undergo, making themselves *into* Americans by education into the symbols and discourses of Americanism. That process, and its global ambitions, was gently satirized at the time by the Hungarian writer George Mikes. In the preface to *How to Scrape Skies*, written "on board RMS *Queen Elizabeth*, May 1947," Mikes wrote:

After the appearance of my little treatise *How to be an Alien*, I was bitterly reproached by a number of people for having written the book at all. "Who wants to be an alien?" people asked me indignantly. "We all want to be Americans. All of us: the thousand million non-American population of this earth, children of all ages, continents, sexes and religious denominations; rich and poor, young and old, black and white, small and great. The coming century is going to be the century of the Americans." "You are wrong"—I objected—"it is going to be the century of the common man." "Same thing," they retorted. "Aren't the Americans common enough?" (Mikes 1966: 9)

For George McKay, American studies, especially that form of it practised *outside* the USA in Europe and the UK especially, was not so much an explanation of the phenomenon of the "two poles" as an interesting example of it. It was "launched on a wave of optimism and pride at the end of World War Two," and inevitably it "bears its own ideological assumptions." But according to McKay it has a poor internal record of admitting to its own history: "The striking thing for me has been the frequency with which discussions of Americanization by Americanists have bypassed the role of their own and their students' discipline, job, career and study area" (McKay 1997: 29). In other words, American studies was no innocent abroad. Even outside the USA its mission was to make the "American century" *American*:

> How far has the "cultural chauvinism" of American Studies actually been unpacked outside the USA? Is it the case that American Studies in Europe simply repeats this "cultural chauvinism" via implicit assumptions of American exceptionalism? . . . Did (does?) American Studies in Europe exist solely or primarily in order to maintain American cultural, economic—even, let's go for it, *imperial*—hegemony? (McKay 1997: 30)

American studies therefore has been seen as both part of American "imperial hegemony," and as an expression of "optimism and pride." McKay wonders if cultural critics from outside the USA have tended to lose some of their critical edge when faced with America. Have they been culturally colonized themselves by getting caught up in a fantasy of Americanness that serves their own desires but does little to explain Americanization? He considers three different areas that have attracted positive evaluation from European Americanists:

(1) America as the zone of liberation or democracy;
(2) American as a locus of pleasure, via popular culture;
(3) America as an invented utopian space, or fantasy zone, as in *Star Trek* (McKay 1997: 37–41).

All these locations cluster near the positive pole of liberatory desire. They do not readily map on to the opposing pole, where the topography might reveal economic supremacism not democracy; cultural imperialism not pleasure; dystopian visions of fragmentation and struggle; fantasies of destruction not identification. It seems that American studies has not always *synthesized* the polar perspectives of imperialism versus liberation, but has served sometimes to *reproduce* them.

For a synthesis it is necessary to make America part of a larger set of concerns—not to exceptionalize it so much as to "provincialize" it. This term is Dipesh Chakrabarty's (1992), although he applied it to Europe as part of the project of subaltern studies. He challenged the long-standing habit in historical and other academic writing of using Europe as the universal subject of discourse and everywhere else—India, for example—as a derivative instance. As noted above, the same problem occurred over America. It was promoted as an exceptional state, exempt from the historical tangles of *anciens régimes*, and simultaneously used as the pattern not only for knowledge about itself but for knowledge in general. How to make America a *province* of knowledge, rather than its *imperium*, was an issue that faced those who sought to explain the opposing tensions.

The cause of the gravitational pull of America was easily identified. What linked the liberationist and imperialist poles was *power*. The USA was the great attractor of the modern socio-cultural universe. For that reason it could prove (or promise) to be liberatory for those whose own powers were increased by identification with it. But that same powerful attraction was imperial for those who sought to maintain independent orbits.

Was America imperial or liberatory? The answer was . . . well, yes! The illogicality of that answer has been one of the great themes of American cultural imaginings. *Star Trek* (original series) was a poeticization of the vicissitudes of the doctrine of manifest destiny. In *Star Wars* the great attractor turned out to be a Death Star, and power was exercised by the "dark side" of an otherwise laudable force. The world looked on.

Power and Culture

Power articulates with culture in practice and in academic discourse in complex ways. "Power" became a central concept in the newly emergent discourses of British cultural studies in the 1970s. During this period, when cultural studies as a whole was increasingly Marxist and certainly leftist in orientation, power was understood as *domination* —it was understood in a straightforward way as something to be *exerted* or *resisted*.

During the same period, the mainstream political sphere was also preoccupied with power. Peace was a fact for the home-populations of advanced nations, economic expansion was a goal, but adversarial politics was increasingly intense. In Britain and elsewhere in Europe struggles dragged on between government and union interests, and industrial disputation reached new high levels. Meanwhile, during the same period, the bitter political divisions created by the Vietnam War were making themselves felt not only in the USA itself, but also in countries such as Australia (which sent troops to Vietnam) and Britain (whose Labour government supported the war). The Cold War seemed a perfect instance of power as a struggle for domination between institutionalized forces engaged in mutual exertion of and resistance to each other's power.

But cultural studies in the British tradition was also influenced by ideas, events, and movements that rejected straightforwardly *political* notions of power. Instead, and in common with other important critical discourses of the period, notably feminism and ethnic or racial politics, it sought to understand power within supposedly apolitical domains such as everyday life, commercial culture, and the private sphere. Cultural and social relations were understood as power relations. Culture was seen as a sphere where class interests, based in the economic sphere, could be exerted via cultural forms and activities. Language, media, and the practices of everyday life were examined to reveal the play of power relations *through* culture. Thus "power" was extended to include "sites of struggle" not traditionally taken into account in political theory. Where exercised in the cultural sphere, power was said to take the form of "hegemony," a term borrowed from the pre-war Italian communist leader Antonio Gramsci.

But the notion of power itself as a relational force expressing inequalities and modes of domination and resistance, was not radically revised. Only after Michel Foucault and his successors would the very concept of power itself be questioned. Here too there were consequences for cultural studies, which began to turn its attention to "regimes of truth" and to the discursive, disciplinary, and institutional sites in which knowledge itself produced effects of power. Foucault's own interests lay in consideration of "total institutions" such as prisons and asylums, of disciplinary discourses in medicine and psychiatry, and of techniques of self-government based on surveillance. He was not himself interested in studying the media or popular culture. But his theorization of power became increasingly influential in British and especially in Australian cultural studies. It was clear that "governmentality" (the management of populations and of the self) did not stop with the government, and that power was distributed into the micro-circuits of everyday life right down to the practices and techniques of self-formation.

During the 1980s and 1990s, the concept of power in the cultural sphere was radically revised via encounters with Foucauldian theory and with the intellectual developments commonly identified as postmodernism. It also responded to more directly activist rethinkings of "power" in the women's, Civil Rights, Black Power, gay and lesbian movements, and in youth culture more generally. The early preoccupation with class as the (British) locus of inequality and struggle gave way to a much more complex set of concerns. The interactions among identity politics, theories of power, and cultural critique led to a reconceptualization of the whole field. Identity could no longer be asserted as a given property of persons (albeit neglected, oppressed, or marginalized by more powerful adversaries) when questions of an even more fundamental kind were raised.

How was subjectivity formed? By what mechanism was identity produced in language, in social and cultural institutions, and in large-scale economic and political arrangements? What was the role of knowledge, of intellectuals, of academic disciplines themselves, in producing selves? What was a person: when and through what activities, techniques, or media was that person rendered a citizen, a consumer, an audience, or a member of the public? Questions of gender, ethnicity, sexuality, age (etc.) inflected and differentiated these questions at every level.

Importation, Indigenization, and Dialogue

Identity (difference), power (knowledge), culture (discourse): it was at this point that *cultural studies* met *American studies*; where the growing disciplinary apparatus of cultural studies, including its preoccupation with identity, power, and the politics of culture, met what Kurt Vonnegut (1982: 13) called the "oompah" of American history.

America was an example of a modern experimental society (though it is not the only one—the USSR and Australia were other instances). It was founded as a nation with no historical alibi for its national form, constitution, and sense of identity. It did not grow haphazardly from ethnic, territorial, and historical roots. It was planted, invented, planned, much like a scientific experiment, using modern techniques of disciplinary knowledge, skills applied as readily to government as to physics, often by the same people—scientist-statesmen such as Jefferson and Franklin. In this context (previously the context of American studies), cultural studies came to town. *American cultural studies* as a specific regional project, then, has been concerned to interrogate some of the legacies of *Americanism* using the critical, theoretical, and analytical tools of *cultural studies*.

The people who started British cultural studies had an ambivalent attitude toward

America. For some, like Richard Hoggart, the perceived Americanization of British culture via television and the cinema was having a negative effect on older traditions of working-class neighborliness, family life, and community. For others working in the same tradition, like Dick Hebdige, America offered an escape route from some of the negative influences of *British* culture, including taste hierarchies based on class and the institutionalization of such class-based preferences as a national culture apparently expressive of eternal verities (see Hebdige 1988: 11). So America had always been there, even in British cultural studies (where it figured as both liberatory and as imperial).

But cultural studies too has a history, an interesting part of which was its importation *into* America. It was a perfect instance of cultural dialogue between two provinces in the semiosphere, as schematized by Yuri Lotman. Speaking of "cultural texts" like literature or cinema films, Lotman described five stages by means of which a cultural form is indigenized by an importing or "receiving" culture (Lotman 1990: 146; see also O'Regan 1996: 214, and Olson 1999: 165–66):

1. "The texts coming in from the outside keep their 'strangeness'." Stage one is where a highly valued foreign import is revered in unchanged form—it does not even have to be translated. This is how British cultural studies first came to the USA. It spoke in its peculiar patois made up from an amalgam of English Marxism, materialist history, modernist literary criticism, and continental high theory, all applied to demotic pursuits and profane culture. Strange, beautiful . . . true! Stage one was represented by the reading of British cultural studies "in the original" by high-status American academics and writers, and by the invitation to the USA of its most charismatic practitioners— Stuart Hall in particular. The themes of British and American cultural studies however remained "asymmetrical" (Lotman's term) or untranslatable: Birmingham England (class, industry, popular culture) did not readily explain Birmingham Alabama (ethnicity, primary production, colonialism). Time for stage two.

2. "The imported text and the home culture . . . restructure each other." Stage two is when this peculiar import begins to be changed by contact with American culture, and American culture changed by contact with it. This was the stage of translations, imitations, and adaptations, of the *application* of the British model (class, ideology, hegemony) to US culture and society. This stage might best be exemplified by John Fiske, a British academic imported to the University of Wisconsin–Madison (via Australia and Iowa). Fiske was very influential in stimulating the field in the USA with his popularizations of media and cultural studies using British paradigms and American examples (see Fiske 1987).

3. "A higher content is found in the imported world-view which can be separated from the national culture of the imported texts." Stage three is the crucial moment of indigenization, when the imported text is held to be merely an *imperfect* attempt at something that could in fact be much better accomplished "over here." The "truth" of the paradigm was its realization in the receiving (US) context. At this stage, the supposed or desired essence of the whole enterprise was held to be rooted not in its British form but in the transplanted soil of America. Perhaps symptomatic of this stage was the moment when British cultural studies, which at the time was very marginally institutionalized in Britain (having its origins in adult education and avant-garde leftist

journals), became installed in American universities as a mainstream subject for under-graduate and graduate study. It had been imported as a discourse about power; it was indigenized as a species of college syllabus-modernization. Its exemplary figure was Lawrence Grossberg at the University of Illinois (latterly at UNC–Chapel Hill): John Fiske's successor as Editor of the journal *Cultural Studies*, and prime mover in holding the 1990 conference that resulted in the big edited collection of the same name (Grossberg, Nelson, and Treichler 1992).

4. "Imported texts are entirely dissolved in the receiving culture." The fourth stage begins the shift from "receiving" to "transmitting": the culture changes to a state of activity, rapidly producing new texts. This was the stage of the "Routledgification of the world" (Hartley 1992: 464; Ray 1995: 7; Morris 1990: 15). It was also the moment when people who were British in origin, such as Dick Hebdige and Andrew Ross (herein), produced work that was recognizably American, and that work began to reconfigure what was done back in Britain.

5. "The receiving culture . . . changes into a transmitting culture directing its product to other, peripheral areas of the semiosphere." The fifth stage is full-on exportation of texts directed outwards to other provinces and regions, which now of course included Britain as part of the semiospherical periphery. Britain imported *American* cultural studies . . . as the opening turn of a new dialogue.

America turned from a receiving to a transmitting culture in the semiosphere of cultural studies. Once again, the world looked on. But again, this was not necessarily evidence of academic or intellectual imperialism. As with all other cultural products that criss-cross the national and regional boundaries of the global semiosphere and the international marketplace, what was *seen* in any remote or peripheral receiving culture is not the same as what was *sent*.

This was in line with the thesis advanced by many recent writers on the theme of international cultural flows; that the importation of any cultural product, from Euro-Disney to cultural theory, was not evidence of direct *power* exerted by the sending country over the receiving one. Instead of power exerted or resisted, a notion of mutual communicative contamination resulting in *hybridity* has emerged from postcolonial studies (see Bhabha 1990). In this vein, Scott Olson has discussed the popularity of American media in overseas markets: "For the most part, their success is a function of their desirability, and their desirability is a function of specific qualities the buyer assigns to them" (Olson 1999: p. x). This accorded exactly with Lotman's stricture that "as with any dialogue, a situation of mutual attraction must precede the actual contact" (Lotman 1990: 146). Olson continued: "whether or not these [American] texts are transforming indigenous cultures into something American, those [global] audiences are transforming the texts into something indigenous" (Olson 1999: 50). Olson called this facility for indigenization in exported texts their "transparency":

> The transparency effect means that American cultural exports . . . manifest narrative structures that easily blend into other cultures. Those cultures are able to project their own narratives, myths, values and meanings into the American iconic media, making those texts resonate with the same meanings they might have if they were indigenous. (Olson 1999: 6)

What went for the products of commercial media could also go for cultural studies. As

American cultural studies switched from a receiving to a transmitting stage, so in turn it was indigenized by other, peripheral, receiving cultures. This occurred all the more successfully where its modes of explanation and analysis could be understood in such places as transparent enough for the resonation of indigenous meanings.

What If They Are Right?

In such a context, even when faced with the global domination of American cultural exports, the traditional notion of power (as direct imperial force) seemed an inadequate explanatory device. Transparency, hybridity, mutual attraction, and dialogue—these terms seemed better suited to the international traffic of the semiosphere, rather than the paranoid Cold War terminology of conventional social and political science. The most helpful terms in cultural studies were derived from *communication* theory not *political* theory. But in fact it was increasingly in the realm of communications that American strength and influence could be identified.

The US economy was strongest, and showed the highest and most sustained growth throughout the Clinton presidency, in the information, communications, media, cultural and knowledge sectors. Traditional manufacturing, primary industry, and commerce were comparatively stagnant. In other words there was, even as American cultural studies evolved as an explanatory discourse, a massive corporatization and capitalization of language, a major investment in meanings, and a shift that brought the doctrine of "cultural exceptionalism" into the economic mainstream.

At the consumer end of these developments, there was a concomitant diversification and hybridization of subject positions, creating new forms and possibilities in citizenship, identity, even in personhood. The confinement of individual and collective political action to the traditional public sphere was a thing of the past. The economy, politics, and public life shifted further towards culture. The realms of the private, of everyday life, of ordinariness, became the arena for political movements and social change. Democratic participation, where exercised, was conducted through commercial institutions, the media and the marketplace as much as it was through public organizations, perhaps more. Segments of highly differentiated populations were made known to each other, and overall public policy was governed, within a virtualized "mediasphere" whose leaders were celebrities, personalities, and stars, not political or business decision-makers, and whose citizens were audiences and readerships, not voters.

Jumbo jets and the Internet were examples of the economic impact of new technologies of communication, both physical and informational. Both were entirely American inventions, with their origins in the same year—1969. As the first commercial jumbo rolled out of its hangar in Seattle, the Internet was being devised in an alliance between the academy and the Pentagon, designed to protect US military computing capacity if the Cold War were ever to heat up. In both cases these major national and commercial investments were subsequently indigenized everywhere in the world, finding uses unimagined by their initial planners. Their growth was not explicable in simple terms of power and domination, whether national (American), or corporate (Microsoft, Boeing). For while they improved American trade balances and enriched certain Americans, they were equally able to serve the purposes of those outside the USA who used them, and of course they were as capable of bringing traffic *into* the States as they were of exporting American bodies and meanings. Even American cultural studies itself began to migrate to the Net (see Eva Vieth, herein), while its better funded practitioners were able to travel to international conferences on jumbos.

Clearly, new understandings were required to account for developments in and of American culture, and of its increasing political and economic significance (see Mark Poster and Manuel Castells, herein). Cultural studies was at a point of generational change (see Jenkins, Shattuc, and McPherson 2000), with less emphasis on identity, and less confidence about the power of oppositional intellectuals to enter the public sphere as defenders of minorities against corporate and state interests. Instead, a more molecular American cultural studies emerged, with affiliative rather than oppositional politics.

Could an emergent American cultural studies prove to be better suited to the conditions of the emergent cultural economy than an earlier adversarial rhetoric? Could it be more sophisticated in its understanding of power? It could certainly explore the extent to which freedom is a *product* of governmentality and power, not their opposing pole. And it could contribute to the surprisingly arduous effort of locating and describing citizenship, even personhood, in *commercial* democracies with *cultural* economies.

Such possibilities require American cultural studies to explain the evolution and working through of "cultural exceptionalism." The usefulness of such an enterprise would not be confined to the world of scholarship and reflection alone. Since "cultural exceptionalism" became the hottest sector of the global economy, and the most intense site of public and commercial policy-making, American cultural studies can help to identify where and what collective and personal decisions might need to follow. America is everyone's indigenous, and culture is power. A question resurfaces that Tom Wolfe asked at the very outset of this intellectual adventure (it is the first reading herein). Despite the "peculiarities of the Americans" in cultural studies, the question remains: *"What if they are right?"*

References

Barthes, Roland (1973). *Mythologies.* London: Paladin.

Bhabha, Homi (ed.) (1990). *Nation and Narration.* New York: Routledge.

Bleuel, Hans Peter (1973). *Strength Through Joy: Sex and Society in Nazi Germany.* London: Pan Books.

Brantlinger, Patrick (1990). *Crusoe's Footprints: Cultural Studies in Britain and America.* London: Routledge.

Chakrabarty, Dipesh (1992). "Provincializing Europe: Postcoloniality and the Critique of History." *Cultural Studies,* 6/3: 337–57.

Chen, (ed.) Kuan-Hsing (1998). *Trajectories: Inter-Asia Cultural Studies.* London: Routledge.

During, Simon (ed.) (1999). *The Cultural Studies Reader* (2nd edn.) London: Routledge.

Fiske, John (1987). *Television Culture.* New York: Routledge.

Frow, John, and Morris, Meaghan (eds.) (1993). *Australian Cultural Studies: A Reader.* Sydney: Allen & Unwin.

Grossberg, Lawrence, Nelson, Cary, and Treichler, Paula (eds.) (1992). *Cultural Studies.* New York: Routledge.

Hartley, John (1992). "Expatriation: Useful Astonishment as Cultural Studies." *Cultural Studies,* 6/3: 449–67.

Hebdige, Dick (1988). *Hiding in the Light: On Images and Things.* London: Comedia/ Routledge.

Jenkins, Henry, Shattuc, Jane, and McPherson, Tara (eds.) (2000). *Hop on Pop: The Politics and Pleasures of Popular Culture*. Durham, NC: Duke University Press.

Lotman, Yuri (1990). *The Universe of the Mind: A Semiotic Theory of Culture*. Bloomington: Indiana University Press.

McKay, George (1997). "Americanization and Popular Culture," in George McKay, (ed.), *Yankee Go Home, (& Take Me With U)*. Sheffield: Sheffield Academic Press, 11–52.

Mikes, George (1966; first published 1948). *How to Scrape Skies: The United States Explored, Rediscovered and Explained*. Harmondsworth: Penguin.

Morris, Meaghan (1990). "Banality in Cultural Studies," In Patricia Mellencamp, (ed.), *Logics of Television: Essays in Cultural Criticism*. Bloomington: Indiana University Press, 14–43.

Olson, Scott Robert (1999). *Hollywood Planet: Global Media and the Competitive Advantage of Narrative Transparency*. Mahwah, NJ: Lawrence Erlbaum Associates.

O'Regan, Tom (1996). *Australian National Cinema*. London: Routledge.

Palumbo-Liu, David (1999). *Asian/American: Historical Crossings of a Racial Frontier*. Stanford, Calif: Stanford University Press.

Ray, Robert B. (1995). *The Avant Garde Finds Andy Hardy*. Cambridge, Mass: Harvard University Press.

Richards, Thomas (1993). *The Imperial Archive: Knowledge and the Fantasy of Empire*. London and New York: Verso.

Rojek, Chris (1998). "Stuart Hall and the Antinominan Tradition." *International Journal of Cultural Studies*, 1/1: 45–65.

Thompson, E. P. (1978). *The Poverty of Theory and Other Essays*. London: Merlin Press.

Tomaselli, Keyan (1998). "African Cultural Studies: Excavating for the Future." *International Journal of Cultural Studies*, 1/1: 143–53.

Turner, Graeme (1990). *British Cultural Studies*. New York: Unwin Hyman/Routledge.

Vonnegut, Kurt (1982). *Palm Sunday: An Autobiographical Collage*. London: Granada.

Wright, Handel K. (1998). "Dare We De-centre Birmingham? Troubling the 'Origin' and Trajectories of Cultural Studies." *European Journal of Cultural Studies*, 1/1: 33–56.

Part One

The Intellectual Context

ists of two parts. Part One delineates some of the
ural studies on three sites: one temporal and the
the New Journalism of the 1960s to establish some
-taking among the contributions. Then there are
and legacies of three different disciplinary projects:

se studies, organized into three chapters under the

que as energetically as have writers, in forms ran-
hotojournalism. A unique component of *American*
on of some "visual cultural studies" from photo-
new things were being said in new ways, and how
s are distributed through the book, tied only loose-
th each one appears. The images are themselves
can in both subject matter and treatment. But they do not simply celebrate
that fact; each one reflects on it, sometimes critically, sometimes quizzically. Using the techniques and traditions of their form, the pictures are themselves a kind of *cultural analysis*,
using the technology of mass communication creatively and sometimes movingly to teach
new truths about "America."

Section I
The New Journalism and Its Legacy

"Muhammad Ali's fist (actual size)", *Esquire*, October 1974. Photo: Pierre Houles.

Section I
The New Journalism and Its Legacy

....

Authors

Tom Wolfe, Susan Sontag, Stokely Carmichael, Vine Deloria, Jr., Marge Piercy, Hunter S. Thompson

Visual Artist

Esquire—Muhammad Ali's fist

We have chosen to confine our major selections to material dating from the 1960s and after. Obviously pre-1960s intellectual discourses are important, but this is one way to limit the material so as to provide the *Reader* with a coherent structure, and the reader with an interesting take on the material.

Despite their almost mythical status in popular culture and also in some academic writing, the 1960s were not at all an originating moment. Culture, politics, and partisan public writing have clashed and intermeshed with each other throughout American history and modernity in general. Nevertheless, during the 1960s there were shifts in cultural discourses and activities at large which bespoke a new centrality for questions of culture in the conduct of American life as a whole. It was at this time that "cultural" forms like music and other media, including television and advertising, converged with politics on a mass scale. The American "whole way of life" became a matter of the highest political controversy, precisely because it could no longer be assumed to be unitary. What "America" meant became controversial—not for the first time, but in a way that has clearly continued to shape and color American culture, both public and private.

At the same time, in the academy, the 1960s witnessed the beginnings of major fractures in modernist disciplinary demarcations that had served intellectual life reasonably well since the late nineteenth century and earlier. This was the decade when "modernist realism" (science, truth, progress, reason) began to be doubted in public, as it were, as well as in philosophical discourses, and when interdisciplinary work began to suggest a new place for the formal study of culture. Changes in consciousness were accompanied by the increasing centrality of culture as a theorized and critical concept. A wide range of work, both formal and journalistic, and both academic and creative, responded to the social, political, and historical changes in the 1960s in ways that directly prefigure what can now be recognized as the abiding preoccupations of American cultural studies.

Although it boasted its champions and "early adopters," cultural studies did not become institutionalized as a separate field of study in the USA until the 1980s. The political and cultural upheaval of the 1960s resulted in transformations in US society, institutions and public writing that in turn led to the possibility of doing cultural studies. It was in the 1960s that culture, and cultural studies too, began to matter to a wider public because cultural politics began to be conducted on the streets and not only in academic journals. It was in the 1960s that some of the most abiding themes of American cultural studies began to find new or refreshed voice. Questions of identity, especially in the crucial areas of gender and race, forced their way into the public arena from various activist movements, and this in turn had an effect on what was done in the academy. American cultural critics have always used journalism to pursue questions of cultural theory and criticism. It is a tradition that began before the USA was founded—and journalism arguably had a hand in assisting that foundation, via the journalistic best-seller of 1775, Thomas Paine's *Common Sense*.

In the 1960s cultural criticism found an active and self-motivated response among whole populations. Journalists such as Hunter S. Thompson and Tom Wolfe, and writers such as Norman Mailer and Joan Didion, abandoned the standard of journalistic "objectivity" to engage in radically subjective critiques of a rapidly changing culture. Thompson "lived" the story he reported in a journalistic equivalent of "going native." Wolfe prioritized his own style and authorial voice over the object of study, whether that was Marshall McLuhan or Modern Art. Didion pursued what may be seen as fictional concerns (with the "imaginary" of American life) by means of true stories. These tendencies all prefigure the "postmodern" refusal to defer to the primacy of any supposed objective reality. Instead, they foreground the agency of the observer, the primacy of discourse in producing knowledge of events, and the importance of banal or non-canonical areas of American life and culture that had previously been outside of the purview of mainstream journalism; the personal, the private, the informal, the counter-cultural. Politically engaged activists included in their analyses of oppression a specifically cultural dimension. After cultural studies it might be said that they spoke of the "dominant" culture's "construction" of "the other." Cultural journalism, and the media-savvy of feminists, black-power activists, and others are all central themes in American cultural studies.

The selection begins with Tom Wolfe's wonderful verbal portrait of Marshall McLuhan, done at the time that McLuhan was just achieving cult status as a guru of the new era of technological communications. Wolfe captures the moment when the world of ideas met the world of PR and advertising; when McLuhan quit grading papers as a provincial college professor to become the hottest property on Madison Avenue. Wolfe's portrait is an example of the New Journalism of which he was a leading exponent, and displays many of its virtues—a strength of realistic reportage that Wolfe himself believed was more "literary" than the fictional literature being produced in America at the time. Certainly this writing was ambitious, exceeding the boundaries of conventional journalism (not least by introducing us to McLuhan via his snap-on tie) but never letting slip its grasp on actuality. If American cultural studies could be as good as this "journalistic" analysis of it, then it would have much to live up to. Wolfe is erudite, funny, and filled with curiosity about everything from McLuhan's theories to his mannerisms, able to sum up a remarkable moment in intellectual and cultural history through an anecdote about how McLuhan's speaking fee leapt from $500 to $25,000 in the course of one phone call.

Like Tom Wolfe, Susan Sontag was not merely an observer of the turbulent 1960s, but a major contributor to the intellectual currents and debates of the time. Here she is one voice in a much larger conversation conducted by the journal *Partisan Review*, which asked a number of leading writers to answer some questions about "America." Sontag's answer is prescient of one of the major themes of subsequent writing in the field (see Hartley's Introduction to this volume)—she interrogates "America" via the notion of "power."

The next three authors interrogate the America of the liberal pluralist orthodoxy of the 1950s, predicated upon the "melting pot" ideology of Americanization and assimilation, from the perspective of an emergent identity politics. In a bold move of cultural politics, Stokely Carmichael, one of the most prominent proponents of Black Power, and Vine Deloria, Jr., Native American activist and scholar, urged African-Americans and Native Americans to recognize and resist the semiotic violence that had been inflicted on them through white representation of their bodies and their cultures. Presaging the position of black cultural studies, Carmichael argues that blacks have internalized their own oppression by accepting white definitions of bodily beauty and of a Western civilization that excludes them. Vine Deloria writes of the white majority's misrepresentation and appropriation of Native American culture, which rendered Native Americans as passive subjects rather than active agents. Marge Piercy, one of America's leading feminist novelists, laments the difficulty of growing up different in the conformist 1950s; the indignities of being female, poor, and non-Anglo in a society that denied the personhood of these categories.

Hunter S. Thompson is one of the best-known exponents of the New Journalism, notorious for his excessive living and language. But here he is in quieter mode, introducing a brief glimpse of Puerto Rico into the "American" mixture represented in the *Reader*. He also introduces a critique of tourism and its discontents as one of the culture industries; another abiding theme of cultural studies thereafter.

The selection of visual images begins with one of the great (and we mean *great*) emblems of the time: Muhammad Ali's fist, published actual size in *Esquire* on the eve of the Ali–Forman world title fight. Muhammad Ali is best known as "The Greatest," the heavyweight boxing champion of the world three times over. He was also a political activist for black rights, via his association with the Nation of Islam. He refused to be drafted to fight in Vietnam, expressing common cause with the "poor people" of that country, and had to do battle up to the Supreme Court over a three-year period to achieve his own civil rights (including the return of his confiscated passport). The fist of the most famous American athlete of all time, clenched in a giant-sized version of the Black Power salute, reproduced actual size in a brilliant journalistic coup, makes a fitting image for the times.

1 What If He Is Right?

Tom Wolfe

I FIRST met Marshall McLuhan in the spring of 1965, in New York. The first thing I noticed about him was that he wore some kind of a trick snap-on necktie with hidden plastic cheaters on it. He was a tall man, 53 years old, handsome, with a long, strong face, but terribly pallid. He had gray hair, which he combed straight back. It was a little thin on top, but he could comb it into nice sloops over the ears. Distinguished-looking, you might say. On the other hand, there were the plastic cheaters. A little of the plastic was showing between his collar and the knot of the tie. I couldn't keep my eye off it. It's the kind of tie you buy off a revolving rack in the Rexall for about 89¢. You just slip the plastic cheaters—they're a couple of little stays sticking out of the knot like wings—you slip them under your collar and there the tie is, hanging down and ready to go, Pree-Tide.

We were having lunch, five of us, out back in the garden of the French restaurant called Lutèce, at 249 East 50th Street. Lutèce is a small place but one of the four or five most fashionable restaurants in New York, I suppose. Certainly it is one of the most expensive. It is so expensive, only your host's menu has the prices listed. Yours just has a list of the dishes. That way you won't feel guilty about it. They put decanters of distilled water on the tables at Lutèce and they have a real wine steward. It is one of those places in the East Fifties in Manhattan where the Main Biggies and the Fashionable Matrons convene for the main event of the weekday, the Status Lunch. Executives, culturati, rich women who are written up in *Women's Wear Daily*, illuminati of all sorts meet there in a marvelous chorale of King Sano and Eastern Honk voices. The women walk in looking an ice-therapy 45, force-starved, peruked and lacquered at the hair-dresser's, wearing peacock-colored Pucci dresses signed "Emilio" up near the throat, taking in "the crowd," sucking their cheeks in for the entrance, and calling Lutèce's owner by his first name, which is André, in a contralto that has been smoke-cured by fifteen to twenty years of inhaling King Sanos, the cigarette of New York Society women. The men come in wearing lozenge-shaped cuff links with real links and precious metal showing on the inside as well as the outside of the cuffs, not those Swank-brand gizmos that stick through and click, and they start honking over André and each other, speaking in a voice known as the Eastern boarding-school honk, a nasal drawl mastered by Nelson Rockefeller, Huntington Hartford, and Robert Dowling, among other eminent Americans. It was grand here, as I say. All honks and smoke-cured droning.

Our table was not the most illustrious, but it was in there trying: a movie actress; the daughter of one of the richest women in America; one of New York's top editors; and, of course, McLuhan. McLuhan, however, was not a celebrity at that time. I doubt that anybody else in the restaurant had ever heard of him.

And vice versa. McLuhan could not have been more oblivious of the special New York grandeur he had landed in. I don't think he noticed the people at all. He was interested in the little garden, or rather its thermodynamics, the way it was set out here in the heat of the noonday sun.

"The warmth steps up the tactile sense and diminishes the visual," he told us presently—as nearly as I can remember his words—I was following the plastic cheater. "It is more involving. It obliterates the distance between people. It is literally more 'intimate.' That's why these so-called 'garden restaurants' work."

Just before he made this sort of statement—and he was always analyzing his environment out loud—he would hook his chin down over his collarbone. It was like an unconscious signal—*now*! I would watch the tie knot swivel over the little telltale strip of plastic. It was a perfect Rexall milky white, this plastic.

At the time I didn't realize that McLuhan had been brought here, to New York, to Lutèce also, to be introduced to *haute New York*. He was about to make his debut, after a fashion. He was about to change from Herbert Marshall McLuhan, 53-year-old Canadian English professor, to *McLuhan*. He certainly didn't act like it, however. It had all been planned, but not by him. To him there was no *haute New York*. It was all past tense in this town. Toward the end of the meal his chin came down, the knot swiveled over the plastic—voices droned and honked richly all around us—and he turned his eyeballs up toward the great office buildings that towered above our little thermo-dynamic enclave.

"Of course, a city like New York is obsolete," he said. "People will no longer concentrate in great urban centers for the purpose of work. New York will become a Disney-land, a pleasure dome . . ."

Somehow, plastic cheaters and all, he had the charisma of a haruspex, the irresistible certitude of the monomaniac. I could see New York turning into a huge Astrodome with raggy little puberteens in white, Courrèges Boots giggling and shrieking and tumbling through the atmosphere like the snow in one of those Christmas paperweights you turn upside down —

What if he's right What . . . if . . . he . . . is . . . right W-h-a-t i-f h-e i-s r-i-g-h-t

		R	
W		I	
H	IF	G	?
A	HE	H	
T	IS	T	

Quite a few American businessmen, it turned out, were already wondering the same thing. There were many studs of the business world, breakfast-food-package designers, television-network creative-department vice presidents, advertising "media reps," lighting-fixture fortune heirs, patent lawyers, industrial spies, we-need-vision board chairmen—all sorts of business studs, as I say, wondering if McLuhan was . . . right. At the time McLuhan was a teacher working out of a little office off on the edge of the University of Toronto that looked like the receiving bin of a second-hand bookstore, grading papers, *grading papers*, for days on end, getting up in the morning, slapping the old Pree-Tide tie on, teaching English, grading more papers —

But what if—large corporations were already trying to put McLuhan in a box. Valuable! Ours! Suppose he *is* what he sounds like, the most important thinker since Newton, Darwin, Freud, Einstein, and Pavlov, studs of the intelligentsia game—suppose he *is* the oracle of the modern times—*what if he is right?*—he'll be in there, in our box.

IBM, General Electric, Bell Telephone, and others had been flying McLuhan from Toronto to New York, Pittsburgh, all over the place, to give private talks to their hierarchs about . . . this unseen world of electronic environment that *only he sees fully*. One corporation offered him $5,000 to present a closed-circuit—*ours*—television lecture on the ways the products in its industry would be used in the future. Another contributed a heavy subsidy to McLuhan's Centre for Culture and Technology at the University of Toronto, which, despite the massive name, was at that time largely McLuhan's genius and some letterhead stationery. One day in New York, McLuhan was staying at Howard Gossage's suite at the Lombardy Hotel. Gossage is a San Francisco advertising man. McLuhan was staying there and representatives of two national weekly magazines called up. Both offered him permanent offices in their buildings, plus fees, to do occasional consulting work. Just to have him in the box, I guess —

"What should I do, Howard?" says McLuhan.

"Take em both!" says Gossage. "You need offices on both sides of town. Suppose you get caught in traffic?"

McLuhan looks puzzled, but Gossage is already off into his laugh. This Gossage has a certain wild cosmic laugh. His eyes light up like Stars of Bethlehem. The laugh comes in waves, from far back in the throat, like echoes from Lane 27 of a bowling alley, rolling, booming far beyond the immediate situation, on to . . .

. . . in any case, McLuhan never failed to provoke this laugh. Perhaps because there were really two contradictory, incongruous McLuhans at this point. Even his appearance could change markedly from situation to situation. One moment he would look like merely the English teacher with the Pree-Tide tie on, naïve, given to bad puns derived from his studies of *Finnegans Wake* and worse jokes from God knows where, a somewhat disheveled man, kindly, disorganized—the very picture of the absent-minded professor. The next moment he would look like what he has, in fact, become: the super-savant, the Freud of our times, the omniscient *philsophe*, the unshakable dialectician. That was whenever the subject was The Theory, which it usually was. On those occasions the monologue began, and McLuhan was, simply, the master. He preferred Socratic dialogues, with six to ten people in attendance. A Socratic dialogue, like a Pentecostal sermon, is a monologue punctuated by worshipful interruptions. "Marshall is actually very polite," said one of his friends, meaning to be kind. "He always waits for your lips to stop moving."

Among his business clients, McLuhan was always that, monomaniac and master. The business studs would sit in their conference rooms under fluorescent lights, with the right air-conditioned air streaming out from behind the management-style draperies. Upward-busting hierarch executives, the real studs, the kind who have already changed over from lie-down crewcuts to brushback Eric Johnston-style Big Boy, haircuts and from Oxford button-downs to Tripler broadcloth straight points and have hung it all on the line, an $80,000 mortgage in New Canaan and a couple of kids at Deerfield and Hotchkiss—hung it all on the line on knowing exactly what this corporation is all about—they sit there with the day's first bloody mary squirting through their capillaries—and this man with a plastic cheater showing at the edge of the collar, who just got through *grading papers*, for godsake, tells them in an *of-course* voice, and with *I'm-being-patient* eyes, that, in effect, politely, they all know just about exactly . . . nothing . . . about the real business they're in —

— Gentlemen, the General Electric Company makes a considerable portion of its profits from electric light bulbs, but it has not yet discovered that it is not in the light bulb business but in the business of moving information. Quite as much as A.T.&T. Yes. *Of-course I-am-willing-to-be-patient.* He pulls his chin down into his neck and looks up out of his long Scotch-lairdly face. Yes. The electric light is pure information. It is a medium without a message, as it were. Yes. Light is a self-contained communications system in which the medium is the message. *Just think that over for a moment—I-am-willing-to-be*—When IBM discovered that it was not in the business of making office equipment or business machines —

——but that it was in the business
of processing
information,
then it began
to navigate
with
clear
vision.
Yes.

Swell! But where did *this* guy come from? What is this—cryptic, Delphic saying: *The electric light is pure information.*

Delphic! *The medium is the message. We are moving out of the age of the visual into the age of the aural and tactile . . . .*

It was beautiful. McLuhan excelled at telling important and apparently knowledgeable people they didn't have the foggiest comprehension of their own bailiwick. He never did it with any overtone of now-I'm-going-to-shock-you, however. He seemed far, far beyond that game, out on a threshold where all the cosmic circuits were programmed. I can see him now, sitting in the conference room on the upper deck of an incredible ferryboat that Walter Landor, one of the country's top package designers, has redone at a cost of about $400,000 as an office and design center. This great package design flagship nestles there in the water at Pier 5 in San Francisco. The sun floods in from the Bay onto the basket-woven wall-to-wall and shines off the dials of Landor's motion-picture projection console. Down below on the main deck is a whole simulated supermarket for bringing people in and testing package impact—and McLuhan says, almost by the way:

"Of course, packages will be obsolete in a few years. People will want tactile experiences, they'll want to feel the product they're getting —"

But! —

McLuhan's chin goes down, his mouth turns down, his eyes roll up in his *of-course* expression: "Goods will be sold in *bins*. People will go right to bins and pick things up and *feel* them rather than just accepting a package."

Landor, the package designer, doesn't lose his cool; he just looks—*what if he is right?*

. . . The human family now exists under conditions of a global village. We live in a single constricted space resonant with tribal drums . . . That even, even, even voice goes on —

— McLuhan is sitting in the Laurent Restaurant in New York with Gibson McCabe, president of *Newsweek,* and several other high-ranking communications people, and McCabe tells of the millions *Newsweek* has put into reader surveys, market research, advertising, the editorial staff, everything, and how it paid off with a huge rise in circulation over the past five years. McLuhan listens, then down comes the chin: "Well . . . of course, your circulation would have risen about the same anyway, the new sensory balance of the people being what it is . . ."

Print gave tribal man an eye for an ear.

McLuhan is at the conference table in the upper room in Gossage's advertising firm in San Francisco, up in what used to be a firehouse. A couple of newspaper people are up there talking about how they are sure their readers want this and that to read— McLuhan pulls his chin down into his neck:

"Well . . . of course, people don't actually *read* newspapers. They get into them every morning like a hot bath."

Perfect! Delphic! Cryptic! Aphoristic! Epigrammatic! With this even, even, even voice, this utter scholarly aplomb—with *pronouncements* —

The phone rings in Gossage's suite and it's for McLuhan. It is a man from one of America's largest packing corporations. They want to fly McLuhan to their home office to deliver a series of three talks, one a day, to their top management group. How much would he charge? McLuhan puts his hand over the receiver and explains the situation to Gossage.

"How much should I charge?"

"What do you usually get for a lecture?" says Gossage.

"Five hundred dollars."

"Tell him a hundred thousand."

McLuhan looks appalled.

"Oh, all right," says Gossage. "Tell him fifty thousand."

McLuhan hesitates, then turns back to the telephone "Fifty thousand."

Now the man on the phone is appalled. That is somewhat outside the fee structure we generally project, Professor McLuhan. They all call him Professor or Doctor. We don't expect you to prepare any new material especially for us, you understand, and it will only be three talks —

"Oh—well then," says McLuhan, "twenty-five thousand."

Great sigh of relief. Well! That is more within our potential structure projection, Professor McLuhan, and we look forward to seeing you!

McLuhan hangs up and stares at Gossage, nonplussed. But Gossage is already off into the cosmic laugh, bounding, galloping, soaring, eyes ablaze—¡*más alla!*—¡*más alla!* just over the next skyline!—El Dorado, Marshall! Don't you understand! —

Looking back, I can see that Gossage, but not McLuhan, knew what was going to happen to McLuhan over the next six months. Namely, that this 53-year-old Canadian English teacher, gray as a park pigeon, would suddenly become an international celebrity and the most famous man his country ever produced.

McLuhan rose up from out of a world more obscure, more invisible, more unknown to the great majority of mankind than a Bantu village or the Southeast Bronx. Namely, the EngLit academic life. Tongaland and the Puerto Rican slums may at least reek, in the imagination, of bloodlust and loins oozing after sundown. EngLit academia, so far as the outside world is concerned, neither reeks, nor blooms; an occasional whiff of rotting tweeds, perhaps: otherwise, a redolence of nothing. It is a world of liberal-arts scholars, graduate schools, *carrels*, and monstrous baby-sitting drills known as freshman English. It is a far more detached life than any garret life of the artists. Garret life? Artists today spend their time calling up Bloomingdale's to see if the yellow velvet Milo Laducci chairs they ordered are in yet.

English-literature scholars start out in little cubicles known as carrels, in the stacks of the university libraries, with nothing but a couple of metal Klampiton shelves of books to sustain them, sitting there making scholarly analogies—detecting signs of Rabelais in Sterne, signs of Ovid in Pound, signs of Dickens in Dostoevsky, signs of nineteenth-century flower symbolism in Melville, signs of Schlegelianism in Coleridge, signs of the Oral-narrative use of the conjunctive in Hemingway, signs, analogies, insights—always *insights*—golden *desideratum*!—hunched over in silence with only the far-off sound of Maggie, a Girl of the Stacks, a townie who puts books back on the shelves—now she is all right, a little lower-class-puffy in the nose, you understand, but . . .—only the sound of her to inject some stray, *sport* thought into this intensely isolated regimen. In effect, the graduate-school scholar settles down at an early age, when the sap is still rising, to a life of little cubicles, little money, little journals in which his insights, if he is extremely diligent, may someday be recorded. A Volkswagen, a too-small apartment, Department Store Danish furniture with dowel legs—before he is 30 his wife will have begun to despise him as a particularly sad sort of failure, once the cultural charisma of *literature* has lost its charm. How much better to have failed at oil prospecting or the diaper-service game than at . . . practically nothing!

. . .

McLuhan, of course, was trained as a literary scholar. He begins *The Gutenberg Galaxy* with three chapters carrying out a somewhat abstruse analysis of *King Lear*. A la Freud's Oedipus, he begins his discussion of "sensory ratios" with Greek legend (the myth of Cadmus: the Phoenician who sowed dragon's teeth—and up rang armed men; and introduced the alphabet to Greece—and up sprang specialism and fragmentation of the senses). It is all quite literary, this neurology. Joyce, Matthew Arnold, Dr. Johnson, Blake, Ruskin, Rimbaud, Pope, Cicero, Dean Swift, Montaigne, Pascal, Tocqueville, Cervantes, Nashe, Marlowe, Shakespeare, Ben Jonson, St. Augustine—they twitter and gleam like celebrities arriving by limousine.

Artists, meanwhile, have precisely the same role in McLuhan's galaxy as in Freud's. They are geniuses who detect the invisible truths intuitively and express them symbolically. They are divine *naturals*, gifted but largely unconscious of the meaning of their own powers. McLuhan sees artists as mankind's "early warning system." They possess greater unity and openness of the senses and therefore respond earlier to the alteration of the "sensory ratios" brought about by changes in technology. McLuhan today is the patron saint of most "mixed-media" artists and of many young "underground" moviemakers (for such dicta as "The day of the story line, the plot, is over"). He was very much the patron saint of the huge "Art and Technology" mixed-media show staged by Robert Rauschenberg and others at the 27th Street Armory in New York in 1967. The artists, incidentally, are apparently willing to overlook McLuhan's theory of how they register their "early warning." It is a rather retrograde performance, as McLuhan sees it. The "avant garde" of each period, he says, is actually always one technology behind. Painters did not discover The Landscape until the early nineteenth century, when the intrusion of machine-age industrialism caused them to see the technology of agriculture—i.e., The Land—as an art form for the first time. They did not discover machine forms (cubism) until the electric age had begun. They did not discover mass-produced forms (pop Art: Roy Lichtenstein's comic strips, Andy Warhol's Campbell Soup cans) until the age of the conveyor belt had given way to the age of electronic circuitry. McLuhan says that this is the early warning, nevertheless—and the idea has made artists happy.

Older literary intellectuals, however, have reacted to McLuhan with the sort of *ressentiment*, to use Nietzsche's word, that indicates he has hit a very bad nerve. The old guard's first salvo came as far back as July, 1964, with a long piece by Dwight Macdonald. It contained most of the objections that have become so familiar since then: the flat conclusion that McLuhan writes nonsense (a typical reaction to Freud), that his style is repetitious and "boring," that he is anti-book and for the new barbarism (TV, electronic brains), or, obversely, that he is amoral, has no values. Once again the example of Freud comes to mind. After Freud's Clark University lectures were published, the Dean of the University of Toronto said: "An ordinary reader would gather that Freud advocates free love, removal of all restraints, and a relapse into savagery." In fact, of course, Freud savaged and very nearly exterminated traditional philosophy, the queen of the sciences throughout the nineteenth century. What was left of the lofty metaphysics of God, Freedom and Immortality, if they were products of the anus and the glans penis?

McLuhan, in turn, has been the savager of the literary intellectuals. He has made the most infuriating announcement of all: You are irrelevant.

He has hit a superannuated target. The literary-intellectual mode that still survives in the United States and England today was fashioned more than 150 years ago in Regency England with the founding of magazines such as the *Edinburgh Review*, the *Quarterly*, *Blackwood's*, the *London Magazine*, the *Examiner* and the *Westminster Review*. They became platforms for educated gentlemen-amateurs to pass judgment in a learned way on two subjects: books and politics. This seemed a natural combination at the time, because so many literati were excited by the French Revolution and its aftermath (e.g., Byron, Wordsworth, Shelley, Hazlitt, Francis Jeffrey). The *Edinburgh Review* had covers of blue and buff, the Whig colors. Remarkably, the literary-intellectual mode has remained locked for more than a century and a half in precisely that format: of books and moral protest, by gentlemen-amateurs, in the British polite-essay form.

McLuhan has come forth as a man with impeccable literary credentials of his own to tell them that the game is all over. He has accused them of "primitivism" and ignorance of the nature of the very medium they profess to value: the book; they "have never thought for one minute about the book as a medium or a structure and how it related itself to other media as a structure, politically, verbally, and so on . . . They have never studied any medium." He has challenged them to come to grips, as he has, with the objective, empirical techniques of exploration developed in the physical and social sciences in the past fifty years; if the literary intellectual continues to retreat from all this into the realm of values, says McLuhan, "he's had it."

This has been the sorest point, for the literary fraternities, as he calls them. During the past five years their response to the overwhelming sweep of scientific empiricism has been *the literary retrenchment*—an ever more determined retrenchment into the moralist stance of the Regency literati ("intellectual" protest against the tyrants and evils of the times). Literary intellectuals even sound the cry in so many words today, asserting that the task of the intellectual in a brutal age is the preservation of sacred values (e.g., Noam Chomsky's manifesto, "The Responsibility of the Intellectuals," in *The New York Review of Books*). Intellectuals thus become a kind of clergy without ordination. Macdonald, for example, has devoted the past two decades of his career to the *retrenchment*. He has been busily digging in against all forms of twentieth-century empiricism, from sociology to linguistics. He even sallied forth against so conservative and benign an intrusion of empiricism into the literary world as the third edition of Webster's Dictionary—on the quaint grounds that it had abdicated its moral responsibility to referee Good vs. Evil in grammar and diction. All the while, from inside the trench, he has been running up the flag of "values."

McLuhan's Nietzschean (*Beyond Good and Evil*) "aphorisms and entr'actes" on this subject have been particularly galling: "For many years I have observed that the moralist typically substitutes anger for perception. He hopes that many people will mistake his irritation for insight . . . The mere moralistic expression of approval or disapproval, preference or detestation, is currently being used in our world as a substitute for observation and a substitute for study. People hope that if they scream loudly enough about 'values' then others will mistake them for serious, sensitive souls who have higher and nobler perceptions than ordinary people. Otherwise, why would they be screaming? . . . Moral bitterness is a basic technique for endowing the idiot with dignity."

Even more galling to the literati, I suspect, is that there is no medium they can turn to, books or otherwise, esoteric or popular, without hearing the McLuhan dicta thundering at them, amid the most amazing fanfare.

Ecce Celebrity.

McLuhan's ascension to the status of international celebrity has been faster than Freud's, due in no small part to the hyped-up tempo of *the media* today—and the fact that the phenomenon of Freud himself had already conditioned the press to exploit the esoteric guru as a star. Freud's ascension was more gradual but quite steady. His emergence, at the Meeting for Freudian Psychology, was in 1908. By 1910 his writings prompted barrages of heated reviews in both American and European intellectual journals, sometimes running to more than a hundred pages apiece. In 1915 his two essays, "Thoughts for the Times on War and Death," were a popular hit and were widely reprinted. By 1924 he was very definitely *Freud*; both the Chicago *Tribune* and the Hearst newspapers offered him huge sums, private ocean liners, etc., to come to the United

States and make a psychoanalysis of the sensational thrill-killers, Leopold and Loeb (he declined).

Both Freud and McLuhan experienced their great publicity booms after trips to the United States, however. Freud's followed a series of lectures at Clark University in Worcester, Massachusetts, in 1909 on the twentieth anniversary of its founding. When his boat landed in New York on August 27, he was mentioned, and merely mentioned, in only one newspaper, and as, "Professor Freund of Vienna," at that. By the time he sailed for Europe on September 21, he had his first honorary doctorate (from Clark) and was well on the way to becoming a proper sensation and outrage.

McLuhan's pivotal trip to the U.S. came in May, 1965. As I say, American corporations had already begun to import him for private lectures. The publication of *Understanding Media* in 1964 had prompted that. There was first of all the sheer intriguing possibility—*what if he is right?* There was also the strange wrong-side-of-the-tracks sense of inferiority such firms seem to feel toward the academic and intellectual worlds. Any scholar with good credentials who will take a serious, vaguely optimistic, or even neutral interest in the matters, of the business world, e.g., technology, will be warmly received. McLuhan's May, 1965, trip to New York, however, was at the behest of two rather extraordinary men from San Francisco, Howard Gossage and Dr. Gerald Feigen.

Gossage is a tall, pale advertising man with one of the great heads of gray hair in the U.S.A., flowing back like John Barrymore's. Feigen is a psychiatrist who became a surgeon; he is dark and has big eyes and a gong-kicker mustache like Jerry Colonna. He is also a ventriloquist and carries around a morbid-looking dummy, named Becky. Gossage and Feigen started a firm called Generalists, Inc., acting as consultants to people who can't get what they need from specialists because what they need is the big picture. Their first client was a man who was stuck with an expensive ski lift in Squaw Valley that was idle half the year. They advised him to start a posh and rather formal restaurant nightclub up the slope that could be reached only by ski lift. So he did. It was named High Camp and immediately became all the rage. One thing that drew Gossage and Feigen to McLuhan was his belief that the age of specialists (fragmentation of intellect) was over.

Gossage and Feigen invested about $6,000 into taking McLuhan around to talk to influential people outside the academic world, chiefly in the communications and advertising industries, on both coasts. Gossage says they had no specific goal (no fragmentation; open field). They just wanted to play it "fat, dumb and happy" and see what would happen.

So in May 1965 they had a series of meetings and lunches set up for McLuhan, at Laurent, Lutèce, and other great expense-account feasteries of the East Fifties in Manhattan, with men of the caliber of Gibson McCabe. The first meetings and a cocktail party in Gossage's suite at the Lombardy were set for a Monday. McLuhan never showed up. Gossage finally got him on the telephone in Toronto that evening. Marshall, what the hell are you doing —

"I'm grading papers."

"Grading papers?"

"And waiting for the excursion rate."

"The excursion rate! What excursion rate?"

— the midweek excursion rate on the airlines. He could save about $12 round-trip if he didn't come to New York until Tuesday morning.

"But Marshall, you're not even *paying* for it!"

— but that was the English prof with the Pree-Tide tie. He had a wife and six children and thirty years behind him of shaving by on an English teacher's pay. So there he was in the bin, grading papers, scratching away —

"Listen," says Gossage, "there are so many people willing to invest money in your work now, you'll never have to grade papers again."

You mean it's going to be fun from now on?" says McLuhan.

"Everything's coming up roses," says Gossage.

By January, 1966, the McLuhan boom was on, and with a force, as I say, that McLuhan himself never dreamed of. I remember seeing McLuhan in August, 1965, in Gossage's firehouse offices in San Francisco. Gossage and Feigen were putting on their own "McLuhan Festival," as they called it. They invited small groups of influential West Coast people in for Socratic dialogues with McLuhan every morning and every afternoon for a week. One afternoon McLuhan was sitting at the round table in Gossage's own big, handsome office with half a dozen people, Gossage, Feigen, Mike Robbins of Young & Rubicam, Herbert Gold the novelist, Edward Keating, then editor and publisher of *Ramparts* magazine, and myself. Someone asked McLuhan what he thought of a large-scale communications conference that happened to be going on in San Francisco at that moment, at the Hilton Hotel, with a thousand scholars in attendance, headed by the renowned semanticist, S. I. Hayakawa.

"Well . . ." said McLuhan, pulling his chin in and turning his eyes up, "they're working from very obsolete premises, of course. Almost by definition."

By definition?

"Certainly. By the time you can get a thousand people to agree on enough principles to hold such a meeting, conditions will already have changed. The principles will be useless."

The Hayakawa conference . . . evaporated.

I thought of this remark four months later. McLuhan had a long-standing invitation to speak before the regular monthly luncheon meeting of a New York advertising group. This group always met in a banquet room off the mezzanine of the Plaza Hotel. Attendance was seldom more than a hundred. Suddenly McLuhan's appearance took on the proportions of a theater opening by a blazing new star. The luncheon had to be transferred to the Plaza's grand ballroom—and was attended by . . . a thousand.

McLuhan, as I look back on it, was magnificent that day. Rather than gratify the sudden popular clamor, he stood up at the podium and became his most cryptic, Delphic, esoteric, Oriental self. He was like a serious-faced Lewis Carroll. Nobody knew what the hell he was saying. I was seated at a table with a number of people from Time-Life, Inc. Several of them were utterly outraged by the performance. They sighed, rolled their eyeballs, then actually turned their chairs around and began conversing among themselves as he spoke. It could not have been more reminiscent of the Freud phenomenon fifty years before. *Many enemies, much honor!*

2   What's Happening to America?

Susan Sontag

1. Does it matter who is in the White House? Or is there something in our system which would force any President to act as Johnson is acting?

2. How serious is the problem of inflation? The problem of poverty?

3. What is the meaning of the split between the Administration and the American intellectuals?

4. Is white America committed to granting equality to the American Negro?

5. Where do you think our foreign policies are likely to lead us?

6. What, in general, do you think is likely to happen in America?

7. Do you think any promise is to be found in the activities of young people today?

Everything that one feels about this country is, or ought to be, conditioned by the awareness of American *power*: of America as the arch-imperium of the planet, holding man's biological as well as his historical future in its King Kong paws. Today's America, with Ronald Reagan the new daddy of California and John Wayne chawing spareribs in the White House, is pretty much the same Yahooland at Mencken was describing. The main difference is that what's happening in America matters so much more in the late sixties than in the twenties. Then, if one had tough innards, one might jeer, sometimes affectionately, at American barbarism and find American innocence somewhat endearing. Both the barbarism and the innocence are lethal, outsized today.

First of all, then, American power is indecent in its scale. But also, the quality of American life is an insult to the possibilities of human growth; and the pollution of American space, with gadgetry and cars and TV and box architecture, brutalizes the senses, making grey neurotics of most of us, and perverse spiritual athletes and strident self-transcenders of the best of us.

Gertrude Stein said that America is the oldest country in the world. Certainly, it's the most conservative. It has the most to lose by change (60 per cent of the world's wealth owned by a country containing 7 per cent of the world's population). Americans know their backs are against the wall, that "they" want to take it away from "us." And I must say America deserves to have it taken away.

Three facts about this country.

America was founded on a genocide, on the unquestioned assumption of the right of white Europeans to exterminate a resident, technologically backward, colored population in order to take over the continent.

America had not only the most brutal system of slavery in modern times, but a

From Susan Sontag, "What's Happening to America?". First appeared in *Partisan Review*, Vol. XXXIV, No. 1, Winter 1967, 51–58.

juridically unique system (compared with other slaveries, say in Latin America and the British colonies) which did not, in a single respect, recognize slaves as persons.

As a country (as distinct from a colony), America was created mainly by the surplus poor of Europe, reinforced by a small group who were just *Europamüde*, tired of Europe (a literary catchword of the eighteen forties) Yet even the poorest knew both a "culture," largely invented by his social betters and administered from above, and a "nature" that had been pacified for centuries. These people arrived in a country where the indigenous culture was simply the enemy and was in process of being ruthlessly annihilated, and where nature, too, was the enemy, a pristine force, unmodified by civilization, that is, by human wants, which had to be defeated. After America was "won," it was filled up by new generations of the poor, and built up according to the tawdry fantasy of the good life that culturally deprived, uprooted people might have at the beginning of the industrial era. And the country looks it.

Foreigners extol the American "energy," attributing to it both our unparalleled economic prosperity and the splendid vivacity of our arts and entertainments. But surely this is energy bad at its source and for which we pay too high a price, a hypernatural and humanly disproportionate dynamism that flays everyone's nerves raw. Basically it is the energy of violence, of free-floating resentment and anxiety unleashed by chronic cultural dislocations which must be, for the most part, ferociously sublimated. This energy has mainly been sublimated into crude materialism and acquisitiveness. Into hectic philanthropy. Into benighted moral crusades, the most spectacular of which was Prohibition. Into an awesome talent for uglifying countryside and cities. Into the loquacity and torment of a minority of gadflies: artists, prophets, muckrakers, cranks and nuts. And into self-punishing neuroses. But the naked violence keeps breaking through, throwing everything into question.

Needless to say, America is not the only violent, ugly and unhappy country on this earth. Again, it is a matter of scale. Only three million Indians lived here when the white man arrived, rifle in hand, for his fresh start. Today, American hegemony menaces the lives not of three but of countless millions who, like the Indians, have never even *heard* of "The United States of America," much less of its mythical empire, "the free world." American policy is still powered by the fantasy of Manifest Destiny, though the limits were once set by the borders of the continent, while today America's destiny embraces the entire world. There are still more hordes of redskins to be mowed down before virtue triumphs; as the classic western movies explain, the only good Red is a dead Red. This may sound like an exaggeration to those who live in the special and more finely modulated atmosphere of New York and its environs. Cross the Hudson. You find out that not just *some* Americans, but virtually all Americans feel that way.

Of course, these people don't know what they're saying, literally. But that's no excuse. That, in fact, is what makes it all possible. The unquenchable American moralism and the American faith in violence are not just twin symptoms of some character neurosis taking the form of a protracted adolescence, which presages an eventual maturity. They constitute a full grown, firmly-installed national psychosis, founded, as are all psychoses, on the efficacious denial of reality. So far it's worked. Except for portions of the South a hundred years ago, America has never known war. A taxi driver said to me on the day that could have been Armageddon, when America and Russia were on collision course off the shores of Cuba: "Me, I'm not worried. I served in the last one, and now I'm over draft age. They can't get me again. But I'm all for letting 'em have it right now. What are we waiting for? Let's get it over with." Since wars always happen Over There, and we always win, why not drop the bomb? If all it takes is pushing a button, even better. For America is that curious hybrid—an apocalyptic country and a valetudinarian country. The average citizen may harbor the fantasies of John Wayne, but he as often has the temperament of Jane Austen's Mr. Woodhouse.

To answer, briefly, some of *Partisan Review's* questions:

1. I do *not* think that Johnson is forced by "our system" to act as he is acting. For instance, in Vietnam, where each evening he personally chooses the bombing targets for the next day's missions. But I think there is something awfully wrong with a *de facto* system which allows the President virtually unlimited discretion in pursuing an immoral and imprudent foreign policy, so that the strenuous opposition of, say, the Chairman of the Senate Foreign Relations Committee counts for—exactly nothing. The *de jure* system vests the power to make war in the Congress—with the exception, apparently, of imperialist ventures and genocidal expeditions. These are best left undeclared.

However, I don't mean to suggest that Johnson's foreign policy is the whim of a clique which has seized control, escalated the power of the Chief Executive, castrated the Congress and manipulated public opinion. Johnson is, alas, all too representative. As Kennedy was not. If there is a conspiracy, it is (or was) that of the more enlightened national leaders hitherto largely selected by the eastern seaboard plutocracy. They engineered the precarious acquiescence to liberal goals that has prevailed in this country for over a generation—a superficial consensus made possible by the strongly apolitical character of a decentralized electorate mainly preoccupied with local issues. If the Bill of Rights were put to a national referendum as a new piece of legislation, it would meet the same fate as New York City's Civilian Review Board. Most of the people in this country believe what Goldwater believes, and always have. But most of them don't know it. Let's hope they don't find out.

4. I do not think white America is committed to granting equality to the American Negro. So committed are only a minority of generous and mostly educated, affluent white Americans, few of whom have had any prolonged social contact with Negroes. This is a passionately racist country; it will continue to be so in the forseeable future.

5. I think that this administration's foreign policies are likely to lead to more wars and to wider wars. Our main hope, and the chief restraint on American bellicosity and paranoia, lies in the fatigue and depoliticization of Western Europe, the lively fear of America and of another world war in Russia and the Eastern European countries, and the corruption and unreliability of our client states in the third world. It's hard to lead a holy war without allies. But America is just crazy enough to try to do it.

6. The meaning of the split between the Administration and the intellectuals? Simply that our leaders are genuine Yahoos, with all the exhibitionist traits of their kind, and that liberal intellectuals (whose deepest loyalties are to an international fraternity of the reasonable) are not *that* blind. At this point, moreover, they have nothing to lose by

proclaiming their discontent and frustration. But it's well to remember that liberal intellectuals, like Jews, tend to have a classical theory of politics, in which the state has a monopoly of power; hoping that those in positions of authority may prove to be enlightened men, wielding power justly, they are natural, if cautious, allies of the "establishment." As the Russian Jews knew they had at least a chance with the Czar's officials but none at all with marauding Cossacks and drunken peasants (Milton Himmelfarb has pointed this out), liberal intellectuals more naturally expect to influence the "decisions" of administrators than they do the volatile "feelings" of masses. Only when it becomes clear that, in fact, the government itself is being staffed by Cossacks and peasants, can a rupture like the present one take place. When (and if) the man in the White House who paws people and scratches his balls in public is replaced by the man who dislikes being touched and finds Yevtushenko "an interesting fellow," American intellectuals won't be so disheartened. The vast majority of them are not revolutionaries, wouldn't know how to be if they tried. Mostly a salaried professoriat, they're as much at home in the system when it functions a little better than it does right now as anyone else.

A somewhat longer comment on the last question.

Yes, I do find much promise in the activities of young people. About the only promise one can find anywhere in this country today is in the way some young people are carrying on, making a fuss. I include both their renewed interest in politics (as protest and as community action, rather than as theory) and the way they dance, dress, wear their hair, riot, make love. I also include the homage they pay to Oriental thought and rituals. And I include, not least of all, their interest in taking drugs—despite the unspeakable vulgarization of this project by Leary and others.

A year ago Leslie Fiedler, in a remarkably wrongheaded and interesting essay (published in *PR* and titled "The New Mutants") called attention to the fact that the new style of young people indicated a deliberate blurring of sexual differences, signaling the creation of a new breed of youthful androgens. The longhaired pop groups with their mass teen-age following and the tiny elite of turned-on kids from Berkeley to the East Village were both lumped together as representatives of the "post-humanist" era now upon us, in which we witness a "radical metamorphosis of the western male," a "revolt against masculinity," even "a rejection of conventional male potency." For Fiedler, this new turn in personal mores, diagnosed as illustrating a "programmatic espousal of an anti-puritanical mode of existence," is some thing to deplore. (Though sometimes, in his characteristic have-it-both-ways manner, Fiedler seemed to be vicariously relishing this development, *mainly* he appeared to be lamenting it.) But why, he never made explicit. I think it is because he is sure such a mode of existence undercuts radical politics, and its moral visions, altogether. Being radical in the older sense (some version of Marxism or socialism or anarchism) meant to be attached still to traditional "puritan" values of work, sobriety, achievement and family–founding. Fiedler suggests, as have Philip Rahv and Irving Howe and Malcolm Muggeridge among others, that the new style of youth must be, at bottom, apolitical, and their revolutionary spirit a species of infantilism. The fact that the same kid joins SNCC or boards a Polaris submarine or agrees with Conor Cruise O'Brien *and* smokes pot and is bisexual and adores the

Supremes, is seen as a contradiction, a kind of ethical fraud or intellectual weak-mindedness.

I don't believe this to be so. The depolarizing of the sexes, to mention the element that Fiedler observes with such fascination, is the natural, and desirable, next stage of the sexual revolution (its dissolution, perhaps) which has moved beyond the idea of sex as a damaged but discrete zone of human activity, beyond the discovery that "society" represses the free expression of sexuality (by fomenting guilt), to the discovery that the way we live and the ordinarily available options of character repress almost entirely the deep experience of pleasure, and the possibility of self-knowledge. "Sexual freedom" is a shallow, outmoded slogan. What, who is being liberated? For older people, the sexual revolution is an idea that remains meaningful. One can be for it or against it; if for it, the idea remains confined within the norm of Freudianism and its derivatives. But Freud *was* a Puritan, or "a fink," as one of Fiedler's students distressingly blurted out. So was Marx. It is right that young people see beyond Freud and Marx. Let the professors be the caretakers of this indeed precious legacy, and discharge all the obligations of piety. No need for dismay if the kids don't continue to pay the old dissenter-gods obeisance.

It seems to me obtuse, though understandable, to patronize the new kind of radicalism, which is post Freudian and post-Marxian. For this radicalism is as much an experience as an idea. Without the personal experience, if one is looking in from the outside, it does look messy and almost pointless. It's easy to be put off by the youngsters throwing themselves around with their eyes closed to the near-deafening music of the discothèques (unless you're dancing, too), by the longhaired marchers carrying flowers and temple bells as often as "Get Out of Vietnam" placards, by the inarticulateness of a Mario Savio. One is also aware of the high casualty rate among this gifted, visionary minority among the young, the tremendous cost in personal suffering and in mental strain. The fakers, the slobs and the merely flipped-out are plentiful among them. But the complex desires of the best of them: to engage and to "drop out"; to be beautiful to look at and touch as well as to be good; to be loving and quiet as well as militant and effective—these desires make sense in our present situation. To sympathize, of course, you have to be convinced that things in America really are as desperately bad as I have indicated. This is hard to see; the desperateness of things is obscured by the comforts and liberties that America does offer. Most people, understandably, don't really believe things are that bad. That's why, for them, the antics of this youth can be no more than a startling item in the passing parade of cultural fashions, to be appraised with a friendly, but essentially weary and knowing look. The sorrowful look that says: I was a radical, too, when I was young. When are these kids going to grow up and realize what we had to realize, that things never are going to be really different, except maybe worse?

From my own experience and observation, I can testify that there is a profound concordance between the sexual revolution, redefined, and the political revolution, redefined. That being a socialist and taking certain drugs (in a fully serious spirit: as a technique for exploring one's consciousness, not as an anodyne or a crutch), are not incompatible, that there is no incompatibility between the exploration of inner space and the rectification of social space. What some of the kids understand is that it's the whole character-structure of modern American man, and his imitators, that needs rehauling. (Old folks like Paul Goodman and Edgar Z. Friedenberg have, of course, been suggesting this for a long time.) That rehauling includes Western "masculinity," too. They believe that some socialist remodeling of institutions and the ascendance, through electoral means or otherwise, of better leaders won't really change any thing. And they are right.

Neither do I dare deride the turn toward the East (or more generally, to the wisdoms of the nonwhite world) on the part of a tiny group of young people—however uninformed and jejune the adherence usually is. (But then, nothing could be more ignorant than Fiedler's insinuation that Oriental modes of thought are "feminine" and "passive," which is the reason the demasculinized kids are drawn to them.) Why shouldn't they look for wisdom elsewhere? If America *is* the culmination of Western white civilization, as everyone from the Left to the Right declares, then there must be something terribly wrong with Western white civilization. This is a painful truth; few of us want to go that far. It's easier, much easier, to accuse the kids, to reproach them for being "non-participants in the past" and "drop-outs from history." But it isn't real history Fiedler is referring to with such solicitude. It's just *our* history, which he claims is identical with "the tradition of the human," the tradition of "reason" itself. Of course, it's hard to assess life on this planet from a genuinely world-historical perspective; the effort induces vertigo and seems like an invitation to suicide. But from a world-historical perspective, that local history which some young people are repudiating (with their fondness for dirty words, their peyote, their macrobiotic rice, their Dadaist art, etc.) looks a good deal less pleasing and less self-evidently worthy of perpetuation. The truth is that Mozart, Pascal, Boolean algebra, Shakespeare, parliamentary government, baroque churches, Newton, the emancipation of women, Kant, Marx, Balanchine ballets, *et al.*, don't redeem what this particular civilization has wrought upon the world. The white race *is* the cancer of human history; it is the white race and it alone—its ideologies and inventions—which eradicates autonomous civilizations wherever it spreads, which has upset the ecological balance of the planet, which now threatens the very existence of life itself. What the Mongol hordes threaten is far less frightening than the damage that Western "Faustian" man, with his idealism, his magnificent art, his sense of intellectual adventure, his world-devouring energies for conquest, has already done, and further threatens to do.

This is what some of the kids sense, though few of them could put it in words. Again, I believe them to be right. I'm not arguing that they're going to prevail, or even that they're likely to change much of anything in this country. But a few of them may save their own souls. America is a fine country for inflaming people, from Emerson and Thoreau to Mailer and Burroughs and Leo Szilard and John Cage and Judith and Julian Beck, with the project of trying to save their own souls. Salvation becomes almost a mundane, inevitable goal when things are so bad, really intolerable.

One last comparison, which I hope won't seem farfetched. The Jews left the ghetto in the early nineteenth century, thus becoming a people doomed to disappear. But one of the by-products of their fateful absorption into the modern world was an incredible burst of creativity in the arts, science and secular scholarship—the relocation of a powerful but frustrated spiritual energy. These innovating artists and intellectuals were not alienated Jews, as is said so often, but people who were alienated *as* Jews.

I'm scarcely more hopeful for America than I am for the Jews. This is a doomed country, it seems to me; I only pray that, when America founders, it doesn't drag the rest of the planet down, too. But one should notice that, during its long elephantine agony, America is also producing its subtlest minority generation of the decent and sensitive, young people who are alienated *as* Americans. They are not drawn to the stale truths of their sad elders (though these are truths). More of their elders should be listening to them.

3 Black Is Good

Stokely Carmichael

P EOPLE said there was no need to come to Pittsburgh because the black people are apathetic. They're lying. You're not apathetic, and you're showing it tonight.

Some people may not like the truth. But the truth is the salvation of black people today. You can't run from it. You've got to embrace it. And I'm here to tell the truth about black people and this country today.

This country has always told *lies* about us. White people believe those lies, and what's bad is that some black people believe those lies too. (Applause)

The first lie this country has told about black people is that we are *lazy*. And some of us go around saying, "yeh, yeh, we lazy." It is our sweat that built this country! (cheers from the audience as Carmichael's voice rises suddenly to a shout) They can't call us lazy. Our mothers feed us and then go feed white babies. (more cheers) You let them tell you you're lazy, and you believe it. And once you believe it you won't ever move to rid yourself of your laziness. We are the ditch diggers in this country. We are the porters. We are the hardest working people. And we are the lowest paid, and that's the truth. (more cheers) We should begin to rid ourselves of that junk. We ain't hardly lazy.

The first thing to rid your minds of—those of you who read the *New York Times* and *Time* magazine and that junk—is "the trouble with them Snick people is that they separatin' us." (a pause, then slowly) You *been* separated. (cheers) We don't have the power to separate you. ("Ain't that the truth") You been separated, and the people who separated you are white. (cheers)

The next thing, some Negroes say, "The trouble is all black. Anything all black is bad." You ought to understand that very carefully. You're talking about yourself because you're black from the bottom of your feet to the nappy hair on the top of your head. You ought not to be saying anything all black is bad. You ought to say anything black is good, it's good! (cheers)

Anybody who'll tell you he's a successful *Neeeeegro* (laughter), the first thing he says is that he moved out of the ghetto from *those* people. (applause) Now that's their success that they've moved away from black people because we hate each other so much that all our lives we try to be white. ("That's right, that's right!")

We hate it so much we try to look white. Because the white people say that in order to be beautiful one has to have thin lips, thin nose and stringy hair. (laughter-cheers) That's right, that's what they say. Black people all their lives try to do that.

They get up their matting-over cream. (cheers-foot stamping)

Not even satisfied with that they wear wigs to cover up their hair. (cheers, laughter)

From Stokely Carmichael, "Black is Good", in David P. Demarest and Lois S. Lamdin (eds.), *The Ghetto Reader* (New York: Random House, 1970), 354–60.

You see our children on buses holding their noses so they won't come open. (laughter-cheers)

My mother didn't want me to drink coffee because it would make me black. You know your mothers said the same thing to you. (more laughter and cheers)

I want you to understand how this country has worked on our minds. On every black college campus in this country . . . if you going to find the homecoming queen, she's light, bright and damned near white. (long applause)

Every magazine you open up, you talk about a beautiful chick, she look white. You got to look again to see, is she one of ours? You got to ask yourself, is she or ain't she? Dig it? (applause)

What we have to recognize is that white and black is different. White people have thin lips, thin noses and stringy hair. We are black. We have broad noses, thick lips, and nappy hair. We are black, and we are beautiful, (cheers) and we are beautiful! (more cheers)

You've got to understand how hard it is to love black. All the books they gave us—what's the name? Dick and Jane—and their little dog, Spot. He was even white. (applause) And the only time you saw us was poor little Sambo eatin' watermelon. You've got to understand the job of educating black people lies with us, not white people. They can't educate us. (applause) We have to begin to educate ourselves, because hating black in this country goes very deep. (applause)

Remember how we used to go to the movies? We all did it. We see Tarzan. Dig it? Here's Tarzan beating up the blacks, and we say, "Git 'em Tarzan—kill 'em Tarzan—go git 'em Tarzan." We go to the movies, and here's this white dumb cracker from England, don't know nuttin' about the jungle, come over and know it better than us and we've been living there all our lives. (laughter and cheers) He couldn't even talk. He say "Aghghghghgh!" (Carmichael beats his chest as the audience roars.) Can you dig that? We would be yelling for him to beat up our black ancestors.

Tarzan is on TV today. I tell all my black children "When y'all see him, y'all yell for the black chiefs to come together and beat that white man to death, beat him up." (more cheers) We say to those black chiefs, beat him up and send him back to Europe where he belong, (applause) and let him take his plants with him because he's exploiting our people in Africa to this day.

The trouble is that the history of the world has been distorted. White people have given it to us and like fools we've swallowed it, hook, line and sinker. Dig it.

We haven't begun to accept in our minds what real history is. White people tell us that we uncivilized, we illiterate, we savages, and they had to come and civilize us. Can you dig that? Can you dig an Eastland comin' to civilize you? Dig it. Do you understand what all that nonsense was about the missionaries? They came to Africa and we were half naked. They said, "cover up your body—you get me excited." (cheers and laughter)

They came to teach about Jesus. We were in Africa. We had the land, and they had the Bible. They left. They had the land, and we still got the Bible. (cheers) Every time a white man says he's helping you he's helping himself. They took the land, they took our sweat, and if we give them a chance they're going to take our bodies. ("That's right, that's right") We (slowly) have to do for ourselves. The trouble with the white world is that nothing is discovered until they set foot on it. Now dig. If they tell you Columbus discovered America in 1492, you'd say, yes, he did. Look how silly you are. When they came here there was already people here, but they don't recognize anybody who's not white.

Columbus was nothing but a dumb cracker. He died thinking he was in India. That's how dumb he was. (laughter and applause) We were there before they got there. It was ours before they got there, and that's what you got to understand, and until you understand, we goin' to be where we are, because we goin' to let the white man define us and how we act. We cannot do that. This is how free people act. (Carmichael's voice sinks to a whisper.) We must define *ourselves*.

Now when we're ready to rewrite the history of this nation, we'll say this nation is a nation of thieves. ("That's right") It stole the United States from the Indians, and wasn't satisfied, killed practically every last one of 'em. But not only were those crackers not satisfied with stealing the Indians and the land, they turned around and stole us from Africa. They started it by calling this the land of the free and the home of the brave, and that's the history we're supposed to follow. And you here talkin' about "My country 'tis of thee."

What we have to begin to do in this country is to develop a concept of *peoplehood*. We don't have a concept of peoplehood. That's because we beat each other, we cut each other, we fight each other, we beat up each other. This country has destroyed that concept in us. We see ourselves as a bunch of individuals plundering on each other, committing violence on each other. Don't nobody talk about violence in our communities. Dig it?

You cut each other, man—the cracker cops stand there and watch you cut each other, and won't even call the ambulance. Dig it? ("That's right") But throw one rock through some dumpy store window, and they bring the whole national guard. And the reason they do that is because property rights is more important than human rights.

Negro leaders talk about non-violence. We need non-violence in the black community first. That's where we need it. We need to love and respect and not beat up each other in the ghetto first.

And then they have their Negro leaders. The only power Negro leaders have in this country is to condemn black people. Because after every rebellion I see some Negro leader get up and say "Oh, oh, black people shouldn't do that, they vagabonds, they hoodlums." (applause) They don't represent you. Uh-uh. Uh-uh. You see them get up and condemn us and call us all sorts of names, as if we don't get it enough from white folks. And you know why—'cause they don't have guts to condemn white folks.

They don't have the guts to tell it like it really is, because that's where it's at. Do they ever tell the people who are charging us high prices? Do they ever call them down and condemn them? Do they ever condemn the slumlords? I will never condemn black people—(applause) never, never, never.

You will never hear Johnson condemn white people. You will never hear any white man get up and condemn white people. But they take our leaders and make them condemn us.

We have to be crystal clear in our minds when we move for our liberation this time around, because this man is not playing with us. And we got to be prepared, 'cause if you think Johnson is talking about crime in the street, he's talking about stopping us. I don't care how nice he makes it sound. When he talks about riot equipment, you know who he talkin' about. And if we don't make up our minds, we going to be like the Jewish people in Germany in the nineteen thirties. (applause)

They only let us respect people who died for their liberation. Have you dug that? They hold up George Washington Carver. Well they need him, because without him white folks would be eating only jelly sandwiches. (applause—cheers) They hold up Booker T. Washington for us.

That means we have to get our own heroes for our children. We can't let them give us heroes any more. Little kid up there talking about George Washington never cut down a cherry tree. You know that cracker sold a black woman for a barrel of molasses? (cheers) What you talkin' about George Washington? You know he denied our existence. How can we call him our hero? He had slaves and sold one of us for a barrel of molasses. And he's their founding father. And you want to know why this country is so full of racism.

And then they hold up Abraham Lincoln. Our hero, Abraham Lincoln. He freed us. You dig him? He freed us, and he didn't free us until 1863, when the war started in 1861. Because the South was winning—that's why he freed us. The slaves were doing labor and let the Southerners free to kill people in the North, and when Lincoln understood it, that's when he freed the slaves. And not only that—when he freed us, he wouldn't let us fight. We weren't fit to fight for our own freedom. Do you know about a great black man named Frederick Douglass? Did you know that it was Frederick Douglass went and straightened that cracker out and told him he better let us fight for our own liberation? Lincoln was getting ready to ship you back to Africa, lock, stock and barrel. He was a leading exponent of the colonization theory. Abraham Lincoln—and he freed us. You dig that?

We will pick our heroes. They will be the Denmark Veseys. He burnt up all the white folks' crops during slavery time. He started a slave revolt and burnt the crops to the ground and killed every white man in his way 'cause they were keeping him in slavery and it's honorable to fight for your liberation. Dig it?

We will raise up to W. E. B. DuBois, who understood what was happening in this country a long time ago. We will raise up to Marcus Garvey, for teaching us pride in our race. We will hold close to the Richard Wrights, and we will make Malcolm X our leader. (applause)

We must give our youth the spirit to fight. This country started off when it said "Give me liberty or give me death." You stand up and say, "Give me my second-class citizenship, or my first-class citizenship whenever you feel like it."

Give me liberty or give me death. It is honorable to say that, and you don't even recognize what they do to you. They take you and train you to kill in Vietnam. They are killing everybody who's in their way, and you are doing their killing for 'em.

Here you killin' the Vietnamese people, who ain't never called you nigger—ain't never made you live with rats—ain't never did nothin' to you! (applause) Dig it? Here's a little yellow man, fighting to save his own land, his own tungsten, his own tin, his own oil. And you over there shooting him because some cracker says shoot. Ain't no other reason you're shooting. What's that man ever done to you. ("Nothing"!)

Cracker get up and say, (mimicking a white voice) we're fighting in Vietnam for democracy and freedom and equality. Here you don't even know what democracy, freedom and equality is. You don't even know what it is and you fighting to give it to somebody. What's democracy? The only equality is in death on the battlefield, and you up there talking about fighting to preserve your country.

A people without its history is like a tree without roots. Have you dug that? We have no history. We don't even concern ourselves about our people. When I see students from Africa, I ask them what they're studying. One says, "I'm studying medicine because my country needs doctors." Another says, "I'm studying agriculture because my country needs agricultural technicians." I see some dumb American Negro, and I ask "Hey, baby, what you takin"? He say, "I'm goin' to be a doctor, man, because that's where the money's at." (applause) They're worried about themselves and their rotten ten-thousand-dollar-a-year job, and we can starve in the ghetto for all they care—they made it. We can't afford to have our children go to college and not come back to the ghetto and help develop it.

He ought to be happy to come back to the ghetto and give us his skills, because the reason he's in college is because of us. That's right, they use him. Whenever we get mad in the ghetto and say "you ain't giving us nothing," they pull this Tom out and say, "look, look, he made it. If you work hard you can make it." Yeah, yeah! That's right. If you work hard you can become senator from Massachusetts. (cheers) Dig it? Dig it?

The white people have been running the world. They have been playing their God. And the reason they have been running the world is because we let them. The playing time is over. That's right. Our ancestors were run by white folks. They ran our grandparents. They ran our parents. This generation is out of breath! (cheers)

4 Indians Today, the Real and the Unreal

Vine Deloria, Jr.

INDIANS are like the weather. Everyone knows all about the weather, but none can change it. When storms are predicted, the sun shines. When picnic weather is announced, the rain begins. Likewise, if you count on the unpredictability of Indian people, you will never be sorry.

One of the finest things about being an Indian is that people are always interested in you and your "plight." Other groups have difficulties, predicaments, quandaries, problems, or troubles. Traditionally we Indians have had a "plight."

Our foremost plight is our transparency. People can tell just by looking at us what we want, what should be done to help us, how we feel, and what a "real" Indian is really like. Indian life, as it relates to the real world, is a continuous attempt not to disappoint people who know us. Unfulfilled expectations cause grief and we have already had our share.

Because people can see right through us, it becomes impossible to tell truth from fiction or fact from mythology. Experts paint us as they would like us to be. Often we paint ourselves as we wish we were or as we might have been.

The more we try to be ourselves the more we are forced to defend what we have never been. The American public feels most comfortable with the mythical Indians of stereotype-land who were always THERE. These Indians are fierce, they wear feathers and grunt. Most of us don't fit this idealized figure since we grunt only when overeating, which is seldom.

To be an Indian in modern American society is in a very real sense to be unreal and ahistorical. In this book we will discuss the other side—the unrealities that face *us* as Indian people. It is this unreal feeling that has been welling up inside us and threatens to make this decade the most decisive in history for Indian people. In so many ways, Indian people are re-examining themselves in an effort to redefine a new social structure for their people. Tribes are reordering their priorities to account for the obvious discrepancies between their goals and the goals whites have defined for them.

Indian reactions are sudden and surprising. One day at a conference we were singing "My Country 'Tis of Thee" and we came across the part that goes:

> *Land where our fathers died*
> *Land of the Pilgrims' pride . . .*

Some of us broke out laughing when we realized that our fathers undoubtedly died trying to keep those Pilgrims from stealing our land. In fact, many of our fathers died because the Pilgrims killed them as witches. We didn't feel much kinship with those Pilgrims, regardless of who they did in.

We often hear "give it back to the Indians" when a gadget fails to work. It's a terrible thing for a people to realize that society has set aside all non-working gadgets for their exclusive use.

During my three years as Executive Director of the National Congress of American Indians it was a rare day when some white didn't visit my office and proudly proclaim that he or she was of Indian descent.

Cherokee was the most popular tribe of their choice and many people placed the Cherokees anywhere from Maine to Washington State. Mohawk, Sioux, and Chippewa were next in popularity. Occasionally I would be told about some mythical tribe from lower Pennsylvania, Virginia, or Massachusetts which had spawned the white standing before me.

At times I became quite defensive about being a Sioux when these white people had a pedigree that was so much more respectable than mine. But eventually I came to understand their need to identify as partially Indian and did not resent them. I would confirm their wildest stories about their Indian ancestry and would add a few tales of my own hoping that they would be able to accept themselves someday and leave us alone.

Whites claiming Indian blood generally tend to reinforce mythical beliefs about Indians. All but one person I met who claimed Indian blood claimed it on their grandmother's side. I once did a projection backward and discovered that evidently most tribes were entirely female for the first three hundred years of white occupation. No one, it seemed, wanted to claim a male Indian as a forebear.

It doesn't take much insight into racial attitudes to understand the real meaning of the Indian-grandmother complex that plagues certain whites. A male ancestor has too much of the aura of the savage warrior, the unknown primitive, the instinctive animal, to make him a respectable member of the family tree. But a young Indian princess? Ah, there was royalty for the taking. Somehow the white was linked with a noble house of gentility and culture if his grandmother was an Indian princess who ran away with an intrepid pioneer. And royalty has always been an unconscious but all-consuming goal of the European immigrant.

The early colonists, accustomed to life under benevolent despots, projected their understanding of the European political structure onto the Indian tribe in trying to explain its political and social structure. European royal houses were closed to ex-convicts and indentured servants, so the colonists made all Indian maidens princesses, then proceeded to climb a social ladder of their own creation. Within the next generation, if the trend continues, a large portion of the American population will eventually be related to Powhattan.

While a real Indian grandmother is probably the nicest thing that could happen to a child, why is a remote Indian princess grandmother so necessary for many whites? Is it because they are afraid of being classed as foreigners? Do they need some blood tie with the frontier and its dangers in order to experience what it means to be an American? Or is it an attempt to avoid facing the guilt they bear for the treatment of the Indian?

The phenomenon seems to be universal. Only among the Jewish community, which has a long tribal-religious tradition of its own, does the mysterious Indian grandmother, the primeval princess, fail to dominate the family tree. Otherwise, there's not much to be gained by claiming Indian blood or publicly identifying as an Indian. The white believes that there is a great danger the lazy Indian will eventually corrupt God's hard-working people. He is still suspicious that the Indian way of life is dreadfully wrong. There is, in fact, something *un-American* about Indians for most whites.

I ran across a classic statement of this attitude one day in a history book which was published shortly after the turn of the century. Often have I wondered how many Senators, Congressmen, and clergymen of the day accepted the attitudes of that book as a basic fact of life in America. In no uncertain terms did the book praise God that the Indian had not yet been able to corrupt North America as he had South America:

It was perhaps fortunate for the future of America that the Indians of the North rejected civilization. Had they accepted it the whites and Indians might have intermarried to some extent as they did in Mexico. That would have given us a population made up in a measure of shiftless half-breeds.

I never dared to show this passage to my white friends who had claimed Indian blood, but I often wondered why they were so energetic if they did have some of the bad seed in them.

Those whites who dare not claim Indian blood have an asset of their own. They *understand* Indians.

Understanding Indians is not an esoteric art. All it takes is a trip through Arizona or New Mexico, watching a documentary on TV, having known *one* in the service, or having read a popular book on *them*.

There appears to be some secret osmosis about Indian people by which they can magically and instantaneously communicate complete knowledge about themselves to these interested whites. Rarely is physical contact required. Anyone and everyone who knows an Indian or who is *interested*, immediately and thoroughly understands them.

You can verify this great truth at your next party. Mention Indians and you will find a person who saw some in a gas station in Utah, or who attended the Gallup ceremonial celebration, or whose Uncle Jim hired one to cut logs in Oregon, or whose church had a missionary come to speak last Sunday on the plight of Indians and the mission of the church.

There is no subject on earth so easily understood as that of the American Indian. Each summer, work camps disgorge teenagers on various reservations. Within one month's time the youngsters acquire a knowledge of Indians that would astound a college professor.

Easy knowledge about Indians is a historical tradition. After Columbus "discovered" America he brought back news of a great new world which he assumed to be India and, therefore, filled with Indians. Almost at once European folklore devised a complete explanation of the new land and its inhabitants which featured the Fountain of Youth, the Seven Cities of Gold, and other exotic attractions. The absence of elephants apparently did not tip off the explorers that they weren't in India. By the time they realized their mistake, instant knowledge of Indians was a cherished tradition.

Missionaries, after learning some of the religious myths of tribes they encountered, solemnly declared that the inhabitants of the new continent were the Ten Lost Tribes of Israel. Indians thus received a religious-historical identity far greater than they wanted or deserved. But it was an impossible identity. Their failure to measure up to Old Testament standards doomed them to a fall from grace and they were soon relegated to the status of a picturesque species of wildlife.

. . .

One of the foremost differences separating white and Indian was simply one of origin. Whites derived predominantly from western Europe. The earliest settlers on the Atlantic seaboard came from England and the low countries. For the most part they shared the common experiences of their peoples and dwelt within the world view which had dominated western Europe for over a millennium.

Conversely Indians had always been in the western hemisphere. Life on this continent and views concerning it were not shaped in a post-Roman atmosphere. The entire outlook of the people was one of simplicity and mystery, not scientific or abstract. The western hemisphere produced wisdom, western Europe produced knowledge.

Perhaps this distinction seems too simple to mention. It is not. Many is the time I have sat in Congressional hearings and heard the chairman of the committee crow about "our" great Anglo-Saxon heritage of law and order. Looking about the hearing room I saw row after row of full-blood Indians with blank expressions on their faces. As far as they were concerned, Sir Walter Raleigh was a brand of pipe tobacco that you got at the trading post.

When we talk about European background, we are talking about feudalism, kings, queens, their divine right to rule their subjects, the Reformation, Christianity, the Magna Charta and all of the events that went to make up European history.

American Indians do not share that heritage. They do not look wistfully back across the seas to the old country. The Apache were not at Runymede to make King John sign the Magna Charta. The Cherokee did not create English common law. The Pima had no experience with the rise of capitalism and industrialism. The Blackfeet had no monasteries. No tribe has an emotional, historical, or political relationship to events of another continent and age.

Indians have had their own political history which has shaped the outlook of the tribes. There were great confederacies throughout the country before the time of the white invader. The eastern Iroquois formed a strong league because as single tribes they had been weak and powerless against larger tribes. The Deep South was controlled by three confederacies: the Creeks with their town system, the Natchez, and the Powhattan confederation which extended into tidelands Virginia. The Pequots and their cousins the Mohicans controlled the area of Connecticut, Massachusetts, Rhode Island, and Long Island.

True democracy was more prevalent among Indian tribes in pre-Columbian days than it has been since. Despotic power was abhorred by tribes that were loose combinations of hunting parties rather than political entities.

Conforming their absolute freedom to fit rigid European political forms has been very difficult for most tribes, but on the whole they have managed extremely well.

Under the Indian Reorganization Act Indian people have generally created a modern version of the old tribal political structure and yet have been able to develop comprehensive reservation programs which compare favorably with governmental structures anywhere.

. . .

Three books, to my way of thinking, give a good idea of the intangible sense of reality that pervades the Indian people. *When the Legends Die* by Hal Borland gives a good picture of Indian youth. *Little Big Man* by Thomas Berger gives a good idea of Indian attitudes toward life. *Stay Away, Joe*, by Dan Cushman, the favorite of Indian people, gives a humorous but accurate idea of the problems caused by the intersection of two ways of life. Anyone who can read, appreciate, and understand the spiritual forces brought out in these books will have a good idea of what Indians are all about.

Other books may be nice, accurate, and historical but they are not really about Indians. In general, they twist Indian reality into a picture which is hard to understand and consequently greatly in error.

Statistical information on Indians can easily be found in other books. What is important, for understanding the present state of Indian Affairs, is to know how tribes are organized today, how they work together, and what they anticipate for the future. And there is no easy way to broach the subject. So let us begin.

In 1934 the Indian Reorganization Act was passed. Under the provisions of this act reservation people were enabled to organize for purposes of self-government. Nearly three-quarters of the reservations organized. These reservations are not known as tribes. Often the remnants of larger historical tribal groups that were located on different pieces of land, they became under IRA officially recognized as "tribes."

There are nineteen different Chippewa tribes, fifteen Sioux tribes, four Potawatomi tribes, a number of Paiute tribes, and several consolidated tribes which encompass two different groups that happened to land on the same reservation.

Examples of consolidated tribes are the Salish and Kootenai of Montana, the Cheyenne-Arapaho of Oklahoma, the Kiowa-Comanche-Apache of Oklahoma, and the Mandan, Hidatsa, and Arikara of the Fort Berthold reservation in North Dakota.

Over the past generation tribes have discovered that they must band together to make themselves heard. Consequently most states have inter-tribal councils, composed of the tribes in that state, that meet regularly and exchange ideas. In some areas, particularly in the Northwest, tribal representation is on a regional basis. The Northwest Affiliated Tribes is an organization made up of tribes from Montana, Idaho, Washington, and Oregon. Its counterpart, the Western Washington Inter-tribal Coordinating Council consists of tribes that live in the Puget Sound area.

Rarely do tribes overlap across state boundaries. While there are fifteen Sioux tribes, the United Sioux is an organization of only South Dakota tribes. Sioux groups in North Dakota, Nebraska, or Minnesota are not invited.

Indians have two "mainstream" organizations, the National Congress of American Indians and the National Indian Youth Council. The NCAI is open to tribes, organizations, and individuals, both red and white. Its major emphasis is on strong tribal membership because it works primarily with legislation and legislation is handled on an individual tribal basis.

The NIYC is the SNCC of Indian Affairs. Organized in 1962, it has been active among the post-college group just entering Indian Affairs. Although NIYC has a short history, it has been able to achieve recognition as a force to be reckoned with in national Indian Affairs. Generally more liberal and more excitable than the NCAI, the NIYC inclines to the spectacular short-term project rather than the extended program. The rivalry between the two groups is intense.

Lesser known but with great potential for the future are the traditional organizations. Primary among these is the oldest continuous Indian-run organization: the League of Nations, Pan American Indians. Its President, Alfred Gagne, incorporates the best of traditional Indian life and national problems into a coherent working philosophy. Should this group ever receive sufficient funding to have field workers, it could very well overturn established government procedures in Indian Affairs. It has long fought the Bureau of Indian Affairs and seeks a return to traditional Indian customs.

From the work of the League of Nations has come the alliance of the traditional Indians of each tribe. In June of 1968 they met in Oklahoma to form the National Aborigine Conference. Discussions ranging from religious prophecies to practical politics were held. From this conference is expected to come a strong nationalistic push on the reservations in the next several years.

Another group well worthy of mention is the American Indian Historical Society of San Francisco. Begun by Rupert Costo, a Cauhilla man, the society has become the publishers of the finest contemporary material on Indians. Excellent research and wide knowledge of Indian people makes it an influential voice in Indian Affairs.

Recently, during the Poor People's March, Indian participants formed the Coalition of American Indian Citizens. A loose and perhaps temporary alliance of disgruntled young people, the Coalition brought to Indian Affairs a sense of urgency. Whether it will continue to function depends on the commitment of its members to goals which they originally stated.

Regional groups are occasionally formed around a specific issue. In the Northwest the Survivors of American Indians, Inc., works exclusively on the issue of fishing rights. In Oklahoma the Original Cherokee Community Organization has been formed to defend hunting and treaty rights of the Cherokees.

Most urban areas have urban centers or clubs composed of Indian people. For the most part these centers provide a place where urban Indians can meet and socialize. The best-known centers are in Los Angeles, Oakland, Chicago, and Minneapolis. New centers are always springing up in different cities. There are probably in excess of thirty functioning centers or clubs at any one time. The urban areas show the most potential for strong lasting organizations, however, and once the urban Indians stabilize themselves they will experience phenomenal growth.

All of these groups are primarily interested in issues and policies. The Indian Council Fire of Chicago works primarily in the field of public relations and Indian culture. The American Indian Development, Inc., works in the field of youth work and economic development of Indian communities.

There are a number of white organizations that attempt to help Indian people. Since we would be better off without them I will not mention them, except to comment that they do exist.

. . .

Individual tribes show incredible differences. No single aspect seems to be as important as tribal solidarity. Tribes that can handle their reservation conflicts in traditional Indian fashion generally make more progress and have better programs than do tribes that continually make adaptations to the white value system. The Pueblos of New Mexico have a solid community life and are just now, with the influx of college-educated Pueblos, beginning large development projects. In spite of the vast differences between the generations, the Pueblos have been able to maintain a sense of tribal purpose and solidarity, and developments are undertaken by the consensus of all the people of the community.

Even more spectacular are the Apaches of the Southwest—the Mescalero, San Carlos, white Mountain, and Jicarilla tribes. Numbering probably less than a dozen college graduates among them, the four tribes have remained close to their traditions, holding ancient ceremonies to be of utmost importance to the future of the tribe. Without the benefit of the white man's vaunted education, these four Apache groups have developed their reservations with amazing skill and foresight. Mescalero Apache owns a ski resort worth over one million dollars. Jicarilla has a modern shopping center. White Mountain has a tremendous tourism development of some twenty-six artificial lakes stocked with trout. San Carlos has a fine cattle industry and is presently developing an industrial park.

Contrast the Chippewas with the Apaches and the picture is not as bright. The Chippewas are located in Minnesota, Wisconsin, and Michigan. They have access to the large cities of Chicago, Minneapolis, Milwaukee, and Detroit. The brain drain of leadership from the Chippewa reservations to the cities has been enormous over the years. Migration to the cities has meant an emphasis on land sales, little development of existing resources, and abandonment of tribal traditions. Only among the Red Lake Chippewa has much progress been made. And Red Lake is probably the most traditional of the Chippewa tribes.

The Sioux, my own people, have a great tradition of conflict. We were the only nation ever to annihiliate the United States Cavalry three times in succession. And when we find no one else to quarrel with, we often fight each other. The Sioux problem is excessive leadership. During one twenty-year period in the last century the Sioux fought over an area from LaCrosse, Wisconsin, to Sheridan, Wyoming, against the Crow, Arapaho, Cheyenne, Mandan, Arikara, Hidatsa, Ponca, Iowa, Pawnee, Otoe, Omaha, Winnebago, Chippewa, Cree, Assiniboine, Sac and Fox, Potawatomi, Ute, and Gros Ventre. This was, of course, in addition to fighting the US Cavalry continually throughout that period. The United States government had to call a special treaty session merely to settle the argument among the tribes in the eastern half of that vast territory. It was the only treaty between tribes supervised by the federal government.

But the Sioux never quit fighting. Reservation programs are continually disrupted by bickering within the reservations. Each election on a Sioux reservation is generally a fight to the finish. A ten-vote margin of some 1,500 votes cast is a landslide victory in

Sioux country. Fortunately strong chairmen have come to have a long tenure on several Sioux reservations and some of the tribes have made a great deal of progress. But the tendency is always present to slug it out at a moment's notice.

. . .

Indian tribes are rapidly becoming accustomed to the manner in which the modern world works. A generation ago most Indians would not have known which way Washington, DC, lay. Today it is a rare tribe that does not make a visit once a year to talk with its Congressional delegation, tour the government agencies, and bring home a new program or project from the many existing programs being funded by the federal government. Many tribes receive the Congressional Record and a number subscribe to leading national publications such as *The Wall Street Journal, Life, Time*, and *Newsweek*. Few events of much importance pass the eyes of watchful tribal groups without comment.

. . .

Some tribes take home upward of ten million dollars a year in government programs and private grants for their reservation people. Many tribes, combining a variety of sources, have their own development officer to plan and project future programs. The White Mountain Apaches are the first tribe to have their own public relations firm to keep tribal relations with the surrounding towns and cities on an even keel.

With a change in Congressional policy away from termination toward support of tribal self-sufficiency, it is conceivable that Indian tribes will be able to become economically independent of the federal government in the next generation. Most tribes operate under the provisions of their Indian Reorganization Act constitutions and are probably better operated than most towns, certainly more honestly operated than the larger cities.

Tribes lost some ten years during the 1950s when all progress was halted by the drive toward termination. Arbitrary and unreasonable harassment of tribal programs, denial of credit funds for program development, and pressure on tribes to liquidate assets all contributed to waste a decade during which tribes could have continued to develop their resources.

Today the Indian people are in a good position to demonstrate to the nation what can be done in community development in the rural areas. With the overcrowding of the urban areas, rural development should be the coming thing and understanding of tribal programs could indicate methods of resettling the vast spaces of rural America.

With so much happening on reservations and the possibility of a brighter future in store, Indians have started to become livid when they realize the contagious trap the mythology of white America has caught them in. The descendant of Pocahontas is a remote and incomprehensible mystery to us. We are no longer a wild species of animal loping freely across the prairie. We have little in common with the last of the Mohicans.

Some years ago at a Congressional hearing someone asked Alex Chasing Hawk, a council member of the Cheyenne River Sioux for thirty years, "Just what do you Indians want?" Alex replied, "A leave-us-alone law!!"

The primary goal and need of Indians today is not for someone to feel sorry for us and claim descent from Pocahontas to make us feel better. Nor do we need to be classified as semi-white and have programs and policies made to bleach us further. Nor do we need further studies to see if we are feasible. We need a new policy by Congress acknowledging our right to live in peace, free from arbitrary harassment. We need the public at large to drop the myths in which it has clothed us for so long. We need fewer and fewer "experts" on Indians.

What we need is a cultural leave-us-alone agreement, in spirit and in fact.

5   Through the Cracks

Marge Piercy

I. A Protracted Adolescence, a Foreshortened Perspective

I think I have some notion how growing up in the fifties compared with growing up in the sixties, because I arranged to have two adolescences, one at the normal age, and one again in the sixties, in SDS. Growing up in the fifties: I never could, exactly. Part of maturing is strengthening a sense of I as an identity and a strong project, and then blending that into some larger We. Being an adult involves a bonding with a community, and therefore of history and progeny, a meshing with time, a sense of struggling and yielding, shaping and being shaped in that river.

In the fifties I found myself a perennial adolescent, isolated, stuck in the alienated pose of an individual in a hostile environment. History had ended in the American apotheosis; it was only a matter of time (and struggle with the forces of evil) before the rest of the world became just like Our Town with cigarette commercials. I remember my best friend's brother-in-law yelling at her, "You aren't satisfied with anything. What do you want, to go live with savages in a cave in Italy?" Changing this country felt inconceivable. Politics was voting. The long ice age of General Motors, General Foods, General Eisenhower, and general miasma: the only choices were conformity or exile. I could not imagine a future. Only sci-fi freaks were into that, and mostly their future looked like the old frontier with shinier gadgets. My own actions of protest against the distribution of wealth, rights, power were doomed to be symbolic and abortive.

Survival was hard enough. It was harder to be poor then than now, I think, although of course that is a snotty judgment eased by the fact that I am no longer poor. There was no support for choosing anything other than a narrowly defined norm. There was no subculture to drop into especially, especially for women. (To an independent woman the enclaves of beat and hep were more piggish than the straight world.) Still, beyond survival or a clubby grouping of nervous politics played by Robert's Rules, the only actions I could see were gesture, bordering on prank. My anger was enormous, when I was in touch with it at all, but the isolated gestures available trivialized it: soapsuds in a fountain, a faked news story, refusing to use footnotes or keep hours, taking off my clothes. Either you got away with it because you didn't get caught so it might as well not have happened, or you did it publicly and were promptly punished.

The end of ideology produced a world in stasis. Actually the fifties represented the last gasp of WASP history as history: the history of the affluent white male Western European and latterly American presence in the world given to us as the history of humankind; Western European culture of the better off sold us as Culture. This battle is

From Marge Piercy, "Through the Cracks". First appeared in *Partisan Review*, Vol. XLI, No. 2, 1974.

still continuing, and most of what is taught in school is still official cult, but at least now it is being challenged. The vast rest of us were deviations from the norm. I call the fifties the end of that but what a fat squat end. What a grey smug tight world. Everything that moved me at first contact (Whitman, Dickinson) turned out to be déclassé or irrelevant to the mainstream, the tradition. It was not, of course, a mainstream that had produced me, a tradition to which I was a natural heir. I would never be a gentleman.

What a need to tidy everything, librarianlike. Everything in art was taught as fitting somewhere in a vast hierarchy. The Great Chain of Being seemed still intact. Even the lawns were Christian. Human nature was a universal constant, each of us with her heart of darkness. In this period of successful identification of ruling class interests seamlessly with the interests of "the people" (who were the images on the cover of the *Saturday Evening Post*) the concept of American classlessness was being pushed at the same time that critics like Lionel Trilling were calling for a novel of manners: meaning literature *interior* to the world of the affluent. The defeat of Marxist literary criticism and theory meant rejection of the class struggle and somehow even of working class experience as a viable theme. Yet class was a fact of my life, something I brooded over constantly in childhood every time I took the Joy Road or Tireman buses in Detroit and noted how if you went downtown there were even more blacks than in our neighborhood and housing got worse and worse, and if you went the other direction there was more space, more trees, yards, single-family brick houses, parks. If I had come to college never having thought about poverty, born out of an egg the day before, going to college was a never-ending education in the finer distinctions of class insult and bias. It kept kicking me in the teeth.

When characters who were not white, male, and affluent appeared in the literature we read, including novels of the time, they were all image and mythology, when not comic relief. When a character was black, generally she represented something in the white writer's psyche—nature, evil, death, life, fecundity. Like Indians. Like women to this day. Such beings were never assumed to have an inner reality equal and coherent to the white male writer. Now we begin to have a diversity of culture to begin to match our different realities, values, lives.

Yes, the world was a dead egg. I felt impacted. Nothing would ever move or change. All that could be imagined was slipping off somewhere special like near Sartre, where things were obviously more vital; or wriggling through the cracks, surviving in the unguarded interstices. There was no support for opting out of the rat race or domesticity. On the other hand, it was easier in some ways to get by; i.e., shoplifting was pitifully easy in the fifties, with none of the organized and increasingly mechanized war between stores and customers that goes on now, only store dicks and a few mirrors. What people conceived of as possible for them to do was small: the possible lives seemed only two or three, like the differences between men's sport jackets or suits. Marry or die! The painfully slow process of work in communities that has produced. a smattering of free clinics, drop-in centers, women' centers, hot-lines, abortion referral services, pregnancy counseling, law communes, food co-ops, switchboards, alternate schools, wasn't even a gleam in an organizer's eye. If you got sick, suicidal, depressed, in trouble, pregnant, hungry, you were on your own. I remember eating flour and water for four days during vacation in the university town, trying to pry my paycheck loose.

Now there would always be someplace I could get a meal. Kids take slightly, slightly more care of each other; the subculture trains folks to pretend at least to care.

· · ·

But I wanted to write. I knew I was writing badly. I could not produce two lines without making five literary allusions, punning in Elizabethan English and dragging in some five-dollar word like *chiaroscuro*. I was assimilating. Graduate school represented the first financial security I had ever known (which may sound weird to you, but meant a meal ticket to me). I knew I could hack it and then I'd be safe, I thought. Actually now I see how shaky are the positions of women in universities, Ph.D. or not, fired just before tenure, shunted into cleanup courses. I didn't have the savvy then to guess that security might not apply to me. But it scared me anyhow and not entirely because I feared success. That wasn't success to me. It was just security.

Success was telling some truth, creating some vision on paper. I had to go back to my own roots somehow before I lost a sense of myself. I lived in Uptown in Chicago, on Wilson Avenue in a poor white neighborhood the JOIN project of SDS was later to work in. I was laboring for a sense of my self, origins, prospects, antecedents, intentions, a renewed sense of a living language natural to my mouth, even a mythology I could use. Some I tried to read from the city streets, some from my grim jobs, some from the library again. On a borrowed card I sought a mythology that centered on women. From 1958 through 1960 I read everything I could get into my hands on the mother goddess religions, mandalas, matriarchy, Crete, Amazons, Isis, Ishtar, Diana, Artemis, Cybele, Demeter. I read Margaret Murray on witches and poured over Jung's illustrations. It was all useless. I could not assimilate it usefully. I could not write out of what soaked dark and wet and fecundating into my brain. I could not make connections. Now of course the emerging women's culture draws on this stuff. But to be interested in Demeter in 1958 wasn't to be a precursor but to be mad, objectively irrelevant. Just as there was no community to mediate for me between individual and mass, there was nobody to write for, nobody to communicate with about matters of being female, alive, thinking, trying to make sense of one's life and times. I wrote novel after novel, poem after poem for no one: to lack a context and to create is to be objectively mad.

Within a year after leaving school I broke out of the box of my marriage. I remember my husband demanding to know what I wanted in leaving him, and yelling that I was pursuing a phoenix. He told me that both he and his shrink agreed I needed help badly, was frigid (I no longer wanted to sleep with him) and pursuing neurotic fancies. I stood there flat-footed and suddenly I could see the cramped, starved, supportive housewife relationship with my husband side-by-side with earlier, freer bondings with other men, and I started to laugh. He tried to tie the divorce to my being willing to go to his shrink or a shrink his shrink would choose, but I just left. I am surprised considering how timid and malleable I was then where the strength emerged to laugh and walk out, to cling to my own flimsy reality against official reality, husband reality, shrink reality, newspaper reality, sociological reality, the reality of everybody I knew telling me I was a self-destructive fool to walk out of such a good marriage. Good for what, I asked? I think only a hunger for reality, a large omnivorous curiosity that had led me to a certain breadth of experience by twenty-two gave me a courage based on having at least some few things to compare other things to.

That comparison was generally lacking: a sense of possibilities, of alternate universes of social discourse, of other assumptions about what was good or primary, of other viable ways of making a living, making love, having and raising children, being together, living, and dying. There was little satisfaction for me in the forms offered, yet there seemed no space but death or madness outside the forms.

II. Femininity as a Persistent Discomfort, like a Headcold

Surely seldom has the role of women been more painful, the contradictions more intense, than they were in the fifties, when the full force of the counterrevolution struck us. Sick was a cant word of the fifties: if you were unhappy, if you wanted something you couldn't have easily or that other people did not want or wouldn't admit to wanting, if you were angry, if you were different, strange, psychic, emotional, intellectual, political, double-jointed: you were sick, sick, sick.

Women's clothing of the fifties, the purchased or stolen trappings of my adolescence: a litany of rubber, metal bands, garters, boning, a rosary of spandex and lycra and nylon, a votive candle of elastic, I consecrate to you. I think you were sick.

The skirts were long and clumsy. How we waded through summer as they hung from us in fat folds muffling our thin hips and flat behinds as if we were matrons vast as car barns. But sweaters were tight. Through the sweater you could see ridges of brassiere like targets for gunnery practice, through the fluorescent pilled nylon (like goose-pimples), the more affluent pastel cashmeres (kept under the bed in trunks by girls in my dormitory, fingered like gold: a nice suburban girl counted her wealth, her worth in cashmeres), the ubiquitous flat lambswool cardigans and pullovers, playing their demure mother and daughter acts under the false teeth of pearls.

Sacky tweed skirts, little grey suits in which no one looked real. What you were supposed to wear to job interviews, along with some hat, white shoes, white gloves. In my drawer were two pairs of white gloves never worn except at job interviews: some mad connection between being paid $1.35 an hour to type and carrying a pair of white gloves. Purity. Virginity. We used to rub chalk on them to make them white.

The other choice besides the acres of swishing skirt was called a sheath. Those were alluring gowns into which we crept, first having squashed flat the belly, the hips, the waist, slowly, slowly, toothpaste cramming back into the tube. If a zipper broke, we spilled out. Bottles filled with our fizzing blood or stale water, it did not matter; they stood alone, their sex so much more definite than our own, hard and horny as the carapace of beetles. Our flesh served them in bondage: the bondage of which all these clothes speak.

What is a woman walking on high heels? What is a giraffe on roller skates? The platform shoes clumping along now depress me. Spike heels used to turn ankles and break legs regularly, catching in gratings, escalators, cracks at elevator doors, stairway treads. Who grows tumid at clumsy mincing, at the warped back of a woman bobbing stiffly—who cannot run if she has to, who is hobbled, distorted, learning to endure pain?

Longline brassieres underneath staved in the ribs, shoved the stomach up into the esophagus, raised the rigid breasts till their padded peaks brushed the chin. Breasts were hard and shiny as the apple stuck in the mouth of the roast suckling pig. Strapless brassieres dug into the skin to leave a red welt encircling. If you reached upward, if you moved suddenly, the bra would remain anchored like a granite ledge. The freed breasts would pop out. Suddenly you stood, Diana of Ephesus with four boobs. I remember my dormitory friend murmuring scorn of the boyfriend who thought he had caressed her breast in the twilit lounge. All he had contacted was Playtex padded perfect circle size 34A.

Girdles: my mother bought me one when I turned twelve saying to me that now I was a woman. I weighed ninety-two pounds and cast no shadow standing sideways. Rubber coffins. They were diving machines that made of air a sticky sea to founder in. Who could eat with pleasure in a girdle? I remember pain at restaurant tables, the squirming, the itching, the overt tweaking and plucking. Who could dance? Run or bend over or climb a ladder? Fuck? Scratch? No, in a girdle you stand and stand. You sit rigidly and nothing jiggles, nothing bounces. You are looked at like an avocado tree in a lobby. The pallid flesh sweats coldly under the rubber mask with its smell of doctors offices and baby cribs.

What do these costumes say with their high, conical breasts, deep waistlines, flat rib cages, and no bellies at all—no wombs, in there, nothing to digest with? Girdles that chafed the thighs raw. It is not trivia, this catalogue of out-of-fashion clothes that arouse lust in middle-aged men. These costumes say that flesh must be confined, must suffer in rigidity. Women must accustom themselves to a constant state of minor pain, binding themselves in a parody of the real body to be constantly "attractive." A woman must never be able to use her body freely.

Before this armory of underwear, flesh was quelled, cowed. It had the shape divine. We didn't have bodies then, we had shapes. We were the poor stuff from which this equipment carved the feminine. Under all this clothing our meat, imprinted with seams and chafed with elastic, shuddered and waited in ignorance. Our bodies were blind worms, helpless under rocks. Secretly they turned to muscle or to flab as they would, but the clothes jailed us, trained us to await babies and cancer and rape, dumb as a center-piece of wax fruit. I feel less vulnerable naked than in those trappings.

III. Daddy, Mommy, and The Bomb

The Bomb: like God, a central presence, hefty as in the Herblock cartoons. With the ever escalating arms race and military budgets, the chances of the world blowing up today are at least as great, but nobody talks of it. It's boring. At least we were obsessed with the probability. But it blocked political thinking. It made us afraid of Them who presum-ably would drop their bomb on us rather than afraid of Us, who were our business to control and who policed us into complicity.

I used to dream eschatologically, New York Harbor choked with charred corpses, the blackened pit that had been Detroit. During my freshman year we spent time, the three of us roommates, fantasizing about what we would do when the bomb fell on Detroit. We had a feeble scheme of stealing horses from a nearby riding stable and heading north to the woods to live off the land—something we had as much idea how to do as construct an atomic pile. That was a big time for lists of necessary supplies to keep in the basement.

I suspect one of the grand sexual fantasies of the fifties was survival with a few choice members of the opposite sex—or same if you were gay. Miraculously saved in Mammoth Cave where you happened to be visiting at the time with a party composed only of you and whomever you wanted. It would be the end of anxiety. The worst would have come true and all the rules gone out the window. Back to the simple life to try it all again. Or wait for the end with fun and games. In any event it too was an outlet, a source of change in a static world. A persistent and obsessive fantasy I found in at least half the men I was involved with in those years.

I think people generally expect less of sex now and that works out better. If a woman obeyed Freud and togetherness and gave up everything for her femininity, she expected the earth to move and the sky to fall in bed. Men who conformed to the corporate image on the job expected to go home to warmth, intimacy, and a personal geisha.

Living was personalized, privatized. You had problems. Everything seemed to go on in small boxes. It was a time dominated by a Freudian theology of biology and childhood as fate. I don't believe there are greater incidences of rape and impotence now than in the fifties. I was a bit outside, and people came to me in crises. It was assumed I would know the abortionist or what to do. I functioned in that way for years, repository of sexual lore, like a crazy bank where people left stuff they didn't really want, to molder and gather slow interest. Then, as now, a great many women were forcibly raped, and then (as now enforced by the society and the law but just beginning to be fought by women), women were ashamed of that violence done to them and believed, as programmed, that to be violently entered was somehow their fault. The incidence of male impotence has always been high among any class of men I've ever known, age, background, race, level of education regardless. I suspect from conversations with much older women that it's held constant since 1910 at least. But nobody talked about it then. Men did not talk honestly to men, women did not talk honestly enough to women. Men talked to women individually but with a mixture of confession, propaganda, blame laying, and demand.

The myth of the vaginal orgasm (big bang theory of femininity) did enormous damage. It not only produced a generation of women alienated from their bodies, trained to deny actual pleasure and to act out fancied orgasms, but alienated from their minds, since generally in order to function and "be happy" in relations with men, women had to believe they were experiencing "fulfillment" in bed.

Mutually exclusive sex roles divided humanity into winners and losers, makers and made, doers and done, fuckers and fuckees, yin and yang, and who the hell wants to be passive, moist, cold, receptive, unmoving, inert: sort of a superbasement of humanity. Women still police each other, to keep each other in line, as men too police women, the range of permissible behavior for women remaining much narrower than for men. But women policed each other in the fifties with a special frenzy, being totally convinced nothing but death and madness lay outside the nuclear family and the baby-doll-mommy roles. How could we have believed that when we saw the toll of death and madness inside the roles?

Even the notion of acceptable beauty was exceedingly limited and marred a whole generation of women who grew up knowing they did not embody it (training in self-hatred) and a whole generation of men who felt they were entitled to it, and any actual woman not resembling the few idols was very second-best: or Everyman has the right to the exclusive possession of Marilyn Monroe. Just as the sex roles have widened, slightly, and loosened, a minute amount, so the range of people who grow up thinking themselves physically acceptable has increased perceptibly. Kinky hair is fine, afros are fine, straight hair is fine, you don't have to wear falsies any more. The common physical conditions still persecuted include being fat and ordinary signs of aging, i.e., flesh being less than brand-new as if from a machine shop.

What we were trained to respond to sexually in men can be roughly divided into two types. One was the Sensitive Hood, mean, destructive, self-destructive, sadistic but suffering. The other was Iceman: now Iceman might be the Cold War cowboy, the suntanned tycoon; or might be the more ectomorphic intellectual with cheekbones and an ascetic air. But he was cold through and through, he was ungiving Daddy, the block of stone, destructive but not usually self-destructive. The perfect tool of empire, whether in his study or his factory or his trenchcoat. The essence of each was the inability to love, to feel in a useful way, while retaining the ability (usually) to act. The Sensitive Hood, the existential darling, feels but only pain or the pleasure of giving pain. A generation of women was raised to impale themselves on knives or pound themselves mushy on rocks, while fantasizing to order about womanly fulfillment, surrender, and the big bang orgasm. It would make me weep if I hadn't had to live through it, wondering what was hitting me. One is the Sinful Son and the other the Terrible Father, basically Puritan ghouls, competitive, alienated, death-dealing and empty, empty in the soul, useless to the preservation of life. Egoistic in quite different styles: insensitivity trained by the grueling rituals of American manhood, or narcissism ogling itself in the shine of a switchblade (usually imaginary).

The only road back from pouring affection down a rat hole lay in your children: creative motherhood. Of course we are approaching the great double bind by which a mother must give all her attention all of the time to her children while they are growing up lest they become drug-dealing preverts, but a possessive mother kills . . .

We had not the active paranoia we have learned through the sixties and seventies, the Pynchonesque government plot involving the CIA, the Mafia, the White House, and ITT: the knowledge that behind the bland or incoherent violent facade of newspaper "events" lie unimaginable writings of interlocked directorates of multinational corporations. No, the facade was entire in the fifties: every Corinthian column in its place and nobody on the white marble steps but the D.A. taking his oath. Our paranoia was, first, petty: that "they," i.e., the FBI, would immediately know if I talked to a Communist or took Engels's *On the Family* out of the library. While I was at Michigan there was a minor furor when a student confessed to her boyfriend that the FBI had scared her into giving them a list of everyone who came to his many parties, for he was . . . an avowed Marxist! When I arranged for Pete Seeger to give his first concert there in many years, I felt incredibly cheeky. It was playing poker with monopoly money. The political dimension had been crushed from our lives, making it impossible to think about community, the state, the economy, history in any vital way.

The paranoia was massive on another level: enemyless. Life would get you. Life was obviously in the employ of J. Edgar Hoover and the *Ladies' Home Journal.* The conception of human nature was narrow: we are only now engaged in trying to knock it more open again. People were cardboard good, or inherently darkly evil. People may kill themselves more now, but they don't jaw endlessly about it.

The fifties, I cannot sentimentalize them. I hardly survived them. The idea that they might come back in some forms appears ahistorical to me but terrifying, like seeing a parade bearing my coffin down the street. They were a mutilating time to grow up female, and an ugly if more complacent time to grow up male. To grow up a gay male was to fit yourself for the closet or a minute bar world. To grow up a lesbian: you didn't exist. Without the dimension of the possibility of loving each other, our friendships among women were doomed to be shelved at the first approach of a male. To say something nice about the fifties. Well, people read less poetry then, but they did read more fiction, and take fiction more seriously. It's hard sometimes to communicate about ideas in the limited vocabulary currently acceptable in conversation. People's unwillingness to look up words they don't know has reached mammoth proportions. Large amounts of time spent with people who don't know how to do much besides roll a joint does inspire me with nostalgic respect for the work ethic (real knowledge about how to do things, like fix machines that break, build walls that stay up, speak Spanish, put in a well, look up something in a library, design a computer language), but I think that knowledge of at least manual skills is beginning to spread. Further, people coming of age now *tend* to be less hierarchical in their ranking of blue-collar, white-collar, black-coat work.

But I can't summon up any honest nostalgia for the fifties. In the fifties when I got pregnant I couldn't get an abortion, had to do it myself at eighteen and almost bled to death. In the fifties I was at the mercy of a male culture terrified of sex and telling me I was either frigid, a nymphomaniac, an earth mother, or stunted with penis envy, and there were no women's experiences available to compare with mine. In the fifties nowhere could I find images of a life I considered good or useful or dignified. Nowhere could I find a way to apply myself to change the world to one I could live in with more joy and utility. Nowhere could I find a community to heal myself to in struggle. Nowhere could I find space in which affluent white men were not the arbiters of all that was good and bad. I could not grow anywhere but through the cracks. I was not *for* anyone, my work burped in a void. I learned survival but also alienation, hostility, craziness, schizophrenia. Not until the slow opening of the sixties was I able to think I might begin to cease to be a victim, an internal exile, a madwoman. I might become an adult. I might be useful, I might speak and be heard, listen and receive. I might be delivered finally to a sense of a past that led to me/us (Harriet Tubman, Sojourner Truth, Mother Jones, Susan B. Anthony, Rosa Luxembourg, Lucy Stone, Louise Michel). I might live in a community, however tacky and bleak at times, however scattered and faddish. I might conceive of my living and my working as a project forward in a struggle, however long and difficult and unlikely, tending toward a more humane society. Of course our recent past and present has also brought me beatings, gassings, danger, repression, fear, separation, demands, condemnation, physical collapse, overwork, exhaustion, petty bickerings, faction fights, fanaticism, hate mail, objectification, a more complicated life than I am at ease with, and a gallery of more judges than I need, presumably on my side but sometimes I despairingly wonder. I would not trade the worst of it for the isolation and dead-endedness of the fifties. To live in the fifties and think that the way this society distributes money, power, resources, prestige, and dirty work was wrong was to stand up in a stadium during a football game and attempt to read aloud a poem.

6   Revisited: The Puerto Rican Problem

Hunter S. Thompson

Two years ago Alfred Kazin, the hard-nosed literary critic, published a searing appraisal of Puerto Rico in the magazine *Commentary*. It did not create much of a stir in the States, but when it was reprinted front page in the *San Juan Star*, all hell broke loose.

Letters poured in, calling Kazin everything from a "crazy Jew" to a "stupid provincial Americano." A few people agreed with him, but to do so in public was to provoke a wild and woolly argument. The dialogue lasted for months—in the press, in bars, in private homes, until eventually the name Kazin evolved into a sort of dirty word from one end of the island to the other.

I was living in San Juan at the time and each day I would sally forth to the fray, defending Kazin more out of sport than any real conviction, and happy in the knowledge that I had a surefire antidote to any dull conversation.

Now all that is changed. If Kazin came back now and wrote the same article it would fall flat. Puerto Rico has made it. The one-time "poorhouse of the Caribbean" is now a blue-chip tourist attraction, and what Alfred Kazin happens to think about it does not make much difference except as a literary curiosity.

This is too bad, in a way, because Puerto Rico, and especially San Juan, is a much duller place than it was two years ago. About the only way to rouse a good argument these days is to gripe about the skyrocketing prices, and of course that's a waste of time. Success has not gone so much to the Puerto Rican's head as to his belly, and a satisfied man is not nearly so quick to take insult as a scrambling neurotic.

There is no longer that defensiveness that marked the Puerto Rico of the formative years. As recently as 1960, the vested interests and even the would-be vested interests were so insecure that most people would fly off the handle at the slightest inference that this island was anything less than a noble experiment and a budding Valhalla. Now the beachhead has been won. The pattern is no longer Boom or Bust, but more along the lines of Organize and Solidify.

For several years the Commonwealth promoted itself with an ad that said: SUDDENLY, EVERYBODY'S GOING TO PUERTO RICO. And as one wag put it, "Suddenly everybody went to Puerto Rico." Which is one of the reasons why the place has gone dull.

All during the fifties San Juan was literally brimming with geeks and hustlers and gung-ho promoters. Absolute incompetents were getting rich overnight, simply because they had stumbled on a good thing at a ripe time. You would meet a man in a bar and he might have $200 to his name: two months later you would meet him again and he'd have more money than he knew what to do with.

From Hunter S. Thompsom, "Revisited: The Puerto Rican Problem," in Hunter S. Thompson, *Songs of the Doomed: More Notes on the Death of the American Dream* (London: Picador, 1991), 1027–5. Reproduced by permission of Macmillan Publishers Ltd.

Gimmicks were paying off with a lunatic consistency. A whole tribe of hustlers got rich selling bowling balls to the natives. Another tribe sold Formica-top tables, and still another pushed transistor radios. Now they are all captains of commerce—and the ones who had the wrong gimmicks went broke and disappeared.

The small operator was often a big wheel in the fifties, but now the Big Boys are moving in—people like Clint Murchison of Texas and Gardner Cowles of *Look* magazine—and the methods are changing. Things are not so rough-edged, so crude as they were before. Everybody has a public-relations man and ready cash is no longer so all-important. They are even giving credit to the natives, which pretty well tells the story.

One of the surest signs of the new status level is that the people who once felt they had a mission here are getting apathetic. Most of those missions are accomplished, and a lot of people who grew up with the island are talking about shoving off to seek what might be called "the challenge of the uncertain."

Chuck New, a columnist for the *San Juan Star*, says he has a feeling that "Puerto Rico doesn't need me anymore." This may or may not be true, but what is beyond any question is the fact that New doesn't need Puerto Rico anymore, either. He came here on a shoestring, started doing a gossip column for the newspaper, and one day found he was sole owner of La Botalla, San Juan's most popular bistro. New is not particularly cunning and offers no explanation for his success except that he claims to lead a Christian life—and that he happened to be in San Juan when things were up for grabs.

Another ex-missionary is Bill Kennedy, managing editor of the *Star* since its beginning in the fall of 1959, who several months ago gave up his job and turned to the writing of fiction. "There was no more challenge on the paper," he says. "The excitement went out of it."

Another man, a promoter who worked for more than five years to make Puerto Rico what it is today, put it a little differently. "You know," he said, "San Juan is getting bourgeois—that's why I'm leaving."

One of the best examples of how Puerto Rico has changed can be seen in the *San Juan Star*. On its first anniversary it had a circulation of 5,000 or so. Now, two years and one Pulitzer Prize later, the figure is 17,000 and climbing steadily. The fact that Gardner Cowles owns it may or may not explain anything, but it is worth noting.

In the beginning the *Star* was staffed largely by drifters, transients who showed up out of nowhere and disappeared with a baffling and unexplained regularity. Some of them left vast debts behind, and others went to jail. On any given night the city editor was just as likely to pick up the phone and get a routine story as he was to hear that half his staff had been locked up for creating a riot.

Nothing like that is very likely to happen now. The wild boys have moved on, and the English-speaking press is pretty staid. This is also what happened to the rest of San Juan—the nuts and the cranks and the oddballs have either fled or stayed long enough to become respectable.

Now the streets of the Old City are full of people who look like New Yorkers wearing ManTan—and most of them are. The streets are also full of American homosexuals—so many that the government has begun an official investigation to find out why this is.

The Old City itself is getting very quaint; whole blocks of slums are being "reconstructed" and knick-knack shops are sprouting everywhere.

In a phrase, San Juan is over the hump, and the rest of Puerto Rico will not be far behind. After ten years of toil and trouble, millions of dollars spent to attract industry and tourists, savage debates and dialogues as to whether all that money and effort was worthwhile—all that is history now, and whatever happens from here on in will very definitely be a second stage. There are still problems, but they are of a different sort, and dealing with them will require different methods and even different men. For better or for worse, it is the end of an era.

San Juan, 1964

Section II
European Cultural Theory and Its Legacy

John Downing, "The King is Dead", *Daily Express*, 1977. Reproduced by permission of Express Newspapers.

Section II
European Cultural Theory and Its Legacy

Authors

Betty Friedan, Marshall McLuhan, Marshall Sahlins, Umberto Eco, Lawrence Grossberg

Visual Artist

John Downing, *The King is Dead*

E UROPEAN cultural and social criticism/theory constituted a crucial precondition for the emergence of a specifically American cultural studies, which did not have a strong tradition of indigenous leftist cultural critique to draw upon. Writers in the British tradition—the not-so-holy trinity of Richard Hoggart, E. P. Thompson, and Raymond Williams, together with Stuart Hall and other "Birmingham" acolytes—contributed a pragmatic empiricism related to a neo-Marxist analytical position. Continental writers—Roland Barthes, Claude Lévi-Strauss, Umberto Eco, Michel Foucault, for instance—contributed theoretical tools for the analysis of culture and cultural texts and others like Jean Baudrillard formulated notions of postmodernity. Some of these writers dealt directly with America (Eco, for one), but for the most part this chapter contains materials from American writers working within—or arguing against—the European tradition.

The chapter opens with a contribution by Betty Friedan—who could easily have appeared in the previous chapter and who carries over its themes into the more formal context of this one. She sets off to *distance* her critique of "the feminine mystique" from the European provenance of Freudian theory. She bases her arguments on the contradiction she observes between the influence of Freudianism on American writers since the 1940s, and her own personal and journalistic observations of women's lives and circumstances in America. Her critical engagement with the legacy of European theory is in fact symptomatic of much of the "legacy" of such imported disciplinary knowledge in the USA. American writers engaged dialogically with it, rejecting as well as assimilating its influence; refusing as well as accepting its applicability to America. Friedan herself was not part of any self-conscious attempt to develop American cultural studies. But the themes of theoretical critique and innovation and of concern with the everyday lives of ordinary women, the strongly argued feminist project, and the politicization of the private sphere, are all moves upon which American cultural studies has continued to build.

Meanwhile, European cultural thought has formed a constant partner in conversation in American cultural studies. One of the most important precursors of the field, Marshall McLuhan, ranges far and wide from his own training in English literature to develop his own highly idiosyncratic formulations on culture and technology.

A more systematic uptake of European theory is undertaken by Marshall Sahlins, an anthropologist partly trained in Paris, who takes up Lévi-Strauss's structural anthropology and applies it to the American clothing system. This is a bold and innovative double move that (a) turns the anthropological gaze on to the home population, and (b) assists in the attempt Sahlins is making to synthesize Marxist (materialist) and anthropological perspectives on culture, so introducing the specific study of the *production of meaning* to American cultural studies.

Umberto Eco was one of the earliest voices in what has sometimes been called the "new humanities." He introduced semiotics to the study not only of literary culture but of the television "message" too. Eco is also well-known as a novelist and columnist, and he combines all these skills of observation, analysis, critical acuity, and narrative brilliance in his writings on the "postmodern" (or, in his terms, neo-medieval) theme of "hyperreality." In the extracts chosen, Eco situates his own position in relation to cultural analysis, and then turns his attention to the home of the hyperreal—America.

Lawrence Grossberg represents one of the earliest cases of full-blown Birmingham cultural studies in the USA (he studied at the Centre for Contemporary Cultural Studies with Stuart Hall). His article herein, however, calls for a reconceptualization of a cultural studies constrained by a conception of essentialist identity categories as the only basis for power struggles, adding his voice to the many within the field who have increasingly come to see identity politics as a bankrupt paradigm.

A different take on the cultural interchange between Europe and America, one where the "legacy" is decidedly American, is offered by John Downing of Britain's *Daily Express* newspaper. His photograph shows a "hard-bitten" fan attending a memorial service in London after Elvis Presley's death in 1977. Here was evidence of how profoundly American popular culture could "influence" Europe. A youthful mourner is evidently overcome with grief. But there is very little about his style or that of his friends to suggest a specifically British or European identity. It is not even clear what decade this is (more than one recent viewer of the picture has presumed that it was taken outside Columbine High School in 1999). Youth culture was already fully international in the 1970s, thanks largely to the pioneering career of "The King". His death was experienced as a personal bereavement by people in far-off countries who weren't born when he first recorded for Sun Records in Memphis. This photograph was a winner of a World Press Photo award, and so in a further dialogic turn the image of Elvis's legacy in Europe itself became a lasting "world" icon.

7 The Sexual Solipsism of Sigmund Freud

Betty Friedan

I⊤ would be half-wrong to say it started with Sigmund Freud. It did not really start, in America, until the 1940s. And then again, it was less a start than the prevention of an end. The old prejudices—women are animals, less than human, unable to think like men, born merely to breed and serve men—were not so easily dispelled by the crusading feminists, by science and education, and by the democratic spirit after all. They merely reappeared in the forties, in Freudian disguise. The feminine mystique derived its power from Freudian thought; for it was an idea born of Freud, which led women, and those who studied them, to misinterpret their mothers' frustrations, and their fathers' and brothers' and husbands' resentments and inadequacies, and their own emotions and possible choices in life. It is a Freudian idea, hardened into apparent fact, that has trapped so many American women today.

The new mystique is much more difficult for the modern woman to question than the old prejudices, partly because the mystique is broadcast by the very agents of education and social science that are supposed to be the chief enemies of prejudice, partly because the very nature of Freudian thought makes it virtually invulnerable to question. How can an educated American woman, who is not herself an analyst, presume to question a Freudian truth? She knows that Freud's discovery of the unconscious workings of the mind was one of the great breakthroughs in man's pursuit of knowledge. She knows that the science built on that discovery has helped many suffering men and women. She has been taught that only after years of analytic training is one capable of understanding the meaning of Freudian truth. She may even know how the human mind unconsciously resists that truth. How can she presume to tread the sacred ground where only analysts are allowed?

No one can question the basic genius of Freud's discoveries, nor the contribution he has made to our culture. Nor do I question the effectiveness of psychoanalysis as it is practiced today by Freudian or anti-Freudian. But I do question, from my own experience as a woman, and my reporter's knowledge of other women, the application of the Freudian theory of femininity to women today. I question its use, not in therapy, but as it has filtered into the lives of American women through the popular magazines and the opinions and interpretations of so-called experts. I think much of the Freudian theory about women is obsolescent, an obstacle to truth for women in America today, and a major cause of the pervasive problem that has no name.

There are many paradoxes here. Freud's concept of the superego helped to free man of the tyranny of the "shoulds," the tyranny of the past, which prevents the child from becoming an adult. Yet Freudian thought helped create a new superego that paralyzes educated modern American women—a new tyranny of the "shoulds," which chains women to an old image, prohibits choice and growth, and denies them individual identity.

Freudian psychology, with its emphasis on freedom from a repressive morality to achieve sexual fulfillment, was part of the ideology of women's emancipation. The lasting American image of the "emancipated woman" is the flapper of the twenties: burdensome hair shingled off, knees bared, flaunting her new freedom to live in a studio in Greenwich Village or Chicago's near North Side, and drive a car, and drink, and smoke and enjoy sexual adventures—or talk about them. And yet today, for reasons far removed from the life of Freud himself, Freudian thought has become the ideological bulwark of the sexual counter-revolution in America. Without Freud's definition of the sexual nature of woman to give the conventional image of femininity new authority, I do not think several generations of educated, spirited American women would have been so easily diverted from the dawning realization of who they were and what they could be.

The concept 'penis envy,' which Freud coined to describe a phenomenon he observed in women—that is, in the middle-class women who were his patients in Vienna in the Victorian era—was seized in this country in the 1940s as the literal explanation of all that was wrong with American women. Many who preached the doctrine of endangered femininity, reversing the movement of American women toward independence and identity, never knew its Freudian origin. Many who seized on it—not the few psychoanalysts, but the many popularizers, sociologists, educators, ad-agency manipulators, magazine writers, child experts, marriage counselors, ministers, cocktail-party authorities—could not have known what Freud himself meant by penis envy. One needs only to know what Freud *was* describing, in those Victorian women, to see the fallacy in literally applying his theory of femininity to women today. And one needs only to know *why* he described it in that way to understand that much of it is obsolescent, contradicted by knowledge that is part of every social scientist's thinking today, but was not yet known in Freud's time.

Freud, it is generally agreed, was a most perceptive and accurate observer of import-ant problems of the human personality. But in describing and interpreting those prob-lems, he was a prisoner of his own culture. As he was creating a new framework for our culture, he could not escape the framework of his own. Even his genius could not give him, then, the knowledge of cultural processes which men who are not geniuses grow up with today.

The physicist's relativity, which in recent years has changed our whole approach to scientific knowledge, is harder, and therefore easier to understand than the social scien-tist's relativity. It is not a slogan, but a fundamental statement about truth to say that no social scientist can completely free himself from the prison of his own culture; he can only interpret what he observes in the scientific framework of his own time. This is true even of the great innovators. They cannot help but translate their revolutionary obser-vations into language and rubrics that have been determined by the progress of science up until their time. Even those discoveries that create new rubrics are relative to the vantage point of their creator.

The knowledge of other cultures, the understanding of cultural relativity, which is part of the framework of social scientists in our own time, was unknown to Freud. Much of what Freud believed to be biological, instinctual, and changeless has been shown by modern research to be a result of specific cultural causes.[1] Much of what Freud described as characteristic of universal human nature was merely characteristic of certain middle-class European men and women at the end of the nineteenth century.

For instance, Freud's theory of the sexual origin of neurosis stems from the fact that many of the patients he first observed suffered from hysteria—and in those cases, he found sexual repression to be the cause. Orthodox Freudians still profess to belive in the sexual origin of all neurosis, and since they look for unconscious sexual memories in their patients, and translate what they hear into sexual symbols, they still manage to find what they are looking for.

But the fact is, cases of hysteria as observed by Freud are much more rare today. In Freud's time, evidently, cultural hypocrisy forced the repression of sex. (Some social theorists even suspect that the very absence of other concerns, in that dying Austrian empire, caused the sexual preoccupation of Freud's patients.)[2] Certainly the fact that his culture denied sex focused Freud's interest on it. He then developed his theory by describing all the stages of growth as sexual, fitting all the phenomena he observed into sexual rubrics.

. . .

In the 1940s, American social scientists and psychoanalysts had already begun to reinterpret Freudian concepts in the light of their growing cultural awareness. But, curiously, this did not prevent their literal application of Freud's theory of femininity to American women.

The fact is that to Freud, even more than to the magazine editor on Madison Avenue today, women were a, strange, inferior, less-than-human species. He saw them as child-like dolls, who existed in terms only of man's love, to love man and serve his needs. It was the same kind of unconscious solipsism that made man for many centuries see the sun only as a bright object that revolved around the earth. Freud grew up with this attitude built in by his culture—not only the culture of Victorian Europe, but that Jewish culture in which men said the daily prayer: "I thank Thee, Lord, that Thou hast not created me a woman," and women prayed in submission: "I thank Thee, Lord, that Thou has created me according to Thy will."

. . .

Freud did not see this attitude as a problem, or cause for any problem, in women. It was woman's nature to be ruled by man, and her sickness to envy him. Freud's letters to Martha, his future wife, written during the four years of their engagement (1882–86) have the fond, patronizing sound of Torvald in *A Doll's House*, scolding Nora for her pretenses at being human. Freud was beginning to probe the secrets of the human brain in the laboratory at Vienna; Martha was to wait, his "sweet child," in her mother's custody for four years, until he could come and fetch her. From these letters one can see that to him her identity was defined as child-housewife, even when she was no longer a child and not yet a housewife.

. . .

That limitless subservience of woman taken for granted by Freud's culture, the very lack of opportunity for independent action or personal identity, seems often to have generated that uneasiness and inhibition in the wife, and that irritation in the husband, which characterized Freud's marriage. As Jones summed it up, Freud's attitude toward women "could probably be called rather old-fashioned, and it would be easy to ascribe this to his social environment and the period in which he grew up rather than to any personal factors."

Whatever his intellectual opinions may have been in the matter, there are many indications in his writing and correspondence of his emotional attitude. It would certainly be going too far to say that he regarded the male sex as the lords of creation, for there was no tinge of arrogance or superiority in his nature, but it might perhaps be fair to describe his view of the female sex as having as their main function to be ministering angels to the needs and comforts of men. His letters and his love choice make it plain that he had only one type of sexual object in his mind, a gentle feminine one. . . .

There is little doubt that Freud found the psychology of women more enigmatic than that of men. He said once to Marie Bonaparte: "The great question that has never been answered and which I have not yet been able to answer, despite my thirty years of research into the feminine soul, is, what does a woman want?"[3]

. . .

Despite the importance of sex in Freud's theory, one gets from his words the impression that the sex act appeared degrading to him; if women themselves were so degraded, in the eyes of man, how could sex appear in any other light? That was not his theory, of course. To Freud, it was the idea of incest with mother or sister that makes man "regard the sex act as something degrading, which soils and contaminates not only the body."[4] In any event, the degradation of women was taken for granted by Freud—and is the key to his theory of femininity. The motive force of woman's personality, in Freud's theory, was her envy of the penis, which causes her to feel as much depreciated in her own eyes "as in the eyes of the boy, and later perhaps of the man," and leads, in normal femininity, to the wish for the penis of her husband, a wish that is never really fulfilled until she possesses a penis through giving birth to a son. In short, she is merely an "homme manqué," a man with something missing. As the eminent psychoanalyst Clara Thompson put it: "Freud never became free from the Victorian attitude toward women. He accepted as an inevitable part of the fate of being a woman the limitation of outlook and life of the Victorian era. . . . The castration complex and penis envy concepts, two of the most basic ideas in his whole thinking, are postulated on the assumption that women are biologically inferior to men."[5]

What did Freud mean by the concept of penis envy? For even those who realize that Freud could not escape his culture do not question that he reported truly what he observed within it. Freud found the phenomenon he called penis envy so unanimous, in middle-class women in Vienna, in that Victorian time, that he based his whole theory of femininity on it. He said, in a lecture on "The Psychology of Women":

In the boy the castration-complex is formed after he has learned from the sight of the female genitals that the sexual organ which he prizes so highly is not a necessary part of every woman's body . . . and thenceforward he comes under the influence of castration-anxiety, which supplies the strongest motive force for his further development. The castration-complex in the girl, as well, is started by the sight of the genital organs of the other sex. She immediately notices the difference and, it must be admitted, its significance. She feels herself at a great disadvantage, and often declares that she would like to have something like that too and falls a victim to penis envy, which leaves ineradicable traces on her development and character-formation, and even in the most favorable instances, is not overcome, without a great expenditure of mental energy. That the girl recognizes the fact that she lacks a penis does not mean that she accepts its absence lightly. On the contrary, she clings for a long time to the desire to get something like it, and believes in that possibility for an extraordinary number of years; and even at a time when her knowledge of reality has long since led her to abandon the fulfillment of this desire as being quite unattainable, analysis proves that it still persists in the unconscious, and retains a con-siderable charge of energy. The desire after all to obtain the penis for which she so much longs may even contribute to the motives that impel a grown-up woman to come to analysis, and what she quite reasonably expects to get from analysis, such, as the capacity to pursue an intellectual career, can often be recognized as a sublimated modification of this repressed wish.[6]

"The discovery of her castration is a turning-point in the life of the girl," Freud went on to say. "She is wounded in her self-love by the unfavorable comparison with the boy, who is so much better equipped." Her mother, and all women, are depreciated in her own eyes, as they are depreciated for the same reason in the eyes of man. This either leads to complete sexual inhibition and neurosis, or to a "masculinity complex" in which she refuses to give up "phallic" activity (that is, "activity such as is usually characteristic of the male") or to "normal femininity," in which the girl's own impulses to activity are repressed, and she turns to her father in her wish for the penis. "The feminine situation is, however, only established when the wish for the penis is replaced by the wish for a child—the child taking the place of the penis." When she played with dolls, this "was not really an expression of her femininity," since this was activity, not passivity. The "strongest feminine wish," the desire for a penis, finds real fulfillment only "if the child is a little boy, who brings the longed-for penis with him. . . . The mother can transfer to her son all the ambition she has had to suppress in herself, and she can hope to get from him the satisfaction of all that has remained to her of her masculinity complex."[7]

But her inherent deficiency, and the resultant penis envy, is so hard to overcome that the women's superego—her conscience, ideals—are never as completely formed as a man's: "women have but little sense of justice, and this is no doubt connected with the preponderance of envy in their mental life." For the same reason, women's interests in society are weaker than those of men, and "their capacity for the sublimation of their instincts is less."

. . .

What was he really reporting? If one interprets "penis envy" as other Freudian concepts have been reinterpreted, in the light of our new knowledge that what Freud
believed to be biological was often a cultural reaction, one sees simply that Victorian
culture gave women many reasons to envy men: the same conditions, in fact, that the
feminists fought against. If a woman who was denied the freedom, the status and the
pleasures that men enjoyed wished secretly that she could have these things, in the
shorthand of the dream, she might wish herself a man and see herself with that one thing
which made men unequivocally different—the penis. She would, of course, have to learn
to keep her envy, her anger, hidden: to play the child, the doll, the toy, for her destiny
depended on charming man. But underneath, it might still fester, sickening her for love.
If she secretly despised herself, and envied man for all she was not, she might go through
the motions of love, or even feel a slavish adoration, but would she be capable of free and
joyous love? You cannot explain away woman's envy of man, or her contempt for herself,
as mere refusal to accept her sexual deformity, unless you think that a woman, by nature,
is a being inferior to man. Then, of course, her wish to be equal is neurotic.

It is recognized now that Freud never gave proper attention, even in man, to growth
of the ego or self: "the impulse to master, control or come to self-fulfilling terms with
the environment."[8] Analysts who have freed themselves from Freud's bias and joined
other behavioral scientists in studying the human need to grow, are beginning to believe
that this is the basic human need, and that interference with it, in any dimension, is the
source of psychic trouble. The sexual is only one dimension of the human potential.
Freud, it must be remembered, thought all neuroses were sexual in origin; he saw
women only in terms of their sexual relationship with men. But in all those women in
whom he saw sexual problems, there must have been very severe problems of blocked
growth, growth short of full human identity—an immature, incomplete self. Society as
it was then, by explicit denial of education and independence, prevented women from
realizing their full potential, or from attaining those interests and ideals that might have
stimulated their growth. Freud reported these deficiencies, but could only explain them
as the toll of "penis envy." He saw women's envy of man *only* as sexual sickness. He saw
that women who secretly hungered to be man's equal would not enjoy being his object;
and in this, he seemed to be describing a fact. But when he dismissed woman's yearning
for equality as "penis envy," was he not merely stating his own view that women could
never really be man's equal any more than she could wear his penis?

. . .

Even if Freud and his contemporaries considered women inferior by God-given,
irrevocable nature, science does not justify such a view today. That inferiority, we now
know, was caused by their lack of education, their confinement to the home. Today,
when women's equal intelligence has been proved by science, when their equal capacity
in every sphere except sheer muscular strength has been demonstrated, a theory
explicitly based on woman's natural inferiority would seem as ridiculous as it is hypo-
critical. But that remains the basis of Freud's theory of women, despite the mask of
timeless sexual truth which disguises its elaborations today.

Because Freud's followers could only see woman in the image defined by Freud—
inferior, childish, helpless, with no possibility of happiness unless she adjusted to being

man's passive object,—they wanted to help women get rid of their suppressed envy, their neurotic desire to be equal. They wanted to help women find sexual fulfillment as women, by affirming their natural inferiority.

But society, which defined that inferiority, had changed drastically by the time Freud's followers transposed bodily to twentieth-century America the causes as well as the cures of the condition Freud called penis envy. In the light of our new knowledge of cultural processes and of human growth, one would assume that women who grew up with the rights and freedom and education that Victorian women were denied would be different from the women Freud tried to cure. One would assume that they would have much less reason to envy man. But Freud was interpreted to American woman in such curiously literal terms that the concept of penis envy acquired a mystical life of its own, as if it existed quite independent of the women in whom it had been observed. It was as if Freud's Victorian image of woman became more real than the twentieth-century women to whom it was applied. Freud's theory of femininity was seized in America with such literalness that women today were considered no different than Victorian women. The real injustices life held for women a century ago, compared to men, were dismissed as mere rationalizations of penis envy. And the real opportunities life offered to women now, compared to women then, were forbidden in the name of penis envy.

The literal application of Freudian theory can be seen in these passages from *Modern Woman: The Lost Sex*, by the psychoanalyst Marynia Farnham and the sociologist Ferdinand Lundberg, which was paraphrased ad nauseam in the magazines and in marriage courses, until most of its statements became a part of the conventional, accepted truth of our time. Equating feminism with penis envy, they stated categorically:

Feminism, despite the external validity of its political program and most (not all) of its social program, was at its core a deep illness. . . . The dominant direction of feminine training and development today . . . discourages just those traits necessary to the attainment of sexual pleasure: receptivity and passiveness, a willingness to accept dependence without fear or resentment, with a deep inwardness and readiness for the final goal of sexual life-impregnation. . . .

It is not in the capacity of the female organism to attain feelings of well-being by the route of male achievement. . . . It was the error of the feminists that they attempted to put women on the essentially male road of exploit, off the female road of nurture. . . .

The psychosocial rule that begins to take form, then, is this: the more educated the woman is, the greater chance there is of sexual disorder, more or less severe. The greater the disordered sexuality in a given group of women, the fewer children do they have. . . . Fate has granted them the boon importuned by Lady Macbeth; they have been unsexed, not only in the matter of giving birth, but in their feelings of pleasure.[9]

Thus Freud's popularizers embedded his core of unrecognized traditional prejudice against women ever deeper in pseudo-scientific cement.

. . .

How could a girl or woman who was not a psychoanalyst discount such ominous pronouncements, which, in the forties, suddenly began to pour out from all the oracles of sophisticated thought?

It would be ridiculous to suggest that the way Freudian theories were used to brainwash two generations of educated American women was part of a psychoanalytic conspiracy. It was done by well-meaning popularizers and inadvertent distorters; by orthodox converts and bandwagon faddists; by those who suffered and those who cured and those who turned suffering to profit; and, above all, by a congruence of forces and needs peculiar to the American people at that particular time. In fact, the literal acceptance in the American culture of Freud's theory of feminine fulfillment was in tragicomic contrast to the personal struggle of many American psychoanalysts to reconcile what they saw in their women patients with Freudian theory. The theory said women should be able to fulfill themselves as wives and mothers if only they could be analyzed out of their "masculine strivings," their "penis envy." But it wasn't as easy as that. "I don't know why American women are so dissatisfied," a Westchester analyst insisted. "Penis envy seems so difficult to eradicate in American women, somehow."

A New York analyst, one of the last trained at Freud's own Psychoanalytic Institute in Vienna, told me:

For twenty years now in analyzing American women, I have found myself again and again in the position of having to superimpose Freud's theory of femininity on the psychic life of my patients in a way that I was not willing to do. I have come to the conclusion that penis envy simply does not exist. I have seen women who are completely expressive, sexually, vaginally, and yet who are not mature, integrated, fulfilled. I had a woman patient on the couch for nearly two years before I could face her real problem—that it was not enough for her to be just a housewife and mother. One day she had a dream that she was teaching a class. I could not dismiss the powerful yearning of this housewife's dream as penis envy. It was the expression of her own need for mature self-fulfillment. I told her: "I can't analyze this dream away. You must do something about it."

This same man teaches the young analysts in his postgraduate clinicum at a leading Eastern university: "If the patient doesn't fit the book, throw away the book, and listen to the patient."

But many analysts threw the book *at* their patients and Freudian theories became accepted fact even among women who never lay down on an analyst's couch, but only knew what they read or heard. To this day, it has not penetrated to the popular culture that the pervasive growing frustration of American women may not be a matter of feminine sexuality. Some analysts, it is true, modified the theories drastically to fit their patients, or even discarded them altogether—but these facts never permeated the public awareness. Freud was accepted so quickly and completely at the end of the forties that for over a decade no one even questioned the race of the educated American woman back to the home. When questions finally had to be asked because something was obviously going wrong, they were asked so completely within the Freudian framework that only one answer was possible: education, freedom, rights are wrong for women.

The uncritical acceptance of Freudian doctrine in America was caused, at least in part, by the very relief it provided from uncomfortable questions about objective realities. After the depression, after the war, Freudian psychology became much more than a science of human behavior, a therapy for the suffering. It became an all-embracing American ideology, a new religion. It filled the vacuum of thought and purpose that existed for many for whom God, or flag, or bank account were no longer sufficient—and yet who were tired of feeling responsible for lynchings and concentration camps and the starving children of India and Africa. It provided a convenient escape from the atom bomb, McCarthy, all the disconcerting problems that might spoil the taste of steaks, and cars and color television and backyard swimming pools. It gave us permission to suppress the troubling questions of the larger world and pursue our own personal pleasures. And if the new psychological religion—which made a virtue of sex, removed all sin from private vice, and cast suspicion on high aspirations of the mind and spirit—had a more devastating personal effect on women than men, nobody planned it that way.

Psychology, long preoccupied with its own scientific inferiority complex, long obsessed with neat little laboratory experiments that gave the illusion of reducing human complexity to the simple measurable behavior of rats in a maze, was transformed into a life-giving giving crusade that swept across the barren fields of American thought. Freud was the spiritual leader, his theories were the bible. And how exciting and real and important it all was. Its mysterious complexity was part of its charm to bored Americans. And if some of it remained impenetrably mystifying, who would admit that he could not understand it? America became the center of the psycoanalytic movement, as Freudian, Jungian and Adlerian analysts fled from Vienna and Berlin and new schools flourished on the multiplying neuroses, and dollars, of Americans.

But the practice of psychoanalysis as a therapy was not primarily responsible for the feminine mystique. It was the creation of writers and editors in the mass media, ad-agency motivation researchers, and behind them the popularizers and translators of Freudian thought in the colleges and universities. Freudian and pseudo-Freudian theories settled everywhere, like fine volcanic ash. Sociology, anthropology, education, even the study of history and literature became permeated and transfigured by Freudian thought. The most zealous missionaries of the feminine mystique were the functionalists, who seized hasty gulps of pre-digested Freud to start their new departments of "Marriage and Family Life Education." The functional courses in marriage taught American college girls how to "play the role" of woman—the old role became a new science. Related movements outside the colleges—parent education, child-study groups, prenatal maternity study groups and mental-health education—spread the new psychological superego throughout the land, replacing bridge and canasta as an entertainment for educated young wives. And this Freudian superego worked for growing numbers of young and impressionable American women as Freud said the superego works—to perpetuate the past.

Mankind never lives completely in the present; the ideologies of the superego perpetuate the past, the traditions of the race and the people, which yield but slowly to the influence of the present and to new developments, and, so long as they work through the superego, play an important part in man's life, quite independently of economic conditions.[10]

The feminine mystique, elevated by Freudian theory into a scientific religion, sounded a single, overprotective, life-restricting, future-denying note for women. Girls who grew up playing baseball, baby-sitting, mastering geometry—almost independent enough, almost resourceful enough, to meet the problems of the fission–fusion era— were told by the most advanced thinkers of our time to go back and live their lives as if they were Noras, restricted to the doll's house by Victorian prejudice. And their own respect and awe for the authority of science—anthropology, sociology, psychology share that authority now—kept them from questioning the feminine mystique.

Notes

1. Clara Thompson, *Psychoanalysis: Evolution and Development* (New York, 1950), pp. 131 ff:

   Freud not only emphasized the biological more than the cultural, but he also developed a cultural theory of his own based on his biological theory. There were two obstacles in the way of understanding the importance of the cultural phenomena he saw and recorded. He was too deeply involved in developing his biological theories to give much thought to other aspects of the data he collected. Thus he was interested chiefly in applying to human society his theory of instincts. Starting with the assumption of a death instinct, for example, he then developed an explanation of the cultural phenomena he observed in terms of the death instinct. Since he did not have the perspective to be gained from knowledge of comparative cultures, he could not evaluate cultural processes as such. . . . Much which Freud believed to be biological has been shown by modern research to be a reaction to a certain type of culture and not characteristic of universal human nature.

2. Richard La Piere, *The Freudian Ethic* (New York, 1959), p. 62.
3. Ernest Jones, *The Life and Works of Sigmund Freud* (New York, 1953) vol. ii, p. 121.
4. Sigmund Freud, "Degradation in Erotic Life," in *The Collected Papers of Sigmund Freud*, vol. iv.
5. Thompson, op. cit., p. 133.
6. Sigmund Freud, "The Psychology of Women," in *New Introductory Lectures on Psychoanalysis*, tr. by W. J. H. Sprott (New York, 1933), pp. 170 f.
7. Ibid., p. 182.
8. Thompson, op. cit., pp. 12 f.
9. Marynia Farnham and Ferdinand Lundberg, *Modern Woman: The Lost Sex* (New York and London, 1947), pp. 142 ff.
10. Sigmund Freud, "The Anatomy of the Mental Personality," in *New Introductory Lectures on Psychoanalysis*, p. 96.

8   The Gutenberg Galaxy

Marshall McLuhan

WHEN King Lear proposes "our darker purpose" as the subdivision of his kingdom, he is expressing a politically daring and *avant-garde* intent for the early seventeenth century:

> Only we still retain
> The name, and all th' additions to a king. The sway,
> Revenue, execution of the rest,
> Beloved sons, be yours; which to confirm,
> This coronet part betwixt you.[1]

Lear is proposing an extremely modern idea of delegation of authority from centre to margins. His "darker purpose" would have been recognized at once as left-wing Machiavellianism by an Elizabethan audience. The new patterns of power and organization which had been discussed during the preceding century were now, in the early seventeenth century, being felt at all levels of social and private life. *King Lear* is a presentation of the new strategy of culture and power as it affects the state, the family, and the individual psyche:

> Meantime we shall express our darker purpose.
> Give me the map there. Know we have divided
> In three our kingdom;

The map was also a novelty in the sixteenth century, age of Mercator's projection, and was key to the new vision of peripheries of power and wealth. Columbus had been a cartographer before he was a navigator; and the discovery that it was possible to continue in a straight-line course, as if space were uniform and continuous, was a major shift in human awareness in the Renaissance. More important, the map brings forward at once a principal theme of King Lear, namely the isolation of the visual sense as a kind of blindness.

. . .

Competitive individualism had become the scandal of a society long invested with corporate and collective values. The role played by print in instituting new patterns of culture is not unfamiliar. But one natural consequence of the specializing action of the new forms of knowledge was that all kinds of power took on a strongly centralist character. Whereas the role of the feudal monarch had been inclusive, the king actually

Extracts from Marshall McLuhan, *The Gutenberg Galaxy: The Making of Typographic Man* (University of Toronto Press), 11–50. Reprinted with permission of the publisher.

including in himself all his subjects, the Renaissance prince tended to become an exclusive power centre surrounded by his individual subjects. And the result of such centralism, itself dependent on many new developments in roads and commerce, was the habit of delegation of powers and the specializing of many functions in separate areas and individuals. In *King Lear*, as in other plays, Shakespeare shows an utter clairvoyance concerning the social and personal consequences of denudation and stripping of attributes and functions for the sake of speed, precision, and increased power.

. . .

King Lear is a working model of the process of denudation by which men translated themselves from a world of roles to a world of jobs

King Lear is a kind of elaborate case history of people translating themselves out of a world of roles into the new world of jobs. This is a process of stripping and denudation which does not occur instantly except in artistic vision. But Shakespeare saw that it had happened in his time. He was not talking about the future. However, the older world of roles had lingered on as a ghost just as after a century of electricity the West still feels the presence of the older values of literacy and privacy and separateness.

The anguish of the third dimension is given its first verbal manifestation in poetic history in *King Lear*

. . .

The stripping of the senses and the interruption of their interplay in tactile synesthesia may well have been one of the effects of the Gutenberg technology. This process of separation and reduction of functions had certainly reached a critical point by the early seventeenth century when *King Lear* appeared. But to determine how far such a revolution in the human sense life could have proceeded from Gutenberg technology calls for a somewhat different approach from merely sampling the sensibility of a great play of the critical period.

 King Lear is a kind of medieval sermon-exemplum or inductive reasoning to display the madness and misery of the new Renaissance life of action. Shakespeare explains minutely that the very principle of *action* is the splitting up of social operations and of the private sense life into specialized segments. The resulting frenzy to discover a new over-all interplay of forces ensures a furious activation of all components and persons affected by the new stress.

 Cervantes had a similar awareness, and his *Don Quixote* is galvanized by the new form of the book as much as Machiavelli had been hypnotized by the special segment of experience that he had chosen to step up to the highest intensity of awareness. Machiavelli's abstraction of the entity of personal power from the social matrix was comparable to the much earlier abstraction of *wheel* from animal form. Such abstraction ensures a great deal more movement. But the Shakespeare–Cervantes vision is of the futility of such movement and of action deliberately framed on a fragmentary or specialist bias.

W. B. Yeats has an epigram which puts the themes of *King Lear* and *Don Quixote* in cryptic form:

> Locke sank into a swoon.
> The garden died
> God took the spinning jenny
> Out of his side.

The Lockean swoon was the hypnotic trance induced by stepping up the visual component in experience until it filled the field of attention. Psychologists define hypnosis as the filling of the field of attention by one sense only. At such a moment "the garden" dies. That is, the garden indicates the interplay of all the senses in haptic harmony. With the instressed concern with one sense only, the mechanical principle of abstraction and repetition emerges into explicit form. Technology is explicitness, as Lyman Bryson said. And explicitness means the spelling out of one thing at a time, one sense at a time, one mental or physical operation at a time. Since the object of the present book is to discern the, origins and modes of the Gutenberg configuration of events, it will be well to consider the effects of the alphabet on native populations today. For as they *are* in relation to the phonetic alphabet, so we once *were*.

The interiorization of the technology of the phonetic alphabet translates man from the magical world of the ear to the neutral visual world

J. C. Carothers, writing in *Psychiatry* (November, 1959) on "Culture, Psychiatry and the Written Word," set forth a number of observations contrasting non-literate natives with literate natives, and the non-literate man with the Western man generally. He starts (p. 308) with the familiar fact that

by reason of the type of educational influences that impinge upon Africans in infancy and early childhood, and indeed throughout their lives, a man comes to regard himself as a rather insignificant part of a much larger organism—the family and the clan—and not as an independent, self-reliant unit; personal initiative and ambition are permitted little outlet; and a meaningful integration of a man's experience on individual, personal lines is not achieved. By contrast to the constriction at the intellectual level, great freedom is allowed for at the temperamental level, and a man is expected to live very much in the "here and now," to be highly extraverted, and to give very free expression to his feelings.

In a word, our notions of the "uninhibited" native ignore the utter inhibition and suppression of his mental and personal life which is unavoidable in a non-literate world:

Whereas the Western child is early introduced to building blocks, keys in locks, water taps, and a multiplicity of items and events which constrain him to think in terms of spatiotemporal relations and mechanical causation, the African child receives instead an education which depends much more exclusively on the spoken word and which is relatively highly charged with drama and emotion. (p. 308)

That is, a child in any Western milieu is surrounded by an abstract explicit visual technology of uniform time and uniform continuous space in which "cause" is efficient and sequential, and things move and happen on single planes and in successive order. But the African child lives in the implicit, magical world of the resonant oral word. He encounters not efficient causes but formal causes of configurational field such as any non-literate society cultivates. Carothers repeats again and again that "rural Africans live largely in a world of sound—a world loaded with direct personal significance for the hearer—whereas the Western European lives much more in a visual world which is on the whole indifferent to him." Since the ear world is a hot hyperesthetic world and the eye world is relatively a cool, neutral world, the Westerner appears to people of ear culture to be a very cold fish indeed.[2]

Carothers reviews the familiar non-literate idea of the "power" of words where thought and behaviour depend upon the magical resonance in words and their power to impose their assumptions relentlessly. He cites Kenyatta concerning love magic among the Kikuyu:

It is very important to acquire the correct use of magical words and their proper intonations, for the progress in applying magic effectively depends on uttering these words in their ritual order. . . . In performing these acts of love magic the performer has to recite a magical formula. . . . After this recitation he calls the name of the girl loudly and starts to address her *as though she were listening.* (p. 309)

It is a matter of "rite words in rote order," as Joyce put it. But once more any Western child today grows up in this kind of magical repetitive world as he hears advertisements on radio and TV.

Carothers next asks (p. 310) how literacy in a society might operate to effect the change from the notion of words as resonant, live, active, natural forces to the notion of words as "meaning" or "significance" for minds:

I suggest that it was only when the written, and still more the printed, word appeared on the scene that the stage was set for words to lose their magic powers and vulnerabilities. Why so?

I developed the theme in an earlier article with reference to Africa, that the nonliterate rural population lives largely in a world of sound, in contrast to western Europeans who live largely in a world of vision. Sounds are in a sense dynamic things, or at least are always indicators of dynamic things—of movements, events, activities, for which man, when largely unprotected from the hazards of life in the bush or the veldt, must be ever on the alert. . . . Sounds lose much of this significance in western Europe, where man often develops, and must develop, a remarkable ability to disregard them. Whereas for Europeans, in general, "seeing is believing," for rural Africans reality seems to reside far more in what is heard and what is said. . . . Indeed, one is constrained to believe that the eye is regarded by many Africans less as a receiving organ than as an instrument of the will, the ear being the main receiving organ.

Carothers reiterates that the Westerner depends on a high degree of visual shaping of spatio-temporal relations without which it is impossible to have the mechanistic sense of causal relations so necessary to the order of our lives. But the quite different assumptions of native perceptual life have led him to ask (p. 311) what has been the possible role of written words in shifting habits of perception from the auditory to visual stress:

When words are written, they become, of course, a part of the visual world. Like most of the elements of the visual world, they become static things and lose, as such, the dynamism which is so characteristic of the auditory world in general, and of the spoken word in particular. They lose much of the personal element, in the sense that the heard word is most commonly directed at oneself, whereas the seen word most commonly is not, and can be read or not as whim dictates. They lose those emotional overtones and emphases which have been described, for instance, by Monrad-Krohn ... Thus, in general, words, by becoming visible, join a world of relative indifference to the viewer—a world from which the magic "power" of the word has been abstracted.

Carothers continues his observations into the area of "free ideation" permitted to literate societies and quite out of the question for oral, non-literate communities:

The concept that verbal thought is separable from action, and is, or can be, ineffective and contained within the man ... has important sociocultural implications, for it is only in societies which recognize that verbal thoughts can be so contained, and do not of their nature emerge on wings of power, that social constraints can, in theory at least, afford to ignore ideation. (p. 311)

Thus, in a society still so profoundly oral as Russia, where spying is done by ear and not by eye, at the memorable "purge" trials of the 1930s Westerners expressed bafflement that many confessed total guilt not because of what they had done but what they had thought. In a highly literate society, then, visual and behavioural conformity frees the individual for inner deviation. Not so in an oral society where inner verbalization is effective social action:

In these circumstances it is implicit that behavioural constraints *must* include constraint of thought. Since all behaviour in such societies is governed and conceived on highly social lines, and since directed thinking can hardly be other than personal and unique for each individual, it is furthermore implicit in the attitude of these societies that the very possibility of such thinking is hardly to be recognized. Therefore, if and when such thinking does occur, at other than strictly practical and utilitarian levels, it is apt to be seen as deriving from the devil or from other external evil influences, and as something to be feared and shunned as much in oneself as in others. (p. 312)

It is, perhaps, a little unexpected to hear the compulsive and rigid patterns of a deeply oral-aural community referred to as "governed and conceived on highly social lines." For nothing can exceed the automatism and rigidity of an oral, non-literate community in its non-personal collectivity. As Western literate communities encounter the various "primitive" or auditory communities still remaining in the world, great confusion occurs. Areas like China and India are still audile-tactile in the main. Such phonetic literacy as has penetrated there has altered very little. Even Russia is still profoundly oral in bias. Only gradually does literacy alter substructures of language and sensibility.

Alexander Inkeles in his book on *Public Opinion in Russia* (p. 137) gives a useful account of how the ordinary and unconscious bias, even of the Russian literate groups, has a direction quite counter to anything a long-literate community would consider "natural." The Russian attitude, like that of any oral society, reverses our stress:

In the United States and England it is the freedom of expression, the right itself in the abstract, that is valued. ... In the Soviet Union, on the other hand, the *results* of exercising freedom are in the forefront of attention, and the preoccupation with the freedom itself is secondary. It is for this reason that the discussions between Soviet and Anglo-American representatives characteristically reach absolutely no agreement on specific proposals, although both sides assert that there should be freedom of the press. The American is usually talking about freedom of *expression*, the right to say or not to say certain things, a right which he claims exists in the United States and not in the Soviet Union. The Soviet representative is usually talking about *access* to the *means* of expression, not to the right to say things at all, and this access he maintains is denied to most in the United States and exists for most in the Soviet Union.

Soviet concern with media *results* is natural to any oral society where interdependence is the result of instant interplay of cause and effect in the total structure. Such is the character of a village, or, since electric media, such is also the character of global village. And it is the advertising and PR community that is most aware of this basic new dimension of global interdependence. Like the Soviet Union, they are concerned about *access* to the media and about *results*. They have no concern whatever about self-expression and would be shocked by any attempt to take over, say, a public advertisement for oil or coke as a vehicle of private opinion or personal feeling. In the same way the literate bureaucrats of the Soviet Union cannot imagine anybody wanting to use public media in a private way. And this attitude has just nothing to do with Marx, Lenin, or Communism. It is a normal tribal attitude of any oral society. The Soviet press is their equivalent of our Madison Avenue in shaping production and social processes.

Schizophrenia may be a necessary consequence of literacy

Carothers stresses that until phonetic writing split apart thought and action, there was no alternative but to hold all men responsible for their thoughts as much as their actions. His great contribution has been, to point to the breaking apart of the magical world of the ear and the neutral world of the eye, and to the emergence of the detribalized individual from this split. It follows, of course, that literate man, when we meet him in the Greek world, is a split man, a schizophrenic, as all literate men have been since the invention of the phonetic alphabet. Mere writing, however, has not the peculiar power of the phonetic technology to detribalize man. Given the phonetic alphabet with its abstraction of meaning from sound and the translation of sound into a visual code, and men were at grips with an experience that transformed them. No pictographic or ideogrammic or hieroglyphic mode of writing has the detribalizing power of the phonetic alphabet. No other kind of writing save the phonetic has ever translated man out of the possessive world of total interdependence and interrelation that is the auditory network. From that magical resonating world of simultaneous relations that is the oral and acoustic space there is only one route to the freedom and independence of detribalized man. That route is *via* the phonetic alphabet, which lands men at once in varying degrees of dualistic schizophrenia. Here is how Bertrand Russell describes (in his *History of Western Philosophy*, p. 39) this condition of the Greek world in the early throes of dichotomy and the trauma of literacy:

Not all of the Greeks, but a large proportion of them, were passionate, unhappy, at war with themselves, driven along one road by the intellect and along another by the passions, with the imagination to conceive heaven and the wilful self-assertion that creates hell. They had a maxim "nothing too much", but they were in fact excessive in everything—in pure thought, in poetry, in religion, and in sin. It was the combination of passion and intellect that made them great, while they were great. . . . There were, in fact, two tendencies in Greece, one passionate, religious, mystical, other worldly, the other cheerful, empirical, rationalistic, and interested in acquiring knowledge of a diversity of facts.

The division of faculties which results from the technological dilation or externalization of one or another sense is so pervasive a feature of the past century that today we have become conscious, for the first time in history, of how these mutations of culture are initiated. Those who experience the first onset of a new technology, whether it be alphabet or radio, respond most emphatically because the new sense ratios set up at once by the technological dilation of eye or ear, present men with a surprising new world, which evokes a vigorous new "closure," or novel pattern of interplay, among all of the senses together. But the initial shock gradually dissipates as the entire community absorbs the new habit of perception into all of its areas of work and association. But the real revolution is in this later and prolonged phase of "adjustment" of all personal and social life to the new model of perception set up by the new technology.

The Romans carried out the alphabetic translation of culture into visual terms. The Greeks, whether ancient or Byzantine, clung to much of the older oral culture with its distrust of action and applied knowledge. For applied knowledge, whether in military structure or industrial organization, depends upon uniformity and homogenization of populations. "It is certain," wrote the symbolist Edgar Allan Poe, "that the mere act of inditing tends in a great degree to the logicalization of thought." Lineal, alphabetic inditing made possible the sudden invention of "grammars" of thought and science by the Greeks. These grammars or explicit spellings out of personal and social processes were visualizations of non-visual functions and relations. The functions and processes were not new. But the means of arrested visual analysis, namely the phonetic alphabet, was as new to the Greeks as the movie camera in our century.

We can ask ourselves later why the fanatic specialism of the Phoenicians, which hacked the alphabet out of the hieroglyphic culture, did not release any further intellectual or artistic activity in them. Meantime, it is relevant to note that Cicero, the encyclopedic synthesizer of the Roman world, when surveying the Greek world, reproves Socrates for having been the first to make a split between mind and heart. The pre-Socratics were still mainly in a non-literate culture. Socrates stood on the border between that oral world and the visual and literate culture. But he wrote nothing. The Middle Ages regarded Plato as the mere scribe or amanuensis of Socrates. And Aquinas considered that neither Socrates nor Our Lord committed their teaching to writing because the kind of interplay of minds that is in teaching is not possible by means of writing.[3]

Does the interiorization of media such as *letters* alter the ratio among our senses and change mental processes?

What concerned Cicero, the practical Roman, was that the Greeks had put difficulties in the way of his own program for the *doctus orator*. In chapters xv–xxiii of the third book of the *De oratore*, he offers a history of philosophy from the beginning to his own time, trying to explain how it came about that the professional philosophers had made a breach between eloquence and wisdom, between practical knowledge and knowledge which these men professed to follow for its own sake. Before Socrates learning had been the preceptress of living rightly and speaking well. But with Socrates came the division between the tongue and the heart. That the eloquent Socrates should have been of all people the one to initiate a division between thinking wisely and speaking well was inexplicable: " . . . quorum princeps Socrates fuit, is, qui omnium eruditorum testimonio totiusque judicio Graeciae cum prudentia et acumine et venustate et subtilitate, tum vero eloquentia, varietate, copia, quam se cumque in partem dedisset omnium fuit facile princeps . . . "

But after Socrates things became much worse in Cicero's opinion. The Stoics despite a refusal to cultivate eloquence, have alone of all the philosophers declared eloquence to be a virtue and wisdom. For Cicero, wisdom is eloquence because only by eloquence can knowledge be applied to the minds and hearts of men. It is applied knowledge that obsesses the mind of Cicero the Roman as it did the mind of Francis Bacon. And for Cicero, as for Bacon, the technique of application depends upon the Roman brick procedure of uniform repeatability and homogeneous segments of knowledge.

If a technology is introduced either from within or from without a culture, and if it gives new stress or ascendancy to one or another of our senses, the ratio among all of our senses is altered. We no longer feel the same, nor do our eyes and ears and other senses remain the same. The interplay among our senses is perpetual save in conditions of anesthesia. But any sense when stepped up to high intensity can act as an anesthetic for other senses. The dentist can now use "audiac"—induced noise—to remove tactility. Hypnosis depends on the same principle of isolating one sense in order to anesthetize the others. The result is a break in the ratio among the senses, a kind of loss of identity. Tribal, non-literate man, living under the intense stress on auditory organization of all experience, is, as it were, entranced.

. . .

Plato shows no awareness of how the phonetic alphabet had altered the sensibility of the Greeks; nor did anybody else in his time or later. Before his time, the myth-makers, poised on the frontiers between the old oral world of the tribe and the new technologies of specialism and individualism, had foreseen all and said all in a few words. The myth of Cadmus states how this King who had introduced the Phoenician script, or the phonetic alphabet to Greece, had sown the dragon's teeth and they had sprung up armed men. This, as with all myth, is a succinct statement of a complex social process that had occurred over a period of centuries. But it was only in recent years that the work of Harold Innis opened up the Cadmus myth fully. (See, for example, *The Bias of Communication* and *Empire and Communications*.) The myth, like the aphorism and maxim, is characteristic of oral culture. For, untill literacy deprives language of his multi-dimensional resonance, every word is a poetic world unto itself, a "momentary deity" or revelation, as it seemed to non-literate men. Ernst Cassirer's *Language and Myth* presents this aspect of non-literate human awareness, surveying the wide range of current study of language origins and development. Towards the end of the nineteenth century numerous students of non-literate societies had begun to have doubts about the *a priori* character of logical categories. Today, when the role of phonetic literacy in the creating of the techniques of enunciation of propositions ("formal logic") is well known, it is still supposed, even by some anthropologists, that Euclidean space and three-dimensional visual perception is a universal datum of mankind. The absence of such space in native art is considered by such scholars to be owing to lack of artistic skill. Cassirer, reporting on the notion of words as myth, (the etymology of *mythos* indicates that it means "word") says (p. 62):

According to Usener, the lowest level to which we can trace back the origin of religious concepts is that of "momentary gods", as he calls those images which are born from the need or the specific feeling of a critical moment. . . . and still bearing the mark of all its pristine volatility and freedom. But it appears that the new findings which ethnology and comparative religion have put at our disposal during the three decades since the publication of Usener's work enable us to go back one step further yet.

Civilization gives the barbarian or tribal man an eye for an ear and is now at odds with the electronic world

This step takes to a more generalized sense of the manifestations of divine potency, away from particular, individualized "archetypes" and epiphanies of "momentary deities." It must often have puzzled the scholars and physicists of our time that just in the degree to which we penetrate the lowest layers of non-literate awareness we encounter the most advanced and sophisticated ideas of twentieth-century art and science. To explain that paradox will be an aspect of the present book. It is a theme around which much emotion and controversy are daily engendered as our world shifts from a visual to an auditory orientation in its electric technology. The controversy, of course, ignores the cause of the process altogether and clings to the "content." Setting aside the effects of the alphabet in creating Euclidean space for the Greek sensibility, as well as the simultaneous discovery of perspective and chronological narrative, it will be necessary to return briefly to the native world with J. C. Carothers. For it is in the non-literate world that it is easiest to discern the operation of phonetic letters in shaping our Western world.

That the Greeks were able to do more with the written word than other communities such as the Babylonian and Egyptian was, according to H. A. L. Fisher (*A History of Europe*, p. 19) that they were not under "the paralysing control of organized priestcraft." But even so, they had only a brief period of exploration and discovery before settling into a *clichéd* pattern of repetitive thought. Carothers feels that the early Greek intelligentsia not only had the stimulus of sudden access to the acquired wisdom of other peoples, but, having none of its own, there were no vested interests in acquired knowledge to frustrate the immediate acceptance and development of the new. It is this very situation which today puts the Western world at such a disadvantage, as against the "backward" countries. It is our enormous backlog of literate and mechanistic technology that renders us so helpless and inept in handling the new electric technology. The new physics is an auditory domain and long-literate society is not at home in the new physics, nor will it ever be.

This, of course, is to overlook the utter discrepancy between the phonetic alphabet and any other kind of writing whatever. Only the phonetic alphabet makes a break between eye and ear, between semantic meaning and visual code; and thus only phonetic writing has the power to translate man from the tribal to the civilized sphere, to give him an eye for an ear. The Chinese culture is considerably more refined and perceptive than the Western world has ever been. But the Chinese are tribal, people of the ear. "Civilization" must now be used technically to mean detribalized man for whom the visual values have priority in the organization of thought and action. Nor is this to give any new meaning or value to "civilization" but rather to specify its character. It is quite obvious, that most civilized people are crude and numb in their perceptions, compared with the hyperesthesia of oral and auditory cultures. For the eye has none of the delicacy of the ear. Carothers goes on (p. 313) to observe that:

So far as Plato's thinking can be considered representative of the thinking of the Greeks, it is very clear that the word, whether thought or written, still retained, for them, and from our point of view, vast powers in the 'real' world. Although at last it was seen as nonbehavioural itself, it now came to be regarded as the fount and origin not only of behaviour but of all discovery: it was the only key to knowledge, and thought alone—in words or figures—would unlock all doors for understanding the world. In a sense, indeed; the power of words or other visual symbols became greater than before . . . now verbal and mathematical thought became the only truth, and the whole sensory world came to be regarded as illusory, except insofar as thoughts were heard or seen.

In his dialogue of the *Cratylus*, named for his teacher of language and grammar, Plato has Socrates say (438):

But if these things are only to be known through names, how can we suppose that the givers of names had knowledge, or were legislators before there were names at all, and therefore before they could have known them?

Cratylus: I believe, Socrates, the true account of the matter to be, that a power more than human gave things their first names, and that the names which were thus given are necessarily their true names.

This view of Cratylus was the basis of most language study until the Renaissance. It is rooted in the old oral "magic" of the "momentary deity" kind such as is favoured again today for various reasons. That it is most alien to merely literary and visual culture is easily found in the remarks of incredulity which Jowett supplies as his contribution to the dialogue.

Carothers turns to David Riesman's *The Lonely Crowd* (p. 9) for further orientation in his queries concerning the effects on writing on non-literate communities. Riesman had characterized our own Western world as developing in its "typical members a social character whose conformity is insured by their tendency to acquire early in life an internalized set of goals." Riesman made no effort to discover why the manuscript culture of the ancient and medieval worlds should not have conferred inner direction, nor why a print culture should inevitably confer inner direction. That is part of the business of the present book. But it can be said at once that "inner direction" depends upon a "fixed point of view." A stable, consistent character is one with an unwavering outlook, an almost hypnotized visual stance, as it were. Manuscripts were altogether too slow and uneven a matter to provide either a fixed point of view or the habit of gliding steadily on single planes of thought and information. As we shall see, manuscript culture is intensely audile-tactile compared to print culture; and that means that detached habits of observation are quite uncongenial to manuscript cultures, whether ancient Egyptian, Greek, or Chinese or medieval. In place of cool visual detachment the manuscript world puts empathy and participation of all the senses. But non-literate cultures experience such an overwhelming tyranny of the ear over the eye that any balanced interplay among the senses is unknown at the auditory extreme, just as balanced interplay of the senses became extremely difficult after print stepped up the visual component in Western experience to extreme intensity.

The modern physicist is at home with oriental field theory

Carothers finds Riesman's classification of "tradition-directed" peoples as corresponding "quite closely to those areas occupied by societies which are non-literate or in which the great majority of the population has been untouched by literacy" (p. 315). It should be understood that to be "touched" by literacy is not a very sudden affair, nor is it a total matter at any time or in any place. That should become very clear as we move through the sixteenth and later centuries. But today, as electricity creates conditions of extreme interdependence on a global scale, we move swiftly again into an auditory world of simultaneous events and over-all awareness. Yet the habits of literacy persist in our speech, our sensibilities, and in our arrangement of the spaces and times of our daily lives. Short of some catastrophe, literacy and visual bias could bear up for a long time against electricity and "unified field" awareness. And the same is true the other way around. Germans and the Japanese, while far-advanced in literate and analytic technology, retained the core of auditory tribal unity and total togetherness. The advent of radio, and electricity generally, was not only for them but for all tribal cultures a most intense experience. Long-literate cultures have naturally more resistance to the auditory dynamic of the total electric field culture of our time.

Riesman, referring to tradition-directed people, says (p. 26):

Since the type of social order we have been discussing is relatively unchanging, the conformity of the individual tends to be dictated to a very large degree by power relations among the various age and sex groups, the clans, castes, professions, and so forth—relations which have endured for centuries and are modified but slightly, if at all, by successive generations. The culture controls behavior minutely, and, . . . careful and rigid etiquette governs the fundamentally influential sphere of kin relationships. . . . Little energy is directed toward finding new solutions of the age-old problems . . .

Riesman points out that to meet even the rigid demands of complex religious ritual and etiquette "individuality of character need not be highly developed." He speaks as a highly literate man for whom "development" means having a private point of view. High development as it might appear to a native would not be accessible to our visual mode of awareness. We can get some idea of the attitude of a member of a tradition-directed society to technological improvements from a story related by Werner Heisenberg in *The Physicist's Conception of Nature*. A modern physicist with his habit of "field" perception, and his sophisticated separation from our conventional habits of Newtonian space, easily finds in the pre-literate world a congenial kind of wisdom.

Heisenberg is discussing "science as a part of the interplay between man and Nature" (p. 20):

In this connection it has often been said that the far-reaching changes in our environment and in our way of life wrought by this technical age have also changed dangerously our ways of thinking, and that here lie the roots of the crises which have shaken our times and which, for instance, are also expressed in modern art. True, this objection is much older than modern technology and science, the use of implements going back to man's earliest beginnings. Thus, two and a half thousand years ago, the Chinese sage Chuang-Tzu spoke of the danger of the machine when he said:

"As Tzu-Gung was travelling through the regions north of the river Han, he saw an old man working in his vegetable garden. He had dug an irrigation ditch. The man would descend into the well, fetch up a vessel of water in his arms and pour it out into the ditch. While his efforts were tremendous the results appeared to be very meagre.

"Tzu-Gung said, 'There is a way whereby you can irrigate a hundred ditches in one day, and whereby you can do much with little effort. Would you not like to hear of it?' Then the gardener stood up, looked at him and said, 'And what would that be?'

"Tzu-Gung replied, 'You take a wooden lever, weighted at the back and light in front. In this way you can bring up water so quickly that it just gushes out. This is called a draw-well.'

"Then anger rose up in the old man's face, and he said, 'I have heard my teacher say that whoever uses machines does all his work like a machine. He who does his work like a machine grows a heart like a machine, and he who carries the heart of a machine in his breast loses his simplicity. He who has lost his simplicity becomes unsure in the strivings of his soul. Uncertainty in the strivings of the soul is something which does not agree with honest sense. It is not that I do not know of such things; I am ashamed to use them.'"

Clearly this ancient tale contains a great deal of wisdom, for "uncertainty in the strivings of the soul" is perhaps one of the aptest descriptions of man's condition in our modern crisis; technology, the machine, has spread through the world to a degree that our Chinese sage could not even have suspected.

The sort of "simplicity" envisaged by the sage is a more complex and subtle product than anything that occurs in a society with specialized technology and sense life. But perhaps the real point of the anecdote is that it appealed to Heisenberg. It would not have interested Newton. Not only does modern physics abandon the specialized visual space of Descartes and Newton, it re-enters the subtle auditory space of the non-literate world. And in the most primitive society, as in the present age, such auditory space is a total field of simultaneous relations in which "change" has as little meaning and appeal as it had for the mind of Shakespeare or the heart of Cervantes. All values apart, we must learn today that our electric technology has consequences for our most ordinary perceptions and habits of action which are quickly recreating in us the mental processes of the most primitive men. These consequences occur, not in our thoughts or opinions, where we are trained to be critical, but in our most ordinary sense life, which creates the vortices and the matrices of thought and action. This book will try to explain why print culture confers on man a lanuage of thought which leaves him quite unready to face the language of his own electro-magnetic technology. The strategy any culture must resort to in a period like this was indicated by Wilhelm von Humboldt:

Man lives with his objects chiefly—in fact, since his feeling and acting depends on his perceptions, one may say exclusively—as language presents them to him. By the same process whereby he spins language out of his own being, he ensnares himself in it; and each language draws a magic circle round the people to which it belongs, a circle from which there is no escape save by stepping out of it into another.[4]

Such awareness as this has generated in our time the technique of the suspended judgment by which we can transcend the limitations of our own assumptions by a critique of them. We can now live, not just amphibiously in divided and distinguished worlds, but pluralistically in many worlds and cultures simultaneously. We are no more committed to one culture—to a single ratio among the human senses—any more than to one book or to one language or to one technology. Our need today is, culturally, the same as the scientist's who seeks to become aware of the bias of the instruments of research in order to correct that bias. Compartmentalizing of human potential by single cultures will soon be as absurd as specialism in subject or discipline has become. It is not likely that our age is more obsessional than any other, but it has become sensitively aware of the conditions and fact of obsession beyond any other age. However, our fascination with all phases of the unconscious, personal and collective, as with all modes of primitive awareness, began in the eighteenth century with the first violent revulsion against print culture and mechanical industry. What began as a "Romantic reaction" towards organic wholeness may or may not have hastened the discovery of electro-magnetic waves. But certainly the electro-magnetic discoveries have recreated the simultaneous "field" in all human affairs so that the human family now exists under conditions of a "global village." We live in a single constricted space resonant with tribal drums. So that concern with the "primitive" today is as banal as nineteenth-century concern with "progress," and as irrelevant to our problems.

The new electronic interdependence recreates the world in the image of a global village

It would be surprising, indeed, if Riesman's description of tradition-directed people did not correspond to Carothers' knowledge of African tribal societies. It would be equally startling were the ordinary reader about native societies not able to vibrate with a deep sense of affinity for the same, since our new electric culture provdes our lives again with a tribal base.

. . .

Reverting to the earlier theme of conformity, Carothers continues (pp. 315–16): "Thought and behavior are not seen as separate; they are both seen as behavioral. Evilwilling is, after all the most fearful type of "behavior" known in many of these societies, and a dormant or awakening fear of it lies ever in the minds of all their members." In our long striving to recover for the Western world a unity of sensibility and of thought and feeling we have no more been prepared to accept the tribal consequences of such unity than we were ready for the fragmentation of the human psyche by print culture.

. . .

When technology extends *one* of our senses, a new translation of culture occurs as swiftly as the new technology is interiorized

Although the main theme of this book is the Gutenberg Galaxy or a configuration of events, which lies far ahead of the world of alphabet and of scribal culture, it needs to be known why, without alphabet, there would have been no Gutenberg. And, therefore, we must get some insight into the conditions of culture and perception that make first, writing, and then, perhaps, alphabet possible at all.[5]

. . .

A recent work by Georg von Bekesy, *Experiments in Hearing,* offers an exactly reverse answer to the problem of space to the one which Carothers has just given us. Whereas he is trying to talk about the perception of non-literate people in terms of literate experience, Professor von Bekesy chooses to begin his discussion of acoustical space on its own terms. As one proficient in auditory spaces, he is keenly aware of the difficulty of talking about the space of hearing, for the acoustical is necessarily a world in "depth."[6] It is of the utmost interest that in trying to elucidate the nature of hearing and of acoustic space, Professor von Bekesy should deliberately avoid viewpoint and perspective in favour of mosaic field. And to this end he resorts to two-dimensional painting as a means of revealing the resonant depth of acoustic space. Here are his own words (p. 4):

It is possible to distinguish two forms of approach to a problem. One, which may be called the theoretical approach, is to formulate the problem in relation to what is already known, to make additions or extensions on the basis of accepted principles, and then to proceed to test these hypotheses experimentally. Another, which may be called the mosaic approach, takes each problem for itself with little reference to the field in which it lies, and seeks to discover relations and principles that hold within the circumscribed area.

Von Bekesy then proceeds to introduce his two paintings:

A close analogy to these two approaches may be found in the field of art. In the period between the eleventh and seventeenth centuries the Arabs and the Persians developed a high mastery of the arts of description. . . . Later, during the Renaissance, a new form of representation was developed in which the attempt was made to give unity and perspective to the picture and to represent the atmosphere. . . .

When in the field of science a great deal of progress has been made and most of the pertinent variables are known, a new problem may most readily be handled by trying to fit it into the existing framework. When, however, the framework is uncertain and the number of variables is large the mosaic approach is much the easier.

The mosaic approach is not only "much the easier" in the study of the simultaneous which is the auditory field; it is the only relevant approach. For the "two-dimensional" mosaic or painting is the mode in which there is muting of the visual as such, in order that there may be maximal interplay among all of the senses. Such was the painterly strategy "since Cézanne," to paint as if you held, rather than as if you saw, objects.

A theory of cultural change is impossible without knowledge of the changing sense ratios effected by various externalizations of our senses

It is very much worth dwelling on this matter, since we shall see that from the invention of the alphabet there has been a continuous drive in the Western world toward the separation of the senses, of functions, of operations, of states emotional and political, as well as of tasks—a fragmentation which terminated, thought Durkheim, in the *anomie* of the nineteenth century. The paradox presented by Professor von Bekesy is that the two-dimensional mosaic is, in fact, a multidimensional world of interstructural resonance. It is the three-dimensional world of pictorial space that is, indeed, an abstract illusion built on the intense separation of the visual from the other senses.

There is here no question of values or preferences. It is necessary, however, for any other kind of understanding to know why "primitive" drawing is two-dimensional, whereas the drawing and painting of literate man tends towards perspective. Without this knowledge we cannot grasp why men ever ceased to be "primitive" or audile-tactile in their sense bias. Nor could we ever understand why men have "since Cézanne" abandoned the visual in favour of the audile-tactile modes of awareness and of organization of experience. This matter clarified, we can much more easily approach the role of alphabet and of printing in giving a dominant role to the visual sense in language and art and in the entire range of social and of political life. For until men have up-graded the visual component communities know only a tribal structure. The detribalizing of the individual has, in the past at least, depended on an intense visual life fostered by literacy, and by literacy of the alphabetic kind alone. For alphabetic writing is not only unique but late. There had been much writing before it. In fact, any people that ceases to be nomadic and pursues sedentary modes of work is ready to invent writing. No merely nomadic people ever had writing any more than they ever developed architecture or "enclosed space." For writing is a visual enclosure of non-visual spaces and senses. It is, therefore, an abstraction of the visual from the ordinary sense interplay. And whereas speech is an outering (utterance) of all of our senses at once, writing abstracts from speech.

At the present time it is easier to grasp this specific technology of writing. The new institutes for teaching speeded-up reading habits work on the separation of eye-movements from inner verbalization. It will be indicated later that all reading in the ancient and medieval worlds was reading aloud. With print the eye speeded up and the voice quieted down. But inner verbalizing was taken for granted as inseparable from the horizontal following of the words on the page. Today we know that the divorce of reading and verbalizing can be made by vertical reading. This, of course, pushes the alphabetic technology of the separation of the senses to an extreme of inanity, but it is relevant to an understanding of how writing of any sort gets started.

In a paper entitled "A History of the Theory of Information," read to the Royal Society in 1951, E. Colin Cherry of the University of London, observed that "Early invention was greatly hampered by an inability to dissociate mechanical structure from animal form. The invention of the wheel was one outstanding early effort of such dissociation. The great spurt in invention which began in the sixteenth century rested on the gradual dissociation of the machine from animal form." Printing was the first mechanization of an ancient handicraft and led easily to the further mechanization of all handicrafts. The modern phases of this process are the theme of *Mechanization Takes Command* by Siegfried Giedion.

However, Giedion is concerned with a minute tracing of the stages by which in the past century we have used mechanism to recover organic form:

In his celebrated studies of the 'seventies on the motions of men and animals, Edward Muybridge set up a series of thirty cameras at twelve-inch intervals, releasing their shutters electromagnetically as soon as the moving object passed before the plate. . . . Each picture showed the object in an isolated phase as arrested by each camera. (p. 107)

That is to say, the object is translated out of organic or simultaneous form into a static or pictorial mode. By revolving a sequence of such static or pictorial spaces at a sufficient speed, the illusion of organic wholeness, or interplay of spaces, is created. Thus, the wheel finally becomes the means of moving our culture away from the machine. But it was by means of electricity applied to the wheel that the wheel merges once more with animal form. In fact, the wheel is now an obsolete form in the electric-missile age. But hypertrophy is the mark of obsolescence, as we shall see again and again. Just because wheel is now returning to organic form in the twentieth century it is quite easy for us to understand how primitive man "invented" it. Any creature in motion is a wheel in that repetition of movement has a cyclic and circular principle in it. Thus the melodies of literate societies are repeatable cycles. But the music of non-literate people has no such repetitive cyclic and abstract form as melody. Invention, in a word, is translation of one kind of space into another.

The twentieth century encounter between alphabetic and electronic faces of culture confers on the printed word a crucial role in staying the return to *the Africa within*

The invention of the alphabet, like the invention of the wheel, was the translation or reduction of a complex, organic interplay of spaces into a single space. The phonetic alphabet reduced the use of all the senses at once, which is oral speech, to a merely visual code. Today, such translation can be effected back and forth through a variety of spatial forms which we call the "media of communication." But each of these spaces has unique properties and impinges upon our other senses or spaces in unique ways.

Today, then, it is easy to understand the invention of the alphabet because, as A. N. Whitehead pointed out in *Science and the Modern World* (p. 141) the great discovery of the nineteenth century was the discovery of the method of discovery:

The greatest invention of the nineteenth century was the invention of the method of invention. A new method entered into life. In order to understand our epoch, we can neglect all the details of change, such as railways, telegraphs, radios, spinning machines, synthetic dyes. We must concentrate on the method in itself; that is the real novelty which has broken up the foundations of the old civilization. . . . One element in the new method is just the discovery of how to set about bridging the gap between the scientific ideas, and the ultimate product. It is a process of disciplined attack upon one difficulty after another.

The method of invention, as Edgar Poe demonstrated in his "Philosophy of Composition," is simply to begin with the solution of the problem or with the effect intended. Then one backtracks, step by step, to the point from which one must begin in order to reach the solution or effect. Such is the method of the detective story, of the symbolist poem, and of modern science. It is, however, the twentieth century step beyond this method of invention which is needed for understanding the origin and the action of such forms as the wheel or the alphabet. And that step is not the backtracking from *product* to starting point, but the following of *process* in isolation from product. To follow the contours of process as in psychoanalysis provides the only means of avoiding the product of process, namely neurosis or psychosis.

It is the purpose of the present book to study primarily the print phase of alphabetic culture. The print phase, however, has encountered today the new organic and biological modes of the electronic world. That is, it is now interpenetrated at its extreme development of mechanism by the electro-biological, as de Chardin has explained. And it is this reversal of character which makes our age "connatural," as it were, with non-literate cultures. We have no more difficulty in understanding the native or non-literate experience, simply because we have recreated it electronically within our own culture. (Yet post-literacy is a quite different mode of interdependence from pre-literacy.) So my dwelling upon the earlier phases of alphabetic technology is not irrelevant to an understanding of the Gutenberg era. . . .

Notes

1. *The Complete Works of Shakespeare*, ed G. L. Kittredge. All quotations from *King Lear*, unless otherwise noted, are from Act I, scene i. Kittredge's edition is cited throughout.
2. See chapter on "Acoustic Space" by E. Carpenter and H. M. McLuhan in *Explorations in Communication*, pp. 65–70.
3. Utrum Christus debuerit doctrinam Suam Scripto tradere. *Summa Theologica*, part III, q. 42, art. 4.
4. Quoted by Cassirer in *Language and Myth*, p. 9.
5. The Koreans by 1403 were making cast-metal type by means of punches and matrices (*The Invention of Printing in China and its Spread Westward* by T. F. Carter). Carter had no concern with the alphabet relation to print and was probably unaware that the Koreans are reputed to have a phonetic alphabet.
6. See "Acoustic Space."

9 Notes on the American Clothing System

Marshall Sahlins

CONSIDERED as a whole, the system of American clothing amounts to a very complex scheme of cultural categories and the relations between them, a veritable map—it does not exaggerate to say—of the cultural universe.[1] The first task will be to suggest that the scheme operates on a kind of general syntax: a set of rules for declining and combining classes of the clothing-form so as to formulate the cultural categories. In a study of *mode* as advertised in several French magazines, Roland Barthes discriminated for women's dress alone some sixty foci of signification. Each site or dimension comprised a range of meaningful contrasts: some by mere presence or absence, as of gloves; some as diversified as the indefinite series of colors (Barthes 1967: 114 ff.).[2] It is evident that with a proper syntax, rules of combination, a formidable series of propositions could be developed, constituting so many statements of the relations between persons and situations in the cultural system. It is equally evident that I could not hope to do more than suggest the presence of this grammar, without pretense at having analyzed it.

There are in costume several levels of semantic production. The outfit as a whole makes a statement, developed out of the particular arrangement of garment parts and by contrast to other total outfits. Again there is a logic of the parts, whose meanings are developed differentially by comparison at this level, in a Saussurean way: as, for example, the value of women's slacks is simultaneously determined by opposition to other garments of that locus, such as skirts or men's pants, as well as by contrast to other examples of the same class (slacks) that differ in color, pattern, or whatever. My concern in discussing this syntax will be more with what is conveyed than with an account of the entire set of rules. It will be enough to indicate that it provides a systematic basis for the the cultural discourse "fashioned" upon it:

"Most people wear some sign, and don't know what it's saying. Choose your sign according to your audience," Malloy said . . . "a good dark suit, white shirt and conservative tie are a young man's best wardrobe friends, if he's applying for a white collar job in a big range of business and professional categories. They're authority symbols. It's that simple," he said. ("Fashion Column," *Chicago Daily News*, 11 Jan. 1974)

But there is another problem, somewhat more difficult. I should like to move down a level to the constituent units composing the discourse: to demonstrate here how particular social meanings are related to elementary physical contrasts in the clothing

From Marshall Sahlins, "Notes on the American Clothing System," in Marshall Sahlins, *Culture and Practical Reason* (Chicago: University of Chicago Press, 1976), 179–204 object. It will be a movement also of rapprochement with totemic thought. For the principle is very much the same: a series of concrete differences among objects of the same class to which correspond distinctions along some dimension of social order—as the difference between blue collar and white is one between manual labor and bureaucratic; the relative saturation or brightness of hue discriminates fall from spring; or, "A sweet disorder in the dress / Kindles in clothes a wantonness" (Herrick). By such means the set of manufactured objects is able to comprehend the entire cultural order of a society it would at once dress and address. (Two words whose derivation from a common root—as Tylor said of "kindred" and "kindness"—expresses in the happiest way one of the most fundamental principles of social life.)

The overall objective in all this, I should stress, is some contribution toward a cultural account of production. It is to this end that I explore the code of object properties and their meaningful combinations. The emphasis on the code implies also that we shall not be concerned at present with how individuals dress. This is not simply a decision for *langue* over *parole*. How people dress is a far more complicated semiotic problem than can be attempted here, including as it does the particular consciousness or self-conceptions of the subject in a specific meaningful "context of the situation:" Again, I touch too briefly on the related question of the manipulation of the fashion code within the clothing industry. However, if all such limitations, which have a common reference to the system in action, render this account regrettably incomplete, they do have the advantage of focusing upon the position it is necessary to establish in advance, and without which all further analysis of action risks relapse into a vulgar pragmatics: that production is the realization of a symbolic scheme.

For notice what is produced in the clothing system. By various objective features an item of apparel becomes appropriate for men or women, for night or for day, for "around the house" or "in public," for adult or adolescent. What is produced is, first, classes of time and place which index situations or activities; and, second, classes of status to which all persons are ascribed. These might be called "notional coordinates" of clothing, in the sense that they mark basic notions of time, place, and person as consti-tuted in the cultural order. Hence what is reproduced in clothing is this classificatory scheme. Yet not simply that. Not simply the boundaries, the divisions, and subdivisions of, say, age-grades or social classes; by a specific symbolism of clothing differences, what is produced are the meaningful differences between these categories. In manufacturing apparel of distinct cut, outline, or color for women as opposed to men, we reproduce the distinction between femininity and masculinity as *known* to this society. That is what is going on in the pragmatic-material process of production.

More specifically, what is going on is a differentiation of the cultural space as between town and country, and within the town between downtown and neighborhood—and then again, a contrast between all of these, as collectively making up a public sphere, and the domestic-familial domain. When a woman goes shopping, she normally "dresses *up*" a domestic costume, at least by the addition of peripheral display of elements such as jewelry; and the more so if she is shopping downtown rather than "in the neighborhood." Conversely, when a man returns home from "a hard day at the office," he dresses down a public style in a way consistent with the "familiarity" of the domestic sphere.[3] At the other extreme are the higher distinctions of national space:

for example, the West Coast and East Coast, of which the marked subclasses are California and the Northeast (cf. Rosencranz 1972: 263–64).

We also substantialize in clothing the basic cultural valuations of time—diurnal, hebdomadal, and seasonal. We have evening clothes and daytime clothes, "little afternoon dresses" and nighttime dress (pajamas). Each references the nature of the activities ordered by those times, in the way that weekday apparel is to Sunday "best" as the secular is to the sacred. The marked seasonal variations are spring and fall, the colors of these seasons usually conceived to parallel the vegetation cycle. (Outdoor color per se, however, seems to be inverted for summer and winter dress: spectral green and red mark the winter solstice [Christmas], whereas white is traditionally appropriate between Memorial Day [May 30] and Labor Day.)

A similar treatment could be made of the class, the sex, and the age-grade of clothing. All these social categories have determinate markers, characteristic variations on the object level. In the common ideology of producers and consumers, this consubstantiality of subject and object is predicated on an identity of essences, such that the silk is "womanly" as women are "silky." "Fine as silk," "soft as silk," the cloth opposes itself on one side to the masculinity of wool and on the other to the inferiority of cotton (cf. Dichter 1959: 104 ff.).[4] But this Veblenesque correlation of the height of luxury with the height of femininity is likely transposed by race, as for American blacks the male seems to be the marked sex whereas whites decorate the female.[5] Yet in turn, the correlation between black male and white female elegance along such dimensions as texture will be differentially inflected by class, insofar as race and class overlap, and it is a commonplace of the homegrown sociology that muted color and minor contrast are upper-class Establishment whereas brilliant color and major contrast are "mass" (Birren 1956). On the other hand, the silken sobriety of the upper-class white woman is exchanged in her daughter's clothes for the textures of youth: which brings us back full circle to wool by the common discrimination of youth and male from the adult female on the attributes of activity/passivity (ceremonial).[6]

Gender and age-grade serve to illustrate another property of the grammar: certain mechanisms of opening the set to make it more complex without, however, a revision in principle. Even in expansion, the system seems to adhere to Sapir's dictum that fashion is custom in the guise of a departure from custom. New species and subspecies are permuted, for example, by a combinatory synthesis of existing oppositions. In designer's categories, the received distinction between infants and schoolchildren has latterly been segmented into "infants," "toddlers," "preschoolers," and "schoolchildren"; adolescents are likewise not what they used to be, but "preteens," "subteens," and "teens" (Rosencranz 1972: 203). In the same way, various categories of homosexuality can be evolved by particular combinations of male and female apparel, to the extent that we now have six more or less clearly distinguishable sartorial sexes. But at the line between adolescent and adult, a second type of permutation is currently in evidence: the adaptation of an existing distinction from elsewhere in the system, a kind of metaphorical transfer, to signify a change of content in a traditional opposition. The received idea of an "adolescent revolution" doubtless predisposed the change, but since the Vietnam War the conflict with the constituted (i.e., adult) authorities has been specifically idiomized politically, and so in apparel by the contrast, adolescent/adult:worker/

capitalist, with youth appropriating the blue jeans and work shirts of *society's under-class*. Perhaps nothing could better prove the absence of practical utility in clothing, since work is one of the last things youth has in mind. But the example serves as well to reveal the singular quality of capitalist society: not that it fails to work on a symbolic code, but that the code works as an open set, responsive to events which it both orchestrates and assimilates to produce expanded versions of itself.

Parenthetically: this view of production as the substantialization of a cultural logic should prohibit us from speaking naively of the generation of demand by supply, as though the social product were the conspiracy of a few "decision-makers," able to impose an ideology of fashion through the deceits of advertising. In Marx's phrase, "The educator himself needs educating." It is not as if the producers' *parole* becomes our *langue*. Nor need one indulge in the converse mystification of capitalist production as a response to consumers' wants: "We always try to adapt," says the head of public relations for the company that has profited most from the recent expansion of blue jeans sales.[7] But who then is dominant, the producer or the consumer? It should be possible to transcend all such subjective representations for an institutional description of capitalist production as a cultural process. Clearly this production is organized to exploit all possible social differentiation by a motivated differentiation of goods. It proceeds according to a meaningful logic of the concrete, of the significance of objective differences, thus developing appropriate signs of emergent social distinctions. Such might well describe the specialization of age differences in clothing, or the metaphoric transfer of blue jeans—especially if it is noted that the iconic integration of social and object distinctions is a dialectic process. The product that reaches its destined market constitutes an objectification of a social category, and so helps to constitute the latter in society; as in turn, the differentiation of the category develops further social declensions of the goods system. Capitalism is no sheer rationality. It is a definite form of cultural order; or a cultural order acting in a particular form. End of parenthesis.

I turn to another type of variation in costume, this corresponding to the division of labor broadly considered, to suggest the presence of systematic rules for social categorization of the clothing form. First, however, we must establish the classification on the social level. In his discussion of the *monde* in the *mode*, Barthes distinguishes two alternate ways in which the social significance of costume is conceived (1967: 249 ff.). These are, in effect, two modalities of social discourse, the active and the passive: doing and being, *faire* and *être*, activity and identity. Adapting the distinction to present purposes, one might say that the first has to do with functions; it indexes costume according to the type of activity, such as sport or manual labor. The second relates to occupational status—the characteristic habit of the industrial worker, the farmer, the waitress, the doctor, the soldier. Again, in the following very general and oversimplified table of functions (Fig. 9.1), I abbreviate a considerable argument, and more than one assumption:

The main assumption is the validity of Veblen's distinction of ceremony and workmanship in American categories of activity and clothing. The key to the entire table is this principle. In each opposition, the marked or ceremonial function is placed to the left, the unmarked and workmanlike to the right, the whole then a set of differentiations of the master distinction between work and leisure (cf. Veblen 1934 [1899]). If this

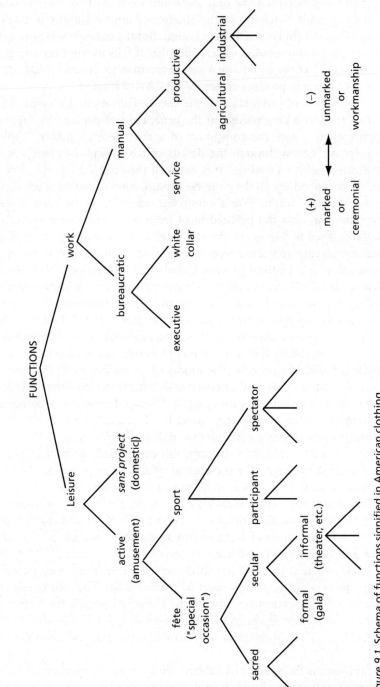

Figure 9.1 Schema of functions signified in American clothing

assumption is allowed as more or less ethnographically correct, and the consequences likewise worked out through the classes and subclasses in a faithful way, two remarkable regularities in the system of clothing are presented to view. The first might be called the *rule of ceremonial correspondence*. It refers to the analogous differentiation of costume in any two functional classes similarly ordered on the opposition of ceremony and workmanship. Consider, for example, the "dress clothes" affected by men on "special occasions" (*fête*), culminating perhaps in formal tuxedo for very ritualized affairs (e.g., marriages, gala) or, slightly less formally, the highly styled dark suit. Notice then that these outfits specifically resemble the "conservative" suits worn by business executives, in a way corresponding to their respective differences from sportive wear in the area of amusement and white-collar dress in the domain of work. The latter two—by their relative "informality," permissible color schemes, and so forth—again resemble each other; indeed, to the extent that a younger office worker may be discriminated from the higher corporate executives precisely by his "sports jacket." Yet exactly the same differences characterize, in a general way, the opposition between the more formal costumes of amusement and the relative undress permitted when "doing nothing; just sitting around the house" (*sans projet*). Or again, it is the difference between the blue jeans or overalls of an industrial worker and the more stylized uniforms of waitresses, deliverymen, and other service workers. This particular opposition also reappears on the leisure side in the sporting outfits of hunting or skiing, which are like uniforms even as they are differentiated from the "casual clothes" of the spectator.[8] It is thus a rule of analogy in the oppositions of ceremony/workmanship, at whatever level they may appear in the system. The terms of any opposition correspond to the terms of any other, such that the marked (ceremonial) costumes of any two classes resemble each other by an analogous differentiation from the unmarked (workmanlike) costumes of their repective classes.

. . .

Besides the similarities in the differences, there are also differences in the similarities—a tuxedo is still more "stylized" than a business suit, as domestic clothes (especially for night) are more "undressed" and "casual" than work clothes—which leads to a second rule: *rule of ceremonial exaggeration*. The rule is that, on one hand, the marked costume in a more ceremonial opposition is itself more ceremonial than its counterpart in some workmanlike opposition: as the uniforms of active sport are more colorful and cut with more flair than the uniform of the waitress or the milkman. On the other hand, the unmarked costume of the ceremonial opposition is even less workmanlike than its counterpart on the more workmanlike side: as the spectator's outfit is more "casual" than the industrial worker's. The same might be said of the opposition of *fête* and sport within the category "amusement," as compared with executive and clerical in the category of managerial work, even as the last pair is at once more ceremonial (the executive suit) and less workmanlike (white collar) than, again, the service versus industrial worker. The rule, therefore, is that the opposition stipulated within a workmanlike class is exaggerated by the corresponding opposition in a more ceremonial class. The exaggeration occurs in both directions: the ceremonial outfit is more ceremonial at its marked pole, less workmanlike at its unmarked pole.

. . .

It seems legitimate to pause at this juncture to explain what claims are being made for exercises of the sort just indulged in. The overall aim is to respond to a question initially posed by Marx, but so far as I know without answer in his or any other Economics: What kind of theoretical account can be given for production as a *mode of life*? I propose here an example of the beginning of such a cultural account: example, because it is concerned only with the system of clothing in modern America; beginning, because it has been concerned so far mostly with the general syntax, social classes of the clothing object, and certain rules of its social declension. But it is necessary to be still more cautious. The claim made for the rules of ceremonial correspondence is only that they suggest such a syntax. To have any higher pretensions, the discussion would have to stipulate the kinds of clothing features to which the rules apply—features of color, color contrast, line and outline, type and congruence of garment pieces, kinds of accessories, qualities of texture—and the modes of their combination. The full scope of the project is very large; this is only an example of the suggestion of a beginning.

. . .

In its economic dimension, this project consists of the reproduction of society in a system of objects not merely useful but meaningful; whose utility indeed consists of a significance. The clothing system in particular replicates for Western society the functions of the so-called totemism. A sumptuary materialization of the principal coordinates of person and occasion, it becomes a vast scheme of communication—such as to serve as a language of everyday life among those who may well have no prior intercourse of acquaintance.[9] "Mere appearance" must be one of the most important forms of symbolic statement in Western civilization. For it is by appearances that civilization turns the basic contradiction of its construction into a miracle of existence: a cohesive society of perfect strangers. But in the event, its cohesion depends on a *coherence* of specific kind: on the possibility of apprehending others, their social condition, and thereby their relation to oneself "on first glance." This dependence on seeing helps to explain, on one hand, why the symbolic dimensions have nevertheless not been obvious. The code works on an unconscious level, the conception built into perception itself. It is precisely the type of thought generally known as "savage"—thought that "does not distinguish the moment of observation and that of interpretation any more than, on observing them one first registers the interlocutor's signs and then tries to understand them; when he speaks, the signs expressed carry with them their meanings" (Lévi-Strauss 1966: 223). On the other hand, this dependence on the glance suggests the presence in the economic and social life of a logic completely foreign to the conventional "rationality." For rationality is time elapsed, a comparison: at least another glance beyond, and a weighing of the alternatives. The relation between logics is that the first, the symbolic, defines and ranks the alternatives by the "choice" among which rationality, oblivious of its own cultural basis, is pleased to consider itself as constituting.

Notes

1. Fashion in clothing is of course frequently commented upon by social scientists and is occasionally given empirical investigation (Barthes 1967; Richardson and Kroeber 1940; Simmel 1904; Stone 1959). But there is a much richer literature upon which one may draw for ethnographic purposes: the direct reflections of participants in the process. Our discussion makes use of the writings of such as admen, market researchers, designers, buyers, fashion editors and critics, and textbooks by teachers of home economics, design, and aesthetics. Moreover, the discussion does not deny itself the advantage of observation and self-reflection in the one situation where the ethnographer finally realizes the privileged position of the participant-observer, namely, in his own village. I do not claim to have exhausted any of these resources—very far from it.

   For a treatment of costume analogous to that attempted here—which, however, came to my attention after this chapter had gone to press—see Bogatyrev 1971.
2. Although Barthes was exclusively concerned with the rhetoric of fashion as written (*le vêtement écrit*) rather than with the symbolic system of the clothing object as such, much of his discussion is pertinent to the present effort, and I have drawn heavily upon it.
3. Cf. Crawley's "principle of adaptation to state": "Dress expresses every social movement, as well as every social grade. It also expresses family, municipal, provincial, regional, tribal, and national character. At the same time it gives full play to the individual. A complete psychology of the subject would analyze all such cases with reference to the principle of adaptation" (Crawley 1931: 172). Some of the objective changes that accompany the fundamental proportion of public/private : impersonal/familial are conjured up by the stereotypic image of the good bourgeois returning home from "a hard day at the office": a banal scene in which the social passage is signified by the man successively removing his hat, kissing his wife, taking off his jacket, stripping away his tie (exaggerated gesture), opening his shirt collar (deep breath), sinking into his favorite armchair, donning the slippers fetched by a well-trained child, spouse, or dog—and breathing a sigh of relief. A whole set of statements about the contrast between kinship and the "larger world" is going on. In Stone's sociological study of clothing in Vansburg, Michigan, it was observed that about 70 percent of manual and white-collar workers arrive at work in what they consider their work clothes, and about 60 percent change when they go home. More than 90 percent of their wives changed clothing before going shopping, and about 75 percent did so again upon returning home (Stone 1959: 109–10). Lynes some lime ago noticed that on weekends, since the (suburban) home has become an arena of do-it-yourself, the white-collar class has affected "workclothes" (e. g., blue jeans) in the domestic sphere—except for the "backyard barbeque," which is distinguished by bright and dashing holiday wear, "symbols of revolt against the conformity imposed on men by the daily routine of business" (1957: 69).
4. Varieties of cotton are again differentiated by sex according to heaviness and stiffness; so the common four-class paradigm in materials:

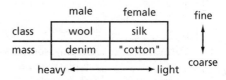

	male	female	
class	wool	silk	
mass	denim	"cotton"	

heavy ←——————→ light

fine ↑ coarse

In a book on advertising technique, Stephen Baker (1961, unpaginated) presents pictures of the same woman draped in four different fabrics He comments: "Fabrics have sexual connotations. Wool is the least feminine of the four materials. . . . It makes a woman appear businesslike, urban, sophisticated. Linen has a mixed image. If it is white, the fabric strongly suggests purity. It is more feminine than wool but has little seductive power. Linen is associated with clean, wholesome fun. The delicacy (and lightness) of lace makes it very much a woman's fabric. Rich in pattern, lace exudes an air of elegance, aloofness, yet soft femininity. Silk is the most sensuous of all materials. It shines and reflects the play of light. It is very soft and clings to a woman's body. This characteristic makes silk (or satin) bring out the seductive qualities of the wearer."

5. Cf. Schwartz (1958) on clothing among American blacks. One observation of this empirical study that seems quite generalizable is that "the least significant motive underlying the selection and wearing of certain items of clothing is protection from the elements" (p. 27).

6. An empirical study of favored costumes of upper-class college and middle-aged women developed contrasts of the following type [see table below] (N. Taylor, cited in Rosencranz 1972: 214–15). From the above information and preceding discussion one could probably make a few guesses about production: for example, that (other things being equal, and they are many), the amount of black silk produced is correlated with the number of middle-aged, upper-class white females in the population—which is itself a product of the total organization of society (notably

including production). The proposition is at once banal and totally unself-evident. It is hardly in the nature of things that silk has some affinity with white middle-aged women, although it is in *the culture of things*.

7. Not to deny that such may be the genuine mode of appearance to the participants in the process: "'I don't think I ever figured it would come to this,'" says Haas, who along with his brother Peter, the (Levi-Strauss) company president, was responsible for molding Levi's into its present structure. "'Basically, what we've tried to do is to serve society's needs.'"

"'The consumer still determines what he wants,'" says Bud Johns, the company's public relations director. "'we always try to adapt'" (Blue jeans: Uniform for a casual world," *Chicago Tribune*, 5 May 1975).

8. Or consider the following example of stylization in relation to ceremonial hierarchy noted by Jacinski in one factory: "'Suntan trousers and shirts but no ties for inspectors; slacks and sport shirts for lead men; slacks, white shirts, and ties for assistant foremen; and the same, plus a jacket, for the foreman'" (Quoted by Ryan 1966: 66)

9. "With briefest visual perception, a complex mental process is aroused, resulting within a very short time, 30 seconds perhaps [*sic*] in judgment of the sex, age, size, nationality, profession and social caste of the stranger together with some estimate of his temperament, his ascendence, friendliness, neatness; and even his trustworthiness" (G. Allport, cited in Horn 1968: 109; cf. Linton 1936: 416).

	Young College Women	Middle-aged Women
Garment	Dark gray wool dress and coat; scarf of gray, black, and red paisley	Black silk ottoman suit
Shoes	Black brogans	Black silk pumps with bow
Hose	"Hint" of gray	Black sheer
Handbag	Black calf	Black silk
Bracelet	Silver with pearls	Gold
Pin	– – – – – –	Diamond sunburst
Ring	Pearl	Pearl and diamond

References

Baker, Stephen (1961). *Visual Persuasion*. New York: McGraw-Hill.

Barthes, Roland (1967). *Système de la mode*. Paris: Seuil.

Berlin, Brent, and Kay, Paul (1956) *Basic Color Terms*. Berkeley: University of California Press.

Birren, Faber (1956). *Selling Color to People*. New York: University Books.

Bogatyrev, Petr (1971 [1937]). *The Functions of Folk Costume in Moravian Slovakia*. Moulton: The Hague.

Crawley, Ernest (1931). *Dress, Drinks, and Drums*. London: Methuen.

Dichter, Ernest (1959). *The Strategy of Desire*. Garden City, New York: Doubleday.

Graves, Maitland (1951). *The Art of Color and Design*. New York: McGraw-Hill.

Horn, Marilyn J. (1968). *The Second Skin: An Interdisciplinary Study of Clothing*. Boston: Houghton Mifflin.

Hurvich, Leo M., and Jameson, Dorothea (1957). "An Opponent-Process Theory of Color Vision." *Psychological Review*, 4: 384–404.

Lévi-Strauss, Claude (1966). *The Savage Mind*. Chicago: University of Chicago Press.

Linton, Ralph (1936). *The Study of Man*. New York: Appleton-Century.

Lynes, Russel (1957). *A Surfeit of Honey*. New York: Harper.

Poffenberger, A. T., and Barrows, B (1924). "The Feeling Value of Lines." *Journal of Applied Psychology*, 8: 187–205.

Pokorny, Joel, and Smith, Vivianne C. (1972). "Color Vision of Normal Observers," in A. M. Potts (ed.), *The Assessment of Visual Function*. Saint Louis: Mosby, 105–35.

Richardson, Jane, and Kroeber, A. L. (1940). "Three Centuries of Women's Dress Fashions." *University of California Anthropological Records*, 5: 111–54.

Rosencranz, Mary Lou (1972). *Clothing Concepts*. New York: Macmillan.

Rudofsky, Bernard (1947). *Are Clothes Modern?* Chicago: Theobold.

Ryan, Mary Shaw (1966). *Clothing: A Study in Human Behaviour*. New York: Holt, Rinehart and Winston.

Schwartz, Jack (1958). "Men's Clothing and the Negro." M.A. diss., Committee on Communication, University of Chicago. (Available at University of Chicago Libraries.)

Simmel, George (1940). "Fashion." *International Quarterly*, 10: 130–55.

Spengler, Oswald (1956). *The Decline of the West*. Vol. 1. New York: Knopf.

Stone, Gregory P. (1959). "Clothing and Social Relations: A Study of Appearance in the Context of Community Life." Ph.D. diss., Sociology, University of Chicago. (Available at University of Chicago Libraries.)

Veblen, Thorstein (1934 [1899]). *The Theory of the Leisure Class*. New York: Modern Library.

10 Travels in Hyperreality

Umberto Eco

Preface to the American Edition

An American interviewer once asked me how I managed to reconcile my work as a scholar and university professor, author of books published by university presses, with my other work as what would be called in the United States a "columnist"—not to mention the fact that, once in my life, I even wrote a novel (a negligible incident and, in any case, an activity allowed by the constitution of every democratic nation). It is true that along with my academic job, I also write regularly for newspapers and magazines, where, in terms less technical than in my books on semiotics, I discuss various aspects of daily life, ranging from sport to politics and culture.

My answer was that this habit is common to all European intellectuals, in Germany, France, Spain, and, naturally, Italy: all countries where a scholar or scientist often feels required to speak out in the papers, to comment, if only from the point of view of his own interests and special field, on events that concern all citizens. And I added, somewhat maliciously, that if there was any problem with this it was not my problem as a European intellectual; it was more a problem of American intellectuals, who live in a country where the division of labor between university professors and militant intellectuals is much more strict than in our countries.

It is true that many American university professors write for cultural reviews or for the book page of the daily papers. But many Italian scholars and literary critics also write columns where they take a stand on political questions, and they do this not only as a natural part of their work, but also as a duty. There is, then, a difference in "patterns of culture." Cultural anthropologists accept cultures in which people eat dogs, monkeys, frogs, and snakes, and even cultures where adults chew gum, so it should be all right for countries to exist where university professors contribute to the newspapers.

The essays chosen for this book are articles that, over the years, I wrote for daily papers and weekly magazines (or, on occasion, monthly reviews, but not strictly academic journals). Some of them may discuss, perhaps over a period of time, the same problems. Others are mutually contradictory (but, again, always over a period of time). I believe that an intellectual should use newspapers the way private diaries and personal letters were once used. At white heat, in the rush of an emotion, stimulated by an event, you write your reflections, hoping that someone will read them and then forget them. I don't believe there is any gap between what I write in my "academic" books and what I write in the papers. I cannot say precisely whether, for the papers, I try to translate into language accessible to all and apply to the events under consideration the ideas I later develop in my academic books, or whether it is the opposite that happens. Probably many of the theories expounded in my academic books grew gradually, on the basis of the observations I wrote down as I followed current events.

At the academic level I concern myself with the problems of language, communication, organization of the systems of signs that we use to describe the world and to tell it to one another. The fact that what I do is called "semiotics" should not frighten anyone. I would still do it if it were called something else.

When my novel came out in the United States, the newspapers referred to semiotics as an "arcane discipline." I would not want to do anything here to dispel the arcanum and reveal what semiotics is to those who perhaps have no need to know. I will say only that if, in these travel notes, these thoughts about politics, these invectives against sport, these meditations on television, I have said things that may interest somebody, it is also because I look at the world through the eyes of a semiologist.

In these pages I try to interpret and to help others interpret some "signs." These signs are not only words, or images; they can also be forms of social behavior, political acts, artificial landscapes. As Charles S. Peirce once said, "A sign is something by knowing which we know something more."

But this is not a book of semiotics. God forbid. There already exist too many people who present as semiotics things that are not semiotics, all over the world; I do not want to make matters worse.

There is another reason why I write these things. I believe it is my political duty. Here again I owe the American reader an explanation. In the United States politics is a profession, whereas in Europe it is a right and a duty. Perhaps we make too much of it, and use it badly; but each of us feels the moral obligation to be involved in it in some way. My way of being involved in politics consists of telling others how I see daily life, political events, the language of the mass media, sometimes the way I look at a movie. I believe it is my job as a scholar and a citizen to show how we are surrounded by "messages," products of political power, of economic power, of the entertainment industry and the revolution industry, and to say that we must know how to analyze and criticize them.

Perhaps I have written these things, and go on writing similar things, for other reasons. I am anxious, insecure, and always afraid of being wrong. What is worse, I am always afraid that the person who says I am wrong is better than I am. I need to check quickly the ideas that come into my head. It takes years to write an "academic" book, and then you have to wait for the reviews, and then correct your own thinking in the later editions. It is work that demands time, peace of mind, patience. I am capable of doing it, I believe, but in the meanwhile I have to allay my anxiety. Insecure persons often cannot delay for years, and it is hard for them to develop their ideas in silence, waiting for the "truth" to be suddenly revealed to them. That is why I like to teach, to expound still-imperfect ideas and hear the students' reaction. That is why I like to write for the newspapers, to reread myself the next day, and to read the reactions of others. A difficult game, because it does not always consist of being reassured when you meet with agreement and having doubts when you are faced with dissent. Sometimes you have to follow the opposite course: distrust agreement and find in dissent the confirmation of your own intuitions. There is no rule; there is only the risk of contra-diction. But sometimes you have to speak because you feel the moral obligation to say something, not because you have the "scientific" certainty that you are saying it in an unassailable way.

Travels in Hyperreality

The Fortresses of Solitude

Two very beautiful naked girls are crouched facing each other. They touch each other sensually, they kiss each other's breasts lightly, with the tip of the tongue. They are enclosed in a kind of cylinder of transparent plastic. Even someone who is not a professional voyeur is tempted to circle the cylinder in order to see the girls from behind, in profile, from the other side. The next temptation is to approach the cylinder, which stands on a little column and is only a few inches in diameter, in order to look down from above: But the girls are no longer there. This was one of the many works displayed in New York by the School of Holography.

Holography, the latest technical miracle of laser rays, was invented back in the 1950s by Dennis Gabor; it achieves a full-color photographic representation that is more than three-dimensional. You look into a magic box and a miniature train or horse appears; as you shift your gaze you can see those parts of the object that you were prevented from glimpsing by the laws of perspective. If the box is circular you can see the object from all sides. If the object was filmed, thanks to various devices, in motion, then it moves before your eyes, or else you move, and as you change position, you can see the girl wink or the fisherman drain the can of beer in his hand. It isn't cinema, but rather a kind of virtual object in three dimensions that exists even where you don't see it, and if you move you can see it there, too.

Holography isn't a toy: NASA has studied it and employed it in space exploration. It is used in medicine to achieve realistic depictions of anatomical changes; it has applica-tions in aerial cartography, and in many industries for the study of physical processes. But it is now being taken up by artists who formerly might have been photorealists, and it satisfies the most ambitious ambitions of photorealism. In San Francisco, at the door of the Museum of Witchcraft, the biggest hologram ever made is on display: of the Devil, with a very beautiful witch.

Holography could prosper only in America, a country obsessed with realism, where, if a reconstruction is to be credible, it must be absolutely iconic, a perfect likeness, a "real" copy of the reality being represented.

Cultivated Europeans and Europeanized Americans think of the United States as the home of the glass-and-steel skyscraper and of abstract expressionism. But the United States is also the home of Superman, the superhuman comic-strip hero who has been in existence since 1938. Every now and then Superman feels a need to be alone with his memories, and he flies off to an inaccessible mountain range where, in the heart of the rock, protected by a huge steel door, is the Fortress of Solitude.

Here Superman keeps his robots, completely faithful copies of himself, miracles of electronic technology, which from time to time he sends out into the world to fulfill a pardonable desire for ubiquity. And the robots are incredible, because their resemblance to reality is absolute; they are not mechanical men, all cogs and beeps, but perfect "copies" of human beings, with skin, voice, movements, and the ability to make decisions. For Superman the fortress is a museum of memories: everything that has happened in his adventurous life is recorded here in perfect copies or preserved in a miniaturized form of the original. Thus he keeps the city of Kandor, a survival from the destruction of the planet Krypton, under a glass bell of the sort familiar from your great-aunt's Victorian parlor. Here, on a reduced scale, are Kandor's buildings, highways, men, and women. Superman's scrupulousness in preserving all the mementoes of his past recalls those private museums; or *Wunderkammern*, so frequent in German baroque civilization, which originated in the treasure chambers of medieval lords and perhaps, before that, with Roman and Hellenistic collections. In those old collections a unicorn's horn would be found next to the copy of a Greek statue, and, later, among mechanical crèches and wondrous automata, cocks of precious metal that sang, clocks with a procession of little figures that paraded at noon. But at first Superman's fussiness seemed incredible because, we thought, in our day a *Wunderkammer* would no longer fascinate anybody. Postinformal art hadn't yet adopted practices such as Arman's crammed assemblage of watchcases arranged in a glass case, or Spoerri's fragments of everyday life (a dinner table after an untidy meal, an unmade bed), or the postconceptual exercises of an artist like Annette Messanger, who accumulates memories of her childhood in neurotically archivistic notebooks which she exhibits as works of art.

The most incredible thing was that, to record some past events, Superman reproduced them in the form of life-size wax statues, rather macabre, very Musée Greévin. Naturally the statues of the photorealists had not yet come on the scene, but even when they did it was normal to think of their creators as bizarre avant-garde artists, who had developed as a reaction to the civilization of the abstract or to the Pop aberration. To the reader of "Superman" it seemed that his museographical quirks had no real connection with American taste and mentality.

And yet in America there are many Fortresses of Solitude, with their wax statues, their automata, their collections of inconsequential wonders. You have only to go beyond the Museum of Modern Art and the art galleries, and you enter another universe, the preserve of the average family, the tourist, the politician.

The most amazing Fortress of Solitude was erected in Austin, Texas, by President Lyndon Johnson, during his own lifetime, as monument, pyramid, personal mausoleum. I'm not referring to the immense imperial-modern-style construction or to the forty-thousand red containers that hold all the documents of his political life, or to the half million documentary photographs, the portraits, the voice of Mrs. Johnson narrating her late husband's life for visitors. No, I am referring to the mass of souvenirs of the Man's scholastic career, the honeymoon snapshots, the nonstop series of films that tell visitors of the presidential couple's foreign trips, and the wax statues that wear the wedding dresses of the daughters Luci and Lynda, the full-scale reproduction of the Oval Office, the red shoes of the ballerina Maria Tallchief, the pianist Van Cliburn's autograph on a piece of music, the plumed hat worn by Carol Channing in *Hello, Dolly!* (all mementoes justified by the fact that the artists in question performed at the White House), and the gifts proffered by envoys of various countries, an Indian feather head-dress, testimonial panels in the form of ten-gallon hats, doilies embroidered with the American flag, a sword given by the king of Thailand, and the moon rock brought back by the astronauts. The Lyndon B. Johnson Library is a true Fortress of Solitude: a *Wunderkammer*, an ingenious example of narrative art, wax museum, cave of robots. And it suggests that there is a constant in the average American imagination and taste, for which the past must be preserved and celebrated in full-scale authentic copy; a philosophy of immortality as duplication. It dominates the relation with the self, with the past, not infrequently with the present, always with History and, even, with the European tradition.

Constructing a full-scale model of the Oval Office (using the same materials, the same colors, but with everything obviously more polished, shinier, protected against deterioration) means that for historical information to be absorbed, it has to assume the aspect of a reincarnation. To speak of things that one wants to connote as real, these things must seem real. The "completely real" becomes identified with the "completely fake." Absolute unreality is offered as real presence. The aim of the reconstructed Oval Office is to supply a "sign" that will then be forgotten as such: the sign aims to be the thing, to abolish the distinction of the reference, the mechanism of replacement. Not the image of the thing, but its plaster cast. Its double, in other words.

Is this the taste of America? Certainly it is not the taste of Frank Lloyd Wright, of the Seagram Building, the skyscrapers of Mies van der Rohe. Nor is it the taste of the New York School, or of Jackson Pollock. It isn't even that of the photorealists, who produce a reality so real that it proclaims its artificiality from the rooftops. We must understand, however, from what depth of popular sensibility and craftsmanship today's photo-realists draw their inspiration and why they feel called upon to force this tendency to the point of exacerbation. There is, then, an America of furious hyperreality, which is not that of Pop art, of Mickey Mouse, or of Hollywood movies. There is another, more secret America (or rather, just as public, but snubbed by the European visitor and also by the American intellectual); and it creates somehow a network of references and influences that finally spread also to the products of high culture and the entertainment industry. It has to be discovered.

And so we set out on a journey, holding on to the Ariadne-thread, an open-sesame that will allow us to identify the object of this pilgrimage no matter what form it may assume. We can identify it through two typical slogans that pervade American advertis-ing. The first, widely used by Coca-Cola but also frequent as a hyperbolic formula in everyday speech, is "the real thing"; the second, found in print and heard on TV, is "more"—in the sense of "extra." The announcer doesn't say, for example, "The program will continue" but rather that there is "More to come." In America you don't say, "Give me another coffee"; you ask for "More coffee"; you don't say that cigarette A is longer than cigarette B, but that there's "more" of it, more than you're used to having, more than you might want, leaving a surplus to throw away—that's prosperity.

This is the reason for this journey into hyperreality, in search of instances where the American imagination demands the real thing and, to attain it, must fabricate the absolute fake; where the boundaries between game and illusion are blurred, the art museum is contaminated by the freak show, and falsehood is enjoyed in a situation of "fullness," of *horror vacui.*

The first stop is the Museum of the City of New York, which relates the birth and growth of Peter Stuyvesant's metropolis, from the purchase of Manhattan by the Dutch from the Indians for the famous twenty-four dollars, down to our own time. The museum has been arranged with care, historical precision, a sense of temporal distances (which the East Coast can permit, while the West Coast, as we shall see, is unable as yet to achieve it), and with considerable didactic flair. Now there can be no doubt that one of the most effective and least boring of didactic mechanisms is the diorama, the reduced-scale reproduction, the model, the crèche. And the museum is full of little crèches in glass cases, where the visiting children—and they are numerous—say, "Look, there's Wall Street," as an Italian child would say, "Look, there's Bethlehem and the ox and the ass." But, primarily, the diorama aims to establish itself as a substitute for reality, as something even more real. When it is flanked by a document (a parchment or an engraving), the little model is undoubtedly more real even than the engraving. Where there is no engraving, there is beside the diorama a color photograph of the diorama that looks like a painting of the period, except that (naturally) the diorama is more effective, more vivid than the painting. In some cases, the period painting exists. At a certain point a card tells us that a seventeenth-century portrait of Peter Stuyvesant exists, and here a European museum with didactic aims would display a good color reproduction; but the New York museum shows us a three-dimensional statue, which reproduces Peter Stuyvesant as portrayed in the painting, except that in the painting, of course, Peter is seen only full-face or in half-profile, whereas here he is complete, buttocks included.

But the museum goes further (and it isn't the only one in the world that does this; the best ethnological museums observe the same criterion): it reconstructs interiors full-scale, like the Johnson Oval Office. Except that in other museums (for example, the splendid anthropological museum in Mexico City) the sometimes impressive reconstruction of an Aztec square (with merchants, warriors, and priests) is presented as such; the archeological finds are displayed separately and when the ancient object is represented by a perfect replica the visitor is clearly warned that he is seeing a reproduction. Now the Museum of the City of New York does not lack archeological precision, and it distinguishes genuine pieces from reconstructed pieces; but the distinction is indicated on explanatory panels beside the cases, while in the reconstruction, on the other hand, the original object and the wax figurine mingle in a continuum that the visitor is not invited to decipher. This occurs partly because, making a pedagogical decision we can hardly criticize, the designers want the visitor to feel an atmosphere and to plunge into the past without becoming a philologist or archeologist, and also because the reconstructed datum was already tainted by this original sin of "the leveling of pasts," the fusion of copy and original. In this respect, the great exhibit that reproduces completely the 1906 drawing room of Mr. and Mrs. Harkness Flagler is exemplary. It is immediately worth noting that a private home seventy years old is already archeology; and this tells us a lot about the ravenous consumption of the present and about the constant "past-izing" process carried out by American civilization in its alternate process of futuristic planning and nostalgic remorse. And it is significant that in the big record shops the section called "Nostalgia," along with racks devoted to the 1940s and the 1950s, has others for the 1960s and 1970s.

But what was the original Flagler home like? As the didactic panel explains, the living room was inspired by the Sala dello Zodiaco in the Ducal Palace of Mantua. The ceiling was copied from a Venetian ecclesiastical building's dome now preserved in the Accademia in Venice. The wall panels are in Pompeiian—pre-Raphaelite style, and the fresco over the fireplace recalls Puvis de Chavannes. Now that real fake, the 1906 home, is maniacally faked in the museum showcase, but in such a way that it is difficult to say which objects were originally part of the room and which are fakes made to serve as connective tissue in the room (and even if we knew the difference, that knowledge would change nothing, because the reproductions of the reproduction are perfect and only a thief in the pay of an antique dealer would worry about the difficulty of telling them apart). The furniture is unquestionably that of the real living room—and there was real furniture in it, of real antiquity, one presumes—but there is no telling what the ceiling is; and while the dummies of the lady of the house, her maid, and a little girl speaking with a visiting friend are obviously false, the clothes the dummies wear are obviously real, that is, dating from 1906.

What is there to complain about? The mortuary chill that seems to enfold the scene? The illusion of absolute reality that it conveys to the more naïve visitor? The "creèche-ification" of the bourgeois universe? The two-level reading the museum prompts with antiquarian information for those who choose to decipher the panels and the flattening of real against fake and the old on the modern for the more nonchalant?

The kitsch reverence that overwhelms the visitor, thrilled by his encounter with a magic past? Or the fact that, coming from the slums or from public housing projects and from schools that lack our historical dimension, he grasps, at least to a certain extent, the idea of the past? Because I have seen groups of black schoolchildren circulating here, excited and entertained, taking much more interest than a group of European white children being trundled through the Louvre . . .

At the exit, along with postcards and illustrated history books, they sell reproductions of historical documents, from the bill of sale of Manhattan to the Declaration of Independence. These are described as "looking and feeling old," because in addition to the tactile illusion, the facsimile is also scented with old spice. Almost real. Unfortunately the Manhattan purchase contract, penned in pseudo-antique characters, is in English, whereas the original was in Dutch. And so it isn't a facsimile, but—excuse the neologism—a fac-different. As in some story by Heinlein or Asimov, you have the impression of entering and leaving time in a spatial-temporal haze where the centuries are confused. The same thing will happen to us in one of the wax museums of the California coast where we will see, in a café in the seaside style of England's Brighton, Mozart and Caruso at the same table, with Hemingway standing behind them, while Shakespeare, at the next table, is conversing with Beethoven, coffee cup in hand.

And for that matter, at Old Bethpage Village, on Long Island, they try to reconstruct an early nineteenth-century farm as it was; but "as it was" means with living animals just like those of the past, while it so happens that sheep, since those days, have undergone—thanks to clever breeding—an interesting evolution. In the past they had black noses with no wool on them; now their noses are white and covered with wool, so obviously the animals are worth more. And the eco-archeologists we're talking about are working to rebreed the line to achieve an "evolutionary retrogression." But the National Breeders' Association is protesting, loudly and firmly, against this insult to zoological and technical progress. A cause is in the making: the advocates of "ever forward" against those of "backward march." And there is no telling now which are the more futurological, and who are the real falsifiers of nature. But as far as battles for "the real thing" are concerned, our journey certainly doesn't end here. *More to come!*

11 Identity and Cultural Studies: Is That All There Is?

Lawrence Grossberg

Identity and Difference in Cultural Studies

Within cultural studies, investigations of the constitution and politics of identity are often predicated on a distinction, nicely articulated by Hall (1990), between two forms of struggle over—two models of the production of—identities. It is important to recognize that Hall offers this, not as a theoretical distinction, although it certainly can be mapped on to the dispute between essentialists and anti-essentialists, but as a historical and strategic distinction. The first model assumes that there is some intrinsic and essential content to any identity which is defined by either a common origin or a common structure of experience or both. Struggling against existing constructions of a particular identity takes the form of contesting negative images with positive ones, and of trying to discover the "authentic" and "original" content of the identity. Basically, the struggle over representations of identity here takes the form of offering one fully constituted, separate and distinct identity in place of another.

The second model emphasizes the impossibility of such fully constituted, separate and distinct identities. It denies the existence of authentic and originary identities based in a universally shared origin or experience. Identities are always relational and incomplete, in process. Any identity depends upon its difference from, its negation of, some other term, even as the identity of the latter term depends upon its difference from, its negation of, the former. As Hall (1991: 21) puts it: "Identity is a structured representation which only achieves its positive through the narrow eye of the negative. It has to go through the eye of the needle of the other before it can construct itself." Identity is always a temporary and unstable effect of relations which define identities by marking differences. Thus the emphasis here is on the multiplicity of identities and differences rather than on a singular identity and on the connections or articulations between the fragments or differences. The fact of multiple identities gives rise to the necessity of what Kobena Mercer has called "the mantra of race, class and gender" (1992: 34). "The challenge is to be able to theorize more than one difference at once." This suggests a much more difficult politics, because the sides are not given in advance, nor in neat divisions. As Michele Wallace (1994: 185) says, echoing June Jordan, "the thing that needed to be said—women are not to be trusted just because they're women, anymore than blacks are to be trusted because they're black, or gays because they're gay and so on." Here struggles over identity no longer involve questions of adequacy or

Reprinted by permission of Sage Publications Ltd from Lawrence Grossberg, "Identity and Cultural Studies: Is That All There Is?," in Stuart Hall and Paul du Gay (eds.), *Questions of Cultural Identity* (London: Sage, 1996), 87–107.

distortion, but of the politics of representation itself. That is, politics involves questioning how identities are produced and taken up through practices of representation. Obviously influenced by Derrida, such a position sees identity as an entirely cultural, even an entirely linguistic, construction. While this model certainly suggests that the identity of one term cannot be explored or challenged without a simultaneous investigation of the second term, this is rarely the case in practice. Most work in cultural studies is concerned with investigating and challenging the construction of subaltern, marginalized or dominated identities, although some recent work has begun to explore dominant identities as social constructions. Rarely, however, are the two ever studied together, as the theory would seem to dictate, as mutually constitutive.

It is obviously this second model which defines work around identity in cultural studies, but I do not mean to suggest that this model defines a singular theoretical position or vocabulary. On the contrary, there are a number of different, overlapping, intersecting and sometimes even competing figures which, taken together, define the space within which cultural studies has theorized the problem of identity. Often, they function together to define specific theories. Interestingly, these figures construct a continuum of images of spatiality, although, as I will suggest, they are, for the most part, structures of temporality. I will describe these figures as: *différance*, fragmentation, hybridity, border and diaspora.

The figure of *différance* describes a particular constitutive relation of negativity in which the subordinate term (the marginalized other or subaltern) is a necessary and internal force of destabilization existing within the identity of the dominant term. The subaltern here is itself constitutive of, and necessary for, the dominant term. The instability of any dominant identity—since it must always and already incorporate its negation—is the result of the very nature of language and signification. The subaltern represents an inherent ambiguity or instability at the center of any formation of language (or identity) which constantly undermines language's power to define a unified stable identity. We can identify two variants of this figure: notions of the "supplement" locate the other outside of the field of subjectivity as it were, as pure excess; notions of "negativity" locate the other within the field of subjectivity as a constitutive exotic other. In the former, the subaltern constitutes the boundaries of the very possibility of subjectivity; in the latter, the subaltern may be granted an incomprehensible subjectivity. There are numerous examples of these two variants of the figure of *différance* in contemporary theories of identity. For example, Lyotard (1990) sees "the Jews" as that which European culture cannot identify because its exclusion, its unnameability, is itself constitutive of European identity. Similarly, Bhabha's (1994) notion of mimicry as an intentional misappropriation of the dominant discourse locates the power of the subaltern in a kind of textual insurrection in which the subaltern is defined only by its internal negation of the colonizer. De Certeau's (1984) attempt to define subordinate populations only by their lack of a place which would entitle them to their own practices or strategies similarly ends up defining the subaltern as pure *différance*. Finally, there is a common reading of Said's *Orientalism* (1978) in which the dominant power necessarily constructs its other as a repressed and desired difference.

The figure of *fragmentation* emphasizes the multiplicity of identities and of positions within any apparent identity. It thus sees a particular concrete or lived identity as "a kind of disassembled and reassembled unity" (Haraway 1991: 174). Identities are thus always contradictory, made up out of partial fragments. Theories of fragmentation can focus on the fragmentation of either individual identities or of the social categories (of difference) within which individuals are placed, or some combination of the two. Further, such fragmentations can be seen as either historical or constitutive. This is perhaps the most powerful image, certainly in British cultural studies, with echoes in Hebdige's notion of "cut 'n' mix" and Gilroy's (1993) notion of syncretism. Donna Haraway (1991: 174) also seems to offer such a figure in the image of a cyborg as "a potent subjectivity synthesized from the fusion of outsider identities." Or, from David Bailey and Stuart Hall (1992: 21): "Identities can, therefore, be contradictory and are always situational. . . . In short, we are all involved in a series of political games around fractured or decentered identities . . . since black signifies a range of experiences, the act of representation becomes not just about decentering the subject but actually exploring the kaleidoscopic conditions of blackness."

The figure of *hybridity* is more difficult to characterize for it is often used synonymously with a number of other figures. Nevertheless, I will use it to describe three different images of *border* existences, of subaltern identities as existing between two competing identities. Images of a "*third space*" (as in Bhabha) see subaltern identities as unique third terms literally defining an "in-between" place inhabited by the subaltern. Images of *liminality* collapse the geography of the third space into the border itself; the subaltern lives, as it were, on the border. In both of these variants of hybridity, the subaltern is neither one nor the other but is defined by its location in a unique spatial condition which constitutes it as different from either alternative. Neither colonizer nor precolonial subject, the post-colonial subject exists as a unique hybrid which may, by definition, constitute the other two as well. Closely related to these two figures of hybridity is that of the "*border-crossing*", marking an image of between-ness which does not construct a place or condition of its own other than the mobility, uncertainty and multiplicity of the fact of the constant border-crossing itself. Often, these three versions of hybridity are conflated in various ways, as in Gloria Anzaldúa's (1987: 37) description of the *Atzlan*: "A borderland is a vague and undetermined place created by the emotional residue of an unnatural boundary. . . . People who inhabit both realities . . . are forced to live in the interface between the two."

Finally, the figure of *diaspora* is closely related to that of border-crossing, but it is often given a more diachronic inflection. This figure has become increasingly visible, through the work of anthropologists such as James Clifford and Smadar Lavie, cultural critics such as Paul Gilroy, and various postcolonial theorists. As Jim Clifford describes it (1994: 308), "the term 'diaspora' is a signifier not simply of transnationality and movement, but of political struggles to define the local—I would prefer to call it place— as a distinctive community, in historical contexts of displacement." That is, diaspora emphasizes the historically spatial fluidity and intentionality of identity, its articulation to structures of historical movements (whether forced or chosen, necessary or desired). Diaspora links identity to spatial location and identifications, to "histories of alternative cosmopolitanisms and diasporic networks". While this figure offers significantly new possibilities for a cultural politics that avoids many of the logics of the modern—by rooting identity in structures of affiliations and ways of belonging, it is, too often, drawn back into the modern. Identity is ultimately returned to history, and the subaltern's place is subsumed within a history of movements and an experience of oppression which privileges particular exemplars as the "proper" figures of identity.

Such theories—built on the range of diverse figures described above—have recently come under attack (e.g. Parry 1987; O'Hanlon 1988): for ignoring the fragmentary and conflictual nature of the discourses of power (different at different places and spaces of course); for ignoring the heterogeneity of power and apparently reducing it to discourses of representation and ignoring its material realities; for ignoring the positivity of the subaltern—as the possessor of other knowledges and traditions; as having their own history in which there are power relations defined within the ranks of the subordinated. And one might add yet another problem concerning the status of the marginal or subordinate in these figures. On what grounds do we assume that a privileged or even different structure of subjectivity belongs to the subaltern? And if, as Hall suggests, the marginal has become central, is it not descriptive of the contemporary subject? The other side of the question is, can one form of subordination become the model of all structural domination? In so far as we have now created a figure of the subaltern, have we not developed another universalizing theory, providing answers to any local struggle before we have even begun, since we know we will always find the production of the other as different?

. . .

Cultural Identity and the Logic of Individuality

Renato Rosaldo (1989: 201) has argued that we need to move away from the tacit assumption "that conflates the notion of culture with the idea of difference" and towards an alternative notion of culture as productive. Deleuze and Guattari (1987: 210) suggest such a notion: "the question . . . is not whether the status of women, or those on the bottom, is better or worse, but the type of organization from which that status results." But I do not believe that the failure to articulate such a theory of culture is the product of the logic of difference; instead, what has prevented the development of a view of culture as production is a particular (modern) logic of individuality which has equated the various processes of individuation and thus collapsed the various planes of effectivity through which individuality is constituted into a single and simple structure.

In political terms, this is the modern invention of what O'Hanlon (1988) calls "the virile figure of the subject-agent," that is, the modern "humanistic individual" which is predicated on the identification of three different planes (and hence, three different issues): (1) the subject as a position defining the possibility and the source of experience and, by extension, of knowledge; (2) the agent as a position of activity; and (3) the self as the mark of a social identity. This equation of different "maps of identification and belonging"—maps which define and produce where and how individuals fit into the world—inevitably gave rise to a paradox, especially when anti-essentialist arguments were mounted against any claims to the unity of both the subject and the self (again, often conflated in these arguments) and when critical arguments were mounted to demonstrate the social construction of both the subject and the self. The paradox is, quite simply, how can the individual be both cause and effect (an old question), both subject and subjected? Or in other words, how and where does one locate agency? This problem has animated the large body of contemporary political and theoretical work on the production of subordinate identities and the possibilities of resistance, whether in the name of the subaltern, feminism, anti-racism or postcolonialism. But the paradox may in fact be a disguise for the operation of modern power, if we see these three aspects of individuality as three distinct individuating productions. In this case, the task is to locate the "machinery" by which each of these planes of identification and belonging is produced and subsequently articulated into structures of individuality (including bodies). Such machines describe the nature of human subjectivity, identity and agency as technologically produced relations which impose a particular organization and a particular conduct on the specific multiplicities operating on different planes of effects.

. . .

While it is clear that structures of subjectivity and self may influence and be articulated to questions of power and the possibilities of agency, there is no reason to assume that they are the same or equivalent. In fact, the question of agency is a matter of action and the nature of change. In its most common form, it is Wittgenstein's question: what is the difference between my raising my arm and my arm rising? It raises questions of intentionality but without assuming a mentalist or voluntarist answer. Obviously, within cultural studies, the question of agency involves more than a simple question of whether or how people control their own actions through some act of will. In classical modern terms, the issue of agency raises questions of the freedom of the will, or of how people can be responsible for their determined actions. But in broader cultural terms, questions of agency involve the possibilities of action as interventions into the processes by which reality is continually being transformed and power enacted. That is, in Marx's terms, the problem of agency is the problem of understanding how people make history in conditions not of their own making. Who gets to make history?

As O'Hanlon (1988: 207, 221) has argued, when the issue shifts to questions of agency and the possibilities of action, "the subaltern is not a social category but a statement of power." She continues:

the subaltern is rendered marginal . . . in part through his inability, in his poverty, his lack of leisure, and his inarticulacy, to participate to any significant degree in the public institutions of civil society, with all the particular kinds of power which they confer, but most of all, through his consequently weaker ability to articulate civil society's self-sustaining myth.

That is, agency involves relations of participation and access, the possibilities of moving into particular sites of activity and power, and of belonging to them in such a way as to be able to enact their powers. In that sense, marginalization is not a spatial position but a vector defining access, mobility and the possibilities of investment. The question of agency is, then, how access and investment or participation (as a structure of belonging) are distributed within particular structured terrains. At the very least, this suggests that agency as a political problem cannot be conflated with issues of cultural identity or of epistemological possibilities. In other words, agency is not so much the "mark of a subject, but the constituting mark of an abode." In Deleuzean terms, agency is the product of a territorializing machine.

. . .

Culture and the Politics of Singularity

Recently, a number of authors have challenged the particular confluence of logics which have defined modern theories of identity. Ahmad (1992), for example, argues that there is often a rather easy slide from an "absence of belonging" to an "excess of belonging" predicated on the assumption of migrancy as an ontological and epistemological condition. Similarly, Dhareshwar (1989: 142–43) warns against the desire for "an identity that fully coheres with the narrative force of theory," which takes the figures of a theoretical system as the "storyline" for narrative identity: "for example, 'decentered subjectivity' as postmodern reality, dissemination as 'immigritude' (my word for the whole narrative of displacement which has become a normative experience in metropolitan politics of cultural description)." I would argue that, in so far as the various theories of identity remain grounded in modern logics of difference, individuality and temporality, the radical implications of the increasingly spatial language of such theories remains unrealized and unrealizable. With Dhareshwar (1989: 146), I wonder whether we need to raise "the possibility and necessity of an entirely different theoretical practice."

I am interested in the implications of the alternative logics of otherness, production and spatiality for a theory of human agency and historical change. In particular, for the moment, I am interested in the possibilities of political identities and alliances. My discussion of agency—and its difference from either subjectivity or "identity" (self)—would seem to suggest the need for a radical rethinking of political identity (and the possibilities of collective agency). It seems to suggest the concept of a belonging without identity, a notion of what might be called *singularity* as the basis for an alternative politics, a politics based on what Giorgio Agamben (1993) has called "the coming community." This project is political at its core, for as Young (1990: 11) says, this quest for the singular can "be related to the project of constructing a form of knowledge that respects the other without absorbing it into the same," or, I might add, the different. As Dhareshwar (1990: 235) points out, "the fetishization and relentless celebration of 'difference' and 'otherness' has displaced any discussion of political identity."

Agamben describes singularity as a mode of existence which is neither universal (i.e. conceptual) nor particular (i.e. individual). He takes as an example of such a mode of existence, the existence of the example *qua* example itself, for the example exists both inside and outside of the class it exemplifies. The example exists "by the indifference of the common and the proper, of the genus and the species, of the essential and the accidental. [It] is the thing with all its properties none of which, however, constitutes difference. Indifference with respect to properties is what individuates and disseminates singularities" (1993: 19). Moreover, the status of the example is not accomplished once and for all; it is a line of becoming, "a shuttling between the common and the singular" (ibid. 20). In other words, the example is defined, not by an appeal to a common universal property—an identity—but by its appropriation of belonging (to the class, in this instance) itself. The example belongs to the set which exists alongside of it, and hence it is defined by its substitutability, since it always already belongs in the place of the other. This is "an unconditioned substitutability, without either representation or possible description" (ibid. 24–25), an absolutely unrepresentable community. This community—that on which the example borders—is an empty and indeterminate totality, an external space of possibilities. Thus, a singularity can be defined as "a being whose community is mediated not by any condition of belonging . . . nor by the simple absence of conditions . . . but by belonging itself" (ibid. 85). To put this all in simpler terms, Agamben is arguing that the example functions as an example not by virtue of some common property which it shares with all the other possible members of the set, but rather by virtue of its metonymical (understood both literally and spatially) relation to the set itself. Any term can become an example of the set because what is at stake is the very claim of belonging to the set.

Agamben turns this to politics by considering the events—the alliance—of Tiananmen Square:

Because if instead of continuing to search for a proper identity in the already improper and senseless form of individuality, humans were to succeed in belonging to this impropriety as such, in making of the proper being—thus not an identity and an individual property but a singularity without identity, a common and absolutely exposed singularity . . . then they would for the first time enter into a community without presuppositions and without subjects. (ibid. 65)

Consider, how one would describe the common identity of those who gathered in Tiananmen Square and, whether intentionally or not, came to define and embody a community of opposition, not only to the Chinese state, but to the state machine itself. In fact, there is no common identity, no property that defines them apart from the fact that they were there, together, in that place. It was the fact of belonging that constituted their belonging together. Such a singularity operates as a "transport machine" following a logic of involvement, a logic of the next (rather than of the proper). It refuses to take any instance as a synecdochal image of the whole. It is only at the intersection of the various lines at the concrete place of belonging that we can identify the different processes of "individuation carried out through groups and people," new modes of individuation and even subjectivation with no identity. Such a community would be based only on the exteriority, the exposure, of the singularity of belonging.

In this sense, we might also reconsider the civil rights movement as a machine of mobilization whose product was a singular belonging rather than a structure of membership. A politics of singularity would need to define places people can belong to or, even more fundamentally, places people can find their way to. Hall and Held (cited in Giroux 1994: 31) describe this as the problem of citizenship: "the diverse communities to which we belong, the complex interplay of identity and identification and the differentiated ways in which people participate in social life." Similarly, Mercer (1992: 33) describes "what was important" about the politics of race of the 1980s as the result of the fact "that we actively constructed an elective community of belonging through a variety of practices." Perhaps Hall and Mercer would assent to the argument that, in specific contexts, identity can become a marker of people's abiding in such a singular community, where the community defines an abode marking people's ways of belonging within the structured mobilities of contemporary life. That would be an identity worth struggling to create.

References

Agamben, Giorgio (1993). *The Coming Community*. Minneapolis: University of Minnesota Press.

Ahmad, Aijaz (1992). In *Theory: Classes, Nations, Literatures*. London: Verso.

Anzaldúa, Gloria (1987). *Borderlands/La Frontera: The New Mestiza*. San Francisco: Spinsters/Aunt Lute.

Bailey, David, and Hall, Stuart (eds.) (1992). "The vertigo of displacement: shifts within black documentary practices," in *Critical Decade: Black British Photography in the 80s, Ten-8*, 3: 15–23.

Bhabha, Homi (1994). *The Location of Culture*. London: Routledge.

Clifford, James (1994). "Diasporas," *Cultural Anthropology*, 9: 302–38.

De Certeau, Michel (1984). *The Practice of Everyday Life*, trans. S. S. Rendall. Berkeley: University of California Press.

Deleuze, Gilles, and Guattari, Felix (1987). *A Thousand Plateaus: Capitalism and Schizophrenia*, trans. B. Massumi. Minneapolis: University of Minnesota Press.

Dhareshwar, Vivek (1989). "Toward a narrative epistemology of the postcolonial predicament," *Inscriptions*, 5.

—— (1990). "The predicament of theory," in M. Kreisworth and M. A. Cheetham (eds.), *Theory between the Disciplines*. Ann Arbor: University of Michigan Press.

Gilroy, Paul (1993). *The Black Atlantic: Modernity and Double Consciousness*. Cambridge, Mass.: Harvard University Press.

Giroux, Henry (1994). "Living dangerously: identity politics and the new cultural racism," in Henry Giroux and Peter McLaren (eds.), *Between Borders: Pedagogy and the Politics of Cultural Studies*. New York: Routledge, 29–55.

Hall, Stuart (1990). "Cultural identity and diaspora," in J. Rutherford (ed.), *Identity: Community, Culture, Difference*. London: Lawrence & Wishart, 222–37.

—— (1991). "The local and the global: globalization and ethnicity," in A. King (ed.), *Culture, Globalization and the World-System*. London: Macmillan, 19–39.

—— (1992). "Race, culture and communications: looking backward and forward at cultural studies," *Rethinking Marxism*, 5: 10–18.

Haraway, Donna (1991). *Simians, Cyborgs and Women: The Reinvention of Nature*. New York: Routledge.

Lyotard, Jean-François (1990). *Heidegger and "the Jews,"* trans. A. Michel and R. Roberts. Minneapolis: University of Minnesota Press.

Mercer, Kobena (1992). "Back to my routes: a postscript to the 80s," in David Bailey and Stuart Hall (eds.), *Critical Decade: Black British Photography in the 80s, Ten–8*, 3: 32–9.

O'Hanlon, Rosalind (1988). "Recovering the subject: subaltern studies and histories of resistance in colonial South Asia," *Modern Asian Studies*, 22: 189–224.

Parry, Benita (1987). "Problems in current theories of colonial discourse," *Oxford Literary Review*, 9: 27–58.

Rosaldo, Renato (1989). *Culture and Truth: The Remaking of Social Analysis*. Boston: Beacon Press.

Said, Edward (1978). *Orientalism*. New York: Vintage.

Wallace, Michele (1994). "Multiculturalism and oppositionality," in Henry Giroux and Peter McLaren (eds.), *Between Borders: Pedagogy and the Politics of Cultural Studies*. New York: Routledge, 180–91.

Young, Robert (1990). *White Mythologies: Writing History and the West*. London: Routledge.

Section III
American Social Science and Its Legacy

Roy Lichtenstein, *Whaam!*, © Estate of Roy Lichtenstein/DACS 2000. Photo © Tate Gallery, London 1999.

Section III
American Social Science and Its Legacy

Authors
Elihu Katz, James W. Carey, George Gerbner, Michael Schudson, Horace Newcomb
and Paul M. Hirsch

Visual Artist
Roy Lichtenstein: *Whaam!*

IN the United States, cultural studies emerged from the shadows of a social science paradigm that had hitherto dominated approaches to the study of everyday life and cultural meaning via the established disciplines of sociology, anthropology, psychology, political economy, and mass communications. Since many of its first practitioners were reacting to (and against) these disciplines' claims to "scientific objectivity" and "value-free" research, an understanding of American cultural studies thus depends upon some knowledge of the social science tradition that had flourished in the USA in the post-war period.

But American social science not only forced cultural studies into a reactive and critical posture, it also contributed to its development. Despite claims to "scientific objectivity" and inevitable ties with culture industries, many social scientists, picking up on earlier European traditions such as those of the Frankfurt School, engaged in radical critiques that still prove useful in the analysis of American society and culture. There is also a strand of work on American media which foregrounds notions of citizenship, the public sphere, and the relation between public and private culture that have recently been taken up again as issues of the "mediasphere" and globalization become increasingly prominent.

It may be noted that there are no women authors represented in this chapter, nor authors who identify with minority speaking positions, including ethnic identity, with the single exception of Jewish writers. There are of course many people working in the social sciences who are both female and from other minorities. But it is nevertheless the case that the overwhelming majority of influential work, especially that which has held dialogue with cultural studies from the perspective of the social sciences, has been published by men. So it is that this chapter represents some of the most interesting work by *social scientists*, and those who have engaged with their work from other disciplinary positions (in this selection, Horace Newcomb). We have taken the decision that a system of "proportional representation" of authors from different backgrounds would fail to give a true picture of the field, of the debates, and of the themes of this "legacy."

Elihu Katz—one of the best-known figures in the sociology of media over many years—describes in his own wonderful phrase the "multidisciplinary armamentarium" that is needed to analyze communications. He brings empirical social science into contact with historical, textual, and other analytic traditions in a call for a broadening of perspective in the analysis of new media technologies, their "content," their institutional productivity and their impact (both textual and sociopsychological) upon audiences. This broad agenda of concerns and approaches has since become well established in media studies especially, but also in more broadly cultural studies work.

James W. Carey, one of the leading figures in the American mass communications tradition, uses the work of anthropologist Clifford Geertz to consider the possibility of a distinctively American cultural studies that would not be bound to the Marxist formulation of ideology so influential upon British cultural studies.

George Gerbner has held his own distinctive place in an area of social science research concerned with the analysis of "cultural indicators." He and his colleagues (associated for a long time with the Annenburg School of Communication) published many studies in "cultivation" theory and analysis, first gaining wide public attention in the 1970s via their research into violence in the media as a "cultural indicator." In this selection, Gerbner provides a useful method he calls "message system analysis." This shows how empirical research into media messages might be conducted via various categories and measures. It also provides an instance of how the cultural field, specially in its large-scale communicative mode, is viewed from a disciplinary perspective that seeks to understand culture and communication *impersonally*, reminding us that culture is also, sometimes, a species of what he calls "industrial behaviour."

In his discussion of television coverage of the American presidency, Michael Schudson, cultural historian as well as mass communications scholar, counters a simplistic technological determinism with one of the key insights of an emergent cultural studies. He argues that textual conventions have as much force in shaping visions of reality as do more tangible factors such as politics and technology. Combining one of the fundamental tools of social science, content analysis, with one of the fundamental tools of cultural studies, narrative analysis, Schudson shows that journalistic fascination with the power of the American presidency long pre-dated the television coverage of the office.

Horace Newcomb is not a social scientist. His training was in the literary field, and he is a TV scriptwriter and critic as well as a noted academic writer. He was one of the earliest American scholars to take television seriously as an object of study in the 1970s. Like Katz, he was interested in interdisciplinary approaches to television (not surprisingly, therefore, there is a network of mutual citation among many of the writers associated with this period of research, several of whom are represented in this *Reader*). In this selection Newcomb collaborated with the sociologist Paul M. Hirsch to produce one of the first attempts to combine close *textual* analysis of popular media forms with much broader social and cultural questions. Their concept of television as a "cultural forum" establishes dialogue with the then emergent work of British cultural studies. It retains from the social sciences a strong interest in social change in the context of mass media and complex culture, and of course maintains a strongly American orientation in the analysis of television programming.

The visual image accompanying this chapter is George Lichtenstein's painting *Whaam!* Lichtenstein was one of the most important of the Pop Artists who came to the fore in the 1960s. As is evident from this image, he was interested in the form of the print-cartoon, taking from it elements of form, composition, color, and theme. *Whaam!* remains an apposite image of those times for its foregrounding of popular culture. But even beyond that the actual image, showing a highly trained operator of high-tech machinery in the act of "analyzing" an anonymous subject to death, is a rather apt exaggeration of some of the tendencies of militant science in action; this is one of a technological society's possible end-points.

12 The Return of the Humanities and Sociology

Elihu Katz

Attention to long-run effects, the notion of genre, and the infusion of semiotics and sociology have inspired methodological, conceptual, and theoretical advances

If communications research is now in ferment, that ferment can be attributed to its invasion by a broader set of multidisciplinary concerns and particularly to a reunion of the social sciences with the humanities. Berelson's requiem for the field, in retrospect, can be seen as valid for the sociopsychological study of the persuasive powers of the mass media and its too narrow definition of "effect."

In the interim, the best thing that has happened to communications research is that it has stopped frantically searching for evidence of the ability of the media to change opinions, attitudes, and actions in the short run. All the recent reviews of work in the field propose a variety of other definitions of effect. The most interesting of these, perhaps, have do with the role of the media in the (long-run) shaping of our images of reality.

While communications research borrowed this focus from philosophy, sociology, and linguistics, it has made some important contributions of its own. Methodologically, communications researchers are trying, in still-too-elementary ways, to study the problem empirically; this is a big step. Conceptually, this thrust gives new status to the classic concept of "reinforcement" in proposing that the absence of change may be a more important effect than its presence. Theoretically, this work gives us insight into process, by relinking mass communications with the study of public opinion from which it had become disconnected. The problem with much of this work, however, is that it has relaxed the stringent criteria that used to guide the examination of alleged effects. It is too easy, so to speak, to give one's name to an (unproven) effect.

This broadening of communications research, with its downgrading of short-run effects, is well reflected in the study of media content. The unit of content analysis is shifting from isolated headlines, persuasive appeals, and acts of violence to the study of genres. Except for a persistent interest in soap opera, social science-based research previously had shown little interest in viewing mass communications as "texts." Thus was the study of cinema and even the study of journalism awarded to the humanists, while the study of broadcasting as stimulus-and-response was given to the social scientists.

From Elihu Katz, "The Return of the Humanities and Sociology," *Journal of Communication*, 33: 3 (1983), 51–52.

But the study of genre is now flourishing in communications research: there are a dozen recent books on television news, a flurry of new interest in entertainment formulae, and several good surveys of the genres of broadcasting. This thrust, best exemplified by the work of Horace Newcomb, reunites the social sciences and the humanities as in days of yore and extends the circle to include anthropology, linguistics, folklore, and the study of popular culture. Most of all, perhaps, interest in genre results from the invasion of social science in the United States by semiotics.

But a still more basic change is the return of *sociology* to communications research

Genre is being talked about as a kind of "contract" in which producers, artists, and audiences join in unwritten agreements to supply and consume certain types of cultural products. The institutions and organizations that implement such agreements, ranging from the pop music industry to the British Broadcasting Corporation, are now attracting the attention of communications researchers. Particularly interesting are the agents of control—inherited culture, establishments, governments, counterculture groups, the market—that relink the study of mass communications to the comparative (and political) study of patron–artist relationships. It is curious that so little work has been done on these institutional aspects; Lasswell's "who" appears to have been poorly conceptualized.

History, too, has rejoined communications research. There is an interest, inspired by Innis and McLuhan, in the social history of the media. And there is an interest in the ideological history of news, entertainment, and advertising. Some of the best talent in the field is now researching these problems. As a result, yet another type of long-run effect has come to the fore: the effect of media technology—printing press, telegraph, newspaper—on social institutions.

These studies, in turn, provide a broadened context for the study of new media technology, which may invigorate the more traditional sociopsychological concerns. Will the tailoring of the new technology to individual needs further atomize modern society? Perhaps we will be in a better position to answer such questions with the multidisciplinary armamentarium now at our disposal.

13 Mass Communication and Cultural Studies

James W. Carey

I

... What is the relationship between culture and society—or, more generally, between expressive forms, particularly art, and social order? For American scholars in general this problem is not even seen as a problem. It is simply a matter of individual choice or one form of determination or another. There is art, of course, and there is society; but to chart the relationship between them is, for a student in communication, to rehearse the obvious and unnecessary. However, in much European work one of the principal (though not exclusive) tasks of scholarship is to work through the relationship of expressive form to social order.

The British sociologist Tom Burns put this nicely somewhere when he observed that the task of art is to make sense out of life. The task of social science is to make sense out of the senses we make out of life. By such reasoning the social scientist stands toward his material—cultural forms such as religion, ideology, journalism, everyday speech—as the literary critic stands toward the novel, play, or poem. He has to figure out what it means, what interpretations it presents of life, and how it relates to the senses of life historically found among a people.

Note what Burns simply takes for granted. There is, on the one hand, life, existence, experience, and behavior and, on the other hand, attempts to find the meaning and significance in this experience and behavior. Culture according to this reading is the meaning and significance particular people discover in their experience through art, religion, and so forth. To study culture is to seek order within these forms, to bring out in starker relief their claims and meanings, and to state systematically the relations between the multiple forms directed to the same end: to render experience comprehensible and charged with affect. But what is called the study of culture also can be called the study of communications, for what we are studying in this context are the ways in which experience is worked into understanding and then disseminated and celebrated (the distinctions, as in dialogue, are not sharp).

Communication studies in the United States have exhibited until recently quite a different intention. They have found most problematic in communication the conditions under which persuasion or social control occurs. Now to reduce the rich variety of American studies to this problematic is, I will admit, a simplification, yet it does capture a significant part of the truth. American studies of communication, mass and interpersonal, have aimed at stating the precise psychogical and sociological conditions under which attitudes are changed, formed, or reinforced and behavior stabilized or redirected. Alternatively, the task is to discover those natural and abstract functions that hold the social order together. Specific forms of culture—art, ritual, journalism—enter the analysis only indirectly, if at all; they enter only insofar as they contribute to such sociological conditions or constitute such psychological forces. They enter, albeit indirectly, in discussions of psychological states, rational or irrational motives and persuasive tactics, differing styles of family organization, sharp distinctions rendered between reality and fantasy-oriented communication, or the role of the mass media in maintaining social integration. But expressive forms are exhausted as intellectual objects suitable for attention by students of communication once relevance to matters of states and rates have been demonstrated. The relation of these forms to social order, the historical transformation of these forms, their entrance into a subjective world of meaning and significance, the interrelations among them, and their role in creating a general culture—a way of life and a pattern of significance—never is entertained seriously.

. . .

II

North American intellectuals are officially committed to a belief in human reason as the instrument of political action. Without that commitment there is little left of a common political life beyond individual taste, choice, and rights. However, as Reinhard Bendix formulated the matter in "Sociology and the Distrust of Reason" (1971), the modern social sciences are equally committed to the view that human action is either the product of individual preference or, more important for this argument, is governed by intrinsic and unconscious or extrinsic and environmental laws and functions. The latter leave little room for the operation of reason, consciousness, or even individually determined choice. Behavior is modeled on laws of conditioning and reinforcement, or prelogical functions, or preconscious urges and scars such as an inferiority complex or will to power. Now the question that immediately arises is this: Where exactly do these laws and functions come from? We have no other choice than to respond: they are either authored by the scientist for his purposes as a member of a controlling class, or they are part of nature and as such control and determine the behavior of the scientist as well as his subjects. But if the activity of the scientist *qua* scientist is determined by conditioning and reinforcement, by the functional necessities of personality and social systems, by the eruption of the demonic and unconscious, what is left of reason? Scientific thought perhaps has no relation to truth because it cannot be explained by truth; it too is a prejudice and a passion, however sophisticated. If the laws of human behavior control the behavior of the scientist, his work is nonsense; if not, just what kind of sense can be made of it?

. . .

Ideology is a scientific term inherited from the philosophers and converted into a weapon. Intellectuals do not generally think of themselves as in the grip of an ideology and don't much like being called ideologists. As a result, we commonly make a distinction between political science or theory, which theoretically and empirically captures the truth, and ideology, which is a tissue of error, distortion, and self-interest, as in "fascist ideology." Consequently, we proclaim the "end of ideology" because we now have a scientific theory of politics. But how does one make the distinction between these forms? The political theory of scientists might be just one more ideology: distortion and fantasy in the service of self-interest, passion, and prejudice.

There is no easy answer to the question. Clifford Geertz calls the dilemma "Mannheim's Paradox" for in *Ideology and Utopia* Karl Mannheim (1965) wrestled heroically with it, though his was a battle without resolution. "Where, if anywhere, ideology leaves off and science begins has been the Sphinx's Riddle of much of modern sociological thought and the rustless weapon of its enemies" (Geertz 1973: 194). But the dilemma is general: Where does conditioning leave off and science begin? Where does class interest leave off and science begin? Where does the unconscious leave off and science begin? The significance of the dilemma for this essay is twofold: first, the study of communication begins when, with the growth of the field of the "sociology of knowledge," the dilemma is faced directly. Second, the principal strategies employed by communication researchers can be seen as devices for escaping Mannheim's Paradox.

Most social scientists do not think much of what they are doing when adopting particular research strategies, and certainly they do not think of themselves as dealing with Mannheim's Paradox. But one important way of looking at the major traditions of social science work is to recognize that there are varying strategies for dealing with "sociology and the distrust of reason." In the study of communication there have been three strategies for attacking the problem, though naturally they parallel the strategies adopted in the other social sciences. The first is to conceive of communication as a behavioral science whose objective is the elucidation of laws. The second is to conceive of communication as a formal science whose objective is the elucidation of structures. The third is to conceive of communication as a cultural science whose objective is the elucidation of meaning. Let me roughly look at these strategies in terms of Geertz's analysis of the perennial problem of ideology.

Two principal explanations of ideology have emerged from the behavioral sciences. Geertz calls them an interest theory and a strain theory, though for us it would be perhaps more felicitous to label them a causal and a functional explanation. A causal explanation attempts to root ideology in the solid ground of social structure. It explains ideological positions by deriving them from the interests of various groups, particularly social classes. It attempts to predict the adoption of ideological positions on the basis of class membership, thereby deriving ideology from antecedent causation. Eventually such an argument starts to creak because it is difficult to predict ideology on the basis of class or, indeed, on any other set of variables. Although ideology is more predictable than many other social phenomena, the net result of causal explanations is relatively low correlations between class position and ideological position. When this form of "essentialism"—one class, one ideology—breaks down, a shift of explanatory apparatus is made. In functional explanations ideology is seen less as caused by structural forces as satisfying certain needs or functions of the personality or society. Geertz calls this latter view a strain theory because it starts from the assumption of the chronic malintegration of the personality and society. It describes life as inevitably riddled by contradictions, antinomies, and inconsistencies. These contradictions give rise to strains, for which ideology provides an answer. If in causal explanations ideology is derived from antecedent factors, in functional explanations ideology is explained as a mechanism for restoring equilibrium to a system put out of joint by the contrariness of modern life. In one model ideology is a weapon for goring someone else's ox; in a functional model it is a device for releasing tension. In the causal model the petit bourgeois shopkeeper's anti-Semitism is explained by class position; in the functional model the same anti-Semitism is explained as catharsis—the displacement of tension onto symbolic enemies.

These same patterns of explanation are found throughout the behavioral sciences. They attempt to explain phenomena by assimilating them to either a functional or a causal law. Both have their weaknesses: causal laws are usually weak at prediction; functional laws are usually obscure in elucidating comprehensible and powerful functions. Moreover, although both explanations are presented as based on empirical data, the data are connected to operative concepts—such as catharsis or interest—by rather questionable and arbitrary operational definitions.

However, the principal concern is not to question the power of the explanations but to see how they deal with Mannheim's Paradox. The behavioral sciences attempt to deal with the paradox in two ways. First, it can be claimed that the behavioral laws elucidated are only statistically true; therefore, although they apply, like the laws of mechanics, to everyone in general, they apply to no one in particular. Because such laws explain only a portion of the variance in the data, it can be asserted that the behavior of the scientist is not governed necessarily by it. A second way to escape the dilemma is simply to claim that the laws do not apply to the scientist *qua* scientist because in the act of comprehending the law he escapes its force. The scientist's knowledge gives him a special purchase to critique the assertions of others, particularly to unmask the illusory and self-serving nature of their ideological assertions.

Now neither of these strategies is particularly effective, but perhaps the greatest disservice they perform for ideology—or, for that matter, for any other symbolic form to which they are applied—is that they dispose of the phenomenon in the very act of naming it. They assume that the flattened scientific forms of speech and prose, that peculiar quality of presumed disinterest and objectivity, are the only mode in which truth can be formulated. What they object to in ideology is hyperbole.

The study of communication in the United States has been dominated by attempts to create a behavioral science and to elucidate laws or functions of behavior. And that study has encountered the same dilemmas that appear throughout the social sciences.

. . .

When popular forms such as ideology enter the study of mass communication, they are usually treated as either a force or a function. Unless a formal analysis of the deep structure of the ideology is undertaken (and none has been particularly successful), one is left with searching out the effects of the ideology or its uses and gratifications. The shift from the former to the latter, the normal trajectory of research, is also a shift from persons conceived as relatively trivial machines to persons as complex systems. This shift from causal and toward functional explanations is not merely the product of the narrow history of communications research but reflects, more importantly, the general history of the social sciences, particularly when those sciences attempt to deal with artifacts and expressions that are explicitly symbolic. There is a sense, of course, in which all human activity in both origins and endings is symbolic. But there is still a useful analytic distinction, to borrow from Geertz, who borrows from Kenneth Burke (1957), between building a house and drawing up a blueprint for building a house, between making love and writing a poem about making love. However much of the symbolic and the artifactual are fused in everyday life, it is nonetheless useful to separate them for analytic purposes. Unfortunately, whenever the symbolic component is inescapably present, a certain theoretical clumsiness overtakes the social sciences. Faced with making some explicit statements about cultural forms, social scientists retreat to obscurantism and reduce their subject matter to social structures or psychological needs. They seem incapable of handling culture in itself—as an ordered though contra-dictory and heterogeneous system of symbols—and treat merely the social and psycho-logical origins of the symbols.

. . .

Mass communication research began as an attempt to explain communication effects by deriving them from some causally antecedent aspect of the communication process. Inspired by both behavioristic psychology and information theory, this explanatory apparatus gave rise to a power model of communication wherein the emphasis was placed on the action of the environment, however conceived, upon a relatively passive receiver. This model was made both possible and necessary by a scientific program that insisted on reducing cultural phenomena to antecedent causes. Some of these causes were explicitly conceptualized as psychological variables—source credibility, appeal of the message—whereas others were rooted in the structural situation of the receiver—class, status, religion, income (Hovland, Janis, and Kelley 1953; Lazarsfeld, Berelson, and Gaudet 1948).

. . .

The entire imagery of culture as a power—the opiate of the people, the hypodermic needle, the product of the environment—denies the functioning of autonomous minds and reduces subjects to trivial machines. The rich history of cultural symbolism, the complex, meaningful transactions of, for example, religion end up no more than shad-owy derivatives of stimuli and structures.

. . .

The difficulty is, of course, the virtual absence in mass communication research of anything more than a rudimentary conception of symbolic processes. There is much talk about escape, finding symbolic outlets, or solidarity being created, but how these miracles are accomplished is never made clear. In such analyses one never finds serious attention being paid to the content of experience. For example, studies of entertainment claim that fantasy is not completely "irrational" because it eases tension, promotes solidarity and promotes learning—claims that seem ridiculous to anyone who has wit-nessed a community divided over the content of movies or personally disturbed by a recurrent film image. What one rarely finds is any analysis of the voice in which films speak. There is an emphasis on everything except what movies are concretely all about.

The link between the causes of mass communication behavior and its effects seems adventitious because the connecting element is a latent function and no attention is paid to the autonomous process of symbolic formation.

. . .

Despite that, I wish neither to gainsay—or to belabor the traditions of work on mass communication. They are indispensable starting points for everyone. I merely wish to suggest that they do not exhaust the tasks of trained intelligence. There is a third way of looking at the goals of intellectual work in communications. Cultural studies does not, however, escape Mannheim's Paradox; it embraces it in ways I hope to show. In doing so it runs the risk of falling into a vicious relativism, though Geertz himself does not see that as a problem. Cultural studies also has far more modest objectives than other traditions. It does not seek to explain human behavior in terms of the laws that govern it or to dissolve it into the structures that underlie it; rather, it seeks to understand it. Cultural studies does not attempt to predict human behavior; rather, it attempts to diagnose human meanings. It is, more positively, an attempt to bypass the rather abstracted empiricism of behavioral studies and the ethereal apparatus of formal theories and to descend deeper into the empirical world. The goals of communications conceived as a cultural science are therefore more modest but also more human, at least in the sense of attempting to be truer to human nature and experience as it ordinarily is encountered. For many students of cultural studies the starting point, as with Geertz, is Max Weber:

Believing with Max Weber, that man is an animal suspended in webs of significance he himself has spun, I take culture to be those webs, and the analysis of it to be therefore not an experimental science in search of law but an interpretive one in search of meaning. It is explication I am after construing social expressions on their surface enigmatical. (Geertz 1973: 5)

That is altogether too arch, so let me explicate the meaning Geertz is after with an artless and transparent example of the type of scene communication researchers should be able to examine. Let us imagine a conversation on the meaning of death. One party to the conversation, a contemporary physician, argues that death occurs with the cessation of brain waves. The test he declares is observable empirically; and so much the better, it makes the organs of the deceased available for quick transplant into waiting patients. A second party to the conversation, a typical middle American, declares that death occurs on the cessation of the heartbeat. This too is empirically available and, so much the better, occurs after the cessation of brain waves. Life is not only prolonged, but because the heart has long been a symbol of human emotions, the test recognizes the affective side of death, the relation of death to the ongoing life of a community. A third party to the conversation, an Irish peasant, finding these first two definitions rather abhorrent, argues that death occurs three days after the cessation of the heartbeat. This too is empirical; days can be counted as well as anything else. In the interim the person, as at the Irish wake, is treated as if he is alive. The "as if" gives away too much; he is alive for three days after the cessation of heartbeats. Death among such peasants occurs with social death, the final separation of the person from a human community. Prior to that he is, for all intents and purposes, alive for he is responded to as a particularly functionless living being. A fourth party to the conversation argues that death occurs seven days prior to the cessation of the heartbeat. He is, let us say, a member of the tribe Colin Turnbull described so vividly in *The Mountain People* (1972). Among these starving people life ceases when food can no longer be gathered or scrambled for. The person is treated as if he were dead during a phase in which we would declare he was alive. Again, ignore the "as if": the definition is as cognitively precise and affectively satisfying as anything put forth by a neurosurgeon. The definition just is: the particular meaning that a group of people assigns to death.

What are we to do with this scene? We certainly cannot choose among these definitions on the basis of the scientific truth of one and the whimsy of the others. Death is not given unequivocally in experience by inflexible biological and social markers, and this has been true since long before the existence of artificial life-support systems. We can, however, show how differing definitions of death point toward differing values and social purposes: fixations on prolonging life by "artificial means," on preserving the continuity of community existence, to reduce the sharpness of the break between life and death. But as to choosing among them on any presumed scientific grounds, we must, at least at this point, remain agnostics.

What more can be done with this scene? Do we want to ask what caused these individuals to hold to these strange definitions? We might naturally inquire after that, but one cannot imagine producing a "lawlike" statement concerning it other than a tautology such as "all people have definitions of death, however varied, because death is something that must be dealt with." The only causal statement that one might imagine is a historical one: a genetic account of how these views grew over time among various people and were changed, displaced, and transformed. But such an analysis is not likely to produce any lawlike statements because it seems intuitively obvious that every people demands a separate history: there are as many reasons for holding differing definitions of death as there are definitions of death.

Could we inquire into the functions these various definitions serve? One supposes so, but that does not seem promising. There is certainly no a priori reason to assume that such definitions serve any function at all. One can imagine elaborate speculations on the role of death in strengthening social solidarity. But this sort of thing runs into the anomaly of all functional analyses: a tribesman starts to figure out if death occurred and ends up strengthening the solidarity of society. There is no necessary relationship between these two activities. "The concept of a latent function," Geertz argues, "is usually invoked to paper over this anomalous state of affairs, but it rather names the phenomenon (whose reality is not in question) than explains it; and the net result is that functional analyses . . . remain hopelessly equivocal" (p. 206).

Might one in such a situation go looking for the deep structure of mind underlying these diverse surface definitions? Again, one might do so, but it is hard to see how such an exercise would help us understand this particular scene. We might, *à la* Lévi-Strauss, go looking for the commonality of semantic structure underlying these definitions of death and therefore out of the variety of definitions produce an elegant vision of a universal meaning of death. But this sort of thing ends up verging on a charade, and as

Geertz (1973: 359) concludes in his essay on Lévi-Strauss, there are enough particular individuals and particular scenes such as I have described to "make any doctrine of man which sees him as the bearer of changeless truths of reason—an 'original logic' proceeding from 'the structure of the mind'—seem merely quaint, an academic curiosity."

I chose an example as simple and simpleminded as death because it is about as universal, transhistorical, and transcultural a phenomenon as one is likely to get. It is also, in its concrete manifestations, as fiercely resistant to reduction to laws, functions, powers and interests as one can imagine. Even in the postmodern age we are going to die in some vividly particular way and in light of some vividly particular set of meanings. Our inability to deal with the ersatz situation I have created and the innumerable ones we are daily called to comment on is not the result of a failure to understand the laws of behavior or the functions of social practices, though insofar as these things can be discovered, it would not hurt us to understand them. Nor does our speechlessness in the face of empirical events result from failure to understand the universal structure of the mind or the nature of cognition—though, again, we could know more of that too. The inability to deal with events such as the death scene derives from our failure, to put it disingenuously, to understand them: to be able to grasp the imaginative universe in which the acts of our actors are signs. What we face in our studies of communication is the consistent challenge to untangle "a multiplicity of complex conceptual structures, many of them superimposed upon or knotted into one another, which are at once strange, irregular, and inexplicit and which he (the student) must contrive somehow first to grasp and then to render" (Geertz 1973: 10). To repeat, we are challenged to grasp the meanings people build into their words and behavior and to make these meanings, these claims about life and experience, explicit and articulate so that we might fairly judge them.

Of course, social scientists do place meanings on their subject's experience: they tell us what thought or action means, what other people are up to. But the meanings such scientists produce have no necessary relation to the subjective intentions or sensed apprehensions of the people they study. As one observer acidly put it, "social scientists go around telling people what it is they [people] think." Geertz is suggesting that the first task of social science is to understand the meaningful structure of symbols in terms of which people bury their dead. This has usually been called, as method, verstehen. However, it is no long-distance mind reading but an attempt to decipher the interpretations people cast on their experience, interpretations available out in the public world.

A cultural science of communication, then, views human behavior—or, more accurately, human action—as a text. Our task is to construct a "reading" of the text. The text itself is a sequence of symbols—speech, writing, gesture—that contain interpretations. Our task, like that of a literary critic, is to interpret the interpretations. As Geertz elegantly summarized the position in an essay on the "Balinese Cockfight":

The culture of a people is an ensemble of texts, themselves ensembles which the anthropologist strains to read over the shoulders of those to whom they properly belong. . . . In the cockfight, then, the Balinese forms and discovers his temperament and his society's temper at the same time. Or more exactly, he forms and discovers a particular face of them. Not only are there a great many other cultural texts providing commentaries on status hierarchy and self regard in Bali; but there are a great many other critical sectors of Balinese life besides the stratificatory . . . that receives such attention. . . . What it says about life is not unqualified nor even unchallenged by what other equally eloquent cultural statements say about it. But there is nothing more surprising in this than in the fact that Racine and Molière were contemporaries, or that the same people who arrange chrysanthemums cast swords (1973: 452–53).

To speak of human action through the metaphor of a text is no longer unusual, though it is still troubling. The metaphor emphasizes that the task of the cultural scientist is closer to that of a literary critic or a scriptural scholar, though it is not the same, than it is to a behavioral scientist. "Texts" are not always printed on pages or chiseled in stone—though sometimes they are. Usually we deal with texts of public utterance or shaped behavior. But we are faced, as is the literary critic, with figuring out what the text says, of constructing a reading of it. Doing communication research (or cultural studies or, in Geertz's term, ethnography) "is like trying to read (in the sense of 'construct a reading of') a manuscript—foreign, faded, full of ellipses, incoherencies, suspicious emendations, and tendentious commentaries but written not in conventionalized graphs of sound but in transient examples of shaped behavior" (p. 10).

To pursue this one a step further, suppose we undress the death scene; that is, deverbalize it, strip it of words. What we observe now is not a conversation but a set of actions. We are interested in the actions because they have meaning—they are an orchestration of gestural symbols. We need to decipher—though it is not so mechanical as cracking a code—what is being said through behavior. What we observe are people silently holding a wake, measuring brain waves, rolling relatives into ravines, and, of course, a good deal more. From such fugitive and fragmentary data we have to construct a reading of the situation: to interpret the meaning in these symbols as gestures. The trick is to read these "texts" in relation to concrete social structure without reducing them to that structure. No one will contend that this is particularly easy. There are enough methodological dilemmas here to keep us occupied for a few generations. But to look at communication as, if you will forgive me, communication—as an interpretation, a meaning construed from and placed upon experience, that is addressed to and interpreted by someone—allows us to concentrate on the subject matter of the enterprise and not some extrinsic and arbitrary formula that accounts for it.

Why do we wish to construct a reading? The answer to this question shows both the modesty and importance of communication as a study of culture. The objective of cultural studies is not so much to answer our questions as, Geertz puts it, "to make available to us answers that others guarding other sheep in other valleys have given and thus to include them in the consultable record of what man has said" (p. 30). This is a modest goal: to understand the meanings that others have placed on experience, to build up a veridical record of what has been said at other times, in other places, and in other ways; to enlarge the human conversation by comprehending what others are saying. Though modest, the inability to engage in this conversation is the imperative failure of the modern social sciences. Not understanding their subjects—that unfortunate word—they do not converse with them so much as impose meanings on them. Social scientists have political theories and subjects have political ideologies; the behavior of social scientists is free and rationally informed, whereas their subjects are conditioned and ruled by habit and superstition—not good intellectual soil for a working democracy.

Geertz is suggesting that the great need of the social sciences and one that cultural studies is able uniquely to perform is the creation of a theory of fictions. Fiction is used here in its original sense—fictio—a "making," a construction. The achievement of the human mind and its extension in culture (though it is as much an abject necessity as an achievement) is the creation of a wide variety of cultural forms through which reality can be created.

. . .

At each point in this circling the task remains the same: to seize upon the interpretations people place on existence and to systematize them so they are more readily available to us. This is a process of making large claims from small matters: studying particular rituals, poems, plays, conversations, songs, dances, theories, and myths and gingerly reaching out to the full relations within a culture or a total way of life. For the student of communications other matters press in: How do changes in forms of communications technology affect the constructions placed on experience? How does such technology change the forms of community in which experience is apprehended and expressed? What, under the force of history, technology, and society, is thought about, thought with, and to whom is it expressed? That is, advances in our understanding of culture cannot be secured unless they are tied to a vivid sense of technology and social structure.

To pull off an effective theory of popular culture requires a conception of persons, not as psychological or sociological but as cultural. Such a model would assume that culture is best understood not by tracing it to psychological and sociological conditions or, indeed, to exclusively political or economic conditions, but as a manifestation of a basic cultural disposition to cast up experience in symbolic form. These forms, however implausible to the investigator, are at once aesthetically right and conceptually veridical. They supply meaningful identities along with an apprehended world.

. . .

III

It is unfortunate that to mention cultural studies to most communications researchers resurrects the image of the arguments concerning mass and popular culture that littered the field a few decades ago. That was part of the disaster Raymond Williams referred to in comments mentioned earlier. Yet many who worked in popular culture were on the right track. The question they both raised and obscured was a simple but profound one: What is the significance of living in the world of meanings conveyed by popular art? What is the relationship between the meanings found in popular art and in forms such as science, religion, and ordinary speech? How, in modern times, is experience cast up, interpreted, and congealed into knowledge and understanding?

The remarkable work of Clifford Geertz—remarkable substantively and methodologically, though the latter has not been explored in this essay—and of many others working in phenomenology, hermeneutics, and literary criticism has served to clarify the objectives of a cultural science of communications and has defined the dimensions of an interpretive science of society. The task now for students of communications or mass communication or contemporary culture is to turn these advances in the science of culture toward the characteristic products of contemporary life: news stories, bureaucratic language, love songs, political rhetoric, daytime serials, scientific reports, television drama, talk shows, and the wider world of contemporary leisure, ritual, and information. To square the circle, those were some of the conventions, forms, and practices Raymond Williams felt had slipped by us when we confidently named our field the study of mass communications.

References

Bendix, Reinhard, and Roth, Guenther (1971). "Sociology and the Distrust of Reason," in *Scholarship and Partisanship: Essays on Max Weber*. Berkeley: University of California Press, 84–105.

Burke, Kenneth (1957). *The Philosophy of Literary Form*. New York: Vintage Books.

Geertz, Clifford (1973). *The Interpretation of Cultures*. New York: Basic Books.

Hovland, Carl, Janis, I., and Kelley, H. (1953). *Communication and Persuasion*. New Haven: Yale University Press.

Lazarsfeld, Paul, Berelson, B., and Gaudet, H. (1948). *The People's Choice*. New York: Columbia University Press.

Mannheim, Karl (1965). *Ideology and Utopia*. New York: Harvest Books.

Turnbull, Colin (1972). *The Mountain People*. New York: Simon and Schuster.

14 Mass Media Discourse: Message System Analysis as a Component of Cultural Indicators

George Gerbner

P ERSONAL tastes and selective habits of cultural participation limit each of us to risky and usually faulty extrapolation about the media experiences of large and diverse populations. The very qualities that draw our attention to exciting plots and to information relevant to our own interests detract from our ability to make representative observations about the composition and structure of large message systems such as mass media discourse.

Mass media discourse reflects policies of media institutions and enters into the cultivation of conceptions in ways that can be investigated. Therefore, informed policy-making and the valid interpretation of social concept formation and response require the development of some indicators of the prevailing winds of the common symbolic environment in which and to which most people respond.

Such indicators are representative abstractions from the collectively experienced total texture of messages. They are the results of analysis applicable to the investigation of the broadest terms of collective cultivation of concepts about life and society. Philosophers, historians, linguists, anthropologists, and others have, of course, addressed such problems before. But the rise of the industrialized and centrally managed discharge of massive symbol-systems into the mainstream of common consciousness has given the inquiry a new urgency and social policy significance. Becoming aware of mass-produced sources of consciousness can also be a liberating experience.

Before we discuss the terms and measures of the analysis, we need to consider the special characteristics of mass media discourse. That consideration will touch upon the nature and distinctive features of public communication in a cultural context whose messages are largely mass-produced and/or distributed by complex industrial structures. The description and definition of the concepts of cultivation and publication, and of their relationships to mass publics created and maintained by mass communication, will complete the background necessary for the development of an approach to message system analysis of mass media discourse.

From George Gerbner, "Mass Media Discourse: Message System Analysis as a Component of Cultural Indicators," in Teun Van Dijk (ed.), *Discourse and Communication* (Berlin: Walter De Gruyter, 1985), 13–25.

Public Communication

Distinctive characteristics of large groups of people are acquired in the process of growing up, learning, and living in one culture rather than another. Individuals may make their own selections through which to cultivate personal images, tastes, views, and preferences. But they cannot cultivate what is not available, and will rarely select what is rarely available, seldom emphasized, or infrequently presented.

A culture cultivates patterns of conformity as well as of alienation or rebellion after its own image. In fact, I define culture as a system of messages that regulates social relationships.

The communications of a culture not only inform but form common images; they not only entertain but create publics; they not only reflect but shape attitudes, tastes, preferences. They provide the boundary conditions and overall patterns within which the processes of personal and group-mediated selection, interpretation, and interaction go on.

Communication is interaction through messages. Messages are formally coded symbolic or representational events of some shared significance in a culture, produced for the purpose of evoking significance. Social interaction through such messages is the "humanizing" process of Homo Sapiens. The terms of this interaction define for members of the species the realities and potentials of the human condition. These terms provide functional perspectives of existence, priority, value, and relationships; they cultivate public notions of what is, what is important, what is right, and what is related to what.

A word on *cultivation*. The term is used to indicate that our primary concern is not with bits of information, education, persuasion, etc., or with any kind of direct communication "effects". It is with the common context into which we are born and in response to which different individual and group selections and interpretations of messages takes place. Instead of measuring change causally attributed to communications injected into an otherwise stable system of messages, our analysis is concerned with assessing the system itself. That assessment is a first step toward investigating the role of message systems in establishing and maintaining stable conceptions of reality. These are conceptions that persuasive and informational efforts are usually "up against."

Public is another word of special significance. It means both a quality of information and an amorphous social aggregate whose members share a community of interest. As a quality of information, the awareness that a certain item of knowledge is publicly held (i.e. not only known to many, but *commonly known that it is known to many*) makes collective thought and action possible. Such knowledge gives individuals their awareness of collective strength (or weakness), and a feeling of social identification or alienation. As an amorphous social aggregate, a public is a basic unit of a requirement for self-government among diverse and scattered groups. The creation of both the awareness and the social structure called public is the result of the "public-making" activity appropriately named *publication*. ("Public opinion" is actually the outcome of eliciting private views and publishing them, as in the publication of polls.)

Publication as a general social process is the creation and cultivation of knowingly shared ways of selecting and viewing events and aspects of life. Mass production and distribution of message systems transforms selected private perspectives into broad public perspectives, and brings mass publics into existence. These publics are maintained through continued publication. They are supplied with selections of information and entertainment, fact and fiction, news and fantasy or "escape" materials which are considered important or interesting or entertaining, and profitable, (or all of these) in terms of the perspectives to be cultivated.

Publication is thus the instrument of community consciousness and of governance among large groups of people too numerous or too dispersed to interact face to face or in any other personally mediated fashion. The truly revolutionary significance of modern mass communication is its broad "public-making" ability. That is the ability to form historically new bases for collective thought and action quickly, continously, and pervasively across previous boundaries of time, space, and culture.

The terms of broadest social interaction are those available in the most widely shared messages of a culture. Increasingly these are mass-produced message systems. Whether one is widely conversant with or unaware of large portions of them, supportive or critical of them, or even alienated from or rebellious of them, these common terms of the culture shape the course of the response.

The institutions producing the most pervasive systems of messages are central to public acculturation, socialization, and the conduct of public affairs. Every society takes special steps to assure that authoritative decision-making in the field of public-making is reserved to the key establishments of the power structure, be that religious, secular, public, private, or some mixture of these. The provisions conferring authoritative control to key establishments may be in the form of state monopoly, public subsidy, tax privileges, protection from public interference with private corporate control (as under the First Amendment to the U.S. Constitution), or some combination of these.

The oldest form of institutionalized public acculturation is what we today call religion, the cultural organization that once encompassed both statecraft and the public philosophy of a community. Two more recent branches are the offspring of the industrial revolution. One of these is public education or formal schooling for all, born of the struggle for equality of opportunity, and sustained by the demand for minimum literacy, competence, and obeisance in increasingly mobile, de-tribalized, de-traditionalized, and non-deferential societies. The other major branch of institutionalized public acculturation is mass communication.

Mass Communication

Mass communication is mass-produced communication. It is the extension of institutionalized public-making and acculturation beyond the limits of handicraft or other personally mediated interactions. It is the continuous mass production and distribution of systems of messages to groups so large, heterogeneous, and widely dispersed that they could never interact face-to-face or through any other but mass-produced and technologically mediated message systems. This becomes possible only when technological means are available and social organizations emerge for the mass production and distribution of messages.

The key to the historic significance of mass communication does not rest, therefore, in the concept of "masses" as such. There were "masses" (i.e. large groups of people) reached by other forms of public communication long before the advent of modern mass communication. The key to the cultural transformation long before the advent of modern mass communication. The key to the cultural transformation which mass communication signifies is the *mass production* of messages forming message systems characteristic of their technological and industrial bases.

The media of mass communications—print, film, radio, television—are ways of selecting, composing, recording, and sharing stories, symbols, and images. They are also social organizations acting as "governments" (i.e. authoritative decision-makers) in the special domain of institutionalized public acculturation. As such, they are products of technology, corporate (or other collective) organization, mass production, and mass markets. They are the cultural arms of the industrial order from which they spring.

Mass media policies reflect and cultivate not only the general structure of social relations but also specific types of institutional and industrial organization and control. Corporate or collective organization, private or public control, and the priorities given to artistic, political, economic or other policy considerations govern their overall operations, affect their relationships to other institutions and shape their public functions. The general context of public consciousness today may have more to do with industrial power, structure and control than with anything else.

Mass Media Message Systems

Mass-produced and/or distributed media discourse is thus both a record and an instrument of industrial behaviour in the cultural field. Its analysis can shed light on its actual controls and functions, independently from policy intentions, rationalizations, and pretentions or from assumptions and claims about its effects. Such analysis is not a substitute for the study of policies and effects. Rather it is a source both of hypotheses for those investigations and of independent results that can help illuminate, support or counter them. But it can also yield strategic intelligence and results that cannot be obtained in any other way, such as explaining why certain issues, problems, courses of action, etc. become salient to large numbers of people at certain times. Message system analysis of mass media discourse is one leg of the three-legged stool of comprehensive cultural indicators, including three types of investigations; institutional policy analysis, message system analysis, and cultivation analysis (see Gerbner et al. 1973).

The Analysis

Message system analysis is thus designed to investigate the aggregate and collective premises presented in mass media discourse. It deals with the "facts of life" and dynamic qualities represented in the systems. Its purpose is to describe the symbolic "world," sense its climate, trace its currents, and identify its functions.

The results make no reference to single communications. They do not interpret selected units of symbolic material or draw conclusions about artistic style or merit. That is the task of essaying works of personal and selective relevance, not necessarily representative of a system of image and message mass-production. Message system analysis seeks to examine what large and heterogeneous communities absorb but not necessarily what any individual selects.

The analysis extracts from the discourse its basic presentation of elements of existence, importance, value, and relationship, and then re-aggregates these elements into larger patterns along lines of investigate purpose. The analysis pivots on the reliable determination of these elements and is limited to clearly perceived and reliably coded items. That limitation does not mean that message system analysis pays attention only to surface structure cues (words, etc.) of discourses. Nor does it leave out the semantic, pragmatic, and other systematically assessible dimensions of messages. It only means that, unlike artistic and literary criticism of a traditional kind, useful for purpose of revealing personal interpretation and unique insight, message system analysis deals with the common elements of discourse such as thematic distribution, propositional context, characterization and action structure, social typing, fate (success, failure) of character types, and other reliably identifiable representations and configurations. If one were to use the perceptions and impressions of casual observers, no matter how sophisticated, the value of the investigation could be reduced, and its purpose confounded. Only an aggregation of unambiguous message elements and their separation from personal impressions left by unidentified clues will provide a valid and reliable standard for comparison with the intentions and claims of policy makers and the perceptions or conceptions of audiences.

What distinguishes the analysis of public, mass-mediated message systems as a social scientific enterprise from other types of observation, commentary, or criticism is the attempt to deal comprehensively, systematically, and generally rather than specifically and selectively or *ad hoc* with patterns of collective cultural life. This approach makes no prior assumptions about such conventionally demarcated functions as "information" and "entertainment," or "high culture" and "low culture." Style of expression, quality of representation, artistic excellence, or the nature of individual experience associated with selective exposure to and participation in mass-cultural activity are not relevant for this purpose. What is informative, entertaining (or both), good, bad, or indifferent by any standard are selective judgments applied to messages in a way that may be quite independent from the functions they actually perform in the context of message systems touching the collective life of a large and diverse population. Conventional and formal judgments applied to selected communications may be irrelevant to general questions about the presentation of what is, what is important, what is right, and what is related to what in mass-produced message systems.

It should be stressed again that the characteristics of a message system are not necessarily the characteristics of individual units composing the system. The purpose of the study of a system *as system* is to reveal features, processes, and relationships expressed in the whole, not in its parts. Unlike most literary or dramatic criticism, or, in fact, most personal cultural participation and judgment, message system analysis focuses on the record of industrial behavior in the cultural field and its symbolic functions.

Symbolic Functions

Symbolic functions are implicit in the way basic elements of a system are presented, weighted, loaded with attributes, and related to each other. Such elements are time, space, characterizations (people) and their fate (success, failure; domination, submission, etc.). Dynamic symbol systems are not maps of some other "real" territory. They are our mythology, our organs of social meaning. They make visible some conceptions of the invisible forces of life and society. We select and shape them to bend otherwise elusive facts to our (not always conscious) purposes. Whether we know it or intend it or not, these purposes are implicit in the way things actually work out in the symbolic world.

On the whole, and in the long run, institutional interests and pressures shape the way things work out in most collective myths, celebrations, and rituals. Mass-produced message systems (as all standardized and assembly-line products) are even more power-ridden and policy-directed. Various power roles enter into the decision-making process that prescribes, selects and shapes the final product. In the creation of news, facts impose some constraints upon invention; the burden of serving institutional purposes is placed upon selection, treatment and display. Fiction and drama carry no presumption of facticity and thus do not inhibit the candid expression of social values. On the contrary, they give free reign to adjusting facts to institutional purpose. Fiction can thus perform social symbolic functions more directly than can other forms of discourse.

Symbolic functions differ from those of nonsymbolic events in the ways in which causal relationships must be traced in the two realms. Physical causation exists outside and independently of consciousness. Trees do not grow and chemicals do not react "on purpose," although human purposes may intervene or cause them to function. When a sequence of physical events is set in motion, we have only partial awareness and little control over the entire chain of its consequences.

The symbolic world, however, is totally invented. The reasons why things exist in the symbolic world, and the ways in which things are related to one another and to their symbolic consequences, are completely artificial. The laws of the symbolic world are entirely socially and culturally determined. Whatever exists in the symbolic world is there because someone put it there. The reason may be a marketing or programming decision or a feeling that it will "improve the story." Having been put there, things not only stand for other things as all symbols do, but also *do* something in their symbolic context. The introduction (or elimination) of a character, a scene, an event, has functional consequences. It changes other things in the story. It makes the whole work "work" differently.

A structure may accommodate to pressure in a way that preserves, or even enhances, the symbolic functions of an act. For example, the first response of television program producers to agitation about violence on television was to eliminate violent women characters, thereby reducing violent acts but also making women involved in violence totally victimized. In other words, we found that when the proportion of violent characterizations was selectively (and temporarily) reduced, the imbalance in the risks of victimization between groups of unequal social power increased, thereby strengthening the symbolic function of violence as a demonstration of relative social powers (Gerbner 1972).

In another study (Nunnaly 1960), the opinions of experts on 10 information questions concerning the mentally ill were compared with mass media (most fictional and dramatic) representations of mentally ill characters. The mass media image was found to diverge widely from the expert image. The "public image," as determined by a attitude survey along the same dimensions, fell between the expert and the media profiles. Thus, instead of "mediating" expert views, the media tended to cultivate conceptions far different from and in many ways opposed to those of the experts. What may be seen in isolation as "ineffective" communication was, on the contrary, powerful media cultivation "pulling" popular notions away from expert views. The symbolic functions of mental illness in popular drama and news may well be to indicate unpredictability, danger, or morally and dramatically appropriate punishment for certain sins—all very different from its diagnostic and therapeutic conceptions.

The study of specific message structures and symbolic functions reveals how these communications help define, characterize, and decide the course of life, the fate of people, and the nature of society in a symbolic world. The "facts" of that world are often different from those of the "real" world, but their functions are those of the real social order. For example, in U.S. television drama, male characters outnumber female characters more than three to one. They dominate the symbolic world, and present more than their share of activities and opportunities. Fiction, drama, and news depict situations and present actions in those realistic, fantastic, tragic, or comic ways that provide the most appropriate symbolic context for the emergence of some institutional and social significance that could not be presented or would not be accepted (let alone enjoyed) in other ways.

Terms of Analysis

Message system analysis thus investigates industrial behaviour in message mass-production for large and heterogeneous populations. The analysis suggests collective and common features and functions of public image formation. The schema and methods of analysis are designed to inquire into those dimensions of mass media discourse that identify elements of *existence*, *importance*, *values*, and *relationships*. Figure 14.1 summarizes the questions, terms, and measures of analysis relevant to each dimension.

The dimension of existence deals with the question "What is?", that is, what is available (can be attended to) in public message systems, how frequently, and in what proportions. The availability of shared messages defines the scope of public attention. The measure of attention, therefore, indicates the presence, frequency, rate, complexity, and varying distributions of items, topics, themes, etc., presented in message systems.

The dimension of *importance* addresses the question, "What is important?" We use measures of *emphasis* to study the context of relative prominence and order or degrees of intensity, centrality, importance. Measures of attention and emphasis may be combined to indicate not only the allocation but also the focusing of attention in a system.

Dimensions	Existence	Priorities	Values	Relationship
Assumptions about	WHAT IS?	WHAT IS IMPORTANT	WHAT IS RIGHT OR WRONG, GOOD OR BAD, ETC.?	WHAT IS RELATED TO WHAT, AND HOW?
Questions	What is available for public attention? How much and how frequently?	In what context or order of importance?	In what light, from what point of view, with what associated judgments?	In what over-all proximal, logical, or causal structure?
Terms and measures of analysis	ATTENTION Prevalence, rate, complexity, variations	EMPHASIS Ordering, ranking, scaling for prominence, centrality or intensity	TENDENCY Measures of critical and differential tendancy; qualities traits	STRUCTURE Correlations, clustering; structure of action

Figure 14.1 Dimensions, questions, terms, and measures of message system analysis

The dimension of *values* inquires into the point of view from which things are presented. It notes certain evaluative and other qualitative characteristics, traits, or connotations attached to themes, events, items, actions, persons, groups, and so on. Measures of *tendency* are used to assess the direction of value judgments observed in units of attention.

The dimension of *relationships* focuses on the associations within and among measures of attention, emphasis, and tendency. When we deal with patterns instead of only simple distributions, or when we relate the clustering of measures to one another, we illuminate the underlying *structure* of assumptions about existence, importance, and values represented in message systems.

The four dimensions, then, yield measures of attention, emphasis, tendency, and structure. *Attention* is the typology or classification of units of discourse into categories of existence (subjects, themes, demographic characteristics, etc.); *emphasis* is the relative importance attributed to each unit attended to within the context of the discourse; *tendency* is the evaluative and other qualities attributed to each unit of attention; and *structure* is the ways in which categories of attention (existence) are related to emphasis (importance) and tendency (values) in the system. For a full and comprehensive analysis, all four dimensions should be included.

Message system analysis begins with the determination of appropriate samples and units of analysis, and the development of an instrument of analysis (coding and recording scheme). The sample should be large enough to permit the development of stable patterns and the assessment of the significance of differences in the distribution of characteristics. The units of analysis should correspond to the units of production as much as possible (newspapers, pages, films, programs, books for context units; stories, scenes, characters, themes, etc., for units of enumeration). The instrument of analysis should be as explicit as possible to facilitate reliable coding and the recording of observations.

The Measures

Let us now discuss each measure in greater detail and illustrate them with examples.

1. Attention indicates the presence (or absence) and frequency of selected elements of existence that a system of messages makes available for public attention. These can be a subject classification, list of themes, typology of characters, or any other category scheme relevant to the purpose of the investigation. The principal issue here is to determine "what is" in the system to which people can attend, and how frequently does each element appear in the system.

Most content analyses use the measure of attention to determine the occurrence of relevant items, themes, and other characteristics in press coverage, dramatic and fictional analyses, thematic study of magazine stories, ads, films, etc. . . . A typical attention item has a subject title or question (i.e. "Foreign News," "Occupation," "Character's Success or Failure," "Character's Age") and several answers, including "cannot code," "uncertain, mixed," and "other-write in," as well as the most relevant substantive categories.

2. Emphasis is a measure of the relative importance of a unit of attention in the

sample. Emphasis directs attention to some units at the expense of attending to other units. The headline or title of a story, its size and placement, the intensity of the mode of communication, the order of presentation, loudness, tone, prominence by other means such as duration, focus, detail, etc. and certain design characteristics are marks of emphasis. Emphasis is always a relative measure and an element of context. Therefore ranks, scales, and other measures of relative value are suitable for indicating emphasis. Frequency (a measure of attention) may also denote emphasis, but there are elements of discourse that are prominent for their relative rarity, while others may receive emphasis by repetition. Therefore, a measure of emphasis that is separate from frequency is sometimes desirable.

The emphasis code (rank order, scale number, etc.) is generally attributed to the unit of attention. It answers the question: now that we have established that something exists in the system and thus may be attended to (attention), let us note how prominent or important it is.

Message system analysis may feature the units of attention that receive the highest emphasis, such as a study of headlines in a comparative investigation of national press perspectives or an investigation of leading characters in television drama. Usually, however, separate and independent measures of attention and of emphasis can illuminate different facets of the system. For example, we have found that one general feature of the representation of women and minorities on American television is that even when their numbers exceeds their proportion of the real population (which is rare), they are more likely to play minor or secondary than major or leading parts (Gerbner and Signorielli 1979).

3. Tendency is a measure of the evaluative or other qualitative characteristics attributed to a unit of attention. It is often a scale defined by such adjectives as good–bad, right–wrong, positive–negative, active–passive, strong–weak, smart–stupid, successful–unsuccessful, or whatever is germane to the purpose of the investigation. A group of such scales may stem from and define a factorial structure of dimension of meaning or personality types such as semantic differential scales. The measure of tendency attempts to answer the question: now that we have established the distribution of attention and emphasis in the system, in what evaluative, qualitative, judgmental light is each unit presented?

Measuring tendency is clearly separate from coding attention and emphasis; whether something is good or bad does not depend on its frequency or prominence. However, the ultimate combination (an element of structure) may determine its meaning. The frequency and prominence of good things certainly impresses us differently from the frequency and prominence of bad things.

Although tendency is thus usually an element of the structure of a message system, presented in conjunction with the other measures, it can also be the principal feature of the investigation. For example, a study of ideological tendencies in the French press showed that different political organs reported a criminal case in different light, even when shifts of attention and emphasis were considered equal.

4. Structure is that aspect of the context of a message system that reveals underlying relationships among the other dimensions. These relationships are "underlying" in that they are not necessarily given in single units but are characteristics of the system as a

whole. A story may present a violent criminal as an "ex mental patient," a doctor as wise and authoritative, and a politician as opportunistic. If the *majority* of stories in a message system present mental patients as violent, doctors as omniscient, and politicians as venal, we are dealing with structural characteristics of the system ("stereotypes") whose meaning for the policies that produce it and the assumption it may cultivate are very different from that of isolated portrayals.

Most of the studies cited in the bibliography and virtually all full-fledged message system analyses investigate the underlaying structure of message systems. Some also relate that structure to theories of the cultural functions of institutions and to theories of cultivation and media effects.

. . .

The analysis of mass media message systems can thus provide a framework in which comprehensive, coherent, cumulative, and comparative mass-cultural information can be systematically assembled and periodically reported. Indicators relevant to specific problems or policies can then be seen in the context of the entire structure of assumptions cultivated at a particular time and place.

These indicators will not tell us what individuals think or do. But they will tell us what most people think or do something *about* and suggest reasons why. They will tell us about industrial policy and process in the cultural field mass-producing shared representations of life and the assumptions and functions embedded in them. They will help understand, judge, and shape the symbolic environment that affects much of what we think and do in common.

References

Gerbner, G. (1972). "Violence in Television Drama: Trends and Symbolic Functions," in G. A. Comstock and E. A. Rubinstein (eds.), *Television and Social Behavior* 1. *Content and Control*. Washington, D.C.: U.S. Government Printing Office, 29–93.

Gerbner G., and Signorielli, N. (1979). "Women and Minorities in Television Drama, 1969–1978." The Annenberg School of Communications, University of Pennsylvania, Philadelphia.

Gerbner, G., and Signorielli, N. (October 1982). "The World According to Television." *American Demographics*, 15–17.

Gerbner, G., Gross, L., and Melody, W. (eds.) (1973). "Cultural Indicators: The Third Voice, " in *Communications Technology and Social Policy*. New York: John Wiley & Sons, 555–73.

Nunnaly, Jr., Jum C. (1960). *Popular Conceptions of Mental Health: Their Development and Change*. New York: Holt, Rinehart and Winston.

15 The Politics of Narrative Form: The Emergence of News Conventions in Print and Television

Michael Schudson

TELEVISION is a central locus of activity in American culture and American politics. It is often cited as a dominant force in changing our political structure—and for the worse, by turning a system of parties into a contest of personalities, shifting a concern with ideas and policies to a preoccupation with images and styles. Further, critics argue that the erosion of congressional government and the growth of the imperial presidency are due in part to television's obsession with the image of a single hero astride the globe. But television has not changed our conception of politics; rather, it crystallizes and expresses a transformation of political narrative that was well established in the print media decades before television appeared.

. . .

The evidence I will present in this essay cannot resolve the debate surrounding the influence of television—the debate between those awed by its power and those inclined to discount it. Instead, it changes the question at issue. While it is true that a new technology can condition politics and society, a new technology appears and comes into use only in certain political and social circumstances. The way the technology is used has a relation to, but is not fully determined by, the technology itself. In light of this, it is somewhat off the mark to ask about the impact of television on the presidency, since there is no way that question can conceivably be answered. We must ask, rather, What is the impact of *this* television, *our* television? To answer that requires more than understanding the new hardware, more even than understanding the social role of the TV set in America's living rooms, dens, and bedrooms. It requires an examination of the national networks as business enterprises; the uneasy relationship of a visible, regulated industry to government agencies; the traditions of American journalism that have shaped the preconceptions and intentions of network news departments; and the decades-long traditions of relations between the president and the press. Our television has a life of its own that plays a role in presidential politics; it is part of the environment that any new development in American politics will be related to. But the form television takes in covering the presidency has been foreshadowed, if not foreordained, by earlier changes in the relationship between print journalism and the presidency.

From Michael Schudson, "The Politics of Narrative Form: The Emergence of News Conventions in Print and Television," *Daedalus*, 111: 4 (1982), 97–112. Reprinted by permission of *Dedalus*, Journal of the American Academy of Arts and Sciences.

In this paper, I will show the changes that have taken place in the way print journalism has treated the presidency since the early days of the Republic, changes that reflect new developments in both politics and journalism. I will suggest that the power of the media lies not only (and not even primarily) in its power to declare things to be true, but in its power to provide the forms in which the declarations appear. News in a newspaper or on television has a relationship to the "real world," not only in content but in form; that is, in the way the world is incorporated into unquestioned and unnoticed conventions of narration, and then transfigured, no longer a subject for discussion but a premise of any conversation at all.

. . .

News is not fictional, but it is conventional. Conventions help make messages readable. They do so in ways that "fit" the social world of readers and writers, for the conventions of one society or time are not those of another. Some of the most familiar news conventions of our day, so obvious they seem timeless, are recent innovations. Like others, these conventions help make culturally consonant messages readable and culturally dissonant messages unsayable. Their function is less to increase or decrease the truth value of the messages they convey than to shape and narrow the range of what kinds of truths can be told. They reinforce certain assumptions about the political world.

I want to examine in detail the emergence of a few of these conventions:

1. That a summary lead and inverted pyramid structure are superior to a chronological account of an event

2. That a president is the most important actor in any event in which he takes part

3. That a news story should focus on a single event rather than a continuous or repeated happening, or that if the action is repeated, attention should center on novelty, not on pattern

4. That a news story covering an important speech or document should quote or state its highlights

5. That a news story covering a political event should convey the meaning of the political acts in a time frame larger than that of the acts themselves

All are unquestioned and generally unstated conventions of twentieth century American journalism; none were elements in journalism of the mid-nineteenth century, nor would any have been familiar to Horace Greeley, James Gordon Bennett, or Henry Raymond. Unlike reporters today, the nineteenth century reporter was not obliged to summarize highlights in a lead, to recognize the president as chief actor on the American political stage, to seek novelty, to quote speeches he reported, or to identify the political significance of events he covered. How, then, did the conventions emerge, and why?

A study of reports of the State of the Union message[1] demonstrates that these conventions, among others, incorporate into the structure of the news story vital assumptions about the nature of politics and the role of the press. They make it plain that American journalists regard themselves, not as partisans of political causes, but as expert analysts of the political world. They make it equally clear that, although as journalists they hold to principles of objective reporting, they nevertheless view their role as involving some fundamental translation and interpretation of political acts to a public ill-equipped to sort out for itself the meaning of events. Further, these conventions institutionalize the journalists' view that meaning is to be found, not in the character of established political institutions, but in the political aims of actors within them. The journalist's responsibility, as they see it, is to discover in the conscious plans of political actors the intentions that create political meaning.

The Constitution of the United States provides that the president shall report to Congress "from time to time" regarding the "state of the Union" and every American president, following the custom inaugurated by Washington, has delivered a message on this subject at the beginning of each winter's congressional session. While the event itself—the way in which the annual message is presented—has changed in some significant respects in the past two centuries, it still provides a reasonably good basis for a comparison of news reporting, having remained more or less constant over the years. Changes in the way the message is reported, therefore, cannot be attributed simply to changes in the event itself, but must be linked to changing precepts in journalism about the nature of politics and what a news story should be.

I

Reports of the State of the Union message have taken three basic forms: the stenographic record of congressional business, from 1790 to about 1850; a chronology and commentary on congressional ritual, from 1850 to 1900; and the report of the message, with an increasing emphasis on its content and its long-range political implications, from 1900 on. Despite journalism's vaunted objectivity, the reporting of the presidential message in each successive period became more interpretative, more divorced from what an ordinary observer could safely assert the message said or that Congress itself heard. This has not made reporting less truthful, but has widened the scope for the journalist's discretion—indicating that, over time, the journalistic function has served rather different intentions.

Early newspaper reports of the message printed it in its entirety, framed as part of congressional proceedings.

. . .

The most significant change in the message as an actual event was initiated by Thomas Jefferson, who felt that for the president to address Congress in person was too imperial a gesture, and so chose to give his State of the Union message in written form. It remained so until Woodrow Wilson reverted to the Federalist precedent of a personal appearance. Despite Jefferson's change, the message continued to be printed in full, either without any reported context or as part of a briefly sketched list of the day's proceedings in Congress. Any commentary on the message was confined entirely to the editorial column, where from the early 1800s on, the message was discussed at length, and the president's statements praised or castigated from an engaged and partisan stance.

By midcentury, and especially after the Civil War, the news report of the president's message was set in a much fuller discussion of Congress. The frame for the message continued to be provided by the congressional ritual of appointing a committee to wait on the president, announcing its readiness to hear a written communication from him read by a clerk. But two additional elements became standard. The first was the coverage devoted to the "spectacle" of the opening of Congress, which typically provided the beginning of the news story. As early as 1852 we read in the *New York Times*: "It is a bright and beautiful day, and the galleries of the House are crowded with ladies and gentlemen; all is gaiety."

. . .

The second change, which became standard from 1870 on, and which was more notable in the long run, was the attention given to congressional reaction to the president's message—several decades before reporters took it upon themselves actually to *report* what the message said.

. . .

In the late 1870s and the 1880s, journalists interviewed individual Congressmen. Reporters on the *Chicago Tribune* and *Washington Post*, for example, did interviews at the reading of the message in 1878, as these papers and others began to publish separate news stories on congressional responses to the message.

. . .

Stories of congressional response to the message grew more elaborate in the 1880s and 1890s. Occasionally there were stories of the response of other bodies, particularly editorial comments in foreign newspapers. But by the end of the century, the attention given to the splendor of the opening of Congress, so prominent in the 1860s and 1870s, seemed to wear on the press. The *Washington Post* drily observed in its December 3, 1878, report that the public showed curiosity at the opening of Congress, "as if it were a new thing." The *Chicago Tribune* teased in its headline of December 4, 1894, "Toil of the Solons/Makers of Laws Resume Business at Washington." Evidently bored, the Washington *Evening Star* announced in its 1890 story, "Here We Go Again."

Thus, at the same time that the press took Congress as its beat, and regarded the opinions of individual Congressman more and more seriously, its respect for the ritual and spectacle of office declined, and it began to delight in the lampooning of congressional affairs. The change taking place in the relation of journalists to officials was part of the new view that journalists took of their own purpose. They began to strain at the tradition of reporting normal occurrences and everyday proceedings. No longer the uncritical reporters of congressional ritual surrounding the reading of the message, they became increasingly uneasy about writing of something that happens again and again, year after year. The uneasiness came out in humor or in self-conscious commentary about how everything is the same as ever but people get involved nonetheless. The notion that the journalist should report original events and not record ongoing institutions grew stronger as the journalists of the 1880s and 1890s found themselves torn between two modes of activity, one might even say two forms of consciousness.

By 1900 the news story had been partially transformed, as the strictly chronological account of the reopening of congressional proceedings gave way to a descriptive account of the reopening of Congress, with a summary lead focusing on the spectacle of

Congress, and some affectionate, jocular remarks about the reassembly of the group. The president's message remained buried within the story on Congress, though always printed in full on another page. The account, beyond the descriptive overview in the lead, tended to be chronological, but it was not as dry and formal as it had been in the early part of the century.

With the establishment of the summary lead as newspaper convention, it becomes clear that journalists began to move from being stenographers, or recorders, to interpreters. Still, in 1900 there was no mention of the content of the president's message in the news story, nor was the president mentioned by name, but referred to simply as "the president." Although he was the author of the message, attention in newspaper reports continued to focus on Congress. Journalists stayed in the here-and-now, reporting on congressional reactions on the floor, and turning to interviews only to supplement the central work of observing the event itself.

After 1900 all of this changed: the president's message, not congressional response to it, became the subject of the lead paragraph, and the president became the chief actor. The highlights of the address were summarized before noting congressional response to the address, as reporters increasingly took it as their prerogative to assert something about the larger political meaning of the message. Although these changes did not happen in all papers simultaneously, or with utter consistency, the trend is unmistakable.

Take, for example, the 1910 account of William Howard Taft's message. The main *New York Times* news story begins: "In the longest message that has been sent to Congress in many a day President Taft today announced the practical abandonment of the unenacted portion of the great legislative programme with which he began his administration." The message, not Congress, is the subject. The content of the message is cited, and the content, not congressional response to it, emphasized. Indeed, rather than taking the message as a litmus test of congressional opinion, congressional response now becomes a way to further characterize the content. The *Times* reporter includes his own observation that the message was "obviously aimed at giving reassurance to business," and supports this comment by reporting that Congressmen regarded the message as "eminently conservative." Further, the president is treated as a person, and is mentioned by name in both the lead paragraph and in the headline, something that happened rarely in the body of the story before 1900, and never in the lead.

This form of the news story is still familiar to us: it incorporates what have become the givens of modern politics into the very form of the story. First, it emphasizes the preeminence of the president; he and his views, not Congress and its reactions or its rituals, are the main theme of the news story. Second, it incorporates the assumption that the president is in some sense a representative of the nation, a national trustee, more than merely the leader of a political party. He speaks for himself to the Congress and the nation, not as the leader of a party to that party in the Congress. After 1910 stories about congressional response to the message continued to emphasize partisan differences, yet the message itself was read, not as a party program, but as an indicator of the president's personal program and political career.

If this form of the news story incorporates, in its very structure, assumptions about our political system, it incorporates as well assumptions about the role and intention of our news media. It takes for granted the journalist's right and obligation to mediate and simplify, to crystallize and identify the key political elements in the news event. It takes for granted that the journalist should place the event in a time frame broader than that immediately apparent to the uninitiated. And it is here that the simplest notion of objectivity—that one should write only what another naive observer on the scene would also have been able to write—is abandoned.

· · ·

The journalist, no longer merely the relayer of documents and messages, has become the interpreter of the news. This new role allows the reporter to write about what he hears and sees, and what is unheard, unseen, or intentionally omitted as well.

· · ·

II

Why have these dramatic changes in reporting presidential addresses occurred, and what might they signify? The changes I have found may not, of course, be representative of news reporting as a whole. Yet, despite the narrow empirical focus of this paper, I believe that similar kinds of transformations have occurred in other types of news stories, and I offer this account as both hypothesis and model against which other researchers might compare changing conventions in other types of news reporting.

The simplest explanation is that news reflects reality, and the political reality itself therefore must have changed. The new conventions of journalism can be viewed as predictable responses to the growing power of the presidency. The form, not just the content, of the news story mirrors the fact that the president and his addresses had, by about 1910, become more important than the Congress and its reactions to presidential policy.

Without question, the power of the presidency grew, and as it did, a shift from a "congressional" to a "presidential" system of government evolved. Theodore Roosevelt, especially, forged a symbolically more central presidency by the force of his personality and by his assiduous efforts at cultivating journalists. Yet, as important as Roosevelt was in bringing new authority to the White House, his actions do not sufficiently explain the changing conventions of journalism. First, some of the most significant changes in the presidency, changes that could be assumed to be causes of new modes of reporting, *followed* the change in news conventions. Woodrow Wilson, for example, revived the precedent, abandoned by Jefferson, of appearing before Congress to deliver the State of the Union address and other messages. In his first such message, he said, "I am very glad indeed to have this opportunity to address the two Houses directly and to verify for myself the impression that the President of the United States is a person, not a mere department of the Government, . . . a human being trying to co-operate with other human beings in a common service." Wilson's action reinforced the centrality of the president and the habit of seeing the president as "a person," but the habit was already being encouraged by journalistic practice.[2]

Another significant change was the establishment of the Bureau of the Budget in 1921 and the beginning of a presidential role in budgetary policy and government-wide policy-making. Until then, governmental agencies submitted budget requests to the secretary of the treasury, who passed them on, with little change, to Congress. The president played, at best, "only a limited role."[3] Despite Teddy Roosevelt's importance, then, in enlarging the prestige of the presidency, his real contribution lay, not in establishing a powerful presidency, but in paving the way for its institutionalization. In this context, the changing conventions of news reporting may have been less a simple result of a change in the political world than a constituent of that process itself.

There is another way to look at the situation. Remember that the press *always* treated the State of the Union address with great seriousness. The full address was always printed and, as in the early 1800s, was sometimes the entire editorial material for a given issue. Later on, though the news story focused on congressional proceedings, the full text continued to be printed, and the editorial—much more the heart of the newspaper in the nineteenth century than it is today—focused on the substance of the president's message itself.

The change in conventions of news reporting, then, while giving greater emphasis to the presidency in describing an altered political reality, more importantly provided a *different form* for describing any political reality at all. It is a very different matter to say the news reflects the social world by describing it, and to say that it reflects the social world by incorporating it into unquestioned and unnoticed conventions of narration. When a changed political reality becomes part of the very structure of news writing, then the story does not "reflect" the new politics but becomes part of the new politics itself. There is not only a narration of politics in the news; the news is part of the politics of narrative form.

In the nineteenth century, reporters had little or no political presence as individuals or as a group. Editors, not Washington correspondents, set the political tone of a paper, and their views were political acts to be reckoned with. In the twentieth century, reporters have taken on a more pronounced political role and acquired political self-consciousness. Although critics bemoan the sensationalism and commercialism of the press and its failure to treat politics with appropriate solemnity, it is still true, as David Riesman observed years ago in *The Lonely Crowd*, that journalists accord politics a prestige that it does not have in the public mind. "They pay more attention to politics than their audience seems to demand. . . . Many of the agencies of mass communications give political news a larger play than might be dictated by strict consideration of market research."[4] In a sense, journalists are the patrons of political life.

To the degree that this is so, the journalism of the national newsweeklies, most large metropolitan newspapers, and the network television news does not mirror the world, but constructs one in which the political realm is preeminent. But what is politics, and how are we to understand it? The changing conventions of reporting State of the Union messages suggest and support a major shift in the public understanding of politics. The changes in story form do not indicate that journalism was once stenographic and is now interpretive, but rather that political commentary, once a partisan activity of the newspaper editor, has become increasingly a professional activity of the journalist. This change, far from being a product of the sixties or of the growing affluence and autonomy of national political reporters in the 1970s, began around the turn of the century.

The transformation of the news story is clearly related to the idea of politics promoted by the Progressive movement. Briefly, progressivism emphasized a "good government" view of the polity; it distrusted political parties and their machinery, and sought more direct public participation in government. The secret ballot; initiative, referendum, and recall; primary elections; direct election of Senators; and other reforms—all were products of the Progressive movement. If there was an effort to remove power from parties, it was not all to be returned to the public. The movement supported "expert" management of the political system, ranging from city-manager municipal government to the establishment of federal administrative agencies for the conservation of natural resources. In the Progressive vision, faction could be avoided, conflict overcome, and politics transformed into technique. Politics itself was to be professionalized. Although the Progressive idea of politics did not cause the changes in conventions of news reporting, it was consonant with them and can be seen as part of the same climate of opinion. As Progressives sought to have politics viewed as technique, so journalists strove to have reporting viewed as political commentary by skilled analysts.

Within journalism itself, three factors may have made this an especially likely ambition. First—and I think most important—reporters as a group were becoming more self-conscious and autonomous. At the end of the nineteenth century, as historian Robert Wiebe has observed, the identification of the middle class with political parties weakened, while their identification with, and allegiance to, occupations and occupational associations grew.[5] In journalism, press clubs began to form in the late nineteenth century, the prestige and the pay of reporters began to rise, professional journals appeared in New York, and at least an elite of reporters like Richard Harding Davis or Sylvester Scovel became quite famous and thereby relatively independent in their work. At the same time, as newspapers became successful big businesses, and publishers increasingly took more interest in making money than in making policy, journalists, freed from the necessity of adhering to their publishers' party lines, came to regard themselves as "professionals." But they did not gain complete autonomy, nor did they achieve all at once the relative independence they now have. What is clear is that editors were losing power relative to reporters as early as the 1890s, when newspapers shifted from reprinting documents to relying on reporters' contacts for news. As Anthony Smith puts it, "The power of brokerage . . . thus passed from news editor to correspondent and specialist reporter, and as a result the editor . . . [could not] wield the same kind of authority he did in previous generations."[6]

Second, newspaper readership grew enormously from the 1880s on, especially among the working class. If this had influenced the conventions of news reporting directly, the expectation would be for the more popular, mass-oriented papers to be the first to adopt the modern interpretive conventions; papers catering to a smaller and better-educated middle-class audience would lag behind. Yet very different papers adopted the new conventions, all at about the same time. Nevertheless, it is plausible to hold that, at some level of consciousness, journalists changed their practice to accommodate the real or presumed demands of a different kind of audience.

Third, the telegraphic transmission of news may have provided a model of how news reporting might be more brief and interpretive. The earliest news reports focusing on the substance of the president's message were stories telegraphed to Midwestern newspapers, as in the *Chicago Tribune*, as early as 1858. These reports did *not* substitute for a full transcript and a largely chronological account of congressional proceedings. These were printed a day later and were clearly regarded as superior. The telegraphed summary of the address was, in fact, offered apologetically, and readers were urged to wait for the full account. So the new format that the telegraph helped to invent did not become the working norm for half a century. When the new conventions finally emerged, there was apparently no overt connection between them and early telegraphic communication. Still, the terse form of news by wire may have lodged somewhere in the literary unconscious of journalists and their readers.

The vital point remains that the modern conventions of news reporting emerged at a time when politics was coming to be thought of as administration. Politicians, then, could be legitimately evaluated according to their efficiency as political leaders rather than on the basis of their political positions. The new conventions of reporting helped take partisanship out of politics. This does not "reflect" a politics grown more independent of party; it incorporates and so helps construct a nearly preconscious set of assumptions about what politics is. The news story today, as in the past, not only describes a world "out there," but translates a political culture into assumptions of representation built into the structure of the story itself.

By the 1920s, a more self-conscious, autonomous journalistic corps covered the president. Reporters felt free to analyze the significance of presidential messages, even if they did not believe it appropriate to comment on the rightness or wrongness of presidential views. They took responsibility for highlighting salient points of the message and for stating how the message related not only to congressional business at hand, but to the president's career and his place in history as well.

It should not be surprising, then, that when television came along, network news departments devoted disproportionate time to covering the presidency. The technology and economics of television make this a likely choice, of course. Since television equipment is expensive and awkward, and can be moved around less easily than the lone reporter with pencil and notepad, film crews tend to be centered in just a few locations, with the result that those locations—especially Washington—gain great emphasis in the TV news. And with the still-current understandings of politics that began decades ago to shift attention from Capitol Hill to the White House, the TV watch on the president was an obvious choice.

. . .

It is not unusual that a new medium comes to serve purposes that older forms are already trying to address. In *On Photography*, Susan Sontag observes that photography enlarges our view of what is worth looking at, until we have come to believe that *anything* may be worth photographing or looking at.[7] This is a far cry from conventional Western image-making. For centuries, only religious subjects were thought worthy of painting; even in the seventeenth and eighteenth centuries, the repertoire of subjects was quite restricted. But in the eighteenth and early nineteenth centuries, the subject matter for painting expanded. In this more democratic era, artists began to paint common people, street life, and a variety of landscapes. For a time, in fact, in the middle of the last century, the range of subject matter for painting was far wider than that of the budding art of photography, which was restricted primarily to portraiture. Within a few decades, however, photography became the more democratic art, as all aspects of life became its subjects. But this could not have been imagined if a profound cultural change was not already underway.

Photography, of course, is not mechanized painting, nor is the news on television only newspaper news with pictures. Television news has its own possibilities. In covering the State of the Union address, TV ironically brings back an abandoned print form: a chronological account of the day's event, the full text of the speech, and the pomp and circumstance, the spectacle and ritual, surrounding the event. Guided by the camera's eye, we see a revival of attention to on-the-scene congressional response to the address, much as the reporters of the late nineteenth century provided. Still, too much has changed in both journalism and politics for this to satisfy the journalists, and presumably the public. The broadcasters provide a "follow-up" that summarizes the high points of the address and suggests the political significance of the message. When the story is retold on the late evening news, the president speaks for himself, *and* the broadcast journalist points out the highlights of the address and uses film of the speech to illustrate them. Television thus inherits the trend toward analytical reporting and nonpartisan political commentary that the print media had already established by the 1920s.

. . .

Notes

1. The data for this study come from examining reports of State of the Union messages in the following newspapers: *New York Times*, every fourth year from 1854 to 1978, and every year from 1900 to 1910; *Chicago Tribune*, every fourth year from 1854 to 1954, and every other year from 1900 to 1910; *Washington Post*, every fourth year from 1878 to 1954, and every other year from 1900 to 1910; Washington *Evening Star*, every fourth year from 1854 to 1954, and every other year from 1900 to 1910. Also, *Boston Gazette*, 1791–1797; *Connecticut Courant*, 1799, 1801, 1802, 1816, 1818; *New-York Evening Post*, 1801, 1802, 1810, 1822, 1826, 1850; *Albany Argus*, 1826; *True Sun* (New York), 1845; *Morning Herald* (New York), 1838; *Philadelphia Daily News*, 1866; *Omaha Daily Republican*, 1886; *San Diego Union*, 1886, 1900, 1908; *Iowa Citizen* (Iowa City), 1894, 1900, 1910.

2. Wilson is quoted in Wilfred E. Binkley, *President and Congress*, 3rd edn. (New York: Vintage Books, 1962), p. 258.

3. Larry Berman, *The Office of Management and Budget and the Presidency, 1921–1979* (Princeton: Princeton University Press, 1979), p. 3. Rexford G. Tugwell cites the establishment of the Budget Bureau as a major event in the growth of a presidential authority in *The Enlargement of the Presidency* (New York: Doubleday, 1960), pp. 396–97.

4. David Riesman, Nathan Glazer, and Reuel Denney, *The Lonely Crowd* (New Haven: Yale University Press, 1950), pp. 197–98.

5. Robert H. Wiebe, *The Search for Order* (New York: Hill and Wang, 1967), p. 129.

6. Anthony Smith, *Goodbye Gutenberg* (New York: Oxford University Press, 1980), p. 186. For more about the rise of the reporter after 1880, see my book, *Discovering the News*, pp. 61–87.

7. (New York: Dell Publishing, 1977), p. 3.

16 Television as a Cultural Forum

Horace Newcomb and Paul M. Hirsch

A CULTURAL basis for the analysis and criticism of television is, for us, the bridge between a concern for television as a communications medium, central to contemporary society, and television as aesthetic object, the expressive medium that, through its storytelling functions, unites and examines a culture. The shortcomings of each of these approaches taken alone are manifold.

The first is based primarily in a concern for understanding specific messages that may have specific effects, and grounds its analysis in "communication" narrowly defined. Complexities of image, style, resonance, narrativity, history, metaphor, and so on are reduced in favor of that content that can be more precisely, some say more objectively, described. The content categories are not allowed to emerge from the text, as is the case in naturalistic observation and in textual analysis. Rather they are predefined in order to be measured more easily. The incidence of certain content categories may be cited as significant, or their "effects" more clearly correlated with some behavior. This concern for measuring is, of course, the result of conceiving television in one way rather than another, as "communication" rather than as "art."

The narrowest versions of this form of analysis need not concern us here. It is to the best versions that we must look, to those that do admit to a range of aesthetic expression and something of a variety of reception. Even when we examine these closely, however, we see that they often assume a monolithic "meaning" in television content. The concern is for "dominant" messages embedded in the pleasant disguise of fictional entertainment, and the concern of the researcher is often that the control of these messages is, more than anything else, a complex sort of political control. The critique that emerges, then, is consciously or unconsciously a critique of the society that is transmitting and maintaining the dominant ideology with the assistance, again conscious or unconscious, of those who control communications technologies and businesses. (Ironically, this perspective does not depend on political perspective or persuasion. It is held by groups on the "right" who see American values being subverted, as well as by those on the "left" who see American values being imposed.)

Such a position assumes that the audience shares or "gets" the same messages and their meanings as the researcher finds. At times, like the literary critic, the researcher assumes this on the basis of superior insight, technique, or sensibility. In a more "scientific" manner the researcher may seek to establish a correlation between the discovered messages and the understanding of the audience. Rarely, however, does the message

From Horace Newcomb and Paul M. Hirsch, "Television as a Cultural Forum," *Quarterly Review of Film Studies*, 8: 3 (1983), 45–55.

analyst allow for the possibility that the audience, while sharing this one meaning, may create many others that have not been examined, asked about, or controlled for.

The television "critic" on the other hand, often basing his work on the analysis of literature or film, succeeds in calling attention to the distinctive qualities of the medium, to the special nature of television fiction. But this approach all too often ignores important questions of production and reception. Intent on correcting what it takes to be a skewed interest in such matters, it often avoids the "business" of television and its "technology." These critics, much like their counterparts in the social sciences, usually assume that viewers should understand programs in the way the critic does, or that the audience is incapable of properly evaluating the entertaining work and should accept the critic's superior judgment.

The differences between the two views of what television is and does rest, in part, on the now familiar distinction between transportation and ritual views of communication processes. The social scientific, or communication theory model outlined above (and we do not claim that it is an exhaustive description) rests most thoroughly on the transportation view. As articulated by James Carey, this model holds that communication is a "process of transmitting messages at a distance for the purpose of control. The archetypal case of communication then is persuasion, attitude change, behavior modification, socialization through the transmission of information, influence, or conditioning."[1]

The more "literary" or "aesthetically based" approach leans toward, but hardly comes to terms with, ritual models of communication. As put by Carey, the ritual view sees communication "not directed toward the extension of messages in space but the maintenance of society in time; not the act of imparting information but the representation of shared beliefs."[2]

Carey also cuts through the middle of these definitions with a more succinct one of his own: "Communication is a symbolic process whereby reality is produced, maintained, repaired, and transformed."[3] It is in the attempt to amplify this basic observation that we present a cultural basis for the analysis of television. We hardly suggest that such an approach is entirely new, or that others are unaware of or do not share many of our assumptions. On the contrary, we find a growing awareness in many disciplines of the nature of symbolic thought, communication, and action, and we see attempts to understand television emerging rapidly from this body of shared concerns.[4]

Our own model for television is grounded in an examination of the cultural role of entertainment and parallels this with a close analysis of television program content in all its various textual levels and forms. We focus on the collective, cultural view of the social construction and negotiation of reality, on the creation of what Carey refers to as "public thought."[5] It is not difficult to see television as central to this process of public thinking. As Hirsch has pointed out,[6] it is now our national medium, replacing those media—film, radio, picture magazines, newspapers—that once served a similar function. Those who create for such media are, in the words of anthropologist Marshall Sahlins, "hucksters of the symbol."[7] They are cultural bricoleurs, seeking and creating new meaning in the combination of cultural elements with embedded significance. They respond to real events, changes in social structure and organization, and to shifts in attitude and value. They also respond to technological shift, the coming of cable or the use of videotape recorders. We think it is clear that the television producer should be added to Sahlins's list of "hucksters." They work in precisely the manner he describes, as do television writers and, to a lesser extent, directors and actors. So too do programmers and network executives who must make decisions about the programs they purchase, develop, and air. At each step of this complicated process they function as cultural interpreters.

Similar notions have often been outlined by scholars of popular culture focusing on the formal characteristics of popular entertainment.[8] To those insights cultural theory adds the possibility of matching formal analysis with cultural and social practice. The best theoretical explanation for this link is suggested to us in the continuing work of anthropologist Victor Turner. This work focuses on cultural ritual and reminds us that ritual must be seen as process rather than as product, a notion not often applied to the study of television, yet crucial to an adequate understanding of the medium.

Specifically we make use of one aspect of Turner's analysis, his view of the *liminal* stage of the ritual process. This is the "in-between" stage, when one is neither totally in nor out of society. It is a stage of license, when rules may be broken or bent, when roles may be reversed, when categories may be overturned. Its essence, suggests Turner,

is to be found in its release from normal constraints, making possible the deconstruction of the "uninteresting" constructions of common sense, the "meaningfulness of ordinary life," . . . into cultural units which may then be reconstructed in novel ways, some of them bizarre to the point of monstrosity. . . . Liminality is the domain of the "interesting" or of "uncommon sense."[9]

Turner does not limit this observation to traditional societies engaged in the *practice* of ritual. He also applies his views to postindustrial, complex societies. In doing so he finds the liminal domain in the arts—all of them.[10] "The dismemberment of ritual has . . . provided the opportunity of theatre in the high culture and carnival at the folk level. A multiplicity of desacralized performative genres have assumed, prismatically, the task of plural cultural reflexivity."[11] In short, contemporary cultures examine themselves through their arts, much as traditional societies do via the experience of ritual. Ritual and the arts offer a metalanguage, a way of understanding who and what we are, how values and attitudes are adjusted, how meaning shifts.

In contributing to this process, particularly in American society, where its role is central, television fulfills what Fiske and Hartley refer to as the "bardic function" of contemporary societies.[12] In its role as central cultural medium it presents a multiplicity of meanings rather than a monolithic dominant point of view. It often focuses on our most prevalent concerns, our deepest dilemmas. Our most traditional views, those that are repressive and reactionary, as well as those that are subversive and emancipatory, are upheld, examined, maintained, and transformed. The emphasis is on process rather than product, on discussion rather than indoctrination, on contradiction and confusion rather than coherence. It is with this view that we turn to an analysis of the texts of television that demonstrates and supports the conception of television as a cultural forum.

This new perspective requires that we revise some of our notions regarding television analysis, criticism, and research. The function of the creator as bricoleur, taken from

Sahlins, is again indicated and clarified. The focus on "uncommon sense," on the freedom afforded by the idea of television as a liminal realm helps us to understand the reliance on and interest in forms, plots, and character types that are not at all familiar in our lived experience. The skewed demography of the world of television is not quite so bizarre and repressive once we admit that it is the realm in which we allow our monsters to come out and play, our dreams to be wrought into pictures, our fantasies transformed into plot structures. Cowboys, detectives, bionic men and great green hulks; fatherly physicians, glamorous female detectives, and tightly knit families living out the pain of the Great Depression; all these become part of the dramatic logic of public thought.

Shows such as *Fantasy Island* and *Love Boat*, difficult to account for within traditional critical systems except as examples of trivia and romance, are easily understood. Islands and boats are among the most fitting liminal metaphors, as Homer, Bacon, Shakespeare, and Melville, among others, have recognized. So, too, are the worlds of the Western and the detective story. With this view we can see the "bizarre" world of situation comedy as a means of deconstructing the world of "common sense" in which all, or most, of us live and work. It also enables us to explain such strange phenomena as game shows and late night talk fests. In short, almost any version of the television text functions as a forum in which important cultural topics may be considered. We illustrate this not with a contemporary program where problems almost always appear on the surface of the show, but with an episode of *Father Knows Best* from the early 1960s. We begin by noting that *FKB* is often cited as an innocuous series, constructed around unstinting paeans to American middle-class virtues and blissfully ignorant of social conflict. In short, it is precisely the sort of television program that reproduces dominant ideology by lulling its audience into a dream world where the status quo is the only status.

In the episode in question Betty Anderson, the older daughter in the family, breaks a great many rules by deciding that she will become an engineer. Over great protest, she is given an internship with a surveying crew as part of a high school "career education" program. But the head of the surveying crew, a young college student, drives her away with taunts and insensitivity. She walks off the job on the first day. Later in the week the young man comes to the Anderson home where Jim Anderson chides him with fatherly anger. The young man apologizes and Betty, overhearing him from the other room, runs upstairs, changes clothes, and comes down. The show ends with their flirtation underway.

Traditional ideological criticism, conducted from the communications or the textual analysis perspective, would remark on the way in which social conflict is ultimately subordinated in this dramatic structure to the personal, the emotional. Commentary would focus on the way in which the questioning of the role structure is shifted away from the world of work to the domestic arena. The emphasis would be on the conclusion of the episode in which Betty's real problem of identity and sex-role, and society's problem of sex-role discrimination, is bound by a more traditional conflict and thereby defused, contained, and redirected. Such a reading is possible, indeed accurate.

We would point out, however, that our emotional sympathy is with Betty throughout this episode. Nowhere does the text instruct the viewer that her concerns are unnatural, no matter how unnaturally they may be framed by other members of the cast. Every argument that can be made for a strong feminist perspective is condensed into the brief, half-hour presentation. The concept of the cultural forum, then, offers a different interpretation. We suggest that in popular culture generally, in television specifically, the raising of questions is as important as the answering of them. That is, it is equally important that an audience be introduced to the problems surrounding sex-role discrimination as it is to conclude the episode in a traditional manner. Indeed, it would be startling to think that mainstream texts in mass society would overtly challenge dominant ideas. But this hardly prevents the oppositional ideas from appearing. Put another way, we argue that television does not present firm ideological conclusions—despite its *formal* conclusions—so much as it *comments on* ideological problems. The conflicts we see in television drama, embedded in familiar and nonthreatening frames, are conflicts ongoing in American social experience and cultural history. In a few cases we might see strong perspectives that argue for the absolute correctness of one point of view or another. But for the most part the rhetoric of television drama is a rhetoric of discussion. Shows such as *All in the Family*, or *The Defenders*, or *Gunsmoke*, which raise the forum/discussion to an intense and obvious level, often make best use of the medium and become highly successful. We see statements *about* the issues and it should be clear that ideological positions can be balanced within the forum by others from a different perspective.

We recognize, of course, that this variety works for the most part within the limits of American monopoly-capitalism and within the range of American pluralism. It is an effective pluralistic forum only insofar as American political pluralism is or can be.[13] We also note, however, that one of the primary functions of the popular culture forum, the television forum, is to monitor the limits and the effectiveness of this pluralism, perhaps the only "public" forum in which this role is performed. As content shifts and attracts the attention of groups and individuals, criticism and reform can be initiated. We will have more to say on this topic shortly.

Our intention here is hardly to argue for the richness of *Father Knows Best* as a television text or as social commentary. Indeed, in our view, any emphasis on individual episodes, series, or even genres, misses the central point of the forum concept. While each of these units can and does present its audiences with incredibly mixed ideas, it is television as a whole system that presents a mass audience with the range and variety of ideas and ideologies inherent in American culture. In order to fully understand the role of television in that culture, we must examine a variety of analytical foci and, finally, see them as parts of a greater whole.

We can, for instance, concentrate on a single episode of television content, as we have done in our example. In our view most television shows offer something of this range of complexity. Not every one of them treats social problems of such immediacy, but submerged in any episode are assumptions about who and what we are. Conflicting viewpoints of social issues are, in fact, the elements that structure most television programs.

At the series level this complexity is heightened. In spite of notions to the contrary, most television shows do change over time. Stanley Cavell has recently suggested that this serial nature of television is perhaps its defining characteristic.[14] By contrast we see that feature only as a primary aspect of the rhetoric of television, one that shifts meaning and shades ideology as series develop. Even a series such as *The Brady Bunch* dealt with ever more complex issues merely because the children, on whom the show focused, grew older. In other cases, shows such as *The Waltons* shifted in content and meaning because they represented shifts in historical time. As the series moved out of the period of the Great Depression, through World War II, and into the postwar period, its tone and emphasis shifted too. In some cases, of course, this sort of change is structured into the show from the beginning, even when the appearance is that of static, undeveloping nature. In *All in the Family* the possibility of change and Archie's resistance to it form the central dramatic problem and offer the central opportunity for dramatic richness, a richness that has developed over many years until the character we now see bears little resemblance to the one we met in the beginning. This is also true of *M*A*S*H*, although there the structured conflicts have more to do with framing than with character development. In *M*A*S*H* we are caught in an anti-war rhetoric that cannot end a war. A truly radical alternative, a desertion or an insurrection, would end the series. But it would also end the "discussion" of this issue. We remain trapped, like American culture in its historical reality, with a dream and the rhetoric of peace and with a bitter experience that denies them.

The model of the forum extends beyond the use of the series with attention to genre. One tendency of genre studies has been to focus on similarities within forms, to indicate the ways in which all Westerns, situation comedies, detective shows and so on are alike. Clearly, however, it is in the economic interests of producers to build on audience familiarity with generic patterns and instill novelty into those generically based presentations. Truly innovative forms that use the generic base as a foundation are likely to be among the more successful shows. This also means that the shows, despite generic similarity, will carry individual rhetorical slants. As a result, while shows like *M*A*S*H*, *The Mary Tyler Moore Show*, and *All in the Family* may all treat similar issues, those issues will have different meanings because of the variations in character, tone, history, style, and so on, despite a general "liberal" tone. Other shows, minus that tone, will clash in varying degrees. The notion that they are all, in some sense, "situation comedies" does not adequately explain the treatment of ideas within them.

This hardly diminishes the strength of generic variation as yet another version of differences within the forum. The rhetoric of the soap opera *pattern* is different from that of the situation comedy and that of the detective show. Thus, when similar topics are treated within different generic frames another level of "discussion" is at work.

It is for this reason that we find it important to examine strips of television programming, "flow" as Raymond Williams refers to it.[15] Within these flow strips we may find opposing ideas abutting one another. We may find opposing treatments of the same ideas. And we will certainly find a viewing behavior that is more akin to actual experience than that found when concentrating on the individual show, the series, or the genre. The forum model, then, has led us into a new exploration of the definition of the television text. We are now examining the "viewing strip" as a potential text and are discovering that in the range of options offered by any given evening's television, the forum is indeed a more accurate model of what goes on *within* television than any other that we know of. By taping entire weeks of television content, and tracing various potential strips in the body of that week, we can construct a huge range of potential "texts" that may have been seen by individual viewers.

Each level of text—the strip as text, the television week, the television day—is compounded yet again by the history of the medium. Our hypothesis is that we might track the history of America's social discussions of the past three decades by examining the multiple rhetorics of television during that period. Given the problematic state of television archiving, a careful study of that hypothesis presents an enormous difficulty. It is, nevertheless, an exciting prospect.

Clearly, our emphasis is on the treatment of issues, on rhetoric. We recognize the validity of analytical structures that emphasize television's skewed demographic patterns, its particular social aberrations, or other "unrealistic distortions" of the world of experience. But we also recognize that in order to make sense of those structures and patterns researchers return again and again to the "meaning" of that television world, to the processes and problems of interpretation. In our view this practice is hardly limited to those of us who study television. It is also open to audiences who view it each evening and to professionals who create for the medium.

The goal of every producer is to create the difference that makes a difference, to maintain an audience with sufficient reference to the known and recognized, but to move ahead into something that distinguishes his show for the program buyer, the scheduler, and most importantly, for the mass audience. As recent work by Newcomb and Alley shows,[16] the goal of many producers, the most successful and powerful ones, is also to include personal ideas in their work, to use television as all artists use their media, as means of personal expression. Given this goal it is possible to examine the work of individual producers as other units of analysis and to compare the work of different producers as expressions within the forum. We need only think of the work of Quinn Martin and Jack Webb, or to contrast their work with that of Norman Lear or Gary Marshall, to recognize the individuality at work within television making. Choices by producers to work in certain generic forms, to express certain political, moral, and ethical attitudes, to explore certain sociocultural topics, all affect the nature of the ultimate "flow text" of television seen by viewers and assure a range of variations within that text.

The existence of this variation is borne out by varying responses among those who view television. A degree of this variance occurs among professional television critics who like and dislike shows for different reasons. But because television critics, certainly in American journalistic situations, are more alike than different in many ways, a more important indicator of the range of responses is that found among "ordinary" viewers, or the disagreements implied by audience acceptance and enthusiasm for program material soundly disavowed by professional critics. Work by Himmleweit in England[17] and Neuman in America[18] indicates that individual viewers do function as "critics," do make important distinctions, and are able, under certain circumstances, to articulate the bases for their judgments. While this work is just beginning, it is still possible to suggest from anecdotal evidence that people agree and disagree with television for a variety of reasons. They find in television texts representations of and challenges to their own ideas, and must somehow come to terms with what is there.

If disagreements cut too deeply into the value structure of the individual, if television threatens the sense of cultural security, the individual may take steps to engage the medium at the level of personal action. Most often this occurs in the form of letters to the network or to local stations, and again, the pattern is not new to television. It has occurred with every other mass medium in modern industrial society.

Nor is it merely the formation of groups or the expression of personal points of view that indicates the working of a forum. It is the *range* of response, the directly contradictory readings of the medium, that cue us to its multiple meanings. Groups may object to the same programs, for example, for entirely opposing reasons. In *Charlie's Angels* feminists may find yet another example of sexist repression, while fundamentalist religious groups may find examples of moral decay expressed in the sexual freedom, the personal appearance, or the "unfeminine" behavior of the protagonists. Other viewers doubtless find the expression of meaningful liberation of women. At this level, the point is hardly that one group is "right" and another "wrong," much less that one is "right" while the other is "left." Individuals and groups are, for many reasons, involved in making their own meanings from the television text.

This variation in interpretive strategies can be related to suggestions made by Stuart Hall in his influential essay, "Encoding and Decoding in the Television Discourse."[19] There he suggests three basic modes of interpretation, corresponding to the interpreter's political stance within the social structure. The interpetation may be "dominant," accepting the prevailing ideological structure. It may be "oppositional," rejecting the basic aspects of the structure. Or it may be "negotiated," creating a sort of personal synthesis. As later work by some of Hall's colleagues suggests, however, it quickly becomes necessary to expand the range of possible interpretations.[20] Following these suggestions to a radical extreme it might be possible to argue that every individual interpretation of television content could, in some way, be "different." Clearly, however, communication is dependent on a greater degree of shared meanings, and expressions of popular entertainment are perhaps even more dependent on the shared level than many other forms of discourse. Our concern then is for the ways in which interpretation is negotiated in society. Special interest groups that focus, at times, on television provide us with readily available resources for the study of interpretive practices.

We see these groups as representative of metaphoric "fault lines" in American society. Television is the terrain in which the faults are expressed and worked out. In studying the groups, their rhetoric, the issues on which they focus, their tactics, their forms of organization, we hope to demonstrate that the idea of the "forum" is more than a metaphor in its own right. In forming special interest groups, or in using such groups to speak about television, citizens actually enter the forum. Television shoves them toward action, toward expression of ideas and values. At this level the model of "television as a cultural forum" enables us to examine "the sociology of interpretation."

Here much attention needs to be given to the historical aspects of this form of activity. How has the definition of issues changed over time? How has that change correlated with change in the television texts? These are important questions which, while difficult to study, are crucial to a full understanding of the role of television in culture. It is primarily through this sort of study that we will be able to define much more precisely the limits of the forum, for groups form monitoring devices that alert us to shortcomings not only in the world of television representation, but to the world of political experience as well. We know, for example, that because of heightened concern on the part of special interest groups, and responses from the creative and institutional communities of television industries, the "fictional" population of black citizens now roughly equals that of the actual population. Regardless of whether such a match is "good" or "necessary," regardless of the nature of the depiction of blacks on television, this indicates that the forum extends beyond the screen. The issue of violence, also deserving close study, is more mixed, varying from year to year. The influence of groups, of individuals, of studies, of the terrible consequences of murder and assassination, however, cannot be denied. Television does not exist in a realm of its own, cut off from the influence of citizens. Our aim is to discover, as precisely as possible, the ways in which the varied worlds interact.

Throughout this kind of analysis, then, it is necessary to cite a range of varied responses to the texts of television. Using the viewing "strip" as the appropriate text of television, and recognizing that it is filled with varied topics and approaches to those topics, we begin to think of the television viewer as a bricoleur who matches the creator in the making of meanings. Bringing values and attitudes, a universe of personal experiences and concerns, to the texts, the viewer selects, examines, acknowledges, and makes texts of his or her own.[21] If we conceive of special interest groups as representatives of *patterns* of cultural attitude and response, we have a potent source of study.

On the production end of this process, in addition to the work of individual producers, we must examine the role of network executives who must purchase and program television content. They, too, are cultural interpreters, intent on "reading" the culture through its relation to the "market." Executives who head and staff the internal censor agencies of each network, the offices of Broadcast Standards or Standards and Practices, are in a similar position. Perhaps as much as any individual or group they present us with a source of rich material for analysis. They are actively engaged in gauging cultural values. Their own research, the assumptions and the findings, needs to be re-analyzed for cultural implications, as does the work of the programmers. In determining who is doing what with whom, at what times, they are interpreting social behavior in America and assigning it meaning. They are using television as a cultural litmus that can be applied in defining such problematic concepts as "childhood," "family," "maturity," and "appropriate." With the Standards and Practices offices, they interpret *and* define the permissible and the "normal." But their interpretations of behavior open to us as many questions as answers, and an appropriate overview, a new model of television is necessary in order to best understand their work and ours.

This new model of "television as a cultural forum" fits the experience of television more accurately than others we have seen applied. Our assumption is that it opens a range of new questions and calls for re-analysis of older findings from both the textual–critical approach and the mass communications research perspective. Ultimately the new model is a simple one. It recognizes the range of interpretation of television content that is now admitted even by those analysts most concerned with television's presentation and maintenance of dominant ideological messages and meanings. But it differs from those perspectives because it does not see this as surprising or unusual. For the most part, that is what central storytelling systems do in all societies. We are far more concerned with the ways in which television contributes to change than with mapping the obvious ways in which it maintains dominant viewpoints. Most research on television, most textual analysis, has assumed that the medium is thin, repetitive, similar, nearly identical in textual formation, easily defined, described, and explained. The variety of response on the part of audiences has been received, as a result of this view, as extraordinary, an astonishing "discovery."

We begin with the observation, based on careful textual analysis, that television is dense, rich, and complex rather than impoverished. Any selection, any cut, any set of questions that is extracted from that text must somehow account for that density, must account for what is *not* studied or measured, for the opposing meanings, for the answering images and symbols. Audiences appear to make meaning by selecting that which touches experience and personal history. The range of responses then should be taken as commonplace rather than as unexpected. But research and critical analysis cannot afford so personal a view. Rather, they must somehow define and describe the inventory that makes possible the multiple meanings extracted by audiences, creators, and network decision makers.

Our model is based on the assumption and observation that only so rich a text could attract a mass audience in a complex culture. The forum offers a perspective that is as complex, as contradictory and confused, as much in process as American culture is in experience. Its texture matches that of our daily experiences. If we can understand it better, then perhaps we will better understand the world we live in, the actions that we must take in order to live there.

Notes

The authors would like to express their appreciation to the John and Mary R. Markle Foundation for support in the preparation of this paper and their ongoing study of the role of television as a cultural forum in American society. The ideas in this paper were first presented, in different form, at the seminar on "The Mass Production of Mythology," New York Institute for the Humanities, New York University, February, 1981. Mary Douglas, Seminar Director.

1. James Carey, "A Cultural Approach to Communications," *Communications*, 2 (December 1975).
2. Ibid.
3. James Carey, "Culture and Communications," *Communications Research* (April 1975).
4. See Roger Silverstone, *The Message of Television: Myth and Narrative in Contemporary Culture* (London: Heinemann, 1981) on structural and narrative analysis; John Fiske and John Hartley, *Reading Television* (London: Methuen, 1978) on the semiotic and cultural bases for the analysis of television; David Thorburn, *The Story Machine* (Oxford University Press: forthcoming) on the aesthetics of television; Himmleweit, Hilda, et al., "The Audience as Critic: An Approach to the Study of Entertainment," in *The Entertainment Functions of Television*, ed. Percy Tannenbaum (New York: Lawrence Erlbaum Associates, 1980) and W. Russel Neuman, "Television and American Culture: The Mass Medium and the Pluralist Audience," *Public Opinion Quarterly*, 46: 4 (Winter 1982), pp. 471–87, on the role of the audience as critic; Todd Gitlin, "Prime Time Ideology: The Hegemonic Process in Television Entertainment," *Social Problems*, 26: 3 (1979) and Douglas Kellner, "TV, Ideology, and Emancipatory Popular Culture," *Socialist Review*, 45

(May–June, 1979) on hegemony and new applications of critical theory; James T. Lull, "The Social Uses of Television," *Human Communications Research*, 7: 3 (1980) and "Family Communication Patterns and the Social Uses of Television," *Communications Research*, 7: 3 (1979), and Tim Meyer, Paul Taudt, and James Anderson, "Non-Traditional Mass Communication Research Methods: Observational Case Studies of Media Use in Natural Settings," *Communication Yearbook IV*, ed. Dan Nimmo (New Brunswick, NJ: Transaction Books) on audience ethnography and symbolic interactionism; and, most importantly, the ongoing work of The Center for Contemporary Cultural Studies at Birmingham University, England, most recently published in *Culture, Media, Language*, ed. Stuart Hall, et al. (London: Hutchinson, in association with The Centre for Contemporary Cultural Studies, 1980) on the interaction of culture and textual analysis from a thoughtful political perspective.

5. Carey 1976.
6. Paul Hirsch, "The Role of Popular Culture and Television in Contemporary Society," *Television: The Critical View*, ed. Horace Newcomb (New York: Oxford University Press, 1979, 1982).
7. Marshall Sahlins, *Culture and Practical Reason* (Chicago: University of Chicago Press, 1976), p. 217.
8. John Cawelti, *Adventure, Mystery, and Romance* (Chicago: University of Chicago Press, 1976), and David Thorburn, "Television Melodrama," *Television: The Critical View* (New York: Oxford University Press, 1979, 1982).
9. Victor Turner, "Process, System, and Symbol: A New Anthropological Synthesis," *Daedalus* (Summer 1977), p. 68.
10. In various works Turner uses both the terms "liminal" and "liminoid" to refer to works of imagination and entertainment in contemporary culture. The latter term is used to clearly mark the distinction between events that have distinct behavioral consequences and those that do not. As Turner suggests, the consequences of entertainment in contemporary culture are hardly as profound as those of the liminal stage of ritual in traditional culture. We are aware of this basic distinction but use the former term in order to avoid a fuller explanation of the neologism. See Turner, "Afterword," to *The Reversible World*, Barbara Babcock, ed. (Ithaca: Cornell University Press, 1979) and "Liminal to Liminoid, in Play, Flow, and Ritual: An Essay in Comparative Symbology," *Rice University Studies*, 60: 3 (1974).

11. Turner 1977, p. 73.
12. Fiske and Hartley 1978, p. 85.
13. We are indebted to Prof. Mary Douglas for encouraging this observation. At the presentation of these ideas at the New York Institute for the Humanities seminar on "The Mass Production of Mythology," she checked our enthusiasm for a pluralistic model of television by stating accurately and succinctly, "there are pluralisms and pluralisms." This comment led us to consider more thoroughly the means by which the forum and responses to it function as a tool with which to monitor the qualify of pluralism in American social life, including its entertainments. The observation added a much needed component to our planned historical analysis.
14. Stanley Cavell, "The Fact of Television," *Daedalus*, 3: 4 (Fall 1982).
15. Raymond Williams, *Television, Technology and Cultural Form* (New York: Schocken, 1971), p. 86 ff.
16. Horace Newcomb and Robert Alley, *The Television Producer as Artist in American Commercial Television* (New York: Oxford University Press, 1983).
17. Ibid.
18. Ibid.
19. Stuart Hall, "Encoding and Decoding in the Television Discourse," *Culture, Media, Language* (London: Hutchinson, in association with The Centre for Contemporary Cultural Studies, 1980).
20. See Dave Morley and Charlotte

Brunsdon, *Everyday Television: "Nationwide"* (London: British Film Institute, 1978) and Morley, "Subjects, Readers, Texts," in *Culture, Media, Language.*

21. We are indebted to Louis Black and Eric Michaels of the Radio–TV–Film department of the University of Texas–Austin for calling this aspect of televiewing to Newcomb's attention. It creates a much desired balance to Sahlin's view of the creator as *bricoleur* and indicates yet another matter in which the forum model enhances our ability to account for more aspects of the television experience. See, especially, Eric Michaels, "TV Tribes," Ph.D. dissertation (University of Texas–Austin, 1982).

Section IV
History and Literature and Their Legacy

Robert Mapplethorpe, "Dolphina Neil-Jones, 1987" © The Estate of Robert Mapplethorpe. Used with permission.

Section IV
History and Literature and Their Legacy

....

Authors
Ward Churchill, Houston A. Baker, Jr., Carroll Smith-Rosenberg, Rita Felski, Janice Radway

Visual Artist
Robert Mapplethorpe: "Dolphina Neil-Jones, 1987"

S CHOLARS in the fields of history and literature have had a profound impact upon the development of American cultural studies. Challenges to textual authority, to conventional models of historical interpretation, to the canon, and to the very organization of the American university have been predicated upon political commitments to multiculturalism and intellectual commitments to post-structuralism and postmodernism. In this chapter, there are very strong themes running through many of the selections to do with identity, difference, and hybridity as concepts around which both literary and historical questions need to be organized.

Ward Churchill, like Vine Deloria, Jr. a Native American scholar and activist, argues that cultural forms, in this case literature, can be every bit as deadly as bullets in conquering indigenous peoples. He analyzes an American literature that, according to him, has consistently misrepresented Native Americans in order to justify their extermination and/or assimilation. Houston Baker, Jr. fires a polemical round in the culture wars of canonicity and civilization, countering the jeremiads of conservative cultural critics who insist on the centrality of the "great books" to Western civilization and American culture, with an impassioned defense of rap. This "poetry for the next society," Baker insists, expresses the hopes and frustrations of young black Americans more fully than could any of the Western Great Books. Feminist historian Carroll Smith-Rosenberg engages with cultural studies' emphasis upon the centrality of language and representation to political struggles centered around class and gender. Her study of an early nineteenth-century women's organization that fulminated against the evils of prostitution reveals that the seizing of semiotic power is not a purely twentieth-century phenomenon.

Rita Felski continues the debate about "identity" by moving beyond that issue towards a systematic critique of "difference." The concept of "difference" gained widespread currency as a "postmodern" replacement for earlier conceptualizations of "identity," including within feminist theory and political work. Felski considers the contributions of postcolonial feminist writers in elaborating useful new possibilities for understanding difference, and analyzes some of the most important concepts resulting from that work, especially the notion of hybridity. Her special strength as a writer however, is her ability to think through the philosophical and theoretical terms of the debate, but to retain a *pragmatic* focus on the "utility of discourse rather than its ontological purity." She wants theorization to remain useful in "can-do" feminist politics.

Janice Radway is perhaps best-known for her work on the reading practices of non-canonical readerships; women readers of romance fiction in particular. She was a major influence on (and participant in) a resurgent form of "audience ethnography" in the 1990s. This approach was itself a prominent component of media and cultural studies during that period, becoming especially popular with people trained in the empirical social sciences who wished nevertheless to investigate cultural questions. In this selection, Radway wears a rather different hat, that of President of the American Studies Association. In this guise, she reflects on many of the issues raised in the Introduction to this *Reader* about the relationships between American studies and cultural studies. Her notion of "intricate interdependencies" allows for a much more open (and sometimes challenging) approach to American national identity, and a preoccupation with the politics of "difference" in culture and in academic writing alike.

Robert Mapplethorpe was one of the best-known photographic artists of his era, bringing to his avant-garde New York milieu an irresistible combination of absolute classicism of form, tone, and composition, with decidedly non-canonical images of homoerotic sexuality. His works became both celebrated and controversial, leading in one case to a very new and surprising (in)version of "Birmingham cultural studies"—the police raided the library of the University of Central England in that city and confiscated one of Mapplethorpe's books, seeking to prosecute the Vice-Chancellor for obscenity. The case reached the high court before it was finally thrown out in 1999. Here however Mapplethorpe is in different mode, and lighter mood. This engaging and optimistic portrait, taken from his study of celebrities and non-celebrities called *Some Women*, catches the light and shade of "identity" in a formal but generous spirit that is both acutely observed by the artist and artfully presented by the "subject."

17 Literature as a Weapon in the Colonization of the American Indian

Ward Churchill

. . .

The Literary Version of Manifest Destiny

Perhaps the first American work which might appropriately be termed a novel (which, along with short stories, novellas, plays and poetry constitutes true literature in the popular conception) concerning American Indians was Charles Brockden Brown's 1799 release, *Edgar Huntley*. It was followed, in reasonably short order for the time, by two chapters "Traits of the Indian Character" and "Philip of Pokanoket." These were devoted to the extermination of the Narragansets during what the colonists called "King Philip's War" in Washington Irving's *Sketch Book*, dating from 1819. The latter absorbs the "noble savage" stereotype associated with Thomas Morton's earlier work:

Even in his last refuge of desperation and dispair a sullen grandure gathers round his [Philip's] memory. We picture him to ourselves seated among his careworn followers, brooding in silence over his blasted fortunes and acquiring a savage sublimity from the wilderness of his lurking place. Defeated but not dismayed, crushed to earth but not humiliated, he seemed to grow more haughty beneath disaster and experience a fierce satisfaction in draining the last dregs of bitterness.[1]

Between 1823 and 1841, James Fenimore Cooper's novels—including *The Pioneers, The Last of the Mohicans, The Deerslayer, The Prairie* and *The Pathfinder*—had firmly established all of the stereotypes denoted above within the popular consciousness. Of course, Cooper had considerable help. During the same period, Chateaubriand's *Atala* appeared, as well as novels by William Gilmore Simms including *The Yamassee* and *Guy Rovers*. As well as novels, there were poems such as John Greenleaf Whittier's 1835 epic, *Mogg Megone* and, by 1855, Henry W. Longfellow's *The Song of Hiawatha, To the Driving Cloud* and *The Burial of Minnisink*. In a less pretentious vein, there was also during this general period the so-called "juvenile fiction" exemplified by Mayne Reid in *The Scalp Hunters* and *Desert Home*. The list is considerable.

The elements of this rapidly proliferating mass of creative output shared several

From Ward Churchill, "Literature as a Weapon in the Colonization of the American Indian," in Ward Churchill, *Fantasies of the Master Race: Literature, Cinema and the Colonization of American Indians*, ed. M. Annette Jaimes (Monroe, Me.: Common Courage Press, 1992), 17–41.

features in common. For instance, none possessed the slightest concrete relationship to the actualities of native culture(s) they portrayed. Hence, each amounted to the imaginative invention of the authors, authors who by virtue of their medium were alien to the context (oral tradition) of which they presumed to write. It can be argued, and has,[2] that such prerogatives rest squarely within the realm of the fiction writer. While this may be true in an aesthetic sense, the practical application of the principle breaks down (for each of these works) on at least two levels:

- The justifying aesthetic rationale is itself an aspect of the European cultural context which generated the literate format at issue. Hence, utilizing aesthetic "freedom" as a justifying basis for the distortive literary manipulation of non-European cultural realities is merely a logically circular continuum. It may perhaps be reasonable that Europe is entitled (in the name of literature) to fabricate whole aspects of its own socio-cultural existence. However, the unilaterally extended proposition that Europeans are entitled to fabricate not only their own reality but also those of other cultures seems arrogant in the extreme, little more than a literary "Manifest Destiny."
- Regardless of the contradictions implied through application of purely European aesthetic values within a cross-cultural context, it must be held in mind that none of the authors in question operated in this abstract sense (such turf being generally reserved for their defenders). In each case, a more or less fictionally intended novel or poetic development was derived from the equally European (Anglo) but ostensibly non-fictive works cited in the previous section. Consequently, each later literary figure could lay claim to the "authenticity" of a firm grounding in the "historical record." That such history utterly ignored the indigenous oral accountings of the people/events thus portrayed, and did so in favor of the thoroughly alien literate record, serves to illustrate the self-contained dynamic through which literature dismisses anything beyond its pale (including the people being written about). Again, the logic describes a perfect circle: product and proof are one and the same.

· · ·

It is relatively easy to perceive how, during the nineteenth century, any valid concept ever possessed by the English-speaking population of North America as to Native Americans being peoples in their own right, peoples with entirely legitimate belief systems, values, knowledge and lifeways, had been lost in distortion presented through popular literature. The stereotypes had assumed a documented authenticity in the public consciousness. Such a process cannot be viewed as meaningless distortion or justified under the guise of aesthetic freedom. For stereotyped and stereotyper alike, it becomes dehumanization and a tool justifying genocide.[3] As Russell Means recently stated:

[W]ho seems most expert at dehumanizing other people? And why? Soldiers who have seen a lot of combat learn to do this to the enemy before going back into combat. Murderers do it before going out to murder. Nazi SS guards did it to concentration camp inmates. Cops do it. Corporation leaders do it to the workers they send into uranium mines and steel mills. Politicians do it to everyone in sight. And what the process has in common for each group doing the dehumanizing is that it makes it alright to kill and otherwise destroy other people. One of the Christian commandments says, "Thou shalt not kill," at least not humans, so the trick is to mentally convert the victims into non-humans. Then you can claim a violation of your own command-ment as a virtue.[4]

Viewed in this way, treatment of the American Indian in the arena of American literature must be seen as part and parcel of the Anglo-American conquest of the North American continent. How else could general Euroamericans have been massively con-ditioned to accept, on their behalf, a system or policy of non-stop expropriation and genocide of the native population throughout U.S. history? The dehumanizing aspects of the stereotyping of American Indians in American literature may be seen as an historical requirement of an imperial process.

The Course of Empire: From the Invasion of the Shock Troops to the Redefinition of Indigenous Culture

> The claim to a national culture in the past does not only rehabilitate that nation and serve as a justification for the hope of a future national culture. In the sphere of socioaffective equilibrium it is responsible for an important change in the native. Perhaps we have not sufficiently demonstrated that colonialism is not simply content to impose its rule upon the present and future of a dominated country. Colonialism is not merely satisfied with holding a people in its grip and emptying the native's brain of all form and content. By a kind of perverse logic, it turns to the past of an oppressed people, and distorts, disfigures and destroys it.
>
> (Frantz Fanon, *The Wretched of the Earth*)

The representation—indeed misrepresentation—is a more accurate word, of indigen-ous people began virtually with the advent of English colonization of the Western hemisphere. Within a relatively short period, styles of exposition emerged which iden-tified primary modes of stereotype. These methods of stereotyping continue in evolved formations today and must rightfully be viewed as having their roots within the literary culture of England itself. This seems true on the basis of the sheer falsity of colonial pronouncements concerning the indigenous American population. The pronounce-ments imply that the notions involved were imported rather than located upon arrival by the colonists, and reflect the prior existence of similar tendencies in "Mother Eng-land." Concerning this last:

Whatever their practical intentions or purposes, the invaders did not confront the native peoples without certain preconceptions about their nature which help shape the way they pursued their goals. Conceptions of "savagery" that developed in the sixteenth and seventeenth centuries and became the common property of Western European culture constituted a distorting lens through which the early colonists assessed the potential and predicted the fate of the non-European peoples they encountered.[5]

The specific stereotypes of American Indians finally deployed in the New England colonies amount to elaboration and continuation of a stream of literary efforts already sanctioned by the Crown and its subjects. In practical terms, the established contours of this writing may be assessed as following a roughly "them vs. us" pathway:

There were two crucial distinctions which allowed Europeans of the Renaissance and Reformation period to divide the human race into superior and inferior categories. One was between Christian and heathen and the other between "civil" and "savage."[6]

The primary stereotypes developed in the Americas did not vary from the established categories. Rather they represent merely the application of the prescribed generalities within a given context, that is, application to the indigenous populations within the territory of the New England colonies.

It is hardly an overstatement that the initial wave of any colonial invasion has been comprised of both the "cutting edge" and "hard core" of empire. These are the shock troops, arrogant, indoctrinated with the ideology of conquest, prepared to undergo hardship and sacrifice in order to actualize the ideal of their own inherent superiority to all that they encounter. Small wonder then that such "pioneers" would be prepared to bear false witness against those inhabitants of alien lands who would dare to stand in the way. A twofold purpose is served. First, in an immediate tactical sense, the overtly physical elimination and expropriation of indigenous peoples is the abrupt necessity of any preliminary colonization. It provides self-justification and even (in the hands of able propagandists) righteousness. The second purpose concerns a longer-term, strategic consideration: a less brutally doctrinaire segment of the "Mother Country" population ultimately must be attracted to the task of settling that which the invaders have conquered.

. . .

At the onset of the nineteenth century, a new process had begun. Revolution had stripped England of its external colonies in the Americas and consolidation of the American nation-state had begun. The emphasis in arts and letters became that of creating the national heritage of the emerging state, a source of patriotism and pride within which history (unless wholly fabricated) played no part. Hence, the preoccupation with histories of the Americas during this period and the historical groundings provided to incipient American fiction. But, and there was never a way to avoid this, the course of the European presence in the hemisphere had always been intertwined with that of the original inhabitants to the most intimate degree. The construction of the U.S. national heritage in terms of history therefore necessarily entailed the reconstruction of American Indian history and reality to conform to the desired image.

. . .

In Fanon's terms, the colonist who had metaphorically stripped the native of his/her present through creation of a surrogate literary reality, defined to the convenience of the colonizer, was now turning the metataphoric/mythic siege guns fully to the past. In this way, the present for the native could be perpetually precluded through the maintenance of this seamlessly constituted surrogate reality as myth. Clearly too, any perpetual "present" must encompass the future as well as the moment. The indigenous reality, the "national culture" of Fanon's thesis, is thereby hopelessly trapped within the definitional power of the oppressor, drifting endlessly in lazy hermeneutic circles, stranded in a pastless/presentless/futureless vacuum. The national identity of the colonizer is created and maintained through the usurpation of the national identity of the colonized, a causal relationship.

The final conquest of the continental land mass by the United States absorbed the whole of the nineteenth century, a period which coincided with the formal creation of American literature. Region by region, tribe by tribe, indigenous cultures were over-whelmed and consigned to the reservation status marking the physical characteristics of U.S. internal colonialism Throughout this era, an overarching theme in American writ-ing, from the embryonic work of Charles Brockden Brown and Washington Irving to the late-century tracts of Charles Leland and Alfred Riggs, was the Indian. Or, rather, a certain image of the Indian which complemented the need of the nation's Euro-american population to supplant the original inhabitants of the land.

Replacing Troops and Guns with Self-Colonization

. . .

The final absorption of the western United States into the national domain was accompanied by a constantly increasing public zeal to civilize the savage, or at least the popular conception of the savage. This latter is of considerable importance insofar as therein lies the primary function of literature within colonialism. The overwhelming preponderance of writing concerning the American Indian during the U.S. expansion was designed to create an image allowing conquest "for the Indians' own good," to effect "betterment" and "progress." The potential for a mass psychology of national guilt at its apparent policy of genocide and theft could be offset in no other conceivable fashion at that time. Further, the imposition of literacy and "education" can be per-ceived as the most effective means to inculcate in the Indians themselves a "correct" understanding (in future generations, at least) of the appropriateness of their physical and cultural demise. As has been noted in this connection:

Since schooling was brought to non-Europeans as a part of empire . . . it was integrated into an effort to bring indigenous peoples into imperial/colonial structures . . . After all, did not the European teacher and the school built on the European capitalist model transmit European values and norms and begin to transform traditional societies into "modern" ones . . . (?)[7]

At this juncture, a truly seamless model of colonialism made its appearance: the training of the colonized to colonize themselves. In this sense, hegemony over truth and knowledge replaces troops and guns finally as the relevant tool of colonization. Litera-ture, always an important property of the European colonial process, assumed an increasingly important centrality to maintenance of the system. As Albert Memmi has observed:

In order for the colonizer to be a complete master, it is not enough for him to be so in actual fact, but he must also believe in its (the colonial system's) legitimacy. In order for that legitimacy to be complete, it is not enough for the colonized to be a slave, he must also accept his role. The bond between the colonizer and the colonized is thus destructive and creative. It destroys and recreates the two partners in colonization into the colonizer and the colonized. One is disfigured into the oppressor, a partial, unpatriotic and treacherous being, worrying about his privileges and their defense; the other into an oppressed creature, whose development is broken and who compromises by his defeat.[8]

Such a view goes far towards answering the obvious questions concerning why, nearly a century after the conclusion of the primary U.S. territorial expansion, American literature still treats the Indian within its own desired framework. Witness the works of Carlos Castaneda, Ruth Beebe Hill and Cash Asher. In the same sense, it explains the nature of the support from publishers, a massive reading audience, and the academic community as a whole.

Removing the Last Vestiges of Literal and Figurative Threat

That which is cannot be admitted. That which will be must be converted by literate logic into that which cannot be. To this end, the publishers publish, the writers invent, the readers consume in as great a portion as may be provided, and the academies sanctify (over and over) the "last word" in true explanation as to where we've been, come and are going. None, or at least few, seem to act from outright malice; most are moved compulsively by internalized forces of fear (of retribution?), guilt and greed.

How then best to deploy the sophistry of literature within such a context? . . . In the post-holocaust era there is no viable ability to justify Sand Creek, the Washita and Wounded Knee. Rather, these are to be purged through a reconstitution of history as a series of tragic aberrations beginning and ending nowhere in time. The literal meaning of such events must at all costs be voided by sentiment and false nostalgia rather than treated as parts of an ongoing process. The literal is rendered tenuously figurative, and then dismissed altogether.

From there, reality can be reconstructed at will. Witness the contemporary obsession with establishing "authenticity." Ruth Beebe Hill requires the services of an aging Indian to verify her every word. Cash Asher requires another aging Indian to step forward and attest the truth of every word. Carlos Casteneda relies upon a truly massive and sustained support from both the publishing and professional academic communities to validate his efforts. Schneebaum, Waldo, Lamb, Storm, all within the past fifteen years, receive considerable support from "reputable" publishers and from some of the most prestigious scholarly establishments in the country.[9]

It is not that they are "ordered" to say specific things about the Indian, although the ancient stereotypes are maintained (albeit in mutated form). Rather, it seems that the current goal of literature concerning American Indians is to create them, if not out of whole cloth, then from only the bare minimum of fact needed to give the resulting fiction the "ring of truth," to those Indians bound to colonialism as readily as to people of European heritage.

At the dawn of English colonization of the New World, Sir Walter Raleigh was able to write that the natives of Guiana, "have their eyes in their shoulders, and their mouths in the middle of their breasts." He was believed then by the English reading public, although his words assume proportions of absurdity today (as, one assumes, they must have to those in a position to know better at the time).

Things have come full circle on the literary front. Where, in the beginning, it was necessary to alter indigenous realities in order to assuage the invading colonial conscience, so it seems necessary today to alter these realities to assure the maintenance of empire. It seems to matter little what American Indians are converted into, as long as it is into other than what they are, have been and might become. Consigned to a mythical realm, they constitute no threat to the established order either figuratively (as matters of guilt and conscience) or literally (in terms of concrete opposition). That which is mythic in nature cannot be or has been murdered, expropriated and colonized in the "real world." The potential problem is solved through intellectual sleight of hand, aesthetic gimmickry and polemical discourse with specters. The objective is not art but absolution. As Vine Deloria, Jr. has observed in another context:

[T]herein lies the meaning of the whites fantasy about Indians—the problem of the Indian image. Underneath all the conflicting image of the Indian one fundamental truth emerges: the white man knows that he is alien and he knows that North America is Indian—and he will never let go of the Indian image because he thinks that by some clever manipulation he can achieve an authenticity which can never be his.[10]

In this sense at least, literature in America is and always has been part and parcel of the colonial process. In this sense too, it has always been that American literature constituted a confused netherworld wherein fictionalized journals met journalized fiction in a jumble of verbiage requisite only to the masking of a disavowed and painful reality.

Notes

1. Washington Irving, *Sketch Book* (1819), as cited in C. F. Ten Kate, "The Indian in American Literature" (1919), *Smithsonian Annual Reports*, 1921, reprinted in *The American Indian Reader: Literature* (American Indian Historical Society, San Francisco, 1973). Citation is from p. 189 of the latter volume.

2. See, as but one example, that subtle justification(s) advanced in Ten Kate.

3. The sense of the definition of dehumanization intended here is as simple as that offered by *The Merriam-Webster Dictionary* (New York, 1974): ". . . the divestiture of human qualities or personality . . ." Surely this is an apt summation of the fate experienced by the native in the literature covered so far.

4. Russell Means, "Fighting Words on the Future of Mother Earth," *Mother Jones* (November 1980), 26–27.

5. George M. Frederickson, *White Supremacy: A Comparative Study in American and South African History* (Oxford University Press, 1981), p. 7.

6. Ibid., pp. 7–8.

7. Martin Carnoy, *Education as Cultural Imperialism* (David McKay and Co., 1974), p. 16.

8. Albert Memmi, *Colonizer and Colonized* (Beacon Press, 1965), p. 89.

9. Some of the specific material intended within this observation includes Cash Asher and Chief Red Fox, *The Memoirs of Chief Red Fox* (Fawcett Books, New York, 1972); Ruth Beebe Hill, with Chunksa Yuha (Alonzo Blacksmith), *Hanta Yo: An American Saga* (Doubleday, New York, 1979); Hyemeyohsts Storm, *Seven Arrows* (Ballantine Books, New York, 1972); Anna Lee Waldo, *Sacajawea* (Avon Books, New York, 1978); Tobias Schneebaum, *Keep the River on Your Right* (Grove Press, New York, 1970); as well as at least the first three books by Carlos Casteneda, the so-called "Castaneda Trilogy."

10. Vine Deloria, Jr. "Foreword: American Fantasy," *The Pretend Indians: Images of Native Americans in the Movies*, ed. Gretchen M. Bataille and Charles L. P. Silet (Iowa State University Press, 1980), p. xvi.

18 Handling "Crisis"

Great Books, Rap Music, and the End of Western Homogeneity (Reflections on the Humanities in America)

Houston A. Baker, Jr.

I Whose "Crisis" Is It, Anyway? A Word on Dire Prophecies and New Sounds in the Humanities

. . .

What seems certain is that an unchallenged sense of global, Western, whitemale superiority, or beauty, or authority, has "had its chance," and we are now engaged with the dynamics of the articulate ascendence of OTHERS. These dynamics are, it seems to me, what many commentators mean when they speak of a "crisis." Finally, as I shall argue later, the "crisis" is one of the OTHER's sound. For the moment, however, we should note that one man's "crisis" can always be an-OTHER's field of dreams, ladder of ascent, or moment of ethical recognition and ethnic identification. Which of us has not heard the amusing account of the moment when Native Americans ride over the hill, causing the masked man to shout: "We're in deep trouble now, Tonto!" A crisis, indeed, seems at hand for the masked man. But the appearance of the riders produces for Tonto an awakening to pronoun-chartings of colonialism: "What do you mean 'WE'?" asks the formerly faithful companion.

This familiar anecdote might prompt the question: "Whose 'crisis' is it, anyway?"

Where the humanities in our present era are concerned, the answer would be too glib and narrow if we designated a single agent, saying the "crisis" is a white, Western, American male exclusive—a gender-coded, mid-life malaise that produces strange fits of passion such as the recent Helms amendment and verbal tantrums about Shakespeare and Zulus. Such single attribution may be solacing, even ethnically gratifying; but it ignores the fact that we OTHERS are not on another planet. . . .

Which is to say, if there is a whitemale "crisis"—one that leads to Star Wars paranoia, arms proliferation, atmospheric pollution, CORE reading-lists in tandem with nuclear reactor CORES—then we might have a *mind* to designate the "crisis" as "their" problem, but our *bodies* are clearly on the line as well. There is, then, a "crisis" that implicates us all.

From Houston A. Baker, Jr., "Handling 'Crisis': Great Books, Rap Music, and the End of Western Homogeneity (Reflections on the Humanities in America)," *Callaloo*, 13: 2 (1990), 173–94. © H. Rowell. Reprinted by permission of the Johns Hopkins University Press.

To the extent that multinational capitalism, shifts in world trade balances, and the decentering of post-World-War-Two geopolitical arrangements of peoples and nations have left whitemale overseers of the United States in the blue-funk of debtors without a cause, one understands why the American condition is projected in dire syllables. For if our economy and Yankee ingenuity are under siege, how can we conceive of our humanity or of our humanities as healthy—even if their current variability, indeterminacy, and hybridity reflect global realignments of value and evaluation? Surely the gloomy sobriety of "crisis thinking" can be read as a symptomatic, if limited, response to real problems faced by the United States.

No one who has surveyed the condition of public education, spent time in secondary and university classrooms, or assessed the status of conventional knowledge and its transmission, reception, and application in the United States can doubt that an old order of literacy has passed. The pastoral, idyllic lyrics of "Schooldays, schooldays, dear old golden rule days," have given way to the postmodern indirection that Spike Lee calls "School Daze." A traditional order of "reading and writing and arithmetic" has yielded—in some cases, to alternative pedagogies and subjects, but more often to deliberate or slovenly indifference. All of these matters seem indisputably true. But the question of their interpretation and address remains very much an open-ended one. There may well exist a dire problem of literacy in our society, but we need seriously to ask in what terms we are to confront this problem. We seem, for example, to have given up on one traditional approach.

"Why Johnny can't read" is not, for example, a serious query today. For if it were a serious query, then the decidedly economic overdetermination of Johnny's plight would not be so consistently ignored, erased, or denied. And we all remember when the "why" phrase was followed by "and what you can do about it." The nostalgia for a seriously-conceived and resolutely economic dedication to Johnny's problem is, perhaps, only a kind of sixties regressiveness. Currently-projected explanations for Johnny's relationship to literacy begin not with serious analysis, informed economics, or a commitment to situational reform.

We are told, instead, that Johnny is a sufferer in the wake of wild-eyed radicals ("thugs" is sometimes the word used) of the sixties who brought the United States to desperate straits by abandoning Western ideals, misreading Nietzsche, and kicking prayer and the hickory stick out of the American classroom.

We are urged to return to old, common ideas that "every American" needs to know, to put a legacy of acknowledged "Great Books" back into place, and to let the philosophers have their head in the maintenance of State affairs.

One virtually hears Barbara Streisand in the background crooning "The Way We Were" as Alan Bloom exhorts a tearful congregation of ex-Cornell professors, and William Bennett passes the collection plate for suggested "required readings" to reclaim a legacy. Meanwhile, Deacon Hirsch counts entries.

Who is there to challenge this new Zion of whitemale literary evangelism? This chosen interpretation of a "crisis" and its solution?

Johnny himself, of course—perhaps not in the voice and guise of Homer and the Classics, but surely in the voice and person of a new hybridity of interests and values. And Johnny, like his sister Johnetta, has a huge stake in such a challenge, because it is, finally, not book-learning, but the bodies of OTHERS that are most decisively in "crisis." That is to say, while whites may have the privilege of endlessly rehearsing a bookish dilemma, what I have described as newly-emergent people and voices have no such luxury. For behind the facade of a "battle of the books," as I have already suggested, lies a terrain of global realignment and multinational economic competition where what Bourdieu calls "cultural capital" has created radically new balances of exchange.

What is expendable in the United States, Johnny and his fellows realize, is *any body* that attempts to ally itself with this current multicultural and shifting flow of world "cultural capital." While Spartan Greek youth wear walkmans from Japan and dance to the hip-hop rhythms of Run DMC, Salt-n-Peppa, N.W.A., and Public Enemy, whitemale cultural literacists nostalgically croon for a return of Homeric highlights and virtually sanction the disappearance of the very bodies that make United States' popular, public culture a valued currency of global exchange—and an informed source of critique for a postmodern world.

In a too shorthanded manner, then, one might say that Johnny and Johnetta can't read "the classics" because neither the classics nor their advocates have realigned themselves and their project to read Johnny or Johnetta—or to listen to them, or to comprehend their postmodern connectedness to a re-formed future. You simply cannot teach a class of people whose life, language, and mores you don't in the least comprehend or respect. Indoctrinate, yes; teach, no. Rather than acknowledge and learn traditions and rhythms that would produce a relational pedagogy—one combining what some hold to be a precious and privileged "legacy" with the long-ignored voices and inheritances that are emerging and being transmitted across cultural frontiers and international, tele-communal viewing spaces today—the American literacists who preach of "crisis" have adopted a strategy of willful ignorance and, ultimately, sanctioned aggression.

Conserving the definite article *the* for humanities conceived only in selective, Western terms is the first move in the dance. Backward glances to a glorious past—one free of colonial expansion, racism, sexism, and self-interested imperialism—a past that never was—is the second move. The third and decisive move is—in a telecommunal age—to couch *the* crisis of *the* humanities in bookish terms, as though reading and writing were not mere technologies that favored an order of privileged ascendency and selective power and ideological control known even to Thoth and his King long ago.

The fourth move in the current "crisis" project is to rid the kingdom of the very bodies of those who represent a "cultural" threat to what the literacists define as "our" national interest. Multiple incidents of campus and university violence against Black and Women, Chicano and Chicana, Asian, Native American, gay and lesbian students by Anglomale perpetrators—incidents that have frequently gone unpunished by Anglo-male administrators and ignored by white academics bent on keeping their heads in cultural sands—testify to the expansiveness of this fourth initiative in the current dance of cultural "crisis." There have been more than 250 incidents of bias-related aggression on American campuses during the past two years alone (1987–1989). Of course, the inner-city public schools of America and the deteriorating, crime-filled neighborhoods in which they fight to serve an educational mission in the absence of adequate funding or enlightened concern from the federal government offer further testimony to a killing indifference of our "crisis" thinkers.

The OTHERS' defense of self is, thus, an inferable necessity of the current "crisis" in the humanities.

Such a defense begins with dramatically reconceptualized self-definitions by people who are products of a history that has yet to be written. (A ritual and transformative drama teaching us our own beauty plays itself out at every turn.) With bodies on the line and life itself at stake, it hardly seems strange that Johnny might regard our current "crisis" advocates of "cultural literacy" as avatars of those white missionaries who paved the way for slavetraders, armies, and curious colonial scholars of the past. Faced with the prospect of such an enslaving and myopic "cultural literacy," Johnny and his fellows have bolted from the schools and given birth to energetic expressive forms such as postmodern hip-hop, interventionist film culture, and radical scholarship into gender, class, and race determinants of power and knowledge in the world we inhabit.

In many ways, the powerful, syncretic, corporally minimalistic urgings of African-American rap music signal this *légitime défense* of a new humanity and a new humanities that will outlast the current "crisis" and create new room for the new people.

One hears Public Enemy cautioning those who might be drawn into a sham "battle of the books" with the injunction: "Don't, don't, don't believe the hype!"

Perhaps it is because rap is so effective in its expressive counters to a bookish "crisis" that those who "have had their chance" seek so forcefully to suppress it. Rap is the metonym for all of those shared sonics that emergent generations have brought to their own defense, to their own expressive soundings of the world. It summons in its urgings *corridos* of the southwest, Native American chant poems, Latin American magical realism, African and Caribbean lyrics, lesbian and gay signifiers, and so very much more that is undreamed of in the philosophies and books of the "crisis" people.

. . .

As the rap group Public Enemy counts the numbers: "It takes a nation of millions to hold us back!" Nobody in America can afford such wasted manpower when our nation is already belated, behind the times and hard-pressed for any future whatsoever. Today's "crisis" will only begin to abate when American whitemale nostalgia for ancient exclusionism gives way to conscientious audition and constructive pedagogy and scholarship based on the sounds of a postmodern world. James Baldwin once asserted in a famous essay about alienation and blackness that it was time for all of those who are nostalgic for prelapsarian days of exclusion to realize that the world "is no longer white, and will never be again." If we add "bookish" or "Great Bookish" to Baldwin's announcement we have, I think, fundamental postulates for listening beyond the thresholds of our present "crisis" to sounds of a safer and more liberating future.

II Practical Philosophy and Vernacular Openings: The Poetry Project and the American Mind

. . .

The battle, in my view, is most decisively not between books ancient and modern, male and female, white and black, but rather between books and bookmen who are hoping to combat and to destroy those occult and instable energies that a postmodern media sensibility has brought to bear in a bookish field of stated male, and well-financed, prerogatives.

One might view this conflict as the polarity between *Piers Plowman* and Chaucer's clerk of Oxenforde—"a field full of folks" versus "twenty bookes." Or: Michael Jackson's momentous, international Victory Tour, attracting millions, versus Bloom's preferred readings for young Platonists in an upper room at Cornell. Run DMC, Salt-n-Peppa, and Public Enemy creating a *lingua franca* that transgresses ethnic barriers and crosses international youth frontiers, versus a specialized, national vocabulary of literacy produced and directed by E. D. Hirsch and William Bennett. American television and motion picture productions energizing millions of households in Europe versus approximately one-hundred square feet of shelf space in Blackwell's Oxford Bookshop housing all of American fiction, drama, poetry, and literary criticism.

At least this can be said: what I have called a postmodern, media sensibility projects globally . . . and in dramatic numbers. Additionally, one might say that this sensibility is youth-oriented, hybrid, and destabillzing in its synergistic collagings of performative sounds and images. . . . I now want to focus on the single category of poetry as a suggestive illustration of the media reorientations of cultural literacy that are being created by the youthful citizens of what might be considered our next society. My observations had their origin in the New York Poetry Project's 1989 symposium entitled "Poetry for the Next Society," about which I will have more to say at the conclusion.

For the moment, I want to turn to the actual text that I presented to The Poetry Project symposium—a text entitled, after the rap ensemble KRS One and Just Ice, "Going Way Back for All the Pioneers." There are two epigraphs from the rap group Public Enemy (of whom I shall speak at the conclusion). First:

> Death row, death row
> What a, what a, what a Brother knows

and:

> Fight, fight
> Fight for your right to fight.

. . .

So I asked my graduate seminar what they considered "poetry for the next society." To a man and woman, they responded "MTV" and "Rap." We didn't stop to dissect their claims, nor did we attempt a poetics of the popular. Instead, we tried to extrapolate from what seemed two significant forms of the present era a description of their being-in-the-world. Terms that emerged included "public," "performative," "audible," "theatrical," "communal," "intra-sensory," "postmodern," "oral," "memorable," and "intertextual." What this list suggests is that my students believe the function of poetry belongs in our era to a telecommunal, popular space in which a global audience interacts with performative artists. A link between music and performance—specifically popular music and performance—seems determinative in their definition of the current and future function of poetry.

They are heirs to a history in which art, audience, entertainment and instruction have assumed profoundly new meanings. The embodied catharsis of Dick Clark's bandstand or Don Cornelius's soultrain would be virtually unrecognizable—or so one thinks—to Aristotle. Thus, Elvis, Chuck Berry, and the Shirelles foreshadow and historically overdetermine the Boss, Bobby Brown, and Kool Moe Dee as, let us say, *People's Poets.*

My students' responses, however, are not nearly as natural or original as they may seem on first view. In fact, they have a familiar cast within a history of contestation and contradistinction governing the relationship between poetry and the State.

The exclusion of poets from the republic by Plato is the ur-Western site of this contest. In Egypt it is Thoth and the King; in Afro-America it is the Preacher and the Bluesman. It would be overly-sacramental to speak of this contest as one between the letter and the spirit, and it would be too Freudian by half to speak of it again as an *agon* between the law and taboo. The simplest way to describe it is in terms of a tensional resonance between homogeneity and heterogeneity.

Plato argues the necessity of a homogeneous State designed to withstand the blue-siness of poets who are always intent on worrying such a line by signifying and troping irreverently on it and continually setting up conditionals. "What if, this?" and "What if, that?" To have a homogeneous line, Plato (like Alan Bloom) advocates that the philosophers effectively eliminate the poets.

If the State is the site of what linguists call the *constative*, then, poetry is an alternative space of the *conditional*. If the State keeps itself in line, as Benedict Anderson suggests, through the linear, empty space of homogeneity, then poetry worries this space or line with heterogeneous performance. If the State is a place of reading the lines correctly, then poetry is the site of audition, of embodied sounding on State wrongs. What, for example, happens to the State Line about the death of the Black Family and the voiceless derogation of Black youth when Run DMC explodes the State Line with the rap: "Kings from Queens / From Queens Come Kings / We're Raising Hell Like a Class When the Lunch Bell Rings! / Kings will be Praised / And Hell Will Be Raised / Suckers try to phase us / But We won't be phased!"

In considering the contestation between homogeneity and heterogeneity, I am drawing on the work of the scholars Homi Bhabha and Peter Stallybrass, who suggest that nationalist or postrevolutionary discourse is always a discourse of the split subject. In order to construct the Nation it is necessary to preserve a homogeneity of remembrance (such as anthems, waving flags, and unifying slogans) in conjunction with an amnesia of heterogeneity. If poetry is disruptive performance, or, in Homi Bhabha's formulation, an articulation of the melancholia of the people's wounding by and before the emergence of the State Line, then poetry can be defined as an audible space of opposition.

Rap is the form of audition in our present era that utterly refuses to sing anthems of, say, whitemale hegemony.

Created by young black people—preeminently males—in their late teens and early twenties, rap situates itself with respect to rhythm and blues, intermixing in its collaged styles the saxophone solos, bridges, and James Brown shouts and energy of that music. Adopting a driving, rhyming, rhythmic format, rappers such as Kurtis Blow, Run DMC, Doug E. Fresh, Rakim and Eric B., LL Kool J, Roxanne Shante, Salt-n-Peppa, Public Enemy, and the Jungle Brothers proceed to take apart the conventional wisdom and skewed ethics of the State Line. Summoning heroes like Malcolm X, Martin Luther

King, Mohammad Ali, Marcus Garvey, and Minister Louis Farrakhan, these young black poets describe cityscapes and an Afro-American existence of the street that are entirely original.

They refigure traditional language, sample and remix conventional history in a sometimes absurdist and completely memorable—almost hypnotic—fashion. Theirs is a poetry of Afro-American pride intended for the people. In its very structure, rap interrogates the politics and technologies of record production in the United States. It is a poetry and music of the voice that originated in New York among black teenagers. Its first-order production requires—like the earliest Afro-American musical productions—only the body of the rapper and his or her "crew" or "posse." The steady back beat can be provided by voice or by bodydrumming equivalent to the hambone.

When rap moves into the studio of record production, what is fascinating about its corporal minimalism is that it signifies on, or deconstructs, the very processes of record production and the mechanics of utilization or instrumentalism in an age of mechanical reproduction. Turntables become mere mechanisms for converting already-produced and fetishized records into cacophonous "scratchings"; microphones are mere voice-boosters (not Midas converters of the black voice unselfconsciously into whitegold) that can be possessed only by the rapper who has proved that he is not a "sucker D.J." in need of "bum rushing."

While there is a marked component of self-aggrandizement and epic boasting in rap, there is also an insistent element of didacticism, polemical challenge, and ethical caution. Drugs and violence are roundly condemned. The State is put on notice that the black community is aware of its "hype."

Rapping as art is endorsed as a challenging form of creativity that converts oppression and lack into a commercial and communal success in which, as Doug E. Fresh states it, one gets "paid in full."

The test of this success vis-à-vis the individual rapper's performance is measured, at least in part, by the danceability of his or her performance. As my student Mark Hunter states in a very suggestive essay on rap: "The test of the lyrics is their link to the consciousness of the streets, usually of life in the hard center of the ghetto where greatest suffering as well as greatest strength and creativity abide . . . the test of the beat is in dancing, whether it can rock you and cause the delight which only a truly hard, tight rhythm can."

Rap is the poetry of youth; it is the continuation in our era of a black musical tradition that has always been syncretic: a collusion of voice and limited instrumentation, social commentary and fortifying entertainment. Rap is also the poetry of what Homi Bhabha calls "melancholia in revolt." Its very form is of heterogeneity—a collaging of all the sources of Afro-American malaise into an energetic sounding. Bits of history combine with boasts of new dress codes, which commingle with juxtapositions between philosophers and teachers, which, in turn, provide a segue into cautionary tales against drug dealing and gang violence, which, in their turn, become an overlay for self-reflexive histories of black music—including rap itself.

Rap is black life unwholly realized, but holy in its fragmentation. It is a spirited critique of a homogeneous State Line.

To say that it is the poetry of the next society is not, finally, to predict, but to describe.

And the description provides a theoretical opening for the refiguration of time frames and expectations that the phrase "poetry for the next society" connotes to an audience of literary-critical aficionados and aspiring literary poets . . . in English. For the recognition of rap *as poetry* by my graduate students is coextensive, it seems to me, with a profound shift in conceptions of art and history that has marked the past twenty years. As Doug E. Fresh puts it:

> Brainwish education
> Of our nation,
> Publicized in its prime,
> To be behind time,
> Verbal abuse,
> Our History's a mystery,
> Or what's the use?

Rap in its general, popular appeal and heterogeneity—in its challenging recovery of both a sociohistorical past and past expressive traditions—is a metonym or an acronym for all of the neglected poetries that are surfacing and competing for audition today. And here, if there were world enough and time, I would enumerate spectacular and specular European, Indian, Latin American, Caribbean, African, and Asian "surfacings." For the attempt is to discover an acronym for a general revolt and not to hug the revolution ceremoniously and chauvinistically to one's own chest. In its unequivocal, questioning of a homogeneous, whitemale harmony, it can be decoded as *R.* (to be pronounced) *A. P.; Recovered Audition of the People.*

. . .

III   Required Questions and Cheney's Book of Hours: A Note on "What Should Be Required?"

What once was an open-ended question has become a holy interrogative today. Two decades ago, in an era scarcely dim or forgotten, we asked: "Should required courses form part of college and university curricula?" In 1990, a new cadre of the Western faithful demands: "What should be required?" The present conservative inquiry tends, among other things, to erase a history of academic debate, contestation, expansion, and revision that has achieved dramatically foregrounded status during recent decades. Today's question—"What should be required?"—also suggests an ontotheology of "required" questions in general: inquiries that take the form: "What doth the Lord *require* of thee?" or "What, then, *must* we do?"

For many, such questions bring an uneasiness akin to that of the man suddenly asked "When, Sir, did you stop beating your wife?" They produce guilt by an absence of association. For when one refuses to respond to required questions, one is immediately branded: willfully obstructionist, blissfully ignorant, coyly evasive, or intellectually retarded. Such is the power and prerogative of interrogative monopolies that produce required questions. The very power to pose and maintain the legitimacy of such questions presupposes both knowledge of and responsibility for their "correct" answers.

"Thou shalt love the lord thy God with all thy heart, and with all thy soul, and with all thy mind." Or, "Thou shalt give to each according to his need, and exact from each according to his ability." Or "thou shalt pursue a core curriculum based upon Western Great Books."

There may be an allowable latitude within such answers (e.g., a tripartite Godhead, a few party leaders who seem to need more than their abilities warrant, a minimal representation of decidedly "other"-than-Western cultures). But the fundamental form and orthodoxy of answers to required questions are implicit in the questions themselves. There exists, then, a closed, ahistorical loop between devout calls for requirements and correct responses from the faithful.

Such ahistorical closure provides merely an interrogative instance of discursive colonization. For surely the colonizer of curriculum discourse in its "normal practice" is the person who speaks from an authoritative site of formation and exercises influence over what might be considered paradigmatic talk about "general education" in the United States. In 1989, one such site is energetically occupied by the Chairman of the National Endowment for the Humanities, Lynne V. Cheney. Mrs. Cheney has set forth her version of "What should be required?" in *50 Hours: A Core Curriculum for College Students. 50 Hours* tellingly illustrates the historical erasure, ontotheological closure, and interrogative monopoly of required questions.

Containing a "Foreword," "Afterword," "Introduction," five sections devoted to large academic subject areas, and a series of "Curriculum Profiles," Cheney's pamphlet is replete with the historical agentlessness of pastoral and the passive-tense constructions of utopian theologism. Here is the sound of the West coming into being as Cheney recounts it in *50 Hours*:

Of those civilizations [of the world in its entirety], the one that has shaped our own culture most profoundly arose in the West. With roots in ancient Israel and Greece, the Western tradition grew to encompass a variety of views, often conflicting, pulling and tugging this way and that. . . . The engagement of ideas, a habit of debate on how people should live and what they should find worthy, assumed a central place. Principles emerged—respect for persons, rule of law, and the right to self government—against which we judge ethical, legal, and political practices today. (22)

Here we have a perfect birth, without trace of ignominy or actual history. We discover Greek and Hebraic origins worthy of Matthew Arnold, place "tab A" into "slot B," and achieve a perfect pop-up picture of the West.

Once such a premiere emergence has been set in place with grammatical passives, it seems uncharitable to ask who the referenced public is for "our own culture," or to inquire about what happened to Africa, Oceania, Native or Latin America in Cheney's account. And it is just as well, because *50 Hours* shows no concern for such matters. The sole African-Americans who find place in the work are Frederick Douglass, Richard Wright, and Martin Luther King, Jr. Chief Joseph stands as the lone Native American representative from "our own culture."

The question of why we need a core curriculum is answered (not surprisingly) in the language of "our own": "A required course of studies—a core of learning—can ensure that students have opportunities to know the literature, philosophy, institutions, and art of our own and other cultures" (11). Perhaps Latin and Native America are "other," joining the thousand notable persons and events that might have been mentioned under the sign African-American? But slowly we come to see, as *50 Hours* unfolds, that everything that is not "great" (a word that vies with "classic" and "monument" for most-often repeated) and "Western" in origin and descent is sharply discounted in Cheney's world of the required question.

First place among "civilizations" has already been awarded to the West, so it follows that, for Cheney, the education of "our own" students should be grounded in the West: "According to this plan, students would take up the West and America—the cultures most accessible to most of them—before study of cultures with which they are less likely to be familiar" (18). Moreover: "All the courses [in Western Civilization] described above reflect an understanding that diverse traditions are best approached by students who are first grounded in one [read: *the West*]" (24).

The idea, then, is to *assume* a premiere civilization's emergence, complete with great men thinking great thoughts and writing them down in great books that answer "enduring human questions" in five large subject categories. After such knowledge, the job of curriculum coring is simple, and forgivably Western. All that remains is to add "diverse" other traditions for variety, erase historical contingency, ignore profound postindustrial and postmodern alterations of human existence, and declare that the resultant plan of study enables students to "encounter classic works and significant ideas" (59).

If testimony to the greatness of the resultant plan is required, it is provided by Cheney's "Curriculum Profiles." These profiles are stories that tell us how collegial interaction and pedagogical inventiveness have utilized Western "monuments" or "classics" in salvific ways to enhance or restore an ailing American education. They are tales of miracles and faith healing. Rather than realistic interludes like Dos Passos's "Camera's eyes," Cheney's "profiles" are churchly witnesses to Western faith.

The most insidious aspects of *50 Hours* are direct products of what I have described as the required question ontotheology. There is no space in the pamphlet for the development of opinion or for conscientious debate. Assumptions of Western greatness sweep all before them. At times, their sweep is almost jingoistic, resounding with a fervid populism. Always, the sweep is Whiggish, moving without a hitch from a great Western past to the florescence of a great Western modernism. (And, of course, the march halts at a modern "something not ourselves" that is distinctively pre-War in flavor and texture, something homogeneously good and noble that "our own" will surely recognize.)

Yes, one can acknowledge the check lists of "other" civilizations and their contents in *50 Hours* without qualifying the pamphlet's Western sweep. After all, such "others" are clearly not "significant" in the manner of "our own." For if they were of genuine significance, then perhaps one of the honorific quotations concerning human learning (which are legion in *50 Hours*) might have been drawn from them. Instead, Cheney quotes one white male praise-singer of the West after another, putting to rest conservative anxieties that the Chairman of "our own" National Endowment might actually be able to cite non-Western sources, illustrating by "thought and deed" (59) her familiarity with "Other Civilizations."

Though Cheney tells us in the "Afterword" to *50 Hours* that "liberal education is a journey" and "the curriculum is a map," the implicit message of her pamphlet is that education is a doxology to the West in which "our own" students must be indoctrinated. Rather than a process of options and cosmopolitan intellectual discovery, *50 Hours* inscribes "education" as a conversion experience, a veritable spiritual rebirth into a blissfully utopian, ahistorical version of Occidental holiness. Cheney's core curriculum begins with the formula "Praise the West from who all blessings flow." *50 Hours* might, thus, be read as a mass-produced "book of hours" designed to lead the faithful back to Plato and the ancient prophets.

Once one has entered the world of required questions, pamphlets such as Cheney's come as no surprise. For, as I have already suggested, such questions are ultimately demands not for debate or dialogue, but for liturgical certainty.

But alas for Western believers! Our current educational dilemmas cannot be solved by conservative hour books or restorationist *autos-da-fé*. And faith—no matter how fervent—in the West and its traditions will not suppress the history and emergence of new people and demands that have produced a crisis for followers of Plato and the prophets in recent decades. To attempt to colonize this history and discourse of postmodern emergence with required questions is to retreat to holy traditions rather than to engage the difficulties of hybridity that confront the academy in the final decade of the twentieth century.

The fact that today's college and university students choose to graduate without taking courses in Western civilization, history, foreign languages, English and American literature, mathematics, or the natural and physical sciences is less a matter for theology and faith than for careful, student-focused inquiry. Is it because such courses are not required that students avoid them, or is it simply that the rapid, postmodernist expansion of specialized information leaves little time for students who wish fully to engage their majors to explore "general education"? Do students of American colleges and universities in the late twentieth century truly compose a body homogeneous enough in Western great bookishness to warrant their group training in a "common" Western discourse of "our own"? Isn't the commonality of college and university students less traditionally bookish than postmodernly telecommunal? Aren't "our" students bonded more in their postmodernity (a global shift completely ignored by *50 Hours*) than in an ahistorical holiness of the Western past stored in Great Books? Isn't it virtually impossible to achieve more than the forced ideological indoctrination of such students if teachers refuse to engage them in their postmodern, hybridly cosmopolitan, telecommunal, popular-cultural, everyday assumptions and bondings? Such queries are designed as counter-interrogatives for required questions. They are meant to suggest that there are questions far more pressing today than the regnant curriculum doxologists allow.

"Why today, more than two decades ago, should any college or university course be *required*?" "What agreed-upon ends are served by *requiring* any course whatsoever?" "Upon what basis should any *required* course build?" Everything today seems as open to question—from a heterodox perspective—as ever. And the current numbers, finances, offices, and intimidations from conservative benches must not compel us to gloss over or to cede to Western orthodoxy the task of aggressively addressing such questions in demandingly secular ways.

We must come realistically to know our students and to participate intellectually and affectively in the sounds of their everyday lives before we can meet them where they are. And it is only by meeting them where they most decidedly are that we can begin instructive conversations about an infinite variety of possible heritages they share in a postmodern, resoundingly hybrid, and increasingly non-white era of study.

Such a prospect does not mean that the West and its Great Books have no role to play as we approach a new century. But it does mean that these minimal aspects of global postmodernism will never suffice as exclusive answers to the next century's questions of requirements. What should first be required, I think, is, at least, a meaningful update of Mrs. Cheney's book of hours—a postmodern facelift that will give it some bearing on the future. At present, there is nothing about *50 Hours* that prevents our mistaking it for a document crafted in an upper room at Cambridge twenty-five to fifty years ago. Still, one is forced to salute the Ulyssean bravado of the pamphlet in its passionate rhetorical sincerity. And Cheney's passion and resolve might be taken as representative of today's conservative ardor for restoration. We can code this fervor in the following words from Tennyson: "We are not now that strength which in old days / Moved earth and heaven, that which we are we are— / One equal temper of heroic hearts / Made weak by time and fate, but strong in will / To strive, to seek, to find, and not to yield."

But, of course, the key lesson of the Eastern martial arts and their attendant philosophies is precisely to yield. Yielding enables a participant to carry the force not only of him or herself but also of opponents into new (and perhaps winning) formations, achieving, at least, a compromise—sometimes an agreed-upon victory. Such new formations of force are precisely what the current crisis in the humanities is centered on, and no exclusive set of requirements, core curricula, or heroic returns to Ithaca will forestall their excitingly hybrid course of production. No discourse of the required will curtail their fruitful disruptions of familiar territories and traditional doxologies. This, it seems to me, is the good news and true historical message of the past two postmodern decades of open-ended questioning.

19 Writing History: Language, Class, and Gender

Carroll Smith-Rosenberg

CAN one write about "Writing History" and not deal with the interaction of writing and history, an interaction so methodologically and philosophically problematic? Writing presumes words, history the world that speaks them. Seemingly distinct, they form a seamless web, for how can we know the world except through the words it constructs? History offers us no exit from this circle of mutual referents, for history itself is part of the circle, a composite of words about words, a narrative of narratives.

Historians' growing sensitivity to the power of words, the product of an active interchange between historians and literary theorists, has greatly enhanced the subtlety with which we explore the past. But it has also encouraged historical nihilism, especially among creative and sophisticated historians. Medievalist Nancy Partner, for example, in a brilliant essay argues that "the whole of historical discourse is calculated to induce a sense of referential reality in a conceptual field with no external reference at all." Historical evidence, Partner suggests, consists of words arbitrarily imposed to make time into chronology, to turn the uncharted chaos of reality into a simple story complete with a beginning, a middle, and an end. It is almost always linguistic, some*one*'s story about reality. Even census returns, the basis of quantitative history, are linguistic constructs, often, Partner insists, relying on "arcane and unexplained measures and procedures" expressed in terms the historian must retranslate. All historical evidence is but "the partial visibilia of an entire invisible world." For Partner, history has become "the definitive human audacity imposed on formless time and meaningless event with the human meaning-maker language."[1]

How ironic if we historians, especially feminist historians, relinquish our grasp on the world behind the words just at the moment when feminist literary critics have begun to look beyond the words to study historical worlds. The text, they insist, can be understood only in terms of the world in which it was written, and read. They have proffered an important invitation to feminist historians, one that we cannot refuse. To do otherwise—to accept historical nihilism as posited by Nancy Partner, Hayden White, and others—would not only deny the knowability of the world, it would lose for us that aspect of the world we are most committed to knowing: women.[2] For women are more than the word *female* contained within (male) quotation marks.

How can feminist historians fascinated with words, and feminist critics intrigued by the world, collectively explore the female experience? We ourselves constitute literal

From Carroll Smith-Rosenberg, "Writing History: Language, Class, and Gender," in Teresa de Lauretis (ed.), *Feminist Studies/Critical Studies* (Bloomington: Indiana University Press, 1986), 31–54.

nodes between words and the world. Rather than seeking to transcend the complexity of our semantic existence, let us meticulously trace it by analyzing the process by which words are formed out of experiences and experiences are shaped by words. It is by rooting our conceptual models in what we do—following words that transpose experience into meaning—rather than what we cannot know—the entirety of the invisible world—that we may best address the principal criticism of White, Partner, and others.

Our sense of our own partiality within a complex world will teach us never to read the part for the whole. And never to forget the transience of words, for the meanings we assign our words, the changing narratives we tell (no story ever exactly replicating a previous story), are themselves so transient. Indeed, as women, our own experience of words will lead us to ask two of the most fundamental questions historians can ask: How does the diversity of language suggest the structure of power? How do words, products of particular power structures, acquire sufficient autonomy to critique and challenge those structures? By applying the critical techniques of close reading to deduce the relations not only of words to words within a literary text but of words in one genre and one social group to the words of quite different genres and social groups—and, lastly and most fundamentally, of words to specific social relations within the ebb and flow of a particular culture—we will begin to re-form history and to hear women's stories with fresh clarity.

To illustrate my point, let me discuss a historical project I am presently engaged in. A historian, I am concerned with the ways in which class identity is formed and maintained. Three aspects of class identity in particular interest me: first, its initial construction; second, the ways in which middle-class American women and men both maintained and altered their identity over time; and third, the diversity and inner conflict that characterize all classes, but, I would argue, the middle class in particular.

I begin in the 1790–1840 period, a time when American women and men had to re-form their senses of self in response to the radical economic and institutional transformations that characterized that period. It was a time when classes first emerged and older social configurations died out. Only just recruited into the new middle class, these women and men had to distinguish themselves from the older mercantile, artisan, and agrarian groups to which they had belonged, from the cultural norms and institutions those groups had espoused, and from the equally new and uncertain working class. They did so gradually, through the construction of elaborate etiquettes and metaphoric "discourses." Through these discourses (the composites of many genres: religious, medical, and legal literature, domestic and child-rearing advice books, political rhetoric, and popular fiction), they expressed their experiences of change and rationalized their new and troubling world. Neither "discourses" nor identities became static; they altered repeatedly as economic and institutional circumstances evolved and as middle-class power became entrenched.

Classes are not monolithic. Many factors divided the nineteenth-century American middle class—ethnicity, religion, regional and generational divisions, and, most especially, gender. Women and men, affected differently by commercialization, urbanization, and industrializaton, situated differently in the power structure, told different stories about the impact of change and developed distinctive styles to discuss their experience of class. They disagreed about which forces threatened middle-class values and, in fact, about what those values were. Gender thus became a fault line undercutting the solidity of class identity.

Class and *gender* are terms that describe social characteristics: occupation, educational levels, consumption patterns, size of family, modes of social interaction. Simultaneously, they constitute conceptual systems, organizing principles, that impose a fictive order upon the complexities of economic and social development. They constitute codes of behavior by which people are expected to structure their lives—or at least their definition of the normative and the "normal."[3] The tension between the two meanings of *gender* and *class* (as sociological description and as cultural prescription) played a critical role in the construction of a middle-class identity. While the one reflected the uncertainties of a world in flux, the other constituted an attempt by new middle-class women and men to impose a sense of order on the economic and demographic disruptions of their time. The "ordered" vision women and men sought to impose differed as widely as their experiences of social change.

As will be clear by now, I have espoused a somewhat controversial definition of class. I have not defined class solely in terms of its relation to production or as a list of definitional variables. In my view, it is that and more. It is a series of relationships, of culturally constructed identities. Only if one accepts such an expanded definition of class can one call "middling" nineteenth-century Americans a class. Many historians and theorists do not. They argue that consensus, not class, characterized nineteenth-century America: that ethnic and religious, not class, identities divided Americans; that the varied and often tenuous relation of its different members to the means of production made the American middle class an "intermediate," not a true, class. Yet some—Anthony Giddens, Mary Ryan, and, most recently, Stuart Blumen—accept its class designation, because, like me, they think of class as a complex exchange between economic forces and cultural identity. To study class, Giddens argues, requires that we examine *"the modes in which* 'economic' relationships become translated into 'noneconomic' social structures."[4]

Yet to quote Blumen, a "critical problem" remains. Many nineteenth-century middle-class Americans, especially men, denied that they constituted a class. Can we talk of an American middle-class identity in the face of this denial? I think we can if we keep two points clearly in mind: first, Roland Barthes's suggestion that the bourgeoisie seeks to deny its own existence, by asserting that what is economically and politically specific to it as a class is, in fact, universal and "natural"; and second, nineteenth-century middle-class men's radical polarization of gender.[5] If Barthes is right, and middle-class men sought consciously and unconsciously to deny their own class identity at the same time that they made class distinctions central to social arrangements and the structure of power, they could do so by displacing the acknowledgment and enactment of class onto middle-class women. Middle-class men used two radically different myths to rationalize middle-class identity in early-nineteenth-century America: "the Myth of the Common Man" and "the Cult of True Womanhood." The one denied class, the other constructed its elaborate etiquette. These apparently opposed yet actually interdependent myths illustrate the ways in which difference, even contradiction, lies at the heart of class identity. They also constitute a paradigm for analyzing the ways in which nineteenth-century American middle-class men simultaneously constructed and denied their class identity.

"Discourse," that is, words are central to my analysis not because they convey "facts" but because, as Michel Foucault argues in *Les Mots et les choses*, they constitute the point of intersection between the world of tangible "things" and the minds that respond to those "things."[6] Words are mental constructs, yet we cannot understand their meanings unless we understand their interaction with "things" such as technology, cities, wealth, work, leisure, and unless we accept that words are themselves in some respects "things." Like the notion of social class itself, words are cultural constructs, imaginative mediations of social experiences. We construct our sense of self out of words.

Words, even more than clothes, make the woman and the man. A nice conceit, but how precisely do they do so? As I have written elsewhere, I am convinced that the varied forms that "words" and "language" take—whether we refer to grammar, dialect, high literary tradition, folk narrative, unconscious metaphor, or sexual or political discourse—reflect the social location and relative power of the speakers. Take black or cockney English, for example, or Scots dialect. Their alternative grammars, the meanings they assign words, their accents and speech patterns deviate from standard American or English in ways that precisely mirror both their speakers' marginality within the American or British political and economic power structure, and the social diversity of those societies. Since "language" affects as well as reflects, the grammatical and accentual deviance of these three dialects reinforces the dominant culture's easy condemnation of each as irregular or anachronistic and, hence, the valuation of its speakers as disorderly or marginal—in either case inferior. While marking their speakers as "Other," they also give expression to "other" experiences, permit coded discourse, and the expression of anger and protest.[7]

If "language" reflects experience, then a multiplicity of "languages" will coexist within any heterogeneous society, reflecting the diversity of experiences across and within gender and class. Radical special transformations and new class formations exacerbate such semantic diversity, producing a profusion both of new social experiences and of resulting social dialects. Divergent, at times conflicting, narratives and imagery will proliferate as marginal social groups, speaking the "language" of their experiences, challenge their culture's "traditional" discourse. At such times, the meaning of words will become problematic. However, disorder is the most transient of social states. A new class, as it assumes political and economic dominance, will inevitably impose a new cultural and linguistic hegemony, seeking to silence voices it can now define as deviant. But the dominant will never completely silence the words of the marginal and the less powerful, within as well as without class. Cacophony, though muted, will persist.

I have just suggested a diachronic view of the interaction of class and "language." A synchronic analysis is also crucial. This time, "language" not only provides the analytic tools, it offers itself as an analytic model. Language construction, like class construction, is dialectical. The need of any group of people for a body of commonly agreed-upon meanings and grammatical constructions wars against the linguistic diversity that characterizes any heterogeneous society. The struggle is ongoing.

"Language," like class, is never static.

As should be clear by now, my ideas are shaped to a significant extent by Bakhtin's literary theories, and in particular by the dialectic he posits between the forces of linguistic diversity (what he calls "heteroglossia") and the need every society and social group feels for a commonly understood grammar and vocabulary (a "unitary language," in Bakhtin's metalinguistic system). Heteroglossia give voice to social differences. Within the term, Bakhtin includes "languages that are socioideological, languages of social groups, professional and 'generic' languages, languages of generations and so forth." The thrust for a unitary language seeks to confine, indeed to outlaw, such linguistic diversity. Linguistic unification thus serves as the handmaiden of ideological unification. It is never politically innocent. It forms, Bakhtin insists, a critical part of the "process of socio-political and cultural centralization."[8]

Bakhtin has provided a linguistic model well suited to the needs of the cultural historian, suggesting the ways in which language both serves and wars against the unifying forces of class cohesion. Language so conceived becomes a synecdochic representation of class itself. It permits us to use the development of language competency as a metaphor for the formation of class identity. The following questions then suggest themselves: Which specific social and gender groups originated the "unitary language" of class identity? Who taught it to whom (that is, to which other social, gender, and generational groups)? What techniques and technologies did they use to disseminate their words? Did those groups who learned the language (rather than originate it) transpose it in the process of learning, so that it more accurately reflected their socio-structural location, their anxieties, and their angers? Did they speak a second language altogether, one that either directly confronted or less overtly subverted the unitary language of class cohesion? If so, were they able to maintain their social dialects against the forces of uniformity? How did the next generation of speakers alter the varied languages they inherited?

Women's popular writing in America during the first half of the nineteenth century offers an ideal body of literature for testing the usefulness of Bakhtin's thesis and of my questions. Since Foucault's early work in *Madness and Civilization*, cultural historians have examined the emergence of a restraining bourgeois "discourse" and have pondered the effect gender had upon that "discourse."[9] Jacques Donzelot, a leading student of Foucault, has insisted that bourgeois women, coopted by the offer of domestic sovereignty, collaborated actively in the dissemination of the new bourgeois ideology (to use Foucault's formulation, they became "enmeshed" in the "new technologies of power").[10] Bonnie Smith, a feminist student of the *bourgeoise*, demurs. Women resisted the new unitary bourgeois discourse, Smith argues; using religious enthusiasm and sexual purity, they constructed a counter "language."[11] Mary Ryan concurs. Demonstrating the initial appeal that male-articulated evangelical enthusiasm held for women just entering the uncertain and rapidly changing world of Utica, she explores the ways in which that appeal, and the women's responses to it, altered as the class structure of Utica became firmly entrenched. Women, she argues, took a male religious "discourse" and transformed it into a female "discourse" that both imposed fictive order on the uncertain world of commercial and industrializing Utica, and demanded their active participation in that world.[12]

Ryan's and Smith's analyses exemplify the contribution historians can make to the analysis of "discourse"—and to historians' exchange with literary critics. Their studies add a contextual richness to the analysis of texts; they demonstrate the dynamic interchange between words and the world that spoke those words. They challenge Foucault's understanding of the constraining force of "discourse" by demonstrating the political and social complexity of "discourse," even of official "discourse." That "discourse," they argue, spoken by those not at the center of power (women in Utica or Rouen, for example), will mean something quite different, socially and politically, because it is spoken by those women rather than by men at the center of power. Ryan's and Smith's studies lay the groundwork for further collaboration.

By positing "language" (and, by extension, class) as the product of an unstable balance between the forces of cohesion and of diversity, Bakhtin may have suggested a next step for our analysis both of "discourse" as a social construction and of the interaction of class and gender. Bourgeois women have always participated in both the unitary and the disruptive aspects of "language" and of "discourse"—in "discourse" as Foucault thought of it, and "discourse" as Ryan and Smith describe it. By carefully tracing women's contributions to each, we may expand our understanding of the complexity of "discourse" and "language" as actors/reactors to social event, and of the role gender plays in class identity formation.

I will now analyze one particular form of nineteenth-century women's writing: bourgeois women's discussion of prostitution, a frequent subject matter in women's writings during the first half of the century. I will argue that it is an example of a female social dialect which, while coexisting with the "unitary language" or ideology, actually worked against that ideology.

. . .

One spring evening in May 1834, a small group of women met at the revivalistic Third Presbyterian Church in New York City to found the New York Female Moral Reform Society. The Society's goals were militantly ambitious: first, to attack urban prostitution and to close the city's brothels; second, to confront the double standard and the male sexual license it condoned.

. . .

Militant in their goals, the Society's members were equally unorthodox in their behaviour. They stationed themselves outside the brothels, carefully recording the names and descriptions of the men who entered, or they marched in, exhorting inmates and clients to reform. Even more aggressively, the Society's first annual report startled respectable New York by asserting that 10,000 prostitutes plied New York City's streets and claimed among their clientele not only the transient and the uncouth but the rich and the respectable.

Who were these women who so defied bourgeois proprieties?

. . .

The members and officers of the American Female Moral Reform Society talked with each other and to the world through the medium of their bimonthly religio-reform magazine; the *Advocate of Moral Reform*. This magazine merged epistolary style and melodrama to create a uniquely American and female composite. What do I mean by epistolary style? The format of the *Advocate's* pages differed significantly from that of contemporary male religious journals (the *New York Evangelist*, for example). Sermons and authoritative articles were largely replaced by letters. Letters from rank-and-file members covered almost all but the front page of the magazine. The reports of auxiliaries frequently took the form of letters to their "sisters," and the Society's editorials that of answering the letters of members and auxiliaries.[13]

All these letters, reports, and editorials endlessly addressed one issue: the origins of urban prostitution. Their answer took the form of a sexual melodrama. They told a tale of invasion, betrayal, and abandonment. Three archetypal figures of strikingly different character and demeanor played the leads: the innocent and vulnerable young woman; the sophisticated and powerful man; the virtuous and religious mother. Fathers and brothers played virtually no role in this melodrama, which focused on a female family of mothers and daughters, a family that was two-generational, uterine, and rural.

The Female Moral Reform Society's melodrama opened with the family farm, a world of mothers, daughters, and sisters. Devoid of crass commercial values and devoted to traditional, preindustrial ways, the farm and its female family were places of relative sexual safety. Yet they contained a problematic figure, the adolescent daughter. She would prove to be the vulnerable member of an endangered family. At first that might seem odd. The women always described the daughter as "innocent," "obedient," "meek," and "gentle." She was a "delicate flower," a "plant" rooted in the country. In true melodramatic fashion, however, she harbored a secret, one that would weaken and ultimately destroy the female family. She was "susceptible" to "enticements," "a very easy prey" to the seductions of men and the blandishments of the city.[14]

Sex differentiated women and men socially as absolutely as it did physically. A source of power and pleasure to men, it brought only misery and desolation to the young woman. Sexual activity, the women contended, made women mere "merchandise," little valued in a crowded market, dependent on the whim of men with money. For the Society's members, prostitution was synonomous with destitution and isolation. If "virtue ... be lost," one member lamented, "oh, what a poor, forlorn, withered, wretched creature you become! Abandoned by your seducer, rejected from your place, disowned by your friends. . . ."[15]

In contrast to the impoverished and abandoned prostitute, the ruthless and sexual man appeared in this script as socially respectable and economically powerful.

. . .

Such male aggression and female vulnerability were new and unexpected. At earlier times, the arm of a male protector and the self-control of the honorable man had stretched over the home and its women. Now this arm, the Society reported, "had been shorn of its strength." Men, who had been women's protectors, had become their assailants. The young woman was suddenly exposed and endangered.

. . .

The female life cycle, as portrayed in the pages of the *Advocate*, took place within two families—the family of origin and the reproductive family. Ideally, the adolescent woman moved from one to the other. Illicit sex, defined as sex outside the family, removed her from both families. It cast her into a familyless world, into the city, onto the streets.

The system that transformed the seduced woman into a familial outcast was the double standard, a system of family organization that imposed a highly restrictive sexual regimen on bourgeois women. The double standard, enforced by British common-law rulings respecting divorce, required women to confine their sexuality within the narrow boundaries of their reproductive family. It permitted men to escape those restrictions. Man's sexuality could thrive within and without the family. He could even invade the family and carry off the innocent daughter—all without social penalties. Women's sexuality was controlled, men's uncontrolled and unbounded. To live beyond boundaries gave man power; it destroyed woman. Outside family boundaries, woman had no legitimate sphere.

· · ·

Boundaries divide the insider from the outcast. The roles of insider (or inmate?) and of outcast were critically important to these middle-class women. They challenged traditional male definitions for the sexual woman as familial outcast, and in this way they challenged the more fundamental male prerogative of naming and defining. Men, they pointed out, by defining the outcast, had been able to set the rules and establish the boundaries of the family. By superimposing a female single moral standard upon the male double sexual standard, the Female Moral Reform Society's women asserted their own right to define the rules of family membership and assert female power over the family.

To define the sexually promiscuous male as the outcast became an essential act in this Jacksonian war between the sexes. Through their organization of thousands of women, they sought to assert real social power and literally to ostracize sexually aggressive men. If female sexuality must be confined to the reproductive family, the male sexual athlete must be excluded from it. All members of the Female Moral Reform Society pledged to bar the known or suspected seducer from their own family circles and their genteel networks. They worked collectively, as well, to pressure merchants to fire clerks accused of seducing young women.

The Society sought to exclude the male seducer on a conceptual and semantic, as well as literal, plane. They defined him as outside of human society. By defying family order, beyond female control, they argued, the seducer had crossed the boundary between the human and the inhuman. From this perspective, the women's extravagant sexual rhetoric assumes social significance. They described him as an "animal," a "wild beast," "a serpent's coil." He was "brutal," a "hideous monster," a "master demon." He existed between states, outside of categories and boundaries. He was alien to woman's world, beyond her control—and dangerous.

· · ·

Two key components of the Victorian double standard—the severity of the restrictions placed upon the sexuality of middle-class women, and the freedom from sexual restraints that it granted middle-class men—expressed, through physiological and sexual rituals, men's demands that women acknowledge men's right to compel social conformity to male laws. The women who challenged those rules faced social ostracism and legal and economic punishment. The Society's demand for a single standard, in contrast, was a demand that men acquiesce to women's rules (or at least to men's rules as women interpreted them). Within the female world of home and family, men must conform to women's power and status within a sphere men had, after all, granted them.

Another way of viewing the conflict over the double standard is to place it in the perspective of class relations. On one very significant level, the debate over the double standard is a debate over who controls the right of sexual access to women: The woman herself? Older women? Older men? Men or women of the same or of a superior class? If the attack upon the double standard is carried on by young women in the name of sexual autonomy, then the entire social hierarchy, that is, men's sexual and economic hegemony, is challenged. These young women would be asserting the rights of women over men, of youth over age and status, of the individual over social and familial demands. If the challenge is brought not by young women in their own name but by older women, then a less thorough challenge to the social system is involved. Then mothers battle with fathers for the control of daughters. The idea of a hierarchy of age, and the subordination of the individual to the demands of family and community, are reinforced. Rules of sexual restraint and purity are not questioned. This battle is not about ultimate social power, but, more narrowly, about who should rule at home.

It is highly significant that the Society depicted the prostitute—and hence the poor farming women, the seamstresses, and the domestic servants whom the prostitute symbolically represented—as daughters, not as sisters. The category sister implies equality, an absolute identification. Daughter implies a hierarchy of power, the right of mothers to criticize and restrain, and of bourgeois women to control the sexual and nonsexual behavior of working-class women. Middle-class matrons identified sufficiently with both the prostitute and the working-class woman to adopt her sexual and economic exploitation as an expression of their own sense of powerlessness in the new commercial system and in relation to the men of their same class. But, they did not take the further and more radical step of transforming their criticism of man's power to exploit women sexually and economically into a fundamental critique of class relations. They strove instead to teach both the prostitute and the working-class woman a sexual language and etiquette adapted to the social and psychological needs of middle-class women. What is truly remarkable is that their educational efforts among the working classes proved as successful as they did.

. . .

For a few brief years, it looked as if bourgeois women had a chance of substituting women's stories for men's in the official ideology of their class. By the late 1840s, however, they had lost their battle for both words and power. Male middle-class economic and ideological hegemony had coalesced. White middle-class women themselves had become more firmly established within the new systems of class power. The old moments of dislocation and of religious disorder (empowering moments for the marginal and powerless) were forgotten or, in fact, were never known by the daughters of the Female Moral Reform Society members. Bourgeois matrons increasingly spoke with male-defined words. But still the match between female and male words never became exact.

Notes

1. Nancy Partner, unpublished paper presented at the 1984 American Historical Association Convention, Chicago.

2. Hayden White, *Metahistory* (Baltimore: Johns Hopkins University Press, 1973) and *Tropics of Discourse* (Baltimore: Johns Hopkins University Press, 1978).

3. See Blumin's discussion of the controversy surrounding definitions of *class* in his "The Hypothesis of Middle-Class Formation in Nineteenth-Century America: A Critique and Some Proposals," *American Historical Review*, 90 (1985): 299–338.

4. Anthony Giddens, *The Class Structure of the Advanced Societies* (New York, 1975), p. 132 and especially pp. 177–97, as cited by Blumin in "The Hypothesis of Middle-Class Formation," p. 307.

5. Roland Barthes, *Mythologies*, trans. Annette Lavers (New York: Hill and Wang, 1972), pp. 137–44. For the pathbreaking and definitive analysis of the Cult of True Womanhood, see Barbara Welter, "The Cult of True Womanhood, 1820–1860," *American Quarterly* (Summer 1966): 151–74.

6. Michel Foucault, *Les Mots et les choses* (Paris: Gallimard, 1966), trans. as *The Order of Things* (New York: Pantheon, 1971). See as well Foucault, *Archeology of Knowledge*, trans. A. M. Sheridan Smith (New York: Pantheon, 1972).

7. Carroll Smith-Rosenberg, *Disorderly Conduct* (New York: Knopf, 1985), chap. 1, "Hearing Women's Words."

8. M. M. Bakhtin, *The Dialogic Imagination: Four Essays*, ed. Michael Holquist (Austin: University of Texas Press, 1981), p. xix; see also "Discourse in the Novel," pp. 259–422.

9. Michel Foucault, *Madness and Civilization* (New York: Pantheon, 1973).

10. Jacques Donzelot, *Policing the Family* (New York: Pantheon, 1979).

11. Bonnie Smith, *The Ladies of the Leisure Class* (Princeton: Princeton University Press, 1981).

12. Mary Ryan, *Cradle of the Middle Class* (New York: Cambridge University Press, 1981), especially chaps. 2 and 3.

13. The most extensive holdings of the *Advocate* can be found at the American Antiquarian Society, Worcester, Massachusetts, and at the New York Historical Society, New York City. I am indebted to the staffs of both institutions. I am indebted, as well, to Maureen Quilligan for pointing out to me the significance of the *Advocate*'s epistolary form.

14. *Advocate*, 1835–37, passim.

15. *Advocate*, vol. 1, p. 15.

20 The Doxa of Difference

Rita Felski

· · ·

EMBLAZONED on book covers, routinely invoked in intellectual debates, "difference" functions as an unassailable value in itself, seemingly irrespective of its referent or context. Difference has become doxa, a magic word of theory and politics radiant with redemptive meanings.

Feminism has its own distinctive version of this story of the triumph of difference over identity. The origins of feminist thought are usually attributed to such figures as Mary Wollstonecraft, who drew on Enlightenment ideals to protest against the subordination of women. Yet such ideals, it soon transpired, were not congenial friends of feminism but merely masks for a phallocentric logic based on the tyranny of identity. Second-wave feminists sought instead to reclaim the feminine; women's liberation lay in the affirmation of their irreducible difference rather than in the pursuit of an illusory goal of equality. This gynocentric ideal in turn has lost much of its power, thanks to the ascent of poststructuralism as well as to extensive criticisms of its political exclusions and biases. As a result, we are now in a postmodern condition, where female difference has fragmented into multiple differences and any appeal to general ideals or norms can only be considered politically questionable and theoretically naive.

This story has been told on numerous occasions and in various registers. For some it is a narrative of progress, as feminism sheds its essentialisms and universalisms to achieve a more sophisticated stage of theoretical consciousness. For others it is a narrative of the fall, as feminism is lured from its true goals by internecine squabbles and the spurious prestige of French avant-garde thought. Many feminist scholars are familiar with this story; we may encounter it in scholarly articles, reproduce it in our classes, repeat it in our own academic writing. Indeed, it undoubtedly contains a grain of truth, at least as a description of the recent trajectory of mainstream feminist theory in the humanities. I want, however, to dislodge at least partially this narrative of feminism's evolution from identity to difference. Its unidirectional structure obscures the actual simultaneity and interdependence of different feminist positions. Like all metanarratives, furthermore, it confuses the internal logic of a particular set of theoretical debates with the condition of the world as a whole. In other words, the political interests and needs of the world's women do not necessarily move in step with the various phases of academic feminist theory.

· · ·

From Rita Felski "The Doxa of Difference," *Signs: Journal of Women in Culture and Society*, 23: 1 (1997), 1–21. © 1997 University of Chicago.

Relatively little attention has been paid to a systematic examination of the theoretical inconsistencies as well as political problems evident in appeals to difference within feminist thought. Indeed, for the most part, the conceptual primacy of difference remains uncontested. While particular notions of difference may be subject to criticism for reproducing an androcentric or imperialist conception of the Other, this critique assumes, if only tacitly, the existence of a "real," more authentic difference existing beyond the deceptive snares of the oppressor's language. One of the aims of this article is to question such visions of alterity as the ultimate truth of feminist theory and politics. My aim is not to polemicize against difference but, rather, to deontologize it by offering a redescription of the status of equality and difference that is framed in prag-matic rather than metaphysical terms. However, I am less interested in arguing that these terms constitute distinct if equally valid choices for feminists (Snitow 1990) than in showing that they exist in a condition of necessary philosophical and political inter-dependence, such that the very pursuit of difference returns one, inexorably, to the seemingly obsolete issue of equality.[1]

. . .

Difference as Dissension: Postcolonial Feminism

Sexual difference feminism results in an impasse. Either feminine difference is given a substantive definition and is thereby subject to charges of essentialism, or it is feted as an asocial principle of alterity and is thereby robbed of any meaningful political con-tent, resulting in the creation of what Laura Donaldson dubs "The Woman without Qualities" (1992: 126). At this point I would like to turn to a discussion of feminist perspectives within postcolonial theory in order to consider some alternative imagin-ings of difference.

Postcolonial feminism is a contested term that would not be unequivocally endorsed by all the writers I discuss. I understand *postcolonial* as designating the historical condi-tion of countries recently liberated from colonial rule, and *postcolonial theory* as addressing the complex dynamics of cultural formation and interchange in such geo-political contexts. Even within these parameters, however, the term has been criticized for homogenizing fundamental differences between national cultures (e.g., India and Australia), for glossing over racial differences and hierarchies within these cultures (Australia may be postcolonial to white settlers, but not to indigenous peoples), and for implying a clear-cut historical transition to a postcolonial condition that ignores ongoing Western influences in the cultural and economic, if not political, realms (Frankenberg and Mani 1993; McClintock 1994). Furthermore, the increasing visibility of postcolonial studies as an academic field has engendered suspicion about the ease with which displays of alterity can be commodified and neutralized with Western institutions (Spivak 1989; Chow 1993). Clearly, *postcolonial* does not function as a neu-tral label for an already existing field but actively demarcates particular processes of inclusion and exclusion.

Like any contested term, then, it can only serve as a starting point, rather than an end point, for inquiry and needs to be combined with conjunctural analyses of specific historical and geopolitical contexts (Frankenberg and Mani 1993). My concern in this article, however, is less with the ultimate value of *postcolonial* as a description of empirical historical realities than with elucidating the ways in which debates within postcolonial feminism help to crystallize the conceptual and political ambiguities of difference. While these discourses are necessarily heterogeneous, they are nevertheless characterized by certain family resemblances and recurring argumentative moves.

One of these moves involves an intensification and further fragmentation of the concept of difference. Criticizing the homogeneous view of the third world woman propagated by Western feminism, postcolonial feminists affirm the irreducible particularity and complex diversities characterizing the lives of non-Western women. For example, Chandra Mohanty's influential article "Under Western Eyes" (1984) critically examines the intersection of feminist theories of women's oppression with a Euro-American conception of the third world to produce the composite image of the "Third World Woman." This woman is depicted as sexually repressed, tradition bound, and uneducated, in explicit contrast to the educated, modern, autonomous, first world feminist. The third world woman is thus appropriated by Western feminism as ultimate proof of the universality of patriarchy and female bondage. She is depicted as both same, part of a putative global sisterhood, and yet mysteriously other, an allegory of enigmatic yet undifferentiated cultural alterity.

Against such an ethnocentric perspective, Mohanty argues for context-specific, differentiated analyses of the ways in which women are produced as a sociopolitical group within particular historical and cultural locations. Such analyses of the complicated intersections of gender with ethnicity, class, religion, and numerous other determinants inevitably undermine an established Western feminist narrative of male power and female powerlessness. In this sense, postcolonial feminist theory articulates a difference from dominant Western feminist conceptions of difference by complicating and further fragmenting the notion of alterity.

Mohanty's emphasis on the specific and the local, as opposed to the homogeneous and the systematizing, seems to indicate skepticism regarding the claims of large-scale social theory. In another context, however, Mohanty insists on the need for a broader perspective on the internationalization of economies and labor forces, emphasizing the value of cross-national and cross-cultural analyses as a way of conceptualizing the systematic socioeconomic and ideological processes within which women of the third world are enmeshed (1991: 2). Here she seeks to retain the category of the "Third World Woman" as a way of demarcating possibilities of political coalition among diversely positioned women through the creation of "imagined communities." Thus the emphasis on particularity is modified by a recognition of the value of systematic analyses of global disparities. In a similar vein, Gayatri Spivak warns of the limitations of microanalyses that remain oblivious to "the broader narratives of imperialism" (1988: 291), and Rey Chow questions the current fetish for cultural/local/ethnic difference as a preordained fact, given that difference cannot be separated from, but is fundamentally related to, the broader structures of communication and domination within which it occurs (1993: 47; see also Trinh 1989).

This suspicion of the Western feminist politics of difference is expressed with particular force and clarity in a recent article by Ien Ang. "As a woman of Chinese descent," Ang writes, "I suddenly find myself in a position in which I can turn my 'difference' into intellectual and political capital, where 'white' feminists invite me to raise my 'voice,' *qua* a nonwhite woman, and make myself heard" (1995: 57). The politics of assimilation, Ang notes, has given way to that of multiculturalism. Yet this seemingly benevolent attentiveness to multiple voices reinforces fundamental hierarchies between women, as feminist discourse reproduces the logic of Western imperialism in its unthinking appropriation of the difference of the other. "Difference is 'dealt with' by absorbing it into an already existing feminist community without challenging the naturalised legitimacy and status of that community *as* a community" (60).

Ang thus complicates an idealized vision of multiple differences by drawing attention to the real, often profound gulf that separates women. This is, in her phrase, "the tension between difference as benign diversity and difference as conflict, disruption, dissension" (68). While the appeal to a common female identity is increasingly untenable within feminism, the turn toward a politics of diversity is an inadequate alternative if it ignores systematic inequalities among women in access to power, knowledge, and material resources. For Ang, such inequalities are fundamentally connected to the structural insurmountability of white, Western hegemony, which she defines as "the systemic consequence of a global historical development over the last 500 years—the expansion of European capitalist modernity throughout the world, resulting in the subsumption of all 'other' peoples to its economic, political and ideological logic and mode of operation" (65).

. . .

In this respect, the field of postcolonial feminism is marked by an ongoing tension between the particular and the universal, between the "thick description" of specific cultural practices and the macrosystemic analysis of transnational structures of inequality. While "local" and "global" may in fact constitute permeable and unstable markers for cultural modalities that thoroughly infiltrate each other (Grewal and Kaplan 1994: 11), there are nevertheless significant differences of emphasis in the work of individual writers. In general, however, postcolonial feminist work is characterized by a refusal to isolate gender from multiple other determinants, including those of race and class, and by a typical (although by no means universal) emphasis on material and institutional, rather than purely linguistic, structures of power (Mohanty 1991).

At the same time, this commitment to the analysis of material inequalities is often combined with a deconstructive critique of identity. Against nativist visions of autonomous racial or cultural difference, postcolonial theorists are likely to note that such distinctions are no longer feasible in an era of pervasive migration, media globalization, and transnational information flow. The colonized's fashioning of an insurgent counteridentity is inevitably shaped by the experience of colonization; the colonizer's culture is irrevocably altered by contact with the native. As a result, a conception of distinct, singular, internally homogeneous groupings gives way to a model of *métissage*, of borrowing and lending across porous cultural boundaries.

Such concepts as hybridity, creolization, and *métissage*, while not uncontested within postcolonial studies, strike me as offering the most viable alternative to the current doxa of difference. I have no particular investment in the word *hybrid* as such. As Robert Young (1995) notes, the term may indeed be compromised by its connections to the discourses of nineteenth-century racist genetics and the assumptions of compulsory heterosexuality. Yet, as Young also acknowledges, the power and value of the term lies in its encapsulation of the logic of both/and. "Hybridity thus makes difference into sameness, and sameness into difference, but in a way that makes the same no longer the same, the different no longer simply different," thereby engendering "difference and sameness in an apparently impossible simultaneity" (26).

Such a reformulation strikes me as a crucial paradigm shift. Metaphors of hybridity and the like not only recognize differences within the subject, fracturing and complicating holistic notions of identity, but also address connections between subjects by recognizing affiliations, cross-pollinations, echoes, and repetitions, thereby unseating difference from a position of absolute privilege. Instead of endorsing a drift toward an ever greater atomization of identity, such metaphors allow us to conceive of multiple, interconnecting axes of affiliation and differentiation. Affiliation, I would stress, does not preclude disagreement but, rather, provides its necessary precondition; it is only in the context of shared premises, beliefs, and vocabularies that dissent becomes possible.

For this reason, while I am sympathetic to much of Ang's argument, I am not fully persuaded by her recourse to the idea of incommensurability to describe the relations between women of different races. This claim arises out of Ang's discussion of competing readings of Madonna as symptomatic of the racial gulf within feminism. While most white feminists, according to Ang, have celebrated Madonna as a symbol of resistive postmodern femininity, black critics such as bell hooks are critical of the racist subtext underpinning such media images of idealized whiteness. Ang comments: "What we see exemplified here is a fundamental *incommensurability* between two competing feminist knowledges, dramatically exposing an irreparable chasm between a white and a black feminist truth. No harmonious compromise or negotiated consensus is possible here" (1995: 64).

Ang's own example, however, surely does not warrant such a strong conclusion. Thus, both black and white feminist readings of Madonna are shaped by overlapping conceptual frameworks and discursive regimes (within which terms such as *identity, the self,* and *oppression* become meaningful and usable), even as they both partake of the distinctive, historically specific "language game" of cultural studies in interpreting a media phenomenon such as Madonna as emblematic of broader social structures and processes. At the same time, their differing political locations result in conflicting interpretations of the resistive potential of this particular cultural icon.[2] The relationship here is surely one of complicated entanglement, overlapping, and disagreement, not a clash of incommensurable discursive universes.

Furthermore, it is precisely this entanglement that makes criticism possible, that allows hooks to point out the contradictions between feminism's claim to represent all women and its actual race blindness, and that enables some white as well as black feminists to explore the racial politics of Madonna (Bordo 1993). Incommensurability, by contrast, does not allow for disagreement, critique, or persuasion because there are no common terms that would allow one argument to latch onto and address another. Furthermore, it is important to realize that the recourse to incommensurability necessarily *works both ways*. It does not simply address the refusal of women of color to have their political concerns subsumed within inappropriate categories but simultaneously legitimates—indeed posits as inevitable—the inaccessibility of such concerns to white women, who are thereby relieved of any need to engage with them. Thus, an actual incommensurability between the positions of white women and women of color would in fact undermine Ang's own argument, making it incomprehensible to those very readers to whom it is ostensibly addressed.

I read Ang's argument as a strategic intervention into a specific debate, a provocation intended to startle white Western feminists out of arrogant assumptions about female commonality beyond racial and cultural difference. While I sympathize with the need for such a provocation, and while I agree that "idealized unity" cannot provide a basis for feminism, the turn toward a model of incommensurability strikes me as counter-productive, as theoretically tenuous and politically defeatist. It is theoretically tenuous because it does not acknowledge actual overlappings of vocabularies, frameworks, and assumptions; it is politically defeatist because it rules out, in advance, the possibility of one discourse acting on and influencing another. Yet how else, one wonders, is politics possible? Of course Ang is right to point out that the vast material and cultural divisions between women cannot be overcome by mere fiat or good intention. Yet her statement, "We might do better to start from point zero and realise that there are moments at which no common ground exists whatsoever, and when any communicative event would be nothing more than a speaking past one another" (1995: 60) seems to offer only the alternative of silence and separatism. It is hard to see how such an a priori conviction of the impossibility of communication can be squared with Ang's own carefully enunciated critique of Western feminism (why bother with such a critique if your audience is incapable of understanding you?) or with the ongoing imperative for political coalitions and alliances among different (unequally) subordinate groups.

At the same time, Ang rightly insists that cultural interchange does not occur on an equal footing, that instances of borrowing and citation are framed by asymmetrical grids of power. In this context, the trope of hybridity has been subject to criticism for effacing material conflicts between the colonizer and the colonized and denying the agency of the oppressed (e.g., Parry 1987). While this criticism may apply to the work of specific writers, it does not, in my view, follow inevitably from its use. To acknowledge the cultural leakages and interconnections between cultures is not necessarily to deny their asymmetrical placement. Neither is it to affirm uncritically a condition of cultural fragmentation and geographical displacement that is often experienced as painful rather than liberating, as has occurred in contemporary celebrations of the nomadic subject. The point is not to idealize and essentialize hybridity as a new source of political value, as a code word for the radically authentic or subversive. It is simply to acknowledge cultural impurity as the inescapable historical backdrop of all contemporary struggles—including those that may invoke politically necessary slogans of tribalism and nativism—in a global culture marked by pervasive and ongoing processes of both voluntary and involuntary cultural interchange.

In other words, the motif of hybridity disrupts the frequent association of political struggle with an assumed need for cultural authenticity free of any taint of the oppressor's culture. Thus, recent postcolonial theory has often stressed the politics of translation, as exemplified in the cultural and temporal specificity of enunciative acts. Rather than demarcate certain concepts (e.g. modernity, equality, technology, the human) as intrinsically "Western" and thus forever tied to the enforcement of an imperialist agenda, recent postcolonial theory has been attentive to the diverse appropriations and rearticulations of such vocabularies across various global sites. The complex intermin-glings of indigenous traditions and external influences are such that discourses once linked to the colonizer may acquire very different meanings when adopted by the colonized to challenge their own condition. Such a pragmatic concern with the utility of discourse rather than its ontological purity strikes me as a more viable—and more hopeful—basis for politics.

Rethinking Difference

In the final section of my article I elaborate the contradictory and impure status of difference as a philosophical category, its necessary imbrication with the very norms and ideals it seeks to negate. I will begin by noting that the common opposition between equality and difference within feminist thought is in fact a false antithesis (Scott 1988). The opposite of equality is not difference but, rather, inequality, a principle to which presumably no feminist would subscribe. Similarly, the antonym of difference is not equality but identity. Thus a difference-based feminism refuses a logic of identity that would subsume women within male-defined norms. It does not, however, reject equality but, rather, argues for an expanded understanding of equality that can simultaneously respect difference. Cornell helpfully refers us to Amartya Sen's notion of equivalence as a way of conceptualizing this vision of "equal differences": "'Equivalence' means of equal value, but not of equal value *because of likeness*" (Cornell 1993: 141).

. . .

It might be objected at this point that my argument continues to reproduce rather than to overturn traditional philosophical oppositions such as difference/identity and universality/particularity. While this reproach is routinely deployed in contemporary theory as a way of disarming one's opponents, its logic is often specious. Specifically, it is frequently based on a misunderstanding of deconstruction (which recognizes by contrast that dualisms cannot be overcome, but at best displaced),[3] as well as on a received reading (or as Gasché would say, misreading) of Hegel, whereby dialectical opposition is seen as a tyrannical logic leading to an inevitable subsumption of differ-ence by identity.

Yet feminist attempts to overcome philosophical dualism, most evident in the work of sexual difference theory, have been spectacularly unsuccessful. They result either in a regression to a reductive monism (the isolation of difference as a foundational cat-egory) or to a reproduction of the same dualism at a more abstract level (the male/female opposition is negated only to be reinstated as a division between phallocentrism and feminine difference). The problem for feminism, I suggest, is less that of dualism per se than of the ways in which particular oppositions have been reified as invariably and ontologically gendered. This problem can be addressed not by reiterating the same oppositions at a more abstract level but, rather, by questioning such a gendering of conceptual oppositions and simultaneously destabilizing them to show their necessary interdependence (recall Young's reference to making difference into sameness and sameness into difference, thereby engendering "difference and sameness in an apparently impossible simultaneity").

In other words, it is surely possible to conceptualize dualistic distinctions in terms of an ongoing oscillation and productive conflict between distinct terms that is not resolved through a Hegelian synthesis. I have sought to discuss the equality/difference distinction in such a light, as a way of demonstrating the necessary interdependence and complex slippage between these terms. Furthermore, I have questioned the assumption that the subject of feminism can be tied to either side of this dialectic by suggesting that particular groups within feminism may ally themselves contingently, variously, and indeed simultaneously to different sides of the equality/difference divide.

Thus, a double strategy comes into play: a *deconstructive* reading of the equality/difference distinction as philosophically unstable and internally independent needs to be combined with a *pragmatic* analysis of the contingent political utility adhering to either side of this dialectic for specific groups of women. For example, some reasons for the current feminist focus on difference might include the unprecedented move of women into traditionally male institutional structures, with a consequent collision of vocabularies, experiences, and forms of life; the impact of poststructuralism on intellectual work in the humanities; and the sustained critique of the exclusionary biases of Western feminism. At the same time, the status of difference as a grounding category for feminism remains radically contested. Many women are unlikely to dismiss equality whether legal, educational, or economic—as passé, as mere male-defined reformism, given the continuing and vast disparities in the global distribution of power and resources. As Chow noted the recent feminist affirmation of female autonomy and its subversive power derives from the specific material and ideological conditions linked to both the achievements and privileges of Western feminism and cannot be carelessly generalized (1993: 66). The status of difference is differentially articulated, just as the political meanings accruing to the struggle for equality are not always equal.

In this context, I conclude by noting that the categories often invoked disparagingly by feminist theorists—equality, reason, history, modernity—are not stable, uniform entities but are reproduced and changed by the specific context of their articulation. It is here that much of feminist philosophy, with its sweeping vision of the *longue durée* of Western history as a history of pathological phallocentrism, reveals its limitations. For example, recent rereadings of modernity have pointed to its internal complexities and uneven temporalities, arguing that white women and people of color have not been outside of the modern, but have been shaped by, and in turn variously have shaped, its political, cultural, and philosophical meanings (Gilroy 1993; Felski 1995). Rather than endorse a metaphysical vision of woman as invariably and eternally other, feminism can more usefully conceptualize the position of women in terms of a difference within sameness and a sameness within difference, a form of *interference* with the purity of such categories that is variously and contingently actualized. Such a perspective remains more open to the multiple and mutable concerns of feminism than does the appeal to incommensurability and otherness, an otherness that necessarily leaves the realm of the same untouched.

Notes

1. Some useful general critiques of the idealization of difference include McGowan 1991; Gasché 1994; Taylor et al. 1994. Helpful feminist discussions include Sypnowich 1993; Collin 1994; Young 1995.
2. I remain unconvinced, furthermore, that race is necessarily the primary or most salient issue in disagreements over Madonna, which are also heavily shaped by generational and disciplinary divisions. While cultural studies has enabled numerous feminist readings of Madonna as sublime parodist, white feminists in other disciplines, and particularly those still affiliated with the movement feminism of the 1970s, are often very critical of Madonna, whom they perceive as buying into, rather than subverting, patriarchal notions of feminine beauty.
3. One might express this recognition by noting that any argument that claims to overcome binary oppositions inevitably sets up a new opposition between binary and nonbinary thought.

References

Ang, Ien (1995). "I'm a Feminist but . . . 'Other' Women and Postnational Feminism," in Barbara Caine and Rosemary Pringle (eds.), *Transitions: New Australian Feminisms*. New York: St. Martin's, 57–73.

Bordo, Susan (1993). *Unbearable Weight: Feminism, Western Culture and the Body*. Berkeley and Los Angeles: University of California Press.

Chow, Rey (1993). *Writing Diaspora: Tactics of Intervention in Contemporary Cultural Studies*. Bloomington: Indiana University Press.

Collin, Françoise (1994). "Plurality, Difference, Identity." *Woman: A Cultural Review*, 5 (1): 13–24.

Cornell, Drucilla (1991). *Beyond Accommodation: Ethical Feminism, Deconstruction and the Law*. New York: Routledge.

—— (1993). *Transformations*. New York: Routledge.

—— (1995). "What is Ethical Feminism?", in Seyla Benhabib, Judith Butler, Drucilla Cornell, and Nancy Fraser, *Feminist Contentions: A Philosophical Exchange*. New York: Routledge, 75–106.

Donaldson, Laura (1992). *Decolonizing Feminisms: Race, Gender and Empire-Building*. Chapel Hill: University of North Carolina Press.

Felski, Rita (1995). *The Gender of Modernity*. Cambridge, Mass.: Harvard University Press.

Frankenberg, Ruth, and Mani, Lata (1993). "Crosscurrents, Crosstalk: Race, 'Post-coloniality' and the Politics of Location." *Cultural Studies*, 7(2): 292–310.

Gasché, Rodolphe (1994). *Inventions of Difference: On Jacques Derrida*. Cambridge, Mass.: Harvard University Press.

Gilroy, Paul (1993). *The Black Atlantic: Modernity and Double Consciousness*. Cambridge, Mass.: Harvard University Press.

Grewal, Inderpal, and Kaplan, Caren (1994). "Introduction: Transnational Feminist Practices and Questions of Postmodernity," in Inderpal Grewal and Caren Kaplan (eds.), *Scattered Hegemonies: Postmodernity and Transnational Feminist Practices*. Minneapolis: University of Minnesota Press, 1–33.

McClintock, Anne (1994). "The Angel of Progress: Pitfalls of the Term 'Post-Colonialism,'" in Patrick Williams and Laura Chrisman (eds.), *Colonial Discourse and Post-Colonial Theory*. New York: Columbia University Press, 291–304.

McGowan, John (1991). *Postmodernism and Its Critics*, Ithaca, NY: Cornell University Press.

Mohanty, Chandra Talpade (1984). "Under Western Eyes: Feminist Scholarship and Colonial Discourse." *boundary 2*, 13(1): 333–57.

—— (1991). "Cartographies of Struggle: Third World Women and the Politics of Feminism," in Chandra Talpade Mohanty, Ann Russo, and Lourdes Torres (eds.), *Third World Women and the Politics of Feminism*. Bloomington: Indiana University Press, 1–47.

Parry, Benita (1987). "Problems in Current Theories of Colonial Discourse." *Oxford Literary Review*, 9(1): 27–58.

Scott, Joan (1988). "Deconstructing Equality-versus-Difference: Or the Uses of Poststructuralist Theory for Feminism." *Feminist Studies*, 14(1): 33–50.

Snitow, Ann (1990). "A Gender Diary," in Marianne Hirsch and Evelyn Fox Keller (eds.), *Conflicts in Feminism*. New York: Routledge, 9–43.

Spivak, Gayatri Chakravorty (1988). "Can the Subaltern Speak?" in Cary Nelson and Lawrence Grossberg (eds.), *Marxism and the Interpretation of Culture*. Urbana: University of Illinois Press, 271–313.

—— (1989). "Who Claims Alterity?" in Barbara Kruger and Phil Mariani (eds.), *Remaking History*. Seattle: Bay, 269–92.

Sypnowich, Christine (1993). "Some Disquiet about 'Difference.'" *Praxis International*, 13(2): 99–112.

Taylor, Charles, Appiah, K. Anthony, Habermas, Jürgen, Rockefeller, Steven C., Walzer, Michael, and Wolf, Susan (1994). *Multiculturalism*. Princeton University Press.

Trinh, Minh-ha (1989). *Woman, Native, Other: Writing Postcoloniality and Feminism*. Bloomington: Indiana University Press.

Young, Iris Marion (1995). "Together in Difference: Transforming the Logic of Group Political Conflict," in Will Kymlicka (ed.), *The Rights of Minority Cultures*. Oxford: Oxford University Press, 155–76.

Young, Robert (1995). *Colonial Desire: Hybridity in Theory, Culture and Race*. London: Routledge.

21 What's in a Name? Presidential Address to the American Studies Association

Janice Radway

. . .

Tᴵᴹᴱ will not permit a full-scale intellectual history of American studies radical traditions nor even of the field's now extensive engagement with the question of difference. In fact virtually every recent president of this association has recounted some aspect of this history. I only want to note here that some of the earliest scholarship on questions of gender, race, ethnicity, and class, and to a certain extent on sexuality, *did* find a hospitable space within American studies, a place where the challenges this work posed to familiar canons and dominant traditions could be formally delivered. Indeed, many scholars working on these questions presented their work at previous American studies conferences. They were able to do so because committed individuals connected with the association have always worked diligently to open the conference proceedings, the organization itself, and the pages of the journal to new modes of thought.

Although the resulting work has varied widely and was differently inflected in order to advance diverse agendas, it seems clear to me that its collective force challenged the earlier consensus view, the notion that the American democratic idea uniformly included within its purview all those who inhabited the United States. By noting the ways in which certain populations were not only *excluded* from the so-called American experiment but also *included* within other communities defined not by national belonging but by gender, race, class, or ethnic affiliation, this scholarship early on centered upon questions of subjectivity—in the parlance of the time, on questions of identity.

The term "identity politics" of course has a complex history, and it has been used both approvingly to delineate various forms of political opposition to an unexamined nationalism and disparagingly as an epithet aimed at questioning the value of so-called "minority" identifications. Within American studies, it seems to me, the causes of identity politics have generally been taken very seriously. Scholars within the field have conscientiously attempted to respond to demands that they examine something more than the activities of educated, middle-class, straight, white men. Important work has been done as a result. In the past, however, these forms of non-national identification sometimes were essentialized and rendered as secondary qualifications to others deemed overarching or primary. What this often amounted to was an additive

From Janice Radway, "What's in a Name? Presidential Address to the American Studies Association, 20 November 1998," *American Quarterly*, 51: 1 (1999), 8–18, 23–24. © The American Studies Association. Reprinted by permission of the Johns Hopkins University Press.

intellectual politics, a politics of inclusion, a move that left intact the assumed privilege of territorial paradigms and the priority of the nationalist community. So-called "minority" identities and projects were construed as having come, not from the core or center, but from the periphery. Since difference thus conceived was assumed to be divisive, a constant reiteration of the need to seek common ground developed in response. American studies was concomitantly envisioned as a more capacious umbrella containing more multitudes than it had been able to encompass before. I take this idea of America as "a stable container of social antagonisms" to be the subject of Nikhil Pal Singh's bracing critique, published in *American Quarterly*, of both past and recent defenses of American liberalism which have sought to justify the idea of common ground against the supposedly divisive claims of multicultural difference.

The liberal solution to the question of difference has increasingly been made untenable, however, by new work on race especially, but also by work on sexuality, ethnicity, gender, and class. Much of this work has made a critical theoretical break with earlier formulations of identity. Sometimes (but not always) informed by post-structuralist understandings of the ways in which subjectivities are constructed, this work has detached the question of difference from various bodily, cultural, and geographic essentialisms and has begun to explore the complex, intersecting ways in which people are embedded within multiple, conflicted discourses, practices, and institutions. Within American studies, this break appeared particularly acute when work on difference explicitly began to engage the question of how American nationalism was actively constructed at specific moments, at specific sites, and through specific practices.

I am thinking here of work like that done by Amy Kaplan, by Lauren Berlant, Lisa Lowe, George Sanchez, Hazel Carby, Wahneema Lubiano, Vicki Ruiz, Eric Sundquist, David Roediger, Carolyn Porter, José Saldívar, Eric Cheyfitz, George Lipsitz, Robyn Weigman, Lisa Duggan, Betsy Erkkila, Gary Okihiro, Robin Kelley, Nancy Hewitt, Dana Nelson, Chandra Mohanty, George Chauncey, and so many others. Although this work is not uniform and is, in fact, animated by quite different theoretical commitments— indeed some of this work is not explicitly post-structuralist—I do think it collectively poses the question of how American national identity has been produced precisely in opposition to, and therefore in relationship with, that which it excludes or subordinates. This work has begun to show that American nationalism is neither autonomously defined—which is to say, exceptional—nor is it internally homogeneous. Rather, it is relationally defined and historically and situational variable because it is dependent upon and therefore intertwined with those affiliations, identities, and communities it must actively subordinate in order to press the privileged claims of the nation upon individuals and groups.

I believe that this work calls for a new way of formulating the "objects" of American studies. Instead of a form of attention that tends to isolate and reify those things that are the focal point of concern, whether a culture, an event, a political subject, or an institution, this new work demands an attention to relationships of connection and dependence, relationships I like to characterize generally as "intricate interdependencies." I use the term "intricate interdependencies" somewhat loosely here to describe a range of radically intertwined relationships that have been brought to the fore in recent attempts to rethink nationalism, race, culture, ethnicity, identity, sex, and gender. Time won't permit a full discussion of the many kinds of intricate interdependencies that have been explored of late, but I would like to point to two sites where the effort to explore the consequences of imperial power relations has foregrounded the need for relational thinking and highlighted the importance of intertwined, material and conceptual dependencies. This work bears portentous implications for the way American studies might be practiced in the future.

There is a large body of work on the social and cultural formation of the subject which attempts to dislodge the question of identity from its attachment to some form of biology. Indeed this desire sits at the heart of a good deal of feminist work on gender, queer work on sex, and anti-racist work on the category of "race." In the interests of time, I have decided only to say a few things about the work on race here as a way of drawing attention to the larger effort to displace essentially defined bodies for complex social subjects produced at the intersection of a number of discourses, practices, and institutions. Some of the key features of this work can be found, I think, in an essay by Wahneema Lubiano entitled "Like Being Mugged by a Metaphor," as well as by the volume she recently edited, *The House that Race Built*.[1]

Neither Lubiano's essay nor the larger volume itself is designed simply to question race as a function of biology or to argue merely that "race" is a socially constructed category. Rather, they aim to argue more radically that the state and the political economy of the United States are themselves entirely dependent on the internal, imperial racialization of the population. What this means is that the American national subject is produced as white and that the process of production takes place in overdetermined fashion through the knotted, inextricably intertwined relationship between practices of symbolic representation and specific economic, educational, and political policies that simultaneously name and subordinate black populations. As Lubiano puts it,

the constructions of our various beings as a group are both material and cultural. The material and the cultural are neither completely separate nor do they operate autonomously. The idea "Black people" is a social reality. Black people are a dominated group politically and economically, even if every member is not always dominated under all circumstances. (73)

The U.S. is thus utterly dependent on its obsession with "blackness." In fact, that obsession is constitutive of the state and the way it functions on behalf of some. The U.S. is intricately intertwined as a national and state entity with those it must dominate in order to establish, in however illusory a fashion, the conceptual stability of, and material security for, a particular ruling group. George Lipsitz has documented in excruciating detail how this is actually managed in his most recent book, *The Possessive Investment in Whiteness*.[2]

The point I am trying to make here is that American national identity is constructed in and through relations of difference. As a conceptual entity, it is intricately intertwined with certain alterities which diacritically define it as something that is supposedly normative, normal, and central. As a material and social entity, it is brought into being through relations of dominance and oppression, through processes of super- and subordination. To take the measure of this national entity, it is necessary, then, to focus on these constitutive relationships, these intricate interdependencies, which are figured ironically as deep fissures and fractures in the national body. America is not an organically unified, homogeneous thing. Nor should it be isolated for simple veneration, as an object in a museum. This, it seems to me is Wahneema Lubiano's important point when she says that the myth of America must be de-aestheticized.

I should point out here that in this article, Lubiano is also raising troubling questions about the political work of intellectuals and university based scholars. She suggests, in fact, that a conceptual instrument like multiculturalism, which she ultimately supports, might function as just another technology for racializing the world if it is used by intellectuals to construct and study blackness without also tracing out how that blackness is wholly functional for the state. This may also be true of the notion of the "American" in American studies. If intellectual practice in the field does not examine the ways in which the construction of a national subject works to the economic and political advantage of some and precisely against the interests of others, then American studies runs the risk of functioning as just another technology of nationalism, a way of ritually repeating the claims of nationalism by assuming it as an autonomous given inevitably worthy of scholarly study.

There is another large body of work on the social and cultural formation of the subject which extends the critique of an aestheticized America by pursuing another set of intricate interdependencies. This work attempts to dislodge the question of identity from its attachment to essentialized notions of culture and geography. Much of this work has been done as part of the examination of the effects of U.S. imperialism around the globe. Because of limited time, I can only comment briefly on the work that has been done in two areas. I would like to acknowledge the important contributions of Chicana/Chicano studies and point as well to the contributions of recent work on the effects of the U.S. presence in the Pacific Rim, especially in Hawaii, Guam, and the Philippines. The nature of these contributions is laid out with exceptional clarity in two essays in the Kaplan–Pease volume, José Saldívar's "Américo Paredes and Decolonization," and Vicente Diaz's "Pious Sites: Chamorro Culture between Spanish Catholicism and American Liberal Individualism."[3] Both of these essays, it seems to me, strain after a new understanding of the concept of culture by seeking to de-reify it. That is, they abandon the conceptualization of culture as an organic, homogeneous thing which is bound to a fixed territory and attempt to reconceptualize it as the result of complex social processes deeply bound up with the exercise of power at specific, concrete sites.

José Saldívar aims to criticize what he calls the "spatial materialism and the politics of cultural identity" that have grounded traditional American studies. He does so by analyzing the influential and generative work of Américo Paredes, whom he characterizes as a "border intellectual." Noting that the Texas-based Paredes refused to be identified as a Mexican immigrant to the United States, Saldívar suggests that Paredes's "antidisciplinary border project" grew out of his desire to acknowledge the fact of U.S. military aggression against the land of his ancestors. In Saldívar's view, Paredes sought to trace out the ways in which the imposition of an Anglocentric economic and cultural hegemony upon the land appropriated from Mexico failed to produce the desired Americanization of the people living there. In his important book on the corrido, *"With His Pistol in His Hand,"* and in his novel, *George Washington Gómez: A Mexicotexan Novel*, Paredes documented the complex ways in which border dwellers produced their own distinctive world and a point of view that acknowledged that they were neither simply Mexican nor American, nor even some third, homogeneous cultural identity.[4] Rather they were deeply and continuously affected by the clash of cultures at a site characterized by a "serious contest of codes and representations." The point of view that this social situation generated, and which Saldívar characterizes as "inbetween-ness," was not equivalent to the simple physical oscillation between two homogeneous and autonomous cultures. Rather, it generated an ambivalent subject, a subject produced not by the simple contiguity of cultures, but by mutual contestation of social histories and habits—by the interleaving and interweaving of cultural practices—a situation achieved through the complex processes of migration, appropriation, domination, and subordination and by the sense of loss, active remembrance, adaptation and borrowing that they produced.

Culture, in this view, is not something one "has" as the consequence of being situated at a particular geographic location. Rather it is a meaning effect produced by hierarchical relationships established between different spaces and the communities that give them significance. Culture becomes remarkable because a sense of alterity is produced through the social confrontations and interdependencies that result from these interconnections. Hence, for Paredes, as Saldívar suggests, "the consensus rhetoric of American studies with its emphasis upon the motto, 'e pluribus unum' had to be negated and supplemented with a more sophisticated sense of 'culture,' as a site of social struggle" (295). This is as true for culture within the boundaries of the U.S. as it is for culture in the borderlands and beyond. The very notion of "the American" is intricately entwined with those "others" produced internally as different and externally as alien through practices of imperial domination and incorporation.

Like Saldívar and Paredes, Vicente Diaz also seeks to "trouble national and cultural boundaries" by examining the complexities of Chamorro cultural history in Guam. He does so by tracing the successive ways in which local histories and practices in the Marianas were deeply affected by the social transactions promoted by the global economic and political policies of imperial states. Thus, he traces the ways in which Chamorro traditions and self-understandings have been transformed by their encounters with Spanish Catholic and U.S. state imperialism. He does this by disentangling the histories embedded in the architectural melange of the capital city, Agana, and by exploring what he calls "the troubled entanglements among indigenous and exogenous ideas and practices" in two nearly contemporaneous events in 1990, the suicide of former governor, Ricardo Bordallo, and the passage of an anti-abortion law by the Guam legislature. What Diaz is able to show is how both places and events in Guam are deeply affected by cultural histories that are neither finished nor past but actively engaged and demonstrably effective in the present through the persistence of memories, dreams, desires, and even spirits.

Through a careful analysis of the intertwined practices and rhetorics that comprised the suicide and the passage of the abortion law, Diaz demonstrates that in both events, indigenous Chamorro, Spanish Catholic, and American liberal beliefs and practices contest each other in ways that act to blur the distinctions among them. Diaz suggests that Chamorro culture has not simply been superseded by Spanish Catholic culture, nor has the latter been displaced by American liberalism. Rather, the practices and representations of which all three are constituted interweave *and* are transformed as a result. He suggests that, because of this it is essential to see "how Chamorro cultural continuity makes a home within intrusive foreign systems . . . that sought to reconsolidate themselves in imperial and evangelical imperatives among people . . . who also sought to reconsolidate their own notions of self and society" (334). Chamorro, Spanish, and American cultures are thus intricately intertwined and dependent upon each other for their mutual self-definition through confrontation *and* exchange.

The point I am trying to make here in discussing the articles of José Saldívar and Vicente Diaz is that much of the work on borderland culture and on the cultural complexities of the Pacific Rim challenges the idea that culture can be adequately conceived as a unitary, uniform thing, as the simple function of a fixed, isolated, and easily mapped territory. Similarly, they suggest that cultural identity can no longer be conceptualized as a naturalized essence or property that thoroughly saturates an individual because of his or her socialization within a particular locale. Instead, identity must be conceptualized as a specific, always changing relationship to multiple, shifting, imagined communities, communities which, despite the fact that they are always imagined, are situated in specific places at particular moments and amidst particular geographies.

This work does not, therefore, diminish the importance of place or geography in the effort to understand societies and culture. Rather, it demands a reconceptualization of both as socially produced through relations of dependence and mutual implication, through relationships established socially and hierarchically between the near and far, the local and the distant. It suggests that far from being conceived on the model of a container—that is, as a particular kind of hollowed out object with evident edges or skin enclosing certain organically uniform contents—territories and geographies need to be reconceived as spatially-situated and intricately intertwined networks of social relationships that tie specific locales to particular histories. The feminist geographer, Doreen Massey, conceptualizes this interweaving of locale and history as a particular "space," that is, as "the sphere of the meeting-up (or not) of multiple trajectories, the sphere where they coexist, affect each other, maybe come into conflict. It is the sphere both of their independence (or) *co*-existence and of their interrelation." Subjects and objects, she adds, "are constructed through the space of those interrelations . . ."[5]

It seems to me that new work on cultural borderlands and hybridities challenges the claims to intellectual validity of fields that unwittingly continue to perpetuate a set of assumptions criticized recently by Akhil Gupta and James Ferguson, assumptions that bounded territories are naturally *dis*connected, that cultures are isomorphically tied to those spaces, and that identities follow necessarily and unitarily from them.[6] This work suggests instead that territories and geographies need to be understood as always hierarchically interconnected, which is tantamount to saying, in the words of Gupta and Ferguson that "spaces are always related to each other through the social relations that control them."[7] Culture needs to be reconceived as a site of perpetual social struggle, as the location where particular forms of power produce opposition and contestation in the very act of trying to control it. Culture is not a matter of coherence and consensus. Rather, it is the always shifting terrain upon which multiple social groups form, actively solicit the identification of some, hinder that of others, and ignore the counterclaims made by still others. Identity is never unitarily achieved, as a result, not even by the claims of nationalism. As David Lloyd points out, it is a paradox of nationalism that though it may often summon into being a 'people' that is to form and subtend the nation-state, it is always confronted with that people as a potentially disruptive excess over the nation and its state—if nationalism calls forth a people for the nation-state, its mode of subjectification still cannot exhaust the identifications available to the individuals thus summoned.[8]

From this perspective, ethnic, queer, feminist, or working-class identities cannot be conceived as separate essences sheltered within a more capacious, ontologically prior American identity. Rather, they must be seen as cross-cutting, insurgent, oftentimes oppositional identifications. Sometimes those identifications are with sub-national communities; at other times, they are with trans- or international communities. In either case, they pose a profound challenge to the integrity of the very idea of an American whose identity is fully accounted for by residence in the territory of the United States.

What does all this mean for American studies at this particular historical moment? If the notion of a bounded national territory and a concomitant national identity deriving isomorphically from it are called into question, why perpetuate a specifically "American" studies? Has enough work been done at this point to complicate and fracture the very idea of an "American" nation, culture, and subject, such that its continued presence in the name of the field and in that of the association no longer functions as a form of premature closure or as an imperial gesture erasing the claims of others to use of the name? In order to promote work that would further reconceptualize the American as always relationally defined and therefore as intricately dependent upon "others" that are used both materially and conceptually to mark its boundaries, would it make sense to think about renaming the association as an institution devoted to a different form of knowledge production, to alternative epistemologies, to the investigation of a different object?

A name change can seem a superficial gesture, or the disrespectful, willful dismissal of a significant past, or it can function as the signifier of something more positive. It is not clear to me whether changing the name of this association would amount to one or another of these possibilities. Would finding another name for this association do little to alter the parameters of the field and the forms of knowledge-production generated within it? Would it amount only to a dangerous and ill-timed denial of the achievements of a field that many believe has done more to foster diversity in personnel and intellectual point of view than have many other scholarly disciplines? Or, would a name change renew the field by pushing scholars to reconceptualize its proper object of study by asking questions about culture for which they do not already have the answers? I am uncertain about how to respond to these questions in part because every name change I can think of produces as many objections to it as it does potentially positive effects. Although I think that in the end, the name "American studies" will have to be retained, I believe it is worthwhile to open up a speculative discussion of the name for several key reasons.

The activity of exploring potential new names is generative because names are never simply descriptives. They also function as directives and sometimes as promises; as such, they have to be enacted and embodied in constitutive practices; their promise demands to be realized. Thinking of possible ways to rename the field and the association can help to identify new practices that might be taken up by participants as a way to institute the relational perspectives I have been recommending here. The act of trying out new names, it seems to me, can therefore work to suggest how a different relation to the name "American studies" might be taken up or realized by those who are seeking to redefine it. If the study of human social interaction is not to be spatialized and essentialized in isomorphic ways at this historical moment, if the boundaries of the "American" are not to be naturalized or taken for granted or mapped onto the United States alone, how should the parameters of the field be delineated, how should objects of study be constituted?

. . .

I come back, then, to American studies, the field, and to the American Studies Association as an organization with a particular name and a complex history, embedded in the contradictions of a particular historical conjuncture. What is to be done? Is it possible to honor the past and to build on the successes of the field and the association even while mounting a responsible but vigorous critique of past myopias and earlier paradigms? I believe that it is. I do not think this field or this association needs to fear change. Together, they have fostered it in the past and embraced its effects; they can do so again. Change, however, won't come on its own. Changes will have to be made deliberately and actively, with an eye to their potential consequences. Although the association probably does not need to be renamed in order to reconfigure for the future, I do believe it should at least seek ways to institutionalize new forms of bifocal vision, a capacity to attend simultaneously to the local and the global *as* they are intricately intertwined. Such a project will entail the fostering of a relational and comparative perspective. It will also require that the association actively pursue the intellectual and political consequences of difference by establishing connections with other organizations, whether they be subnational in focus, differently national, transnational, or regional. It will entail a recognition of the *theoretical* centrality of working class and ethnic studies, women's studies, queer studies, and Native American studies to a reconceived American studies project. At the same time, it will require conversations with others who have very different points of view, a fact that will require even greater disciplinary and political openness. I believe the association must promote multilingualism within American studies programs and departments and within its conference proceedings. Finally, as a way of foregrounding the complexity of the social relations that produce the cultural flows, transactions, and exchanges that are now to be highlighted, the association must seek ways to foreground the intricate calibrations between the structural and the cultural. This will require more extensive attention to social theory and to the new work being done in the social sciences. Attention to the complexity of cultural construction will require renewed and refined thinking about the intricacies of social behavior and social action. This is a complex agenda, I know, but it seems to me that this field and this association, which have both changed dramatically since their inception, can embrace further change and actively seek to bring it about in order to face the challenges of the future.

Notes

1. Wahneema Lubiano, "Like Being Mugged by a Metaphor," in *Mapping Multiculturalism*, ed. Avery F. Gordon and Christopher Newfield (Minneapolis, 1996), 64–75 and *The House That Race Built* (New York, 1997).

2. George Lipsitz, *The Possessive Investment in Whiteness: How White People Profit from Identity Politics* (Philadelphia, 1998).

3. José Saldívar, "Américo Parades and Decolonization," in *Cultures of United States Imperialism*, ed. Amy Kaplan and Donald Pease (Durham, NC, 1993), 292–311 and Vicente M. Diaz, "Pious Sites: Chamorro Culture between Spanish Catholicism and American Liberal Individualism," in *Cultures of United States Imperialism*, 312–339.

4. Américo Paredes, *"With His Pistol in His Hand": A Border Ballad and Its Hero* (Austin, 1958); *George Washington Gómez: A Mexicotexan Novel* (Houston, 1990).

5. Doreen Massey, "Spaces of Politics," unpublished paper delivered at the University of North Carolina, 1998.

6. Akhil Gupta and James Ferguson, "Beyond 'Culture': Space, Identity and the Politics of Difference," in *Culture, Power, Place: Explorations in Critical Anthropology*, ed. Akhil Gupta and James Ferguson (Durham, NC, 1997), 33–51.

7. Gupta and Ferguson, 35.

8. David Lloyd, "Nationalisms Against the State," in *The Politics of Culture in the Shadow of Capital*, ed. Lisa Lowe and David Lloyd (Durham, NC, 1997) 173–200.

Part Two

Cultural Sites

The subdivision of this part of the book into "Identities," "Practices," and "Media" is primarily one of convenience: it is hard to see how any one category can appear without invoking and involving the others. Generally speaking, however, work on identities, practices and media constitutes much of current cultural studies research in the USA. These case studies deal with all aspects of American culture—past and present, "high" and "low"—and relate to the theoretical materials in Part One.

Section V
Identities

Hulleah Tsinhnahjinnie, "Damn! There goes the Neighborhood!". © 1998 Hulleah J. Tsinhnahjinnie.

Section V
Identities

....

Authors

Cindy Patton, Herman Gray, James Holston and Arjun Appadurai, Jean Franco,
Marjorie Garber

Visual Artist

Hulleah Tsinhnahjinnie: "Damn! There goes the Neighborhood"

IDENTITY became one of the most important sites of work in American cultural studies, but, at the same time, in the face of post-structuralist notions of the fragmented subject, the concept has itself been questioned. British cultural studies initially privileged class as the primary determinant of oppression. The work of feminists and persons of colour challenged this privileging but led to debates over what might be termed the hierarchy of oppression: How do we account for the complex interactions among race, gender and class? Many scholars now choose to acknowledge, if not solve, this problem by invoking the sometimes ritualized mantra of 'race, gender, class' but the increased awareness of issues around sexual identity, diasporic cultures, post-colonialism, and indigeneity renders this an ever more inadequate solution. The material in this section addresses these categories as well as their interactions in both a contemporary and historical perspective and includes articles on specific "cultures" and on identity politics more generally. We have also included material that shows how arguments about identity and developments beyond "identity politics" may be projecting a new focus for the future.

As does Grossberg in an earlier article, Cindy Patton, one of the leading queer theorists, questions cultural studies' commitment to what might seem an increasingly outdated identity politics. Her analysis of the polemical interface between the American new right and the gay community shows that the achievement of political goals in the twenty-first century may depend more upon the postmodern performance of identity than through modernist claims to the rights of subjects constituted within essentialist identity categories.

Herman Gray analyses the interactions between postmodern theory and Afrocentric nationalist discourses on the other. He specifies essentialist and anti-essentialist elements in these encounters, and points out that there is often a gulf between the insights gained in theoretical work and the material conditions and experiences of different sections of the black community in America. As a result, Gray observes a return to essentialism in street-level politics and culture at the very moment when anti-essentialism is holding sway in theoretical discourses. Like Felski in an earlier selection, Gray calls for a more strategic and pragmatic utility for the theoretical and analytical work of cultural studies.

James Holston and Arjun Appadurai offer a new dimension, location, and concept to the unfolding work of cultural analysis. Writing in the journal *Public Culture*, they introduce the perspective of "cultural geography," focusing on the place of cities and of citizenship in the development and transformations of modernity. Citizenship is of course a long-standing theme in sociology and political science, and it has become increasingly important in more recent cultural studies. They consider the "wedge" that transnational flows have driven between national space and urban centers, and reflect on the importance of identity and difference in the spatial context of multicultural and multi-ethnic cityscapes. Their article provides a broad introduction to many of the themes relevant to the contemporary study of citizenship, which is still rooted in urban life, they argue, even as it evolves into cyber-space.

In her comparison of United States and Mexican romance narratives, Jean Franco builds on previous analysis by feminist literary critics such as Janice Radway, Tania Modleski, and others. Her intervention offers further proof that the genre can be neither simply condemned as oppressive nor celebrated for its liberatory potential. Careful scholarship must account for the significant variations in the romance genre and its putative effects within specifically delineated national contexts of class, gender, and ideology.

Marjorie Garber reflects on a theme animating much work in cultural studies: the way that groups or identities presumed in orthodox thinking to be other or different, derivative, marginal or deviant, are on closer analysis not in such positions at all. Garber argues for transvestism not as a departure from the norm in popular culture, but as something at the very centre of representation in its most theatrical mode. She analyses the "consternation of gender" she identifies in the image and work of three apparently very different performers—Liberace, Valentino, and Elvis Presley. This allows her not only to re-read their own careers, but also to offer an innovative and intriguing approach to bodily performance more generally.

Hulleah Tsinhnahjinnie is a Native American photographic artist whose "Damn!" series makes accessible, witty, but also very sharp criticisms of the relations between Native peoples and "America." One of the series shows a very clichéd image of a Western desert landscape, captioned "This is not a commercial, this is my homeland." The image selected, "Damn! There Goes the Neighborhood," collages a monochrome (historic) image of a Native man holding a smoking gun with a color picture of a wiener-mobile hot-dog car (showing bullet holes along the side). The caption steals a classic white racist quip to express reaction to the expansion of suburbanized American culture from the point of view of Native people. Tsinhnahjinnie has said in an interview that she "claims photographs as her primary language," and that in "creating images of Native thought, her emphasis is art for Indigenous communities." She said, "Many times Native people will let their pictures be taken while thinking, 'Damn! Another tourist.' Not too many people will say it aloud. I enjoy giving voice to the apprehensions of those who are being observed."[1]

Note

1. See Jane Alison (ed.) *Native Nations: Journeys in American Photography* (London: Barbican Art Gallery, 1998), 240–42, 282, 315.

22 Tremble, Hetero Swine!

Cindy Patton

T HIS essay is *outré*, madness, a tragic, cruel fantasy, an eruption of inner rage, on
how the oppressed desperately dream of being the oppressor. We shall sodom-
ize your sons, emblems of your feeble masculinity, of your shallow dreams and
vulgar lies . . . All laws banning homosexual activity shall be revoked. Instead, legislation shall be passed which engenders love between men . . . We will raise vast,
private armies, as Mishima did, to defeat you . . . The family unit . . . will be destroyed . . . Perfect boys will be conceived and grown in the genetic laboratory . . .
Tremble, hetero swine, when we appear before you without our masks.[1]

For many readers, the above will be evident as a gay revenge fantasy. Because the author
constructs his parodic identity through a campy desire to reverse the roles of oppressor
and oppressed rather than arguing for the ordinariness of homosexuality, we might
surmise that the author is a gay liberationist or Queer Nationalist. The arch style works
because we also recognize the essay's foil: paranoid new-right conspiracy theories.

. . .

It is ironic that the new right seems to have gained power in part in response to the
moderate gains of the gay civil rights movement and the increased visibility it has
afforded many lesbians and gay men. But similarly, the gay movement capitalized on the
bold and vicious opposition to it that was generated by a general societal homophobia,
even if this strategy and the movement's rhetoric could not erase the reality that violence was exacted on gay people by homophobes, but not the reverse. Using texts from
the new right, I will argue in a moment that the mutual focus on the new-right/gay-
movement oppositional dyad not only helped consolidate the internal identities of each
group, but was also used by each to promote general societal *dis*identification with the
other: if neither group could reasonably hope to recruit many outsiders to its identity,
promoting disidentification produced at least temporary allies.

The form of this deadly dance suggests that what is at stake is not the content of
identities but the modes for staging politics through identity. The identity claimed in
post-World War II discourses of civil rights is performative, less a discovery of self by
people who were once shackled by a false consciousness than an effect of a rhetoric
designed to reshape the ways in which political subjects are formed. Instead of understanding identity in an ego-psychological or developmental framework, I will argue that
identity discourse is a strategy in a field of power in which the so-called identity
movements attempt to alter the conditions for constituting the political subject.

From Cindy Patton, "Tremble, Hetero Swine!" in Michael Warner (ed.), *Fear of a Queer Planet: Queer Politics and Social
Theory* (Minneapolis and London: University of Minnesota Press, 1993), 143–77.

Gay and new-right identities define each other relationally, by a rhetorical reversal and counterreversal. Rhetorical reversal is one of the fundamental principles of the identity discourses of the post-World War II movements. Black, women's, and gay liberation typically "reclaimed" derogatory terms that were considered part of the hegemonic vocabulary and symptomatic of pervasive, stereotypical, negative societal attitudes. For example, the slogans "black is beautiful" and "gay is good" were designed to reverse the perception that African Americans could not conform to (white) standards of beauty and that homosexuals were bad citizens. Sometimes the appropriations take the form of recontextualizing terms—nigger, queer, girls, bitches—when used inside the group to which these terms once signified submission.

The new right performs a second reversal that is more than merely restating the position of the hegemony against which the progressive minorities stage their identities. Although using the hegemonic significations—"white, heterosexual, family-oriented" — the new right takes up its position as another minority, but one constituted in relation to the homophile and feminist Rainbow Coalition of minorities now read by the new right as the dominant society. The new right must perpetually reestablish the dominance of this implausible aggregation of special-interest groups; the new right incites homosexual speech in order to create a simulacrum homosexual movement whose epistemological structure is the speaking out of its inner (if perverse) certainty about its homosexual nature. The evidence (speeches, chronologies) of this phantom movement is then reversed to constitute the new right's objectivating knowledge structure—the new right images the public declarations of gay coming out as purloined information consolidated and managed through conspiracy theories. Thus, gay and new-right identities are lopsided counterparts. Gay identity comes from spilling the beans, from coming out of the closet to claim the other's derogatory speech as one's inverted reality. New-right identity cloisters self-revelation, reinterprets proud gay speech as confessions to the distinctive perversion that gay liberation's reversal sought to expose as fraud. If coming out says, "We're queer, we're here, get used to it," new-right identity appropriates this to say, "We knew it" and to society, "We told you so." What operates as a performative act of identity assertion for "queers" is read by the new right as *descriptive*, as not performative at all.

A second fundamental principle of identity discourse seems to have been lost from view in the debate about postmodernism and postidentity politics. Implicit in the differing modes of identity construction are claims about political formation, about forms of governmentality, about the difference between modernity and postmodernity. To the extent that groups like ACT UP or Queer Nation have, largely due to their sophisticated use of cynical media practices, been associated with postmodernism,[2] other forms of gay political labor have been implicitly identified as "bad old modernist." But more than standing for the discovery of a self, identities suture those who take them up to specific moral duties. Identities carry with them a requirement to act, which is felt as "what a person like me does." There is a pragmatic, temporal aspect to identities, whether we believe in them or not: the requirement to *act* implicit in even transient identities means that those who inhabit them feel they must do some thing and do it now. This produces a kind of closure, but that does not mean that identities are or become effectively essential: the stabilization of identities appears to be ineluctably essentialist only when we treat them in the realm of the imaginary, with its apparent promise of infinite possibilities for performance and reperformance. Instead, I propose here that we treat identities as a series of rhetorical closures linked with practical strategies, implicit or consciously defined, alliances and realliances that in turn affect the whole systems for staging political claims. As I will show, it is most importantly in the play of shifting pragmatics of alliance formation (what I will call deontic closures in order to indicate the performative and pragmatic dimensions, rather than imaginary dimensions) that identity rhetorics perform their work.

There are at least two forms of group identity, affiliative and exclusionary. The first is characterized by strategies of identification while the second is characterized by strategies of disidentification. Particular social identities (African-American, gay) will combine affiliative and exclusive identities—a person can inhabit either, or a mix of identifications and disidentifications—and it is from the relations of these identity procedures and the closures they produce that political subject formation occurs in postmodernity.

When I suggest that identities operate deontologically in a field of power, I mean field in Bourdieu's sense of a domain in which there are shifting, ongoing, and appropriative constructions of difference, in this case, differences of moral duty signified by proposing attributes as proper to contended identities. If it has seemed impossible to arbitrate between accomplished identities, this is because identities refer to each other to create distinctions of moral duty. This is why gay liberation and new-right rhetorics haunt each other, perpetually shifting their identificatory alliances. It is crucial to recognize these reorganizations, and in a moment I will detail a shift in new-right identity that simultaneously opposes homosexuality and embraces black conservatism. In this redistribution of moral duty the new right reconstructs its identity to oppose both white supremacist identity and black racial identity, to which gay liberation identity is likened.

"Resistance" in the context of these problematics of the subject might best be understood as a battle over the grammar of identity construction rather than a process of stabilizing the production of particular, individually appropriable identities. While resistance may occur through arch rearrangements of established identities, identity must be understood as performatively linking signifiers of social identity with duties to act: identity operates performatively in a practical and temporary space, a situation, if you will. Thus, identity constitution is less an achievement than an effect and is symptomatic of the shifts occurring in postmodern governmentality. A "real" state no longer simply institutes categories for political engagement; instead, competing rhetorics of identity interpellate individuals to moral positions that carry with them requirements for action. Identity is an issue of deontology, not ontology; it is a matter of duties and ethics, not of being.

. . .

The New Right: Refiguring Identity

Howard Winant[3] has noted that the right has a range of politics in regard to race, and this is true of rightist positions in relation to homosexuality. What is crucial for our purposes here is to note that the far right, with its militarist associations like the Klan and neo-Nazi groups, is centrally organized around an oppositional identity that from the Reconstruction through the New Deal has been articulated in terms of racial purity.[4] In the post-World War II era, this began to be articulated directly as a "white" identity. While it may seem paradoxical to mark the unmarked category in this way, it is crucial for neo-fascist racist discourse to produce as a rhetorical effect a white identity that sees itself as distinct from the unmarked nonidentity of the (white) hegemonic middle class. This racist white identity operates as importantly against the nonvigilant "race-mixing" white as it does against the "nonwhite."

The new-right and neo-conservative movements have a rather different view of race. The new right and neo-conservatives have courted conservative African Americans and "Hispanics" since the 1970s: Justice Clarence Thomas is only one of the recruits. Thomas had been writing for new-right and neo-conservative periodicals for over a decade, and is listed as an important black leader in Richard Viguerie's 1981 new-right manifesto, which has a "coming out" feel in listing the names and "rightist" credentials of dozens of people he considers the current and rising leaders of a new movement to reclaim the social space of America. The free-market ethos of the new right and neo-conservative permits the assimilation of people of color if race is erased as an issue. The civil rights movement is gingerly embraced through a kind of octoroon approach to history in which a partial racial heritage can be "made white" through persistent re-breeding/ reading. The role of the far right in sustaining racial hatred is suppressed in favor of constructing the liberals and their welfare state as the cause of black underdevelopment.

This rhetorical co-optation of the black civil rights movement is crucial in holding the line against *gay* claims to civil rights. In the following passage, David Pence invokes a popular memory of black resistance, then deploys it as a trope in transhistorically linked biblical and contemporary holocaust, both neatly "explained" by the attempt of homosexuals to attain civil status:

Most individuals who were not involved in the civil rights movement against racism tend to lump the traditional civil rights movement with the later feminist and gay liberation campaigns. This hijacking of the freedom train by middle class careerists and sexual adolescents has virtually destroyed the real civil rights movement . . . The early civil rights movement did not try to build identity on skin color but affirmed the common humanity, the common Creator and the common citizenship of each of us . . . [T]he gay lobby [is] a middle class special interest group which has squandered the moral authority of the old civil rights movement and captured many of the government jobs in human rights agencies formerly held by racial minorities . . . The road to Selma did not lead to the right to sodomy.[5]

Notice the reconstruction of black identity as a *non*racial identity constituted through "common humanity" rather than "skin color." Pence clearly sees gay liberation as based in a "trait" like skin color; the assertion of trait-loyalty is *opposed* to common citizenship. To make matters worse, queers are supposed to have taken minority jobs.

The invocation of Selma is crucial: the new right and neo-conservatives generally promote a long view of Western tradition. In *Cultural Conservatism: Toward a New National Agenda*, the popular manifesto of what has evolved into the political correctness debates, William Lind and William Marshner argue that

cultural conservatism is the belief that there is a necessary, unbreakable, and causal relationship between traditional Western Judeo-Christian values, definitions of right and wrong, ways of thinking and ways of living—the parameters of Western culture—and the secular success of Western societies: their prosperity, their liberties, and the opportunities they offer their citizens to lead fulfilling, rewarding lives . . . [T]raditional values and virtues are required not only to create a society that is free and prosperous, but also for individual fulfillment.[6]

In the context of this now well-articulated notion of survived forms of morality (the "Western" or "Judeo-Christian tradition"), the invocation of Selma (oddly enough, site of civil rights accomplished) serves to reconstruct a powerful popular memory of resistance. This incorporates African Americans into the traditional values, if they choose to join, but refuses a place for feminists and gays. The triple historical citation in Pence—Western civilization generally, black civil rights, the biblical destruction of Sodom—is collapsed into the linear figure of a road: the crumbled metanarrative of Western progress appears humbly here as common humanity in a common creator, which should embody the "true" rights achieved in a reorganized memory of the black civil rights movement. And the sibilant, stunning double metonymy, Selma/Sodom, is metaphorized as opposite ends of a road: if the destruction of Sodom somehow marked the beginning of true (black) civil rights, then to situate Sodom and Selma in the same place reverses (in fact, implodes) the progress of black civil rights. This rendering of the imputed map of a moral terrain in which Sodom and Selma marked opposite places asks the reader to bend the map, to entertain moving Sodom(y) to Selma.

. . .

Identity and Postmodern Governmentality

A new form of governmentality, concerned with the rules by which groups may claim subject status is emerging. The identitarian politics now stressed by the apprehension of multiple and conflicting identities within movement members as well as by the claims of once mainstream persons (white, middle-class, heterosexual men) to be a "minority" were born in a modernist and essentializing impulse. Identity served as a useful strategy for extending representation, both expanding the content of what might count as a subject and increasing channels of access to an already constituted polis and quickly became the principal means of staging political claims. However, with the emergence of group identities that make no reference to a transcendent essence (as in both Queer Nation and the new right) the political presence no longer requires the pretense of representing some prediscursive constituency. Identity now functions not so much to retain a representational space or define a trajectory toward cultural autonomy as it operates as a holograph of what the appropriate subject of a new form of governance might look like. The referents of identities are now less important than the capacity to look like an identity at all.

The battle over identity has been misunderstood by critics and practitioners alike. When identity-based politics are understood as related to modernist political forma-tions, they do seem to employ an essentialist understanding of the identity as a psycho-logical and communal accomplishment. However, a slight change of angle to explore the interrelation between claims to identity constitution suggests that identity politics is coextensive with (perhaps both constitutive of and constituted by) a shift from the modernist state to a postmodern condition of governmentality.

Current theory and, as I will argue in a moment, especially queer theory have become confused about the issue of identity because there are a range of competing populist and academic concepts of identity, as well as important differences between European and U.S. political experiences of calls to identity. I want to propose a more specific understanding of identity in the U.S. context, which is linked with larger issues of governmentality and social theory. As I suggested in my discussion of new-right identity, identity is a rhetorical effect that (1) elides its construction, (2) implies or re-narrates a history, (3) produces a deontic closure, and (4) operates performatively within a field of power in which citational chains link symbols and political subject position.

Metasocial Claims

There are multiple forms of identity, some linked with radically liberationist efforts, and some linked with radically fascist, genocidal efforts. European theorists, I think, are more conscious of the ambivalence of the idea of identity, not least because identity there is more recently, and currently, associated with both Nazism and "progressive" neo-nationalisms linked to territorial claims. Alain Touraine describes "two faces of identity" that appear to emerge in postindustrial society, both of which oppose the existing social roles, but one form of which is popular and one of which originates in the state:

In the case of most societies, the appeal to identity relies upon a metasocial guarantor of social order, such as the essence of humanity or, more simply, one's belonging to a community defined by certain values or by a natural or historical attribute. But in our society the appeal to identity seems more often to refer not to a metasocial guarantor but to an infrasocial and natural force. The appeal to identity becomes an appeal, against social rules, to life, freedom, and creativity. Finally, the State itself appeals to identity against social roles, and attempts to impose the idea of a unity above all forms of particular belongings. A national State, for example, appeals to citizenship, and, through it, to patriotism against all social, professional, and geographical differences. The individual or collective appeal to identity is thus the obverse of social life. Whereas the latter is a network of relations, the locus of identity is all at once that of individuals, communities, and States.[7]

Touraine's argument that both state and local identities are antisocial undercuts social constructionist sociology, which focuses on identities in relation to social roles consti-tuted *against* nature or the state. In Touraine's view, there are both essentialist and antiessentialist concepts of identity. In general, suggests Touraine, "infrasocial" prin-ciples (including nature) are the court of appeals for identity claims that appear to be "essential"; however, it is important to distinguish between claims to transcendent, foundational categories and claims *against* social roles. The idea of social roles seems to arise within late modernity and in part to facilitate reintegration into the social whole of fracturing identities (especially geopolitical and national) through naturalizing things like race and gender. This naturalization of modernity's social roles seems to have promoted an identity strategy (still existing in pluralist liberal and left discourse) that copes with the proliferation of subject-linked differences through a teleological narrative that can collapse everyone into a transcendental subject. The "metasocial guarantor" here is the metanarrative of modernity itself. To stage claims to identity, however ineluctably sutured to the claimants' personal sense of psychic integrity, is to stage a claim *against* the self-naturalizing *social* roles that social constructionists have so eloquently described. That is as long as identity is deconstructed within the framework of modernity, identities will appear to be claims to a natural self underneath the tyranny of modernity's own social roles. But this is to take the "native story" of identity claimants too seriously; it is to accept the story identities must tell in order to stand up within the modernist metanarrative as the only story they have to tell. If identities, however crude the translation, are allowed to speak not against the social roles within the modernity that birthed them, but against social integration as a whole, it begins to appear that identities are claims against the modern governmentality altogether. As content-empty spaces of signification designed strategically to link through rhetorics of moral duty, identities oppose rather than operate through ontological claims. The fact that the identity rhetorics associated with civil rights movements emphasize "being who we are" is a matter of strategic gloss. Queer Nationalists, the new right, and the homeys of East Los Angeles don't "be"—they "do" what they have to and by any means necessary (echoing Malcolm X).

The state forms of identity, while similar to older integrative appeals to the nation, are also importantly different and postmodern. As Touraine notes, patriotism (conserving an already existent national) and neo-nationalism (claims to a new national) are appeals against the integrative social order.[8] Severed from their earlier role of defining the relation between local and national interests and between the interests of competing collectivities defined as nations, nationalist rhetorics can now float free from the geopolitical boundaries they once referenced. Touraine's discussion goes some distance in explaining why, for example, Queer Nation read as a kind of nationalist identity causes concern for other gay activists who are still haunted by the deployment of national identity in Nazism, or, for that matter, in the United States's own Aryan Nation. We may be able to sort out some of these political differences and develop a postidentitarian political strategy if we understand how the state has begun to shift under the pressure of both the claims to and deconstructions of identity in the post-World War II era.

. . .

Governmentality and Gay Identity: The Space of Queerness

The modern liberal state has an overt concern with coordinating and integrating different claims on resources and power. In this organic notion of governmentality, it makes sense to differentiate interests in order to place them under different forms of control that can be generally subsumed under a governing body whose legitimacy is staged through the appearance of consent in democratic representation. Here, "politics" is equated with state management and the direct process of achieving representation (elections, certainly, but also the hiring power—"affirmative action"—through which elective positions assert power under the illusion of representativeness). The "social" means issues affecting daily life, extrarepresentational issues like equitable distribution of resources ("poverty"), the environment, and "lifestyle."

If the modern state's business was to legitimate its existence in the absence of theological justification, to produce itself as a visible, secular, central organizational force Foucault describes so well, then the postmodern state seems concerned to recede from visibility, to operate blindly as a purely administrative apparatus to an apparent market democracy. If the modern state had to describe its existence in terms of reason, suggesting in one way or another that it was an outcome of the social contract, capable of organizing consent and policing deviation, the postmodern state has to pose itself as capable of administering an incoherent, incommensurable plurality of interests. The modern state integrates social factions to resolve conflict; the postmodern state holds pluralities apart. Instead of invoking an organicist logic that links the nation to the individual through increasingly smaller collectivities like the province, the township, and the family, the postmodern state proposes lateral linkages, communities or consumption units held in relation to one another and operating through the commercial logic of a free market at circulates rather than negotiates freedoms.

If modernity conceived power in blocks that operate entropically, postmodern power circulates, disperses, intensifies. The fields of power operative in postmodernity may be more importantly about the constitution of governable subjectivities than they are about the constitution of a governing state. Certainly, the two are connected, ideologically and practically. However, the crucial difference lies in the constitution of identities: it may be that essentialist and social constructionist claims are unadjudicable because accession to power—the constitution of governmentality—is now accomplished through, rather than a precondition of, making good on claims to identity.

The crucial battle now for "minorities" and resistant subalterns is not achieving democratic representation but wresting control over the discourses concerning identity construction. The opponent is not the state as much as it is the other collectivities attempting to set the rules for identity constitution in something like a "civil society." The problem is not one of cognitive or psychic dissonance—that is, that the right, for example, will not allow us to feel or be who we want to be, but that the terms for asserting identity *are* the categories of political engagement. The discursive practices of identity and the actors who activate them produce the categories of governmentality that engender the administrative state apparatus, not vice versa. It is as important to look at the battles taking place within the field of power in which accomplishment of "identities" operates as political capital—say, between the right and gays—as it is to see how their variously constituted identities interact with the administrative units.

Thus, identity as an effect comes into play at the threshold of what de Certeau,[9] following Derrida,[10] calls "the proper," at the threshold of engagement with constituted social and political institutions. As I have tried to show, this narrower sense of identity involves performativity, the ability to operate through citation within a field of power in which oppositional pairs are discernible against a backdrop of institutions and spaces. Institutions could be history or the courts, and spaces could be the social, gender, the nation. This is the place in which the new right invokes homophobia but a homophobia contingent on the continued construction of isolatable "gay identities."

If agents in possession of gay identities make demands for minority status within the political sphere, this is not because acquisition of gay identity strips away ideology and allows a homosexual body to realize its desire for civil rights that are simply waiting around for the asking. Rather, the demand for civil rights is an intrinsic effect of coming-out rhetoric, altering both the meaning of civil rights and the meaning of homoerotic practices. Coming-out rhetoric, in effect, articulates gay identity to civil rights practices, articulates homoerotic practices to the political concept of minority. The person who takes up a post-Stonewall gay identity feels compelled to act in a way that will constitute her or himself as a subject appropriate to civil rights discourse, and thus, deserving of the status accruing to successful claims to minority status. In the process of queer enunciation, the meaning of civil rights, indeed, the capacity to hold apart the political and social, the public and private, have been radically altered.

The innovation of gay identity was not so much in making homosexuality seem acceptable to the homosexual, but in creating a crisis of duty in gays who could "come out" (in some sense, leave the private/social). In linking the demand for acceptance by society with the instantiation of identity in oneself, gay liberationists want society to take a stand for or against specific or specifiably "gay" persons. All identities effect these deontic closures: in fact, as I have argued above, the achievement of identities is precisely the staking out of duties and alliances in a field of power. Postmodern mininarratives of individual and collective moral legitimacy are replacing the rational metanarratives—like the social contract, pluralism, and democracy—that characterized state legitimation in modernity.

. . .

Notes

1. "The Homoerotic Order," *Gay Community News*; cited in "The Homosexual Mentality," *New Dimensions*, 1989, 28–29.

2. Douglas Crimp and Adam Rolston, *AIDS Demo Graphics* (Seattle: Bay Press, 1990); Cindy Patton, *Inventing AIDS* (New York: Routledge. 1990).

3. Howard Winant, "Postmodern Racial Politics: Difference and Inequality," *Social Review*, 20: 1 (1990).

4. Michael Omi and Howard Winant, *Racial Formation in the United States from the 1960s to the 1980s* (New York: Routledge and Kegan Paul, 1986).

5. David Pence, "Address to Physicians, Grand Rapids, Michigan, November 4, 1987," in *Vital Speeches*, December, 1987.

6. William Lind and William Marshner, *Cultural Conservatism: Toward a New National Agenda*, Free Congress Research and Educational Foundation (Lanham, Md.: UPA Inc., 1987), 8.

7. Alain Touraine, *The Return of the Actor* (Minneapolis: University of Minnesota Press, 1988), 75–76.

8. Ibid.

9. Michel de Certeau, *The Practice of Everyday Life* (Berkeley: University of California Press, 1988).

10. Jacques Derrida, *Positions* (Chicago: University of Chicago Press, 1981).

23 African-American Political Desire and the Seductions of Contemporary Cultural Politics

Herman Gray

Wᴵᵀʜᴵɴ contemporary African-American cultural and political discourse, identity politics in general and disputes about "Blackness" in particular have become the site of stimulating and sometimes acrimonious debate — among the focal points of many of these debates are the positions articulated around the issues of diversity, affirmative action and political correctness on university campuses around the country, the efficacy of the liberal welfare state, the behavioral and moral fitness of the so called urban "underclass" and more recently the appeal of Afrocentric discourses and nationalism.[1]

What does all of this have to do with the minority discourse in general and black self-representation in particular? I am less interested in developing a definite response as much as I want to explore the consequence of this situation in terms of theorizing and understanding the present condition of black Americans. I am also less concerned with directly taking up the issues of nationalism, post-modernism, anti-essentialism and identity politics than understanding how they and the discourses in which they are embedded have had important consequences for our present circumstance, especially the conceptualization and representation of that circumstance.

Indeed, it seems to me that for all of the poststructuralist insights and theorization about multiple subject positions and transgressive identities, we are experiencing something of a return to so-called essentialist ways of constructing and imaging ourselves (as black people). These days territorial imperatives, especially in the United States, seem stronger than ever. There seem to be greater racial, sexual, class-based suspicions and assaults on vast sectors of the black community in the United States. Statistics about death, destruction, immiseration, poverty and powerlessness continue to indicate that in many respects, large sectors of black Americans, especially the poor, continue to experience the very worst that this society has to offer (Hacker 1992; Johnson and Oliver 1991). And as we are well aware these assaults do not only come from outside black communities; antagonisms and conflicts between blacks are also as intense as ever.[2] In the face of this kind of assault, suspicion, and antagonism, Afrocentric perspectives and nationalist constructions of identity are increasingly attractive to various sectors of the black community. For an increasing number of blacks these perspectives serve as com-

From Herman Gray, "African-American Political Desire and the Seductions of Contemporary Cultural Politics," *Cultural Studies*, 7: 3 (1993), 364–73. Taylor & Francis Ltd, PO Box 25, Abingdon, Oxfordshire, UK.

pelling guides for action, as utopian visions of possibility, and as ways of making sense of the world and their experience of it.

Ironically then, the very possibilities that discourses and debates about essentialism, postmodernism and identity opened have also produced this "return" or turn if you will, toward essentialism. I think that this "return" or turn represents the very contingency to which Stuart Hall alludes when he suggests that we cannot have a politics of guarantees. In the face of debates and discourses about essentialism, postmodernism, and identity on the one hand and the appeals and expressions of nationalism in black communities (especially among significant segments of black students on university campuses) on the other, how are we to think about these developments and the political difficulties as well as possibilities they pose? As Cornel West (1990a) so cogently put it, as critical black intellectuals how do we theorize and build political strategies across and within racial, sexual, class, and gender difference? That is to say, one of the possibilities of any kind of politics forged at the site of contradictory cultural practice, which sees ideology as lived and culture as a site of struggle, is precisely that those whom one seeks to organize and direct may in fact constitute themselves and be drawn to other ways of making sense of their lives and circumstance (Hall 1985, 1986, 1988).

It seems to me that discursively we have moved quite a way to revealing and specifying the complex terms and articulations of difference within blacks communities (hooks 1990; West 1990a; White 1990). In these ways postmodernism, anti-essentialism, and poststructuralism have provided key insights. Conceptions that emphasize the centrality of images, the power of the mass media, the fragmentary and constructed nature of reality, have provided signal contributions from these quarters. These notions have challenged and exposed totalizing discourses and their hegemonic power. In the best instances, critical black intellectuals use these insights to open up and examine the rich and often contradictory construction and self-representation of blacks (West 1990a).

At the same time I want to argue that in many instances these insights have been misapplied and misdirected. We have too often remained at and needlessly confined our analysis to the level of textual representation and taken too little account of the material locations and practices of different sectors of the black community as well as the cultural desires through which they are constructed. For I believe that no small part of the attraction and persistence of essentialized constructions like nationalism for large numbers of blacks rests in part with the material and social conditions they face.

Thus, for example, while the recent interventions of Henry Louis Gates, Jr. (1991, 1992) on the question of inaccuracies, silences, and anti-Semitism in certain strains of nationalist and Afrocentric discourses, is if nothing else bold, it does, nevertheless, illustrate my central point. The totalizing impulses, mythological constructions of an African past and scapegoating of Jews described by Gates are to be sure elements which underwrite this discourse. And, like others, he is quite right to name these and expose the empirical and historical fallacies on which they are built.[3]

This is an important part of the critical labors of cultural politics to be sure, but far from the only part since, as Cornel West (1991, 1992) points out, these impulses and the resonance they signal have deep and enduring histories and produce different political effects within and outside African-American communities. And they are histories built on and circumscribed by unequal power relationships expressed through race and ethnicity, culture, class, neighborhood, patronage and so on. (The relationships through which such antagonisms are expressed are built on histories of co-operation and alliance against oppression as well.) Attention alone to the discursive manifestations, inaccuracies, and myths of the nationalist and Afrocentric discourse of Afrocentrism (especially the volatile antagonisms between Blacks and Jews) without contextualizing, historicizing or attending to the material conditions and political desires from which they spring and to which they are directed, as a political project, simply forces a choosing of sides from two equally unappealing options. Moreover, it is not the political ground on which to forge new alliances, articulations and progressive politics.

However factually inaccurate and culturally romantic, these discourses continue to have resonance for different sectors of African-American people. And that resonance cannot be effectively contested or explained away by deconstructing and discrediting the work of its leading figures or by casting its adherents as simple-minded, untutored or misguided. We must own up to the hard fact that in certain progressive quarters of African-American counter-discourse, important political ground has been ceded and too often been absorbed into a privileged and often narrow network of academic discourse. The persistence and pervasiveness of certain versions of nationalism says as much about the discourses and (class) locations of progressive critical intellectuals as it does about the people who desire it (West 1990a). In other words, to account for the appeal and persistence of various forms and expressions of nationalism, we must carefully attend to social locations and material circumstances of African Americans as well as the character, orbit and terms of these debates within black America.

Hence, I want to signal and try to specify the localities and relationships of critical black intellectual engagements with postmodernism and especially essentialism (e.g., the university and the academy), the social locations of those involved, and the tensions, gulfs and focus of the objects of these debates (West 1990b). It seems to me that part of what has occurred is that the object of postmodernist debates, anti-essentialist discourses and identity politics has been and remains in large measure divorced and disarticulated from the experiences, practices, and locations of significant segments of blacks in the United States. Consequently, the strategic appeal of discourses such as nationalism and Afrocentricity, remain compelling insofar as they fill significant voids created by the desire, indeed imperative, to make sense of daily encounters, suspicions and hostilities experienced by blacks in the United States.

My position on this point is not a move to tolerate or excuse the silence, marginalization, and policing of these totalizing discourses (especially their renderings in popular culture). Rather it is to suggest that we carefully interrogate and critically understand the force of such attractions and the circumstances in which they find resonance. Similarly, I am not ready to completely abandon some of the key insights suggested by postmodernism and anti-essentialism for understanding identity within African-American cultural discourse. I do want to suggest, however, that we put these insights to more strategic use (Gramsci 1971); that we deploy them more directly in terms of the material conditions and social locations of people's lives; that we see culture and representation as both an important site within which our struggles take place and as an object over which we struggle (Lipsitz 1990: 16–17).[4] Such strategic and critical engagement perhaps would help avoid confusing and misusing the relevant insights of these discourses.

African-American Identity and the Material Condition(s) of Black Life in Modern America

No matter how strong the temptation to make them so, the attraction to and desire for nationalist and Afrocentric discourses (including the critiques they generate) do not exist in isolation. Even if figured this way these discourses and the desires to which they respond are not generated and sustained out of a simple longing for some golden moment of a rich African past. That is a serious misreading and underestimation of both the discourse and the material conditions and strategies out of which they emerge and in which they circulate.

Even the most cursory reading of any daily newspaper or weekly news magazine in the United States would indicate that in the current moment there are zones in the social and cultural landscape of American society that remain deeply inflected and characterized by racial inequality, suspicion and hostility. These conflicts and inequalities, which are expressed at the intersections of race, class, gender and sexuality, are experienced at various levels and sites of everyday life.[5] Expressions of these conflicts and their policing and containment by the state are evident everywhere: in the data on prison populations and police brutality; in family violence, abandonment and sexual abuse of children; in violence against women; in racial violence and confrontations such as those evidenced by recent incidents in New York City (painting Latino children white) and Denver (the confrontations at a MLK rally between the Klan and King supporters); in the local and national fallout of the David Duke candidacy for governor of Louisiana; in the salience of race in the 1980, 1984, 1988 and 1992 presidential campaigns (the Willie Horton phenomena); in failed and abandoned public educational systems in urban communities across the country, and in the attacks on and attempts to de-legitimate affirmative-action policies in general and blacks who are their beneficiaries in particular (Edsall and Edsall 1991; Hacker 1992; Tagaki 1993).

Exacerbating these expressions of a racialized American society are the broad, but surely no less significant, transformations and crises in capitalism, especially the damaging consequences for blacks and other communities of color in the recession-plagued US economy. National economic restructuring, dismantling of the welfare state and unemployment, all of which constantly threaten middle- and working-class stability, have served to exacerbate racial hostilities and suspicion (Davis 1991; Edsall and Edsall 1991; Johnson and Oliver 1989, 1991).

To this state of affairs we might also add the social and political construction of immigration and its material effects — reconfigurations of neighborhoods, schools, workplaces, and public space (Davis 1989, 1991; Miles 1992). Together these constructions and their effects have increased resentment and competition over access and entitlements to public services. Such demographic and economic shifts, especially their representation by politicians and the press, have heightened intraracial suspicions and hostilities between Blacks and Latinos, Blacks and Koreans, blacks and other recent immigrants who compete for already scarce resources and rewards (Johnson and Oliver 1989). As the Los Angeles riots of April 1992 demonstrate territorial boundaries such as neighborhood, sites of economic exchange and so on become the material site and cultural expression of struggle over community and identity (Davis 1989; Johnson *et al.* 1992; Miles 1992). In short, these material, social and cultural conditions have heightened the appeal and resonance of nationalist identities among various sectors of the black community.[6]

Essentialism, Nationalism and Black Self-Representation

Across the United States, African Americans, especially the youth, are explicitly walking, wearing and speaking their blackness. The most general and cursory survey of recent popular self-representations of blacks in film, popular music and television easily reveals persistent and pervasive nationalist constructions of self and community. As Kimberlé Crenshaw (1991), Marlon Riggs (1991), bell hooks (1990), Francis White (1990) and others have argued, these nationalist and masculinist representations in film, popular music and television are contradictory and come with the hidden but consequential costs of silencing, policing, marginalization and violation of the voices and experiences of women and gays and lesbians within black communities.

In some of the most notable and commercially successful television shows, music videos and films the construction of blackness and community is mobilized through various emblems of the imagined black nation, a mythic African past, and heroic black masculinity. These are expressed in the dress, hairstyles, language, bodies of young black (mostly) males who wear, speak and look the part of "real brothers". From *Do the Right Thing* to *Boyz 'n the Hood*, such self-constructions and representations are impossible to miss. Where internal differences of social class, social location, sexuality and gender are represented in many contemporary black self-representations, they have nevertheless been criticized because such differences are the objects rather than the subjects of cinematic representation.[7]

Perhaps the most controversial and pervasive example of this contemporary black self-representation is rap music.[8] Expressed with a compelling (and for some disturbing) "in your face" immediacy and urgency and cleverly rooted in the rich tradition of African-American oral vernacular practice, rap has become one of the most contested and influential contemporary sites of black self-representation and identity. Explicit about its symbolic (and for some literal) call to arms in defense of the nation, hip-hop's most forceful and articulate (male) practitioners continue to seize upon and speak about the(ir) "realities" of being black in America in the 1990s. Such contradictions and policing notwithstanding, these conceptions and representations of the black nation seem to strike a resonant cord for many black youth.[9]

These expressive self-representations and critiques of white racism are by no means confined to the popular culture and mass media. Indeed, many of these same impulses and attractions are evident in the university, professional associations, and conferences.[10] The interventions of Molefi Asante, Ron Karenga, and others, the adoption of Afrocentric school curricula in public schools and universities around the country, together indicate that as political visions Afrocentrism and nationalism gathered a certain discursive force as an intellectual formation (*Newsweek* 1991).

Similarly, the anti-essentialist challenge to unifying categories of identification and identity such as race, gender, and heterosexuality have produced forceful critiques of essentialist and totalizing versions of nationalism. These critiques which have come from black feminist theorists, literary critics and other critical intellectuals concerned with the totalizing dimensions of identity rooted in "blackness", "heterosexuality" and "masculinity" have gained wide circulation in universities, professional organizations and conferences. Such critiques have produced an impressive body of critical scholarship, especially criticism concerned with black self-representation in texts and cultural practices such as films, novels, and popular music, and television. Curiously, unlike some of the essentialist and nationalist impulses that circulate across various segments of black communities, much of this critical writing and commentary remains confined to academic and professional communities. As a political issue, this circulation and confinement to the locality of the professions and academy raises the question of where these discourses circulate, to whom they are directed and their efficacy for social transformation.

Essentialist discourses, expressed most powerfully in totalizing forms of nationalism, have aggressively sought out and intervened in those zones and public arenas, especially mass mediated expressive culture, where black men and women do not enjoy the material privilege or the social space to construct themselves differently. Critiques of essentialism and the debates around difference in black self-representation, remain for the most part confined to very specific discursive sites, especially the publishing industry, the university, conferences, and other alternative spaces of cultural production.

Conceptualizing cultural struggles and identity politics in terms of differentially positioned and enabled zones helps in part to explain the persistence and attraction for many African Americans of nationalist discourses in the popular media, everyday life and, increasingly, the academy. It is not just that the large number of blacks for whom nationalism remains attractive are incapable of imagining themselves or living their lives differently: rather I contend that the social and material conditions of their lives may not permit them to. In contrast, critical black intellectuals may, indeed often do, live and work in worlds where such possibilities are not constrained in the same way.[11] Hence all of these localities constitute important sites of contestation and struggle. But they remain one among many such sites of contestation.

Essentialism, Postmodernism and (Identity) Politics

It is fair to say that we are all differently positioned and constrained by the circumstance of our locations and the discourses in which we are positioned. Moreover, we experience and negotiate these positions differently. Theoretically, both essentialist and anti-essentialist categories for constructing ourselves and perceiving the world are available to all of us; however our discursive as well as institutional access to these categories and material sites are not always evenly distributed and available to each of us in the same way.

If this is indeed the case, as critical black intellectuals we must take up, in very serious and urgent ways, the desires and circumstances that make the various forms and expressions of nationalism appealing and resonant. We must not simply read on to those desires the arrogance and privilege of our own location. As Gramsci's insights and Hall's extensions of them show, politically, it is important to concretely specify those zones and circuits of social life and practice where anti-essentialist and postmodern possibilities and impulses are possible and those where they are not (at least in the current material, political and social condition) (Gramsci 1971; Hall 1988). For example, the university as a social and political site where many critical black intellectuals work and form friendships, professional relationships and circulate is, under certain social conditions, perhaps a site of greater transgressive possibilities (West 1990b). It is, indeed, often possible for those of us operating in these spaces to experience ourselves and others more fully in terms of the multiple and complex subject positions that character-ize all of our lives. Just as often, of course, many of us experience (and struggle against) the confinements, rigidities, and inequalities of these institutions.

Social and cultural life (and the discourses of identity which circulate) within black communities are characterized by multiple and intersecting cultural zones and social sites. Within these conditions, black self-representations and the political desires they express are contingent, uneven and contradictory: often they are totalizing, closed, constrained, oppressive and fortified at borders; at other times they are open, fluid and transgressive. Of course this kind of theoretical and political specification implicates critical black intellectuals in our own critical practice. The point is that, whatever their manifestations and circuits, we as critical intellectuals must specify these (and our own) as *sites* of everyday life and not just read political identifications and desire from our privileged locations.

Our critical concepts and the labors they produce must specify and interrogate more carefully where and under what conditions the expressions of essentialist thinking operates as well as those possibilities for anti-essential thinking. I think the work of Francis White, Patricia Hill-Collins, Robin D. G. Kelly, Kimberlé Crenshaw, Cornel West and John Brown Childs among others are exemplary in this respect. These critical black intellectuals do not excuse or justify the resonance of these categories and constructions so much as they open discursive spaces for strategic interventions (political and ana-lytic) that allow us to struggle in and over such sites. Totalizing conceptions and con-demnations rather than critical and strategic interventions and deployment simply up the ante without actively moving the debates into those zones where they enlist and mobilize complexly positioned African-American subjects and subjectivities. This means that we too have to remain aware of our own locations and relationships to others. We must be prepared to make critical examinations and interventions across multiple sites of struggle, to struggle in and over culture and to articulate (and dis-articulate) those discursive struggles with the material conditions of people's lives.

Notes

Thanks to Rosa Linda Fregoso, John Brown Childs, Tommy Lott, Ruth Frankenberg, Richard Yarborough, Kobena Mercer, Lata Mani, Lawrence Grossberg, and Melvin Oliver. Many of the ideas discussed in this paper were clarified through their lively discussion and critical insights. An earlier version of this paper was presented at a 1992 UCLA conference entitled "Speaking for the Subject": My thanks also to the organizers and participants in this conference.

1. Here I refer to recent publications such as *Tenured Radicals, The Closing of the*

American Mind, and *Illiberal Education*. I also have in mind media coverage of these debates in weekly news magazines such as *Newsweek, Time, The Village Voice, The New York Times* and news shows such as *Nightline* and *The McNeil/Leher Newshour*.

2. For example, recent press reports abound about the escalating homicide rates and violent crimes in urban black communities throughout the nation. In particular, cities like Washington DC, Oakland, Detroit, Los Angeles, Houston, and Miami are rapidly surpassing record highs for homicide rates and violent crimes.

3. In an interesting and slightly different intervention into this debate, legal scholar Derrick Bell notes, "[W]ere I a Jew, I would be damned concerned about the latent—and often active— anti-semitism in this country. But to leap with a vengence on inflamatory comments by Blacks is a misguided effort to vent justified fears on black targets of opportunity who are the society's least powerful influences and —I might add— the most likely to be made the scapegoats for deeply rooted anti-semitism that they didn't create and that will not be cured by their destruction." See Bell (1992: 121).

4. See Lipsitz (1990: 16–17).

5. Here I refer to the public and personal sites such as the state and corporations as well as family and interpersonal relations.

6. For example, the imperatives of territoriality and nationalism is evident in the black and Korean struggles that occurred in New York and Los Angeles.

7. On the other hand, where such differences are the subjects of black film representation in projects such as *Looking for Langston, Tongues Untied, Paris is Burning*, to name only three films that address the issue of sexuality and race, the issue of the subordination of race is usually the object of criticism.

8. In television one finds this badge of blackness from across a wide range of genres and programs: from television talk, sports events and advertisements to music television, to situation comedy (e.g., *True Colors, Family Matters, It's a Different World, The Cosby Show*), similar codes and emblems of membership in the nation are abundant, clearly identifiable and available to real and imagined members of the nation. In addition, given the circuits of television (e.g., music television, sports and advertisement) the nationalist sensibilities of rap are also found in television.

9. Both at Northeastern in Boston, my former university, and UCSC, my current one, I have found a number of graduate and undergraduate students interested in pursuing papers, thesis and dissertations on nationalism and rap.

10. I think particularly of the activities and controversies at City College in New and San Francisco State in California.

11. Thanks to John Brown Childs for his clear insights on this issue.

References

Bell, Derrick (1992). *Faces at the Bottom of the Well: The Permanence of Racism*. New York: Basic.

Crenshaw, Kimberlé (1991). "Beyond racism and misogyny: Black feminism and 2 Live Crew". *Boston Review*, 16: 6.

Davis, Mike (1989). "Homeowners and homeboys: Urban restructuring in LA" *Enclitic*, 9–16.

—— *City of Quartz*. London: Verso.

Edsall, Thomas Byrne, and Edsall, Mary (1991). *Chain Reaction: The Impact of Race, Rights, and Taxes on American Politics*. New York: Norton.

Gates, Henry Louis (1991). "Beware of the new pharaohs." *Newsweek*, 23 September: 47.

—— (1992). "Black demagogues and pseudo-scholars." *New York Times*, 20 July: A15.

Gramsci, Antonio (1971). *Selections from The Prison Notebooks*, trans. Q. Hoare and

G. Nowell Smith. New York: International Publishers.

Hacker, Andrew (1992). *Two Nations: Black and White, Separate, Hostile, and Unequal.* New York: Scribner's Sons.

Hall, Stuart (1985). "Signification, ideology, and representation: Althusser and the post-structuralist debate." *Critical Studies in Mass Communication*, 2: 91–114.

—— (1986). "On postmodernism and articulation: An interview." *Journal of Communication*, 10: 45–60.

—— (1988). "Toad in the garden: Thatcherism among the theorists," in C. Nelson and L. Grossberg (eds.), *Marxism and the Interpretation of Culture.* Urbana-Champaign: University of Illinois, 35–57.

hooks, bell (1990). *Yearnings: Race, Gender and Cultural Politics.* Boston: South End Press.

Johnson, Jr., James H., and Oliver, Melvin (1989). "Inter-ethnic minority conflict in urban America: The effects of economic and social dislocation." *Urban Geography*, 10: 449–63.

—— (1991). "Economic restructuring and black male joblessness in U.S. metropolitan areas." *Urban Geography*, 12: 542–62.

Johnson, Jr., James H., *et al.* (1992). "The Los Angles rebellion, 1992: A preliminary assessment from ground zero." UCLA Center for the Study of Urban Poverty, Occasional Working Paper Series. Institute for Social Science Research, Los Angeles: UCLA.

Lipsitz, George (1990). *Time Passages: Collective Memory and American Popular Culture.* Minneapolis: University of Minnesota Press.

Miles, Jack (1992). "Blacks vs. Browns." *The Atlantic*, October: 41–70.

Newsweek (1991). 23 September.

Riggs, Marlon (1991). "Black macho revisited: Reflections of a snap queen." *Black American Literature Forum*, 25: 389–95.

Tagaki, Dana (1993). *The Retreat from Race: The Asian American Admissions Controversy.* New Brunswick: Rutgers University Press.

West, Cornel (1990a). "The new cultural politics of difference," Russell Ferguson, Martha Gever, Trinh T. Minh-ha, and Cornel West (eds.) *Marginalization and Contemporary Cultures.* Cambridge, Mass: MIT Press, 19–39.

—— (1990b). "Theory, pragmatism, and politics," in Barbara Johnson and Jonathan Arac (eds.), *The Consequence of Theory.* Baltimore: Johns Hopkins University Press.

—— (1991). "Black anti-semitism and the rhetoric of resentment." *Tikkun* 7: 15–17.

—— (1992). "Learning to talk of race." *The New York Times Magazine*, 2 August: 24–26.

White, E. Francis (1990). "Africa on my mind: Gender, counter discourse and African American nationalism." *Journal of Women's History*, 2: 73–97.

24 Cities and Citizenship

James Holston and Arjun Appadurai

$\mathbf{W}$HY cities? Why citizenship? Since the eighteenth century, one of the defining marks of modernity has been the use of two linked concepts of association — citizenship and nationality — to establish the meaning of full membership in society. Citizenship rather than subjectship or kinship or cultship has defined the prerogatives and encumbrances of that membership, and the nation-state rather than the neighborhood or the city or the region established its scope. What it means to be a member of society in many areas of the world came to be understood, to a significant degree, in terms of what it means to be a right-bearing citizen of a territorial nation-state. Undeniably, this historical development has been both revolutionary and democratic, even as it has also been conservative and exclusionary. On the one hand, for persons deemed eligible, nation-states have sought to establish citizenship as that identity which subordinates and coordinates all other identities — of religion, estate, family, gender, ethnicity, region, and the like — to its framework of a uniform body of law. Overwhelming other titles with its universal *citoyen*, citizenship thus erodes local hierarchies, statuses, and privileges in favor of national jurisdictions and contractual relations based in principle on an equality of rights. On the other hand, the mobilizations of those excluded from the circle of citizens, their rallies against the hypocrisies of its ideology of universal equality and respect, have expanded democracies everywhere: they generate new kinds of citizens, new sources of law, and new participation in the decisions that bind. As much as anything else, these conflicting and disjunctive processes of change constitute the core meaning of modern citizenship, constantly unsettling its assumptions.

· · ·

But if cities have historically been the locus of such tumult, they experience today an unsettling of national citizenship which promises unprecedented change. In some places, the nation itself is no longer a successful arbiter of citizenship. As a result, the project of a national society of citizens, especially liberalism's twentieth-century version, appears increasingly exhausted and discredited. In other places the nation may maintain the envelope of citizenship, but the substance has been so changed or at least challenged that the emerging social morphologies are radically unfamiliar and force a reconsideration of the basic principles of membership. Such transformations have generated profound uncertainties about many aspects of citizenship which only recently seemed secure: uncertainty about the community of allegiance, its form of organization, manner of election and repudiation, inclusiveness, ethical foundations, and

From James Holston and Arjun Appadurai, "Cities and Citizenship," *Public Culture*, 8: 2 (1996), 187–204. © Duke University Press. All rights reserved. Reprinted with permission.

signifying performances; uncertainty about the location of sovereign power; uncertainty about the priorities of the right and the good; uncertainty about the role of cultural identities increasingly viewed as defining natural memberships.

. . .

Our point is not to argue that the transnational flow of ideas, goods, images, and persons—intensified by recent developments in the globalization of capital—is obliterating the salience of the nation-state. Rather, it is to suggest that this flow tends to drive a deeper wedge between national space and its urban centers. There are a growing number of societies in which cities have a different relationship to global processes than the visions and policies of their nation-states may admit or endorse. London today is a global city in many ways that do not fit with the politics of the United Kingdom, just as Shanghai may be oriented to a global traffic beyond the control of the government of the People's Republic of China, as Mogadishu may represent a civil war only tangentially tied to a wider Somali politics, and as Los Angeles may sustain many aspects of a multicultural society and economy at odds with mainstream ideologies of American identity. Cities have always been stages for politics of a different sort than their hinterlands. But in the era of mass migration, globalization of the economy, and rapid circulation of rights discourse, cities represent the localization of global forces as much as they do the dense articulation of national resources, persons, and projects.

. . .

The conventional distinction between formal and substantive aspects of citizenship is helpful in sorting out various dimensions of these proposals. In particular, it suggests why cities may be especially salient sites for the constitution of different citizenships, or at least for considering the exhaustion of national modes. If the formal refers to membership in the nation-state and the substantive to the array of civil, political, socio-economic, and cultural rights people possess and exercise, much of the turmoil of citizenship derives from the following problem: although in theory full access to rights depends on membership, in practice that which constitutes citizenship substantively is often independent of its formal status. In other words, formal membership in the nation-state is increasingly neither a necessary nor a sufficient condition for substantive citizenship. That it is not sufficient is obvious for many poor citizens who have formal membership in the state but who are excluded in fact or law from enjoying the rights of citizenship and participating effectively in its organization.

. . .

That formal citizenship is less necessary for access to substantive rights is also clear: although it is required for a few rights (like voting in national elections), it is not for most. Indeed, legally resident noncitizens, and even illegally resident ones, often possess virtually identical socio-economic and civil rights as citizens. Moreover, the exclusive rights of citizens are often onerous, like jury duty, military service, and certain tax requirements. Thus, people tend to perceive them more as burdens than as rights. It is not surprising, therefore, that recent surveys indicate that many immigrants are not as anxious as they once might have been to embrace the citizenship of their new countries, thereby compromising their right of return.

Such disjunctions between the form and substance of citizenship have made defining it in terms of membership in the nation-state less convincing and have thus devalued this form of association for both members and nonmembers alike. As a result, there have been two general responses. One tries to make citizenship more exclusive. Hence, we witness a host of reactionary movements: some aim to deny social services to various categories of noncitizens or to legislate the exclusive use of one language or another. Others employ urban incorporation to gain the powers of local government. Their objective is to privatize or dismantle public spaces and services and to implant zoning regulations which in effect keep the undesired out. Other exclusionary movements (some militia-backed) attack federalism and the idea of national government itself, advancing the priority of local, small-scale communities. All of these movements tend to emphasize private security and vigilantism as acceptable forms of self-determination. Most are tinged with racism if not outright violence.

The other kind of response has gone in the opposite direction. It tries to make citizenship more inclusive. It aims to reconceive citizenship in supranational and non-local terms in which rights are available to individuals regardless of national origins, residence, or place of work. Examples include movements for human rights, trans-national citizenship, and continental associations (e.g., EEC, Nafta, and Mercosur). But if both types of response aim to reinvigorate citizenship, they both typically have their perverse outcomes: in the one case, localism can generate xenophobic violence; in the other, the elimination of local community as the ground of citizenship tends to pre-clude active participation in the business of rule. Instead, it leads to the replacement of that civic ideal with a more passive sense of entitlement to benefits which seem to derive from remote sources. Far from renewing citizenship, violence and passivity further erode its foundations.

As such erosion spreads, it threatens the very notion of a shared community and culture as the basis of citizenship. The extension of the shared beyond the local and the homogeneous is, of course, an essential part of citizenship's revolutionary and demo-cratic promise. This extension of citizenship is corrosive of other notions of the shared precisely because its concept of allegiance is, ultimately, volitional and consensual rather than natural. Yet, one would be hard-pressed to find a major urban population today which felt compelled, except in extraordinary moments like war, by "a direct sense of community membership based on loyalty to a civilization which is a common posses-sion," to use a phrase from T. H. Marshall's classic study of citizenship (1977[1949]:94). The exhaustion of this sense over the half century forces us to reconsider not only the national basis of citizenship but also its democratic ideals of commonwealth, participa-tion, and equality.

. . .

Among the most vocal critics of liberal citizenship are groups organized around specific identities—the kind of prior differences liberalism relegates to the private sphere—which affirm the importance of these identities in the public calculus of citizenship. That is, they affirm the right to difference as an integral part of the foundation of citizenship. Feminism launched this critique by arguing that liberalism depends in fact on an ideology of difference because its supposedly universal citizen is, historically, of a particular type, namely, a white, European, propertied, male. The ideology of universal equality arises because members of this referent group have never had to assert their difference, but only their equality, to claim citizenship. From the perspective of the rest who are excluded, this assertion looks like one of difference, not equality. In any case, it will not work for those not already equal in these terms. Hence, for the excluded, the political question is to change the terms. Therefore, the politics of difference becomes more important and potentially incompatible with that of universal equality as the real basis for citizenship.

For example, this politics argues that although different treatment (e.g., with regard to gender) can produce inequality, equal treatment, when it means sameness, can discriminate against just the kinds of values and identities people find most meaningful.

. . .

As in the case of gender, many other distinguishing identities have given focus to organized groups who challenge established, difference-neutral conceptions of citizenship. These include national and cultural minorities, sexual-orientation groups, and racial, religious, and ethnic organizations. They demand different treatment on the basis of their inalienable right to retain and realize their unique qualities, contributions, and histories. Their core argument usually entails the claim they have been denied respect and opportunity because they are different. That difference in fact constitutes their authentic and original character, which they have every right to develop to full capacity. Thus, they demand citizenship rights as person who have authentic needs and interests which must be met if they are to live fully human lives. As Taylor demonstrates, the argument from authenticity leads to a politics of difference rather than to a politics of universalism or equalization of rights (1992:3–73). It results in a claim upon others to recognize special qualities and to accord them rights on that account which will ensure their survival and well-being. Although this kind of demand would seem contradictory and incompatible with citizenship as an ideology of equality, there is nevertheless a growing sense that it is changing the meaning of equality itself. What it objects to is the equation that equality means sameness. It rejects citizenship as a homogenizing identity with the charge that homogenization reduces and impoverishes. Rather, it would take equality to mean equal opportunity. Thus, it would define citizenship on the basis of rights to different treatment with equal opportunity.

Identity politics of this sort is having a major impact because the identities of difference are competing more successfully for people's time and passion than the tired identity of formal, national citizenship. Without doubt, this impact is divisive. Identity politics tends to disrupt established ideologies of civic unity and moral solidarity in ways which often make people angry and anxious. For example, the politics of difference challenges the basic premise of liberal citizenship that the principles of justice impose negative restrictions on the kinds of goods individuals can pursue. Hence, when Muslim women in France demand the right to use the veil in public schools, or American Fundamentalists to include creationism in the curriculum, they contest that priority and the plural public sphere it supposedly creates. By demanding the right to pursue their definitions of the good and proper life in the public sphere, they challenge the liberal democratic conviction that the *res publica* should articulate all interests according to conditions which subscribe to none in particular. Precisely because their demands are opposed, they show that Western liberal republics neither achieve nor in fact subscribe to such a procedurally neutral articulation. Thus, they debunk a fundamental premise of liberal ideology. The politics of difference has become so intense precisely because it suggests a basic change in the historical role of citizenship: it indicates the increasing disarticulation of formal citizenship as the principal norm for coordinating and managing the simultaneity of modern social identities in highly differentiated societies. In that suggestion, it ignites deep anxieties about what form such coordination might take, both juridically and symbolically, if citizenship no longer has that primary role.

Immigration is a central link between classical issues of citizenship—imaged as a right-bearing form of membership in the territorial nation-state and the city as this dense and heterogeneous lived space. Immigrants typically congregate and work in cities because the demands for their labor tend to be generated by urban commerce, infrastructure, and wage-differentiation. Moreover, immigrants tend to rely on previous networks of knowledge and affiliation for jobs and basic amenities. Thus, the politics of immigration is closely tied to the politics of cities, and the violence surrounding immigration is intimately connected with urban youth, gangs, slums, and politics. In the recent hunt for Islamic terrorists in the subways of Paris, or the recent expulsion of Bangladeshi immigrants from Bombay (which also involved the deportation of many Indian Muslims by "accident"), we see that in cities the politics of quality (in particular of difference) meets the politics of quantity (and of the anxieties of density). Immigration politics cannot be abstractly conducted evenly across all national space. It tends to be implosive (Appadurai, in press) and its most intense points of implosion are cities.

. . .

The great turmoil of citizenship in cities derives in large measure from new concentrations of wealth and misery among nationals related to industrialization. Where the shanties of migrants sprout next to the mansions, factories, and skyscrapers of industrial-state capitalism, new kinds of citizens engage each other in struggles over the nature of belonging to the national society. Such struggles are particularly evident in the social movements of the urban poor for rights to the city. They are especially associated with the emergence of democracy because they empower poor citizens to mobilize around the redistributive right-claims of citizenship. These movements are new not only because they force the state to respond to new social conditions of the working poor—in which sense they are, indeed, one of the significant consequences of massive urban poverty for citizenship. They are also unprecedented in many cases because they create new kinds of rights outside of the normative and institutional definitions of the state and its legal codes. These rights generally address the new collective and personal spaces of the modern metropolis, especially its impoverished residential neighborhoods. They affirm access to housing, property, sanitation, health services, education, child care, and so forth on the basis of citizenship. In this assertion, they expand the scope and understanding of entitlement. Is adequate housing a right? Is employment?

In this sense, the development of the economy itself fuels the growth of citizenship as new areas of social and economic life are brought under the calculus of right.

This expansion amounts to more than multiplying the number and beneficiaries of socio-economic rights, itself no small achievement. In addition, it changes the very conception of right and citizenship. Right becomes more of a claim upon than a possession held against the world. It becomes a claim upon society for the resources necessary to meet the basic needs and interests of members rather than a kind of property some possess and others do not. It is probably the case that this change applies mostly to socio-economic and political rights rather than to civil rights. In the emerging democracies of the developing world, the latter tend to remain decidedly underdeveloped. But in terms of rights to the city and rights to political participation, right becomes conceived as an aspect of social relatedness rather than as an inherent and natural property of individuals. This sort of claim is often based on the deeply felt capacity of new urban workers to contribute morally and politically to the public sphere because they do so economically. That is, even though poor, even if illegal squatters, they have rights because they are consumers and taxpayers. Moreover, in the development of this mode of reasoning, it is also possible to discern the beginnings of a more radical argument: people have rights to a minimum standard of living which does not depend on their relative economic or market worth but on their absolute rights as citizens to a measure of economic well-being and dignity. Potentially, this argument is radically redistributive of a society's wealth because it breaks down entrenched, elite-based explanations for relative worth and inequality.

. . .

To the extent that we have theories of citizenship that link these factors of globalization, economic change, immigration, and cities, they tend to focus either on the labor/immigration nexus or on the narrative of the erosion of Fordist ideas about industrial production. Yet, to deal with the range of cities in which dramas of citizenship are today played out, we need a broader image of urban processes that breaks out of the constraints of the Fordist (and post-Fordist) narrative. The histories of many cities in Africa, Asia, and Latin America have little to do with industry, manufacture, or production. Some of these cities are fundamentally commercial and financial, others are military and bureaucratic, and yet others are monumental and recreative of nationalist historiographies. This variety of cities generates a variety of dramas of citizenship, and in each of them the relationship between production, finance, labor, and service is somewhat different. We need more images and narratives of urban economies so that we can better identify the various ways in which such cities spawn class fragments, ethnic enclaves, gang territories, and varied maps of work, crime, and kinship.

. . .

As we have suggested citizenship concerns more than rights to participate in politics. It also includes other kinds of rights in the public sphere, namely, civil, socio-economic, and cultural. Moreover, in addition to the legal, it concerns the moral and performative dimensions of membership which define the meanings and practices of belonging in society. Undeniably, people use violence to make claims about all of these dimensions of belonging. In this sense, violence is a specific type of social action. Moreover, different social processes have their stock expressions of violence. This is not to say that industrialization features one repertoire of violence and globalization another. It is rather to suggest, that social processes instigate their own forms of violence in a given social and historical context, the meanings of which consolidate around specific problems, for example, of cultural identity, labor, or residence.

Thus, it is possible to observe that in many countries today democratization brings its own forms of violence. Moreover, as democratization is always a disjunctive process, in which citizenship rights expand and erode in complex arhythmic ways (Holston, forthcoming), it is possible to discern the effects of disjunction on the forms of violence. As discussed earlier, many transitions to democracy included a sustained expansion of political and socio-economic rights for the urban poor. Strikes which are violently repressed and turn into riots, land invasions and expulsions, destruction of public transportation, and political assassinations typically express the conflicts of this expansion. But even where the political and socio-economic components of citizenship are relatively consolidated in these transitions to democracy, the civil component which guarantees liberty, security, and above all justice is often inchoate and ineffectual. This disjunction is common to many countries undergoing democratization today. Where it happens, the majority cannot expect the institutions of state—the courts and the police especially—to respect or guarantee their individual rights, arbitrate their conflicts justly, or control violence legally. In other words, there is massive support for market forms of justice on the one hand (private security, vigilantes, enforcers) and, on the other, for extralegal and even illegal measures of control by state institutions, particularly the police (and related death squads) who kill large numbers of "marginals." This kind of violence further discredits the justice system and with it the entire project of democracy and its citizenship.

. . .

Surely, violence is not city-bound. But coincidence does not have to be absolute or exclusive to establish correspondence. The point is that people use violence to make claims upon the city and use the city to make violent claims. They appropriate a space to which they then declare they belong; they violate a space which others claim. Such acts generate a city-specific violence of citizenship. Its geography is too legible, too visible to be missed in the abandoned public spaces of the modern city, in its fortified residential enclaves, its division into corporate luxury zone's and quarantined war zones, its forbidden sectors of gangs and "armed response" security, its bunkers of fundamentalists, its illegally constructed shanties, its endless neighborhoods of unemployed youth.

With the breakdown of civility and nationality thus evident, many are seeking alternatives in the post-, trans-, de-, re-, (and plain con) of current speculations about the future of the nation-state. It is a heady moment, full of great creativity and uncertainty. Many proposals are circulating for new kinds of public spheres, third spaces, virtual communities, transnations, and diasporic networks. The results are surely contradictory. It may be that cybercitizenship draws some into a more tolerant and accessible public realm. But it also seems to drive others further into the recesses of the private and the market. The failure of nation-states to produce convincing fantasies of the commensurability of its citizens ("The People") compels some to imagine recombinant forms of nonterritorial, life-world sovereignties, while it forces others into even more primordial and violent affiliations of territory, religion, and race. The grand theories that were once used to explain pushes and pulls of such magnitude have themselves splintered, in keeping with the nations which gave them sustenance. Contemporary theory seems as displaced and dislocated, as hybrid and diasporic, as so many of the world's populations.

In all of this commotion, it is perhaps understandable to treat the city, that old form of human society, as irrelevant. But until transnations attain more flesh and bone, cities may still be the most important sites in which we experience the crises of national membership and through which we may rethink citizenship. It may even be, after all, that there is something irreducible and nontransferable, necessary but not quite sufficient, about the city's public street and square for the realization of a meaningfully democratic citizenship. If we support the latter, we may have to do much more to defend the former.

References

Appadurai, Arjun (forthcoming). *Modernity at Large: Cultural Dimensions of Globalization*. Minneapolis: University of Minnesota Press.

Dietz, Mary (1992). "Context Is All: Feminism and Theories of Citizenship," in Chantal Mouffe (ed.), *Dimensions of Radical Democracy: Pluralism, Citizenship, Community*. London: Verso, 63–85.

Holston, James (1989). *The Modernist City: An Anthropological Critique of Brasilia*. Chicago: University of Chicago Press.

—— (forthcoming) "Justice in a Disjunctive Democracy: Judicial Reform, Alternative Law, and Social Conflict in Brazil." *Latin American Research Review*.

Marshall, T. H. (1977 [1949]). "Citizenship and Social Class," in *Class, Citizenship, and Social Development*. Chicago: University of Chicago Press, 71–134.

Okin, Susan Moller (1992). "Women, Equality, and Citizenship." *Queens's Quarterly*, 99 (1): 56–71.

Pateman, Carole (1989). *The Disorder of Women*. Stanford: Stanford University Press.

Taylor, Charles (1992). "Multiculturalism and the Politics of Recognition," in Charles Taylor, edited with commentary by Amy Gutmann, *Multiculturalism and the Politics of Recognition*. Princeton University Press, 3–73.

25 Plotting Women

Popular Narratives for Women in the United States and in Latin America

Jean Franco

. . .

THE exportability of mass culture (and particularly U.S. mass culture) is a factor of major importance in contemporary Latin American societies. In the first place, it provides a common cultural repertoire that crosses national boundaries and thus tends, superficially at least, to blur the local idiosyncracies on which the idea of national character formerly depended. Second, most mass culture forms use formulas that can readily be adjusted to local circumstances. Third, as I shall point out in this comparison between women's popular romance in the United States and Mexico, mass culture has clearly a didactic function and operates as a socializing system that is now as powerful as schooling and religion, though its methods are vastly different from the methods of these institutions.

The use of formulas—that is, ready-made plots and ready-to-hand symbols—is both a major feature of mass culture and the target of most of the critical attacks from academics and high-culture critics. Theodore Adorno's analysis of jazz (by which he meant popular American music) was prototypical in this respect.[1] More recently, the attacks have tended to isolate the "closed narratives" that are characteristic of nineteenth-century "classical realism" as well as of modern mass literature, in which plotting toward a felicitous conclusion (and therefore a closure of meaning) is the major structural device, producing functional characters, situations, and descriptions. Although there are many subgenres of formula literature both in the United States and in Latin America, women's literature seems to have attracted the most attention because of its overwhelming popularity, on the one hand, and its repetitive poverty of form, on the other. These critical speculations range from the denunciation of mass literature for women as degraded to claims that the audience "reads" in a way that is different from, though not necessarily inferior to, the reading of the "high-culture" audience.

. . .

The study of popular fiction in the United States and Mexico makes abundantly clear not only that the plotting of women into gender roles takes on new forms when they are

From Jean Franco, "Plotting Women: Popular Narratives for Women in the United States and in Latin America," in Bell Gale Chevigny and Gari Laguardia (eds.), *Reinventing the Americas: Comparative Studies of Literature of the United States and Spanish America* (Cambridge: Cambridge University Press, 1986), 249–68.

considered both as consumers and as reproducers of the labor force but also that the international division of labor between privileged industrialized societies and Third World societies affects the way that corporate society regulates its fictions of the subject and of socialization.

. . .

What has made mass literature of interest to critics (particularly feminists), however, is not its repetitive and anachronistic form but its popularity. Ann Barr Snitow, for instance, mentions the colossal sales figures of Harlequins and popular romances in the United States and justifies her study of books that are not art but "leisure activities that take the place of art," on the grounds that "it would be at best grossly incurious, and at worse sadly limited, for literary critics to ignore a genre that millions and millions of women read voraciously."[2] Janice Radway, in an important study of romance literature, illustrates how the corporate takeover of publishing encouraged the promotion of what she calls "category literature." Corporate publishers "believe it is easier to introduce a new author by fitting his or her work into a previously formalized chain of communication than to establish its uniqueness by locating a special audience for it. The trend has proven so powerful, in fact, that as of 1980, 40 to 50 percent of nearly every house's monthly releases were paperback originals."[3]

In their efforts to find reasons for these large sales, many feminist critics have turned to psychological explanations. Ann Barr Snitow, for instance, argues that these romances "feed certain regressive elements of female experience,"[4] but is reluctant to come down from the fence and either condemn or celebrate them: "To observe that they express primary structures of our social relations is not to claim either a cathartic usefulness for them or a dangerous power to keep women in their place." Rosalind Coward, writing on romance as an expression of women's desire, believes that such fiction "restores the childhood world of sexual relations and suppresses criticism of the inadequacy of men, the suffocation of the family, or the damage inflicted by patriarchal power. Yet it simultaneously manages to avoid the guilt and fear which might come from that childhood world. Sexuality is defined firmly as the father's responsibility and fear of suffocation is overcome because women achieve a sort of power in the romantic fiction."[5] Thus, for Coward, women pay a high price for fictional power and enjoyment —a price that involves evading the pain of self-assertion by remaining perpetual children. Furthermore, any power that the heroine or reader is likely to attain, according to Coward's interpretation, has little effect on the larger structures of authority that determine the heroine's path to the paradise of consumption. In fact, most feminist critics want to have their cake and eat it, want to show that the formula is restrictive, yet want to find that it offers space for resistance. For instance, in an illuminating analysis that owes much to Freudian criticism, Tania Modleski suggests that the very tightness of the plot indicates the scope of women's resentment, which can be controlled only by making the heroine perform a "disappearing act."[6] The reader, for her part, is forced into a kind of schizoid reaction, being the surveyor of the heroine while also being invited to identify with her and hence to be the surveyed. Modleski argues that, far from achieving undiluted escape, the reader experiences a compulsion to repeat the reading because there is no real-life resolution of these contradictory feelings.[7] Though Janice

Radway criticizes such literary readings of romance in her book *Reading the Romance* and tries to correct them by showing how the romances are read and evaluated by real readers, her conclusions bear out some of Modleski's assertions. Radway's readers invariably stressed enjoyment of repeated readings, their need for escape from family and daily routine, and their preference for the kind of romance in which satisfactory characters and resolutions remove the anxieties and enigmas posed by the plot. In short, what we discover in recent criticism in the United States is the tendency not to blame the reader and to stress women's active participation in reading.

. . .

Both Harlequins and Mexican *libros semanales* (i.e., weekly comic-strip books) present a manifest reader's plot and an authorial plot. The first can be described as a plot that incorporates elements from everyday experience, such as resentment and violence; the authorial plot resolves these tensions in a publicly acceptable form, so that plot resolution is not intended to thwart the reader's expectations but rather to suggest forms of system incorporation that not only allow women a social role but also promise social recognition. The brevity of this essay obliges me to select a single example of the Harlequins for discussion even though this appears to privilege one instance of a repetitive plot structure. Fortunately, other critics (e.g., Janice Radway) have read exhaustively in order to isolate the invariable elements. I shall therefore concentrate on one popular Harlequin, *Moonwitch* by Ann Mather. I choose this example because it explicitly plots women into corporate society.

Sara, the heroine of *Moonwitch*, has a humble background. She is an orphan, brought up by a grandfather who, on his deathbed, bequeaths her to the Kyle Textile Corporation, believing this to be controlled by his old friend J. K. In fact, the corporation has been taken over by J. K.'s son Jarrod, and the father is living in retirement in the Kyle manor house. Despite his misgivings, Jarrod accepts Sara as his ward but turns her over to J. K., who becomes her companion and guides her through the unfamiliar social world she has now entered. It is no accident that this social world is represented by the manorial space of the Kyle house, for this is the anachronistic space of patriarchy that is based on a feudal master-slave relationship. Sara's training is essentially a programming into corporate society. At the same time, she faces the typical double binds of the Harlequin heroine—that is, she is seductive and yet cannot afford to give in when Jarrod attempts to seduce her.

It should be stressed that, although the sexual encounters in such books as the Candlelight Ecstasy romances are often more titillating and "modern," the archaic formula of postponement of pleasure used by the Harlequin is still a powerful attraction to women readers all over the world. Thus, though prevented from responding sexually before marriage, Sara appears in seductive situations (half-naked on a beach in Jamaica), and it is always she, rather than the male, who must exercise self-control in order to reach the final goal of marriage. Furthermore, though she will attain upward mobility through marriage, she is not allowed to be ambitious for money. Indeed, Jarrod treats her badly as long as he believes her to be seducing him for his wealth. This double bind is transcended only when the patriarch J. K. dies, leaving Sara his valuable porcelain collection. Overcome by grief, she spurns the collection, thus proving that she is not simply after money. Disinterestedness is the shortest road to wealth for the Harlequin heroine.

The function of the Harlequin plot is twofold. In the first place, it reproduces anxiety situations that are insoluble, but this insoluble plot is then overcoded by a second plot —that is, the plot we read in the light of the successful outcome. The two plots center mainly on the hero's character, which in the first plot is enigmatic and hostile, just as adult society is enigmatic and hostile to most women, who are forced to learn how to behave by trial and error. This hostility is likely to cause resentment. The second plot ensures that we read the story in order to correct any misunderstanding as to the hero's character. The corporate hero is, in reality, benign and considerate and when success-fully "read" will lift the heroine up to her proper place as reproducer of consumer society. This clearly suggests that anxiety is an essential element in consumer society and shows how women are taught to use the tactics of the weak—seduction—in order to negotiate a modest place in a society whose rules they have not made and from which they are initially estranged.

As Tania Modleski points out, the first plot is presented as an incorrect reading, that is, the misunderstanding of the hero's true character. Thanks to the ending and the marriage contract, this misunderstanding can be corrected. Thus the marriage contract is itself of dual significance since it recognizes that the heroine is worthy to take her "true" place in society, while showing that this acceptance must come from outside, from the patriarchal order itself. Misreading marks women's accession to the symbolic order; that is to say, misrecognition is a basic part of their training. Men are repressive, cruel, and powerful, and the only way to get by is to learn what society says women "truly" want. What is unpleasant and even unnatural can be tamed by the right tactics. Thus the second plot maps the paths that allow the first plot to be controlled. The powerful male figure has to be "reread" not as an oppressive tyrant but as a master of social rules that the heroine must learn, just as the hero has to learn to soften his will to power. At the same time, Harlequins exploit the preconstructed expectations that stem from the reader's experience of unequal gender relations in order to negotiate a more satisfactory contract with corporate consumerism. However, it is a contract that one can negotiate only by falling back on the tactics of the weak—that is, on seduction rather than outright confrontation.

If women's popular fiction offers an oddly hedged response to self-indulgence in the United States, this hedging is even more apparent in literature produced in societies of scarcity. Mexico is particularly interesting as a vantage point from which to monitor this literature, both because it is a major producer of "photonovels" and other types of popular fiction and because the productions of corporate Mexico conflict in significant ways with an older nationalist ideology.

. . .

The trend away from the reformist state (*el estado de compromiso*) to a deregulated society that made scarcity the major incentive of the work force has generally been presented under the euphemistic label "modernization." Because women were now a major factor in the development of new industries, women, too, had to be modernized. Magazines and popular literature all over Latin America played a major role by showing the desirability of "modernity," as Michèle Mattelart pointed out in a study of women's magazines sold in Chile during the early 1970s.[8] In a study of "photonovels" (i.e., novels that use photographic stills and a brief text to tell the story), Cornelia Butler Flora and Jan Flora likewise argued that this literature was an instrument for integrating the population into the labor force as well as into a consumer culture. The authors divide photonovels into three categories: (1) disintegrative/integrative, that is, as to the way they break down old patterns and integrate readers into new ways of thinking; (2) pure escape; and (3) consumer-oriented. Obviously, these are not narrative categories and, as content categories, they are not clearly distinguishable. Nevertheless, the Floras' conclusion is persuasive, for it gives this literature a performative role. "Seen as an evolutionary process, these stories separate a woman from her actual environment and prepare her to accept the necessity of marginal participation as consumption is added to her function of reproduction of household labor."[9]

In contrast to photonovels, *libros semanales*, or comic-strip novels, have attracted little critical attention,[10] despite the somewhat idiosyncratic manner in which the modernization plot is written. There are two major publishers of these comic-strip novels. The novels I shall discuss here are published by Novedades Editores, a subsidiary of Mex-Ameris, which is controlled by the powerful O'Farrill interests.

. . .

The comic strips are crudely drawn and often use the shorthand indices of emotion conventionalized in U.S. comics, which are left untranslated in Spanish. For instance, "Snif, Snif," indicates weeping. The color of the comics is a monotonous sepia, and the covers are often unattractive. They have neither the glossy appeal of the photonovel nor the escapist fantasy provided by the romance fiction produced under the name of Corín Tellado. Precisely because the *libros semanales* are so unglamorous and are so clearly intended for women who are integrated or about to be integrated into the work place, they require a different kind of modernization plot, one that cannot simply hold out the carrot of consumption.

The distinctive feature of the *novela semanal* is its explicit moral, a moral that often strikingly conflicts with the apparent plot. In *Los nuevos ricos* (The Nouveaux Riches, vol. 32, no. 1541, March 9, 1984), the plot appears to focus on adultery. The wife of Luis Felipe, who has married him only for his money seduces his brother Luciano. The novel begins at the dramatic moment when Luciano, shocked at his own conduct, commits suicide. The family and Luis Felipe, who know nothing of the affair, are baffled by this tragedy, but before they discover its cause, there is an unexpected and apparently disconnected flashback to Luis Felipe's father, whose origins are now explained in some detail.

Luis Felipe's father is a *nuevo rico* who began life as a peasant. One day as he returns from work in the fields accompanied by an aunt, he finds the family home destroyed and his parents dead. A Mexican reader might immediately connect this destruction to the revolution or the Cristero War, but the novel avoids such historical specificity and turns it into an accidental tragedy. Soldiers, in search of a fugitive, had mistakenly caused the deaths. The novel thus manages at once to allude to the violence of the past without indicating that this violence brought about social change and to suggest that violence comes from the forces of the state. The "accident" drives the father and his aunt from the village and into the city, where they make a fortune selling fruit. They become the "new rich" of the title; in due time, the father marries and has two sons, Luciano and Luis Felipe, whose upbringing he neglects because of his concern with money. At the end of this flashback, we return to the adultress, who is now haunted by the dead Luciano and who dies in remorse. This second "accident" will have the same result as the first. Luis Felipe decides that he can no longer live with his parents and must make his own way in life, starting from scratch.

Now the best that can be said about this plot is that it is incoherent. Certainly, if the reader were to draw a moral lesson, it might concern the evils of adultery. Yet the adultery turns out to be a side issue. The explicit moral printed at the end of the story is "Money and social position kill even the sincerest feeling. Luciano and Luis Felipe's parents forgot that they owed their children love and instead amassed a large fortune which, as the novel shows, was of no use to them." What seems to be the plot of the story, a plot that arouses anger at the conduct of an unscrupulous temptress, turns out to be a secondary matter that is punished by supernatural means. The "sin" of the older generation—their egoism—has to be dealt with on the level of everyday life. Egoism and moral blindness prevent them from being suitable guides for their children, who have to seek their satisfaction outside the traditional family.

This seems a strange conclusion for a country like Mexico in which the family has, at least in theory, always provided a network of support. It also contrasts in startling fashion with the Victorian treatment of sexually aberrant behavior, which was often exposed and punished, the better to cement the ties between generations. *La Traviata* is a classic example of a father-son relationship cemented by the sacrifice of the courtesan, whose death allows the family to triumph over sexuality. In the Mexican *novela semanal*, the family is an obstacle to individual progress, and adultery is one of the consequences of members of the same family inhabiting the same house. Unlike Freudianism, which makes "separation" from the mother and the oedipal conflict a crucial stage in childhood development, this novel stresses separation as an *adult* process that frees the individual from the weight of the past represented by the older generation. Though never officially stated, the official ideology of postrevolutionary Mexico, which was, at least in theory, based on the desirability of state-directed (paternalistic) reform with each generation building on the contribution of the prior generation, is here undermined by an individualistic self-help philosophy.

Though I cannot claim to have read more than a small number of these novels, I have read a sufficient number to make it clear that the attack on the older generation in *Los nuevos ricos* is not an isolated example. Again and again, such stories exploit violence, rape, and sensation only to place the blame in the end squarely on the shoulders of the older generation. In one of the novels, *Las abandonadas* (The Abandoned Girls, vol. 32, no. 1537, February 10, 1984), the children of a "fallen" mother and a cruel father eventually escape from the father's house and find work in the city. The moral states: "Parents must never betray their children's trust. Children are soft wax which can be molded. Unhappy children become unhappy adults but happy children will form homes that are filled with peace and love."

Clearly this moral does not follow from the logic of the conclusion, since "the abandoned girls" should be as evil as their parents. Once again the conclusion we might naturally draw from the life story is thwarted, this time because the moral of the story suggests a culture of poverty thesis according to which the older generation passes on its defects to the next. If children are "soft wax," how can they escape from evil parenting? In this case, we can only conclude that children can break the cycle by making a break with the family and going to work in the city.

In both the examples I have discussed, the focus is not so much on women as on the family as an institution. Mexican postrevolutionary policy had encouraged the secularization of public life while leaving the traditional patriarchal family untouched and absorbing machismo into its national image. The Mexican family is thus an extremely complex institution, not only a source of considerable tensions, especially among the poor, but a source of support and daily communication that the state and its institutions cannot replace. It is interesting, therefore, that many of the *novelas semanales* place less emphasis on romance than on working or on marriage as a working partnership. In *Lo que no quiso recordar* (What She Did Not Want to Remember, vol. 22, no. 1557, June 29, 1984), the heroine Chelo marries a friendly architect after some misadventures with an unscrupulous brother-in-law, who had tried to blackmail her into a relationship. The moral declares that "true love means faith and trust in one's partner and the knowledge that, despite hardship, trouble and economic difficulty, their mutual love will make them confident that all will turn out right in the end."

Though, in this case, the reader might have reached this conclusion without prompting, the suggestion that marriages face economic hardship is not reflected in the plot. Yet it is not a totally gratuitous observation, for it serves as a warning that the romantic element should not blind the reader to the fact that marriage is a working relationship. It underlines the fact that in this Mexican popular literature, unlike the Harlequin, romance is not the issue and readers are expected to use real-life experience to evaluate the story.

One explanation of the disjunction between plot and explicit moral message may be rooted in the origin of the stories—that is, everyday life as told in readers' letters or in the popular press. The latter provides a diet of violence and sensationalism that has few parallels in the rest of Latin America. Why violence should be so popular among Mexicans is not altogether clear, unless it has to do with the desire to dramatize lives that may otherwise seem pointless. At the same time, since the violence is attributed in the novels mainly to a regressive mentality, it clearly belongs to the past that the novel condemns and not to the modern life toward which the readers are supposed to aspire. In the modernization tale, it is the ingrained habits of the "typical" Mexican—violence, machismo, and drunkenness—that have to be repudiated, and since men of the older generation do not seem likely to reform themselves, women must simply break away from the traditional family and embrace the work ethic.

. . .

It should be stressed here that the organization of plot material in the *novela semanal* is different from that in the Harlequin novel. The *novela semanal* is not written exclusively from the female point of view and does not incorporate itself into the social norm. Rather, women are invited to see themselves as victims of a plot, the plot of the old

Mexico that has passed on the tradition of machismo and thus harmed them. If, instead of reading themselves into the plot as helpless victims, they turn their resentment against the older generation of men and separate themselves from this influence, they can expect to succeed. The solution suggests the need for struggle rather than escapism. The determinism of one generation transmitting its defects to the next can be transcended, and women can start life anew as members of the work force.

It is therefore not surprising to find an explicitly feminist ideology in some of the *libros semanales*. In *Una mujer insatisfecha* (An Unsatisfied Woman, vol. 32, no. 1580, December 7, 1984) the heroine is married to a boring and impotent businessman who believes in patriarchy and the traditional values of family life. Luisa is repelled by his puritanical attitude to marital relations and quarrels with her Italian mother-in-law, whose ideas on marriage are strictly traditional. She sets up her own consultancy as a designer and meets another man but refuses to enter into a relationship that promises to be as oppressive as the one with her husband. Back in her mother's home, she hangs up the telephone when her new lover calls, feeling "free, happy and without ties." More surprising is the plot of *Desprestigiada* (The Disgraced Woman, vol. 32, no. 1572, October 12, 1984), in which the heroine, a flirt who likes to pick up male visitors to the Pyramids, is raped by a "foreigner" (probably a Central American) who works in the post office. When she discovers that she is pregnant, she has an abortion thanks to the help of a traditional *curandera* and a woman doctor. But the foreigner rapes her a second time, because he wants a child he can adopt and take back to his own country. The rape (which is a somewhat unusual adoption procedure) is, however, less germane to the conclusion than the birth of the illegitimate child. The foreigner's plan to seize the baby is thwarted when he is picked up as an illegal immigrant, and it is Luisa who brings the baby up until the child is weaned. The reader might expect this to be the ending, but this is not a story about a girl's redemption through motherhood. Rather, as soon as the child is old enough to be left with another person, she is handed over to Luisa's mother and Luisa goes back to her old life, picking up men at the Pyramids. The only moral lesson is that in the future she must be more careful.

There is considerable irony in this attack on machismo in the guise of liberation. It plays on the sentiments of 1968, plays on the difference between the modernity of the young and the blind conformity of the old. It does so thanks to the anachronistic melodramatic plot, in which random acts of violence can be justified only on the grounds of the heroine's final social integration. Even so, the moral and the ending are often so arbitrary in relation to the sequence of events that they highlight the arbitrary nature of all narratives, including the master narrative of nationalism with its appeal to rootedness, to place, and to community.

In older forms of social narrative, the "story" tended to be woven out of lived experience. This term, now rightly treated with suspicion because of its empirical bias, must nevertheless be introduced because the process of human life ("the logic of mortality") cannot help but be the most powerful of paradigms. We fell in love and married and had children, and all this seemed to happen naturally. Of course, we were still woven into a social plot in which marriage and the family not only satisfied our needs for affection and recognition but also contributed to social reproduction. Nevertheless, this plot was built on events—childhood, adolescence, maturation—that appeared to be natural. The modernization plot works against this formerly "natural" state of affairs, showing that life stories are not what they seem. In Harlequins, romance is a prize available only to those who learn the conditions under which female power can be exercised. In the *libros semanales*, the family is not seen as the inevitable source of satisfaction for women.

. . .

Mass culture narrative thus deals with problems that go far beyond entertainment. By addressing itself to serialized readers, it can appeal to private feelings and private lives. Yet this literature commutes private sentiments into stories that map out (plot) the way different sectors of the population can be incorporated into the international division of labor. Whereas the Harlequin romances use the powerful parallel between the stages of socialization and a ritual of passage from adolescence to womanhood, the *libros semanales* often depict a violent break between women as workers and women as family members. The plots of both, however, seem to depend on the fact that women experience considerable anxiety and uncertainty as to where they stand in relation to society. The *libros semanales* reveal that there is not a single model for the sex-gender system under capitalism, but rather multiple options. Furthermore, when these options contradict women's everyday practices or beliefs, they have to be plotted as a simulation of real life in order to persuade the readership to change its attitudes. The *libro semanal* thus bears some resemblance to the CIA guerrilla manual, which, since it could not appeal to the real-life situations of Nicaraguans, resorted to simulating events (e.g., an execution) in order to provide such experience.[11]

. . .

Women, then, are plotted in different ways according to their position in the international division of labor. Curiously, it is women in the most affluent sectors (or those who can aspire to that affluence) who are invited most vigorously to give up their cultural capital (that which would permit them to "think like a man") and find security in their own narcissistic image. In the lower strata of the international division of labor, work or individual emancipation takes the place of romance. These novels suggest that "love" is a luxury, a fantasy not for all women but for middle- and upper-class women seeking the complementary man who will heal the split in their personality. What women want is provided by the Harlequin romance in a very efficient way, but it disguises the fact that this is the only way of being truly "incorporated." If the *libro semanal* is more problematic, it is because it does not address what women want, but rather disguises economic oppression as emancipation from the violence and oppression of working-class men. Significantly missing from mass literature is any form of female solidarity; it reinforces the serialization of women, which is the very factor that makes their exploitation both as reproducers of the labor force and as cheap labor so viable even in corporate society.

Plotting is a social as well as a literary device, and clearly, although it is important to recognize that reading the plot does not mean being committed to the social system it maps out, it is also important to understand the perplexing disjunction that is now taking place at the level of morality. "The area of belief which concerned religion, sexual and personal morality, and the sanctity and social significance of the family, has collapsed in modern bourgeois culture," according to one group of critics.[12] Harlequins map out the conditions for consumerism and *libros semanales* for incorporation into the work force, but whereas the former retain traditional morality in almost nostalgic fashion within the ethical vacuum of consumerism, the latter insist on emancipation from the restraints of a family that is now a hindrance to capitalist development in Mexico.

Both kinds of mass literature I have examined seem to indicate that women find a great deal of satisfaction in stories that promise an illusory form of social recognition and provide a parenthesis to everyday life in which that recognition is withheld. Thus, even though this literature plots women's lives with regard to system integration, it also points to personal needs that arise from the ethical vacuum of late capitalism, which offers little more than raw competition, the fetishism of the commodity, or in Mexico, the exploitation of the runaway shop.

Notes

1. Theodor Adorno, "On popular music," *Studies in Philosophy and Social Science* (New York) 9 (1941): 17–28.
2. Ann Barr Snitow, "Mass Market Romance: Pornography for Women Is Different," in Ann Snitow, Christine Stansell, and Sharon Thompson (eds.), *Powers of Desire: The Politics of Sexuality* (New York: Monthly Review Press, 1983), p. 246.
3. Janice A. Radway, *Reading the Romance: Women, Patriarchy and Popular Literature* (Chapel Hill: University of North Carolina Press, 1984), p. 36.
4. Snitow, "Mass Market Romance," p. 247.
5. Rosalind Coward, *Female Desire: Women's Sexuality Today* (New York: Palladin, 1984), p. 196.
6. Tania Modleski, *Loving with a Vengeance: Mass Produced Fantasies for Women* (Hamden, Conn.: Archon Books, 1982), p. 37.
7. Ibid., p. 57.
8. Michèle Mattelart, "Notes on 'Modernity': A Way of Reading Women's Magazines," in Armand Mattelart and Seth Siegelaub (eds.), *Communication and Class Struggle* (New York: International General, 1979), pp. 158–70.
9. Cornelia Butler Flora and Jan Flora, "The Fotonovela as a Tool for Class and Cultural Domination," *Latin American Perspectives*, issue 16, vol. 5, no. 1 (Winter 1978): 134–50.
10. Except for Charles Tatum and Harold E. Hinds, "Mexican and American Comic Books in a Comparative Perspective," in Juanita Luna Lawhn, Juan Bruce-Novoa, Guillermo Campos, and Ramón Saldívar (eds.), *Mexico and the United States: Intercultural Relations in the Humanities* (Texas: San Antonio College Press 1984), pp. 67–83.
11. *Psychological Operations in Guerrilla Warfare*, with essays by Joanne Omang and Aryeh Neier (New York: Vintage Books, 1985).
12. Nicolas Abercrombie, Stephen Hill, and Bryan S. Turner, *The Dominant Ideology Thesis* (London: Allen & Unwin, 1980), p. 138.

26 The Transvestite Continuum Liberace–Valentino–Elvis

Majorie Garber

THE more I have studied transvestism and its relation to representation the more I have begun to see it, oddly enough, as in many ways normative: as a condition that very frequently accompanies theatrical representation when theatrical self-awareness is greatest. Transvestite theater from Kabuki to the Renaissance English stage to the contemporary drag show is not—or not only—a recuperative structure for the social control of sexual behavior, but also a critique of the possibility of "representation" itself.

In order to make such large claims for transvestism as a social and theoretical force—in order to argue that there can be no culture without the transvestite because the transvestite marks the entry into the Symbolic—I need to test out the *boundaries* of transvestism, to see it or read it in places other than where it is most obvious. I need to argue, in other words, for an *unconscious* of transvestism, for transvestism as a language that can be read, and double-read, like a dream, a fantasy, or a slip of the tongue. In the domain of theater, the self-reflexive locus of much transvestite activity, I want to hypothesize what might be called "unmarked" transvestism, to explore the possibility that some entertainers who do not overly claim to be "female impersonators," for example, may in fact signal their cross-gender identities onstage, and that this quality of crossing—which is fundamentally related to other kinds of boundary-crossing in their performances—can be more powerful and seductive than explicit "female impersonation," which is often designed to confront, scandalize, titillate, or shock.

. . .

I would like to turn to three figures from popular culture in whom a certain consternation of gender is, to use a distinction from Roland Barthes, "received" but not "read."[1] ("The rhetorical or latent signified," says Barthes, discussing the ideology of fashion, is "the essential paradox of connoted signification: it is, one might say, a signification that is *received* but not *read.*") This is another opportunity to look *at* rather than *through* the transvestite, in this case by regarding the unconscious of transvestism as a speaking symptom, a language of clothing which is, tacitly, both dress and address. Unlike professional female impersonators, or comedians who affect travesty for particular theatrical ends (Milton Berle, Flip Wilson as Geraldine, Dana Carvey as the Church Lady), these performers do not think of themselves as transvestites. But—as we will see—the way they are received and discussed in the media, and, increasingly, the way they emphasize

From Marjorie Garber, "The Transvestite Continuum: Liberace–Valentino–Elvis," in Marjorie Garber, *Vested Interests: Cross-Dressing and Cultural Anxiety* (New York and London: Routledge, 1992), 353–74.

their own trademark idiosyncrasies of dress in response to audience interest all suggest that the question of cross-dressing, whether overt or latent, is central to their success, and even to the very question of stardom.

My first example may strike you as a bit too obvious to be considered completely unmarked, but he is, I think, at the origin of a certain theatrical worrying of exactly that borderline. I refer, of course, to the figure "known variously as Mr. Showmanship, the Candelabra Kid, Guru of Glitter, Mr. Smiles, The King of Diamonds, and Mr. Box-office," and described as "undoubtedly America's most beloved entertainer"[2]: Liberace.

Liberace, pianist, singer, tap dancer, and fashion plate, clearly regarded himself as a direct influence upon the pop stars of the eighties, citing Prince, Michael Jackson, Boy George, and Madonna as among those who had learned from him about "escapism and fantasy."[3] "There was a time," he reminisced, "when one woman might say to another, 'May I borrow your lipstick?' Now, it's not unusual for one male rocker to say to another, 'May I borrow your eyeliner?' And practically no man is above borrowing his best friend's skin bronzer" (Liberace, 222). "I was the first to create shock waves," he said. "For me to wear a simple tuxedo onstage would be like asking Marlene Dietrich to wear a housedress."[4]

The genial campiness of these remarks offers the retrospective view of a survivor. Yet Liberace's crossover career in fact tested boundaries with a singular combination of business acumen and purported self-revelation. Strikingly illustrating the notion I have developed above of the transvestite who emerges as sign of a "category crisis" located in a domain other than that of gender, he straddled the line between classical and popular music, all the while keeping his costume changes one jump (or one jumpsuit) ahead of the competition. A black diamond mink cape lined with Austrian rhinestones, weighing 135 pounds, so heavy that it gave one backstage worker a hernia. An ostrich-feather cape. A hundred-pound cape of pink-dyed turkey feathers for the Radio City Music Hall Easter Show, in which he planned to emerge from a giant Fabergé egg. "Quite frankly," grumped one critic, "all that pink and feathers make him look like a female imperson-ator auditioning for 'An Evening at La Cage.'"[5] A white fox fur cape with a long train which he wore for a command performance for the Queen. A matador's outfit that prefigures George Michael's—and Grace Jones's. A fancy-dress uniform with epaulets and gold braid that anticipates Michael Jackson in "We Are the World." Red, white, and blue hot pants that made him look like a drum majorette. His rings and jewelry were as extravagant as his furs and sequins. "To shake his hand," said the New York Times, "was to flirt with laceration."[6]

Liberace's appeal is often thought to have been largely or exclusively to older women, but at the peak of his popularity he was a culture hero to "girls and women of all ages—ready to squeal or swoon when they thought the occasion required it of them," and who responded with "hysterical adoration" to his appearance in 1956 at the Festival Hall—at least according to the customarily staid Times of London.[7] When the Liberace family—Lee, George, and their mother—arrived in London in 1956, he was welcomed by a crowd of over 3,000, mostly young girls and women, though the Times also notes the presence of "a few amused policemen [and] some ardent young men."[8] The British reviews are cautiously admiring, of his "resourceful" piano playing and "agreeable" singing and tap dancing as well as his "fancy dress": "with all his finery and his almost natural peaches and cream complexion," one noted, "he is a shy, quiet little man . . . He did not swank or slobber, or flash diamond rings shaped like grand pianos at his admirers" (*Times*, October 2, 1956).

His performances were more like fashion shows than piano recitals. Parading up and down the stage in outfit after outfit ("Pardon me while I go slip into something more spectacular") he was in effect the first to mainstream "voguing"—the eighties dance craze borrowed from male transvestite drag shows in Harlem in the sixties, that incorporates exaggerated fashion model poses. Liberace dressed for the stage, he said himself, "just one step short of drag" (Thomas, 215).

Displacing sexual questions onto sartorial ones with practiced ease, Liberace used the word "straight" to describe his "civilian" or offstage *clothes* (Liberace, 179). Although in his stage performances of the eighties he joked that he'd never wear in the street the clothes he wore on the stage, "or I'd get picked up, for sure," he preserved a theatrical space in which he could both assert and put in teasing question his heterosexuality and his biological or anatomical maleness. Thus the gag lines in his nightclub act about "streaking" with sex-symbol Burt Reynolds ("I've got the diamonds, he's got the jewels") and about the necessity of getting up from the piano from time to time ("it straightens the shorts").[9]

. . .

It was not Peter Pan, however, who was Liberace's ideal, but rather a male star who had remained forever young by the unlooked-for expedient of dying early—his namesake, Rudolph Valentino. Liberace's mother, a great fan of the Latin lover, named her son Wladziu Valentino Liberace and, for good measure, also named his younger brother Rudolph. In many ways Liberace seems to have been haunted by the phantom of Valentino, "my namesake," as he described him to reporters (Thomas, 100). He had some of Valentino's elaborate costumes copied for stage performance. He bought Valentino's bed and put it in one of his guest rooms; he collected and exhibited at the Liberace Museum a pair of silver goblets said to have been intended as wedding gifts to Valentino and Pola Negri.

Furthermore, Valentino appears as a major figure in Liberace's personal social history of crossover style: "Years ago, both male and female movie legends influenced the fashion and cosmetic industries. All over the world, you could find copies of Dietrich's eyebrows, Joan Crawford's shoulder pads and shoes, Valentino's slave bracelet, as well as his slicked-back, glossy patent-leather hairstyle" (Liberace, 222). All of these, we might note, are cross-dressed or cross-gendered examples: a woman's shoulder pads, a man's bracelet, Dietrich's eyebrows.

He-man, heartthrob, movie idol, Valentino seems about as distant from Liberace—and from transvestism, marked or unmarked—as it would seem possible to get. Yet he is in fact an exemplary figure of unmarked transvestism, at once feminized and hypermale. His appearance in Arab robes, eyebrow pencil and mascara as the title character in *The Sheik* (1921), as we have noted, set off a frenzy of response among (largely female) filmgoers with its drama of sexual sadism amidst the tents of a "Middle Eastern" locale.

In fact the cross-dressing elements in Valentino's story are stronger and more omnipresent than the eye-makeup and the flowing robes. A notorious photograph of him as a faun, dressed in fake fur tights and playing a flute was exhibited in court. Valentino apparently tried to explain it as a "costume test" for a never-produced film called *The Faun through the Ages*, but it is more probable that he was posing in the Nijinsky role from *L'Après-midi d'un Faune* at the behest of his wife, the dancer Natacha Rambova. But then his wife or rather, his wives—were part of his image problem, at least with men. For Rudolph Valentino, ballyhooed as the Great Lover, had married two women reputed to be lesbians, both members of the coterie surrounding the celebrated Alla Nazimova.[10] Rambova, his second wife, apparently had him prancing about in fur shorts; his first wife, Jean Acker, who according to one account "favoured a short, very masculine hairstyle, and wore a white blouse and tie under a rather severely cut suit,"[11] had locked him out of the marital bedroom and refused to consummate the marriage.

His unusual marital history, coupled with the masterful and pleasurable sadism of the original *Sheik* and the masochism and misogyny of its sequel have led some recent commentators to speculate about Valentino's own sexual orientation: "The obvious pleasure he sought from the company of young men, often as handsome as himself," writes one observer, "should not make us suppose he was homosexual." And, from the same source, "There is always something inherently feminine in the 'Great Lover,' for it is his own narcissistic reflection he seeks in the depths of his beloved's eyes" (Walker, 119). The campy appeal of Valentino to film audiences today exposes an inherent bisexuality in his self-presentation, again emphasized, if not in fact made possible, by the Arab dress he wore in his most famous film.

Valentino, as an immigrant from Italy who had worked as a gardener and a dance partner before making it in films, was first read as a foreign interloper replacing the image of the "All-American [i.e. Anglo] boy." This young Italian actor, despite the European specificity of his origins, became the prototype of the so-called "Latin lover"—the category to which, without saying so explicitly, the wits at "Saturday Night Live" had consigned the contestants for their "macho" contest, Fernando Lamas and Ricardo Montalban. (The Anglo television actor Jack Lord, star of "Hawaii Five-O," apparently won the contest.) In this catch-all categorization ethnic and racial distinctions become invidiously blurred, as Latino, Hispanic, Italian and presumably other dark complected, dark-haired men are deliberately conflated as "Latin"—smooth, seductive, predatory, irresistible to women. And once again "hypermale" and "feminized" become, somehow, versions of the same description: these men are too seductive to be "really" men. As Miriam Hansen has noted, "the more desperately Valentino himself emphasized attributes of physical prowess and virility, the more perfectly he played the part of the male impersonator, brilliant counterpart to the female 'female' impersonators of the American screen such as Mae West or the vamps of his own films."[12] The mythical "Latin lover," like the "Third World," was an entity that could be simultaneously invented and manipulated. And chief among these fantasy figures, in the puritanically xenophobic imagination, was the dangerous Valentino. In other words, Rudolph Valentino was himself a significant figure of *crossover*, disruption, rupture.

· · ·

We have been looking at Rudolph Valentino as the unlikely role model for Liberace and as the equally unlikely object of what might be called "transvestification." Where Liberace was complicit with his cultural classification as a transvestite figure, instinctively understood its relationship to "star quality," and made it work for him, Valentino was both surprised and appalled, challenging the editorial writer to a boxing match to prove "which is the better man." But there is a third figure who stands in significant relation to these two, uncannily linked by circumstances that seem both bizarre and overdetermined, and that is the figure of Elvis Presley.

We have already noted that Liberace thought of himself as the precursor of glitter rock. But of all the show business "copies" to which Liberace laid claim, the one he most insisted upon was Elvis Presley. In his testimony in a British court in 1959 he maintained that he had to "dress better than the others who were copying me. One was a young man named Elvis Presley" (Thomas, 131). He made the same claim to the media on the occasion of his twenty-fifth anniversary in show business: "Because of Elvis Presley and his imitators, I really have to exaggerate to look different and to top them."[13] Elvis became a *cause* of feminine virile display.

There is a famous moment, a kind of sartorial primal scene, in which Elvis and Liberace themselves change clothes, become each other's changelings. In 1956 they met in Las Vegas, when Elvis appeared in the audience at Liberace's show. Liberace invited the young singer backstage, where, apparently at the suggestion of a press agent, Elvis put on Liberace's gold sequinned tuxedo jacket, and Liberace donned Elvis's striped sport coat. They then swapped instruments, Liberace on guitar, Elvis on piano, and jammed together for twenty minutes on two of their signature tunes, "Hound Dog" and "I'll Be Seeing You." "Elvis and I may be characters," commented Liberace, "me with my gold jackets and him with his sideburns—but we can afford to be" (Thomas, 117).

This crossover moment between two crossover stars (Liberace traversing the boundary between pop and classical, Elvis between "white" and "black" music) has important implications beyond those of local publicity. The *New York Times* obituary for Liberace says, succinctly, about his gold lamé jacket, "Soon Elvis Presley was wearing a suit of gold lamé. Soon Elvis impersonators were wearing suits of gold lamé"[14](So that Elvis impersonators are really Liberace impersonators.)[15]

Predictably, the keepers of the Elvis legend are less forthcoming about any Liberace connection.[16] The film *This Is Elvis* shows a shot of the Riviera Hotel marquee proclaiming "Liberace" in large letters, presumably to show what kind of entertainment Las Vegas was used to before the arrival of the King. An off-screen narrator impersonating the voice of Elvis says, "Liberace and his brother were one of the top acts of the time. I wasn't sure the place was ready for Elvis Presley." The point is contrast, disruption, not continuity.

Thirteen years later Elvis returned to Las Vegas, heavier, in pancake makeup, wearing a white jumpsuit with an elaborate jeweled belt and cape, crooning pop songs to a microphone: in effect, he had become Liberace. Even his fans were now middle-aged matrons and blue-haired grandmothers, who praised him as a good son who loved his mother; Mother's Day became a special holiday for Elvis's fans as it was for Liberace's.

A 1980 videotape of *Liberace in Las Vegas* (made, therefore, three years after Elvis's death), opens with a lush videotour of his home, including a tour of his closet. This is surely in part a camp joke, but the racks and racks of sequins, rhinestones, and furs—all of which we will shortly see him model onstage—will be oddly but closely echoed in the 1981 Elvis retrospective film, *This Is Elvis*, in which—also quite early in the film—

attendants are shown readying his wardrobe for the show. Once again there are racks of clothes, jumpsuits with spangles and rhinestones, a whole rolling rack of jeweled belts. Watching the two films in succession it is difficult to tell whose closet is whose.

But something else, even more uncanny, ties Elvis and Liberace together. Both of them, remarkably, were twins, each born with a twin brother who immediately died. Both, that is to say, were—in the sense in which I have been using the term—changelings, changeling boys, substitutes for or doubles of something that never was.

Elvis Aron and Jesse Garon. *The Rolling Stone Illustrated History of Rock & Roll* notes that "His twin, Jesse Garon, died at birth, and he was always to be reminded of this absence ('They say when one twin dies, the other grows up with all the quality of the other, too . . . If I did, I'm lucky'), as if he were somehow incomplete, even down to his matching name,"[17] and almost all his biographers make some version of the same point.[18] Had Elvis's own child, Lisa Marie, been a boy, the parents intended to call him John Baron, continuing the rhyming line.

One biography of Liberace begins with a dramatization of the entertainer's momentous birth:

"One of the babies was born under the veil," said the midwife in a voice shaded with sadness. "But the other one, my dear . . . her voice suddenly joyful. "A *big* baby boy!"

How pitiful the dead infant looked, its tiny body almost a skeleton, a film of placenta over its shriveled face like a cloth for burial . . .

But the other baby—what a pulsing, squalling, robust piece of humanity. (Thomas, 1)

Uncannily enough, here is a *third* version of this changeling scenario, from the opening paragraphs of yet another biography.

Just before the turn of the present century, two bouncing babies were born who were to bring untold happiness into the lives of men and women all over the world.

One was the fledgling cinema. . . .

The other was Rudolph Valentino. . . .

As the babes grew up together, it was tragically ordained that so they would die.[19]

Jesse Garon Presley, Liberace's unnamed twin, the silent movie: three ghosts that haunt, and perhaps shape, the very notion of contemporary stardom.

Furthermore, Elvis, like Liberace, was obsessed with Rudolph Valentino, to whose celebrity (and spectacular funeral) his own were inevitably compared. The son of his promoter in the early Memphis days remembers that Elvis "aspired to be a second Rudolph Valentino" (Goldman, 129). Hence the sideburns, the "sullen, sultry leer" (the adjectives are those of Albert Goldman, a highly unsympathetic biographer), the photo sessions from this period stripped to the waist, the claim to friends that he had Italian blood.[20]

But it is the delicacy and vulnerability of the two men's visual images, as much as their sheer sexual power, that binds them. The pout, the curled lip (about which Elvis would joke onstage in his later Las Vegas years, "This lip used to curl easier"), the cool stare and contained sexuality, an auto-voyeurism incredibly provocative—all of these can be seen in Valentino's *Son of the Sheik,* an uncanny phantom of Elvis. Indeed Elvis made his own Sheik movie, *Harum Scarum* (1965), in which, dressed in "Arab" robes and headdress, pursuing the Princess Shalimar (played by Miss America Mary Ann Mobley), he is clearly intended to evoke memories of Valentino. Even the antics of the midget Billy Barty seemingly gratuitous to the plot—echo, as if for emphasis, the hapless dwarf in *Son of the Sheik*. In an earlier—and better—film, *Jailhouse Rock* (1957), Elvis is stripped to the waist and beaten, in another clear citation from the popular Valentino film. In fact, the example of Valentino is one reason why he chose a movie career, and thus missed out on the early great days of what he himself had started—the theatricalization of rock and roll.

. . .

Elvis, like Valentino, seemed to take the world by erotic surprise. Contrasted, again like Valentino, with a notion of the clean-cut all-American boy (represented in his case by Pat Boone), Elvis seemed for a time to stand as the personification of sex. But what does it mean to personify sex? And which sex?

The famous Ed Sullivan story—of how the camera filmed Elvis only from the waist up —has been told and retold, debunked as myth and explained as titillating publicity, a displacement upward that increased desire for a peek below. But what would that peek disclose?

"Is it a sausage? It is certainly smooth and damp-looking, but whoever heard of a 172-lb sausage 6 ft. tall?" This is the beginning of *Time* magazine's review of the film *Love Me Tender* in 1956. The referent, it soon becomes clear, is Elvis himself, not—as one might think—only a part of his anatomy. But Elvis as part-object, Elvis the Pelvis, became, not only a fan's fantasy and fetish but also, perhaps inevitably, his own. "The Pelvis "—an anatomical region which seems at first specific, but is in fact both remarkably vague and distinctly ungendered—became the site of speculation and spectatorship.

Thus, for example, an admiring male rock critic writing in 1970 praised Elvis as "The master of the sexual simile, treating his guitar as both phallus and girl . . . rumor had it that into his skin-tight jeans was sewn a lead bar to suggest a weapon of heroic proportions.[21]

But a boyhood friend of Elvis's tells it somewhat differently, describing a stage ploy from the singer's early career, around 1955: "He would take the cardboard cylinder out of a roll of toilet paper and put a string in one end of it. Then, he'd tie that string around his waist. The other end, with the cardboard roller, would hang down outside his drawers, so as when he got onstage and reared back with that guitar in his hand, it would look to the girls up front like he had one helluva thing there inside his pants."[22]

. . .

What I am going to claim—is that transvestism *on the stage*, and particularly in the kind of entertainment culture that generates the phenomenon known as "stardom," is a symptom for the *culture*, rather than the individual performer. In the context of popular culture these transvestic symptoms appear, so to speak, to gratify a social or cultural scenario of desire. The onstage transvestite is the fetishized part-object for the social or cultural script of the fan.

One of the hallmarks of transvestic display, as we have seen repeatedly, is the detachable part. Wig, false breasts, the codpiece that can conceal male or female parts, or both, or neither. In the Elvis story the detachable part is not only explicitly and repeatedly described as an artificial phallus but also as a trick, a stage device, and a sham. Not for the first time the phallus itself becomes an impersonator—and, moreover, a female impersonator, for only a female would lack the phallus and need a substitute.

Elvis as female impersonator? Let us look further.

Elvis's appearance at the Grand Ole Opry, at the very beginning of his career, provoked a double scandal. His music was too black, and he was wearing eyeshadow. He was not asked back. For Chet Atkins, soon to become the organizer of Elvis's recording sessions in Nashville, the one lingering memory of Elvis at the Opry was his eye make-up. "I couldn't get over that eye shadow he was wearing. It was like seein' a couple of guys kissin' in Key West."[23] (Notice here once again the conflation of cross-dressing, theatricality, and homosexuality.)

Elvis's hair created even more of a furor. It was like a black man's (Little Richard's; James Brown's); it was like a hood's; it was like a woman's. Race, class, and gender: Elvis's appearance violated or disrupted them all. His created "identity" as the boy who crossed over, who could take a song like "Hound Dog" from Big Mama Thornton or the onstage raving—and the pompadour, mascara, and pink and black clothing—from Little Richard, made of Elvis, in the popular imagination, a cultural mulatto, the oxymoronic "Hillbilly Cat," a living category crisis. Little Richard, defiantly gay, his conked pompadour teased up six inches above his head, his face and eyes brilliantly made-up, his clothes and capes glittering with sequins, appearing, as we have already noted "in one show dressed as the Queen of England and in the next as the pope,"[24] was vestimentary crossover incarnate,[25] not passing but trespassing. To put it another way, Elvis mimicking Little Richard is Elvis as female impersonator—or rather, as the *impersonator* of a female impersonator. And it is worth remembering that Richard attributes his adoption of bizarre costume in this period to *racial* crossover. "We were breaking through the racial barrier. . . . We decided that my image should be crazy and way-out so that the adults would think I was harmless" (White, 65–66). The year was 1956.

Elvis was the white "boy" who could sing "black," the music merchandiser's dream. And that crossover move was (perhaps inevitably) read as a crossover move in gender terms: a move from hypermale to hyperfemale, to, in fact, *hyperreal* female, female impersonator, transvestite.

It was in 1970, only two years after his much-heralded television "Comeback" performance, that Elvis made a striking vestimentary crossover in Las Vegas:

Not since Marlene Dietrich stunned the ringsiders with the sight of her celebrated legs encased from hip to ankle in a transparent gown had any performer so electrified Las Vegas with his mere physical appearance. Bill Belew [the costume designer], who had been very cautious up to this point about designing any costume that would make Elvis look effeminate, decided finally to kick out the jams. Now Elvis faced the house encased in a smashing white jumpsuit, slashed to the sternum and lovingly fitted around his broad shoulders, flat belly, narrow hips and tightly packed crotch. And then there were his pearls—loads of lustrous pearls, not sewn on the costume but worn unabashedly as body ornaments. (Goldman, 448)

"Not since Marlene Dietrich." This—in the voice of Elvis debunker Goldman—is Elvis precisely as female impersonator. Critic after critic notices that his sexuality is subject to reassignment, consciously or unconsciously, though the paradox—male sex symbol as female impersonator—remains perplexing and unexamined. "As for Elvis himself," writes one biographer, "he'll be gradually castrated into an everlasting pubescent boy. And as movie follows movie, each one worse than the last, he will actually start resembling a eunuch: a plump, jittery figure."[26]

Elvis moves in the course of his career along a curious continuum from androgyne to transvestite. This male sex symbol is insistently and paradoxically read by the culture as a boy, a eunuch, or a "woman"—as anything but a man.

His ex-wife Priscilla, the executive producer of the recent television series depicting Elvis's life, wanted in fact to repress, or expunge, the memory of his later years. "The problem," wrote one critic sympathetically, "is that Elvis left in such bad shape: overweight, forgetting the words to his songs, wearing clownish rhinestone-covered jumpsuits. It's *that* Elvis—the one who keeps cropping up in books and TV-movies—that Priscilla wants to get out of people's minds." And, "if only Elvis had paid more attention to his image. Maybe he would have made it through the '70s, checked into the Betty Ford Center, turned on to aerobics. . . ."[27]

Overweight. Reviews and commentaries on Elvis in his last years speak frequently of him as having a "weight problem," as looking fat, not being able to keep the weight off. Of which gender do we usually speak in these terms? We may think of Elizabeth Taylor and her constant battle with extra pounds: Liz fat, Liz thin, Liz in and out of the Betty Ford Center. This is the spirit in which Elvis watchers watched Elvis watching his weight, as if the eternal boy within could be disclosed by the shedding of pounds, the disappearance of a telltale paunch. The comparable corpulence of wonder-boys Orson Welles and Marlon Brando, though remarked by the press, is not feminized in this way.

Yet the feminization and/or transgendering of Elvis begins much earlier than the Las Vegas jumpsuit days.[28] Whether through his mascara, his dyed hair, or his imitation of black music and style, Elvis was always already crossing over.

The 1990 debut of a weekly TV series on the life of Elvis Presley broke new ground for television programming, as John J. O'Connor noted in the *New York Times*. "It is," he points out, "the first weekly series built around the life of an actual entertainment personality"; "a decided rarity—a half-hour format devoted not to a sitcom but to straightforward biography." "Can," he wondered in print, "episodic biographies of Marilyn, Chaplin, Dean, et al., be far behind?"[29]

. . .

Newsweek read Warhol's interest in Elvis as the recognition of "an almost androgynous softness and passivity in his punk-hood persona,"[30] and the claim to androgyny, as we have seen, is not infrequently made as an explanation of Elvis's powerful appeal to women and men. But one of the things Andy Warhol may have seen in Elvis was the perfection of his status as a pop icon in his condition as always already multiple and replicated. The phenomenon of "Elvis impersonators," which began long *before* the singer's death, is one of the most startling effects of the Elvis cult.

. . .

"The woman of fashion," writes Roland Barthes, is a "collection of tiny, separate essences." "The paradox," he says, "is a generality of accumulation, not of synthesis: in Fashion, the *person* is thus simultaneously impossible and yet entirely known" (Barthes, 254–55.) Here Barthes says "person," but, earlier, "woman." It is "woman" whom fashion creates as this illusion of parts. And "woman" is what can be known, exhibited, disseminated, replicated—while at the same time remaining "impossible."

Elvis, too, is simultaneously impossible and entirely known. Much as he is exhibited, he is also withheld from view: in the army, in Hollywood, holed up at Graceland. At the end of every performance, while his fans screamed for more, an announcer would solemnly intone, "Ladies and gentlemen, Elvis has left the building." Like the changeling boy, Elvis is always absent or elsewhere. Indeed as always already absent, Elvis himself was the best, and the most poignant, of Elvis impersonators, staging a much-heralded "comeback" in 1968 at the age of 30, and, in another comeback, revisiting his classic crossover rock songs of the fifties from the curious vantage point of Hawaii or Las Vegas in the middle seventies. Like a revenant, he just never stops coming back. (Here we might recall the story of the phantom hitchhiker in the film *Mystery Train*—who turns out, of course, to be the ghost of Elvis heading for Graceland.)

We have briefly noted the fact that Elvis in effect sat out the rock revolution that he himself had started. Instead of taking to the concert stage like the Beatles, he went to Hollywood to become a "movie star," following the game plan of Colonel Parker, but also, presumably, his own dream of being a Valentino. Like Flaubert writing for the French theater, he was a genre behind. He missed his own moment—the moment that he had engendered—and spent the rest of his career as he had spent the beginning, being always too early or too late to be the Elvis that he was.

Is it possible that this is the essence of stardom, of superstardom? To be simultaneously belated and replicated; not to be there, and to cover up that absence with representations?

In a recent essay on camp, Andrew Ross has suggested that "in popular rock culture today, the most 'masculine' images are signified by miles of coiffured hair, layers of gaudy make-up, and a complete range of fetishistic body accessories, while it is the clean-cut, close-cropped, fifties-style Europop crooners who are seen as lacking masculine legitimacy" (Ross, 164). As a cultural observation this is shrewd, yet it reinscribes the binary *within* the reassuring domain of the masculine. Ross underestimates the power of the transvestite as that spectral other who exists only in representation—not a representation of male or of female, but of, precisely, itself: its own phantom or ghost.

The argument from "masquerade" tries to establish "woman" as artifactual, gestural, a theatrical creature who can be taken apart and put back together. But what has become clearer and clearer is that "man"—the male person—is at least as artifactual as "woman." Mechanical reproduction is the displacement into its opposite of the fear of artifactuality and dismemberment.

"Which is most macho?" The answer can come only from the impersonator. For by enacting on the stage—or the video screen—the disarticulation of parts, the repetition of images that is the breakdown of the image itself, it is only the impersonator who can theorize gender. Let me quote once again from Roland Barthes.

As for the human body, Hegel had already suggested that it was in a relation of signification with clothing: as pure sentience, the body cannot signify; clothing guarantees the passage from sentience to meaning; it is, we might say, the signified par excellence. But which body is the Fashion garment to signify? (Barthes, 258)

What are the choices? An article in the gay and lesbian journal *Out/Look* called attention to the power of "The Drag Queen in The Age of Mechanical Reproduction," because the drag queen foregrounds illusion and falsehood as material reality: "being a drag queen means the constant assertion of the *body.*[31] But again, *which* body? The fashion garment of the drag queen signifies the absent or phantom body. Paradoxically, the body here is no body, and nobody, the clothes without the Emperor.

It is epistemologically intolerable to many people—including many literary and cultural critics—that the ground should be a figure. That gender exists only in representation. But this is the subversive secret of transvestism, that the body is not the ground, but the figure. Elvis Presley watching *his* figure, as his weight balloons up and down, Elvis deploying his lips and his hips to repeat by an act of will and artifice the "natural" gestures that once made them seem to take on an uncanny, transgressive life of their own, Elvis Presley, male sex symbol as female impersonator, becomes the fascinating dramatization of the transvestite effect that underlies representation itself.

Notes

1. Roland Barthes, *The Fashion System,* trans. Matthew Ward and Richard Howard (New York: Hill and Wang, 1983), 231–32.
2. Dustjacket copy for *The Wonderful Private World of Liberace,* by Liberace (New York: Harper & Row, 1986).
3. Liberace, *The Wonderful Private World of Liberace,* 171.
4. Bob Thomas, *Liberace* (New York: St. Martin's Press, 1987), 243.
5. Dick Maurice, *Las Vegas Sun,* March 1986. Thomas, *Liberace,* 254.
6. William E. Geist, "About New York: Liberace Is Here, with His Glitter Undimmed," *New York Times,* April 3, 1985: B5.
7. *Times* of London, October 2, 1956: 3.
8. *Times* of London, September 26, 1956: 6.
9. Videocassette, *Liberace: Behind the Music.*
10. Alexander Walker, *Rudolph Valentino* (London: Elm Tree Books/Hamish Hamilton, 1976), 32–33, 99. The desire of critics to accept allegations that Acker and Rambova were lesbians may suggest something of their own ambivalence toward Valentino's love-god image; thus one biographer comments, for example, on Valentino's statement that "a man may admire a woman without desiring her." "It has been reported that Natacha construed this as a veiled reference to her Lesbianism, and, on reading it, slapped Valentino's face. But such a report is necessarily hard to confirm" (Walker, 99).
11. Noel Botham and Peter Donnelly, *Valentino: The Love God* (London: Everest Books, 1976), 70.
12. Miriam Hansen, "Pleasure, Ambivalence, Identification: Valentino and Female Spectatorship," *Cinema Journal,* 25: 4 (Summer 1986): 25. Hansen also has excellent things to say about the Latin Lover, the discourse of exoticism, and the "repressed desire of miscegenation" in the U.S.
13. *Time,* the *New York Times,* and the *Los Angeles Times* all carried articles on him. Thomas, *Liberace,* 173.
14. James Barron, "Liberace, Flamboyant Pianist, Is Dead," *New York Times,* February 5, 1987: B6.
15. There have, in fact, been numerous Liberace imitators, as Dick Alexander

notes in the *San Francisco Examiner*, July 22, 1990: T4.

16. Although at least one, Jac L. Tharpe, points it out in passing. Tharpe, "Will the Real Elvis Presley . . .", in Tharpe, *Elvis: Images and Fancies* (Jackson: University Press of Mississippi, 1979), 4.

17. Peter Guralnick, *The Rolling Stone Illustrated History of Rock & Roll*, ed. Jim Miller (New York: Random House/ Rolling Stone Press, 1980), 21.

18. Nik Cohn's novel, *King Death* (1975), speculates on what would have happened had Jesse lived. Albert Goldman comments that "This spirit brother is one of the most important characters in the life of Elvis Presley." Albert Goldman, *Elvis* (New York: McGraw-Hill, 1981), 65.

19. Norman A. Mackenzie, *The Magic of Rudolph Valentino* (London: The Research Publishing Co., 1974), 11.

20. "This surprising identification with the film idol of the silent era, a man who was dead before Elvis was born," writes Albert Goldman, "is the first unmistakable sign that Elvis had discovered the essence of his appeal and was starting to cultivate a corresponding image. It is also a sign of prescience, for nothing better defines Elvis' future role than the formula: teen Valentino. If you add to the basic image of the sultry Latin lover the further garnishings of an erotic style of music and dance, the tango for the twenties, rock 'n' roll for the fifties, the parallel is perfect. Soon Elvis would even have crow-black hair" (Goldman, *Elvis*, 129).

21. George Melly, *Revolt into Style* (Harmondsworth: Penguin, 1970), 36–37.

22. David Houston. Goldman, *Elvis*, 157.

23. Goldman, *Elvis*, 122. Patsy Guy Hammontree, *Elvis Presley. A Bio-Bibliography* (Westport, Connecticut; Greenwood Press, 1985), 13.

24. Charles White, *The Life and Times of Little Richard* (New York: Pocket Books, 1984), 66, 69.

25. Charles White, *The Life and Times of Little Richard* (New York: Pocket Books, 1984), 69.

26. William Allen Harbinson, *The Illustrated Elvis* (New York: Grosset & Dunlap, 1977), 93.

27. J. David Stern, "The King Is Back," *TV Guide*, 38: 7 (February 17, 1990), 6–7.

28. Albert Goldman, whose view of Elvis often borders on the vitriolic, puts the turning point at his army experience, which was traditionally supposed to make a man of him: "The Elvis who had appeared on the Dorsey, Berle, and Sullivan shows, who had starred in *Loving You* and *Jailhouse Rock*, was butch. He had a chunky, clunky aura. . . . After the army, Elvis appears very delicate and vulnerable. . . . With his preposterous Little Richard conk, his limp wrist, girlish grin, and wobbly knees, which now turn out instead of in, he looks outrageously gay" (Goldman, *Elvis*, 329–30). Goldman targets, especially, what he describes as "his queer showing on *Frank Sinatra's Welcome Home Party for Elvis Presley*." "When he confronts the much smaller but more masculine Sinatra, Elvis's body language flashes, 'I surrender, dear.' "
    Goldman's hostility toward (and fascination with) his subject is clear, as is his desire to pop-psychoanalyze and re-gender him. Thus he describes the 21-year old Elvis's "Girlish boudoir," full of Teddy bears (picture caption, Goldman 289ff.), observes that "throwing things like a hysterical woman was one of Elvis's more dangerous habits" (Goldman, 337) and claims that he was so sensitive about his uncircumcised state that "instead of pissing in a urinal . . . he would always go inside, like a woman" (Goldman, 339). When it comes to accounting for the singer's popularity, Goldman has recourse again to gender and to a kind of instant cultural criticism. "Much of Elvis's power over young girls came not just from the fact that he embodied their erotic fantasies but that he likewise projected frankly feminine traits with which they could identify. This AC/DC quality became in time characteristic of rock stars in general, commencing with Mick Jagger and the Beatles (who had such ravishingly girlish falsettos) and

going on to include Jim Morrison, David Bowie, Elton John and many figures of the punk pantheon" (Goldman, 345).

29. John J. O'Connor, "'Elvis' the Series: Poor Boy Makes Good," *New York Times*, February 6, 1990: B1.

30. *Newsweek*, August 29, 1977. Cited in Tharpe, *Elvis: Images*, 4.

31. Mark Leger, "The Drag Queen in the Age of Mechanical Reproduction," *Out/Look*, 6 (Fall 1989): 29.

Section VI
Practices

Sally Mann, "Jesse Bites, 1985", © Sally Mann. Courtesy: Edwynn Houk Gallery, New York.

Section VI
Practices

....

Authors
Andrew Ross, George Lipsitz, Susan Willis, Paula A. Treichler, Toby Miller

Visual artist
Sally Mann: *Immediate Family.*

AMERICAN scholars have drawn upon the formulations of French theorists such as Foucault and de Certeau as well as the more empirically oriented work of British scholars such as Hebdige and McRobbie to engage in detailed analyses of the material practices of everyday life. While recognizing that such a distinction is of necessity blurred, materials in this chapter deal with "direct" rather than "mediated" experiences: what people do with their bodies, rather than what they watch on their screens.

Andrew Ross, a Scottish transplant now practicing a distinctively American cultural studies, outlines a distinctively American debate about the numerical representation of minority artists in art museums. Such practices attest to the deep imbrication of culture and politics in a late twentieth-century United States, where even the wealthiest bastions of the highest culture are subject to claims to cultural justice by hitherto excluded populations. George Lipsitz relates the prominence of black and Latino musicians in rock and roll and the music's popularity among white teenagers to the rapid reconfiguration of American politics and culture that would follow on in the 1960s and subsequent decades. His article focuses more specifically upon the hitherto neglected contribution of Chicano artists and audiences to this reconfiguration. Susan Willis investigates one of the most bodily of all bodily practices, the workout, from a feminist perspective, arguing that the practice is simultaneously liberatory (through its empowerment of the female body) and oppressive (through its imposition of male cultural norms on the female body).

Sexual practices are central to many representational systems and to the lives of communities as such. They are unusually fertile ground for discourses both factual and fictional. In the era of AIDS, they suddenly also became potentially lethal practices; here the predominant discourse used to represent them was, as Paula A. Treichler observes, scientific. In such a "discursive jungle," Paula A. Treichler seeks to find a path to understand the AIDS epidemic as a discursive construction. Her conclusion about the importance of understanding discourses that organize practices is a general defense of cultural studies at its best, and her article is certainly an exemplary achievement.

The selection from Toby Miller's work returns to the "practice" of citizenship, a theme also broached by Holston and Appadurai in a previous chapter. Miller's conceit here is to intersect "truth, Latin America and US television" in order to analyze relations among "the Americas." *The Americas* turns out to be an "educational" TV series, and "the citizen" turns out to be the TV audience. Miller subjects a certain kind of Americanism abroad to a very cogent critique, showing how the politics of citizenship and realities of US regional policy do in fact intersect in the virtual space, and among the virtual practices, of citizenship formation.

Sally Mann's *Immediate Family* provides the image of another kind of practice, that of artistically imagined domestic life. "Jessie Bites" is one of a series of photographs Mann took of her own children as they grew up in rural Virginia. Her own practice as an artist became controversial, since for some observers the use of her children raised questions of consent and exploitation, while for others the age of the children and their often rather casual attitude to the wearing of clothes raised issues about whether the images were sexualizing children, and whether this was appropriate. In the context of this book, Sally Mann's work represents not only the issues it has raised among cultural and moral critics, but also the "method" devised by Mann herself to analyze the truth and beauty of everyday American life. Her sumptuous prints and "narrative" pictures (in which something has happened or is happening) is what she has called "truth told slant."

27 The Great Un-American Numbers Game

Andrew Ross

For many folks in the New York art world, the most telling facts you needed to know about the 1995 Biennial Exhibition at the Whitney Museum of American Art were on the Guerrilla Girl statistic sheet distributed around town and to those attending the opening (see Fig. 27.1).

These statistics became a serviceable shorthand for public opinion, since they coincided so neatly with the indifferent critical reception of the exhibition. The numbers showed a plunge in the percentage of women and artists of color represented in the show, as compared with the all-time high of 1993. For some, the statistics served as a transparent index of institutional injustice. For others, citing the numbers offered a welcome relief from the tiresome obligation to offer a detailed judgment about the show. For still others, they were crude emblems of the great un-American quota mentality, and therefore an affront to the principle of aesthetic meritocracy. For almost everyone, it seemed as if the Guerrilla Girls' body count had finally become an integral and unavoidable part of the response to the most important periodic survey of contemporary North American art. Of course, there were other components to be accounted for in explaining the tenor of the selections, such as the curator Klaus Kertess's own powerful belief in pure aesthetics, or his predilection for painting and formal sculpture—each seen as regressive elements in a critical climate that had so depreciated the modernist canon of taste and the art media with which it had been most associated. But the numbers were the proverbial last word, serving as some kind of lightning rod to channel and ground the turbulent atmospheric energies that had been released by the North American Culture Wars. This was a strange moment, although in many ways it simply brought to the surface and reduced to a statistical format the shifting undercurrents of anxieties and resentments about exclusion from the pantheon of recognition that biennial surveys have fostered and encouraged in recent decades. Who's in, who's out, what kinds of media are favored, how many dead artists, how many Latin Americans, and so on.

It was also a moment of triumph for the Guerrilla Girls themselves, self-styled "conscience of the art world," after ten years of agitprop badgering of galleries and museums for their underrepresentation of women and minority artists. The lineage of this activity dates from the first protests against the Whitney's surveys, initiated by Faith Ringgold in November 1968, continued, along with Lucy Lippard, Poppy Johnson, and

From Andrew Ross, "The Great Un-American Numbers Game," in Andrew Ross, *Real Love: In Pursuit of Cultural Justice* (London: Routledge, 1998), 117–48.

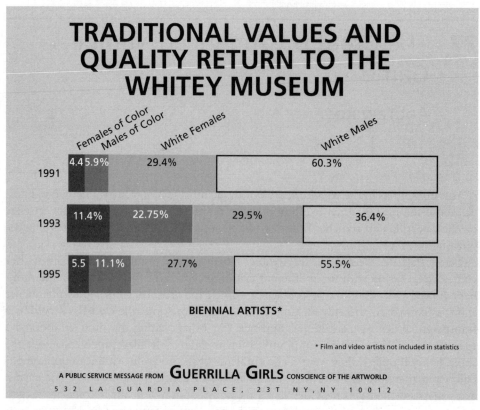

Figure 27.1 Guerrilla Girls poster.

Brenda Miller, in an organized form as the Ad Hoc Women Artists Committee in 1970 and 1971, and extended under the rubric of Artists Meeting for Cultural Change, formed in 1975 to protest the Whitney's bicentennial offering. Other groups active during this period were the Women Artists and Students for Black Art Liberation, the Black Emergency Cultural Coalition, and, in California, the Council of Women Artists, who threatened a civil rights suit against Los Angeles County Museum of Art. The original umbrella organization had been the Art Workers' Coalition, founded in 1969, from which emerged the feminist artists group Women Artists in Revolution and the Guerrilla Art Action Group. Today the Guerrilla Girls' allies include Godzilla, the Asian American artists pressure group, and PESTS, a coalition of artists of color. The Guerrilla Girls have long since established a permanent identity in the art world, largely through their media-savvy tactics, analogous to the new generation of public and institutional activism forged by ACT UP and its artists' collectives like Gran Fury and DivaTV. Indeed, their use of statistical weaponry was adopted as an activist model by the art world group WAC (Women's Action Coalition), which left a legacy of chronicled injustices to women in the form of a book, *WAC STATS*. Alternately, tne GG posters have been hung as works of art in the museums they have targeted—striking evidence, depending on your point of view, of their success or their failure to combat the ceaseless capacity of postmodern institutional life to absorb all forms of criticism. All the

1970s politically alternative art groupings and spaces—Colab, AIR, JAM, Taller Boricua, Fashion Moda, Group Material, Political Art Documentation/Distribution—wrestled with the dismal paradox that their critiques of institutional art were more likely to become institutionalized than to generate lasting alternatives. This facility to incorporate dissent can be seen even in the formative years of art activism; after the Art Worker's Coalition picketed the Metropolitan Museum of Art in 1967, some of the activists were offered employment by the Met. All the same, it is still disquieting to consider Elizabeth Hess's suggestion that "there are . . . more advantages to being a Guerrilla Girl today than there are to being a woman artist."[1]

There are many lessons to be drawn from the history of art world activism in the period since the late 1960s. My interest here lies primarily in the use of statistics to organize moral and political dissent in general, and to make arguments about selection and representation in exhibitions in particular. How do we explain the current urgency of this phenomenon in cultural affairs, in that realm of social activity where quantitative reasoning is supposed to have least influence and where aesthetic taste and qualitative value hold most sway? Although it is far from restricted to the hothouse of the North American art world, it's fair to say that in the example of the Guerrilla Girls we have one of the cleanest, most concise, and most visible displays of this criterion of judging by the numbers. To many eyes, it has produced a standoff between a disinterested principle of selection and one based on accountability to particular group identities. For the most part, this is perceived as a confrontation that has emerged only very recently—the inevitable result of a clash between the upsurge in identity politics, whereby different minority groups demand recognition and parity of representation in the public sphere, and an older, prevailing tradition of assessment that was less conscious of, or intrinsically blind to, its record of exclusions. On the contrary, the discrepancy between these two principles of selection is not simply of recent origin; it can be traced back to the goals articulated in the foundation of the great public museums in the nineteenth century. For the most part, I will focus my discussion on the art museum.

In two recent influential books, Tony Bennett (*The Birth of the Museum*) and Carol Duncan (*Civilizing Rituals*) have documented how the public museums were instituted by bourgeois reformers with the intent of providing a means of self-improvement to the mass of the population.[2] At a time when culture was being drawn into the province of government, museums and other public institutions like parks, libraries, and symphony halls were intended to serve as instruments of peaceable self-reform for urban populations that were becoming increasingly unmanageable. To perform their function in an educative manner, museum collections had to be fully representative of art history: their precursors had been the collections of Renaissance princes, absolute monarchs, and aristocratic gentlemen, which had aimed more at the singular, the exotic, and the wondrous—the Cabinet of Curiosities—rather than at extensive historical coverage. In many instances (in the Met as well as in more provincial institutions) this coverage would be provided initially by plaster-of-paris replicas. Thus was born not only the principle of universal representation, according to the canons of art-historical taste, but also the impossible ideal of the complete collection, as defined, again, by the prevailing aesthetic sense. According to Bennett, this goal of telling the story of Man on the basis of his universality could never be satisfied by any particular display of Man, which would always fall short, as a result of exclusions and bias. So too, there was a contradiction between the use of the museum as a vehicle for universal education and its use as a means of reforming the manners and conduct of its new audiences; one goal addressed its audience as an undifferentiated group, the other actively differentiated its audience according to their level of social and cultural refinement.[3] Despite its universalist intentions, usage of the art museum, then and now, has always been confined to socially upscale populations. Casual visitors to Washington's museum mall soon discover that the big draws are the Air and Space Museum, the most popular in the world, and the Natural History Museum, where the main attraction—the spectacle of the Hope Diamond in a display case—generates the longest line of all. By contrast, one can stroll unimpeded through the miles of uncluttered art gallery corridors and enjoy the relative solitude that art appreciation is supposed to foster and that truly popular art education can only disturb and despoil. The nineteenth-century story was not terribly different. Despite conservatives' fears that the newly admitted masses would desecrate the art on display and generally run riot, the forbidding architectural milieu of the temple-museums and the austere tenor of their educational paternalism were sufficiently off-putting to the majority, while trustee elites privately fostered policies that discouraged popular use. It did not help matters, for example, that the religiously minded trustees of institutions like the Met closed the museum on Sundays, the only day of recreation for the working class. Bending to criticism of this twenty-year policy, the trustees opened the doors in 1891 with the public aim of seducing people away from Coney Island. No doubt they were relieved, but hardly surprised, when the initially large Sunday attendance fell off rather quickly, and the museum resumed its air of an exclusive preserve for urban elites.

Unlike in France, where the king's royal collection had become nationalized in the Louvre, or in England, where bourgeois reformers created national museums *in opposition to* the vast collections of the aristocracy (King Charles's collection had been dispersed by the Puritans), the great American civic museums of New York, Boston, Chicago, and Philadelphia were created by prosperous Protestant elites intent on securing their country's symbolic prestige in the world of industrial nations. The collections were built up through extraordinary gifts from those storied tycoons who effected a massive relocation of art objects from Europe in the later decades of the century. The major museum bequests of the millionaires made front page news and brought them great social status. Thus was the WASP heritage of high European culture established as the American national patrimony.[4]

While the great museums had to retain their public credibility—building on public land, accepting public monies, and advertising their role in public education—they were dependent on the private bequests and were controlled by the interests of their millionaire benefactors. These moguls were accustomed to sit on the self-perpetuating boards of trustees, and many of them maintained their own rooms, with the right to display their own art, in an arrangement that made buildings like the Met appear more like mausoleums to enshrine their benefactors' fame than the people's museums they were supposed to be. The public excesses of the Gilded Age tycoons were eventually curbed in the nation at large. As Duncan notes, one result was the new policy in most museums of discouraging restricted bequests (revived again in recent decades), and, more generally, the advent of professional curatorial control over collections.[5] But there was little decline in the influence of the family names associated with bequests to the nation's blue-chip cultural establishments—Astor, Vanderbilt, Girard, Lowell, Peabody, Rockefeller, Carnegie, Morgan, Stanford, Frick, Corcoran, Gardner, Getty, Mellon, Huntingdon, Widener, Kress, and Altman. For this class, ties to the elite institutions of the arts and higher education have continued to be an obligatory mark of prestige and social standing. Policing of taste in many of these institutions was preserved through the board of trustees, where, in New York City to this day, the same Social Register names appear on the boards of the likes of MOMA, the Metropolitan, the Juilliard, the New York Philharmonic Orchestra, Lincoln Center, the New York Public Library, and the big-league foundations. They are accustomed to dining regularly, after hours, amid the opulent furniture of palaces like the Met, at fund-raising parties that are as integral to the social season of the wealthy as to the economic health of the high-end arts. It is hardly surprising, then, that the intimate involvement of these institutions with wealthy patrons has sustained the latter's often arbitrary influence over taste and exhibition selection, and that the public mandate of the museums often appears to be a facade.

This historical tradition of sustaining private interest in the name of public enlightenment was extended to the art world as a whole with the creation of an international art market as early as the 1930s. Under modernism's aesthetic banner of pure formalism, works of art would now work their way from one autonomous sphere to another—from the commerce-free studio through the commodity-saturated market-place and prestige-rich collection into the canonical museum—without becoming soiled with the taint of dollar value.[6] No doubt this system also depended on the development of advanced security systems. Electronic surveillance has only recently displaced an armed security presence in some galleries and museums.

. . .

Indeed the entire tradition of art appreciation and connoisseurship, as it has evolved, is exemplary of the self-discipline and self-surveillance that are the favored modes of behavioral management in advanced liberal societies.

But security is not there simply to protect art or regulate moral behavior through self-fashioning, it is also there to boost the spectator's estimate of the value of art. Who hasn't heard the story that the Mona Lisa became a truly valuable work of art only after it had been stolen? In the age of the grand purchase, the huge sums of money raised by museums to acquire art treasures are presented as acts of public service, often attended by a sense of nationalistic urgency if the work is able to augment the nation's cultural capital. This nationalism is ever more pronounced in excolonizing countries, whose patrimony is partly a result of the imperial pillage of other countries' artifacts. (To this day the illicit antiquities trade continues this plunder, particularly of the Third World, and often in the service of providing cultural diversity for Western institutions.) The patrimony principle also supports the tax-evasive habits of the wealthy, for whom their collection of art is often supervised by a lawyer's assessment of the future state of taxation policies and death duties. In this way the principle of accumulation is fully aided and abetted by the state's fiscal recognition of the art world as a medium for transferring, circulating, and generating capital. At the heart of this process is the use of art institutions to negotiate private investments in the name of public interest. Under these circumstances, it is clear how and why a bullish art market, of the sort sustained in the 1980s, requires an increase in the number of museums. Indeed, the museum-building boom of the last two decades has been matched only by the growth of prisons in certain countries and regions. Almost every North American city and many in Europe initiated a museum-building or renovation project during the 1980s, usually in the name of civic-mindedness or provincial pride, but also in response to the demands created by the collectors' market. Indeed, the new museum became the prestige building type of the era, identified with a star architect—Meier, Pei, Hollein, Kahn, Sterling, Venturi.[7] In many cases the building opens with virtually no collection and functions as a lavish advertisement for prospective bequests.

One of my reasons for outlining this history of private influence on the development of museums is to remind us that the business of cultural advocacy is not a recent tendency in the history of museums. Cultural claims, in both the public and private interest, have always been strongly promoted and endorsed by and through the museum. Initially, these were presented in the universalist guise of displaying the glories of national or world civilizations. The favored version was an evolutionary, and hence scientific, narrative of aesthetic and technological progress. This presented a linear, affirming genealogy for the currently existing nation-state, with its currently existing racial and class hierarchies.[8] No less disinterested were museum officials' conceptions of their public culture as a mass civilizing medium, in direct competition with other institutions. Some of these rivals were public, in the case of universities, but most were commercial, in the case of palaces of consumption like the grand department store, or spectacles of performance like the popular theater, circus, and fairground. This public mission of the nineteenth-century museum no more stood on its own then than it does today, where the museum's place in the tourist circuit of airport, hotel, restaurant, and shopping is as important as its place at the end of the institutional circuit that runs through the artist's studio, the gallery, the auction house, and the private collection. Nor were the boundaries of public, commercial, and popular so distinct that they constituted entirely separate spheres. With Sears, Bonwit Teller, Filene's, Marshal Field's, Macy's, Montgomery Ward, and Saks on one side and Barnum and Bailey on the other, the competition for mass taste was too attractive for museum administrators to pass up.[9] Nostalgia and spectacle contended with historical aura for the audience's attention. Didacticism made its bed alongside the diorama, integrating what had been separated to some degree, at the great fairs, where the popular genres of burlesque and carnival that flourished on the fringe in the midway often commented parodically on the official exhibits inside the gates.

Above all, the state has always been an interested agent in this process, from the early nineteenth century need for national collections to compete in the league of civilized nations to the most recent flaps over "historical revisionism" in the nation's official institutions of record at the Smithsonian. Bennett argues that the opening of the nineteenth-century museum's doors to the public was a significant administrative move in the modern state's bid to employ culture as a means of social management. The good conduct of the popular classes must come from self-reform, many reformers concurred, and libraries and museums were designated to be as necessary to moral health as good sanitation. Such public facilities would distract the dissolute away from the alehouse and other disorderly sites of free assembly. The museum was to be a "passionless reformer," in the words of George Brown Goode, assistant secretary of the Smithsonian in 1895 at the time he wrote the influential *Principles of Museum Administration*.[10]

Concomitant with the development of liberal society, the vital mission of such institutions was to educate the citizens of popular classes in the habits of self-discipline and self-regulation. This could succeed only if the artifacts of power were on permanent display—nothing could be hidden from view in this transfer of culture from the aristocratic few to the many. In this respect, the museum's commitment to exhibition and display had more in common with the fairs and Great Expositions than with the library or the public park. Bennett's analysis of the function of public exhibition runs parallel with Foucault's discussion of the institutions of punishment and incarceration. For Foucault, the spectacle of trial and sentencing had become newly public at a time when the spectacle of punishment was being withdrawn from public display behind the penitentiary walls. Bennett places the emergence of the museum in the context of public health policy, alongside the state's programs of sanitation. In accord with the administrative principle of "governing at a distance," these programs were designed to harness the concept of the free, self-civilizing individual to a policy of morally reforming the otherwise ungovernable populace. The unruly sphere of popular recreation was vilified in favor of civic instruction, moral uplift, and refinement of taste. Bennett, then, shows how the nineteenth-century museum was introduced as a space where the reform of taste and manners could be presented as a voluntary revision of behavior. Even better, this would take place in environments where costly property would be imbued with new levels of respect.

Thus was the new etiquette of cultural power established. It has not been altered sustantially.

. . .

As for the etiquette of behavior within the museum, most of its codes are still extant and have become refined over the years. Let me quote from the opening of a popular manual, entitled *How to Visit a Museum*:

There is no right or wrong way to visit a museum. The most important rule you should keep in mind as you go through the front door is to follow your own instincts. Be prepared to find what excites you, to enjoy what delights your heart and mind, perhaps to have aesthetic experiences you will never forget. You have a feast in store for you and you should make the most of it. Stay as long or as short a time as you will, but do your best at all times to let the work of art speak directly to you with a minimum of interference or distraction.[11]

The book offers commonsense advice about how to match the conventions of art appreciation with the physical constraints of the museum environment. In general, the tips are about how to manage your time to maximum aesthetic effect by individualizing each available moment, breaking away from the oppressive, mechanistic routines of the tour guide, or avoiding the press of the crowd:

It is difficult to stand in front of an individual work for longer than a few seconds when people are milling around you, pushing and shoving to get on with the show. . . . Kandinsky once wrote scornfully of the "vulgar herd" that strolls through museums and pronounces the pictures "nice" or "splendid." Then they go away, he added, "neither richer nor poorer than when they came." Whenever you feel that way, do your best to shut out the sense of being with other people. It takes concentration, but it can be done. It helps when there are breathing spaces in the crowd, and for a minute or two you can be alone. It is wise to take advantage of these "gaps," moving across a room quickly and forgetting about seeing each work in sequence. There are also tricks one can try, like going to a popular exhibition a half-hour before it closes, when audiences will have thinned out.

Enlisting the support of a great artist's disdain for the "vulgar herd," this text illustrates well the principle of the self-maximization of the civilizing effect—the aim being to become "richer" rather than "poorer" as a result. The reader is encouraged to emulate those connoisseurs who shun the museum literature and guides and who are comfortably at home in these vast, templed environments. Less well educated visitors are likely to feel alienated by the sanctimonious atmosphere, tending to stick close to family or friends while their visits, so vital to the museums' attendance figures, are mass processed by guides.[12] Nothing is more clear than that the public's visits are differentiated by cultural class, even in minority or community arts museums. For each social group, a calculus of profit is at play, at once individualizing and massifying, whereby maximum use is extracted from managing quality aesthetic time.

   Bennett locates the origins of this principle in the nineteenth-century school of utilitarianism, according to which public institutions were viewed as a means of multiplying the utility of culture. Statistical accounting was paramount in ensuring the maximum distribution of culture among the populace, especially in the provinces, where curators circulated artifacts from metropolitan museum collections in order to spread the effect. In this context, the museum's function ran parallel with the flood of data collecting and numerical analysis that sustained the demographic inquiries of the Victorian period. The United States in particular was undergoing the largest documented population growth of modern times. The warm patriotism associated with surging numbers, seen as the engine of democracy in the first century of the Republic, was joined now by a post-Malthusian suspicion about the burdens and potential dangers posed by population growth, reinforced by a nativist hostility to the new urban working class, swelling with immigrants.

Counting by Numbers

To assess how museums today are responding to claims based on statistics of group representation, we might note, first of all, the many contexts in which "the numbers game" is played out in North American public life in the 1990s. Casual perusal of any daily newspaper will reveal the steady attention to the authority of quantitative analysis, from the blizzard of data breakdowns in the financial pages to the latest cost-benefit analysis from a medical expert showing exactly how many years longer we will live if we run two and a half miles more each week. The current fiscal climate, devotionally bound to the gospel of the balanced budget, is the prevailing pressure system, deeply affecting the treatment of almost every story in the news. The bruises left by the cruel passage across the political landscape of *The Bell Curve*'s linking of race and IQ are all too apparent. The debate about the role of Scholastic Aptitude Test scores in education simmers on. As a legacy of the "regulatory reform" initiatives of the Contract with America, Congress has established statistical risk assessment at the heart of government as the new primary form of administrative rationality. We have recently been informed, without too much fanfare, that 1 percent of the U.S. population owns 40 percent of its wealth—a sobering statistic redolent of the days of the robber barons in the late nineteenth century. On the culture front, the much disputed 69 cents a year that taxpayers used to set aside for funding of the arts through the NEA and the NEH has long since attained a bizarre status in public opinion. And on the museum front, the furor about historical revisionism bears the memory of the flap over the *Enola Gay* exhibit at the Smithsonian's Air and Space Museum, which revolved around a revised estimate of the number of Americans allegedly spared by the decision to use the atomic bomb in the war against Japan. Drawing on current historical scholarship, curators of the exhibit had suggested a number of 63,000 instead of the quarter million estimate preferred by the Air Force Association and by veterans in general, in an incident that had incinerated over 140,000 Japanese civilians after the Second World War had ended in all but name. The Smithsonian unconditionally surrendered to pressure from the vets to edit the narrative, and another act of what scholars have labeled "historical cleansing" was accomplished.

The most significant level of attention to numbers, however, has been in the prolonged backlash against affirmative action programs, selected as a "wedge" issue by the New Right to appeal to white voters. Affirmative action, the statistical machinery that emerged from reformed race policy in the 1960s, successfully broke open the occupational caste system but arguably failed, in the abdication of the liberal will to push any further, to break up the de facto segregation of so many sectors of social and economic life. While corporate institutions and businesses have benefited by acquiring a dash of diversity for their statistical profiles, national social statistics continue to show a marked deterioration in the quality of life—income, health, housing, educational opportunity—for most minority communities. Nonetheless, affirmative action and other claims for group cultural rights are seen by many as a natural extension of the representative democratic process, by which the demographics of gender, race, or ethnic characteristics are more equitably represented in public, institutional life.

Those of us employed in North American higher education are all too aware that our own workplace has been established as a front line in some of the most significant struggles over these claims to cultural justice. Notwithstanding the initial benefits achieved in education by policies of affirmative action, it pains to watch the lifeblood of institutional racism and sexism pulsing on, in tune to the heartbeat of corporate logic, which increasingly governs the administrative direction of our colleges and universities. All of us also know what a genuine difference it makes to have a threshold number of students and faculty of color in formerly white classrooms and faculty meetings. The conversation *is* different, in ways that diverge from comparable shifts in gender ratios. In 1997, when the first decisions against affirmative action went into effect in state university systems in California and Texas, it became clear what a disastrous effect these legal changes had wrought, not just on minority acceptance rates, but also on minority applications.

While the principle of group representation and participation has had some impact on all cultural institutions, those under the aegis of the arts are predominantly governed by principles of *taste*, and therefore do not carry quite the same legal (however now besieged) commitment to opportunity associated with public education. Consequently, the Guerrilla Girls' numbers have been taken as a direct assault on the traditions of connoisseurship. While numbers cannot speak for themselves, they carry moral power as a stand-in for some vision of cultural justice that is still incomplete and ideally would no longer have to respond to number-based demands for group representation. On the other hand, their proximity to the quantitative mentality of modern bureaucracy resonates with the history of the state's use of statistics as a medium of social control, stabilizing disorder, normalizing behavior, rationalizing inequality, and, most relevant here, managing diversity by defining identities and their share of public resources and representation. In the United States, the exemplary statistical state, the dominion of numbers has come to pervade institutional life, masquerading (like its judicial counterpart, the rule of law) as a neutral arbiter of competing claims on resources and rights. Consequently, such claims are often obliged to appeal to the statistical format in advance of any other moral language. Numbers invariably speak louder than opinions.

While the democratic validity of a principle like threshold representation is obvious, inclusion by numbers is no guarantee of cultural accountability. No one, for example, can expect women artists to automatically represent the experience of their gender (or of women of different ethnicities and classes) any more than they can be assumed to lack the capacity to speak to male experience. As in other areas of social life, naturalizing the link between the identity of artists and the content of their work erodes the challenge of empathy across our cultural differences that is so crucial to a multiethnic society.

. . .

The Principles of Exhibition

If the nineteenth-century museum was intended as an agent of cultural administration for an emergent mass urban population, there's no evidence that its principles of exhibition acknowledged in any way the claims for group cultural rights that have become such a contested feature of cultural institutions in the last twenty-five years. The nineteenth-century museum had no such brief for cultural pluralism, and even less for the principle of demographic representation. After all, it evolved in an institutional climate where scientific racism prevailed—sanctioning a hierarchy of races and ethnic identities—and indeed was actively championed by the officers and curators of institutions like Chicago's Field Museum, the American Museum of Natural History, and the Smithsonian itself. Nonetheless, the museum's promise of a complete field of representation in its displays and its mandate to be universally accessible to the public provided the framework for later claims about cultural rights and equal representation. These claims became more and more visible in the climate of cultural politics that evolved in the wake of the civil rights movement.

The use of political arithmetic in government has not changed in the last century. Then as now, the federal system used census numbers as the proportional basis for distributing resources and political representation. What *is* new is the concept of using that same principle as a basis for claims to cultural rights and representation.

Proportional entitlement and representation is now applied to the sphere of culture, not without much resistance, but nonetheless with considerable success. Why is this so? At least three reasons apply.

First is the democratic significance of numbers. Despite the fact that the culture of the arts is still governed by concepts of aesthetic *taste* and *quality*, and that the sphere of culture in general is supposed to be exempt from the numerical bottom line applied in most other sectors of society, the democratic connotation of numbers is too powerful to resist. Just as the arithmetic of the state was described by early statisticians like Adolphe Quétlet as the creation of "moral statistics," so the principle of demographic representation is applied to cultural institutions today as a moral corrective in the direction of numerical equality. If, in the nineteenth century, the useful effects of art on the population could be quantified, then it is not such a great leap to suggest that the quantitative spread of the population be reflected in the selection and public display of art itself. What could be the moral basis, in a statistical democracy, for any other principle of representation?

The second reason relates to the history of cultural rights claims in the period since the Civil Rights Act. From the time of the passing of the Fourteenth Amendment in 1868 until the first affirmative action programs a century later, a dominant civil claim was the putative right of the individual to be treated apart from his or her race. This interpretation, while rarely observed in practice, is now nostalgically upheld by opponents of affirmative action as the true liberal basis of the so-called color-blind Constitution. Since the introduction of affirmative action programs designed to breach the walls of occupational racial exclusion, race- and gender-based interpretations of group rights have become more common. Consequently, proportional representation has been sanctioned either through affirmative action's appeal to the compensatory principle of remedial justice or, more radically, according to some principle of mirror representation whereby the distribution of opportunity and representation is seen to be proportionate to the existing racial and gender composition of society; and any deviation from that ratio is perceived as discriminatory. While these principles have been besieged in recent years, their appeal to the statistical ethos of representative government is a very powerful one. All institutions that depend on the public status of their activities have been obliged to respect this ethos in their attempts to create more diversity among their participants.

The third reason involves the claim of cultural institutions like the museum to represent the world, the nation, the community, or some surveyable field of the arts. In the case of the art museum, the claim to universal representation has always been shaky but intrinsic to its public function. In the last two decades, as critical anti-institutional art has flourished, the institutional authority of the museum has been rather successfully demystified, along with its curatorial powers to represent and exhibit art with unimpeachable taste. With the collapse of the claim to represent according to authoritative taste, pressure to acknowledge some principle of representative diversity, proportional or not, has been unceasing.

Most of the controversy that results from this pressure has been associated with temporary exhibits, or with the kind of periodic surveys presented by the various Biennales and by *documenta* at Kassel. At the Whitney, for example, much of the controversy was defused after the selection of its Biennial artists was entrusted to the singular, subjective taste of an individual staff curator, or in the case of the 1997 Biennial, to one insider—Lisa Phillips from the Whitney—and one outsider—Louise Neri from *Parkett* magazine. One result of the increased political significance of the temporary exhibit or survey has been that the role of the curator has been transformed from aesthetic arbiter to cultural mediator, brokering the interests of artists, dealers, collectors, and trustees. Ultimately, the curator can act as a broker for cultural ethnicity if he or she has ties to ethnic communities pushing for greater representation.[13] This is less likely to happen at the blue-chip museums than at minority museums operating under the wing of large institutions, like the Smithsonian's Anacostia Museum, or functioning autonomously as neighborhood or community museums, like New York's Museo del Barrio, the Studio Museum in Harlem, the Afro-American Historical and Cultural Museum in Philadelphia, the Museum of the National Center of Afro-American Artists in Boston, or the Rhode Island Heritage Society. While the growth of the latter has inspired the community arts movement and given legitimacy to the principle of community self-representation, it has also served the cause of diversity management all too well, relieving establishment institutions like MOMA and the Met of the obligation to confront cultural diversity more fully within their own walls.

Recent talk about the crisis of the museum has been tied to the crisis of the principle of institutional representation, urgently felt across the spectrum of education as in the arts. As I have argued, this crisis ought to be seen in the light of the modern history of representative democracy in the United States, with its vast statistical machinery. In modern times, that process has proven faithful to the precept of proportional demographics on the one hand, while exercising care, on the other, not to disturb the liberal credo of meritocratic entitlement with any suggestion of a system of opportunity tied to quotas—currently the dirtiest word in U.S. political culture. Just as important, however, the crisis over institutional representation has its roots in the museum's origins and its ambitious goal of universal coverage.

The Strange Death of Public Culture

The museum's predicament is also typical of the plight of public culture in the age of privatization. One of the most abused terms in our political lexicon, the concept of the public has long been associated with decline, depreciation, and loss—there always is a more expansive public that was enjoyed in days of yore. Many of the institutions perceived as guardians of public culture have often appealed cynically to evidence of cultural decline—usually by vilifying popular culture—in order to reinforce their access to subsidies, resources, and privileges. It's also true that if these institutions have cried wolf once too often in the past, there really is a new kind of wolf at the door today, as the race toward privatization quickens. While public culture in the United States has usually depended on a mix of government, nonprofit, and private funding, the market-driven tilt toward corporate sponsorship is now transforming the face of the arts and education. In response to the massive cuts in social services, nonprofit sponsors are increasingly inclined to encourage art that is community-oriented or that addresses social problems from which the state has withdrawn the aid of its depleted welfare service agencies. On the other hand, the pressure of corporate sponsorship has boosted the merchandizing of culture, even through cable shopping networks (now in the business of serving as museum stores), to a degree that public art may soon be seen as a series of branding opportunities.

In response, the defense of the *status quo ante bellum* in public arts funding has all too often rested on hackneyed appeals to the Romantic safe haven of "artistic freedom," eternally secure against philistines and barbarians. Whatever its worth as a measure of protection for artists against the interests of the state or the powerful and wealthy, the cult of artistic freedom has also nurtured the myth of the "artist in quarantine," regally immune to public accountability and accessible public dialogue. It has also sustained the arrogant gulf that separates fine arts communities from those who work in the cultural marketplace, in media, fashion, graphic arts, design, and journalism—that sphere of cultural labor that, in spite of its commercial overlordship, has released some of the most vital social and political energies of this century at the same time it has marginalized so many others.

With the evaporation of any substantial challenge to market civilization, economic elites have less and less need for public culture to serve as a cloak of respectability for their wealth and status. Nor does the transnational nature of their power require public culture to assume a national form in order to compete for prestige in the league of nations. So too, the reliance of anti-imperialist nationalists on their national cultures to resist the global flows of cultural product has often served as a way to suppress internal minorities or preserve the power balance between metropolitan and provincial culture. Such attempts to defend the national patrimony have been outflanked by the omnivorous appetite of the globalizing culture industries for incorporating local and regional differences.

In response, some versions of public culture have gone supranational—utilizing preexisting networks of communication, like the international art market/circuit, or new technologies, like the Internet. Within the nation-state itself, where the cynical use of the Culture Wars to villainize dissenters shows no sign of abating, the response cannot be single minded. Even for those who decide to devote their energies exclusively to the preservation of public cultural institutions, public culture will never be the same, nor should it be. The current crisis of its institutions should not be regarded as an occasion for retrenchment, but as an opportunity for us to overhaul, modernize, redefine, and fully democratize their structures. You don't have to be a conspiracy theorist to see that the race to privatization is occurring at the very moment when genuine attempts are being made to democratize public culture and diversify its participants, its content, and its reach into a wide range of communities. Claims for diversity and cultural equity are less likely to be met by corporate sponsorship, unless they coincide with a particular multicultural profile suggested by the market research division.

Some elements of the older version of public culture have to remain in place. Without the appeal to universal representation, however impossible and incomplete in practice, we will lose the basis, in a statistical democracy, for demanding that exhibits, collections, and programs be inclusive and diverse. In this respect, the effective graphic impact of the Guerrilla Girls report cards are indispensable billboards for advertising the progress (or retrenchment) of claims for equity. Such notices are a public reminder of how much remains to be done to attain anything close to a critical mass of under-represented artists and voices. Ultimately, however, these claims have a limited effect on the business structure of the art world—the gallery system, the art market, the glorification of authorship, the control of access and participation, and the use of fine art values to police class divisions. From this angle, elevating women and minority artists into the pantheon of the masters may be a matter of fine-tuning rather than a structural overhaul. The fact that the memory, let alone the vestigial reality, of the alternative arts space movement has taken such a beating makes it all the more difficult to imagine and reconstruct alternatives. The perils of co-option—relentlessly cautioned by the alternative arts movement—are no longer even fit for discussion among younger artists whose formation postdates the early 1980s.

On the one hand, then, we must be conscious of the injustices involved in propping up institutions like museums that have a history of transforming cultural rights into social privileges and treating open access as a means of behavior control, and that are even now recruiting the voices of the socially marginalized to pretty up the statistics required by diversity managers. On the other hand, we must be opportunistic, as always, under conditions not of our own making, in making use of the resources that are available. This has to involve creative attempts to use the new patterns of sponsorship to change the frankly elitist relationship between institutions and their audiences, between artists and their publics, between art and popular culture. These new funding patterns offer a potential vehicle for democratizing those relationships at the same time as they threaten to deliver the art world into exactly the kind of corporate overlordship that governs aesthetics in the culture and media industries. From the perspective of the state, public culture is no longer viable as an instrument of popular reform. The evolution of highly controlled and managed forms of popular entertainment, from Coney Island to pay-per-view televised sport, has resolved the problems of civic disorder posed by unsupervised free assembly. Having entered the field in the nineteenth century with a fierce reforming mission that has long since lost its zeal, government is retreating from the province of culture in a manner not unlike that of a colonial power withdrawing from its provincial possessions in the hope that regional market brokers will remain friendly to its will. The national patrimony will remain a concern—the legacy of the *Enola Gay* will not fade quickly. In the meantime, we will continue to lock horns over the politics of inclusion—who's in, who's out. We must also continue to ask whether the vast resources of museums might be better utilized than in authoritative presentations of exhibits to passive spectators. But the larger task will be to create and promote new versions of the "public" that are inclusive, that have popular appeal, and that are elastic enough to accommodate the vast energies of a strong democracy of opinion.

Notes

1. Elizabeth Hess, "Guerrilla Girl Power: Why the Art World Needs a Conscience," in Nina Felshin (ed.), *But Is It Art? The Spirit of Art as Activism* (Seattle: Bay Press, 1995), 327.

2. Tony Bennett, *The Birth of the Museum: History, Theory, and Politics* (London: Routledge, 1996); and Carol Duncan, *Civilizing Rituals: Inside Public Art Museums* (London: Routledge, 1995). My

descriptive account of the nineteenth-century museum draws liberally on their work.

3. Bennett, *Birth of the Museum*, 91 ff.
4. Duncan, *Civilizing Rituals*, 48–71.
5. Ibid., 63.
6. Michael Fitzgerald, *Making Modernism: Picasso and the Creation of the Market for Twentieth-Century Art* (New York: Farrar, Straus and Giroux, 1995).
7. Reesa Greenberg, "The Exibition Redistributed," in Reesa Greenberg, Bruce Ferguson, Sandy Nairne (eds.), *Thinking about Exhibitions* (New York: Routledge, 1995), 362.
8. Neil Harris, "A Historical Perspective on Museum Advocacy," in *Cultural Excursions: Marketing Appetites and Cultural Tastes in Modern America* (Chicago: University of Chicago Press, 1990), 82–95.
9. Neil Harris, "Museums, Merchandising, and Popular Taste," in *Cultural Excursions*, 56–81.
10. Bennett, *Birth of the Museum*, 59–87. George Brown Goode's classic volume is *The Principles of Modern Administration* (York: Coultas and Volans, 1895).
11. David Finn, *How to Visit a Museum* (New York: Harry Abrams, 1985), 10.
12. The different kinds of social access experienced in museum going by disparate groups is examined in Pierre Bourdieu, Alain Darbel, et al., *The Love of Art: European Art Museums and Their Public* (Palo Alto: Stanford University Press, 1969).
13. Maria Ramirez, "Brokering Identities: Art Curators and the Politics of Cultural Representation," in Greenberg, Ferguson, and Nairne (eds.) *Thinking About Exhibitions*, 21–38.

28 Land of a Thousand Dances: Youth, Minorities, and the Rise of Rock and Roll

George Lipsitz

... perhaps the zoot suit conceals profound political meaning; perhaps the symmetrical frenzy of the Lindy-hop conceals clues to great political power.[1]

(Ralph Ellison)

O NE of the most persistent preoccupations in popular culture in the 1970s and 1980s has been nostalgia for the 1950s and 1960s. Although severe inaccuracies and over-simplifications pervade these images, their focus on the birth of rock and roll as an important shared memory reveals a sensitive appreciation of the recent past. The true story of the "Happy Days" of the 1950s and 1960s is every bit as significant as current nostalgic imagery suggests. In that era, young people identified themselves as a self-conscious and rebellious social group, they made music that reflected all unprecedented crossing of racial and class lines, and their actions posed serious challenges to traditional American cultural attitudes and values. The calculated foolishness of the 1950s and 1960s was quite serious; its imagination and sense of play went a long way toward transforming American culture from the domain of a privileged elite into a "land of a thousand dances."

The retrospective approval of rock and roll music pervading so much of popular culture in the 1970s and 1980s stands in sharp contrast to rock and roll's reputation in its early years. The music industry resisted rock and roll, despite its demonstrated popularity with a mass audience, and civic and church leaders condemned it as immoral and debilitating. Intellectuals and moralists during those years tended to see rock and roll music as just another facet of an alienating and potentially anarchic society, one suffering from too many unsocialized youths and too much populist energy. Subsequent social critics, themselves raised amid the mass popularity of rock and roll, have shown more appreciation for the important racial and social implications of the music's mass appeal, yet these critics have rarely connected rock and roll music to the social history that gave it determinate shape. They have underestimated the significance of a mass popular music capable of speaking the language of everyday life and articulating the experiences and activities of the streets. Awed by the formal properties or commercial successes of rock and roll, these critics have overlooked the reasons for

From George Lipsitz, "Land of a Thousand Dances: Youth, Minorities, and the Rise of Rock and Roll," in Larry May (ed.), *Recasting America: Culture and Politics in the Age of Cold War* (Chicago and London: University of Chicago Press, 1989), 267–84.

the music's successful challenge to elite culture as well as its mobilization of youth across racial, class, and ethnic lines.

The acceptance of rock and roll music as a core icon in popular memory stems from its historical significance as a conduit for cultural change in postwar America. Rock and roll's popularity reflected changes in race relations as white teenagers accepted as their own a music that originated among racial minorities. It reflected changes within minority communities as black and brown musicians staked unprecedented claims for themselves as participants in shaping American popular culture. Finally, rock and roll music reflected the rich cultural interactions in American cities in the wake of social changes emanating from war mobilization and mass migrations during World War II. This inquiry revolves around the relationship between rock and roll music and those social changes. But, instead of exploring art disengaged from social context, this study will examine its subject historically—in one specific community over a period of time. My point of entry will be "Land of a Thousand Dances," the mid-1960s song revived by the recent wrestling promotional video. A hit song for black singers Chris Kenner, Round Robin, and Wilson Pickett, "Land of a Thousand Dances" established itself as a conduit for the many cultural streams flowing through rock and roll music in 1965, when it was recorded by Cannibal and the Headhunters, a Chicano group from East Los Angeles.[2] Recent writing about popular music has acknowledged the significance of rock and roll as a shared creation by young whites and young blacks in postwar America, but little has been written about the contribution of Chicano artists and audiences to that fused culture. To understand the era in which rock and roll emerged, we must also understand the complex cultural mediations taking place in communities like the East Los Angeles barrio where Cannibal and the Headhunters developed their musical aspirations and ambitions. The rock and roll music made by Mexican-American musicians like Cannibal and the Headhunters reveals important connections among music, memory, class, ethnicity, and race, and it illumines the enduring usefulness of rock and roll as a vehicle for collective popular memory.

Frankie "Cannibal" Garcia and the other members of his group grew up in a public housing project in East Los Angeles. They originally learned to play music as folk artists in Mexican *mariachi* and *jarocho* bands, but like other brown, black, white, red, and yellow youths all across America, they blended the traditional music of their community with the sounds they heard on records and radio, drawing inspiration from the diversity of urban life and the excitement of the city streets. The Los Angeles environment that nurtured and shaped their music reflected the oppressive and exploitative hierarchies that had done so much to distort American culture in the past, but the postwar years brought radically new social formations that encouraged the development of alternative forms of cultural expression.

During the 1940s, defense spending and war mobilization changed the face of Los Angeles, stimulating a massive in-migration of whites, blacks, and Chicanos. Traditional residential segregation confined Afro-Americans to the south-central area while limiting Chicanos largely to housing near downtown and in east-side neighborhoods.[3] Private bankers and government planners encouraged housing segregation by class and race, viewing ethnic heterogeneity in Los Angeles (as in other cities) as a defect of urban life rather than as one of its advantages.

. . .

The Federal Housing Authority gave its lowest possible rating to Boyle Heights in East Los Angeles because its mixture of Chicano, Jewish, and Eastern European residents convinced the appraisers that "This is a 'melting pot' area and is literally honeycombed with diverse and subversive racial elements. It is seriously doubted whether there is a single block in the area which does not contain detrimental racial elements and there are very few districts which are not hopelessly heterogeneous. . . ."[4]

Yet the opening of new shipyards and aircraft-assembly plants combined with Los Angeles's severe housing shortage to produce unprecedented interethnic mixing in Los Angeles. Official segregation gave way bit by bit as Chicanos and European ethnics lived and worked together in Boyle Heights and Lincoln Park and blacks and Chicanos lived in close proximity in Watts and in the San Fernando Valley suburb of Pacoima.[5]

. . .

Recruiting performers from the communities they knew best, small-scale local record producers responded to trends in the streets. In addition, the proliferation of local radio stations in the postwar years offered exposure to new audiences. Juke-box operators, furniture-store owners, and musicians responded to the consumer demand for a popular music that reflected the folk roots and multiracial ethos of the new urban streets. For example, a 1948 hit record by Los Angeles's Don Tosti Band titled "Pachuco Boogie" sold more than two million copies, an extraordinary total for any Spanish-language record in the United States, but especially for one that glorified one of the barrio's more reviled subcultures—the pachucos.[6]

In many ways, pachucos embodied the defiance of conventional authority that came to symbolize the appeal of rock and roll. Pachucos were teenage gang members sporting zoot suits, ducktail haircuts, and distinctive tattoos; they had attracted public attention during the war years when newspaper stories blamed them for much of the youth crime in Los Angeles. Tensions peaked in June 1943, when hundreds of sailors invaded the East Los Angeles community to beat up Mexican-American youths who wore zoot suits. The police, prosecutors, and city council joined forces to praise this criminal attack, lauding the sailors for their efforts to "clean up" the city. But the racism manifest in the attacks caused many Mexican-Americans to start looking at the pachucos as defenders of the community against outside encroachment and as symbols of Chicano victimization and marginality.[7]

The Don Tosti Band's "Pachuco Boogie" captured the spirit of that new-found admiration for street rebels. The song's lyrics employed *calo*, the street slang associated with pachucos but considered vulgar by "respectable" Mexican-Americans. "Pachuco Boogie" blended Mexican speech and rhythms with Afro-American scat singing and blues harmonies to form a provocative musical synthesis. Some Spanish-language radio stations refused to play the song, but Anglo disc jockeys programming black rhythm-and-blues shows aimed at white teenagers put it on their playlists, to the delight of their listeners. Itself a blend of Chicano, Anglo, and Afro-American musical forms, "Pachuco Boogie" garnered commercial success by uniting a diverse audience into a new synthesis—a "unity of disunity."[8]

"Pachuco Boogie" signaled the start of creative new links among previously divided groups. Anglo youth, especially, imitated the distinctive dress of Mexican-American "cholos" with their khaki pants and long-sleeved Pendleton shirts over sleeveless white undershirts, and "cholo" became a hip slang word with larger meanings. The word "cholo" probably derives from an Aztec word meaning servant, and it connotes someone with low status, usually a recent immigrant from a rural area. Cholos spoke a bilingual slang, displayed elaborate tattoos, and staked their claims to urban neighborhoods by covering walls with stylized graffiti. The studied disinterest and cultivated detachment affected by cholos echoed the oppositional postures of other postwar subcultures, including bop musicians and Beat poets. But in Los Angeles, the cholo relationship to rock and roll made that subculture the most accessible model of "otherness" for middle-class white youths. When Anglo, black, or even Chicano youths embraced the cholo image, they flaunted their alienation by openly identifying with one of society's most depised groups.[9]

. . .

Perhaps the artist who best exemplifies the new cultural fusions engendered by rock and roll music is Johnny Otis. The son of a Greek immigrant grocer and shipyard worker from northern California, Otis first came to Los Angeles in 1943 as the white drummer in a black band playing at the Club Alabam on Central Avenue in Watts. Otis had developed his interest in black music while growing up in a mixed but mostly black neighborhood in Berkeley, where he accompanied his friends to "sanctified" churches to listen to the gospel preachers, singers, and choirs. "This society says no white kid can stay in black culture," Otis observes, "but see, that culture had captured me. I loved it and it was richer and more fulfilling and more natural. I thought it was mine."[10] When a high school teacher suggested that he spend less time with blacks and associate more with whites, Otis capped a long battle with his teachers and principals by dropping out of school in disgust. He became a drummer with Count Otis Matthews's West Oakland House Rockers and then went on the road to tour with a variety of Afro-American bands, including Lloyd Hunter's Territory Jazz Band.

In Los Angeles, Otis worked with black musicians, married a black woman, and thought of himself as "black by persuasion." But part of the consciousness of the black community he joined there involved staking a claim for full participation in American life and culture, and that claim led to interactions with other groups and other cultures. "I got here in '43 and at that time the Avenue [Central] was just swinging. It was like a transplanted Harlem Renaissance," Otis remembers.[11] One night at the Lincoln Theater, he saw the blues singer and piano player Charles Brown win a talent contest by playing "Clair de Lune." Otis recalls,

He kind of apologized for what he played, but they loved him, they made him do an encore— "Rhapsody in Blue"—he just broke it up. And it was a good lesson for me, because in later years people would tell me that "You can't take Big Mama Thornton to New York because she's too rough and bluesy, and you can't take Sally Blair to the Apollo because she's not bluesy enough." Well, bullshit on both counts. The people just liked it. If it's really strong and it has artistry, they like it.[12]

Otis began promoting rhythm and blues shows for mixed audiences, offering

Chicano and white youths a chance to hear the music of the black community. He promoted and starred in weekly rhythm and blues shows at Angeles Hall on the east side that demonstrated the powerful appeal of black music for Mexican-American audiences and that helped stimulate the growth of rock and roll music within the barrio.[13] Otis had rock and roll television programs on three Los Angeles television stations in the early 1950s and promoted dances all over the city, despite harassment from local authorities upset about a music that crossed racial and class lines. "The cops would come and hassle the kids standing in line to get into the television show," Otis recalls. "They see black kids and Hispanic kids and Asian kids and they don't like it. They just didn't want to see that. If it were all Asian and Hispanic and black they wouldn't care, but there were whites there, and they're mixing with the blacks and what not."[14] But despite the official harassment, the teenagers kept coming out to Otis's shows, and, despite rumors of gang violence and racial incidents about to happen, Otis remembers that "We never had any trouble, the people got along great."[15]

Exemplifying the fusion of small entrepreneur and musician that often brought rock and roll to the public, Otis started a small record label and recording studio in the mid-fifties featuring many of Los Angeles's leading rhythm and blues singers, including L'il Julian Herrera, the city's first commercially successful Chicano rock and roller. Otis produced Herrera's 1956 local hit "Lonely, Lonely Nights," a classic do-wop ballad, and featured him in his stage shows as part of a special effort to attract Chicano audiences. As Otis tells it, "L'il Julian came to me as a kid, a young Mexican-American guy and sang. He wasn't great, but he could sing and he was charming and it was nice and real. I put him on stage, and the little Mexican girls loved him, and our Chicano audience was a big part of our audience in those days. I put him in the band, and then he lived in my house."[16]

Herrera's relationship with Johnny Otis illustrates the ways in which rock and roll music became a common ground for people from diverse backgrounds in Los Angeles in the early 1950s. After all, "Lonely, Lonely Nights" presented a Chicano's rendition of a black vocal style on a record produced by a white man who thought of himself as black. But Otis found out that the story of L'il Julian Herrera was even more complicated than he knew. One day, a juvenile officer walked into Otis's record company in search of Ron Gregory, a runaway youth from the East. When the officer showed Otis a picture, he realized that Ron Gregory was L'il Julian Herrera. "He ran away from home, hitchhiked out here, and this Mexican lady in Boyle Heights takes him in and raises him as her son," Otis relates.[17] It turned out that Los Angeles's first Chicano rock and roll star was born a Hungarian Jew and became "a Chicano by persuasion," just as Johnny Otis had become "black by persuasion."[18]

The pinnacle of this brown-white-black mixing in rock and roll music in Los Angeles came with the enormous popularity of Ritchie Valens, East Los Angeles's best-selling and most significant rock and roll artist. Independent record producer Bob Keane discovered Valens when he noticed that the car-club cholos of East Los Angeles responded to a band called the Silhouettes and their lead singer, Richard Valenzuela. Shortening (and Anglicizing) the youth's last name to Valens, Keane signed him to a contract and recorded the singer with the same back-up musicians that Keane used on sessions by the black gospel and rock singer Sam Cooke. These session musicians brought a wealth of musical experience to Valens's recordings—bass player Red Callendar had played with jazz great Art Tatum, and drummer Earl Palmer had recorded with rhythm and blues artists in New Orleans, including Roy Brown, Fats Domino, and Little Richard.[19] But Ritchie Valens did not have to learn his cultural pluralism in a studio; life in postwar Los Angeles had already prepared him well for the mixing of forms and styles that would come to characterize his recorded music.

More than any other artist, Valens brought the folk traditions of Mexican music to a mass audience through rock and roll, but his music also reflected an extraordinary blending of traditions and styles from other cultures. Born in 1941 in the San Fernando Valley suburb of Pacoima, Valens learned music listening to his relatives sing Mexican songs as they gathered at each other's homes in the evenings. At the age of five, Valens made a toy guitar out of a cigar box and learned to fret it with the help of an uncle who taught him how to play his first song—the traditional Mexican *huapango*, "La Bamba." In Pacoima, Valens met William Jones, a black musician who lived across the street from the youth's Aunt Ernestine. Jones taught Valens how to tune a guitar and play chords. After building a green and white electric guitar for himself in his junior high school wood-shop class, Valens began to experiment with the Afro-American rhythm and blues songs that he heard on the radio. In 1957, he joined the Silhouettes, a band put together by Chicano vibraphonist Gil Rocha that featured Valens on guitar, William Jones's sons Conrad and Bill on drums and clarinet, and Japanese-American Walter Takaki on tenor saxophone. Valens became the featured vocalist with the band, and his tributes to the black rhythm and blues singer Little Richard moved his admirers to start calling him "Little Ritchie."[20]

In the brief period between Valens's emergence on the best-selling record charts and his death in a plane crash early in 1959, he brought an extraordinary range of musics before pop audiences. He borrowed from white rockabilly, black blues, and Mexican folk musicians because they all made up parts of his cultural environment in postwar Los Angeles. "La Bamba" and "Come On, Let's Go" featured variations on melodies and harmonies common to Mexican fiesta music, while "Ooh My Head" employed the boogie-woogie form and vocal mannerisms common to Afro-American music. One of Valens's unfinished records included an attempt to lay the rhythm popularized by blues guitarist Bo Diddley underneath the Latin guitar standard "Malaguena." Radio programs and phonograph records made Eddie Cochran's rockabilly and Bo Diddley's rhythm and blues songs an organic part of barrio life, and the limited but nonetheless real cultural mixing in working-class neighborhoods enabled young people to explore the culture of their neighbors. Valens wrote his big hit song "Donna" about a failed romance with an Anglo classmate whose father ordered her to stop going out with "that Mexican," and he recorded a version of his favorite rhythm and blues song "Framed," which had originally been recorded by a Los Angeles rhythm and blues group, the Robins, but which had been written by Mike Stoller and Jerry Leiber.[21]

Valens's tragic death at age seventeen deprived the Los Angeles Chicano community of its biggest star, and it cut short the career of one of rock and roll's most eclectic synthesizers. But other artists carried on his propensity for blending the folk musics of the barrio with the styles and forms circulating within popular music. In the late 1950s and early 1960s, groups such as the Salas Brothers, Carlos Brothers, Rene and Ray, and the Romancers had regional and national hit songs that reflected the barrio's dialogue with mainstream rock and roll music. Just as Ritchie Valens established himself as a commercial performer by playing rhythm and blues-styled versions of Anglo and Mexican songs for a mixed audience, later Chicano musicians played a combination of different musics for a combination of audiences. In concerts at East Los Angeles College and at El Monte Legion Stadium, at dances held in youth centers and union halls, and at popular nightclubs like the Rhythm Room and Rainbow Gardens, Chicano rock and rollers learned to blend Mexican and rock musics into a synthesis that won them admirers both inside and outside the barrio.[22]

Nothing illustrates this synthesis more completely than the song "Land of a Thousand Dances" by Cannibal and the Headhunters. Garcia got his start as a rock singer when the lead vocalist for the Royal Jesters (another East Los Angeles rock group) became sick, and the band recruited Garcia to take his place "because I sang in school with a mariachi band, doing traditional Mexican music."[23] Garcia later joined with some friends from the Ramona Gardens Housing Project to form Cannibal and the Headhunters, taking their name from Garcia's "street" (gang) name of "Cannibal," gained when he bit an opponent in a fight. One of their most effective songs in live performances had been Chris Kenner's "Land of a Thousand Dances," but at one show Garcia forgot the words at the beginning of the song and ad-libbed "na-na-na-na-na," to the delight of the crowd. In the studio, they retained Cannibal's accidental improvisation to give the record a captivating introduction that helped it become one of the best-selling records of 1965. They also borrowed the double drum sound prominent in Stevie Wonder records to forge a synthesis that attracted the attention of audiences all over the country.

Other Chicano musicians in the 1960s combined a fusion of popular and Mexican musics with lyrics that addressed one facet of their lives that distinguished them from previous generations—a fascination with the automobile. They celebrated cars as a means to pleasure, joy, and excitement, not as transportation to work or as a means of accomplishing mundane tasks.

. . .

The car culture's quest for fun and good times expressed a desire for the good life of material success, but it also provided a means for satirizing and subverting ruling icons of consumer society. Just as Chicano car customizers "improved" upon the mass-produced vehicles from Detroit, Chicano rock songs like "Whittier Boulevard" celebrated Mexican-American appropriations of automobiles as part of a community ritual. By the late 1960s, that dialogue between the images of mass culture and the realities of barrio life increasingly took on an expressly political cast. At that time, changes in urban economics and politics threatened to destroy the social basis for the cultural pluralism of Los Angeles rock and roll by undermining the social and economic infrastructure of the central city. The cumulative effects of postwar highway and housing policies had subsidized suburban growth at the expense of the inner city, had exacerbated racial and class polarizations, and had encouraged residential segregation. For Chicanos, increased migration from Mexico, inadequate access to decent housing, and discrimination in a segmented labor market all combined to help create a new consciousness.[24]

The failures of 1960s social programs including the War on Poverty, the effects of the Vietnam War on poor and working-class youths, and the repressive policies of the Los Angeles Police Department all contributed to a growing political activism and cultural nationalism. On August 29, 1970, the Chicano community mobilized for a massive antiwar demonstration that expressed anger over many pent-up grievances and complaints. Taking their opposition to the war and their growing nationalism to the streets, demonstrators relied on their cultural traditions to give form to their protest activity. As one participant chronicled the start of that day's events, "The boulevard was filled with *gente*, doing Latino chants and playing musica right in the streets. It started taking on the atmosphere of a carnival. Some even danced."[25] This demonstration involved an attempt to reclaim city streets as a terrain for culture, politics, and celebration. But its aggressive festivity provoked a violent reaction from the authorities. Los Angeles police officers used force against the demonstrators; one officer shot and killed *Los Angeles Times* columnist Ruben Salazar. The Salazar killing outraged many people in the Mexican-American community and helped mobilize subsequent activism and demonstrations.[26]

The political ferment surrounding the 1970 demonstration found its way into Mexican-American rock and roll music in significant ways. Thee Midnighters recorded a song titled "Chicano Power" in 1970, and the group the V.I.P.'s changed their name that same year to El Chicano. In the early 1970s, East Los Angeles musicians began to feature Latin musical forms and Spanish-language lyrics more prominently in their songs, and they attached themselves to a variety of community icons and subcultures. A series of outdoor music festivals, known popularly as "Chicano Woodstocks," showcased the community's musicians and provided a forum for displaying and celebrating diverse images of Chicano identity. The band Tierra emerged as a favorite of the "lowrider" car customizers in the early 1970s, while Los Lobos got its start with an album recorded under the aegis of Cesar Chavez's United Farm Workers union. Mixing images from the past of pachucos and cholos with contemporary ones like low riders, these bands and their audiences placed current struggles in historical perspective, preserving a measure of continuity in a period of extraordinary change.[27]

Yet the music of East Los Angeles still had significant influence on artists and audiences outside the barrio. In 1975, for example, a mostly Afro-American jazz/funk ensemble from Long Beach calling themselves War recorded "Low Rider," a tribute to Chicano car customizers, cruisers, and musicians.[28] One of the year's best-selling records, "Low Rider" expressed War's own experiences playing dances and concerts for Mexican-American audiences throughout southern California, but the song also reflected demographic trends in Los Angeles that encouraged black-Chicano cultural interaction. In 1970, more than 50,000 Hispanics lived in the traditionally black south-central area of Los Angeles; by 1980 that figure had doubled, with Chicanos making up 21 percent of the total population of the south-central area.[29] The clear Latin influence on the subject and style of "Low Rider" testifies to the importance of Chicano music to American popular music, even when Chicano artists themselves might not enjoy access to a mass audience.

In striking contrast to previous eras when the music and experiences of racial minorities remained largely inaccessible to youths from comfortable economic backgrounds, Chicano and black music in the postwar years played a major role in defining the worldview of Anglo artists and audiences. Mass popular culture and especially radio offered young people an opportunity to expand their cultural tastes in private, away from the surveillance of adult authority.

. . .

Even outside Los Angeles, white rock and roll musicians playing to largely middle-class audiences recognized and acknowledged their debt to Chicano rock and roll. The popular British band Led Zeppelin remade Ritchie Valens's "Ooh My Head" in 1976, and the New York "punk" group, the Ramones, recorded his "Come On, Let's Go." Rock critic Lester Bangs saluted Valens's "La Bamba" as the original punk-rock song, and he identified it as the forerunner of the Ramones' "Blitzkrieg Bop."[30] The national and international respect for Chicano music among rock and punk musicians made itself felt in Los Angeles in the late 1970s when Chicano groups emerged as an important part of the local punk-rock scene. Ruben Guevara told a reporter in 1980 that the Chicano punk groups attained popularity because of their ability to involve audiences in basic feelings and emotions that rarely surfaced in mainstream popular music. "This music has a particular quality that's missing in most of the stuff that's playing around town," Guevara noted. "For lack of a better word, it's raw, primitive. Which reminds me of something Stravinsky said which I think is relevant. When a culture loses its primitive music it dies."[31]

Chicano rock and roll music extended the perceptions of the Mexican-American community to a mass audience that included young people raised in affluent circumstances, cushioned by the privileges of white skin. The tendency for the culture of aggrieved communities to form the core of significant strains in popular culture characterized the vital center of an unprecedented youth culture in postwar America, one that made a definitive break with the historically sanctioned hierarchies of American life. The increased purchasing power of the middle class and the likelihood of postponed entry into the work force gave middle-class youths the resources to begin experimenting with cultural forms that challenged sexual repression, racial oppression, and class suppression. At the same time, the cultures and subcultures of seemingly marginalized outsiders held a fascinating attraction for privileged youths looking for alternatives to the secure but stifling and limited sexual roles and identities of middle-class life.

The kinds of ethnic and class interactions common to industrial cities like Los Angeles in the 1940s and 1950s provided the subtext for the emergence of rock and roll as the central force in American popular music. Even though a combination of public and private policies worked to destroy the very kinds of cities that made that music possible, a nostalgia for the heterogeneity of the postwar industrial city has provided the impetus for all the "great leaps" that have marked the history of rock and roll from the 1950s to the present. Elvis Presley and Chuck Berry rose to popularity in the 1950s by immortalizing in song the racial interactions they had experienced as young workers in Memphis and St. Louis (respectively) during the late 1940s and early 1950s. The "British Invasion" spearheaded by the Beatles and Rolling Stones in 1964 resonated with the echoes of the lost cultural fusions of the 1950s forged by Presley, Berry, and Bill Haley.

. . .

Above all, the experience of rock and roll music in East Los Angeles over the past forty years illumines the social and cultural basis for a major shift in American life. By the mid-fifties, rock and roll music became a conduit for racial and class grievances as well as a determinate force in middle-class youth culture. As such, it was more than play. Real historical experiences and aspirations lay within rock and roll music, inside the life histories of individual musicians, and inside the collective memory of the audience. Often unacknowledged, these sedimented layers did much to undermine an older cultural hierarchy, and they shed light on where America has been, as well as where it may yet go. As demonstrated by the rock and roll music created in East Los Angeles over the years, seemingly neutral and frivolous forms of popular culture can contain the history of concrete communities of creation and reception. So, when popular films, television programs, and phonograph records hark back to the early days of rock and roll, they engage in something more than nostalgia for the carefree days of youth. They touch a resonant chord in collective popular memory because they recall the exhilaration of years when popular culture began to cross previously insurmountable barriers of race, class, and ethnicity—a time when young artists and audiences transformed the dissonance and noise of urban life into a chorus of many voices. In the face of an increasingly standardized manipulation of urban spatial and cultural relations, they carved out a place in popular culture for a vision of America as a land of a thousand dances.

Notes

1. Ralph Ellison, "Editorial Comment," *Negro Quarterly*, 1 (Winter–Spring 1943): 301.
2. Bob Shannon and John Javna, *Behind the Hits* (New York: Warner, 1986), 94–95.
3. Eshrev Shevky and Marilyn Williams, *The Social Areas of Los Angeles* (Berkeley: University of California Press, 1949); Ricardo Romo, *East Los Angeles* (Austin: University of Texas Press, 1983). Romo also reveals some long-standing ethnic interactions between blacks and Chicanos in Los Angeles neighborhoods.
4. City Survey Files, Los Angeles, 1939, 7, Home Owners Loan Corporation Papers, National Archives, Washington, D.C., D–53.
5. Gilbert G. Gonzales, "Factors Relating to Property Ownership of Chicanos in Lincoln Heights, Los Angeles," *Aztlan*, 2 (Fall 1971): 111–14.
6. Lindsey Haley, "Pachuco Boogie," *Low Rider* (June 1985): 34. *Los Angeles Times*, Calendar Section (October 12, 1980). Roberto Caballero-Robledo, "The Return of Pachuco Boogie," *Nuestro* (November 1979): 4–17.
7. Mauricio Mazon, *Zoot Suit Riots* (Austin: University of Texas Press, 1984); George Lipsitz, *Class and Culture in Cold War America: A Rainbow at Midnight* (South Hadley, Mass.: Bergin and Garvey, 1982), 26–28.
8. Marshall Berman, *All That Is Solid Melts into Air* (New York: Simon and Schuster, 1982), 15.
9. Ruben Guevara, "The View from the Sixth Street Bridge: The History of Chicano Rock," in *Rock 'n' Roll Confidential Report*, ed. Dave Marsh (New York: Pantheon, 1985), 118. Marjorie Miller, "Cholos Return to Their Roots and Find They Bloom," *Los Angeles Times* (September 9, 1984): pt. 1, 3.

10. Johnny Otis, interview with author, Altadena, California, December 14, 1986.
11. Ibid.
12. Ibid.
13. Ibid. Steven Loza, "The Musical Life of the Mexican-Chicano People in Los Angeles, 1945–1985," Ph.D. diss. (University of California–Los Angeles, 1985), 124.
14. Johnny Otis, interview with author.
15. Ibid.
16. Ibid. Guevara, "The View from the Sixth Street Bridge," 118.
17. Johnny Otis, interview with author.
18. Johnny Otis, *Listen to the Lambs* (New York: Norton, 1968). *Los Angeles Times*, Calendar Section (April 3, 1985). Joe Sasfy, "Johnny Otis' Fifth Decade," *Washington Post* (June 24, 1985): sect. B, 7.
19. Jim Dawson and Bob Keane, "Ritchie Valens—His Life Story," Rhino Records insert, 1981.
20. Jim Dawson, "Valens, the Forgotten Story," *Los Angeles Times* (February 3, 1980): 100. Dawson and Keane, "Ritchie Valens."
21. Dawson and Keane, "Ritchie Valens." Jim Dawson, "Valens, the Forgotten Story."
22. Don Snowden, "The Sound of East LA.,

1964," *Los Angeles Times* (October 28, 1984): 6.
23. Ethlie Ann Vare, "Cannibal and the Headhunters," *Goldmine* (November 1983): 26, 53. Don Snowden, "The Sounds of East L.A., 1964," 7.
24. For a detailed explanation of the urban crisis of the 1960s and 1970s, see John Mollenkopf, *The Contested City* (Princeton: Princeton University Press, 1983).
25. Luis Rodriguez, "La Veintineuve," in *Latino Experience in Literature and Art* (Los Angeles: Los Angeles Latino Writers Association, 1982), 9.
26. Guevara, "The View from the Sixth Street Bridge," 120.
27. Ibid. *Los Angeles Times*, Calendar Section (November 9, 1980): 69. El Larry, "Los Lobos," *Low Rider* (March–April 1984): 34.
28. Joel Whitburn, *The Billboard Book of Top 40 Hits* (New York: Billboard, 1984).
29. Melvin Oliver and James Johnson, Jr., "Inter-Ethnic Conflict in an Urban Ghetto," *Research in Social Movements: Conflict and Change*, 6: 57–94.
30. Dawson and Keane, "Ritchie Valens—His Life Story."
31. *Los Angeles Times*, Calendar Section (October 12, 1980): 7.

29 Work(ing) Out

Susan Willis

The Workout

Many young women today do not realize that exercise for women as a widely available and socially acceptable endeavour represents a recent victory in women's struggle for equality with men.

. . .

One of the positive outgrowths of the women's movement in the 1960s was the invigorating of the female body coupled with the acceptability for women to appear in public activity engaged in vigorous physical activity. Sixty-minute aerobics workouts four or five times a week or a jogging program aimed at twenty-five miles a week, these are the exercise standards many women set for themselves. Most are white middle-class, professional women, although many younger black women students and professionals are beginning to enter the exercise lifestyle. Racial equality and class mobility are synonymous with the professions and professional workouts. While for the working class in general, and particularly black women who work outside the home, freedom means liberation from effort, "why exercise when you kill yourself working all day?"

I want to look at women's exercise, bearing in mind its narrowly defined constituency, but realizing at the same time that middle-class white America defines the model and the look of consumer capitalism. I also want to maintain a sense of all the positive features exercise for women generates including the development of independence and the possibility for bonding between women; but I want particularly to scrutinize the way exercise has evolved in a commodified society so as to contain or limit these positive features.

In the 1960s many women had begun to make exercise a part of their daily lives with Jack LaLanne. A TV entrepreneur of exercise and health products, LaLanne mixed rhythmic stretching, bouncing and bending with brazen exhortations to "Bertha" and "Gertie" to get up off their bulgy behinds, work their baggy thighs, and strengthen their flabby underarms. "Come on now, Clara, do just one more". LaLanne's daily half-hour exercise program was immensely popular during the 1960s. It underscored a moment when many women found themselves bound up in domestic space and work, with the TV something of a companion during the hours when kids and husband were out of the house. LaLanne's exercise had the practicality of offering women a wide range of movements that could be performed with no more fancy equipment than a

From Susan Willis, "Work(ing) Out," *Cultural Studies*, 4: 1 (1990), 1–18. Taylor & Francis Ltd, PO Box 25, Abingdon, Oxfordshire, UK.

straight-legged wooden chair. Women at the time did not seem to consider the jarring incongruity of shaping their movements to the video image of a very muscled man, whose bulging pectorals and biceps they could not hope to achieve even if they performed every movement ten times as directed. In the early 1960s, women who sought autonomy through exercise had to put up with patronizing male attitudes towards women's "lesser" physical capabilities, outright condescension toward flab, and exaggerated macho images of male physical prowess. LaLanne is reported to have swum from Alcatraz to the mainland, his hands manacled behind him, and towing a small boat. This may be a figure for liberation, but it's not one any of the male prisoners on Alcatraz ever duplicated, nor is it one the 1960s housewife could readily emulate.

Today LaLanne has been replaced by a new male TV guru of exercise for women: Richard Simmons, who was once proportioned like the Pillsbury Dough Boy and now offers his slimmer, trimmer body as an example of what every overweight woman can achieve. With a round baby face and somewhat childish voice, Simmons offers women a lot less machismo than LaLanne but he serves up equal doses of condescension toward flab. Where LaLanne aggressively chided women for being overweight, Simmons cajoles and preaches. Of course, neither ever mentions that male domination, which restricts many women to home life or body-restricting clerical jobs, is a major flab-producing factor. Both LaLanne and Simmons define the woman viewer as offensive to the male gaze and helpless—if not altogether mindless—for having gotten a too-large body in the first place.

In the face of overt male domination of exercise for women, Jane Fonda's *Workout*, and particularly her "Prime time workout" for women in midlife, represent something of a feminist alternative in the exercise market. Published in 1981, the *Workout* book was on the bestseller charts for two years and continues to be newly discovered and widely read by women. Its diffusion has subsequently been extended by a videotape version available in every home video rental store. In her 40s when the book first appeared, with photos of herself throughout, Fonda undertook the task of "womanizing" exercise. She made it clear that women of all ages can strive for and attain health, strength—and a good-looking body (although many women drew the line at doing back flips *à la* Fonda).

The "Prime time workout" included in the book of essays, *Women Coming of Age*, is an excellent model for understanding how far a feminist approach to exercise can go in a culture that continues to be defined by men and capitalism. I see this book as an exercise in contradiction whose tentatives towards defining women-centered notions about the female body bring to light in equal measure the limitations our society places on the full realization of such alternatives. The title, "Prime time workout", is a good case in point. Fonda explains her choice of words by underscoring the double meaning of prime time. A woman's "prime of life"—her middle years—elides with the notion of network prime time. Fonda makes the comparison in order to emphasize a simple point about sexism. That is, men in their prime times are like the 9:00 slot on CBS. They are the most sought after, most successful, most esteemed. In contrast, women at age 40 are made to feel like a 4:00 sitcom rerun. (AM or PM, take your pick.)

The book is written to stake women's claim on the future and on future definitions of womanhood. But as Fonda explains in her introduction, *Women Corming of Age* documents a moment of transition. It is not yet clear to Fonda writing the book or any of us following its guidelines what sort of women will emerge as the 1980s and post-1980s come to be defined more and more by women over 40 in the workforce and in the public eye. The problem Fonda confronts is how to shape the transition, deeply burdened as she is with twentieth-century male-dominated ideas of womanhood where beauty is synonymous with youth. Proclaiming that the physical characteristics of a woman's aging are "negotiable" (Fonda 1984: 39) Fonda defines a thin line between recapitulating the quest for beauty (how to combat facial wrinkles, for instance) and affirming some wholly new and autonomous notion of womanhood whose precursors are the fifty-year-old marathoners and swimmers whose photos crop up throughout the book and function as reality principles to the more glamorous dance-pose photos of Fonda herself.

. . .

This brings me to the consideration of the other half of the book's exercise title: the notion of the "workout", itself. My hypothesis is that the workout, as the contradictory synthesis of work and leisure, may well represent the most highly evolved commodity form yet to appear in late-twentieth-century consumer capitalism. The workout isolates the individual for the optimal expenditure of selectively focussed effort aimed at the production of the quintessential body object. Nevertheless, I would maintain that the workout, and particularly the nautilus workout, includes utopian dimensions as well. In seeking to reveal how the workout embodies production and consumption in capitalist society and the desire for their utopian transformation, I am elaborating on Fredric Jameson's dictum that "even the most degraded type of mass culture has a [utopian dimension] which remains implicitly, and no matter how faintly, critical of the social order from which (as a commodity) it springs" (Jameson 1979: 144).

The workout represents the culmination of the trend in exercise towards privatization. The process originated at the turn of the century with "males only" health clubs and terminates in today's unisex exercise spas. It is abundantly clear that exercise is a commodity with the advent of TV exercise shows and the now more individualized mode of consumption: the video cassette. In today's big-money exercise market, the only possible antithesis to the commodity form are local community exercise classes offered in school gymnasiums and church recreation hails. However, the burgeoning of glitzy private clubs and spas has made the YMCA and community recreation programs appear lackluster and old fashioned—something for the elderly and middle-age-spread cases. The difference between a workout in a private spa and an exercise class at the "Y" is the way the latter promotes bonding between women and a sense of community that cut across the generations and socio-economic strata. Women who participate in community-organized programs generally comment that they most appreciate getting to know, and to laugh and sweat with, other women. Community-sponsored exercise programs do not sever their participants from their lives with families and friends. Rather, the exercise class creates an opportunity for women to develop themselves in community with other women. Such opportunities are absolutely negated when exercise is channelled by the media into private living rooms. The private spa, then, offers escape from job or domestic space, but it severely limits the possibility for conversation and community. This is because a woman who participates in aerobatics at a spa is made to see herself as an isolated individual. The atmosphere of the spa promotes an aura of body rivalry. Mirrors are everywhere. Women compare, but do not share themselves with others. They see themselves as bodies. They scrutinize their lines and curves and they check out who's wearing the hottest leotard.

The workout focuses women's positive desires for strength, agility, and the physical affirmation of self and transforms these into competition over style and rivalry for a particular body look and performance. Body rivalry has long been a feature of men's exercise. Men flexing for themselves and each other in front of a mirror is the single most expressive metaphor of masculinity and exercise. The workout puts women in contention with one another for the right look. For women, poised body line and flexed muscles are only half the picture. Achieving the proper workout look requires several exercise costumes, special no-smudge makeup, and an artfully understated hairdo.

The workout produces the gendered look of exercise: long Barbie-doll legs; strikingly accentuated by irredescent hot pink tights; set off by a pair of not too floppy purple leg warmers (worn even when the weather is warm); a willowy body poured into a plum-colored leotard whose leg openings define the thigh at waist level; and finally a color-co-ordinated headband (or wristbands)—teasing reminders that in order to look the way it does the body must sweat. Many women now wear their exercise costumes while doing errands to and from the spa. I have seen women in dazzling workout costumes on line at McDonald's, getting cash at the bank's instant teller, picking their kids up at day care, pushing a shopping cart at the supermarket, and on city streets from coast to coast. Most women who appear in public *à la* exercise choose not to cover up their luminescent body socks with blouse, skirt or dungarees. In so doing, they unabashedly define themselves as workout women. In making a public body statement, a woman affirms herself as someone who has seized control over the making and shaping of her body. She demonstrates her right to participate in professional body toning, an endeavor previously felt to be a man's prerogative. However, all these affirmative, apparently liberatory aspects of a woman's public-exercise statement are negated by the simple fact that men do not appear in public similarly clad. Why should they? Being male is synonymous with having muscles, just as it is synonymous with having a penis. The workout, notwithstanding its co-ed classes and equal access to the nautilus, substantiates male domination through the gendered look of exercise. As with most things in our society, having gender generally comes to mean being female. By the simple reason of being dominant, men need not proclaim themselves as gendered subjects. Women, who define their struggle for equality solely at the level of gender, stand to gain little more than the right to appear as gendered subjects. The image of the workout woman articulates the fundamental contradiction between the desire for dramatic transformation shackled to the desire for gender identity, in a society where only one gender needs definition.

. . .

Working

Many women who workout today, work at managerial jobs; part-time jobs, clerical jobs, micro-assembly jobs, and professional sit-down, body restricting, stress-producing jobs.

For such women the not-so-distant remembrance of "Rosie the Riveter" must summon up striking alternative notions of women in the workforce. "Rosie the Riveter" is an icon intimately associated with industrial labor during the Second World War. Clad in overalls, toting tools and a metal lunch box, "Rosie the Riveter" represents the explosive moment when women as a group appropriated not just the uniforms and roles traditionally reserved for men, but actually seized the single most important symbol of male-dominated industrial capitalism: the machine. The image of "Rosie the Riveter" astride the tremendous fuselage of a B-52 gives feminist reversal to the privileged relationship of man to machine defined a century earlier by Emile Zola in his apocalyptic railroad epic, *La Bête Humaine*. Zola's portrayal of the engineer who forces bone, muscle and passion to control a hurtling locomotive epitomizes man's integral relationship with the machine, unbroken till the 1940s.

Unlike "Rosie the Riveter" who dramatically defined women as a productive force, most working women today have difficulty perceiving their labor in terms of production. Many working men also feel disassociated from producing but the experience is more largely a woman's experience because women predominate in service-sector employment as well as unskilled and micro-assembly jobs. If we consider the broad history of women in the workplace from the Second World War to the present, we would begin with women's appropriation of industrial jobs in the 1940s, their return to domesticity in the 1950s, and their reinduction into the labor force during the 1970s and 1980s as a low-skilled and low-paid component of the labor force. The image of women actively engaged in production and intimately associated with machinery has been erased from popular inconography. Even if she works a forty-hour week, a woman will probably never be thought of as having anything to do with machinery other than labor-saving kitchen devices (like the food processor ironically named "La Machine") and the family car.

In the context of women's labor history, the nautilus machine is a capitalist wish-fulfillment. It gives a woman access to the machine but denies access to production. It requires energy and effort and negates the experience of labor. It isolates the individual from other women who workout and defines her body as an assemblage of body areas and muscle functions, each requiring a specialized machine and machine function. The nautilus machine and the woman who works out on it is the distorted 1980s equivalent of "Rosie the Riveter" astride the body of an aircraft. As an icon in the popular imagination, the nautilus metaphorizes women's relationship to self and to labor. Nothing is produced but the body itself.

"You practically crawl inside it." This is how my son characterized working out on the nautilus as compared to the now old-fashioned weight-lifting equipment where your strength is pitted against the machine's resistance. When asked to describe the nautilus, most people have expressed similar feelings of being assimilated into the machine. Rather than the direct expenditure of effort out of your body, along a wire, over a pulley to lift a weight, the nautilus incorporates your body into its function. The woman inside the nautilus machine is the object produced by the machine even while she is at the same time the producer producing herself as product of the machine. The allusion to production is enhanced by the layout of the room housing the nautilus. Anyone who has ever visited a machine shop will see in the nautilus' division of labor, where separate machines are designed and situated in order to accomplish specific tasks, a mirrored and chrome version of a tool-and-die shop. The woman who works out has the illusive gratification of being in the workplace, where she can experience first-hand the reduction of labor into repetitive, narrowly defined tasks.

What I find most striking about mass culture today is that many of the features that define a particular mass cultural object, such as those that typify the aerobics workout, are reiterated in other cultural objects, some of them from the realm of "high" art. A good example is the photographic artist, Cindy Sherman, whose work has for some time been acclaimed by the New York art world and has more recently come to the attention of the popular press, such as *Vogue* magazine. Cindy Sherman's photography enacts the same relationship to production and consumption as do women who work-out on the nautilus machine. The majority of Sherman's photos are of herself. Most of the earlier work resembles black and white movie stills with Sherman depicted as someone either in a Fellini landscape or in a Hollywood B movie. Curiously enough, many of Sherman's photos bear a strong resemblance to the photos of Jane Fonda that appear in the movie star's workout books.

Sherman's photos of herself are not self-portraits in the traditional sense of the term because each photo reveals an entirely different Cindy Sherman. Each is a discrete photo object whose singular subject is made-up, costumed and depicted as somehow autonomous and separate from Cindy Sherman the photographer. Sherman is both the photographer and the subject photographed. She is inside the production/reproduction circuit. She is the product produced and hung on the gallery wall for public consumption and at the same time she is the producer producing the body image product. There is a famous woodblock print by Albrecht Dürer that many students encounter in an introductory art history course. It depicts a male artist in the process of capturing on paper the reclining figure of a nude female. Between the artist and his subject is a grid, through which the artist gazes and whose lines and spaces dissect the supine female body, thus allowing the artist to reproduce her in detail and perspective. By appropriating the camera, the mechanism for reproduction, Cindy Sherman occupies the privileged position of Dürer's artist and is at the same time the objectified model. Indeed, in one of her photos, Sherman mimics the reclining pose of Dürer's nude which she could only have captured by defining her gaze at herself along the line of sight first used by Dürer's artist.

Sherman's art, like women working at the nautilus, is the most appropriate image for the era after the struggle to appropriate male-dominated production has been won and then summarily reabsorbed by capitalism Not unlike industrial machinery, the machine for photographic production, the camera, was originally associated with great *male* artists; Cartier-Bresson, Stieglitz, Hine. The influx of women photographers in an art world previously dominated by men is fundamentally related to the development of photography as a leisure-time commodity. Only after the camera was domesticated largely by Eastman Kodak to tap the tremendous profitability of home photography did it become accessible to women and children, female photographers and housewives alike.

If the Luddites urged breaking the machinery of capitalism, and "Rosie the Riveter" represented a temporary feminist usurpation of the machine, then Cindy Sherman, the nautilus of photography, defines intimate oneness with the machine and assimilation into the production process. In the nineteenth century, Marx wrote against the worker's alienation. He demonstrated that in selling labor power, the worker was separated both from control over production and from the fruits of labor, the commodities and profits from their sale. The contradiction of the commodity is that it can be absolutely divorced from the worker while at the same time it is the container of the worker's alienated labor. Alienation informs the entire circuit of production and consumption under capitalism. In such a system, the utopian impulse often finds expression in the very forms that simultaneously articulate its containment. The image of a woman producing herself on the nautilus machine and Cindy Sherman dramatically posing into her self-activated camera are both expressions of women's deep desire to deny alienation. Both articulate the desire to seize control over production and the commodity. Both demonstrate the utopian desire to be in control, to activate the machine. And they express the highly reified desire to be absorbed into the machine's function. Both express the utopian longing to no longer see one's alienated labor in the commodity, but do so by the dystopian formula of making the self into the commodity.

The libertory impulses are in every instance contained within the larger capitalist system which gives the lie to the notion of feminized production. Cindy Sherman and the nautilus are epiphenomenal metaphors for an era when more and more women are being brought into the workforce. Many now derive from the middle strata whose women in the past would have been frozen in the domestic sphere. This means that whatever notions of alterity that previously informed the bourgeois family and home as separate from production are now collapsed as the home, office, and highway merge into every woman's production/reproduction circuit. Then, too, because most women are brought into production as part-time or service workers, their wage labor is as devalued as their domestic labor was (and is) invisible. Images of women at one with the machine, collapsed into a system where production is simultaneous with reproduction are not alternatives, but rather sublime metaphors for the working woman's place in commodity capitalism.

Jem and the Holograms

"The simulacrum is the truth." This is Jean Baudrillard's brilliantly succinct way of summarizing all the phenomena of late capitalism, including the receding significance of the referent, the loss of the subject, and the endless flow of mass-produced and fetishized commodities (Baudrillard 1981). By affirming "the simulacrum" as "the truth," Baudrillard metaphorizes the relationship between production and consumption in late capitalism. Indeed there is a popular new doll marketed for young girls whose name is Jem and who is a simulacrum, not in the old sense of the term as every doll is a mimetic representation of a real child or baby, but a simulacrum totally divorced from any possible referent whose only truth is itself. Physically, Jem is a Barbie lookalike: long, thin legs and torso; accentuated breasts; hard, stiff body (made not for play or cuddling, but for posing in her myriad fashions); blue eyes; and synthetic blond hair. Unlike Barbie, whose media appearances are limited to TV commercials for Barbie, Jem is the star of a weekly cartoon series and her own two-hour video, as well as being a toy marketed from coast to coast. "Record company executive by day, rock star by night", this is the advertising hype for Jem. Actually Jem's transformations are more frequent than the Wolfman's. This is because she doesn't require the moon in order to change, but regularly flip-flops between rock star and executive at least three or four times a day. Jem's dual personality brings together all the cultural connotations associated with transformation and identity. She is the schizoid personality, she is also Cinderella, she is the simulacrum who produces her own referent (who, as it turns out, is also a simulacrum), and she is also a very good example of the nautilus/Cindy Sherman syndrome: the woman inside the circuit of production and consumption.

The story of Jem is a little complicated, but most 6-year-old girls can give a fair account of how Jem and her alter ego came about. The greatest difficulty for the child narrator is in attempting to tell which personality is real and why. The story begins with Jerrica, whose mother is long dead and whose father has just died, leaving his daughter heir to the Starlight Record Company, which he owned, and the orphanage, which he acquired as a tax shelter. As executrix and philanthropist, Jerrica quickly runs head on into opposition: the unscrupulous Eric Raymond, who is executor of her father's will and Jerrica's official guardian. Raymond's aim is to take over the record company, thus leaving Jerrica penniless and unable to keep the orphanage going.

However, all is not lost because Jerrica's father has left her another bequest, a marvel of high technology; "a complete music synthesizer and holographic machine!" Cynergy is the machine's name. Endowed with a feminine voice, personality and face that appears on her video screen matrix, the machine is Jerrica's fairy godmother. This is where the story becomes difficult to tell for the child who is most likely to base her narrative on the story of Cinderella. In both the Grimm and the Disney versions of the fairy tale, Cinderella's transformation is enacted at the level of appearance. As the brothers Grimm tell it, Cinderella chants over her mother's grave and a little bird throws down a gold and silver dress and slippers. In Disney's animation, Cinderella cries over her mother's grave and her fairy godmother (a pre-Baby M form of surrogate motherhood) transforms a pumpkin into a coach, mice into horses, and Cinderella's ragged dress into a bouffant ball gown. Transformations such as these do not pose a problem for the child narrator whose experience of stories is apt to include all the traditional forms, particularly those like fairy tales that involve magical explanations. After all, Cinderella, notwithstanding her fancy dress, is still Cinderella.

However, Jerrica's transformation to Jem is another matter altogether because she really becomes someone else. And if that weren't enough, the high-tech holographic machine thoroughly eases all but the most residual traces of those factors that in the Cinderella story function as a reality principle (like the pumpkin and Cinderella's grimy face). Cynergy does not just dress Jerrica up in new attire and give her an acoustic guitar, she produces Jem as a holographic image, who completely replaces her referent, Jerrica. What's more, the machine can also make a holographic image of Jerrica. This means that once the process begins, Jem and Jerrica are simultaneously defined as simulacra and as real. "The simulacrum is the truth."

While watching the Jem video with my 8-year-old daughter, I found myself struggling to define what was real and what wasn't. In one scene, Jem is about to be run over by a speeding car. "Is that Jem a projection from the machine, or is she really there", I asked.

"She's really there", said Stacy, "but Jerrica, when she was standing by the side of the road, was a projection . . . that time". Of course, the whole thing—Jem, Jerrica, their respective projections, the fairy godmother machine—are all animations, which, if we recall the relationship of animation to the film industry, represents something of a technological simulacrum with respect to the cinematic reality of film. What's more, these particular animations are all computer-produced, making them the synthetic antitheses of the original hand drawn, painted and inked animations produced by the Disney Studio in the 1930s.

The production of art is at stake in the creation of Jem just as it is for Cindy Sherman. This Cinderella is a world-famous musician and lead singer accompanied by the female rock group, the Holograms. Composed of former orphans from Jerrica's home for the homeless, the Holograms have similarly been transformed by the holographic machine. Jem and the Holograms travel around the world cutting gold records, playing to sellout concerts, and winning every rock music competition they enter. Throughout, they are doggedly pursued and snafued by a rival female rock band, the Misfits. This gang of rowdy evildoers loses all its music competitions to Jem, and consequently tries to sabotage Jem and her success. What's interesting about the Misfits is that the loud and clearly bad music they play is real. It's their own music, played by themselves on their instruments. Whereas Jem's music, which wins all the prizes and sounds good, is no less a simulacrum than Jem herself. As one of the orphans exclaims when they all first discover Cynergy, "Wow, this is a complete music synthesizer!" From its composition, through realization, to sales, Jem's music, her art, is a product of the machine. This is where Jem as artist and producer rejoins Cindy Sherman and the nautilus machine. Jem is inside the producing machine, playing at being producer and object consumed. She produces her art, and she and her art are produced.

Jem allows us to grasp a larger picture of production not available to us when we focus more narrowly on Cindy Sherman and recognize in her work the positive aspect of a woman artist's appropriation of a field previously defined by men. What we see with Jem is the feminization of production. Cynergy is the machine as woman. She is a surrogate mother for whom there is no difference between creation and procreation. Cynergy offers the young child born into an era when women's rights to economic and social equality are supposed to have been won, the appearance of a production system defined by women and run by women. This, however, is an illusion more false than any simulacrul truth. The absent father who made the machine, bequeathed it to his daughter, and probably controls her through it from the grave defines the bottom line in capitalist production. The invisible fatherly mastermind suggests a new way of looking at Cynergy—now as father surrogate in drag.

From Fairy Tale to Romance

As storytellers, young girls will find enough similarities between Jem and Cinderella to structure a tale along the lines of the traditional fairy tale. Besides the fairy godmother, and the new rock star dresses, there is also a pair of sparkling rose-colored earrings, Jem's equivalent of the Cinderella slippers. These stay with her from one transformation to the next and function as a magical, techno-cybernetic hookup with Cynergy.

Whenever Jerrica finds herself in trouble, she puts her finger to her earring and chants, "Show time, Cynergy". Immediately, she becomes Jem, who solves the problem and closes the episode by reversing the chant. "Show's over, Cynergy", and Jem becomes Jerrica again.

As they form an audience, young girls who watch Jem on TV function not as tellers, but as readers. From this perspective they are put in a position where they are instructed on how to read a different popular form, one that will shape their lives as adults to a much greater extent than the fairy tale. This is the romance. For every Cinderella component Jem includes an equally significant narrative feature derived from Harlequin romances. In bringing together the two traditions, Jem extinguishes the contradictions that are more apparent in the older tales by assimilating them to the romance where contradiction is more thoroughly managed. Grimm's version of Cinderella is a tension-wrought text. In the relationship between Cinderella and her dead mother, the tale demonstrates the potential for strong, nurturing bonding between women, whose antithesis is the equally strong dissension and rivalry between Cinderella and her stepmother. The fairy tale allows young girls to experience both sides of women's contradictory relationships fully and to realize that the way women are— either caring or competitive—is largely determined by their relationship to absent or superficially defined male figures. The deepest contradiction of the fairy tale is the strength of male domination which need not be described in full in order for the Prince to be the solution to Cinderella and the resolution of the tale.

Tania Modleski has written an important essay on the Harlequin romance. Whereas these novels have long been felt to be little more than trashy reading for self-indulgent women, Modleski shows that the romance articulates women's deepest hostilities towards men as well as their own ill-defined longings for autonomy. The romance is, then, the form for the containment of women's aspirations and for the management of social contradiction. Inferring from the texts and their portrayal of women, Modleski concludes on an optimistic note focussed on the untapped strength of women's desire: "the fact that the novels must go to such extremes to neutralize women's anger and to make masculine hostility bearable testifies to the depths of women's discontent" (Modleski 1982: 58).

Jem goes to such extremes to manage the young girl's awareness of the contradictions embedded in the allusion to Cinderella and likely to become freshly activated at a time when young girls expect to fulfill all their aspirations and have not yet learned that, while times have changed, the structures of domination that contained their grandmothers continue to the present and may well contain them. Jem's machine-generated talent, success, and body allow her to experience the fruits of her aspirations without ever having to confront the social opposition that any other young girl would have to deal with in order to become a corporate executive, successful musician, and beautiful, many-costumed star. However, the most potent device for the management of contradiction in Jem is the erasure of all adult women figures and the subsequent function of men as the young girl's only socializing influence. The young girl's total dependence (both economic and emotional) on a dominant male figure (whether he be cast as benign or sinister) without recourse to a counter-balancing female character is a fundamental feature of romance. Besides the father and his holographic machine, Jem is conditioned by her relationship to her boyfriend, Rio, a sort of ineffectual Prince Charming; and her combative relationship to Eric Raymond, a stock Harlequin character who is as evil as he is handsome. In usurping the young heroine's rightful place as head of Starlight Music, Raymond forms a direct link with the father and demonstrates that while men may pay lip service to women's equality, real power is still in the hands of men, who may appear to be antagonistic (the one good, the other evil), but are in fact co-conspirators. In developing a comparison between Harlequins in North America and the Latin American photonovels and *libros semanales,* Jean Franco coined a succinct pun for the way Anglo women are managed and brought into control by the male-dominated network. As she put it, they are "incorporated" [see Chapter 25 in this *Reader*]. This is definitely the case for Jem as it is for many of the Harlequin heroines who strive for careers only to find themselves brought into the corporation as mascots, play pretties, dependent nieces, and finally wives.

Jem's "incorporation" extends into her love relationships, negating the possibility for developing and experiencing her sexuality. In her life and identity as Jerrica, she is defined as girlfriend to Rio, her age-mate and buddy who helps out at the orphanage and in the daily concerns of rock music administration. They are like old-fashioned high-school "steadies" whose relationship will never become sexual simply because Jerrica is always vanishing, usually at a moment that would have brought her closer to Rio, in order to become Jem. Jem, of course, is extremely attractive and usually in some dire situation, requiring Rio to come to her rescue. Hence Jem is constantly seducing Rio who undergoes deep torment over his emotional infidelity for Jerrica. However, the relationship between Jem and Rio will also never be sexual because as soon as the escapade ends, "Show's over" and Jem becomes Jerrica. On the surface this all looks like a complicated way to keep sex out of children's Saturday morning cartoons. Read more deeply and from a liberal perspective, we might be tempted to say that cutting off the development of both love relationships helps teach young girls not to see themselves wholly defined by a man, love and marriage. However, read more profoundly and in the context of the way patriarchal power dominates the corporation and works through the machine, Jem's inability to continue either her "steady" relationship or her seductive relationship can only be interpreted as an abrupt negation of her adult sexuality. The machine that controls her passage from one identity to another has her perpetually locked at the level of pubescent child. Allowed to establish budding relationships with another man, she is finally and foremost her father's daughter.

Jem as a contemporary women's allegory is a horrific tale. In it, the desire for self-hood is met with a machine-produced body and machine-produced art. While the desire for autonomy is solved by "incorporation" into the corporation. This is patriarchy nautilus-style. It allows women the false gratification of seeing themselves in the self-made products they constitute. However, because real power lies elsewhere in the larger corporate structure, Jem who activates the holograph and is the hologram, like you or I, when we activate the nautilus and become its finely honed body, enact the expropriation of ourselves as producers and the alienation of ourselves as consumers.

References

Baudrillard J. (1981). *Simulacres et Simulation.* Paris: Edition Galilee; also "Simulations," in *In the Shadow of the Silent Majorities and Other Essays,* trans. P. Foss, 1983. New York: Semiotext(e).

Fonda, J. (1984). *Women Coming of Age.* New York: Simon & Schuster.

Jameson, F. (1979). "Reification and utopia in mass culture." *Social Text,* I.

Modleski, T. (1982). *Loving with a Vengeance.* London: Methuen.

Vogue (1988) "The Image Culture," March.

30 AIDS, Homophobia, and Biomedical Discourse: An Epidemic of Signification

Paula A. Treichler

An Epidemic of Signification

In multiple, fragmentary and often contradictory ways we struggle to achieve some sort of understanding of AIDS, a reality that is frightening, widely publicized, and yet finally neither directly nor fully knowable. AIDS is no different in this respect from other linguistic constructions which, in the commonsense view of language, are thought to transmit pre-existing ideas and represent real-world entities and yet in fact do neither. For the nature of the relationship between language and reality is highly problematic; and "AIDS" is not merely an invented label, provided to us by science and scientific naming practices, for a clear-cut disease entity caused by a virus. Rather, the very nature of AIDS is constructed through language and in particular through the discourses of medicine and science; this construction is "true" or "real" only in certain specific ways—for example, in so far as it successfully guides research or facilitates clinical control over the illness. The name "AIDS" in part *constructs* the disease and helps make it intelligible. We cannot therefore look "through" language to determine what AIDS "really" is. Rather we must explore the site where such determinations *really* occur and intervene at the point where meaning is created: in language.

Of course, AIDS is a real disease syndrome, damaging and killing real human beings. Because of this, it is tempting—perhaps in some instances imperative—to view science and medicine as providing a discourse about AIDS closer to its "reality" than what we can provide ourselves. Yet the AIDS epidemic—with its genuine potential for global devastation—is simultaneously an epidemic of a transmissible lethal disease and an epidemic of meanings or signification. Both epidemics are equally crucial for us to understand, for, try as we may to treat AIDS as "an infectious disease" and nothing more, meanings continue to multiply wildly and at an extraordinary rate. This epidemic of meanings is readily apparent in the chaotic assemblage of understandings of AIDS that by now exists. The mere enumeration of some of the ways AIDS has been characterized suggests its enormous power to generate meanings.

1 An irreversible, untreatable and invariably fatal infectious disease which threatens to wipe out the whole world

From Paula A. Treichler, "AIDS, Homophobia and Biomedical Discourse: An Epidemic of Signification," *Cultural Studies*, 1: 3 (1987), 263–305. Taylor & Francis Ltd, PO Box 25, Abingdon, Oxfordshire, UK.

2 A creation of the media which has sensationalized a minor health problem for its own profit and pleasure

3 A creation of the state to legitimize widespread invasion of people's lives and sexual practices

4 A creation of biomedical scientists and the Centers for Disease Control to generate funding for their activities

5 A gay plague, probably emanating from San Francisco

6 The crucible in which the field of immunology will be tested

7 The most extraordinary medical chronicle of our times

8 A condemnation to celibacy or death

9 An Andromeda strain with the transmission efficiency of the common cold

10 An imperialist plot to destroy the Third World

11 A fascist plot to destroy homosexuals

12 A CIA plot to destroy subversives

13 A capitalist plot to create new markets for pharmaceutical products

14 A Soviet plot to destroy capitalists

15 The result of experiments on the immunological system of men not likely to reproduce

16 The result of genetic mutations caused by 'mixed marriages'

17 The result of moral decay and a major force destroying the Boy Scouts

18 A plague stored in King Tut's tomb and unleashed when the Tut exhibit toured the US in 1976

19 The perfect emblem of twentieth-century decadence; of *fin-de-siècle* decadence; of postmodern decadence

20 A disease that turns fruits into vegetables

21 A disease introduced by aliens to weaken us before the takeover

22 Nature's way of cleaning house

23 America's Ideal Death Sentence

24 An infectious agent that has suppressed our immunity from guilt

25 A spiritual force that is creatively disrupting civilization

26 A sign that the end of the world is at hand

27 God's punishment of our weaknesses

28 God's test of our strengths

29 The price paid for the sixties

30 The price paid for anal intercourse

31 The price paid for genetic inferiority and male aggression

32 An absolutely unique disease for which there is no precedent

33 Just another venereal disease

34 The most urgent and complex public health problem facing the world today

35 A golden opportunity for science and medicine

36 Science fiction

37 Stranger than science fiction

38 A terrible and expensive way to die

Such diverse conceptualizations of AIDS are coupled with fragmentary interpretations of its specific elements. Confusion about transmission now causes approximately half the US population to refuse to *give* blood. Many believe you can "catch" AIDS through casual contact, such as sitting beside an infected person on a bus. Many believe that lesbians—a population relatively free of sexually transmitted diseases in general—are as likely to be infected as gay men. Other stereotypes about homosexuals generate startling deductions about the illness: "I thought AIDS was a gay disease," said a man interviewed by *USA Today* in October 1985, "but if Rock Hudson's dead it can kill anyone."

We cannot effectively analyze AIDS or develop intelligent social policy if we dismiss such conceptions as irrational myths and homophobic fantasies which deliberately ignore the "real scientific facts." Rather they are part of the necessary work people do in attempting to understand—however imperfectly—the complex, puzzling and quite terrifying phenomenon of AIDS. No matter how much we desire, with Susan Sontag, to resist treating illness as metaphor, illness *is* metaphor, and this semantic work—this effort to "make sense of" AIDS—has to be done. Further, this work is as necessary and often as difficult and imperfect for physicians and scientists as it is for "the rest of us."

I am arguing, then, not that we must take both the social and the biological dimensions of AIDS into account, but rather that the social dimension is far more pervasive and central than we are accustomed to believing. Science is not the true material base generating our merely symbolic superstructure. Our social constructions of AIDS (in terms of global devastation, threat to civil rights, emblem of sex and death, the "gay plague", the postmodern condition, whatever) are based not upon objective, scientifically determined "reality" but upon what we are told about this reality: that is, upon *prior* social constructions routinely produced within the discourses of biomedical science. (AIDS as infectious disease is one such construction.) There is a continuum, then, not a dichotomy, between popular and biomedical discourses (and, as Latour and Woolgar (1985: 281) put it, "a continuum between controversies in daily life and those occurring in the laboratory"), and these play out in language. Consider, for example, the ambiguities embedded within this statement by an AIDS expert (an immunologist) on a television documentary in October 1985 designed to *dispel* misconceptions about AIDS:

> The biggest misconception that we have encountered and that most cities throughout the United States have seen is that many people feel that casual contact—being in the same room with an AIDS victim—will transmit the virus and may infect them. This has not been substantiated by any evidence whatsoever. . . . [This misconception lingers because] this is an extremely emotional issue. I think that when there are such strong emotions associated with a medical problem such as this it's very difficult for facts to sink in. I think also there's the problem that we cannot give any 100 percent assurances one way or the other about these factors. There may always be some exception to the rule. Anything we may say, someone could come up with an exception. But as far as most of the medical–scientific community is concerned, this is a virus that is actually very *difficult* to transmit and therefore the general public should really not worry about casual contact—not even using the same silverware and dishes would probably be a problem.

Would you buy a scientific fact from this man? Can we expect to understand AIDS transmission when this is part of what we have to work with? The point is not merely that this particular scientist has not yet learned to "talk to the media" (see Fain 1985; Check 1985) but that ambiguity and uncertainty are features of scientific inquiry which must be socially and linguistically managed. What is at issue here is a fatal infectious disease which is simply not fully understood; questions remain about the nature of the disease, its etiology, its transmission, and what individuals can do about it. It does not seem unreasonable that in the face of these uncertainties people give birth to many different conceptions; to label them "misconceptions" implies what? Wrongful birth? Only "facts" can give birth to proper conceptions and only science can give birth to facts? In that case, we may wish to avert our eyes from some of the "scientific" conceptions that have been born in the course of the AIDS crisis:

AIDS could be *anything*, considering what homosexual men do to each other in gay baths. (cited in Leibowich 1985)
Heroin addicts won't use clean needles because they would rather get AIDS than give up the ritual of sharing them. (cited in Barrett 1985)
Prostitutes do not routinely keep themselves clean and are therefore "reservoirs" of disease. (cited in Langone 1985)
AIDS is homosexual; it can only be transmitted by males to males.
AIDS in Africa is heterosexual but uni-directional; it can only be transmitted from males to females. (cited in Langone 1985)
AIDS in Africa is heterosexual because anal intercourse is a common form of birth control. (cited in L. Altman 1985)

The point here is that no clear line can be drawn between the facticity of scientific and non-scientific (mis)conceptions. Ambiguity, homophobia, stereotyping, confusion, doublethink, them-versus-us, blame-the-victim, wishful thinking: none of these popular forms of semantic legerdemain about AIDS is absent from biomedical communication. But scientific and medical discourses have traditions through which the semantic epidemic as well as the biological one is controlled, and these may disguise contradiction and irrationality. In writing about AIDS, these traditions typically include characterizing ambiguity and contradiction as "non-scientific" (a no-nonsense, lets-get-the-facts-on-the-table-and-clear-up-this-muddle approach), invoking faith in scientific inquiry, taking for granted the reality of quantitative and/or biomedical data, deducing social and behavioral reality from quantitative and/or biomedical data, setting forth fantasies and speculations as though they were logical deductions, using technical euphemisms for sensitive sexual or political realities, and revising both past and future to conform to present thinking.

Many of these traditions are illustrated in an article by John Langone in the December 1985 general science journal *Discover*. In this lengthy review of research to date, entitled "AIDS: the latest scientific facts", Langone (1985: 40–1) suggests that the virus enters the bloodstream by way of the "vulnerable anus" and the "fragile urethra"; in contrast, the "rugged vagina" (built to be abused by such blunt instruments as penises and small babies) provides too tough a barrier for the AIDS virus to penetrate. "Contrary to what you've heard," Langone concludes (52)— and his conclusion echoes a fair amount of medical and scientific writing at the time—"AIDS isn't a threat to the vast majority of heterosexuals. . . . It is now and is likely to remain—largely the fatal price one can pay for anal intercourse." (This excerpt from the article also ran as the cover blurb.) It sounded plausible; and detailed illustrations demonstrated the article's conclusion.

But by December 1986 the big news—what the major US news magazines were running cover stories on—was the grave danger of AIDS to heterosexuals. No dramatic discoveries during the intervening year had changed the fundamental scientific conception of AIDS. What had changed was not "the facts" but the way in which they were now used to construct the AIDS text and the meanings we were now allowed—indeed, at last encouraged—to read from that text. The AIDS story, in other words, is not merely the familiar story of heroic scientific discovery. And until we understand AIDS' dual life as both a material and a linguistic reality—a duality inherent in all linguistic entities but extraordinarily exaggerated and potentially deadly in the case of AIDS—we cannot begin to read the story of this illness accurately or formulate intelligent interventions.

Intelligent interventions from outside biomedical science have helped shape the discourse on AIDS. Almost from the beginning, members of the gay community, through intense interest and informed political activism, have repeatedly contested the terminology, meanings and interpretations produced by scientific inquiry. Such contestations had occurred a decade earlier in the struggle over whether homosexuality was to be officially classified as an illness by the American Psychiatric Association (see Bayer 1981). Gay men and lesbians in the succeeding period had achieved considerable success in political organizing. AIDS, then, first struck members of a relatively seasoned and politically sophisticated community. The importance of not relinquishing authority to medicine was articulated early in the AIDS crisis by Michael Lynch (1982):

Another crisis exists with the medical one. It has gone largely unexamined, even by the gay press. Like helpless mice we have peremptorily, almost inexplicably, relinquished the one power we so long fought for in constructing our modern gay community: the power to determine our own identity. And to whom have we relinquished it? The very authority we wrested it from in a struggle that occupied us for more than a hundred years: the medical profession.

To challenge biomedical authority—whose meanings are part of powerful and deeply entrenched social and historical codes— has required considerable tenacity and courage from people dependent in the AIDS crisis upon science and medicine for protection, care and the possibility of cure. These contestations provide the model for a broader social analysis which moves away from AIDS as a "lifestyle" issue and examines its significance for this country, at this time, with the cultural and material sources available to us. This, in turn, requires us to acknowledge and examine the multiple ways in which our social constructions guide our visions of material reality.

AIDS and Homophobia: Constructing the Text of the Gay Male Body

Whatever else it may be, AIDS is a story, or multiple stories, read to a surprising extent from a text that does not exist: the body of the male homosexual. It is a text people so want—need—to read that they have gone so far as to write it themselves. AIDS is a nexus where multiple meanings, stories and discourses intersect and overlap, reinforce and subvert each other. Yet clearly this mysterious male homosexual text has figured centrally in generating what I call here an epidemic of signification.

. . .

Ironically, a major turning point in US consciousness came when Rock Hudson acknowledged that he was being treated for AIDS. Through an extraordinary conflation of texts, the Rock Hudson case dramatized the possibility that the disease could spread to the "general population". In fact this possibility had been evident for some time to anyone who wished to find it: as Jean Marx summarized the evidence in *Science* in 1984 (147), "Sexual intercourse both of the heterosexual and homosexual varieties is a major pathway of transmission." But only in late 1986 (and somewhat reluctantly at that) did the Centers for Disease Control (1986b) expand upon their early '4-H list' of high-risk categories: HOMOSEXUALS, HEMOPHILIACS, HEROIN ADDICTS and HAITIANS, and the sexual partners of people within these groups. The original list, developed during 1981 and 1982, has structured evidence collection in the intervening years and contributed to a view that the major risk factor in acquiring AIDS is being a particular kind of person rather than doing particular things.

. . .

This commitment to categories based on stereotyped identity filters out information. Shaw (1986) argues that, when women are asked in CDC protocols "Are you hetero-sexual?", "this loses the diversity of behaviors that may have a bearing on infection." Even now, with established evidence that transmission can be heterosexual (which begins with the letter H after all), scientific discourse continues to construct women as "inefficient" and "incompetent" transmitters of HIV ("the AIDS virus"), passive recept-acles without the projectile capacity of a penis or syringe—stolid, uninteresting barriers that impede the unrestrained passage of the virus from brother to brother. Exceptions include prostitutes, whose discursive legacy—despite their longstanding professional knowledge and continued activism about AIDS—is to be seen as so contaminated that their bodies are virtual laboratory cultures for viral replication. Other exceptions are African women, whose exotic bodies, sexual practices or who knows what are seen to be so radically different from those of women in the US that anything can happen in them. The term *exotic*, sometimes used to describe a virus that appears to have originated "elsewhere" (but "elsewhere," like "other" is not a fixed category), is an important theme running through AIDS literature (Leibowich 1985: 73). The fact that one of the more extensive and visually elegant analyses of AIDS appeared recently in the *National Geographic* (Jaret 1986) is perhaps further evidence of its life on an idealized "exotic" terrain.

The early hypotheses about AIDS, when the first cases appeared in New York, Los Angeles and Paris, were sociological, relating it directly to the supposed "gay male lifestyle." In February 1982, for example, it was thought that a particular supply of amyl nitrate (poppers) might be contaminated. "The poppers fable", writes Jacques Leibow-ich (1985: 5), becomes

a Grimm fairy tale when the first cases of AIDS-without-poppers are discovered among homo-sexuals absolutely repelled by the smell of the product and among heterosexuals unfamiliar with even the words *amyl nitrate* or *poppers*. But, as will be habitual in the history of AIDS, rumors last longer than either common sense or the facts would warrant. The odor of AIDS-poppers will hover in the air a long time—long enough for dozens of mice in the Atlanta epidemiology labs to be kept in restricted cages on an obligatory sniffed diet of poppers 8 to 12 hours a day for several months, until, nauseated but still healthy, without a trace of AIDS, the wretched rodents were released—provisionally—upon the announcement of a new hypothesis: *promiscuity*.

This new perspective generated numerous possibilities. One was that sperm itself could destroy the immune system. "God's plan for man", after all, "was for Adam and Eve and not Adam and Steve". Women, the "natural" receptacles for male sperm, have evolved over the millennia so that their bodies can deal with these foreign invaders; men, not thus blessed by nature, become vulnerable to the "killer sperm" of other men. AIDS in the lay press became known as the "toxic cock syndrome". While scientists and physicians tended initially to define AIDS as a gay sociological problem, gay men, for other reasons, also tended to reject the possibility that AIDS was a new contagious disease. Not only could this make them sexual lepers, it didn't make sense: "How could a disease pick out gays? That had to be medical homophobia" (Black 1986).

. . .

Another favored possibility in the early 1980s (still not universally discarded, for it's plausible so long as the cases of AIDS among monogamous homebodies are ignored) is the notion of "co-factors": no *single* infectious agent causes the disease; rather, someone who is sexually active with multiple partners is exposed to a kind of bacterial/viral tidal wave that can crush the immune system. Gay men on the sexual "fast-track" would be particularly susceptible because of the prevalence of specific practices that would maximize exposure to pathogenic microbes. What were considered potentially relevant data came to be routinely included in scientific papers and presentations, with the result that the terminology of these reports was increasingly scrutinized by gay activists.

. . .

Out of this dense discursive jungle came the "fragile anus" hypothesis as well as the vision of "multiple partners". Even after sociological explanations for AIDS gave way to biomedical ones involving a transmissible virus, these various images of AIDS as a "gay disease" proved too alluring to abandon. It is easy to see both the scientific and the popular appeal of the "fragile anus" hypothesis: scientifically, it confines the public health dimensions of AIDS to an infected population in the millions—merely mind-boggling, that is—enabling us to stop short of the impossible, the unthinkable billions that widespread heterosexual transmission might infect. Another appeal of thinking of AIDS as a "gay disease" is that it protects not only the sexual practices of heterosexuality but also its ideological superiority. In the service of this hypothesis, both homophobia and sexism are folded imperturbably into the language of the scientific text. Women, as I noted above, are characterized in the scholarly literature as "inefficient" transmitters of AIDS; Leibowich (1985: 36) refers to the "refractory impermeability of the vaginal mucous membrane". A study of German prostitutes that appeared to demonstrate female-to-male transmission of AIDS was interpreted in the *Journal of the American Medical Association* as actually representing "quasi-homosexual" transmission: Man A, infected with HIV, has vaginal intercourse with Prostitute; she, "[performing] no more than perfunctory external cleansing between customers" (quoted by Langone 1985: 49), then has intercourse with Man B; Man B is infected with the virus via the semen of Man A. The prostitute's vagina thus functions merely as a reservoir, a passive holding tank for semen that becomes infectious only when another penis is dipped into it—like a swamp where mosquitoes come to breed.

But the conception and the conclusion are inaccurate. It is not monogamy or abstention *per se* that protects one from AIDS infection but practices and protections that prevent the virus from entering one's bloodstream. Some evidence suggests that prostitutes are at greater risk not because they have multiple sex partners but because they are likely to use intravenous drugs; at this point "they may be better protected than the typical woman who is 'just going to a bar' or a woman who thinks of herself as not sexually active but who 'just happens to have this relationship'. They may be more aware than women who are involved in serial monogamy or those whose self-image is 'I'm not at risk so I'm not going to learn more about it'" (Shaw and Paleo 1986: 144). Indeed, COYOTE and other organizations of prostitutes have addressed the issue of AIDS rather aggressively for several years.

. . .

Rendezvous with 007

"Interpretations", write Bruno Latour and Steve Woolgar in *Laboratory Life* (1985), their analysis of the construction of facts in science, "do not so much *in*form as *per*form." And nowhere do we see interpretation shaped toward performance so clearly as in the issues and controversies surrounding the identification and naming of "the AIDS virus."

As early as 1979, gay men in New York and California were coming down with and dying from illnesses unusual in young healthy people. One of the actors whose help created the San Francisco *A.I.D.S. Show* (1986) recalled that early period:

I had a friend who died way way back in New York in 1981. He was one of the first to go. We didn't know what AIDS was, there was no name for it. We didn't know it was contagious—we had no idea it was sexually transmitted—we didn't know it was anything. We just thought that he—alone—was ill. He was 26 years old and just had one thing after another wrong with him . . . He was still coming to work 'cause he didn't *know* he had a terminal disease.

The oddness of these nameless isolated events gave way to an even more terrifying period in which gay men on both coasts gradually began to realize that too many friends and acquaintances were dying. As the numbers mounted, the deaths became "cases" of what was informally called in New York hospitals WOGS: the Wrath of God Syndrome. It all became official in 1981, when five deaths in Los Angeles from *Pneumocystis* pneumonia were described in the 5 June issue of the CDC's bulletin *Morbidity and Mortality Weekly Report* with an editorial note explaining that

The occurrence of pneumocystosis in these 5 previously healthy individuals without a clinically underlying immunodeficiency is unusual. The fact that these patients were all homosexuals suggests an association between some aspect of a homosexual lifestyle or disease acquired through sexual contact and *Pneumocystis* in this population. (Centers for Disease Control 1981a)

Gottlieb's 1981 paper in the *New England Journal of Medicine* described the deaths of young, previously healthy gay men from another rare but rarely fatal disease. The deaths were attributed to a breakdown of the immune system which left the body utterly unable to defend itself against infections not normally fatal. The syndrome was provisionally called GRID: gay-related immunodeficiency. These published reports drew similar information from physicians in other cities (see Centres for Disease Control 1981b), and before too long these rare diseases had been diagnosed in non-gay people (for example, hemophiliacs and people who had recently had blood transfusions). Epidemiological follow-up interview over the next several months confirmed that the problem—whatever it was—was growing at epidemic rates, and a CDC task force was accordingly established to coordinate data collection, communication and research. The name AIDS was selected at a 1982 conference in Washington (GRID was no longer applicable now that non-gays were also getting sick): acquired immune deficiency syndrome ("reasonably descriptive", said Curran, "without being pejorative"—Black 1986: 60).

. . .

By 1986, five years after the initial article in the *Morbidity and Mortality Weekly Report*, a Human Retrovirus Subcommittee empowered by the International Committee on the Taxonomy of Viruses was at work "to propose an appropriate name for the retrovirus isolates recently implicated as the causative agents of the acquired immune deficiency syndrome (AIDS)"—to consider, that is, what "the AIDS virus" should officially be named. After more than a year of deliberation, the nomenclature subcommittee published its recommendations in the form of a letter to scientific journals (it appeared in *Science* 232, 9 May 1986: 697). Their task has been made crucial, they note, by the widespread interest in AIDS and the multiplicity of names now in use:

LAV:	lymphadenopathy-associated virus (1983—Montagnier, Pasteur)
HTLV-III:	human T-cell lymphotropic virus type III (1984—Gallo, NCI)
IDAV:	immunodeficiency-associated virus
ARV:	AIDS-associated retrovirus (1984—Levy, UCSF)
HTLV III/LAV and	
LAV/HTLV-III:	compound names used to keep peace (the CDC's use was perhaps a reprimand to the NCI for its perceived uncooperativeness in sharing data)
AIDS virus:	popular press

The subcommittee proposes HIV, "human immunodeficiency viruses". They reason that this conforms to the nomenclature of other viruses in which the first slot signals the host species (human), the second slot the major pathogenic property (immunodeficiency) and the last slot V for virus. (For some viruses, though not HIV, individual strains are distinguished by the initials of the thus "immortalized" patient from whom they originally came and in whose "daughter cells" they are perpetuated.) The multiple names of "the AIDS virus" point toward a succession of identities and offer a fragmented sense indeed of what this virus, or family of viruses, "really" is. The new name, in contrast, promises to unify the political fragmentations of the scientific establishment and certify the health of the single-virus hypothesis. The subcommittee argues in favor of its proposed name that it does not incorporate the term AIDS, on the advice of many clinicians; it is distinct from all existing names and "has been chosen without regard to priority of discovery" (not insignificantly, Montagnier and Levy signed the subcommittee letter but Gallo and Essex did not); and it distinguishes the HI viruses from those with distinctly different biological properties, for example the HTLV line (HTLV-I and HTLV-II), which this subcommittee calls "human t-cell leukenua viruses", perhaps to chastise Gallo for changing the 'L' in the nomenclature of the HTLVs from *leukemia* to *lymphotropic* so that HTLV-III (the AIDS virus) would appear to fit generically into the same series (and bear the stamp of his lab). In the same issue of *Science* (Marx 1986a: 699–700), the editors chose to discuss this letter in their "News and comment" column: "Disputes over viral nomenclature do not ordinarily command much attention beyond the individuals immediately involved in the fray"; but the current dissension, part of the continuing controversy over who should get credit for discovering the virus, "could provide 6 months' of scripts for the television series 'Dallas'".

Why such struggles over naming and interpretation? Because there are high stakes where this performance is concerned—not only patent rights to the lucrative test kits for the AIDS virus (Gallo fears that loss of the HTLV-III designation will weaken his claims) but the future and honor immunology. Modern immunology, as Donna Haraway (1979, 1985) observes, moved into the realm of high science when it reworked the military combat metaphors of World War II (battles, struggle, territory, enemy, truces) into the language of postmodern warfare: communication command control—coding, transmission, messages—interceptions, spies, lies. Scientific descriptions for general readers, like this one from the *National Geographic* article on the AIDS virus (Jaret 1986: 709), accentuate this shift from combat to code:

Many of these enemies [of the body, or self] have evolved devious methods to escape detection. The viruses that cause influenza and the common cold, for example, constantly mutate, changing their fingerprints. The AIDS virus, most insidious of all, employs a range of strategies, including hiding out in healthy cells. What makes it fatal is its ability to invade and kill helper T cells, thereby short-circuiting the entire immune response.

No ground troops here, no combat, not even generals: we see here the evolution of a conception of the AIDS virus as a top-flight secret agent—a James Bond of secret agents, armed with "a range of strategies" and licensed to kill. "Like Greeks hidden inside the Trojan horse", 007 enters the body concealed inside a helper T-cell from an infected host (Jaret 1986: 723 and see Anderson and Yunis 1983); but "the virus is not an innocent passenger in the body of its victims" (Krim 1985):

In the invaded victim, helper T's immediately detect the foreign T cell. But as the two T's meet, the virus slips through the cell membrane into the defending cell. Before the defending T cell can mobilize the troops, the virus disables it. . . . Once inside an inactive T cell, the virus may lie dormant for months, even years. Then, perhaps when another, unrelated infection triggers the invaded T cells to divide, the AIDS virus also begins to multiply. One by one, its clones emerge to infect nearby T cells. Slowly but inexorably the body loses the very sentinels that should be alerting the rest of the immune system. Phagocytes and killer cells receive no call to arms. B cells are not alerted to produce antibodies. The enemy can run free. (Jaret 1986: 723/4).

But on no mundane battlefield. The January 1987 *Scientific American* column "Science and the citizen" (58–9) warns of the mutability—the "protean nature of the AIDS virus"—that will make very difficult the development of a vaccine as well as the perfect screening of blood. "It is also possible", the column concludes, "that a more virulent strain could emerge"; indeed, even now "the envelope of the virus seems to be changing." Clearly, 007 is a spy's spy, capable of any deception: evading the "fluid patrol officers" is child's play. Indeed, it is so shifting and uncertain we might even acknowledge our own historical moment more specifically by giving the AIDS virus a postmodern identity: a terrorist's terrorist, an Abu Nidal of viruses.

. . .

Reconstructing the AIDS Text: Rewriting the Body

There is now broad consensus that AIDS—"plague of the millennium", "health disaster of pandemic proportions"—is the greatest public health problem of our era. The epidemic of signification that surrounds AIDS is neither simple nor under control. AIDS exists at a point where many entrenched narratives intersect, each with its own problematic and context in which AIDS acquires meaning. It is extremely hard to resist the lure, familiarity and ubiquitousness of these discourses. The AIDS virus enters the cell and integrates with its genetic code, establishing a disinformation campaign at the highest level and ensuring that replication and dissemination will be systemic. We inherit a series of discursive dichotomies; the discourse of AIDS attaches itself to these other systems of difference and plays itself out there:

self and not-self
the one and the other
homosexual and heterosexual
homosexual and "the general population"
active and passive, guilty and innocent, perpetrator and victim
vice and virtue, us and them, anus and vagina
sins of the parent and innocence of the child
love and death, sex and death, sex and money, death and money
science and not-science, knowledge and ignorance
doctor and patient, expert and patient, doctor and expert
addiction and abstention, contamination and cleanliness
contagion and containment, life and death
injection and reception, instrument and receptacle
normal and abnormal, natural and alien
prostitute and paragon, whore and wife
safe sex and bad sex, safe sex and good sex
First World and Third World, free world and iron curtain
capitalists and communists
certainty and uncertainty
virus and victim, guest and host

As Brooke-Rose (1986) demonstrates, one must pay close attention to the way in which these apparently fundamental and natural semantic oppositions are put to work. What is self and what is not-self? Who wears the white and who the black hat? (Or, in her discussion, perhaps, who wears the pants and who the skirt?) As Turner (1984: 221) observes with regard to sexually transmitted diseases in general, the diseased are seen not as "victims" but as "agents" of biological disaster. If Koch's postulates must be fulfilled to identify a given microbe with a given disease, perhaps it would be helpful, in rewriting the AIDS text, to take "Turner's postulates" into account (1984: 209): (1) disease is a language; (2) the body is a representation; and (3) medicine is a political practice.

There is little doubt that for some people the AIDS crisis lends force to their fear and hatred of gays; AIDS appears, for example, to be a significant factor in the increasing violence against them, and other homophobic acts in the U.S. (Greer 1986). But to talk of "homophobia" as though it were a simple and rather easily recognized phenomenon is impossible. When we review the various conceptions of the gay male body produced within scientific research by the signifier AIDS, we find a discourse rich in signification as to what AIDS "means". At first, some scientists doubted that AIDS could be an infectious disease because they could not imagine what gay men could do to each other to transmit infection. But intimate knowledge generated quite different conceptions:

AIDS is caused by multiple and violent gay sexual encounters: exposure to countless infections and pathogenic agents overwhelms the immune system.
AIDS is caused by killer sperm, shooting from one man's penis to the anus of another.
Gay men are as sexually driven as alcoholics or drug addicts.
AIDS cannot infect females because the virus can't penetrate the tough mucous membranes of the vagina.
Women cannot transmit AIDS because their bodies do not have the strong projectile capacity of a penis or syringe.
Prostitutes can transmit the virus because their contaminated bodies harbor massive quantities of killer microbes.

Repeated hints that the male body is sexually potent and adventurous suggest that homophobia in biomedical discourse may play out as a literal "fear of the same". The text constructed around the gay male body—the epidemic of signification so evident in the conceptions cited above and elsewhere in this essay—is driven in part by the need for constant flight from sites of potential identity and thus the successive construction of new oppositions that will barricade self from not-self. The homophobic meanings associated with AIDS continue to be layered into existing discourse: analysis demonstrates ways in which the AIDS virus is linguistically identified with those it strikes: the penis is "fragile", the urethra is "fragile", the virus is "fragile"; the African woman's body is "exotic", the virus is "exotic". The virus "penetrates" its victims; a carrier of death, it wears an "innocent" disguise. AIDS is "caused" by homosexuals; AIDS is "caused" by a virus. Homosexuality exists on a border between male and female, the virus between life and non-life. This cross-cannibalization of language is unsurprising. What greater relief than to find a final refuge from the specter of gay sexuality where the language that has obsessively accumulated around the body can attach to its substitute: the virus. This is a signifier that can be embraced forever.

The question is how to disrupt and renegotiate the powerful cultural narratives surrounding AIDS. Homophobia is inscribed within other discourses at a high level, and it is at a high level that they must be interrupted and challenged.

. . .

The fact is that any separation of not-self ("AIDS victims") from self (the "general population") is no longer possible. The US Surgeon General and National Academy reports make clear that "that security blanket has now been stripped away" ("Science and the citizen" 1987: 58). Yet the familiar signifying practices that exercise control over meaning continue. The *Scientific American* column (59) goes on to note fears that the one-to-one African ratio of females with AIDS to males may foreshadow US statistics: "Experts point out, however, that such factors as the prevalence of other venereal diseases that cause genital sores, the use of sterilized needles in clinics and the lack of blood-screening tests may explain the different epidemiology of AIDS in Africa." Thus the African data are reinterpreted to reinstate the "us"/"them" dichotomy and project a rosier scenario for "us". (Well, maybe it improves on comic Richard Belzer's narrative: "A monkey bites some guy on the ass in Africa and *he* balls a guy in Haiti and now we're all gonna fuckin' die. THANKS A LOT!")

. . .

In AIDS, where meanings are overwhelming in their sheer volume and often explicitly linked to extreme political agendas, we do not know whose meanings will become "the official story". We need an epidemiology of signification – a comprehensive mapping and analysis of these multiple meanings – to form the basis for official definition that will in turn constitute the policies, regulations, rules and practices that will govern our behaviour for some time to come.

. . .

The discursive structures I have talked about in this essay are familiar to those of us in "the human sciences". We have learned that there is a disjunction between historical subjects and constructed scientific objects. There is still debate about whether, or to what extent, scientific discourse can be privileged—and relied upon to transcend contradiction. My own view is unequivocal: it cannot be privileged in this way. Of course, where AIDS is concerned, science can usefully perform its interpretive part: we can learn to live—indeed, *must* learn to live—as though there are such things as viruses. The virus—a constructed scientific object—is also a historical subject, a "human immuno-deficiency virus", a real source of illness and death that can be passed from one person to another under certain conditions that we can apparently—individually and collectively—influence. The trick is to learn to live with this disjunction, but the lesson is imperative. Dr Rieux, the physician-narrator of Camus's novel, acknowledges that by dealing medically with the plague he is allowing himself the luxury of "living in a world of abstractions". But not indefinitely; for "when abstraction sets to killing you, you've got to get busy with it."

But getting busy with it may require us to relinquish some luxuries of our own: the luxury of accepting without reflection the "findings" science seems effortlessly able to provide us, the luxury of avoiding vigilance, the luxury of hoping it will all go away. Rather we need to use what science gives us in ways that are selective, self-conscious and pragmatic ("as though" they were true). We need to understand that AIDS is and will remain a provisional and deeply problematic signifier. Above all we need to resist, at all costs, the luxury of listening to the thousands of language tapes playing in our heads,

laden with prior discourse, that tell us with compelling certainty and dizzying contradiction what AlDS "really" means.

References

"AIDS: Deadly but hard to catch" (1986).
   Consumer Reports, (November 724–8.
"AIDS funding boost requested: Increase
   would bring $200 million to bear on
   the disease" (1985). *Daily Illini* (27
   September): 7.
"AIDS hearing" (1984). Committee on Energy
   and Commerce, Subcommittee on Health
   and the Environment, US House of
   Representatives, 17 September. Serial No.
   98–105. Washington, DC: US Government
   Printing Office.
"AIDS: Public health and civil liberties"
   (1986). *Hastings Center Report*, Special
   Supplement, 16: 6 (December).
"AIDS: Science, ethics, policy" (1986). Forum,
   Issues in Science and Technology, 2:
   2 (Winter): 39–73.
*The A.I.D.S. Show—Artists Involved with
   Death and Survival* (1986). Documentary
   video produced by Peter Adair and Rob
   Epstein, directed by Leland Moss; based on
   theater production at Theater Rhinoceros,
   San Francisco; aired on PBS, November.
"AIDS: What is to be done?" (1985). Forum,
   Harper's Magazine (October): 39–52.
Altman, Lawrence K. (1985). "Linking AIDS to
   Africa provokes bitter debate." *New York
   Times* (21 November): 1, 8.
American Medical Association Council on
   Scientific Affairs (1984). "The acquired
   immunodeficiency syndrome:
   Commentary." *Journal of the American
   Medical Association*, 252: 15 (19 October):
   2037–43.
Anderson, D. J., and Yunis, E. J. (1983).
   "'Trojan Horse' leukocytes in AIDS."
   New England Journal of Medicine, 309:
   984–5.
Associated Press (1986). "571 AIDS cases tied
   to heterosexual cases." *Champaign-Urbana
   News-Gazette* (12 December): A-7.
Barret, Wayne (1985). "Straight shooters: AIDS
   targets another lifestyle." *Village Voice* (26
   October): 14–18.

Bayer, Ronald (1981). *Homosexuality and
   American Psychiatry: The Politics of
   Diagnosis.* New York: Basic Books.
Black, David (1986). *The Plague Years: A
   Chronicle of AIDS, the Epidemic of Our
   Times.* New York: Simon &Schuster.
Brooke-Rose, Christine (1986). "Woman as a
   semiotic object," in Susan Rubin Suleiman
   (ed.), *The Female Body in Western Culture:
   Contemporary Perspectives.* Cambridge,
   Mass.: Harvard University Press: 305–16.
Centers for Disease Cotrol (1981a).
   "*Pneumocystic* pneumonia—Los Angeles."
   Morbidity and Mortality Weekly Report, 30:
   250–2.
——(1981b). "Kaposi's sarcoma and
   Pneumocystis pneumonia among
   homosexual men." *Morbidity and Mortality
   Weekly Report*, 30: 305–8.
——(1986a). "Positive HTLV-III/LAV
   antibody results for sexually active female
   members of social/sexual clubs—
   Minnesota." *Morbidity and Mortality
   Weekly Report*, 35: 697—99.
——(1986b) "Update: Acquired
   immunodeficiency syndrome—United
   States." *Morbidity and Mortality Weekly
   Report*, 35: 757–60, 765–66.
Check, William (1985). "Public education on
   AIDS: Not only the media's responsibility."
   Hastings Center Report, Special Supplement
   (August): 27–31.
Fain, Nathan (1985), "AIDS: An antidote to
   fear." *Village Voice* (1 October): 35.
Gottlieb, M. S., Schroff, R., Schanker, H. M., *et
   al.* (1981). "*Pneumocysits carinii* pneumonia
   and mucosal candidiasis in previously
   healthy homosexual men." *New England
   Journal of Medicine*, 305: 1425–31.
Greer, William R. (1986). "Violence against
   homosexuals rising, groups say in seeking
   protections." *New York Times* (23
   November): 15.
Haraway, Donna (1979). "The biological
   enterprise: Sex, mind, and profit from

human engineering to sociobiology."
Radical History Review, 20 (Spring/
Summer): 206–37.

—— (1985) "A manifesto for cyborgs,
science, technology, and social feminism in
the 1980s." *Socialist Review*, 80 (March/
April): 65–108.

Jaret, Peter (1986). "Our immune system: The
wars within." *National Geographic* (June):
702–35.

Krim, Mathilde (1985). "AIDS: the challenge
to science and medicine." *AIDS: The
Emerging Ethical Dilemmas: A Hastings
Center Report*, Special Supplement
(August): 2–7.

Langone, John (1985). "AIDS: The latest
scientific facts." *Discover* (December):
27–52.

Latour, Bruno, and Woolgar, Steve (1985).
*Laboratory Life: The Construction of
Scientific Fact*. Cambridge: Cambridge
University Press.

Leibowich, Jacques (1985). *A Strange Virus of
Unknown Origin*, trans. Richard Howard,
introduction Robert C. Gallo. New York:
Ballantine.

Lynch, Michael (1982). "Living with Kaposi's."
Body Politic, 88 (November).

Marx, Jean L. (1984). "Strong new candidate
for AIDS agent." "Research news," *Science*
(4 May): 146–51.

—— (1986a). "AIDS virus has new name—
perhaps." "News and comment," *Science*,
232 (9 May): 699–700.

—— (1986b). "New relatives of AIDS virus
found." "Research news," *Science*, 232 (11
April): 157.

"Science and the citizen" (1987). *Scientific
American*, 256: 1 (January): 58–9.

Shaw, Nancy S. (1986). "Woman and AIDS:
Theory and politics." Presented at the
annual meeting of the National Woman's
Studies Association, University of Illinois,
Urbana (June).

—— and Paleo, Lyn (1986). "Woman and
AIDS," in Leon McKusick (ed.), *What to do
about AIDS*. Berkeley: University of
California Press: 142–54.

Sontag, Susan (1978). *Illness as Metaphor*. New
York: Farrar, Straus & Giroux.

Turner, Bryan A. (1984). *The Body and Society*.
New York: Basil Blackwell.

31 The Truth is a Murky Path

Toby Miller

. . .

The Americas

> Chile and Peru are narrow coastal territories, and they have no culture of their own. . . . it did possess an indigenous culture when it was first discovered by the Europeans. . . . We do have information concerning America and its culture, especially as it had developed in Mexico and Peru, but only to the effect that it was a purely national culture which had to perish as soon as the spirit approached it.
>
> (Hegel 157, 163)

The intersection of truth, Latin America, and U.S. television forms the remainder of this chapter. General news coverage of the region in the United States is rare by contrast with reports of disaster and revolution, and there is normally no ongoing media presence or background to stories. *The Americas* television series, which screened in prime time in January–March 1993, was designed to rectify this problem. A coproduction of WGBH Boston for PBS and Britain's Central Television Enterprises for Channel 4, it was funded by Annenberg and other foundations (including Carnegie and Rockefeller). The series and its ancillary written materials were authorized by academics from Tufts, Columbia, and Florida International Universities. To participate in the passage of the broadcast text into social and pedagogic space by enrolling in a course for credit, viewers merely required access to the inevitable touch-tone phone: "To find out more about any of these features, call our friendly customer service staff at 1-800-LEARNER" (Day 306; Corporation).

Promotional material for *The Americas* includes *Biographical Notes* that contain, inter alia, information about the achievements of Yezid Campos and Marc de Beaufort, who jointly produced the ninth episode of the series, "Fire in the Mind," an investigation of recent military struggles in El Salvador and Peru. Their short biohistories speak of a recent film "for British television" called *The People of the Shining Path*: "the first report from the inside on Peru's revolutionary organization, the Sendero Luminoso" in the data on Campos, and a film made "with inside access" in the case of de Beaufort (WGBH *Biographical* 2).

There are three reasons for attaching significance to these facts. First, they are indications of the filmmakers' quality and experience that legitimate the series. Second, the form of words describing *The People of the Shining Path* is a complex generic

From Toby Miller, "The Truth is a Murky Path," in Toby Miller, *Technologies of Truth: Cultural Citizenship and the Popular Media* (Minneapolis and London: University of Minnesota Press, 1998), 206–15.

classification of texts that are, indeed, made "from the inside." The third reason is that, effectively, *The People of the Shining Path* was produced as half of 'Fire in the Mind." It was recut for American broadcast without the producers' endorsement, but screened in the original version back in the United Kingdom as part of the *Dispatches* series. This to-ing and fro-ing took place because Campos and de Beaufort's work was said to portray a one-sided view of the Peruvian revolutionaries, what the North American screen establishment calls "point-of-view" documentary. (Much, perhaps, as *Cathy Come Home* failed to consider the needs of landholders in 1960s Britain and the first *Four Corners* reports on Aboriginal living conditions did not consult adequately with government officials in 1960s Australia.) This fantasy about value-free film has very interesting constitutional ramifications. The U.S. Information Agency has litigated, unsuccessfully, to deny customs benefits to documentary filmmakers whose work it deems propagandist, not educational, because of "point-of-view" nonsense. The courts have derided any such neat separation of positionality from learning, but censorship is frequently internalized by filmmakers anyway ("Panel" 351).

The academic advisers to *The Americas* decided a positive presentation of Sendero Luminoso (the Shining Path) was unacceptable. It is now left to the Berkeley-based Committee to Support the Revolution Peru to distribute *The People of the Shining Path* in the United States. (The more available sign is the Che Guevara lookalike who rules a netherworld of 2013 on Sendero Luminoso principles in *John Carpenter's Escape from L.A.* [1996].) But remarkably, the very partiality of the suppressed documentary, the quality that required its alteration, resurfaces in publicity material for *The Americas*. Perhaps this should not surprise us in a series that claims to offer "An Insider Perspective on Contemporary Latin American and Caribbean Society," even as it distances itself from de Beaufort's film (WGBH *Series* 1; Winn Introductory).

This controversy, publicly paraded in the *Boston Globe*, sheds light on the ethical zoning procedures of screen citizenship. A major educational-TV initiative lies before us: all fifty U.S. states offer such programs of study with more than half a million students enrolled in "telecourses" each year. This is not a textual-analytic debate over ideology but a problem in a textual career, an occasion of critique. Nor is it Robinson Crusoe: WGBH's career also includes notorious interventions into *Korea: The Unknown War*, jointly funded with Thames Television in 1988, again involving multiple publishing spin-offs and opportunities for asinine mystification. Here, Bostonians were concerned with the cosmetic horror of "thick British accents," as well as "anti-Western bias," according to WGBH producer Austin Hoyt. So they hired Richard Stilwell, a retired U.S. general who had been in charge of covert operations during the Korean War to make what he called "accuracy checks." Stillwell found the original text "not appropriate for an American audience." And Ali A. Mazrui's 1986 BBC–PBS series *The Africans: A Triple Heritage* ran into problems in the "New Gods" episode, where he referred to Marx as "the last of the great Jewish Prophets." This phrase was safely broadcast to audiences in Israel, Jordan, Australia, Finland, and Nigeria, but not the United States, where PBS thought it might offend viewers. That did not prevent the press from attacking the network and Mazrui for creating a program that included this message in other versions, accusing him of being anti-Western. The National Conservative Foundation urged readers of *Broadcasting*, a trade magazine, to watch *The Africans* and then "threaten to withdraw financial support for public broadcasting" (Orr xix; Cumings 231–67; Stilwell quoted in Jacobsen 47 and Cumings 231; Mazrui 90; Matabane and Candy 6, 14 n. 1).

The Nation Abroad

> At what precise moment did Peru fuck itself up?
> (Stavans 18)

> Peru, Peru, Peru—Macy's Bridges the Americas.
> (store advertisement in 1930s
> New York quoted in Hamburger 290)

A specter is haunting educational TV—the specter of citizenship. It has been difficult to bring into discourse. We ask questions—Is this propaganda? Is it balanced? Who is its author? Is it true?—presuming there is an ontological space of metacritique alongside experiential knowledge and intentionality. Such activity is beyond me, for I am a viewer. That position inclines me a few degrees, toward more modest space. This space poses certain questions of statements made, but it does not do so in terms of a *non dit*, the secreted unconscious of deceit and mystification that can be related to a subject position or absolute distinctions between truth and falsehood. Rather, this space says, "You cannot tell me the statements I have heard deny their true meaning if you also wish to use them as evidence of that denial, for that indicates these statements say something you claim they do not say." (See the formulations of Foucault *Archaeology* 109–10).

This will *not* be a symptomatic reading, but a reassemblage of the materiality of the event called "Fire in the Mind." I do this as an outsider, an engaged but unenrolled viewer, in the knowledge that the Shining Path has been locked in a struggle with sovereign and not-so-sovereign authorities for more than a decade. More than twenty-five thousand lives have been lost, with violence on all sides and accusations of "narcoterrorism" problematizing the group's left-revolutionary claims (Poole and Rénique; Tarazona-Sevillano; Winn *Americas* 537). I shall refrain from comparing these films with the *real* Americas. But I "know" a great deal about *The Americas*, thanks to a *Series Backgrounder*:

The 10 programs focus on themes that often draw together several countries. The film on racial identity, for example, moves smoothly from Bolivia to the Dominican Republic to Haiti, illuminating the unique ethnic and racial problems of each country through human stories, a filmmaking style that succeeds through the deceptively simple means of looking and listening.

Behind those images, however something quite complicated is going on. Entire armies of scholars, researchers, producers and production staff are, in effect, on the march. "I sometimes feel like a general," says [the executive producer]. (WGBH *Series* 2)

This process is meant to produce an innovative amalgam of diegetic individuation, whereby experiential narratives personalize public history and extradiegetic academicism serves as a pedagogic warrant. Promotional descriptions make this quite apparent: "The series presents personal stories that highlight the issues behind the limited images and incomplete information that capture public attention in newspapers and popular magazines" (WGBH *Fact* I). Popular culture distorts, but it can be pursued and utilized homeostatically to educate (as per video and the Bulger murder). But to say what?

Cultural technologies such as the TV series analyzed here create, and sometimes inhabit, the masks of an other. Countries of the region are defined as different but similar. "The Americas" emphasizes certainty (the definite article) and difference (the plural form). And just after the programs' identificatory humanism quoted earlier, self-promotional material adds an assurance from academic director Peter Winn that the "complex arguments and historical background," which "books are better at present-ing," will promote reason rather than tourism. But wait; if books can argue and provide history, and film is good for what he terms "images and sounds," then the original account of the Shining Path was not worth recutting. Its material always already lacked complexity, depending on "images and sounds" immune to subtle agonistics. But the material *was* reedited into an acceptable form. Winn himself said of the sanitized version that it was a "better film . . . significantly improved throughout." Was the film's content improved through a telegenics of truth that satisfied the Star Chamber of Historiography? The answer to this question resides in the contingent protocols of the academy. For instance, Ken Burns's 1994 *Baseball* series, another PBS venture into pedagogy for fun and profit, is advertised in *American Quarterly*, the key American studies journal, as "Directly Correlated to the New Standards in U.S. History" ("Teach"; WGBH *Backgrounder* 2; Winn quoted in P. Bennett B30). And no doubt it is. But are those standards shared by Dianne Feinstein, Peter Winn, and *dependistas*?

These questions relate to publicity for the *Americas* series that authenticated it through the carefully rewritten promotion of two producers who made "insider" texts for the United Kingdom: traces of value that *are* only traces, because *what* they pro-duced is deemed unsuitable. A cosmic ambivalence is at play here in the chalking of territory. Uneasy marks of extraterritoriality characterize the United States as a military, economic, diplomatic, and intellectual seeker of a self riven by the fault lines of an immigrant but export culture and the lost project of its own invention: civics. The formula for the surface, diegetic truth making of the series, "personal stories," simply doesn't work with the original Peruvian footage. Even when Shining Path members are in-shot—imprisoned, masked, or caught on home video—they speak ideological lan-guage unsuited to the series and contemporary world politics. Time is out of joint, if not coca. In short, these folk appear antediluvian to the Whiggish narrative that overcame the series during the ten years it took to produce, as the politics of the continent shifted welcomely from the horrors of the 1980s. With that shift, North American policy—part *of*, as much as a reaction *to*, these transformations—recast itself, adopting a new posture toward those it had once abjured in El Salvador. But such revisionism was not applied to the Shining Path.

The Day of the Citizen

> Lloyd DeGrane's recent book of photographs is called *Tuned In: Television in Ameri-can Life*. It retails for U.S. $11.95 from the University of Illinois Press. The front cover depicts three television viewers watching a large-screen set. To the left of the frame a woman is in an armchair. A man is sitting directly opposite her. The central position in the photograph and in front of the TV is taken by a llama, attached to the man's left hand by a leash.

By now my intent will be clear. This section of the chapter does not center Peru or El Salvador. Nor is my referent the Byzantine—but structurally predictable—rent-seeking wars of university intellectuals versus media intellectuals. My concern is the stalked creature whose imaginary presence animates those conflicts: the much sought, oft-analyzed, but never-subdued creature encountered in the introduction, the television audience. Specific to this case, I am concerned with tracking how various telegenic protocols inscribe viewing positions for that audience together with the extratelevisual pedagogic objects created for *The Americas*, producing ethical zones of historical citizenship. But where should I, the armchair analyst lacking a green card that is reportedly pink, begin? Is there a text in this chapter?

"Fire in the Mind" is decidedly not "a" text. Peter Winn and his team of advisers could not control its production or circulation in the United Kingdom. Marc de Beaufort and his team of technicians could not control its postproduction or circulation in the United States in the face of what he called "a particular generation of academics." The text itself is set up to be interpreted through study guides, the seminar of the mind, and teaching manuals. As *The Americas* series' executive producer, Judith Vecchione, said, it "seems a shame to do all that work and broadcast the results only once. . . . I really like the idea that we're doing programming both for prime time general audiences *and* for student audiences" (de Beaufort quoted in P. Bennett B30; Vecchione quoted in Maurer 3). This is a *series of events*, in need of explanation as such.

I shall not go into a detailed empirical contrast of the Channel 4 and WGBH versions. Suffice it to say that such an account might refer to the excision in the United States of narration that describes the Path as "a highly organized political party" with "rapidly growing support," in favor of its nomination as "one of the deadliest revolutionary groups in the world." And it would probably note *military* atrocities displaced by *party* atrocities, plus the removal of scenes showing Shining Path peasants peacefully herding llamas. The American version locates resistance to the ruling regime and the Shining Path in organic community opposition, whereas the British version centers the Path as the organ of dissonance. I shall concentrate on the call to citizenship that occurs at the elision between the two halves of the American version to establish an equilibrium-disequilibrium struggle across two unrelated histories: El Salvador and Peru did not need to be seen together, but they were *brought* together, through a "Monroe" strategy of narration.

Consider the interpellative address that begins the film: "The Americas"—an atmospheric, apolitical, geographic syntagm—accompanies an image track of the sublime through a mountainous establishing shot. Then "a rich, vibrant region" is matched by the shot of a twirling dancer (in itself perhaps amenable to a politicized reading, but here reduced to the "rich cuisine" end of multiculturalism). This is soon supplanted by "close to our borders," accompanied by a close-up on a Shining Path woman in uniform—that most disturbing of *Mädchen*—marching and charging under the sign of the red flag. You will be astonished to learn that "their choices will change our lives." And guess what? "All of them are as much Americans as we are."

The Monroe strategy works either because we know the terrain or can reshape it to *look* familiar. I refer here to the words spoken by Raul Julia, the offscreen narrator, for it is his voice, the script, and perhaps the authenticity offered by Julia's public *persona* as a

Puerto Rican and the feature-film lead of both *Romero* (John Duigan, 1989) and *Kiss of the Spider Woman* (Hector Babenco, 1985) that merge these essentially unconnected stories. We begin with the tragedy of El Salvador. Blame is equally apportioned: the violence is set in play and reinforced by a combination of the state, rebels, and U.S. foreign policy. The horrors we enter into, particularly shocking in the death that was felt around the world, the death of Archbishop Romero (an occurrence that, even at this distance and in this film, makes my eyes water), are very retroactive, bundled together as a history lesson for future policy makers, participants in the viewing public sphere. They are about former errors. Specifically, it is acknowledged that previous disasters made revolutionary violence inescapable. Or, put another way, as U.S. policy on El Salvador recognizes its complicity in this past horror, that insurrectionary violence is made understandable. The new, improved U.S. foreign policy means there is no need for such activity anymore. Equilibrium is restored to country, film, and viewer: El Salvador is a democracy, the screen sequence is over, and the citizen-spectator has an exemplary instance of former foibles to read against current wisdoms.

Halfway through "Fire in the Mind," there is a cut between armchair prognostications about the settlement in El Salvador and a political march through the hills of Peru. One site is individuated, named, and subordinated to the intellectual space of argument. The other is visceral, demotic, and namelessly threatening. Unlike in Hollywood, where we might expect a dream sequence to articulate this shift in diegetic space, there are no concessions to continuity outside Julia's narration: "In the 1990s, the unfolding drama of Peru might be a grim indication of more radical ways of revolution." There is an absolute logic splicing Peru into El Salvador in this chillingly arrogant manner. Regardless of authorial intentionality, matching the two situations sets up a particular ethical practice available only to Monrovians (and you know whom I mean when I use that term). We are shifted from the site of former revolutionary violence. At its zenith, this violence was considered illegitimate by the United States. The film takes it to be reasonable now that it has ended (partly *because* the United States ceased to regard it as illegitimate). The crossover takes us to contemporary violence, which—surprise, surprise—is rendered simultaneously illegitimate by both the U.S. government and the narration of the program. The edit achieved by Julia's voice track connects a *historic* violence that was *right*—rather like the American and French Revolutions—with a *current* violence that is *wrong*.

In the 1990s, most of Latin America became democratic, much to the satisfaction of the United States. With major trading blocs emergent across the globe, often working against North American investment interests, the prospect of economic growth in the region was equally pleasurable, leading George Bush to propose a free-trade zone through his "Initiative of the Americas." When Peruvian president Alberto Fujimori suspended the Constitution and dissolved Congress and the Supreme Court in his April 1992 *autogolpe*, the economic portfolios in Washington lobbied for inaction. Bush suspended financial aid, but when the rest of the continent remained comparatively silent, pressure on Fujimori from the United States diminished. The maintenance of good relations between Washington and other capitals in the region was reasserted as a priority. The Clinton administration was only marginally more prepared to criticize the regime (Vargas Llosa 126–30, 141 n. 4; Madalengoitia). Meanwhile, Fujimori was offering powerful experiential narratives of his encounters with the oppressed and the efforts he makes on their behalf:

> On weekends, I generally try to go out to the slum areas of Lima and the poverty-stricken areas elsewhere in the country—precisely those areas where Shining Path is supposed to be present—to see with my own eyes what they are living through.
>
> My car has been stuck in the mud many times in such places, where I've seen that water costs an unaffordable one dollar per container. Having seen that, I immediately put the armed forces to work to build the necessary infrastructure so that water will cost half as much. (II)

Perhaps the water has scarcity value because vast amounts are needed to make the mud to bog down his limousines.

Such issues are superficially far from students of *The Americas*; you don't need to know about the economy of Peru, the beliefs of its peoples, or the activities of the state to pass *The Americas*. The book guiding students in their work begins with a two-step operation that articulates the Monroe strategy by its paragraphic slippage. The first thing to know is that the next century will find Latin American and Caribbean people as the biggest minority group in the United States, the second thing that "our relationship with this vital region" is of great importance. The "our" is suddenly historical and yet contemporary: "we" are about to be internally differentiated, so now is the time for "us" to learn about the process, but also to influence it by adopting a knowledgeable position on U.S. foreign policy (one of the course's principal educational goals) (Orr xi; xii, 134).

There is a crucial choice in the "Test Bank" of questions for viewers enrolled in college courses associated with the series. In that splendid false syntagm, the multiple-choice section, questions 17 and 20 are concerned with Sendero Luminoso. The account of the party's leadership offers the following possibilities: (a) opposed to violence against the peasantry, (b) inspired by other regional revolutionaries, (c) opposed to drug trafficking, and (d) favoring violent overthrow of the state. There is one right answer. The other question has *two* correct answers, which tell us that the movement adheres to Maoist principles "despite the discrediting of international Communism" and "has used terrorist tactics against the civilian population." The essay question on the topic asks students to find ways of dissociating the Peruvian crisis from other revolutionary conflicts in the history of the region (Orr 125–27). An ethical zone is upon us. It is not a zone of active, engaged citizenship, I fear, but a homology between liberal-humanist textual strategies and governmental policies. Ongoing academic debate about the Shining Path indicates its complexity (L. Taylor). The address and narration of *The Americas* are massively conditional even as they seem to rest on an unsignifying native turf of personal and collective memories and rights and absolutist professional history.

Perhaps, however, the artificiality of that turf, its contingent dependency on a policy consensus, is ironically made available to redress by the little cut between otherwise disparate countries and struggles, through Julia's voice of authority, for surely that cut alerts us to silliness. Contrasting the British and American versions of truth in Peru stresses that, as the materials could so easily be rearranged to make a different point for the sensitive eyes and ears of North American viewers, they could have been added to in another way: left as they were diegetically, but accompanied by additional discussion and debate, if necessary heated—an encounter between differing positions on the film, a "live" advisory. Alternatively, might a way be found to add information and critique that makes academic study and prime-time television performatively dialogic, rather than disassembling the work of documentarists? There are two immediate options for doing this: conflictual voices inside the primary text, a multiperspectival narration, and associational editing; or a hypertext variant on the studio-discussion model, with software enabling viewers to "choose their line" (e.g., "Would you like to hear a pro/anti-government position on these topics?"). At least something could be done to alert viewers that the multiple-choice and essay questions make sense *only* if this readership shares the concerns of U.S. foreign policy at the moment the questions were written. Such thoughts come as a consequence of that little opening, the space between El Salvador and Peru that Julia's butterfly vocal suture could not close. And if this gesture toward reconsidering that hinge of truth has been suggestive, then I shall feel satisfied.

References

Bennett, Philip (1993). "The Fractious Making of a WGBH Film." *Boston Globe* (10 January): B25, B30.

Corporation for Public Broadcasting. *1993 Annenberg/CPB Collection Video Series.* N.p., n.d.

Cumings, Bruce (1992). *War and Television.* London: Verso.

Day, J. Laurence (1987). "United States News Coverage of Latin America: A Short Historical Perspective." *Studies in Latin American Popular Culture*, 6: 301–9.

Foucault, Michel (1974). *The Archaeology of Knowledge*, trans. A. M. Sheridan Smith. London: Tavistock.

Hamburger, Estelle (1939). *It's a Woman's Business.* New York: Vanguard.

Hegel, Georg Wilhelm Friedrich (1988). *Lectures on the Philosophy of World History. Introduction: Reason in History*, trans. H. B. Nisbet. Cambridge: Cambridge University Press.

Jacobsen, Kurt (1993). "WGBH Makes History." *Bulletin of Concerned Asian Scholars*, 25 (2): 46–49.

Magdalengoitia, Laura (1991). "Paradoxes in the Relations between the United States and Perú." *International Journal of Political Economy*, 21 (2): 26–45.

Matabane, Paula W., and Gandy, Jr., Oscar H. (1988). "Through the Prism of Race and Controversy: Did Viewers Learn Anything from *The Africans*?" *Journal of Black Studies*, 19 (1): 3–16.

Maurer, Richard (1992). Interview with Judith Vecchione. WGBH series feature.

Mazrui, Ali A. (1990). *Cultural Forces in World Politics.* London: James Currey.

Orr, Bernadette M., with Cruz, Bárbara (1993). *Americas Study Guide.* New York: Oxford University Press.

"Panel Discussion" (1992). *Journal of Arts Management and Law*, 21 (4): 349–54.

Poole, Deborah, and Rénique, Gerardo (1992). *Peru: Time of Fear.* London: Latin America Bureau.

Stavans, Ilan (1993). "Two Peruvians: How a Novelist and a Terrorist Came to Represent Peru's Divided Soul." *Transition*, 61: 18–39.

Tarazona-Sevillano, Gabriela, with Reuter, John B. (1990). *Sendero Luminoso and the Threat of Narcoterrorism.* New York: Praeger.

Taylor, Lewis (1993). "Peru's 'Time of Cholera': Economic Decline and Civil War, 1985–1990." *Third World Quarterly*, 14 (1): 173–79.

"Teach America's History" (1994). *American Quarterly*, 46 (3).

Vargas Llosa, Alvaro (1994). *The Madness of Things Peruvian: Democracy under Siege.* New Brunswick, NJ: Transaction.

WGBH (1992). *Americas Biographical Notes.* Boston.

—— (1992). *Americas Fact Sheet/Listings.* Boston.

—— (1992). *Americas Series Backgrounder.*

"Discovering AMERICAS: A Look behind the Scenes." Boston.

—— (n.d.). *Americas Series Press Release.* Boston.

Winn, Peter (1992). *Americas: The Changing Face of Latin America and the Caribbean.* New York: Pantheon.

Section VII
Media

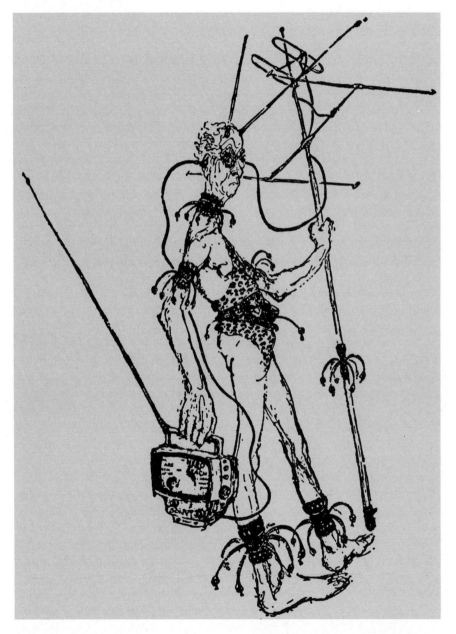

Section VII
Media

Authors
John Fiske, Lynn Spigel, Robert Stam, Henry Jenkins, Mark Poster, Manuel Castells

Visual Artist
Tom Wolfe: *What if he is right?*

SINCE many US cultural studies scholars have backgrounds in literary or cinema studies, media analysis constitutes a large proportion of American research, much of which focuses on textual analysis. Researchers have also borrowed from political economy in their investigations of media production and from sociology/anthropology in their investigations of media audiences. We accept that a full understanding of the media's relationship to culture depends upon the analysis of the circuit of production, "texts," and audiences. The articles selected address the inevitable theoretical and methodological dilemmas that such a position entails, while also serving as exemplary studies in this burgeoning area. Again, materials will be both of a contemporary and a historical nature.

John Fiske is one of the best known exponents of American cultural studies. His work on television in particular has been widely influential, and his early forays into the politics of culture on behalf of "audience liberation" proved both entertaining and controversial. In this selection, however, his attention is drawn to the print media, and to the category of news. He identifies a genre of "popular news" that is distinct from and frequently at odds with official or even alternative news. Inevitably a large part of the analysis concerns questions of knowledge and truth. But Fiske does not take tabloid journalism to task for its lapses in objectivity. Rather he shows how the imperatives of the "cultural sphere" differ from those of the "public sphere." While they may display few of the traditionally looked-for virtues of "serious" journalism, the popular or tabloid press are nevertheless important, not least because they may contribute to the extension of democracy to places that other media have trouble reaching.

Lynn Spigel's cultural history of the relationships among the seemingly distinct discursive realms of television, the suburbs and the space race uses sources as diverse as *Life Magazine*, science fiction novels and presidential speeches. The article shows that television programmes can only be fully understood within the plenitude of a fully delineated specific cultural and historical moment. Robert Stam addresses the specific cultural and historical moment of the quincentennial of Columbus' "discovery" of the "new world." His painstaking textual analyses of films and television programs produced around this moment reveal a frightening continuity between dominant texts depicting Columbus as hero and indigenous populations as depraved or invisible. But his discussion of indigenous peoples' own media productions offers hope that dominant representations will not always remain dominant. In similar fashion, Henry Jenkins discusses how gay *Star Trek* fans have contested the program's exclusion of gay characters, protesting the implicit homophobia of a utopic vision of the future that fails to recognize diversity of sexual orientation. Jenkins' article typifies the celebratory strain of cultural studies that emphasizes the ageny of receivers over the domination of producers.

Mark Poster theorizes one of the newest media technologies, the Internet. He distances himself from both Marxist and postmodernist traditions of cultural criticism, neither of which have much to say about democracy. He characterizes the Net as an improvable community, capable of democratic practices whose shapes may be imperfectly understood via existing theoretical paradigms. His combination of political and cultural concerns, and of public-sphere with technological analysis, produces an interesting vision of "postmodern politics" that takes American cultural studies to new questions on new sites.

The last selection comes from Manuel Castells, whose magisterial work on the "network society" provides yet another set of new possibilities for American cultural studies. He contends that the social transformations effected by new technologies, new patterns of capital and labour flow, and the establishment of "the network society," "deeply affect culture and power." Understanding how this can be, and what political, personal, and mediated consequences follow from it, is where cultural studies first came in.

Full circle, perhaps: certainly a chapter on "media" is aptly illustrated by Tom Wolfe's witty sketch of Marshall McLuhan as the media guru of the "global village," wrapped in his "tribal" outfit and lugging the high-tech extensions of his senses into the virtual sphere. Risible certainly; a vision of the future—possibly. But as ever, the question is still: *What if he is right?*

32 Popularity and the Politics of Information

John Fiske

T HIS chapter addresses the problem of understanding which forms of news can be popular in a late capitalist society such as the US. There is a paradox at the heart of the problem in that news traditionally is produced by the power-bloc whereas popularity is the product of the people. This paradox has been well formulated by Stuart Hall.

> The people versus the power-bloc: this, rather than "class-against-class", is the central line of contradiction around which the terrain of culture is polarized. Popular culture, especially, is organized around the contradiction: the popular forces versus the power-bloc. (Hall 1981: 238)

. . .

Popular politics tend towards those domains where popular interests may be best promoted. In our current conditions, the public sphere has been so thoroughly, and often corruptly, colonized by the power-bloc that the people are channelling their political energies elsewhere. This may be a worrying shift, but at least it is a shift of politics, not its extinction.

I propose now to turn to an analysis of some of the forms taken by popular news in the contemporary US. First, I must distinguish it from official news and alternative news, which I locate and characterize fairly briefly as they are not the main focus of this chapter.

Official news is the news of the "quality" press and network television. It is extended in current affairs shows such as *60 Minutes* or *Larry King Live* and in magazines such as *Time* or *Newsweek* in the US. It presents its information as objective facts selected from an empiricist reality wherein lies a "truth" that is accessible by good objective investigation. Its tone is serious, official, impersonal and is aimed at producing understanding and belief. It is generally the news which the power-bloc wants the people to have.

Alternative news differs from official news first in its selection of events to report, and second in the way it makes the selection and, therefore, repression of events explicitly political. It flourishes better in print journalism than electronic—neither television nor radio in the US has the equivalent of radical journals such as *The Nation, In These Times* or *The Progressive*, though National Public Radio will carry alternative stories, and Black Entertainment Television will give news of black people and events, particularly from Africa, that is never seen on the white networks, and the Discovery Channel will sometimes do the same for Latin America and other areas of the Third World. But this

From John Fiske, "Popularity and the Politics of Information," in Peter Dahlgren and Colin Sparks (eds.), *Journalism and Popular Culture* (London, Newbury Park, and New Delhi: Sage Publications, 1992), 45–63. Reprinted with permission of Sage Publications and John Fiske.

alternative news, valuable though it is, particularly in its politicization of the selection of events and, in its radical forms, of the discursive strategies by which events are made-to-mean, differs from popular news. Much of it circulates among a fraction of the same educated middle classes as does official news and, in these cases, its political struggle is conducted between class fractions rather than between classes, or, to avoid such a vulgar Marxist model, it is a struggle between more central and more marginalized allegiances within the power-bloc, rather than between the power-bloc and the people.

Popular news, whether electronic or printed, is often given the disparaging label "tabloid" and is regularly subject to vehement scorn and disapproval by both official and alternative news (see Glynn 1990). Yet despite, or perhaps because of, such disapproval it flourishes in the market-place. Indeed, the defining innovations of the last two seasons of US television have been in the development of "tabloid television" which, as its name suggests, is television's equivalent of the tabloid press.

Tabloid journalism's economic success is beyond question, but its popularity has hardly been investigated and its defining characteristics are remarkably hard to pin down with any precision. Its subject matter is generally that produced at the intersection between public and private life: its style is sensational, sometimes sceptical, sometimes moralistically earnest; its tone is populist; its modality fluidly denies any stylistic difference between fiction and documentary, between news and entertainment.

Typical American print tabloids are the *Weekly World News* and the *National Enquirer.* TV programmes in the genre include *COPS*, where a minicam travels with police officers on routine patrols, or *Rescue 911*, which consists of re-enactments of spectacular rescues, usually by the people involved, interspersed with interviews and first-person narratives. *America's Most Wanted* is a mix of re-enactments of usually violent or sexual crimes, together with an appeal to the public to join in the search for the criminal. Unlike official news, tabloid news rarely admits of any distinction between the factual and the fictional. In all these tabloid shows, suddenly, in exceptional circumstances, the lives of ordinary people enter the public domain of law and order or public safety. Almost always this entry into the public is in the role of victim—a spectacular exaggeration of their normal social position. These crime-centred tabloids seem to tend towards a reactionary populism, characterized by a simplistic moral earnestness and by an individualistic reduction of crime and protection to a singular cause and effect model. But, as Hall et al. (1978) have pointed out, it is difficult to maintain a progressive stance towards crime when the weak are its victims. It is equally difficult to maintain a sense of social difference in the face of disaster or danger when the forces of power are manifest in rescue and protection rather than oppression.

Another type of programme in the genre is the sensationalized current affairs or news show such as *A Current Affair* or *Hard Copy* in the US. Any clear generic distinction between these tabloid shows and more respectable, established ones like *60 Minutes* is blurred by newer, slightly more sensational but still "responsible" ones such as *The Reporters. A Current Affair*, however, is generically tabloid wherever the boundary between tabloid and official is drawn, and is characterized by its sensational subject matter, populist and sceptical tone and general offensive vulgarity.

Both these types of show are recent, and are widely accepted as tabloid television. But there is a third type of programme, traditional and well established, and not usually thought of as tabloid, which is also an agent in the popular circulation of information, and that is the chat show, particularly the daytime one's such as those hosted by Phil Donahue, Oprah Winfrey or Geraldo.

What I do in this chapter is base an analysis of some examples of tabloid journalism upon the insights into popular taste that have been afforded us by the work of Bakhtin (1968) and Bourdieu (1984), and which I have elaborated elsewhere (Fiske, 1989a, 1989b). Any basic definition of news, whether official or tabloid, must include its informational function. But information is not simply a set of objective facts to be packaged and delivered around the nation: informing is a deeply political process. To inform is simultaneously to circulate knowledge and to give form to something: and what information "forms" is both reality and identity. We are what we know and what we do not know we cannot be. Similarly it is the known and knowable world that constitutes our reality: the unknowable is the unreal. Information, in a reciprocal movement, produces both social subjects and social reality, so the control of information is a vital cog in the mechanism of social discipline. A top-down definition of information is a disciplinary one, and it hides its disciplinarity under notions of objectivity, responsibility and political education. What the people ought to know for a liberal democracy to function properly is a concept that hides repression under its liberal rhetoric and power under its pluralism. The knowledge it proposes as proper is that required for the smooth operation of the public sphere and of governmental party politics. It is a generalized knowledge of policy, of broad social events and movements that is distanced from the materiality of everyday life. It is a knowledge required by public, not private life, it is a knowledge of society in general rather than of the particularities of daily life. The social reality it produces is the habitat of the masculine, educated middle class, the habitat that is congenial to the various alliances formed by the power-bloc in white patriarchal capitalist societies. A manifestation of these alliances in practice is the Washington social circuit in which the leaders of government, the military, industry, the judiciary and the press mingle at party after party, turning structural social relations into personal social relationships.

But the subjectivity produced by this knowledge is even more significant than the reality. It produces a believing subject, and this is one of the defining differences between official and tabloid news. The last thing that tabloid journalism produces is a believing subject. One of its most characteristic tones of voice is that of a sceptical laughter which offers the pleasures of disbelief, the pleasures of not being taken in. This popular pleasure of "seeing through" them (whoever constitutes the powerful *them* of the moment) is the historical result of centuries of subordination which the people have not allowed to develop into subjection.

. . .

Unlike official news, popular news makes no attempt to smooth out contradictions in its discourse: indeed it exploits them, for unresolved contradictions are central to popular culture. The experience of the people in capitalist societies is contradictory to its core, for not only is their life lived at the various points of conflict between the interests of the subordinate and those of the dominant, but those interests themselves are full of contradictions. The system that subordinates the people can also sustain and protect them (cf. *Rescue 911* and *America's Most Wanted*), it can offer the resources by which to struggle against the constraints it imposes. So the interests of the people may at certain times and in certain areas of experience be served best by acceding to the forces of domination, and, at others, by opposing or evading them. Knowing when to dissemble and go along with the system and when not to is a crucial tactic of everyday life. The contradictions between the reactionary populism of *America's Most Wanted* and the more progressive scepticism found sometimes on *A Current Affair* are both a product and a performance of this structural conflict within popular experience. In elaborated capitalism neither the opposition of social interests nor the interests themselves can ever be pure and unconflicted, so the everyday life of the people necessarily involves the constant negotiation of unresolved contradictions.

Recognizing this requires us to view the people as social agents rather than social subjects. The multiplicity of contradictions and their lack of resolution debars any of the coherence necessary to produce and position unified or even divided subjectivities: instead they require active social agents to negotiate them. There is, therefore, a necessary creativity of the people exercised in producing a felt equilibrium that is theirs and within which they can live their lives with a degree of ease. It is an equilibrium that makes the contradictions liveable, for everyday life could not be lived in a state of constant consciousness of antagonism of interest—the anxiety produced would be dysfunctional. But such equilibrium is never secure, it has to be constantly re-achieved and renegotiated; it is always in process as the people chart their paths through the social determinations that both constrain and empower them. In the realm of the social, therefore, popular agency works to produce points of equilibrium between the contradictory interests of the power-bloc and of the people, and of the contradictory forces within both.

Tabloid journalism not only transgresses norms, it also exceeds them. Excess is a popular stylistic device that is similar to transgression in that it also allows for a conflicted reading position. As the sceptical transgression of norms requires the negotiation between belief and disbelief, so exceeding them requires a negation between acceptance and rejection.

. . .

Sensationalism, a frequently criticized characteristic of popular news, is a display of excess, a sort of mega-normality which writes large and visibly that which is normally taken for granted and whose political effectivity depends precisely upon its status as uninspected common sense. Norms exceeded are made visible and by being thus abnormalized are made available for subversion and criticism. Parody, which Bakhtin (1968) defines as a typical stylistic device of popular art, is a form of abnormalizing excess, for it works by exaggerating conventions and thus exposes what is normally tacitly accepted to subversive laughter. This headline is simultaneously excessive, sensational and parodic; indeed, the three adjectives are finally only different descriptors for the same stylistic feature. Like transgression, excess works on the contradictory play of forces between the normal and its rejection. Like transgression, therefore, it reproduces in reading relations the contradictoriness which is the defining feature of the social relations of the subordinate, and calls up sceptical reading competencies that are the equivalent of the social competencies by which the people control the immediate conditions of their everyday lives.

The politics of all this is a difficult question. While I believe that the pleasures of scepticism and of parodic excess can be progressive I do not wish to suggest that they are always or necessarily so. The politics of popular culture are as deeply conflicted as the experience of the people.

. . .

This sort of tabloid journalism, unlike its official counterpart, makes no effort to present its information to us as an objective set of facts in an unchanging universe: for it, information is not an essentialist knowledge system but is a process that works only in a political relationship to other knowledges. Its politics lies in its oppositionality to the normal, the official. It is a popular knowledge and a repressed knowledge, just as the people are repressed social formations, and its definition, like that of the people, must be sought in the relations of repression not in any objective category of what is repressed. This knowledge is a sociopolitical process in action.

Its politics, therefore, are generalized: it is an agent in the production of a politicized stance towards social relations in general; it rarely engages in politics that are issue centred. In particular, unlike the alternative press, it rarely offers repressed information on issues that the power-bloc have placed on the political agenda. This does not mean that its politics are of a lesser order, but that they are different. It also means that they are not sufficient in themselves—they are a politics of potential rather than of actualization.

The tabloid television that takes the form of chat show can, however, extend this sceptical stance and this oppositional information into the agenda set not by itself but by the power-bloc. Phil Donahue's program on "The drug business" (23 February 1990) is a case in point. His main guest is Michael Levine a former undercover agent in Reagan's Drug Enforcement Agency who has just written a "tell-all" book on his experiences. His information has the same ontological status as official information—that is it is presented as objective truth—but its political repression is explicit. Its oppositionality is foregrounded as is its intention to produce a disbelief in the official knowledge, though not in its own. It does not produce, as does the *Weekly World News*, a scepticism towards "their" explanation of the world in general, but a confrontational disbelief of their explanation of this specific issue. Part of the discussion runs thus:

Michael Levine (Former DEA Agent): The drug war is a fraud. Our government does not want to win it. And for a DEA agent working overseas, the biggest danger in the world is the Pentagon, CIA, and the Drug Enforcement Administration, and the secret powers that are more interested in keeping the drug economy strong.

Donahue: And in fighting communism.

Levine: And in fighting communism, and third-world banking, and everything else you can imagine, the last priority of which is winning the drug war.

Donahue: Let's just talk about fighting communism for a moment. It was fighting communism that kept us in bed with Noriega, wasn't it?

Levine: There are a thousand Noriegas out there right now. The case that I just did was a nightmare, and it culminated 10 years of nightmarish undercover experiences, where the biggest drug dealers in the world were protected by our own government. And we just don't want to win, but the show is there for all of you to believe that there really is a drug war.

Donahue: And the show is standing by the table with all the cocaine, the biggest bust in the history of the universe, 11 o'clock news, action news, pictures at 11. And it looks like we're winning, and you're saying that's a phony.

Levine: Absolutely, Phil. If I were a rich man, I would give my book to everyone in this country, just so that they could look at these victory speeches—drug war victory speeches—and say, "We know they're lying."

Levine went on to give specific examples, and concluded:

In each three cases, our government moved to destroy the case, and it stopped right there.

Donahue: And they did so because?

Levine: They did so because there are other interests that are much more important than that [drug running].

Donahue: And what would they be, communism?

Levine: Communism is one, but the commissioner—the ex-commissioner of customs, William von Rabb, in his letter of resignation, said to the President of the United States, Bush, that the reason he's resigning is that third-world banking schemes are more important than the drug war. Well, what that means, simply, is that we have an estimated problem that amounts to about $200 billion a year flowing out to third-world countries in drug money. The Andean nations, for instance, owe $42 billion in debt. What happens if the drug flow is cut off? They can't pay our bankers. Now, you don't take it from Mike Levine. Take it from van Rabb, the ex-commissioner of customs, who resigned because of it. It's about time, I think, that Americans got wise and stopped believing these victory drug—

Donahue: So profit motives on the part of 'suits', as you disparagingly call the bureaucrats—

Levine: Yeah, very disparagingly.

Donahue: Profit motives, then, and good old-fashioned capitalism is getting in the way of effective drug enforcement.

Levine: Exactly.

Later on in the discussion, when the topic turns to rehabilitation, Donahue underscores the same point: "You can get money for hardware that makes money for giant, multinational corporations. You can't get money for drug rehabilitation. There's no missile involved. You can't sell a Jeep or an Ml or anything else around the world."

As in many chat shows, "ordinary" people join in to question the panellists, to recount their own everyday experiences and to offer their own opinions and solutions. The show is tabloid not only in its invitation to disbelief and its promotion of repressed information, but also in its focus on the point where the official meets the popular and, where consequently, its inadequacy is exposed.

So relatives of drug users, many of whom have died, tell of the failures of the limited rehabilitation programmes that exist, and former dealers talk about the racial aspects—how the government was only stirred to declare a drug war when drug abuse extended beyond the coloured communities into the white. Various populist solutions are offered. Some audience members voice the authoritarian populism of simplistic morality and muscular action—precisely the populism which Bush attempts to articulate in his drug war rhetoric—jail or execute the suppliers but, unlike Bush and Bennett, the people here speak with a class-aware accent: the enemy is not simply the wicked Latin Americans. As one audience member put it: "Instead of bombing the [drug] fields, why don't we fly over the million-dollar mansions and bomb them . . . you bomb the 20 million-dollar home every time they build one."

There were also voices of a more democratic, progressive populism which located the source of the problem squarely within the social order that makes people want to change their consciousness, by legal or illegal drugs, in order to be happy. These voices recognized that the solution to the problem could never come from above, and there were a number of calls for popular action which varied from the conventional one of voting the current politicians out of office to a call for an organized popular movement:

15th Audience member: Bring them together. Group up. Tell these people, "Get off our streets. We don't want you people selling drugs to our kids!"

Donahue: How do you do that?

15th Audience member: By joining together, as people uniting to one. Never mind the government.

16th Audience member: What we're doing on a national, on a state, and on a local level—the government—the suits, as he calls it—have got to give the power back to the people. They're the ones that are going to make the difference.

Levine: The people can take the power back.

16th Audience member: Yes, and we're doing it.

Panellist: [*off camera*] The people have the power.

The show ends, as most chat shows do, with a fade out as the studio debate continues passionately, there is no attempt to close off the story, as there is in official news, no attempt to finalize the truth. I have argued elsewhere (Fiske 1989*b*) that for news to be popular it needs to provoke conversation, it is by taking up and recirculating the issues of news orally that the people construct aspects of the public sphere as relevant to their own. The oral recirculation of news is a typical way of re-informing it into popular culture.

It is neither easy nor prudent to attempt to predict just which of the doings of the public sphere may, under which conditions, be taken up and made popular by which formations of the people, though the drug issue is clearly a prime candidate, for drugs figure prominently in much popular experience It may be easier, however, to make some tentative predictions about which forms of information or ways of informing invite this popular adoption. Popular culture is participatory (Bakhtin 1968; Bourdieu, 1984) and forms such as the open-ended chat show, where populist voices have been allowed to clash among themselves, and whose populism has articulated itself in oppositional knowledge, are textually incomplete. They can be made adequate only if and when they are continued and reworked in oral circulation. So, too, scepticism is an unstable stance that requires the participation of the people to anchor it at various moments in the play of belief–disbelief: it, too, invites a continuation and a reworking in oral culture. Such invitations are risky because they lie beyond the control of the knowledge that informs the text and, therefore, of the social power that informs that knowledge. In oral circulation, in specific and different formations of the people, information becomes reformed, the people are re-informed and participate in that re-information. Top-down, or official news, has to be re-informed by popular productivity if it is to be made relevant to everyday life.

Bourdieu (1984) has shown how popular taste requires its cultural forms to have a relevance and a use. He argues that the distancing of art from the mundanities of daily life is a bourgeois luxury that is a sign of the bourgeois freedom from material necessity and financial constraint. For those whose social position disadvantages them both materially and politically, however, there is an inescapable necessity to use whatever resources are available to combat deprivation, constraint and disempowerment.

These social conditions are reproduced textually; so top-down texts, such as official news, tend to constrain the meanings which can be made from them and repress alternative or oppositional knowledges. These conditions of constraint (social and textual) may be generalizable in discourse, but in practice they are experienced concretely and differently. The social system that produces deprivation and subordination is structurally the same one for all who live within it, but the actual conditions under which that deprivation is lived and experienced vary enormously. The lived experience of the people consists more imperatively of concrete specificities than of an abstracted or generalized system, it is micro- rather than macro-social. It is in these specificities that we find the contribution of the people to their conditions of existence, and it is these specificities that are the sites of struggle for control over those conditions. The people may be unable to exert much influence over the system that produces social conditions in general, but they can and do strive to control their own immediate conditions of existence.

In the cultural sphere of meanings, information and pleasure this control works first in the selection of which mass-mediated resources to use and then in the use that is made of them. In both stages of the cultural process, relevance plays a vital role. And relevance can only be produced from the bottom-up: while it may in itself be a generalized criterion, what constitutes relevance is not, but varies according to the concrete specificities of the immediate social relations of its production. Information can be evaluated as relevant according to either or both the reality it produces (roughly, its content) and the social relations or identities it promotes (roughly, its form). Relevance of form, with its production of appropriate stances towards the power-bloc, is at least as important in popular news as relevance of content. Indeed, it may be the primary relevance, for it is this popular stance which is most generally transposable over the variety of social conditions of the people. A sceptical mobility, the pleasure of playing with belief and disbelief, the parodic inversion of *their* norms in *our* experience—all these informed social orientations can translate relatively easily into the specific and various formations within which subordination is experienced.

Relevance of content, however, because of its reference to specific events and people may be more limited to those social formations to which the issues involved are already pertinent. One of the techniques by which tabloid journalism attempts to overcome these limitations is to represent this "content" in the experience of ordinary people. So Donahue mixes the information of the DEA agent with that of the studio audience, and opposes both to that of the power-bloc. The *Weekly World News* typically shows ordinary people experiencing the breakdown of social norms, or living beyond the limits of the explanatory power of official knowledge. The reality informed by such journalism is that of the extraordinary experience of ordinary people, and it is from its ordinariness (whether extra- or not) that its relevance can be constructed.

For official news, however, the ordinary becomes newsworthy only under abnormal conditions, such as those of crime or disaster. More typically, official news concerns itself with the doings of elite people in elite or distant places and its informed reality is not so readily constructed as relevant by many formations of the people. Under certain conditions, however, it may be. One such condition is when it contains a representation of subordination or repression, for instance, black Americans may find news of black African leaders relevant because blackness is, in our society, a condition of disempowerment. Similarly, women may construct relevance from the news of elite women (the wife of the president, or the British Queen, for example) for femininity is also a condition of disempowerment. But the activities of white males as such are less likely to be made relevant to the people (even to white men among them) because whiteness and masculinity are not conditions of disempowerment and thus do not resonate so readily with the experience of the people. It is not surprising, then, that the audience of TV network news and the readership of the "serious" press is largely composed of white, educated men, for this privileged social position facilitates reading positions which are in alliance with the interests of the power-bloc rather than those of the people.

Neither the content nor the form of official news makes many concessions to popular relevance. The professional ideology of objectivity—the production of a value-free, depoliticized truth—produces a form of news narrative that works to produce subjected, believing reading relations. So both the form and content of this information work to position it within what de Certeau (1984) calls the "scriptural economy" which attempts to discipline its readers into "deciphering" its texts rather than "reading" them. Deciphering a text is subjecting oneself to its truth, much as the priesthood taught the congregation to decipher the scriptures: reading, however, involves bringing to the text oral competencies developed in the immediate conditions of the reader's social history. Reading is thus a negotiation (typically for de Certeau an antagonistic one) between a text produced from the top and its reading from below. Unresolved contradictions, unstable, unfinished knowledge, scepticism, parody and excess all invite reading: truth and objectivity invite decipherment. Reading is participatory, it involves the production of relevance; decipherment, the perception and acceptance of distance (social and aesthetic). Both the *Weekly World News* and *The Donahue Show* require reading—the network news, on the other hand, invites decipherment.

. . .

Of course, any democracy needs a full flow of information, but the conventional forms of official news can actually limit rather than facilitate that flow. Knowledge about the political world needs to be transformed into popular information, that is into information that forms the world and those who know it as part of the conditions of the everyday life of the people. The difference between official and popular information lies not only in the events of which it makes sense, but also in its cultural process of informing. It may be too simple to suggest that we need the informing of the *Weekly World News* applied to the events and issues in the *New York Times*, but I do believe that official journalism has much to learn from the tabloid's way of informing both their social reality and their social readers. Like many others, I am deeply concerned at the gap between the micro-politics of popular everyday life and macro-political action. I believe it is in the interests of the power-bloc to maintain this gap while simultaneously deploring it, so I want to know more about those instances when the people do make relevant connections between the immediate conditions of everyday life and the larger structures which determine those conditions and about what sort of information encourages or enables this. I am interested in the possible points of intersection between information about events at the macro-structural level of organized political life and the information that the people desire in order to extend their control over the conditions of their lives within that macro-political order. The two informational sets may coincide, may conflict or may not touch each other at all. Our current conditions of popular alienation will necessarily produce many informational sets that are quite separate, but they can also produce valuable moments of overlap such as on *The Donahue Show*.

I have no conclusion to these tentative analyses. I believe the tabloid press constantly attempts to incorporate popular tones of voice and popular stances towards official knowledge. I see some evidence that this informed popular scepticism can be, if all too rarely, turned towards events in the public, political sphere, though I do not wish to overemphasize this. Much of the tabloid press attempts to turn this scepticism to its own immediate commercial advantage, and has little or no interest in attempting to harness it so that the people can use it to their advantage. Equally, however, I do not wish to join either official or alternative journalism in denigrating tabloid journalism, for it seems to me that they both have much to learn about conversing with subordinated social formations. Because their commercial viability does not depend upon reaching the disempowered, there is little motivation for them to attempt to do so. This is particularly regrettable in the case of the alternative press, whose political interests would clearly be best served if it could bridge this gap between what we might call macro-structural informing and micro-practical informing.

. . .

References

Bakhtin, M. (1968). *Rabelais and His World.* Cambridge, Mass.: Massachusetts Institute of Technology Press.

Bourdieu, P. (1984). *Distinction: A Social Critique of the Judgement of Taste.* Cambridge, Mass.: Harvard University Press.

Fiske, J. (1989a). *Understanding Popular Culture.* Boston: Unwin Hyman.

—— (1989b) *Reading the Popular.* Boston: Unwin Hyman.

Foucault, M. (1979). *Discipline and Punish: The Birth of the Prison.* London: Allen Lane.

Glynn, K. (1990). "Tabloid television's transgressive aesthetic: *A Current Affair* and the 'shows that taste forgot.'" *Wide Angle*, 12 (2): 22–44.

Hall, S. (1981). "Notes on deconstructing 'the popular,'" in R. Samuel (ed.), *People's History and Socialist Theory.* London: Routledge and Kegan Paul, pp. 227–40.

Hall, S., Critcher, C., Jefferson, T., Clarke, J., and Roberts, B. (1978). *Policing the Crisis: Mugging, the State and Law and Order.* London: Macmillan.

33 From Theatre to Space Ship
Metaphors of Suburban Domesticity in Postwar America

Lynn Spigel

IN 1956, a year before the Soviet launching of Sputnik, Shakespeare travelled to the planet of the Krel in the science fiction classic *Forbidden Planet*. An adaptation of *The Tempest*, the film presents the fantastic tale of Mobius, an earthling who lands on an alien world where he builds a suburban dream house complete with modernist decor and the latest in robotic home appliances. As the film unfolds, this Technicolor version of suburban bliss becomes a stage not only for Shakespearean drama, but also for the darker side of suburban domesticity. The audience soon discovers that this marvellous space-age home contains a threatening underworld of perverse sexual pleasure. As it turns out, Mobius has an obsessive need to keep his daughter for himself by maintaining her innocence of sexual difference and desire—a need that is destroyed when a team of swarthy astronauts arrives on his planet and awakens the sexual longings of the girl. In his jealous state, Mobius begins to conjure up a series of threats to deter the advances of her suitor. But, as in Shakespeare's famous play, the father's stormy rage is placed in check when the young woman, now fully aware of her sexuality, embraces her astronaut lover and takes off on his rocket bound for earth.

As a film that restages Shakespeare's Oedipal drama in the better homes and gardens of outer space, *Forbidden Planet* is symptomatic of a transition in the language used to represent suburban family life during the postwar period. This transition entailed a shift from metaphors that presented domesticity as theatre—a stage on which predefined gender and generational roles were played—to a competing set of images that presented suburban family life in terms of space travel. As in the case of *Forbidden Planet*, the new metaphor of space travel was typically quite ambiguous. On the one hand, it functioned to glorify the high-tech Family utopias promised by the developers of the postwar suburbs; on the other, space travel offered an escape from the perverse homogeneity of suburban life and toward an imaginary elsewhere where difference (sexual and otherwise) was possible to sustain.

This conceptual shift certainly was not smooth or even. Instead, following Raymond Williams's classic formulation, I would argue that the metaphors of "home as theatre" and "home as space ship" are better conceived as dominant, residual, and emergent forms. These metaphors existed in a kind of parallel universe, and sometimes—as in the

From Lynn Spigel, "From Theatre to Space Ship: Metaphors of Suburban Domesticity in Postwar America," in Roger Silverstone (ed.), *Visions of Suburbia* (London and New York: Routledge, 1997), 217–39.

case of *Forbidden Planet* where domestic gender roles were performed theatrically in outer space—these worlds did collide. What interests me particularly here is the way these conceptions of suburban domesticity competed for cultural legitimacy during the late 1950s and through the 1960s. What was at stake in this discursive competition? And how did it relate to wider social and political attitudes about the ideal design for living during a decade marked by intense social change?

In asking these questions, I am not simply interested in the "poetics" of suburbia or even just in describing an ideological shift. Thinking about suburban domesticity in terms of the language used to describe it is, I believe, a necessary step in understanding the way people have represented *and also lived* their social relationships. Criticism of the suburbs has generally been divided between the culturalists interested in "meanings" and the structuralists interested in economic and political policy. More recently, the field of critical geography and suburban history has complicated this culture/structure split. Feminist historians such as Margaret Marsh and Elizabeth Wilson, and Marxist writers such as Mike Davis, have provided ways to see the connections between language systems and the structural policies the affect urban and suburban design. Cultural representations of the suburbs, I want to argue, were deeply implicated in the policies and practices of suburban social life. These metaphors were not merely symptomatic of those deep structures, but also helped to create a language for domestic and suburban space—a spatial language in which people lived their lives and through which economic and political struggles were also formulated.

Staged Domesticity: The Home as Theatre

In the American housing boom after the Second World War, the mass-produced suburbs provided a practical alternative to the rising costs and diminishing space in urban areas. Towns like Chicago's Park Forest and New York's Levittown offered urban Americans of the white middle (and sometimes working) class a new design for living, largely devoid of the extended families and ethnic ties in the city. These new mass-produced suburbs were funded by Federal Housing Administration (FHA) building loan starts, which included strict "red-lining" zones that effectively kept these new neighbourhoods confined to whites of European descent (many of whom were second-generation immigrants). Because the FHA issued GI loans to returning soldiers, many of the occupants were young couples, poised to raise families. The architectural layouts of the homes as well as the neighbourhoods themselves were designed for this form of nuclear family life and thus tended to exclude the interests and lifestyles of people not living in such arrangements.

Most interesting for my purposes is the way these mass-produced suburbs were modelled on notions of everyday life as a form of theatre, a stage on which to play out a set of bourgeois social conventions.

. . .

Postwar Americans—especially those being inducted into the ranks of middle-class home ownership—must, to some degree, have been aware of the artifice involved in suburban ideals of family life. For people who had lived through the Depression and the hardships of the Second World War, the new consumer dreams must have seemed somewhat pretentious. Leaving ethnic and working-class areas for mass produced suburbs, these people must have been aware of the new roles they were asked to play in a prefabricated social setting. This perception is suggested by sociologists of the era, whose studies showed that people were sensitive to the theatrical quality of everyday life.

The strongest case was made in 1955 by sociologist Nelson Foote. In his article "Family Living as Play," Foote claimed that "family living in a residential suburb has come to consist almost entirely of play." While he admitted that the "popular recognition of this fait accompli is only partial," he went on to detail how "the family home may be most aptly described as a theatre." The members of the family, he argued, were all performers: "The husband may be an audience to the wife or the wife to the husband, or the older child to both."[1] If Foote used theatricality as a metaphor for family relations, other sociologists concentrated on the wider drama of social relations, showing how families transformed their homes into showcases for their neighbours. In his study of the mass produced suburbs, Harry Henderson suggested that "constant attention to external appearance 'counts for a lot' and wins high praise from neighbors." While residents decorated their homes in distinctive ways, none strayed far from the predictable standards exhibited in middle-class magazines—in fact, Henderson argued that "what many [new home owners] sought in their furniture was a kind of 'approval insurance.'"[2] Sociologist William H. Whyte described the social conformity of interior decor in the suburban home, noting one woman who was "so ashamed of the emptiness of her living room that she smeared the picture window with Bon Ami; not until a dinette set arrived did she wipe it off."[3] For this woman the picture window itself became a venue of theatrical display in which furniture took on the status of props.

· · ·

The theatrical quality of everyday life became a major organizing principle of the emerging television sitcom. Family sitcoms highlighted the performative nature of middle-class life on a weekly basis, and, like the Victorian parlour theatrical, such programmes were extremely self-reflexive in nature. By far the most self-reflexive was *The George Burns and Gracie Allen Show* (1950–8), whose entire premise revolved around a real-life couple (ex-vaudevillians George Burns and Gracie Allen) who played themselves playing themselves as real-life performers who had a television show based on their lives as television stars. If this is a bit confusing, it should be because the entire show was based on the paradox involved in transforming everyday life into a play for television. Designed to be the television version of *Our Town*, and set for most of its run in the *nouveau riche* suburb of Beverly Hills, the programme featured George Burns as part-time narrator/part-time character, who continually stepped out of his role in the family scene, reflecting on the stage business and the plot.

Although *Burns and Allen* was an extreme example, its self-reflexive theatricality was symptomatic of a general trend in domestic comedies. Sitcoms such as *The Adventures of Ozzie and Harriet* (1952–66), and *I Love Lucy* (1951–7) featured celebrity couples who seemed to be living their family lives on television. Furthermore, a cycle of "showbiz family sitcoms," such as *I Love Lucy*, *The Danny Thomas Show* (1953–64), and *The Dick*

Van Dyke Show (1961–6) worked much like the backstage musical as episodes revolved around families with careers in show business, ambiguously staging performances for a diegetic audience [a fictional audience inside the show] as well as the actual viewer at home.

. . .

In addition to the premises of all of these programmes, the family sitcoms developed formal conventions that presented the home as a proscenium, theatrical space where performances took place. In *Burns and Allen* the domestic space was often revealed to be a stage set as George walked out of the home setting (and his place in the story) in order to go on to a theatre stage where he addressed the camera in first person. Moreover, in numerous family sitcoms, the domestic set was often ambiguously a "realist" element of the story world in which characters interacted and a theatrical stage on which star talents were featured. In suburban sitcoms such as *I Married Joan* (1952–5) and *The Ruggles* (1949–52), the story was often completely derailed as the home was turned into a vaudeville performance space. For example, in a *Ruggles* episode entitled "Charlie's Lucky Day," the domestic setting is suddenly transformed into a stage as numerous comedians, who play highly stereotyped roles reminiscent of stock characters in vaudeville sketches (a policeman, an inventor, and an insurance agent), knock on the door, enter the living room, and begin performing short sketches full of comic banter and broad physical humour. Even in the more "folksy" naturalist comedy of *Ozzie and Harriet*, the interior space of the Nelson home served as a proscenium space in which the celebrity family performed their talents.

. . .

The Voyage Home

By the beginning of the 1960s another metaphor for domesticity began to have increased cultural currency. A perfect example of this transition is a 1959 episode of *Men Into Space* (1959–60) a popular science fiction anthology that was produced with the assistance of the Department of Defense. The episode begins as astronaut Captain Hale returns from the space lab to his suburban home and invites his wife Renza to join him on a voyage that will make her the "first woman on the moon." The excited housewife immediately wonders how many clothes she will be able to bring, how she'll live without her hairdresser, and whether she'll be able to fit the fancy china into the rocket's luggage compartment. As it turns out, her feminine imaginings aren't far from wrong. In fact, once on the moon Renza learns that she is not allowed to go out of the capsule, but instead must stay home and cook anti-gravity Yorkshire puddings for the boys. Isolated and distraught over her inability to get the pudding to rise, Renza finally breaks out on her own. When Captain Hale discovers her moon-walking out of radio-control range he becomes enraged and rails, "Your place is on earth at home." While initially furious, the feisty Renza finally does return to the ship, at least after the couple metaphorically "kiss" and make up by rubbing their space helmets together.

This episode is symptomatic of a shift in the language used to represent suburban domesticity. Now the home was depicted as a space ship that promised to carry occupants away from the conventional roles played in domestic space to the new and exciting frontiers of outer space. Even while this episode ends conservatively, with Renza accepting her role as space wife on the ship, the new metaphor of rocketry serves as a narrative vehicle through which Renza, and by implication the audience, can (at least temporarily) break loose into an imaginary elsewhere, beyond the boundaries of domestic (or in this case space ship) confinement.

. . .

This transition from "home as theatre" to "home as space ship" was, I want to repeat, not smooth or even. Still, the idea of the "home as space ship" gained popular currency during the late 1950s, and through the 1960s it served as a compelling metaphor for suburban family life. Its emergence can be seen in the context of a set of historical transitions, both at the micro-level of everyday life and the level of macroeconomics and politics.

By the end of the 1950s, utopian dreams for consumer prosperity and domestic bliss that the suburbs had once represented were revealing their limits in ways that could no longer be brushed aside. Social criticism of suburbia had become a genre of its own. John Keats's *A Crack in the Picture Window* (1956) presented unflattering pictures of the new suburbanites, with characters like John and Mary Drone, whose lives were spent deciding how to buy washing machines and avoid their busybody neighbours. William Whyte's *The Organization Man* (1956) was a damning critique of the new company boys, whose willingness to conform to job expectations was mirrored by the peer pressure politics of their suburban lifestyles. In *The City in History* (1961), Lewis Mumford criticized the new organization of social space and the homogeneous living arrangements it encouraged. Meanwhile, in women's culture, Betty Friedan's *The Feminine Mystique* (1963) indicted mass media and a host of other social institutions for forcing women to accept the role of "occupation housewife."

What Friedan perhaps didn't notice, however, is that the mass media had already been offering their own criticisms of postwar domesticity and suburban entrapment for women (and men). Science fiction novels such as Philip K. Dick's *Time Out of Joint* (1959) used the suburbs as a trope for the uncanny horrors of banality, while Hollywood genres from science fiction/horror to melodrama to social problem films presented suburbia as a paranoid, claustrophobic space where perverse social relationships reigned in the suburban family sitcom, the housewife's enslavement became a common theme as female characters searched for roles outside the home. For example, an episode of *Father Knows Best* (1954–63) entitled "Margaret's Vacation" shows wife Margaret fed up with her housework and wandering from the family home to a downtown club where she flirts with becoming a beatnik.

Such depictions of suburban domesticity continued throughout the 1960s and into the 1970s. Perhaps in this respect it is no surprise that a new cycle of television sitcoms which represented single girls and later "new liberated women" did so largely by having them move to the city. For example, in *That Girl* (1966–71), the first single girl sitcom to picture a woman living alone, Ann Marie moves from her middle-class suburban town of New Rochelle to New York City. On *The Mary Tyler Moore Show* (1970–7) which is generally seen to inaugurate a cycle of "new woman" sitcoms, Mary Richards moves from her small town suburban life to Minneapolis where she chooses a career over marriage. Significantly, both of these shows (as well as several others of the genre) contained credit sequences that narrativized scenarios of female autonomy through a glorification of city life in which forms of transportation were central narrative vehicles. In *That Girl*, Ann Marie frolics through the streets of New York City as a bus drives by with a picture of her on it. And in the now famous credit sequence of *The Mary Tyler Moore Show*, Mary is shown driving her car to her new Midwestern metropolis as the lyrics remind us that she might just "make it on her own." A similar driving sequence is seen in the second season of *The Doris Day Show* (1968–73) when single mother Doris commutes from her small town to her job in San Francisco.

. . .

As all of these "driving" sequences indicate, the widespread disillusionment with suburban lifestyles that began to mount at the end of the 1950s gave way to a newfound fascination with the trope of transportation in popular media. At least at the level of fantasy, transportation offered a way out of the confines of suburban domesticity and into more exciting locales. Considering the fact that the postwar suburbs were themselves constructed around new transportation systems—i.e. freeways—this is no small irony. Now, in cultural fantasies the freeway system provided a great escape from the very suburban communities that were enabled and perpetuated by it. It is in this context of transportation and its peculiar relation to the suburbs that we might begin to understand how domestic space came to be associated with rocketry over the course of the 1960s.

. . .

I want to suggest that fantasies of suburban domesticity, as well as the escape from it, were translated into the hardware of rocket science during the period of America's space race.

That period, of course, was inaugurated with the advent of Sputnik in October 1957. The Russian launching of the rocket precipitated the most stunning technological embarrassment of the times. Cold War logic was predicated upon America's ability to prevail in all technological endeavours, especially those associated with national security. Thus, the advent of a Russian rocket soaring into orbit sharply contrasted with previous conventions for representing American relations with the Soviets. Sputnik quickly became a media panic, and two months later when America's own rocket, Vanguard I, fell to the ground, the media called it such derisive names as "Flopnik," "Kaputnik," and "Stayputnik." More generally, critics expressed anxieties about the nation's technological agenda, claiming that American science had put its faith in consumer durables rather than concentrating on the truly important goals of national security. As Henry Luce of *Life* said, "For years no knowledgeable U.S. scientist has had any reason to doubt that his Russian opposite number is at least his equal. It has been doubted only by people—some of them in the Pentagon—who confuse scientific progress with freezer and lipstick output."[4] By using freezers and lipstick as examples, Luce not too implicitly suggested that America had put its faith in femininity and domesticity as opposed to the scientific arena more typically associated with men.

. . .

It is in the documentary coverage of the space race that we can begin to see how the trappings of suburban family life came to be communicated through the new image of rocketry and outer space.

. . .

The imagery of space travel obviously captured the attention of the American public. The A. C. Nielsen rating service estimated that the average home was tuned in for five hours and fifteen minutes of the ten-hour coverage of John Glenn's orbital flight on 20 February 1962. This was, according to A. C. Nielsen, "by far the largest audience ever tuned to daytime TV"; even at its "low" moments the programme reached "5 million more homes than typically tuned to the highest rated network [prime time] program, WAGON TRAIN."[5] Presumably, the public's fascination with the new frontier had far surpassed its passion for the old.

It is perhaps no coincidence that the rocket launchings served as an exciting replacement for the quintessial form of televised images of family life—the daytime soaps. Indeed, more generally, the Kennedy administration's notion of satisfying news coverage tended towards family melodrama rather than scientific data. The "documentary" coverage of the space race gave way to an intensive exploration of spectacularized family life with astronaut stars and their wives appearing on the airwaves, in newspapers, and on the covers of national consumer magazines. In these media spectacles, ideals of suburban domesticity and the fantastic voyage to outer space were intricately bound together.

The discursive merger between domestic and outer space found its standard form in *Life*'s biographical essays, which presented technical information alongside multi-page spreads depicting family scenes and life histories of the astronauts. In the 18 May 1962 issue, Scott Carpenter was pictured with his wife Rene on the cover, while the inside story showed family photos of Scott as a child with his grandfather, his pony, his friends, and his modern-day wife and children. The snapshots showed them as the ideal American family: playing at home, enjoying a family vacation, and finally, in the last pages of the essay, saying their farewells just before the space flight. In this way, the photographic narrative sequence suggested that Scott Carpenter's flight to the moon was one more in a series of "everyday" family activities.[6] This became the conventional narration of *Life*'s astronaut profiles in the years to come.

In a practical sense, this essay format allowed the magazines to appeal to diverse audiences because it conveyed technical, scientific information in the popular format of family drama. Discussions of domesticity made space familiar, offering a down-to-earth context for the often abstract reasoning behind space flights. When astronaut John Young went into space in 1965, this merger of science and domesticity was taken to its logical extreme. *Life* reported his flight by telling the story of his wife and children, who witnessed the event on television while sitting in their suburban home:

The Youngs watch. In John Young's home outside Houston, the astronaut's family sits at the TV set as the seconds crawl toward launch time. Barbara Young fidgets, Sandy fiddles with a bit of string and Johnny, still getting over chicken pox, stares unsmiling at the screen. At lift off Mrs. Young hugs Sandy. "Fantastic," she crows . . . as ship soars skyward.[7]

The accompanying photographs show the Young Family sitting before their television set in their suburban home, much as other Americans would have done that day. Here as elsewhere, the "fantastic" is communicated through the domestic, and space technology is itself mediated through the more familial technology of television.

. . .

While the merger of science fiction fantasies and domesticity often served to make outer space seem familiar, it also accomplished the opposite purpose of making the familiar seem strange. As Fredric Jameson has argued, science fiction tends less to imagine the future than to "defamiliarize and restructure our experience of our own present."[8] While Jameson is speaking about literary and filmic texts, we can apply the same rule to other forms of material culture, including the geographical and domestic spaces of the suburbs. The redecoration of suburban towns with "outer-space" architecture and building ornamentation, as well as the new penchant in furniture design and home decor for the space-age look, suggests a profound reorganization of the familiar through the strange. This estrangement of domesticity worked as the central propeller for a model of suburban family life that took transportation—and space travel in particular—as its central metaphor.

Within this new symbolic regime, television's portrayal of family life also looked to the planets. Like Captain and Renza Hale in *Men into Space*, numerous television families were renegotiating their roles through the fantastic possibilities of space science. Programmes such as *My Favorite Martian* (1963–6), *It's About Time* (1966–7), the cartoon sitcom *The Jetsons* (1962–3), and the more "family-drama" oriented (by now cult classic) *Lost in Space* (1965–8) were part of a genre cycle of fantastic family sitcoms in which the suburban family sitcom and science fiction fantasy (or sometimes horror) were joined into a hybrid form.[9] This collision of two unlikely forms gave rise to the moment of "hesitation" which Tzvetan Todorov identifies as the "fantastic."[10] According to Todorov's account, the fantastic often occurs at the point at which the hero or heroine doubts the credibility of the narrative situation (can this be happening, or am I dreaming this?). In addition to this hesitation within the mind of a character, the fantastic also makes the reader uncertain about the status of the text. The story calls its own conventions of representation into question and makes the reader wonder whether the narrative situation is possible at all. In the fantastic family sitcom, the elements called into question are not the supernatural elements of the story (we are never made to question whether genies or Martians exist). Rather, the moment of hesitation takes place in the realm of the natural. We are, in other words, made to question the "naturalness" of middle-class suburban ideals, especially as those ideals had been communicated through the genre conventions of previous suburban sitcoms such as *Ozzie and Harriet* or *Donna Reed*. In place of the suburban sitcom's friendly next-door neighbours and heterosexual nuclear family, the programmes offered neighbourhood snoops and unconventional couples like a talking horse and his master *(Mr. Ed*, 1961–5) or a man and his mother who had been reincarnated as a car *(My Mother the Car*, 1965–6).

The sitcoms with outer space themes were equally unusual. *My Favorite Martian*, for example, was premised on the idea of a Martian who landed in the yard of a young man's suburban home. The Martian took on the double identity of earthling Uncle

Martin, moved in with young man, and hid his true Martian self from suspicious folks around the neighbourhood. This premise not only allowed for a comedic exploration of the social conformity demanded in suburban neighbourhoods, it more specifically can be seen as a programme that worked through nagging anxieties about bachelors, especially bachelors who lived with other men. Uncle Martin was constantly thwarting the advances of his overzealous landlady, who could not understand why he preferred bachelorhood to her womanly ways.

As a companion piece for *My Favorite Martian*'s homophobic nervousness about single men in suburbia, *I Dream of Jeannie* presented anxieties about the single girl. Based on the exploits of astronaut Tony Nelson, who finds a beautiful genie (named Jeannie) after crashing his rocket on a beach, this programme also dealt with the closeted sexuality that suburban social conventions demanded. When Tony brings Jeannie back to his suburban home, he has to hide his live-in supernatural girlfriend from the boys at NASA. But while he tries literally to bottle up Jeannie's powers, she typically escapes the rational logics of masculine science by using her feminine supernatural power to wreak havoc at home and at the space lab. And unlike NASA, which spends billions to get men up to the moon, Jeannie is able to wish her way there in a matter of seconds. The programme thus functions as a contradictory mix of contemporary discourses on swinging singles (with Jeannie as the ultimate playmate who lies around in harem garb and calls her live-in boyfriend "master") and the emerging discourses of women's liberation (with Jeannie as a supernatural and superpowerful woman).

Anthologies such as *The Twilight Zone* (1959–65), *The Outer Limits* (1963–5), and *Science Fiction Theater* (1955–7) also presented stories that linked suburban domesticity to space travel. A central theme was the paranoid fear of difference in suburbia, played out (as in much science fiction of the times) through the figure of the alien. At the height of the Cold War and anti-communist sentiments, *The Twilight Zone*'s "The Monsters on Maple Street" depicted a suburban town where citizens suspected someone in their midst to be a space alien, while the premiere episode of *The Outer Limits*, "The Galaxy Being," showed how suburbanites demonized a kindly extraterrestrial whose only wish was to communicate peacefully with them. And in a period when FHA building policies were predicated on keeping racial "others" out of white suburbs, *Science Fiction Theater*'s "The People from Planet Pecos" presented a space scientist whose suburban home was located next door to a family suspected of being from another planet. Such liberal cautionary tales about interplanetary race relations often included didactic narration that encouraged audiences to question the more familiar acts of racism and xenophobia (as well as other types of social exclusion) in their own everyday suburban towns.

. . .

A Cautionary Tale for Cybernauts

Today, as everyone is caught up in the electronic sublime of cyberspace and the postmodern communities it proposes, it seems especially useful to consider the way suburban living and community space has been imagined in modern times. In one utopian sense, these metaphors of theatricality and space travel have come to stand for the dream places people wish to inhabit; in another way these metaphors have been used to defamiliarize the "lived" suburban spaces that are oppressive in their homogeneity and rigid social expectations; and finally these metaphors have been deployed in blatantly racist, classist, homophobic, and sexist ways to keep the suburbs clean of those "aliens" that won't or can't play the "roles" required of them.

. . .

Hopefully, however, it is by now clear that my point is not that everyday life is distinct from the images used to describe it. Instead, the metaphors by which we live our lives often result in the structures we build to contain them. The metaphors of suburban domesticity that circulate in popular culture serve as a foundational myth for the housing policies and community designs in which we live or cannot live.

Despite the fact that these metaphors are often used in ways that conserve property values at the expense of human justice, there is a positive side to thinking about social life in terms of language. After all, metaphors, as Haraway has taught us, are "software." As such, with some imaginative play, they can be recast and turned into rhetorical tools that we might use to dismantle those very community planning and building policies that have often rendered suburbia a hostile and alienating terrain. From this point of view, thinking about the poetics of suburbia is not merely a literary critic's pastime. Instead, by understanding the language used to represent domestic and community space, we might be able to refashion the cultural myths that organize those spaces. In so doing, we might begin to build more joyous environments in which to lead our everyday lives.

Notes

1. Nelson Foote, "Family Living as Play," *Marriage and Family Living*, 17: 4 (November 1955), pp. 297, 299.
2. Harry Henderson, "Rugged American Collectivism," *Harpers*, November 1953, p. 81 and "The Mass Produced Suburbs, Part II," *Harpers*, December 1953, p. 27.
3. William H. Whyte, Jr, *The Organization Man* (1956: reprint, Garden City, NY: Doubleday, 1957), p. 133.
4. Henry Luce, "Common Sense and Sputnick," *Life*, 21 October 1957, p. 35.
5. Erwin H. Ephron, A. C. Nielson Company Press Release, "News Nielsen: 40 Million Homes Follow Telecast of First U.S. Orbital Flight," White House Central Staff Files, Box 655: File 054, c. 21 March 1962, John Fitzgerald Kennedy Library, p. 1.
6. Loudon Wainwright, "Comes a Quiet Man to Ride Aurora 7," *Life*, 18 May 1961, pp. 32–41.
7. Miguel Acoca, "He's On His Way . . . And It Couldn't Be Prettier," *Life*, 2 April 1965, pp. 36–37.
8. Fredric Jameson, "Progress vs. Utopia: Or Can We Imagine the Future?," *Science Fiction Studies*, 9: 27 (1982), p. 151.
9. See my "From Domestic Space to Outer Space: The 1960s Fantastic Family Sitcom," in *Close Enconters: Film, Feminism, and Science Fiction*, edited by Constance Penley, Elizabeth Lyon, Lynn Spigel, and Janet Bergsrom (Minneapolis: University of Minnesota Press, 1991), pp. 205–35.
10. Tzvetan Todorov, *The Fantastic: A Structural Approach to a Literary Genre*, trans. Richard Howard (Ithaca, NY: Cornell University Press, 1970).

34 Eurocentrism, Polycentrism, and Multicultural Pedagogy: Film and the Quincentennial

Robert Stam

B OTH inside and outside the academy, recent years have witnessed energetic debates about the interrelated issues of Eurocentrism, racism, and multiculturalism. These debates have focused on diverse questions—the historical debate about Columbus, the academic debate about the literary canon, the pedagogical debate about Afrocentric schools—and have invoked many buzzwords: "political correctness," "identity politics," "postcoloniality."

. . .

Although neoconservatives often caricature multiculturalism as calling for the violent jettisoning of the classics and of Western civilization as an area of study, the more radical versions of multiculturalism constitute an assault not on Europe but on Eurocentrism, definable as the procrustean forcing of cultural heterogeneity into a single paradigmatic perspective. Eurocentrism sees Europe as the privileged source of meaning, as the world's center of gravity, as ontological "reality" to the rest of the world's shadow. Eurocentrism, like Renaissance perspective in painting, envisions the world from a single privileged point. It maps the world in a cartography that centralizes and augments Europe while literally "belittling" Africa, and organizes everyday language in binaristic cultural hierarchies implicitly flattering to Europe (our nations/their tribes; our religions/their superstitions; our culture/their folklore).

. . .

As an ideological substratum common to colonialist, imperialist and racist discourse, Eurocentrism is a form of vestigial thinking that permeates and structures contemporary practices and representations even after the formal end of colonialism. Although colonialist discourse and Eurocentric discourse are intimately intertwined, the terms have distinct emphases. While the former explicitly justifies colonialist practices, the latter embeds, takes for granted, and "normalizes" the hierarchical power relations generated by colonialism and imperialism, without necessarily even thematizing those issues directly. Although generated by the colonizing process, Eurocentrism's links to that process are obscured in a kind of buried epistemology.

Eurocentric discourse is complex, contradictory, historically unstable. But in a kind

From Robert Stam, "Eurocentrism, Polycentrism, and Multicultural Pedagogy: Film and the Quincentennial," in Román de la Campa, E. Ann Kaplan, and Michael Sprinker (eds.), *Late Imperial Culture* (London and New York: Verso, 1995), 97–121.

of composite portrait or "ideal type," Eurocentrism as a mode of thought might be seen as engaging in a number of mutually reinforcing intellectual tendencies or operations. (1) Eurocentric discourse projects a linear historical trajectory leading from the Middle East and Mesopotamia to classical Greece (constructed as "pure," "Western," and "democratic") to imperial Rome and then to the metropolitan capitals of Europe and the United States. It renders history as a sequence of empires: Pax Romana, Pax Hispanica, Pax Britannica, Pax Americana. In all cases, Europe, alone and unaided, is seen as the "motor" for progressive historical change: democracy, class society, feudalism, capitalism, the industrial revolution. (2) Eurocentrism attributes to the "West" an inherent progress toward democratic institutions (Torquemada, Mussolini and Hitler must be seen as aberrations within this logic of historical amnesia and selective legitimation). (3) Eurocentrism elides non-European democratic traditions, while obscuring the manipulations embedded in Western formal democracy, and masking the West's part in subverting democracies abroad. (4) Eurocentrism minimizes the West's oppressive practices by regarding them as contingent, accidental, exceptional. Western colonialism, slave trading, and imperialism are not seen as fundamental causes of the West's disproportionate power. (5) Eurocentrism appropriates the cultural and material production of non-Europeans while denying both their achievements and its own appropriation, thus consolidating its sense of self and glorifying its own cultural anthropophagy. In sum, Eurocentrism sanitizes Western history while patronizing and even demonizing the non-West; it thinks of itself in terms of its noblest achievements—science, progress, humanism—but of the non-West in terms of the latter's deficiencies, real or imagined.

. . .

What is missing in much of the discussion of multiculturalism is a notion of ethnic relationality and community answerability. Neoconservatives accuse multiculturalists of Balkanizing the nation, of emphasizing what divides people rather than what brings them together. That the inequitable distribution of power itself generates violence and divisiveness goes unacknowledged; that multiculturalism offers a more egalitarian vision of social relations is ignored. A radical multiculturalism calls for a profound restructuring and reconceptualization of the power relations between cultural communities. Refusing a ghettoizing discourse, it links minoritarian communities, challenging the hierarchy that makes some communities "minor" and others "major" and "normative." Thus, what neoconservatives in fact find threatening about the more radical forms of multiculturalism is the intellectual and political regrouping by which different "minorities" become a majority seeking to move beyond being "tolerated" to forming active intercommunal coalitions.

I would distinguish, therefore, between a co-optive liberal pluralism, tainted at birth by its historical roots in the systematic inequities of conquest, slavery and exploitation, and what I see as a more relational and radical *polycentric multiculturalism*. The notion of polycentrism, in my view, globalizes multiculturalism. It envisions a restructuring of intercommunal relations within and beyond the nation-state according to the internal and partially overlapping imperatives of diverse communities. Within a polycentric vision, the world has many dynamic cultural locations, many possible vantage points.

The emphasis in "polycentrism" is not on spatial relations or points of origin but on fields of power, energy and struggle. The "poly" does not refer to a finite list of centers of power but rather introduces a systematic principle of differentiation, relationality, and linkage. No single community or part of the world, whatever its economic or political power, is epistemologically privileged.

Polycentric multiculturalism differs from liberal pluralism in the following ways. First, unlike a liberal-pluralist discourse of ethical universals—freedom, tolerance, charity—polycentric multiculturalism sees all cultural history in relation to social power. Polycentric multiculturalism is not about "touchy-feely" sensitivity toward other groups; it is about dispersing power, about empowering the disempowered, about transforming institutions and discourses. Polycentric multiculturalism calls for changes not just in images but in power relations. Second, polycentric multiculturalism does not preach a pseudo-equality of viewpoints; its sympathies clearly go to the under-represented, the marginalized, and the oppressed. Third, whereas pluralism is premissed on an established hierarchical order of cultures and is grudgingly accretive—it benevolently "allows" other voices to add themselves to the mainstream—polycentric multiculturalism is celebratory. It thinks and imagines "from the margins," seeing minoritarian communities not as "interest groups" to be "added on" to a preexisting nucleus but rather as active, generative participants at the very core of a shared, conflictual history. Fourth, polycentric multiculturalism grants an "epistemological advantage" to those prodded by historical circumstance into what Du Bois called "double consciousness," to those familiar with both "margins" and "center" (or even with many margins and many centers), and thus ideally placed to "deconstruct" dominant or narrowly national discourses. Fifth, polycentric multiculturalism rejects a unified, fixed, and essentialist concept of identities (or communities) as consolidated sets of practices, meanings and experiences. Rather, it sees identities as multiple, unstable, historically situated, the products of ongoing differentiation and polymorphous identifications and pluralizations. Sixth, polycentric multiculturalism goes beyond narrow definitions of identity politics, opening the way for informed affiliation on the basis of shared social desires and identifications. Seventh, polycentric multiculturalism is reciprocal, dialogical; it sees all acts of verbal or cultural exchange as taking place not between essential discrete bounded individuals or cultures but rather between mutually permeable, changing individuals and communities. (Henceforth, I will use the term "multiculturalism" in the radical sense outlined here.)

. . .

Our collective goal as educators, at this point, should be to "deprovincialize" our students, and this in both temporal and spatial terms. To understand present-day representations, students need to understand the longer history of a colonialist discourse accreted and sedimented over centuries, traceable in part to typically Western binarisms and hierarchies but also traceable historically to the grand encounter of an expanding Europe with its African, Asian aud American "others." A polycentric audiovisual pedagogy, in this sense, might play off Eurocentric self-idealizations against alternative perspectives, using film and video in order to deconstruct and subvert the Eurocentrism whose fundamental operations have just been outlined.

Columbus and Audiovisual Pedagogy

For just one example of such an audiovisual pedagogy, we might think about the recent quincentennial debates about the historical legacy of Columbus.

. . .

The Columbus story is crucial to Eurocentrism, not only because Columbus was a seminal figure within the history of colonialism, but also because idealized versions of his story have served to initiate generation after generation into the colonial paradigm. For many children in North America and elsewhere, the tale of Columbus is totemic; it introduces them not only to the concepts of "discovery" and the "New World," but also to the idea of history itself. The vast majority of school textbooks, including very recent ones, as Bill Bigelow points out, describe and picture Columbus as handsome, studious, pious, commanding, audacious. Young pupils are induced to empathize with what are imagined to be his childhood dreams and hopes, so that their identification with him is virtually assured even before they encounter the New World others, who are described variously as friendly or as fierce, but whose perspective is rigorously elided.[1] Only some voices and perspectives, it is implied, resonate in the world.

. . .

The quincentennial period brought not only two adulatory Hollywood superproductions and a Public Broadcasting Service (PBS) special, but also a number of critical, revisionist features and protest documentaries whose titles reveal their anti-Columbus thrust: *Surviving Columbus* (1990); *Columbus on Trial* (1992); *The Columbus Invasion* (1992); and *Columbus Didn't Discover Us* (1991). Cinematic recreations of the past reshape the imagination of the present, legitimating or interrogating hegemonic memories and assumptions. The mainstream films devoted to Columbus prolong the pedagogic role of the pro-Columbus textbooks. Indeed, such films exercise more influence over the representation of Columbus (and thus over perceptions of colonial history) than any number of debates and protests. There is surprisingly little difference, in this respect, between the 1949 (British) David Macdonald film *Christopher Columbus* and the recent (1992) Salkind superproduction *Columbus: the Discovery*. Although almost a half-century separates the two films, their idealizations of Columbus are virtually identical. Both films portray Columbus as a man of vision, an avatar of modernity and the Christian faith struggling against obstacles of superstition, ignorance, and envy. Both films relay the old chestnut that "they all laughed at Christopher Columbus, when he said the world was round," when in fact most educated Europeans (and Arabs) knew very well the world was round. Both emphasize European antagonists, and especially the aristocrat Bobadilla, and thus displace attention from the more fundamental antagonism of Europe and the indigenous peoples. In both films, Columbus is charismatic, attractive, and a loving father, a man whose fundamental motivations are not mercantile but religious—to convert the "heathen"—and scientific—to prove his thesis about the shape of the globe.

The 1949 film, featuring Fredric March as Columbus, is almost comically teleological, in that it has Columbus speak anachronistically of the "new world" at a time when the historical Columbus was unaware of its existence. Millions of benighted "heathens," the dialog informs us, are simply "waiting to be converted." Commentative music translates the film's Manicheanism into contrastive harmonies; the music associated with Columbus is choral/religious, that associated with the natives is ominous, provoking an acoustic sense of menace and encirclement. (The music's orientalizing overtones replay Columbus's own transfer of cultural stereotypes from East to West.) When Columbus arrives in the Caribbean, the mass of natives spontaneously applaud the conquest of their own land and seem to acquiesce in their own enslavement. They immediately abandon their beliefs and their culture, it is implied, and embrace those of Europe as irresistibly and charismatically true. Their spontaneous genuflections translate Columbus's own phantasy—namely, that his reading of a text in Spanish to uncomprehending natives signifies a legitimate transfer of ownership—into veristic representation.

Although Columbus's greed led him to demand, upon pain of hanging, that every Taino man, woman and child over fourteen deliver, every three months, a hawk's bell crammed with gold, the film makes Columbus himself the outspoken critic of unfair trade practices. "We are here to convert the natives," he tells a greedy underling, "not to exploit them;" Although the natives are supposedly played by indigenous people from the "Carib reserve" on Dominica island, they never achieve the status of characters, nor is their acting credited. They literally have no voice, no language, no dialog, and no apparent point of view beyond cheerful collaboration with European designs. Exhibited in the Spanish Court alongside the New World parrots, the Tainos show no discomfort with their role. Indeed, the parrots are granted more voice than the natives; they are allowed to squawk: "Long Live the King! Long Live the Queen! Long Live the Admiral!"

. . .

The very title of the 1992 Salkind film—*Columbus: The Discovery*—betrays its makers' contempt for all those who have objected to the term "discovery." According to its producer, the film is an "adventure picture" combining "aspects of *Lawrence of Arabia* and *Robin Hood*" and featuring "no politics." The generic choice of adventure film, the intertextual reference to an orientalist classic, and the tendentious use of "no politics" to mean "no opposition politics," are in keeping with the general tone of the film. That the Salkinds were the producing team behind the first *Superman* films (1978, 1981), *The Three Musketeers* (1974) and *Santa Claus—the Movie* (1985), and that the chosen director (John Glen) was a veteran of several James Bond films, might have forewarned us about the heroic paradigm into which Columbus was about to be placed. Since the film covers only Columbus's campaign to win Queen Isabella's support, his first voyage, and his return in glory to Spain, it can ignore the death by massacre or disease that befell thousands of Indians after Columbus's second voyage. From the beginning, Columbus is portrayed as the personification of individual initiative overcoming bureaucratic inertia. Despite the historical Columbus's arcane views about so many subjects (mermaids, cannibals, devils), he is portrayed as the voice of modern rationality. That the role is incarnated by a handsome actor (George Corraface) further enforces spectatorial identification. Symphonic European music constantly supports the swelling ambition of Columbus's enterprise whilst virtually every scene adds a humanizing touch. At one point, Columbus gives a young Jewish cabin boy a free ticket out of anti-Semitic Spain. The natives, meanwhile, are reduced to mute, admiring witnesses who regard white men as gods. They barely speak to one another, and seem to have no vibrant culture. The film portrays the native women as flirtatious toward the Europeans, while the *mise-en-scéne* exploitatively places their nudity center-screen. No full picture of indigenous life, or of their reaction to the conquest, is developed.

Ridley Scott's *1492: The Conquest of Paradise*, meanwhile, is erratically revisionist, yet fundamentally protective of Columbus's good name. Here the scintillating beauty of the cinematography enfolds the violence of conquest into the ideology of the aesthetic. The film makes token acknowledgements of the present-day controversies surrounding Columbus, but in highly ambiguous ways. Once again, Columbus (Gerard Depardieu) is the central figure, subjectivized through voiceover, sycophantic close-ups, and empathetic music; and once again, he is the voice of faith, science, and modernity. *1492* covers a greater number of Columbus's voyages (although the four voyages are reduced to three) and portrays him as being occasionally brutal as well as magnanimous. With sets built in Seville and Grenada, the film shows the final siege of the Moors in Grenada, and portrays Columbus, on the basis of no known historical evidence, as outraged by the Inquisition. Throughout we are sutured into his vantage point, while the music encodes a binarist perspective; choral music with ecclesiastical overtones cues sympathy for Columbus, while brooding dissonance subliminally instructs us to fear the natives despite an otherwise positive portrayal. And indeed, on some levels the film does pay respect to indigenous culture. The Indians speak their own language, and complain that Columbus has never learned it. A native shaman takes care of the European sick, and in general the natives act with gentleness and dignity, although there is no hint that Columbus helped eradicate complex civilizations. What looks like forced labor is shown, but Columbus's crucial role in it is obscured, while the film scapegoats an underling figure (a scheming Spanish nobleman who happens to look very much like an Indian) as the racist, and Columbus as his antagonist. With the upgrading of the native image goes a parallel upgrading of Columbus. An enlightened version of the traditional figure, he sympathizes with the Indians and treats them just as he treats Spanish noble-men. It is as if the film combined the personalities and ideologies of Columbus and Bartolome de las Casas; as if the "discoverer" had been retroactively endowed with the conscience of the radical priest.

The seven-hour PBS documentary *Columbus and the Age of Discovery* (1991), mean-while, careens between occasional liberal-sympathetic images of indigenous people and a generally conservative glorification of Columbus's enterprise. The opening image of the ocean, followed by a caravelle, already positions the spectator within the perspective of the voyagers, those who made the "encounter" possible. The orienting questions are: "Who was the man Columbus?" and: "Should we celebrate Columbus's achievement as a great discovery . . . or should we mourn a world forever lost?" The series thus con-fronts us with a dubious choice—celebrate Columbus or mourn a presumably vanished civilization—leaving no room for activism or solidarity in the present. Although the film does sporadically show some of the suffering generated by the Conquest, it explicitly exhorts us, in the final episode, to "celebrate Columbus." More important, the series is structured as a voyage/inquiry into the mind of Columbus. There is no attempt to explore the cognition and understanding of the indigenous people. The series's subplot, meanwhile, revolves around the mobilization of the energies of the modern participants (shipbuilders, navigators, cartographers, historians) who reenact Columbus' first voyage in replica vessels under the auspices of the Spanish Navy. Why would people today be so psychically and financially "invested," one wonders, in literally following in Columbus's tracks, if his voyage did not speak to them in quasi-mythic terms? Attitudes, one suspects, are being replicated along with the ships. (Entrepreneurs have often replicated the *Niña*, the *Pinta* and the *Santa María*; did they ever replicate a slave ship?)

. . .

Revisionist Film and the Quincentennial

Only recently have films begun to offer a critical perspective on the conquest. A proleptic anti-quincentennial film, Glauber Rocha's *Land in Anguish* (1967), an allegory about contemporaneous Brazilian politics, satirically reenacts the arrival of Brazil's Columbus—Pedro Cabral—on the shores of Brazil in the year 1500. The right-wing figure of the film (named Porfino Diaz after the Mexican dictator who slaughtered thousands of "Indians") arrives from the sea, suggesting a myth of national origins. Carrying a black banner and a crucifix and dressed in an anachronistic modern-day suit, he is seen alongside a priest in an old Catholic habit, a sixteenth-century conquistador, and a symbolic feathered Indian. A huge cross is fixed in the sand as Diaz approaches it to kneel and perform a ritual evoking, for the Brazilian spectator, the famous "first mass" celebrated in the newly "discovered" land, but in an anachronistic manner that stresses continuities between the *conquista* and modern oppression. Yoruba religious chants pervade the soundtrack, evoking the "transe" of the Portuguese title and suggesting, perhaps, an Afro-indigenous link.

Land in Anguish anticipated a number of more recent revisionist historical films, set in the initial period of conquest, which relativize and even invert colonialist perspectives on the Conquest. The Mexican film *Cabeza de Vaca* (1989) tells the story of Alvar Nuñez Cabeza de Vaca, the shipwrecked Spaniard who went by foot from Florida to Texas. The film's source text, Alvar Nuñez's *Relación de los Naufragios*, already relates the Conquest as a story of failure. Inverting the usual roles, Nuñez portrays the Spaniards as vulnerable, as losing control, weeping, supplicating. And while a phantasmatic cannibalism usually serves to justify European exploitation, here it is the Spanish, as occasionally did occur, who cannibalize one another, and the natives who watch in horror. Although the film version fails to humanize the Indians, it does expose the underside of European religious proselytizing, and shows the conquistadores, not the natives, as the real cannibals. The Venezuelan film *Jericó*, meanwhile, largely adopts the indigenous perspective, while respecting the languages, histories, and cultural styles of the indigenous groups portrayed. Jericho's story evokes what was actually a not infrequent occurrence during the first centuries of conquest—the case of the European who "goes native." In Mexico, Gonzalo Guerrero, a Spaniard kidnapped by Indians in the Yucatan, ultimately became a Cacique with tattooed face and pierced ears.[2] And in North America, as Hector de Crèvecoeur noted, thousands of Europeans became "white Indians" (to the point that some colonies passed laws against "indianizing"), while "we have no examples of even one of these Aborigines having from choice become Europeans."[3]

Jericó concerns a Franciscan priest, Santiago, the lone survivor of a sixteenth-century expedition led by the cruel conquistador Gascuna, in search of the mythic Mar del Sur. Although Santiago hopes to spiritually conquer the Indians, he is in fact spiritually conquered by them. While their captive, he comes to question European attitudes toward religion, the body, the earth, and social life, and finally renounces his evangelical mission. Whereas most Hollywood films have the "Indians" speak a laughable pidgin English, here the natives laugh at the priest's garbled attempt to speak *their* language. In the end, Santiago is retaken by the Spaniards, who regard his "going native" as a form of madness and heresy. What makes this revisionist captivity narrative so subversive is that it transforms what official Europe regarded with fear and loathing—indigenous culture—into a seductive pole of attraction for Europeans.

. . .

The most remarkable recent development in relation to the larger relations between Europeans and the native peoples of the Americas has been the emergence of "indigenous media," that is the use of audiovisual technology (camcorders, video cassette recorders—VCRs) for the cultural and political purposes of indigenous peoples. The phrase "indigenous media" itself, as Faye Ginsberg points out, is oxymoronic, evoking both the self-understanding of aboriginal groups and the vast institutional structures of television and cinema. Within indigenous media, the producers are themselves the receivers, along with neighboring communities. Occasionally, videos are sent to distant cultural institutions or festivals. The two most active producers of indigenous media production in the Americas are native (especially Arctic) North Americans (Inuit, Yup'ik) and the Indians of the Amazon Basin (Nambiquara, Kayapo). Indigenous media, while not a panacea for the social ills afflicting native peoples, is an empowering vehicle for communities struggling against geographical displacement, ecological and economic deterioration, and cultural annihilation.

In Brazil, the *Centro de Trabalho Indigenista* (Center for Work with Indigenous Peoples) has been working in collaboration with indigenous groups since 1979, teaching videomaking and editing, and offering technologies and facilities in order to protect indigenous land and consolidate resistance. In Vincent Carelli's *The Spirit of TV* (1991), the Waiapi people, newly introduced to television, reflect on ways that video can be used to make contact with other peoples and defend themselves against the encroachments of federal agents, goldminers, and loggers. Taking an eminently pragmatic approach, the Waiapi ask the filmmakers to hide their weakness to the outside world; "exaggerate our strength," they say, "so they won't occupy our land." In *Arco de Zo'e* (Meeting Ancestors, 1993), Chief Wai-Wai recounts his visit to the Zo'e, a recently contacted group whom the Waiapi had known only through video images. The two groups compare hunting and weaving techniques, food, rituals, myths and history. The film communicates the diversity of indigenous cultures—Chief Wai-Wai has difficulty adjusting to the total nudity of his hosts, for example. *Like Brothers* (1993), lastly, recounts the cultural exchange between the Parakateje of Para and their relatives the Kraho of Tocantins. The two groups exchange information and strategies for maintaining their language and identity and for resisting Euro-Brazilian domination. In all the films, the "outside" spectator is no longer the privileged interlocutor; video is primarily a facilitator for exchange between indigenous groups. On a secondary level, "outsiders" are welcome to view these exchanges and even support the cause in financial or other ways, but there is no romantic narrative of redemption whereby the raising of spectatorial consciousness will somehow "save the world." In these videos, the First World spectator must become accustomed to "Indians" who laugh, who are ironical, and who are quite prepared to speak of the absolute necessity of killing non-Indian invaders.

Among the most media-savvy of the indigenous groups are the Kayapo, a Go-speaking people of central Brazil who live in fourteen communities scattered over an area roughly the size of Great Britain. When a documentary crew from Granada Television went to Brazil to film the Kayapo in 1987, the Kayapo demanded videocameras, VCR, monitor and videotapes as the quid pro quo for their cooperation They have subsequently used video to record their own traditional ceremonies, demonstrations, and encounters with whites (so as to have the equivalent of a legal transcript). They have documented their traditional knowledge of the forest environment, and plan to record the transmission of myths and oral history. For the Kayapo, as Terry Turner puts it, video media have become "not merely a means of representing culture . . . but themselves the ends of social action and objectification in consciousness."[4] The Kayapo not only sent a delegation to the Brazilian Constitutional Convention to lobby delegates debating indigenous rights, but also videotaped themselves in the process, winning international attention for their cause. Widely disseminated images of the Kayapo wielding video cameras, appearing in *Time* and the *New York Times Magazine*, derive their power to shock from the premiss that "natives" must be quaint and allochronic ("real" Indians don't carry camcorders).

In the Granada Television documentary *Kayapo: Out of the Forest* (1989), we see the Kayapo and other native peoples stage a mass ritual performance to protest the planned construction of a hydroelectric dam. One of the Kayapo leaders, Chief Pombo, points out that the name of the proposed dam, *"Kararao,"* is taken from a Kayapo war cry. Another, Chief Raoni, appears with the rock star Sting in a successful attempt to capture international media attention. At one point a woman presses a machete against the company spokesman's face as she scolds him in Kayapo. Another woman, in a remarkable reversal of colonialist *écriture*, tells the spokesman to write down her name, reminding him that she is one of those who will die. The spectator enamored of "modernity" comes to question the reflex association of hydroelectric dams with an axiomatically good "progress."

The case of the Kayapo reminds us that polycentric multiculturalism cannot simply be "nice," like a suburban barbecue or teaparty. Any substantive multiculturalism has to recognize the existential realities of pain, anger and even rage, since the multiple cultures invoked by the term multiculturalism have not historically existed within relations of equality and mutual respect. A polycentric perspective would recognize not only difference but even irreconcilable difference. The Native American view of the land as a sacred and communal trust, as Vine Deloria points out, is simply not reconcilable with the European view of land as alienable property. The descendants of the slave ships and the descendants of the immigrant ships cannot look at the Washington Monument, or Ellis Island, through exactly the same viewfinder. But these gaps in perception are not unbridgeable; they do not preclude community answerability, alliances, dialogical coalitions, intercommunal identifications and affinities.

Central to polycentric multiculturalism is the notion of mutual and reciprocal relativization, the idea that the diverse cultures in play should each come to perceive the limitations of their own cultural perspective. Each group offers what Bakhtin calls its own "excess seeing;" hopefully they come not only to "see" other groups, but also, through a salutary estrangement, to see how it is itself seen, not in order to completely embrace the other perspective but at least to recognize it, acknowledge it, take it into account. By counterpointing cultural perspectives, we practice what Michael Fischer calls "defamiliarization by crosscultural juxtaposition." But historical configurations of power and knowledge generate a clear asymmetry within this relativization. The powerful are not accustomed to being relativized; most of the world's representations are tailored to the measure of their narcissism. Thus a sudden relativization by a less flattering perspective is experienced as a shock, an outrage, giving rise to the hysterical neoconservative discourse of victimization and reverse discrimination. Subaltern groups, in contrast, are not only historically accustomed to being relativized, they also display a highly relativizing, even irreverent attitude toward the dominant culture. Multiculturalism should not be seen as a favor, something intended to make other people feel good about themselves; it also makes an epistemological contribution. More than a response to a demographic challenge, multiculturalism is a long-overdue course correction, a gesture toward historical lucidity, a matter not of charity but of simple justice; it is not a gift, but an indispensable part of the global decolonization of cultural life.

Notes

1. Bill Bigelow, "Discovering Columbus, Re-reading the Past," in *Rethinking Columbus,* a special quincentenary issue of *Rethinking Schools* (1991).

2. Quoted in Stephen Greenblatt, *Marvelous Possessions: The Wonder of the New World* (Chicago: University of Chicago Press, 1991), p. 141.

3. From Hector St John de Crèvecoeur, *Letters from an American Farmer,* quoted in James Axtell, *The European and the Indian: Essays in the Ethnohistory of Colonial North America* (New York: Oxford, 1981), p. 172.

4. See Terence Turner's fascinating account of his longstanding collaboration with the Kayapo in "Visual Media, Cultural Politics and Anthropological Practice," *Independent,* 14: 1 (January/February 1991).

35 "Out of the Closet and into the Universe"

Queers and *Star Trek*

Henry Jenkins

Star Trek celebrates its 25th anniversary in 1991. In that quarter century, one of the most important aspects of the series . . . has been the vision that humanity will one day put aside its differences to work and live in peace together. *Star Trek*, in its various television and motion picture forms, has presented us with Africans, Asians, Americans and Andorians, Russians and Romulans, French and Ferengi, Hispanics and Hortas, human and non-human men and women. In 25 years, it has also never shown an openly gay character.

> (Franklin Hummel, *Gaylactic Gazette*)[1]

Perhaps someday our ability to love won't be so limited.

> (Dr Beverley Crusher, "The Host,"
> *Star Trek: The Next Generation*)

"2, 4, 6, 8, how do you know Kirk is straight?" the Gaylaxians chanted as they marched down the streets of Boston on Gay Pride day. "3, 5, 7, 9, he and Spock have a real fine time!" The chant encapsulates central issues of concern to the group: How do texts determine the sexual orientation of their characters and how might queer spectators gain a foothold for self-representation within dominant media narratives? How has *Star Trek* written gays and lesbians out of its future, and why do the characters and their fans so steadfastly refuse to stay in the closet?

. . .

The Boston Area Gaylaxians is a local chapter of the international Gaylactic Network Inc., an organization for gay, lesbian and bisexual science fiction fans and their friends.[2] Founded in 1987, the group has chapters in many cities in the United States and Canada. Adopting the slogan, "Out of the closet and into the universe", the group has sought to increase gay visibility within the science fiction fan community and "to help gay fans contact and develop friendships with each other".[3] The group hosts a national convention, Gaylaxicon, which brings together fans and writers interested in sexuality and science fiction. Although only recently given official recognition from the Network, group members have organized a national letter-writing campaign to urge Paramount

From Henry Jenkins, "'Out of the Closet and into the Universe': Queers and *Star Trek*," in J. Tulloch and H. Jenkins, *Science Fiction Audiences: Watching "Dr Who" and "Star Trek"* London and New York: Routledge, 1995), 237–65.

to acknowledge a queer presence in the twenty-fourth-century future represented on *Star Trek: The Next Generation*. Their efforts have so far attracted national attention from both the gay and mainstream press and have provoked responses from production spokespeople and several cast members. Gene Roddenberry publicly committed himself to incorporate gay characters into the series in the final months before his death, but the producers never delivered on that promise. The series *has* featured two episodes which can loosely be read as presenting images of alternative sexuality, "The Host," and "The Outcast." Although the producers have promoted these stories as responsive to the gay and lesbian community's concerns, both treat queer lifestyles as alien rather than familiar aspects of the Federation culture and have sparked further controversy and dissatisfaction among the Gaylaxians.

The fans' requests are relatively straightforward—perhaps showing two male crew members holding hands in the ship's bar, perhaps a passing reference to a lesbian lover, some evidence that gays, bisexuals and lesbians exist in the twenty-fourth century represented on the programme. Others want more—an explicitly gay or lesbian character, a regular presence on the series, even if in a relatively minor capacity. As far as the producers are concerned, homosexuality and homophobia are so tightly interwoven that there is no way to represent the first without simultaneously reintroducing the second, while for the fans, what is desired is precisely a future which offers homosexuality without homophobia.

. . .

Intervention Analysis and Fan Culture

This chapter, thus, documents the Gaylaxians' struggles with Paramount over the issue of queer visibility on *Star Trek*, their efforts to gain a public acknowledgement that gay, lesbian and bisexual people belong within the programme's utopian community. I write from a partisan position within this debate as a *Star Trek* fan and a member of the Gaylaxians. John Hartley has called upon media scholars to engage in what he calls intervention analysis: "Intervention analysis seeks not only to describe and explain existing dispositions of knowledge, but also to change them.[4] Hartley advocates that media scholars write from the position(s) of media audiences, recognizing and articulating the interpretive work which viewers perform, documenting their creative engagement with the media content. Hartley continues:

Intervention analysis certainly needs to take popular television more or less as it finds it, without high-culture fastidiousness or right-on political squeamishness, but it needs to intervene *in* the media and in the production of popular knowledges *about* them.[5]

Intervention analysis, Hartley argues, speaks from, about and for the margins of popular culture.

My goal is thus to intervene in the debates about queer visibility on *Star Trek*, to trace the discursive logic by which producers have sought to exclude and fans have sought to include queer characters, to situate this issue within a larger social and cultural context of queer reception of science fiction and network representation of alternative sexuality. My goal is not to instruct or politicize audience response, since I believe that fans already exercise a form of grassroots cultural politics which powerfully reflects their interests in the media and their own ideological stakes. We need to create a context where fan politics may be acknowledged and accepted as a valid contribution to the debates about mass culture.

. . .

Children of Uranus[6]

> During the course of our production, there have been many special interest groups who have lobbied for their particular cause. It is Gene Roddenberry's policy to present *Star Trek* as he sees it and not to be governed by outside influences.
>
> (Susan Sackett, executive assistant to Gene Roddenberry)[7]
>
> We had been the target of a concerted, organized movement by gay activists to put a gay character on the show.
>
> (Michael Piller, *Star Trek* writing staff supervisor)[8]
>
> In the late 1960's, a "special interest group" lobbied a national television network to renew a series for a third season. If those networks had not listened to those with a special interest, *Star Trek* would not have returned and today *Star Trek* might very likely not be all of what it has become. You, Mr. Roddenberry, and *Star Trek* owe much to a special interest group: *Star Trek* fans. Perhaps you should consider listening to some of those same fans who are speaking to you now.
>
> (Franklin Hummel)[9]

The people who organized the national letter-writing campaign to get a queer character included on *Star Trek: The Next Generation* were not "outside influences," "special interest groups" or "gay activists." They saw themselves as vitally involved with the life of the series and firmly committed to its survival. As Hummel asserts, "we are *part* of *Star Trek*." They saw their goals not as antagonistic to Roddenberry's artistic vision but rather as logically consistent with the utopian politics he had articulated in *The Making of Star Trek* and elsewhere.

. . .

The fans reminded Roddenberry that he had said:

To be different is not necessarily to be ugly; to have a different idea is not necessarily wrong. The worst possible thing that can happen to humanity is for all of us to begin to look and act and think alike.[10]

When, they asked, was *Star Trek* going to acknowledge and accept sexual "difference" as part of the pluralistic vision it had so consistently evoked? They cited his successful fight to get a black woman on the *Enterprise* bridge and his unsuccessful one to have a female second-in-command, and wondered aloud "why can't *Star Trek* be as controversial in educating people about our movement as they were for the black civil rights movement?" (James).[11]

The people who organized the letter-writing campaign were *Star Trek* fans and, as such, they claimed a special relationship to the series, at once protective and possessive, celebratory and critical.

. . .

The producers' refusal to represent gay and lesbian characters cut deeply:

Frank: They betrayed everything *Star Trek* was—the vision of humanity I have held for over 25 years. They betrayed Gene Roddenberry and his vision and all the fans. They didn't have the guts to live up to what *Star Trek* was for.

. . .

To understand the intensity of the Gaylaxians' responses, we need to consider more closely what science fiction as a genre has offered these gay, lesbian and bisexual fans. David, a member of the Boston group, described his early experiences with the genre:

I wasn't very happy with my world as it was and found that by reading science fiction or fantasy, it took me to places where things were possible, things that couldn't happen in my normal, everyday life. It would make it possible to go out and change things that I hated about my life, the world in general, into something that was more comfortable for me, something that would allow me to become what I really wanted to be. . . . Being able to work out prejudices in different ways. Dealing with man's inhumanity to man. To have a vision for a future or to escape and revel in glory and deeds that have no real mundane purpose. To be what you are and greater than the world around you lets you be.

Lynne, another Gaylaxian, tells a smiliar story:

I wasn't very happy with my life as a kid and I liked the idea that there might be someplace else where things were different. I didn't look for it on this planet. I figured it was elsewhere. I used to sit there in the Bronx, looking up at the stars, hoping that a UFO would come and get me. Of course, it would never land in the Bronx but I still had my hopes.

What these fans describe is something more than an abstract notion of escapism—the persistent queer fantasy of a space beyond the closet doorway. Such utopian fantasies can provide an important first step towards political awareness, since utopianism allows us to envision an alternative social order which we must work to realize ("something positive to look forward to") and to recognize the limitations of our current situation (the dystopian present against which the utopian alternative can be read).

. . .

Writers like Marion Zimmer Bradley, Joanna Russ and Samuel R. Delany were writing science fiction novels in the 1960s which dealt in complex ways with issues of sexual orientation and envisioned futures which held almost unlimited possibilities for gays and lesbians.[12] These writers' efforts opened possibilities for a new generation of queer authors, working in all subgenres, to introduce gay, bisexual and lesbian characters within otherwise mainstream science fiction stories. A key shift has been the movement from early science fiction stories that treated homosexuality as a profoundly alien sexuality towards stories that deal with queer characters as a normal part of the narrative universe and that treat sexuality as simply one aspect of their characterization.[13]

. . .

Nobody had expected the original *Star Trek* series, released in a pre-Stonewall society, to address directly the concerns of gay, lesbian and bisexual fans. They had taken it on faith that its vision of a United Federation of Planets, of intergalactic cooperation and acceptance, included them as vital partners. Yet, when *Star Trek: The Next Generation* appeared, at a time when queer characters had appeared on many American series, they hoped for something more, to be there on the screen, an explicit presence in its twenty-fourth century.

. . .

Where No [Gay] Man Has Gone Before

> Mr. Roddenberry has always stated that he would be happy to include a character of *any* special interest group if such a character is relevant to the story.
>
> (Susan Sackett)[14]
>
> Were Uhura and LeForge included because the fact they were black was relevant to a story? Was Sulu included because the fact he was Asian was important to the plot? Were Crusher and Troi and Yar included because the fact they were female was relevant to an episode? I do not think so. These characters were included because they were important to the *spirit* of *Star Trek*.
>
> (Franklin Hummel)[15]

"We expected *Star Trek* to do it because we expected more of *Star Trek* than other series," one fan explained. They looked around them and saw other series—*LA Law, Heartbeat, Thirtysomething, Quantum Leap, Northern Exposure, Days of Our Lives, Roseanne*—opening up new possibilities for queer characters on network television, while their programme could only hint around the possibility that there might be some form of sexuality out there, somewhere beyond the known universe, which did not look like heterosexuality. *Star Trek* was no longer setting the standards for other programmes.

"Sooner or later, we'll have to address the issue," Roddenberry had told a group of Boston fans in November 1986, while *Star Trek: The Next Generation* was still on the drawing boards: "We should probably have a gay character on *Star Trek*."[16] "For your information, the possibility that several members of the Enterprise crew might be gay has been discussed in a very positive light. It is very much an area that a show like *Star Trek* should address," acknowledged David Gerrold, the man assigned to prepare the programme Bible for *Star Trek: The Next Generation*.[17]

What were the Gaylaxians to make of the absence of gays and lesbians in the pro-gramme universe, of Roddenberry's silence on the subject, as season after season came and went? Steve K., writing in *The Lavender Dragon*, a fan newsletter, saw only two possibilities consistent with the fan community's realist reading of the series:

As a U.S. Navy veteran, I have had firsthand experience with the military's discrimination against gays and lesbians. It could be that the United Federation of Planets also bans homosexuals from serving in Starfleet. . . . That would explain the large number of never-married officers on board the Enterprise. Except for Dr. Crusher, none of the regular officers have been married (chiefs, e.g. Chief O'Brian, are non-commissioned officers like sergeants). Does Starfleet have a huge closet? Still, this does leave the problem of civilian homosexuals. Since many of the episodes involve interaction with non-Starfleet characters, you would think that occasionally a gay or lesbian character would be somewhere in the 24th century. Has the Federation found a "cure" for homosexuality?[18]

Invisibility meant either that gays were closeted or that they had ceased to exist. Neither was an attractive alternative to a group, whose motto, after all, is "Out of the closet and into the universe."

If they had listened more carefully, the fans might have recognized the slippage in Roddenberry's original comments, from including gay people as *characters* to dealing with homosexuality as an *issue*. What the Gaylaxians wanted was to be visible without being an "issue" or a "problem" which the script writers needed to confront and resolve.

. . .

As Theresa M. wrote:

I want to see men holding hands and kissing in Ten-Forward. I want to see a smile of joy on Picard's face as he, as captain, joins two women together in a holy union, or pain across his face when he tells a man that his same-sex mate has been killed in battle. I want to hear Troi assure a crew member, questioning their mixed emotions, that bisexuality is a way to enjoy the best of what both sexes have to offer. I want to see crew members going about their business and acting appropriately no matter what their sexual orientation in every situation.[19]

Such moments of public affection, community ritual or psychological therapy were common aspects of the programme text; the only difference would be that in this case, the characters involved would be recognizably queer. The fans wanted to be visible participants within a future which had long since resolved the problem of homophobia. They felt this utopian acceptance to be more consistent with the programme's ideology than a more dystopian representation of the social problems they confronted as gays, lesbians and bisexuals living in a still largely homophobic society.

The programme's producers would seem to agree, since their public responses to the letter-writing campaign often presuppose that queers would have gained tolerance and acceptance within *Star Trek*'s future, yet they evaded attempts to make this commitment visible on the screen.

. . .

One can identify a series of basic assumptions about the representation of gay identities which underlie the producers' responses to the letter-writing campaign:

1. The explicit representation of homosexuality within the programme text would require some form of labelling while a general climate of tolerance had made the entire issue disappear. As Roddenberry explained in a statement released to the gay newspaper, *The Advocate*, "I've never found it necessary to do a special homosexual-theme story because people in the time line of *The Next Generation*, the 24th century, will not be labeled."[20]

2. The representation of homosexuality on *Star Trek* would necessarily become the site of some form of dramatic conflict. As Richard Arnold, the man appointed to serve as *Star Trek*'s liaison with the fan community, explained:

In Gene Roddenberry's 24th century *Star Trek* universe, homosexuality will not be an issue as it is today. How do you, then, address a non-issue? No one aboard the starship could care less what anyone else's sexual preference would be. . . . Do not ask us to show conflict aboard the Enterprise when it comes to people's choices over their sex, politics or religion. By that time, all choices will be respected equally.[21]

The producers, in a curious bit of circular logic, were insisting that the absence of gays and lesbians in the *Star Trek* universe was evidence of their acceptance within the Federation, while their visibility could only be read as signs of conflict, a renewed eruption of homophobia.

3. Representation of homosexuality on *Star Trek* would make their sexuality "obvious" and therefore risk offence. As Arnold explained,

Although we have no problem with any of our characters being gay, it would not be appropriate to portray them as such. A person's (or being's) sexual preference should not be obvious, just as we can't tell anyone's religious or political affiliations by looking at them.[22]

The signs of homosexuality, if they are there to be seen at all, automatically become too "obvious" in a homophobic society while the marks of heterosexuality are naturalized, rendered invisible, because they are too pervasive to even be noticed.

4. Representation could only occur through reliance on easily recognizable stereotypes of contemporary gay identities. With a twist, the group which the producers didn't dare to offend turns out to be not the religious right (which has often put pressure on producers to exclude gay or lesbian characters) but the gay fans who are demanding representation within the programme: "Do you expect us to show stereotypical behaviour that would be more insulting to the gay community than supportive?[23] Arnold asked a room of 1,200 *Star Trek* fans at Boston's Sheraton Hotel: What would you have us do, put pink triangles on them? Have them sashay down the corridors?"[24]

5. Representation of gay characters would require the explicit representation of their sexual practice. Arnold asked, "Would you have us show two men in bed together?[25] Since a heterosexist society has reduced homosexuals to their sexuality, then the only way to represent them would be to show them engaged in sexual activity.

6. Representation of gay characters and their relationships would be a violation of genre expectations. Adopting a suggestively feminine metaphor, Arnold asked, "Would you have us turn this [*Star Trek*] into a soap opera?" To deal with homosexuality as part of the character's lifestyle would be to transform (and perhaps, emasculate) *Star Trek* while to deal with heterosexuality as part of the character's lifestyle would be to leave its status as a male-targeted action-adventure programme unchanged. Any sort of concerted effort to respond to this logic requires an attempt to make heterosexuality rather than homosexuality visible, to show how its marks can be seen on the characters, the plots, and the entire environment:

Frank: How do we know any of the characters are heterosexual? How do you know? Because you see them interact with other people, especially in their intimate relations. *Star Trek* has done that over and over and over again. You know Picard is heterosexual. You know Riker is heterosexual. Why? Because they've had constant relationships with people of the opposite sex. This has been done systematically as character development. Why not this same development of a gay character?

7. As a last resort, having failed to convince the Gaylaxians with their other arguments, the producers sought to deny their own agency in the production of the programme and their own control over its ideological vision. "Should a *good* script come along that allows us to address the problems that the gay and lesbian community face on the planet today, then it will very likely be produced.[26] But, in fact, there had been a script, called "Blood and Fire," written by David Gerrold, in the very first season of *Star Trek: The Next Generation* at a time when producers were desperately looking for material to keep the fledgling series on the air. Gerrold's script used Regalian Blood Worms as a metaphor to deal with the issue of Aids and included a gay couple as secondary characters. . . .

Gerrold's script went through multiple revisions before being scuttled. The producers have consistently insisted that their decision not to produce "Blood and Fire" was based on its merits, not its inclusion of gay themes and characters. Gerrold, who parted company with Roddenberry shortly after this incident, has repeatedly challenged this account, charging that the episode was never filmed because the producers were uncomfortable with his attempts to introduce the issue of homosexuality into the *Star Trek* universe: "People complained the script had blatantly homosexual characters. Rick Berman said we can't do this in an afternoon market in some places. We'll have parents writing letters."[27]

Gerrold told his story at science fiction conventions, on the computer nets, and to lots and lots of reporters. Copies of the script have circulated informally among Gaylaxians and other fans. "Blood and Fire" became part of the fan community's understanding of the programme history and was a key factor in motivating the Gaylaxians to adopt more aggressive strategies in lobbying for their cause. "Good scripts are accepted, and this script was deemed not to be a good script," said Ernest Over, an assistant to the executive producer.[28]

The producers had said, repeatedly, in so many different ways, that the only ways that queers could become visible within *Star Trek* was by becoming a problem, and so, gay, lesbian and bisexual *Star Trek* fans became a problem for the producers. They organized a national letter-writing campaign; they posted notices on the computer nets; they went to the queer press and made their dissatisfaction with the producers' responses a public issue. Ernest Over, himself a gay community activist, told *The Advocate* that the *Star Trek* office had received "more letters on this than we'd had on anything else".[29]

In the midst of the publicity, just a few months before his death, Gene Roddenberry issued a statement: "In the fifth season of *Star Trek: The Next Generation*, viewers will see more of shipboard life in some episodes, which will, among other things, include gay crew members in day-to-day circumstances".[30] An editorialist in the *Los Angeles Times* reported,

This season, gays and lesbians will appear unobtrusively aboard the Enterprise. . . . They weren't "outed" and they won't be outcasts; apparently they'll be neither objects of pity nor melodramatic attention. Their sexual orientation will be a matter of indifference to the rest of the crew.[31]

· · ·

When the Gaylaxians sought confirmation of Roddenberry's statements, they received no response. When reporters from the *Washington Blade* called, they received only a tape recorded message from executive producer Rick Berman: "The writers and producers of *Star Trek: The Next Generation* are actively exploring a number of possible approaches that would address the issue of sexual orientation."[32] Once again, "the issue of sexual orientation" had substituted for the promise of queer characters. And, as the new season premièred, queer fans learned that they would become "outcasts", after all.

A Human Failing

> [Roddenberry] had discussed with us before his death the possibility of having two men hold hands in some scene, which was totally irrelevant to the issue of homosexuality. . . . So we decided to tell a story that was about sexual intolerance.
>
> (Writing Staff Supervisor Michael Piller)[33]

· · ·

There is a curious footnote in Gene Roddenberry's novelization of *Star Trek: The Motion Picture*, one which members of the female fan writing community have long read as the producer's wink towards Kirk/Spock fiction. "Because *t'hy'la* [a term Spock used to refer to Kirk] can be used to mean *lover*, and since Kirk's and Spock's friendship was unusually close, this has led some to speculate over whether they had actually indeed become lovers," Roddenberry explained, acknowledging for the first and only time within a canonical *Star Trek* story that the concept, at least, of homosexuality still existed within his twenty-fourth-century universe.[34] Homosexuality is still the subject of "speculations," "rumors," perhaps of blackmail. Yet, Roddenberry allows Kirk to set the record "straight":

I was never aware of this *lovers* rumor, although I have been told that Spock encountered it several times. Apparently he had always dismissed it with his characteristic lifting of his right eyebrow which usually connoted some combination of surprise, disbelief, and/or annoyance. As for myself, although I have no moral or other objections to physical love in any of its many Earthly, alien and mixed forms, I have always found my best gratification in that creature *woman*. Also, I would dislike being thought of as so foolish that I would select a love partner who came into sexual heat only once every seven years.[35]

So, just as quickly as he makes it appear, Roddenberry begins to make homosexuality disappear again. Yet Roddenberry doesn't totally close the door here. With an extra bit of effort, we can peek into Kirk's closet and find hints of something perverse. What exactly does Kirk, this man of multiple worlds, mean when he says that his "best gratification" came through heterosexuality? How has he come to be in a position to make such an evaluation? He doesn't, after all, say that it was his only gratification. What experiences had Kirk had with "physical love in any of its many Earthly, alien and mixed forms"? And, so, Roddenberry, at one and the same time, authorizes a space for fan speculation and explicitly, directly, denies the possibility that homosexual desire might run between Kirk and Spock.

In an important contribution to queer media theory, D. A. Miller has traced the ways that Alfred Hitchcock's *Rope* makes its characters' homosexuality a matter of connotation rather than denotation, something which is suggested but never said. "Connotation will always manifest a certain semiotic insufficiency," Miller notes, allowing "homosexual meaning to be elided even as it is also being elaborated."[36] While the homosexuality of *Rope*'s major characters has been taken for granted by almost all critics writing about the film, their sexual preference is never explicitly stated and thus remains a matter of interpretation. The truth of denotation (i.e. the explicit representation or statement of homosexuality) is self-evident while the truth of connotation (i.e. suggestion or implication) remains open to debate and re-interpretation. Connotation has, as Miller suggests, "an abiding deniability." A play with connotation is often a way to work around censorship, but by its very nature, it denies the queer visibility the Gaylaxians sought from *Star Trek*'s producers. Rather, the play with connotation, as Miller suggests, teaches only the importance of remaining silent.

"The Host" and "The Outcast," the two *Star Trek: The Next Generation* episodes which brush across the issue of sexual preference can be seen as similar plays with connotation, often threatened with being swamped by some larger, more "universal" concern. Here, for example, is director Marvin Rush describing the *Star Trek* episode, "The Host":

Male/female male/male, female/female relationships exist in life in various forms and they're fair game for drama. I think "The Host" was about an aspect of that. But to me it was more about the nature of love, and [whether] the packages makes a difference.[37]

Writing staff supervisor Michael Piller acknowledges that "The Outcast" was a conscious response to the letter-writing campaign but it was, in truth, a "story that addressed the issue of sexual intolerance. . . . that was really the broader issue."[38]

In "The Host," the *Enterprise*'s doctor, Beverley Crusher, falls in love—with a man. Odan, an alien ambassador, beams aboard, charms the pants off her, and the two become romantically, and, it is strongly suggested, sexually, involved. Only then, after the fact, does Crusher learn that the body she has been sleeping with is actually simply the host while the "man" with whom she has fallen in love is an extraterrestrial symbiont. The host body is dying. The symbiont is temporarily transplanted into Riker's body, the body of a man she considers as a "brother." After much soul-searching, Crusher again falls in love with Odan and it is again suggested that she goes to bed with him. In the final scene, Odan's new host, a woman, arrives to receive the transplant. Odan, in this body as in all of his previous bodies, still desires "Doctor Beverley," but Beverley backs away from embracing him in his female form. "Perhaps it is a human failing but we are not accustomed to those kinds of changes," Dr. Beverley says with a cold stare and a distant voice. "I can't keep up. . . . I can't live with that kind of uncertainty. Perhaps someday our ability to love won't be so limited." Odan kisses her on the wrist and then walks away, before the camera fades away on a cold, expressionless close-up of the good doctor contemplating, no doubt, the "nature of love." "Perhaps it was a human failing," she confessed, safe in the knowledge that on *Star Trek*, human failings like compassion, friendship, emotion, altruism, love, have long been validated in the face of alien challenge. It is, after all, in our failings that we are most decidedly human.

The Gaylaxians were sharply divided about "The Host." Christine, president of the Boston chapter, wrote a letter praising the episode: "The story was powerful, sensitive, well-acted and intelligent, and clearly illustrates *Trek*'s continuing commitment to explore and present important issues regardless of how controversial they might be."[39] Her praise was tempered by her recognition of what could be expected to be said on television rather than what it might be desirable for the programme to actually say. *Star Trek*, she suggested, had found a way to explore alternative sexuality without running the "risk that the entire midwest would immediately switch off their TVs." Christine's acceptance of "The Host" thus balances multiple reading formations: one which interprets the programme's ideology in relation to Roddenberry's activist image and the other which recognizes the fans as a "powerless elite" which must reconcile its desires with what is practical in reaching a larger viewing public. Similarly, she negotiates between the appreciation of allegory as a form of social commentary and the fans' desire for recognition in terms acceptable within fandom's realist aesthetic.

. . .

Not surprisingly, however, given the precarious balance she achieves between these differing reading formations, other group members did not share Christine's endorsement of the episode. The ambiguities of the closing scene particularly provoked discomfort and debate. Why does Crusher pull back from Odan when he appears to her as a woman, yet she was able to sleep with him when he took the form of her "brother"? Is it, as she says, because she can't keep up with the changes or because, as is strongly implied, she can't deal with the possibility of lesbian desire? What is it that the people of the Federation have not yet learned to accept, parasites in host bodies or queer visibility? And, is homosexuality even what's on offer here, given the programme's careful efforts to situate Odan as quite literally a man's mind trapped inside a woman's body? Consider, for example, this exchange during one of the interview sessions, a debate which recurred in a similar form each time I discussed this episode with group members:

Betty: I liked it but I wanted it to go on for another half hour. If the third body—the woman— had come in fifteen or twenty minutes before the end of the show and Beverley had to deal with her.

Lynne: But they don't have the guts to do that yet. . . .

Betty: If Beverley had to deal with the person she loved in the body of a woman, the whole gay issue would have been raised and you would have lost sight of the issue you raised—is it the shell or the personality that you love?

Even here, heterosexuality is seen as universal, abstract, while homosexuality is too particular and concrete to carry the weight of such a global concern as "the nature of love." Straights can stand for all lovers, while lesbians are more specialized signifiers.

. . .

Lynne: I think Beverley would have responded almost similarly if Odan came back as a young blond male but a total stranger. "I can't do this again." That's the feeling I got. But on top of it all, it's a woman and she's not usually inclined that way. I can't deal with you changing bodies on me. You don't look like you did before. First she had to deal with

> Riker. My God! Riker's body! Blech! She dealt with that but it took her a good twenty minutes of the episode. She would have needed another twenty minutes of episode to deal with this female body. But I saw the little smile on her face at the end and that's what clued me in that the writer's left it open-ended.

Homosexuality survives as a "little smile," an ambiguous gesture, which is readable as homophobic, foreclosing all future possibilities or as tolerant, "open-ended" and subject to multiple interpretations. So much weight to put on a "little smile" but sometimes that's all you have.

The following season, *Star Trek* tried again to confront and resolve the "problem" of homosexuality. If "The Host" wasn't really about homosexuality, even if it visually represented the possibility, however fleetingly, on the screen, "The Outcast" was to be "*The* gay episode." Supervising producer Jeri Taylor explains, "'The Host' was really more about the nature of what is the basis of a love relationship. 'The Outcast,' though, is a gay rights story. It absolutely, specifically and outspokenly dealt with gay issues."[40] "The Outcast" would put the issue behind them once and for all, carefully containing its implications within a single story set on an alien world which had no previous contact with the Federation and, under the circumstances, probably wouldn't want to get into communication again.

The J'naii are an androgynous race who have outlawed the very concept of gender. (The J'naii, predictably enough, were played entirely by women.)[41] Riker meets Soren, a J'naii technician, while working together to rescue a space ship which has been lost in "null space." The appearance of a woman without gender invites a constant investigation of the wonders of heterosexuality. "What kind of a woman do you find attractive?" she asks Riker. "Tell me, is that the kind of woman all human males prefer?" she asks again. "It is up to the woman to attract the man?" Soren inquires of Dr Crusher. Repairing a disabled shuttle craft, Riker and Soren discuss their feelings towards each other. "What is involved with two sexes? Mating?" she wants to know, and each time, both her questions and their responses assume that heterosexuality is the only possibility. After all, in a world with two sexes, why settle for only one? "Perhaps it is that complexity which makes the differences in the sexes so interesting," she exclaims, amid Riker's knowing talk about "snips and snails and puppy dog tales" and "sugar and spice and everything nice". Soren confesses that she has, in fact, come to think of herself as female and to have an "unnatural" preference for men, even though such a sexual identity is outlawed in her culture:

> I am taking a terrible risk telling you that. . . . Some have strong inclinations for maleness. Some have urges to be female. I am one of the latter. . . . In our world, these feelings are forbidden. Those who are discovered are shamed and ridiculed. . . . Those of us who have these urges lead secret and guarded lives. We seek each other out. Always hiding, always terrified of being discovered.

The two disobey the laws of her culture and dare to express their "deviant" heterosexual desires for each other, but Soren is made to defend her heterosexuality before the council of Androgynies: "What we do is not different from what you do. . . . What makes you think you can dictate how people love each other?" After much soul-searching, Riker and Worf decide to disobey Star Fleet's Prime Directive and attempt to rescue Soren from the therapy which will "cure" her of her outcast sexuality. For once, on a programme famous for its split-second escapes from certain doom, they arrive too late. Soren, who has been cured, rejects Riker's advances and so he flies away aboard *the Enterprise*, leaving her behind.

. . .

If allegory depends upon the readers' abilities to fill its silences with their own voices, to complete the statements the text has left unfinished, the fans saw only the gaps and the evasions. Nowhere do any of the characters make explicit reference to the possibility of homosexuality nor do they directly confront homophobia. Homosexuality remains a connotative ghost, still that form of sexual desire that dares not speak its name.

The Gaylaxians recognized that what made this episode particularly dangerous was its insubstantiability, its refusal to state directly and explicitly what its message was intended to be:

The depiction of Soren's society seemed to be something taken right from Rush Limbaugh's show or Pat Buchanan's campaign literature. If you listen to those people, you'll hear them talking about how the feminist and homosexual political agendas want to destroy the traditional family and make society into a sexless, genderless collection of politically correct clones, and if you don't toe the line, you'll be censored. Soren's society was a depiction of those people's worst nightmares. It seems to me that if you were of that mindset to begin with, this show did nothing but confirm those unfounded fears, and nothing to challenge them. . . . It was so ambiguous, so valueless and empty, as to leave it open for this interpretation.[42]

The denotative dimensions of the story—the literal level of the narrative had such force, they feared, that it would completely swamp the connotative meanings of the allegory. What appears on screen, at the most basic denotative level, is an "outspoken" defence of heterosexuality, including that daring moment when Riker and Soren, Jonathan Frakes and Melinda Culea, break all social taboos and kiss each other on the lips, right there on television.

. . .

But, pull back from the denotative, take the allegory on its own connotative terms, and what do you have?

If I were a gay teenager trying to come out, this episode would have done nothing for me. I would have left with exactly what I came in with. Yeah—I suppose there are gay people out there. I don't know how or why I'm going to find them and I don't have any kind of sense that things are going to be okay. (Gaylaxian group discussion)

. . .

But then again, given the instability of this allegory, perhaps some people missed the point altogether, perhaps some straight people didn't even realize that the episode was supposed to be about "gay rights." This story was oft-repeated:

There was a discussion where I work in an almost completely straight environment and a lot of people who watched it didn't connect it to the gay issue at all. . . . The thing that was interesting, they were still outraged by what was done to Soren. They felt it was a generic freedom of choice issue. She wasn't allowed to live the life she wanted regardless of what that was. That this might be treated as a gay-related issue was quite a surprise to them. (Gaylaxian group discussion)

What happened when you pointed it out to them? "They argued with it. They still felt that it was more a human rights issue." And they did not perceive that a gay rights issue might also be a human rights issue? "Well, I couldn't really go into it because I'm only out to half of the group I was talking with and so it wasn't something I could pursue."

And, so, maybe, all the episode said was that heterosexuality ought to exist everywhere in the galaxy, hardly a ground-breaking statement. As staff writer Brannon Braga said, "We were advocating tolerance. What's so risky about making a statement that intolerance is bad?"[43] The allegorical nature of the story allowed the producers to place the risk of "coming out" onto the backs of viewers rather than taking on that responsibility for themselves. "It was a very special episode. There are no subject[s] taboo for this show," Braga brags.[44] Gay fans noted that this was not the same way the series had tackled civil rights issues in the 1960s:

Frank: "Let That Be The Last Battlefield" was a statement against racial discrimination. There was no need to make that statement. Star Trek had been making a statement against prejudice from the first episode when they had a multi-racial crew. If they had done "Battlefield" exactly as they did it as a statement against racial prejudice and every person on the ship was white, it would have been insulting—hypocrisy. But that's exactly what "The Outcast" did. They said basically, "we should be accepting and tolerant of people who have different sexual preferences but we aren't going to show any on our show. We aren't going to include any on the crew."

Q for Queer?

What about non-human species homosexuality? A Klingon male in drag would surely be a highlight of the TV season. Or maybe a lesbian Vulcan, who logically decided that sex with men was unnecessary. Or even a Betazoid chicken hawk after the virginal Wesley Crusher. The ST:NG Enterprise has been the home of some homosexual stereotypes. Tasha Yar was at times the ultimate in butch female, not afraid of any man. Data is more anally retentive than even the Odd Couple's Felix Unger. And Worf sometimes wears more leather than an entire issue of Drummer.

(Steve K., The Lavender Dragon)[45]

. . .

If Paramount and Berman thought that "The Outcast" would safely contain the spectre of homosexuality on the far-strung planet of the J'Naii, then they misunderstood the power of connotation to grow, like ivy, all over a text once it has been planted there. As D. A. Miller writes, queer connotation has the

inconvenience of tending to raise this ghost all over the place. For once received in all its uncertainty, the connotation instigates a project of confirmation. . . . Connotation thus tends to light everywhere, to put all signifiers to a test of their hospitality.[46]

The constant promise and deferral of a gay character coloured the Gaylaxians' relationship to the series and invited them to constantly read a gay subtext into the episodes.

Star Trek seemed always on the verge of confessing its characters' sexual preferences, only to back away yet again.

If the producers have trouble thinking of ways to make homosexuality visible within *Star Trek*, if they couldn't seem to find a "good script" to tell that particular story, the Gaylaxians have no trouble locating possibilities. Watch any episode with them and they will show you the spot, the right moment, for a confession of previously repressed desire to come out from hiding:

Lynne: "Geordi realizes that the reason he can't seem to work things out with women is that he's gay. . . . Picard goes on shore leave and meets this great woman. Why can't he go on shore leave and meet this great man? It doesn't mean he always prefers men. He can mix it up a little. . . . And it [bisexuality] would probably flourish on board the *Enterprise*. They're real open minded there.

Soon the entire group is participating within this carnival of outlaw signifiers.

. . .

For these fans, the text's silences about characters' sexuality or motives can be filled with homosexual desire, since, after all, in our society, such desire must often go unspoken. Straight fans, on the other hand, are apt to demand conclusive evidence that a character is homosexual and otherwise, read all unmarked characters as straight by default. What's at stake is the burden of proof and the nature of evidence within a culture where homosexuality most often appears within connotation rather than denotation. Such speculations cannot sustain direct challenge and often are not taken literally by those who advance them, but open up a fleeting possibility of imagining a different text existing in the margins of that which Paramount delivers.

Sometimes, the possibilities seem to cohere around a particular character, who appears to embody the richest potential for queer visibility, who builds upon the iconography and stereotypes of queer identity. Here, bids for character sexuality can be more strongly maintained since the text offers precisely the type of evidence that is most commonly presented within popular culture to indicate a character's potential homosexuality. Rumours surrounded the arrival of Tasha Yar as a character in *The Next Generation's* first season. Maybe this is the queer character Roddenberry had promised: "Tasha Yar—an obvious bisexual character. Considering what she went through as a child, she should be a lesbian" (Betty). Tasha Yar—tough, independent, security chief with short-cropped hair, from a planet where she was repeatedly gang-raped by men, able to fight against any and all adversaries, was the classic Amazon: "She could easily be conceived as being a lesbian" (David). But, as the fans are quick to note, she goes to bed with Data in the programme's second episode, "The Naked Now": "When they decided to straighten her, they used an android. So we ended up heterosexualizing two perfectly wonderful characters. . . . Even if they had left the character alone and not heterosexualized Tasha Yar, we would have been farther ahead than we are now" (David).

The marks of heterosexuality, normally invisible, are made "obvious" by this interpretation, an act of violence committed against otherwise potentially queer characters, a reaction of homosexual panic which seeks to stabilize (or even to deny) their sexuality. Characters' sexualities do not remain unmarked for long within the world of *Star Trek* or, for that matter, the world of popular culture, which insists that characters be undeniably heterosexual even if their sexual preference is totally irrelevant to their narrative actions.[47] "Data has been assigned a sexual orientation, basically" (James). Data has been "heterosexualized". Yar has been "straightened".

Yet, again, how stable is that orientation? "Data is someone where bisexuality can be explored" (James). And, soon, the speculations are all open again:

. . .

Cultural studies' embrace of the model of resistant reading is a logical response to theoretical traditions which spoke of readers only in terms of textually constructed subject positions. Resistant reading, as a model, addresses many important questions about the ideological power of the mass media and the relationship between "the viewer and the viewed." Resistant reading, however, only describes one axis of a more complex relationship between readers and texts. The reading practices characteristic of fandom are never purely and rarely openly resistant to the meanings and categories advanced by programme producers. Often, as we have seen, the fans' resistant reading occurs within rather than outside the ideological framework provided by the programme and is fought in the name of fidelity to the programme concepts. The consummate negotiating readers, fan critics work to repair gaps or contradictions in the programme ideology, to make it cohere into a satisfying whole which satisfies their needs for continuity and emotional realism. Fandom is characterized by a contradictory and often highly fluid series of attitudes towards the primary text, marked by fascination as well as frustration, proximity as well as distance, acceptance of programme ideology as well as rejection. The fans feel a strong identification with the programmes, the characters, the producers and their ideological conceptions, even when they feel strong frustration with the failure of the producers to create stories they would like to see told.

. . .

Moreover, we need to identify ways in which resistant reading is not necessarily a sufficient response to dissatisfaction with the images currently in circulation. As many writers have noted, resistant reading risks becoming a catch-all solution for all the problems within popular culture, a way of escaping the need for ideological criticism or research into the political economy of media institutions. A model of resistant reading quickly becomes profoundly patronizing if it amounts to telling already socially mar-ginalized audiences that they should be satisfied with their ability to produce their own interpretations and should not worry too much about their lack of representation within the media itself. Resistant reading can sustain the Gaylaxians' own activism, can become a source of collective identity and mutual support, but precisely because it is a subcultural activity which is denied public visibility, resistant reading cannot change the political agenda, cannot challenge other constructions of gay identity and cannot have an impact on the ways people outside of the group think about the issues which matter to the Gaylaxians. Slash, or K/S fiction, represents a long-standing tradition in the women's fan-writing community which poses ways of constructing homo-erotic fan-tasies employing the series characters.

. . .

Cultural studies' embrace of the model of resistant reading, then, only makes sense in a context which recognizes the centrality of issues of media access and media owner- ship. Resistant reading is an important survival skill in a hostile atmosphere where most of us can do little to alter social conditions and where many of the important stories that matter to us can't be told on network television. It is, however, no substitute for other forms of media criticism and activism. The Gaylaxians' reception of *Star Trek* points to the importance of linking ethnographic research on resistant readers or sub- cultural appropriations with a political economy of media ownership and control and with the ideological analysis of programme content. If earlier forms of ideological analysis worked from the assumption that texts constructed reading subjects, this new mixture would assume that readers play an active role in defining the texts which they consume but: (a) they do so within a social, historical and cultural context that shapes their relative access to different discourses and generic models for making sense of the programme materials; (b) they do so in relation to institutional power that may satisfy or defer audience desires; and (c) they do so in regard to texts whose properties may facilitate or resist the readers' interpretive activities. The relationship between readers, institutions and texts is not fixed but fluid. That relationship changes over time, constantly shifting in relation to the ever-changing balance of power between these competing forces.

Notes

1. Franklin Hummel, "Where None Have Gone Before." *Gaylactic Gayzette,* May 1991, p.2. I am indebted to John Campbell for his extensive assistance in recruiting members of the Gaylaxians to participate in the interviews for this chapter. Interviews were conducted both in informal settings (members' homes) as well as more formal ones (my office), depending on the size and the needs of the groups. As it evolved, the groups were segregated by gender.

2. For more information on the Gaylaxian Network, see Franklin Hummel, "SF Comes to Boston: Gaylaxians at the World Science Fiction Convention," *New York Native,* 23 October 1989, p. 26.

3. Gaylaxians International, recruitment flier.

4. John Hartley, *Tele-ology: Studies in Television* (New York: Routledge, Chapman and Hall, 1992), p. 5.

5. Hartley 1992, p. 7.

6. The nineteenth-century word, Uranian, was coined by early German homosexual emancipationist Karl Ulrichs and used popularly through the First World War to refer to homosexuals. As Eric Garber and Lyn Paleo note, "It refers to Aphrodite Urania, whom Plato had identified as the patron Goddess of homosexuality in his Symposium."

7. Susan Sackett, executive assistant to Gene Roddenberry, letter to Franklin Hummel, 12 March 1991.

8. Mark A. Altman, "Tackling Gay Rights," *Cinefantastique,* October 1992, p. 74.

9. Franklin Hummel, Director, Gaylactic Network, letter to Gene Roddenberry, 1 May 1991.

10. Ibid.

11. The analogy John and other Gaylaxians draw between the black civil rights movement of the 1960s and the queer civil rights movement of the 1990s is a controversial one. But it is hardly unique to these fans. This analogy has been part of the discursive context surrounding Bill Clinton's efforts to end the American military's ban on gay and lesbian enlistment.

12. Several of the writers associated with the

original *Star Trek* series made important contributions to the development of gay and lesbian science fiction: Theodore Sturgeon, who wrote "Amok Time" and "Shore Leave," two of the best-loved episodes, had been dealing with issues of alien sexuality and homosexuality in his fiction as early as 1957; David Gerrold, who wrote "Trouble with Tribbles" and was closely involved in the development of *Star Trek: The Next Generation*, was the author of a 1973 science fiction novel, *The Man Who Folded Himself*, which dealt with the auto-erotic and homoerotic possibilities of time travel; Norman Spinrad, the author of "The Doomsday Machine," wrote stories which dealt, not always sympathetically, with alternative sexualities and had included gay characters in his fiction prior to his involvement in *Star Trek*.

13. Clearly, these newer representations of gay characters, rather than the older representations of the problem or issue of gay sexuality, set expectations about how *Star Trek* might best address the concerns of its gay, lesbian and bisexual viewers.

14. Sackett, op. cit. Roddenberry has, at various times, acknowledged that he saw his inclusion of Uhura on the original series as a contribution to the civil rights movement, that he had added Chekhov in response to a *Pravda* editorial calling for an acknowledgement of Soviet accomplishments in space, and that he introduced the blind character, Geordi, on *Star Trek: The Next Generation* as a response to the many disabled fans he had encountered through the years. Given such a pattern, it was not unreasonable for the Gaylaxians to anticipate a similar gesture towards gay, lesbian and bisexual viewers.

15. Hummel, *Gaylactic Gayzette*, op. cit.

16. Edward Gross, *The Making of The Next Generation* (Las Vegas: Pioneer Books) as reprinted in *Gaylactic Gayzette*, May 1991.

17. David Gerrold, letter to Frank Hummel, 23 November 1986.

18. Steve K., "Gays and Lesbians in the 24th Century: *Star Trek—The Next Generation*," *The Lavender Dragon*, August 1991, 1: 3, p. 1.

19. Theresa M., ibid.

20. "*Star Trek:* The Next Genderation," *The Advocate*, 27 August 1991, p. 74.

21. Richard Arnold, letter to J. DeSort, Jr, 10 March 1991.

22. Richard Arnold, letter to J. DeSort, Jr, 10 September 1989.

23. Ibid.

24. Mark A. Perigard, "Invisible, Again," *Bay Windows*, 7 February 1991, p. 8.

25. Richard Arnold, letter to J. DeSort, Jr, 10 March 1991.

26. Ibid.

27. Altman (1992), p. 72. Note that Berman or the other producers have never made similar arguments in their public statements about the controversy, always suggesting other reasons for their failure to introduce gay, lesbian or bisexual characters into the series.

28. Clark, p. 74.

29. Ibid.

30. Ibid.

31. Ruth Rosen, "*Star Trek* Is On Another Bold Journey," *Los Angeles Times*, 30 October 1991.

32. John Perry, "To Boldly Go . . . These Are the Not-So-Gay Voyages of the Starship Enterprise," *The Washington Blade*, 20 September 1991, p. 36.

33. Altman (1992) p. 74.

34. Gene Roddenberry, *Star Trek: The Motion Picture* (New York: Pocket Books, 1979), p.22.

35. Ibid.

36. D. A. Miller, "Anal *Rope,*" in Diana Fuss (ed.), *Inside/Out: Lesbian Theories, Gay Theories* (New York: Routledge, Chapman and Hall, 1991), p. 124. For other useful discussions of this subject, see Danae Clarke, "Commodity Lesbianism," *Camera Obscura*, 25–6, January–May 1991, pp. 181–202; Eve Kosofsky Sedgwick, *Epistemology of the Closet* (Berkeley: University of California Press, 1990).

37. Altman (1992), p. 73.

38. Altman (1992), p. 74.

QUEERS AND *STAR TREK* 401

39. Christine M. Conran, letter to Gene Roddenberry, 23 May 1991.

40. Altman (1992), p. 74.

41. Jonathan Frakes: "I don't think they were gutsy enough to take it where they should have. Soren should have been more obviously male." Rick Berman: "We were either going to cast with non-masculine men or non-feminine females. We knew we had to go one way or the other. We read both men and women for the roles and decided to go with women. It might have been interesting to go with men, but that was the choice we made." Brannon Braga: "If it would have been a man playing the role would he have kissed him? I think Jonathan would have because he's a gutsy guy." "Episode Guide," *Cinefantastique*, October 1992, p. 78. Gays might find some solace in the fact that it clearly takes more "guts" to be a homosexual than a heterosexual.

42. E-mail posting, name withheld.

43. Altman (1992), p. 74.

44. Ibid.

45. Steve K., *The Lavender Dragon*, p. 2.

46. Miller (1991), p. 125.

47. The Gaylaxians note, for example, a similar pattern in the introduction and development of Ensign Ro in *Star Trek: The Next Generation*'s fifth season: Ro, like Yar, drew on iconography associated with butch lesbians, and appearing in the midst of the letter-writing campaign was read as the long-promised queer character. Within a few episodes of her introduction, however, the programme involved her in a plot where the *Enterprise* crew loses its memory and Riker and Ro become lovers. As one Gaylaxian explained during a panel discussion of the series at Gaylaxicon, "Oops! I forgot I was a Lesbian!"

36 CyberDemocracy: Internet and the Public Sphere

Mark Poster

....

> I am an advertisement for a version of myself.
>
> (David Byrne)

...

Decentralized Technology

My plea for indulgence with the limitations of the postmodern position on politics quickly gains credibility when the old question of technological determinism is posed in relation to the Internet. For when the question of technology is posed we may see immediately how the Internet disrupts the basic assumptions of the older positions. The Internet is above all a decentralized communication system. Like the telephone network, anyone hooked up to the Internet may initiate a call, send a message that he or she has composed, and may do so in the manner of the broadcast system, that is to say, may send a message to many receivers, and do this either in "real time" or as stored data or both. The Internet is also decentralized at a basic level of organization since, as a network of networks, new networks may be added so long as they conform to certain communications protocols. As a historian I find it fascinating that this unique structure should emerge from a confluence of cultural communities which appear to have so little in common: the Cold War Defense Department which sought to insure survival against nuclear attack by promoting decentralization, the counter-cultural ethos of computer programming engineers which had a deep distaste for any form of censorship or active restraint of communications and the world of university research which I am at a loss to characterize. Added to this is a technological substratum of digital electronics which unifies all symbolic forms in a single system of codes, rendering transmission instantaneous and duplication effortless. If the technological structure of the Internet institutes costless reproduction, instantaneous dissemination and radical decentralization, what might be its effects upon the society, the culture and the political institutions?

There can be only one answer to this question and that is that it is the wrong question. Technologically determined effects derive from a broad set of assumptions in which what is technological is a configuration of materials that effect other materials and the relation between the technology and human beings is external, that is, where human beings are understood to manipulate the materials for ends that they impose

From Mark Poster, "CyberDemocracy: Internet and the Public Sphere," in David Porter (ed.), *Internet Culture* (London and New York: Routledge, 1997), 201–17.

upon the technology from a preconstituted position of subjectivity. But what the Internet technology imposes is a dematerialization of communication and in many of its aspects a transformation of the subject position of the individual who engages within it. The Internet resists the basic conditions for asking the question of the effects of technology. It installs a new regime of relations between humans and matter and between matter and non-matter, reconfiguring the relation of technology to culture and thereby undermining the standpoint from within which, in the past, a discourse developed—one which appeared to be natural—about the effects of technology. The only way to define the technological effects of the Internet is to build the Internet, to set in place a series of relations which constitute an electronic geography. While this may be true as well for other communications technologies, none but the Internet so drastically reconfigures the basic conditions of speech and reception.

Put differently the Internet is more like a social space than a thing so that its effects are more like those of Germany than those of hammers. The effects of Germany upon the people within it is to make them Germans (at least for the most part); the effects of hammers is not to make people hammers, though Heideggerians[1] some others might disagree, but to force metal spikes into wood. As long as we understand the Internet as a hammer we will fail to discern the way it is like Germany. The problem is that modern perspectives tend to reduce the Internet to a hammer. In this grand narrative of modernity, the Internet is an efficient tool of communication, advancing the goals of its users who are understood as preconstituted instrumental identities.

The Internet, I suppose like Germany, is complex enough so that it may with some profit be viewed in part as a hammer. If I search the database functions of the Internet or if I send e-mail purely as a substitute for paper mail, then its effects may reasonably be seen to be those on the order of the hammer. The database on the Internet may be more easily or cheaply accessed than its alternatives and the same may be said of e-mail in relation to the Post Office or the FAX machine. But the aspects of the Internet that I would like to underscore are those which instantiate new forms of interaction and which pose the question of new kinds of relations of power between participants. The question that needs to be asked about the relation of the Internet to democracy is this: are there new kinds of relations occurring within it which suggest new forms of power configurations between communicating individuals? In other words, is there a new politics on the Internet? One way to approach this question is to make a detour from the issue of technology and raise again the question of a public sphere, gauging the extent to which Internet democracy may become intelligible in relation to it. To frame the issue of the political nature of the Internet in relation to the concept of the public sphere is particularly appropriate because of the spatial metaphor associated with the term. Instead of an immediate reference to the structure of an institution, which is often a formalist argument over procedures, or to the claims of a given social group, which assumes a certain figure of agency that I would like to keep in suspense, the notion of a public sphere suggests an arena of exchange, like the ancient Greek agora or the colonial New England town hall. If there is a public sphere on the Internet, who populates it and how? In particular one must ask what kinds of beings exchange information on this public sphere? Since there occurs no face-to-face interaction, only electronic flickers[2] on a screen, what kind of community can there be in this space? What kind of peculiar, virtual embodiment of politics are inscribed so evanescently in cyberspace? Modernist curmudgeons may object vehemently against attributing to information flows on the Internet the dignified term "community." Are they correct and if so what sort of phenomenon is this cyberdemocracy?

The Internet as a Public Sphere?

The issue of the public sphere is at the heart of any reconceptualization of democracy. Contemporary social relations seem to be devoid of a basic level of interactive practice which, in the past, was the matrix of democratizing politics: loci such as the agora, the New England town hall, the village church, the coffee house, the tavern, the public square, a convenient barn, a union hall, a park, a factory lunchroom, and even a street corner. Many of these places remain but no longer serve as organizing centers for political discussion and action. It appears that the media, especially television but also other forms of electronic communication isolate citizens from one another and substitute themselves for older spaces of politics. An example from the Clinton health-care reform campaign will suffice: the Clinton forces at one point (mid-July 1994) felt that Congress was less favorable to their proposal than the general population. To convince the Congress of the wisdom of health-care reform, the adminstration purchased television advertising which depicted ordinary citizens speaking in favor of the legislation. The ads were shown *only in Washington D.C.* because they were directed not at the general population of viewers but at congressmen and congresswomen alone. The executive branch deployed the media directly on the legislative branch. Such are politics in the era of the mode of information. In a context like this, one may ask where is the public sphere, where is the place citizens interact to form opinions in relation to which public policy must be attuned? John Hartley makes the bold and convincing argument that the media *are* the public sphere: "Television, popular newspapers, magazines and photography, the popular media of the modern period, are the public domain, the place where and the means by which the public is created and has its being."[3] The same claim is offered by Paul Virilio: "Avenues and public venues from now on are eclipsed by the screen, by electronic displays, in a preview of the 'vision machines' just around the corner."[4] "Public" tends more and more to slide into "publicity" as "character" is replaced by "image." These changes must be examined without nostalgia and the retrospective glance of modernist politics and theory.

Sensing a collapse of the public sphere and therefore a crisis of democratic politics, Jürgen Habermas published *The Structural Transformation of the Public Sphere* in 1962.[5] In this highly influential work he traced the development of a democratic public sphere in the seventeenth and eighteenth centuries and charted its course to its decline in the twentieth century. In that work and arguably since then as well, Habermas' political intent was to further "the project of Enlightenment" by the reconstruction of a public sphere in which reason might prevail, not the instrumental reason of much modern practice but the critical reason that represents the best of the democratic tradition. Habermas defined the public sphere as a domain of uncoerced conversation oriented toward a pragmatic accord. His position came under attack by poststructuralists like

Lyotard who questioned the emancipatory potentials of its model of consensus through rational debate.[6] At issue was the poststructuralist critique of Habermas' Enlightenment ideal of the autonomous rational subject as a universal foundation for democracy. Before deploying the category of the public sphere to evaluate democracy on the Internet, I shall turn to recent developments in the debate over Habermas' position.

In the 1980s Lyotard's critique was expanded by feminists like Nancy Fraser who demonstrate the gender blindness in Habermas' position.[7] Even before the poststructuralists and feminists, Oskar Negt and Alexander Kluge began the critique of Habermas by articulating the notion of an *oppositional* public sphere, specifically that of the proletariat. What is important about their argument, as demonstrated so clearly by Miriam Hansen, is that Negt and Kluge shifted the terrain of the notion of the public sphere from an historico-transcendental idealization of the Enlightenment to a plurality and heterotopia of discourses. This crucial change in the notion of the public sphere assumes its full significance when it is seen in relation to liberal democracy. The great ideological fiction of liberalism is to reduce the public sphere to existing democratic institutions. Habermas' critique of liberalism counterposes a radical alternative to it but one that still universalizes and monopolizes the political. Negt and Kluge, in contrast, decentralize and multiply the public sphere, opening a path of critique and possibly a new politics.[8]

The final step in the development of the concept of the public sphere came with Rita Felski's synthesis of Negt/Kluge with both feminist gender analysis and the poststructuralist critique of the autonomous subject. For Felski the concept of the public sphere must build on the "experience" of political protest (in the sense of Negt and Kluge), must acknowledge and amplify the multiplicity of the subject (in the sense of poststructuralism) and must account for gender differences (in the sense of feminism). She writes:

Unlike the bourgeois public sphere, then, the feminist public sphere does not claim a representative universality but rather offers a critique of cultural values from the standpoint of women as a marginalized group within society. In this sense it constitutes a *partial* or counter-public sphere. . . . Yet insofar as it is a *public* sphere, its arguments are also directed outward, toward a dissemination of feminist ideas and values throughout society as a whole.[9]

Felski seriously revises the Habermasian notion of the public sphere, separating it from its patriarchal, bourgeois and logocentric attachments perhaps, but nonetheless still invoking the notion of a public sphere and more or less reducing politics to it. This becomes clear in the conclusion of her argument:

Some form of appeal to collective identity and solidarity is a necessary precondition for the emergence and effectiveness of an oppositional movement; feminist theorists who reject any notion of a unifying identity as a repressive fiction in favor of a stress on absolute difference fail to show how such diversity and fragmentation can be reconciled with goal-oriented political struggles based upon common interests. An appeal to a shared experience of oppression provides the starting point from which women as a group can open upon the problematic of gender, at the same time as this notion of gendered community contains a strongly utopian dimension. . . . (pp. 168–9)

In the end Felski sees the public sphere as central to feminist politics. But then we must ask how this public sphere is to be distinguished from any political discussion? From the heights of Habermas' impossible (counter-factual) ideal of rational communication, the public sphere here multiplies, opens and extends to political discussion by all oppressed individuals.

The problem we face is that of defining the term "public." Liberal theory generally resorted to the ancient Greek distinction between the family or household and the polis, the former being "private" and the latter "public." When the term crossed boundaries from political to economic theory, with Ricardo and Marx, a complication set in: the term "political economy" combined the Greek sense of public and the Greek sense of private since economy referred for them to the governance of the (private) household. The older usage preserved a space for the public in the agora to be sure but referred to discussions about the general good, not market transactions. In the newer usage the economic realm is termed "political economy" but is considered "private." To make matters worse, common parlance nowadays has the term "private" designating speeches and actions that are isolated, unobserved by anyone and not recorded or monitored by any machine.[10] Privacy now becomes restricted to the space of the home, in a sense returning to the ancient Greek usage even though family structure has altered dramatically in the interum. In Fraser's argument, for example, the "public" sphere is the opposite of the "private" sphere in the sense that it is a locus of "talk," ". . . a space in which citizens deliberate about their common affairs. . ." and is essential to democracy.[11] There are serious problems then in using the term "public" in relation to a politics of emancipation.

This difficulty is amplified considerably once newer electronically mediated communications are taken into account, in particular the Internet. Now the question of "talk," of meeting face-to-face, of "public" discourse is confused and complicated by the electronic form of exchange of symbols. If "public" discourse exists as pixels on screens generated at remote locations by individuals one has never and probably will never meet, as it is in the case of the Internet with its "virtual communities," "electronic cafés," bulletin boards, e-mail, computer conferencing and even video conferencing, then how is it to be distinguished from "private" letters, printface and so forth. The age of the public sphere as face-to-face talk is clearly over: the question of democracy must henceforth take into account new forms of electronically mediated discourse. What are the conditions of democratic speech in the mode of information? What kind of "subject" speaks or writes or communicates in these conditions? What is its relation to machines? What complexes of subjects, bodies and machines are required for democratic exchange and emancipatory action? For Habermas, the public sphere is a homogeneous space of embodied subjects in symmetrical relations, pursuing consensus through the critique of arguments and the presentation of validity claims. This model, I contend, is systematically denied in the arenas of electronic politics. We are advised then to abandon Habermas' concept of the public sphere in assessing the Internet as a political domain.

Against my contention, Judith Perrolle turns to a Habermasian perspective to look at conversations on bulletin boards and finds that the conditions of the ideal speech situation do not apply. She contends that these conversations are "distorted" by a level of machine control: here validity ". . . claims of meaningfulness, truth, sincerity and appropriateness . . . appear to be physical or logical characteristics of the machine rather than an outcome of human negotiation." [12] The basic conditions for speech are configured in the program of the virtual community and remain outside the arena of discussion. She continues: "Most computer interfaces are either not designed to allow the user to question data validity, or else designed so that data may be changed by anyone with a moderate level of technical skill" (p. 354). While this argument cannot be refuted from within the framework of Habermas' theory of communicative action, the question remains if these criteria are able to capture the specific qualities of the electronic forms of interaction.

Now that the thick culture of information machines provides the interface for much if not most discourse on political issues, the fiction of the democratic community of full human presence serves only to obscure critical reflection and divert the development of a political theory of this decidedly postmodern condition. For too long critical theory has insisted on a public sphere, bemoaning the fact of media "interference," the static of first radio's then of television's role in politics. But the fact is that political discourse has long been mediated by electronic machines: the issue now is that the machines enable new forms of decentralized dialogue and create new combinations of human–machine assemblages, new individual and collective "voices," "specters," "interactivities" which are the new building blocks of political formations and groupings. As Paul Virilio writes, "What remains of the notion of things 'public' when public *images* (in real time) are more important than public space?" [13] If the technological basis of the media has habitually been viewed as a threat to democracy, how can theory account for the turn toward a construction of technology (the Internet) which appears to promote a decentralization of discourse if not democracy itself and appears to threaten the state (unmonitorable conversations), mock at private property (the infinite reproducibility of information) and flaunt moral propriety (the dissemination of images of unclothed people often in awkward positions)?

A Postmodern Technology?

Many areas of the Internet extend pre-existing identities and institutions. Usenet newsgroups elicit obnoxious pranks from teenage boys; databases enable researchers and corporations to retrieve information at lower costs; electronic mail affords speedy, reliable communication of messages; the digitization of images allows a wider distribution of erotic materials, and so it goes. The Internet then is modern in the sense of continuing the tradition of tools as efficient means and in the sense that prevailing modern cultures transfer their characteristics to the new domain. These issues remain to be studied in detail and from a variety of standpoints, but for the time being the above conclusion may be sustained. Other areas of the Internet are less easy to contain within modern points of view. The examination of these cyberspaces raises the issue of a new understanding of technology and finally leads to a reassessment of the political aspects of the Internet. I refer to the bulletin board services that have come to be known as "virtual communities," to the MOO phenomenon and to the synthesis of virtual reality technology with the Internet.

In these cases what is at stake is the direct solicitation to construct identities in the course of communication practices. Individuals invent themselves and do so repeatedly and differentially in the course of conversing or messaging electronically. Now there is surely nothing new in discursive practices that are so characterized: reading a novel,[14] speaking on CB radio, indeed watching a television advertisement, I contend, all in varying degrees and in different ways encourage the individual to shape an identity in the course of engaging in communication. The case of the limited areas of the Internet I listed above, however, goes considerably beyond, or at least is quite distinct from, the latter examples. The individual's performance of the communication requires linguistic acts of self-positioning that are less explicit in the cases of reading a novel or watching a television advertisement. On the Internet, individuals read and interpret communications to themselves and to others and also respond by shaping sentences and transmitting them. Novels and TV ads are interpreted by individuals who are interpellated by them but these readers and viewers are not addressed directly, only as a generalized audience and, of course, they respond in fully articulated linguistic acts. (I avoid framing the distinction I am making here in the binary active/passive because that couplet is so associated with the modern autonomous agent that it would appear that I am depicting the Internet as the realization of the modern dream universal, "active" speech. I refuse this resort because it rests upon the notion of identity as a fixed essence, presocial and prelinguistic, whereas I want to argue that Internet discourse constitutes the subject as the subject fashions him or herself. I want to locate subject constitution at a level which is outside the oppositions of freedom/determinism, activity/passivity.) On the Internet individuals construct their identities, doing so in relation to ongoing dialogues not as acts of pure consciousness. But such activity does not count as freedom in the liberal-Marxist sense because it does not refer back to a foundational subject. Yet it does connote a "democratization" of subject constitution because the acts of discourse are not limited to one-way address and not constrained by the gender and ethnic traces inscribed in face-to-face communications. The magic of the Internet is that it is a technology that puts cultural acts, symbolizations in all forms, in the hands of all participants; it radically decentralizes the positions of speech, publishing, film-making, radio and television broadcasting, in short the apparatuses of cultural production.

Gender and Virtual Communities

Let us examine the case of gender in Internet communication as a way to clarify what is at stake and to remove some likely confusions about what I am arguing. In real-time chat rooms, MOOs and MUDs, participants must invent identities which consist, as a minimum, of a name and a gender. Gender, unlike age or ethnicity, is thus a general attribute of Internet identities. This gender however bears no necessary relation to one's gender in daily life. The gendered body is replaced by the gendered text. Studies have pointed out that the absence of bodily gender cues in bulletin board discussion groups does not eliminate sexism or even the hierarchies of gender that pervade society generally.[15] The disadvantages suffered by women in society carries over into "the virtual communities" on the Internet: women are underrepresented in these electronic places (although this is changing as in 1998 more women than men went on line for the first time in the U.S.) and they are subject to various forms of harassment and sexual abuse. The fact that sexual identities are self-designated does not in itself eliminate the annoyances and the constraints of patriarchy. Yet Internet social relations are often taken seriously by participants, so much so that gender problems in daily life take on new dimensions in cyberspace. There is an articulation of gender on the Internet that goes beyond the reproduction of real life hierarchies to instantiate new conditions of inscription.

The case of "Joan" is instructive in this regard. A man named Alex presented himself on a bulletin board as a disabled woman, "Joan," in order to experience the "intimacy" he admired in women's conversations. Alex wanted to talk to women as a woman because of the limitations he perceived in real life masculine identities. Van Gelder reports that when his "ruse" was unveiled, many of the women "Joan" interacted with were deeply hurt. But Van Gelder also reports that their greatest disappointment was that "Joan" did not exist.[16] The construction of gender in this example indicates a level of complexity not accounted for by the supposition that cultural and social forms are or are not transferrable to the Internet. Alex turned to the Internet virtual community to make up for a perceived lack of feminine traits in his masculine sexual identity. The women who suffered his ploy regretted the "death" of the virtual friend "Joan." These are unique uses of virtual communities not easily found in "reality." In cyberspace, one may create and live a gendered identity that differs from one's daily life persona; one may build friendships within this identity and experience joy and sadness as these relations develop, change and end. Still in the "worst" cases, one must admit that the mere fact of communicating under the conditions of the new technology does not cancel the marks of power relations constituted under the conditions of face-to-face, print and electronic broadcasting modes of intercourse.

Nonetheless the structural conditions of communicating in Internet communities do introduce resistances to and breaks with these gender determinations, including sexual preferences The fact of having to decide on one's gender and sexual preference itself raises the issue of individual identity in a novel and compelling manner. If one is to be masculine, one must choose to be so. Further, one must enact one's gender choice in language and in language alone, without any marks and gestures of the body, without clothing or intonations of voice. Presenting one's gender is accomplished solely through textual means, although this does include various iconic markings invented in electronic communities such as, for example, emoticons or smilies [:-)]. Also one may experience directly the opposite gender by assuming it and enacting it in conversations.[17] Finally the particular configuration of conversation through computers and modems produces a new relation to one's body as it communicates, a cyborg in cyberspace who is different from all the embodied genders of earlier modes of information. These cyborg genders test and transgress the boundaries of the modern gender system without any necessary inclination in that direction on the part of the participant.[18]

If Internet communication does not completely filter out pre-existing technologies of power as it enacts new ones, it reproduces them variably depending on the specific feature of the Internet in question. Some aspects of the Internet, such as electronic mail between individuals who know each other, may introduce no strong disruption of the gender system. In this case, the cyborg individual does not overtake or displace the embodied individual, though even here studies have shown some differences in self presentation (more spontaneity and less guardedness).[19] From email at one end of the spectrum of modern versus postmodern identity construction, one moves to bulletin board conversations where identities may be fixed and genders unaltered but where strangers are encountered. The next, still more postmodern example would be that where identities are invented but the discourse consists in simple dialogues, the case of "virtual communities" like the Well. Further removed still from ordinary speech is the Internet Relay Chat[20] in which dialogue occurs in real time with very little hierarchy or structure. Perhaps the full novelty enabled by the Internet are the Multi-User Dimensions, Object Oriented or MOOs, which divide into adventure games and social types. More study needs to be done on the differences between these technologies of subject constitution.

On the MOOs of the social variety, advanced possibilities of postmodern identities are enacted. Here identities are invented and changeable; elaborate self-descriptions are composed; domiciles are depicted in textual form and individuals interact purely for the sake of doing so. MOO inhabitants, however, do not enjoy a democratic utopia. There exist hierarchies specific to this form of cyberspace: the site administrators who initiate and maintain the MOO have abilities to change rules and procedures that are not available to most regular players. After these "Gods" come the players themselves who, by dint of experience in the electronic space and with the programming language, accumulate certain skills, even privileges for ease of access to an array of commands. These regular members are distinguished from "guests" who, as a result of their temporary status, have fewer privileges and fewer skills in negotiating the MOO.[21] Another but far more trivial criterion of political differentiation is typing skill since this determines in part who speaks most often, especially as conversations move along with considerable speed. Even in cyberspace, asymmetries emerge which could be termed "political inequalities." Yet the salient characteristic of Internet community is the diminution in different ways of prevailing hierarchies of race,[22] age, status and especially gender. What appears in the embodied world as irreducible hierarchy, plays a lesser role in the cyberspace of MOOs. And as a result the relation of cyberspace to material human geography is decidedly one of rupture and challenge to existing identity configurations. In this sense Internet communities function as places of difference from and resistance to modern society. In a sense, they serve the function of a Habermasian public sphere, however reconfigured, without intentionally or even actually being one. They are places not of the presence of validity claims or the actuality of critical reason, but of the inscription of new assemblages of self-constitution. As audio and video begin to enhance the current textual mode of conversation the claims of these virtual realities may even become more exigent.[23] The complaint that these electronic villages are no more than the escapism of white, male undergraduates may then become less convincing.

Cyborg Politics

The example of the deconstruction of gender in Internet MOO communities illustrates the depth of the stakes in theorizing politics in the mode of information. Because the Internet inscribes the new social figure of the cyborg and institutes a communicative practice of self-constitution, the political as we have known it is reconfigured. The wrapping of language on the Internet, its digitized, machine-mediated signifiers in a space without bodies,[24] introduces an unprecedented novelty for political theory. How will electronic beings be governed? How will their experience of self-constitution rebound in the existing political arena? How will the power relations on the Internet combine with or influence power relations that emerge from face-to-face relations, print relations and broadcast relations? Assuming the U.S. government and the corporations do not shape the Internet entirely in their own image and that places of cyberdemocracy remain and spread to larger and larger segments of the population, what will emerge as a postmodern politics?

If these conditions are met, one possibility is that authority as we have known it will change drastically. The nature of political authority has shifted from embodiment in lineages in the Middle Ages to instrumentally rational mandates from voters in the modern era. In each case a certain aura becomes fetishistically attached to authority holders. In Internet communities such aura is more difficult to sustain. The Internet seems to discourage the endowment of individuals with inflated status. The example of scholarly research illustrates the point. The formation of canons and authorities is seriously undermined by the electronic nature of texts. Texts become "hypertexts" which are reconstructed in the act of reading, rendering the reader an author and disrupting the stability of experts or "authorities."[25] Similar arguments have been made by Walter Benjamin regarding film and Roland Barthes regarding novels.[26] But the material structure of Internet relations instantiates the reversibility of authorial power at a much more fundamental level than that in film and the novel.

If scholarly authority is challenged and reformed by the location and dissemination of texts on the Internet, it is possible that political authorities will be subject to a similar fate. If the term "democracy" refers to the sovereignty of embodied individuals and the system of determining office-holders by them, a new term will be required to indicate a relation of leaders and followers that is mediated by cyberspace and constituted in relation to the mobile identities found therein.

Notes

1. When I wrote this I had forgotten that Heidegger uses the example of the hammer in his discussion of technology in *Being and Time*, trans. John Macquarrie and Edward Robinson (New York: Harper and Row, 1962) pp. 69ff. I was reminded of this while reading Don Ihde's illuminating work, *Technology and the Lifeworld: From Garden to Earth* (Bloomington: Indiana University Press, 1990), pp. 31–34. Heidegger does not exactly speak of human beings becoming hammers as I suggest but something pretty close: *Dasein* is "absorbed" in equipment (p. 102).

2. See N. Katherine Hayles, "Virtual Bodies and Flickering Signifiers," *October*, 66 (Fall 1993), pp. 69–91.

3. For a study of the role of the media in the formation of a public sphere, see John Hartley, *The Politics of Pictures: The Creation of the Public in the Age of Popular Media* (New York: Routledge, 1992), p. 1. Hartley examines in particular the role of graphic images in newspapers.

4. Paul Virilio, *The Vision Machine*, trans. Julie Rose (Bloomington: Indiana University Press, 1994), p. 64.

5. Jürgen Habermas, *The Structural Transformation of the Public Sphere*, trans. Thomas Burger (Cambridge, Mass.: MIT Press, 1989).

6. Jean-François Lyotard, *The Postmodern Condition*, trans. Brian Massumi et al. (Minneapolis: University of Minnesota Press, 1984).

7. Nancy Fraser, "Rethinking the Public Sphere," *Social Text*, 25/26 (1990), pp. 56–80 and *Unruly Practices* (Minneapolis: University of Minnesota Press, 1989), esp. ch. 6, "What's Critical about Critical Theory? The Case of Habermas and Gender." For a critique of Habermas' historical analysis, see Joan Landes, *Women and the Public Sphere in the Age of the French Revolution* (Ithaca, NY: Cornell University Press, 1988).

8. Oskar Negt and Alexander Kluge, *Public Sphere and Experience: Toward an Analysis of the Bourgeois and Proletarian Public Sphere*, trans. Peter Labanyi et al. (Minneapolis: University of Minnesota Press, 1993). The foreword by Miriam Hansen (pp. ix–xli) is essential and important in its own right.

9. Rita Felski, *Beyond Feminist Aesthetics: Feminist Literature and Social Change* (Cambridge, Mass.: Harvard University Press, 1989), p. 167.

12. See the discussion of privacy in relation to electronic surveillance in David Lyon, *The Electronic Eye: The Rise of Surveillance Society* (Minneapolis: University of Minnesota Press, 1994), pp. 14–17.

11. Nancy Fraser, "Rethinking the Public Sphere," p. 57.

12. Judith Perrolle, "Conversations and Trust in Computer Interfaces," in Charles Dunlop and Rob Kling, eds., *Computerization and Controversy* (New York: Academic Press, 1991) p. 351.

13. Paul Virilio, "The Third Interval: A Critical Transition," in Verena Conley (ed.), *Rethinking Technologies* (Minneapolis: University of Minnesota Press, 1993), p. 9.

14. Marie-Laure Ryan, "Immersion vs. Interactivity: Virtual Reality and Literary Theory," *Postmodern Culture*, 5: 1 (September 1994) presents a subtle, complex comparison of reading a novel and virtual reality. She does not deal directly with MOOs and Internet virtual communities.

15. Lynn Cherny, "Gender Differences in Text-Based Virtual Reality," *Proceedings of the Berkeley Conference on Women and Language, April 1994* (forthcoming) concludes that men and women have gender specific communications on MOOs. For an analysis of bulletin board conversations that reaches the same pessimistic conclusions, see Susan C. Herring, "Gender and Democracy in Computer-Mediated Communication," *Electronic Journal of Communications*, 3: 2 (1993). Herring wants to argue that the Internet does not foster democracy since sexism continues there, but she fails to measure the degree of sexism on bulletin boards against that in face-to-face situations, nor even to indicate how this would be done. The essay may be found at info.curtin.edu.au in the directory Journals/curtin/arteduc/ejcrec/ Volume_03/Number_02/herring.txt.

16. Lindsy Van Gelder, "The Strange Case of the Electronic Lover," in Charles Dunlop and Rob Kling (eds.), *Computerization and Controversy* (New York: Academic Press, 1991), p. 373.

17. One example of education through gender switching is given by K. K. Campbell in an e-mail message entitled, "Attack of the Cyber-Weenies." Campbell explains how he was harassed when he assumed a feminine persona on a bulletin board. I wish to thank Debora Halbert for making me aware of this message.

18. For an excellent study of the cultural implications of virtual communities, see Elizabeth Reid, "Cultural Formations in Text-Based Virtual Realities" an Electronic essay at ftp.parc.xerox.com in / pub/Moo/Papers also appearing as "Virtual Worlds: Culture and Imagination," in Steve Jones (ed.), *Cybersociety* (New York: Sage, 1994), pp. 164–83.

19. In "Conversational Structure and Personality Correlates of Electronic Communication" Jill Serpentelli studies the differences in communication pattern

on different types of Internet structures. (Electronic essay at ftp.parc.xerox.com in /pub/Moo/Papers) Sara Kiesler, Jane Siegel, Timothy McGuire, "Social Psychological Aspects of Computer-Mediated Communication," in Charles Dunlop and Rob Kling (eds.), *Computerization and Controversy* (New York: Academic Press, 1991), pp. 330–49 report that spontaneity and egalitarianism are trends of these conversations.

20. For a fascinating study of the IRC, see Elizabeth Reid, "Electropolis: Communication and Community on Internet Relay Chat," an Electronic essay at ftp.parc.xerox.com in /pub/Moo/Papers also published in *Intertek*, 3: 3 (Winter 1992), pp. 7–15.

21. I wish to thank Charles Stivale for pointing this distinction out to me and for providing other helpful comments and suggestions.

22. See Lisa Nakamura, "Race In/For Cyberspace: Identity Tourism and Racial Passing on the Internet," in *Works and Days*, 13: 1–2 (Spring–Fall 1995), pp. 181–93, who argues that race persists on MOOs but is constructed differently from "real life."

23. For a discussion of these new developments see "MUDs Grow Up: Social Virtual Reality in the Real World," by Pavel Curtis and David A. Nichols (Electronic essay at ftp.parc.xerox.com in /pub/MOO/Papers).

24. On this issue, see the important essay by Hans Ulrich Gumbrecht, "A Farewell to Interpretation," in Hans Ulrich Gumbrecht and K. Ludwig Pfeiffer (eds.), *Materialities of Communication*, trans. William Whobrey (Stanford Calif.: Stanford University Press, 1994), pp. 389–402.

25. "The Scholar's Rhizome: Networked Communication Issues" by Kathleen Burnett (kburnett@gandalf.rutgers.edu) explores this issue with convincing logic.

26. Walter Benjamin, "The Work of Art in the Age of Mechanical Reproduction," *Illuminations*, trans. Harry Zohn (New York: Schocken, 1969), p. 232 ". . . the distinction between author and public is about to lose its basic character . . . At any moment the reader is ready to turn into a writer . . ." See also Roland Barthes, *S/Z*, trans. Richard Miller (New York: Hill and Wang, 1974) for the concept of readerly texts (*texte lisible*) and writerly texts (*texte scriptible*), p. 4 for another way of theorizing the reversibility of positions.

37 Materials for an Exploratory Theory of the Network Society

Manuel Castells

. . .

THE NETWORK SOCIETY: AN OVERVIEW

In the last two decades of the twentieth century a related set of social transformations has taken place around the world. While cultures, institutions, and historical trajectories introduce a great deal of diversity in the actual manifestations of each one of these transformations, it can be shown that, overall, the vast majority of societies are affected in a fundamental way by these transformations. All together they constitute a new type of social structure that I call the network society for reasons that hopefully will become apparent. I shall summarize below the main features of these transformations, in a sequential order that does not imply hierarchy of causation in any way.

We have entered a new *technological paradigm*, centred around microelectronics-based, information/communication technologies, and genetic engineering. In this sense what is characteristic of the network society is not the critical role of knowledge and information, because knowledge and information were central in all societies. Thus, we should abandon the notion of 'Information Society', which I have myself used sometimes, as unspecific and misleading. What is new in our age is a new set of information technologies. I contend they represent a greater change in the history of technology than the technologies associated with the Industrial Revolution, or with the previous Information Revolution (printing). Furthermore, we are only at the beginning of this technological revolution, as the Internet becomes a universal tool of interactive communication, as we shift from computer-centred technologies to network-diffused technologies, as we make progress in nanotechnology (and thus in the diffusion capacity of information devices), and, even more importantly, as we unleash the biology revolution, making possible for the first time, the design and manipulation of living organisms, including human parts. What is also characteristic of this technological paradigm is the use of knowledge-based, information technologies to enhance and accelerate the production of knowledge and information, in a self-expanding, virtuous circle. Because information processing is at the source of life, and of social action, every domain of our eco-social system is thereby transformed.

From Manuel Castells, 'Materials for an Exploratory Theory of the Network Society', *British Journal of Sociology*, vol. no. 51, no. 1 (January/March 2000) pp. 5–24. © London School of Economics 2000. Reproduced with permission of the *British Journal of Sociology* and Taylor and Francis Ltd, http://www.tandf.co.uk/journals.

We live in *a new economy*, characterized by three fundamental features. First, it is *informational*, that is, the capacity of generating knowledge and processing/managing information determine the productivity and competitiveness of all kinds of economic units, be they firms, regions, or countries. While it took two decades for the new technological system to yield its productivity dividend, we are now observing substantial productivity growth in the most advanced economies and sectors, in spite of the difficulty in measuring informational productivity with the categories of the industrial era.

Second, this new economy is *global* in the precise sense that its core, strategic activities, have the capacity to work as a unit on a planetary scale in real time or chosen time. By core activities I mean financial markets, science and technology, international trade of goods and services, advanced business services, multinational production firms and their ancillary networks, communication media, and highly skilled speciality labour. Most jobs are in fact not global, but all economies are under the influence of the movements of their globalized core. Globalization is highly selective. It proceeds by linking up all that, according to dominant interests, has value anywhere in the planet, and discarding anything (people, firms, territories, resources) which has no value or becomes devalued, in a variable geometry of creative destruction and destructive creation of value.

Third, the new economy is *networked*. At the heart of the connectivity of the global economy and of the flexibility of informational production, there is a new form of economic organization, the *network enterprise*. This is not a network of enterprises. It is a network made from either firms or segments of firms, and/or from internal segmentation of firms. Large corporations are internally de-centralized as networks. Small and medium businesses are connected in networks. These networks connect among themselves on specific business projects, and switch to another network as soon as the project is finished. Major corporations work in a strategy of changing alliances and partnerships, specific to a given product, process, time, and space. Furthermore, these co-operations are based on sharing of information. These are information networks, which, in the limit, link up suppliers and customers through one firm, with this firm being essentially an intermediary of supply and demand, collecting a fee for its ability to process information.

The unit of this production process is not the firm, but the business project. The firm continues to be the legal unit of capital accumulation. But since the value of the firm ultimately depends on its valuation in the stock market, the unit of capital accumulation (the firm) itself becomes a node in a global network of financial flows. In this economy, the dominant layer is the global financial market, where all earnings from all activities and countries end up being traded. This global financial market works only partly according to market rules. It is shaped and moved by information turbulences of various origins, processed and transmitted almost instantly by telecommunicated, information systems, in the absence of the institutional regulation of global capital flows.

This new economy (informational, global, networked) is certainly capitalist. Indeed, for the first time in history, the whole planet is capitalist, for all practical purposes (except North Korea, but not Cuba or Myanmar [Burma], and certainly not China). But it is a new brand of capitalism, in which rules for investment, accumulation, and reward, have substantially changed (see Giddens and Hutton 2000). Besides, since nothing authorizes capitalism as eternal, it is essential to focus on the characteristics of the new economy because it may well outlast the mode of production where it was born, once capitalism comes under decisive challenge and/or plunges into a structural crisis derived from its internal contradictions (after all, statism died from its self-inflicted flaws).

Work and employment are substantially transformed in/by the new economy. But, against a persistent myth, there is no mass unemployment as a consequence of new information technologies. The empirical record is conclusive on this matter (Carnoy 2000). Yet, there is a serious unemployment problem in Europe, unrelated to technology, and there are dramatic problems of underemployment in the developing world, caused by economic and institutional backwardness, including the insufficient diffusion and inefficient use of information technologies. There is a decisive transformation of work and employment. Induced by globalization, and the network enterprise, and facilitated by information/communication technologies, the most important transformation in employment patterns concerns the development of flexible work, as the predominant form of working arrangements. Part-time work, temporary work, self-employment, work by contract, informal or semi-formal labour arrangements, and relentless occupational mobility, are the key features of the new labour market. Feminization of paid labour leads to the rise of the 'flexible woman', gradually replacing the 'organization man', as the harbinger of the new type of worker. The key transformation is the individualization of labour, reversing the process of socialization of production characteristic of the industrial era, still at the roots of our current system of industrial relations.

The work process is interconnected between firms, regions, and countries, in a stepped up spatial division of labour, in which networks of locations are more important than hierarchies of places. Labour is fundamentally divided in two categories: self-programmable labour, and generic labour. Self programmable labour is equipped with the ability to retrain itself, and adapt to new tasks, new processes, and new sources of information, as technology, demand, and management speed up their rate of change. Generic labour, by contrast, is exchangeable and disposable, and co-exists in the same circuits with machines and with unskilled labour from around the world. Beyond the realm of employable labour, legions of discarded, devalued people form the growing planet of the irrelevant, from where perverse connections are made, by fringe capitalist business, through to the booming, global criminal economy. Because of this structural divide in terms of informational capacities, and because of the individualization of the reward system, in the absence of a determined public policy aimed at correcting structural trends, we have witnessed in the last 20 years a dramatic surge of inequality, social polarization, and social exclusion in the world at large, and in most countries, particularly, among advanced societies, in the USA and in the UK (see UNDP 1999; Hutton 1996; Castells 2000, for sources).

Shifting to the *cultural realm*, we see the emergence of a similar pattern of networking, flexibility, and ephemeral symbolic communication, in a culture organized primarily around an integrated system of electronic media, obviously including the Internet. Cultural expressions of all kinds are increasingly enclosed in or shaped by this electronic hypertext. But the new media system is not characterized by one-way, undifferentiated messages through a limited number of channels that constituted the world of mass media. And it is not a global village. Media are extraordinarily diverse, and send targeted messages to specific segments of audiences responding to specific moods of audiences. They are increasingly inclusive, bridging from one another, from network TV to cable TV or satellite TV, radio, VCR, video, portable devices, and the Internet. The whole set is coming together in the multimedia system, computer-operated by the digitalized set-top box that opens up hundreds of channels of interactive communication, reaching from the global to the local. While there is oligopolistic concentration of multimedia groups, there is, at the same time, market segmentation, and the rise of an interactive audience, superseding the uniformity of the mass audience. Because of the inclusiveness and flexibility of this system of symbolic exchange, most cultural expressions are enclosed in it, thus inducing the formation of what I call a culture of 'real virtuality'. Our symbolic environment is, by and large, structured by this flexible, inclusive hypertext, in which many people surf each day. The virtuality of this text is in fact a fundamental dimension of reality, providing the symbols and icons from which we think and thus exist.

This growing enclosure of communication in the space of a flexible, interactive, electronic hypertext does not only concern culture. It has a fundamental effect on *politics*. In almost all countries, media have become the space of politics. To an overwhelming extent people receive their information, on the basis of which they form their political opinion and structure their behaviour, through the media and particularly television and radio. Media politics needs to convey very simple messages. The simplest message is an image. The simplest, individualized image is a person. Political competition increasingly revolves around the personalization of politics. The most effective political weapons are negative messages. The most effective negative message is character assassination of opponents' personalities, and/or of their supporting organizations. Political marketing is an essential means to win political competition, including, in the information age, media presence, media advertising, telephone banks, targeted mailing, image making and unmaking. Thus, politics becomes a very expensive business, way beyond the means of traditional sources of political financing, at a time when citizens resist giving more of their tax money to politicians. Thus, parties and leaders use access to power as ways to obtain resources for their trade. Political corruption becomes a systemic feature of information age politics. Since character assassination needs some substance from time to time, systemic political corruption provides ample opportunity, as a market of intermediaries is created to leak and counter-leak damaging information. The politics of scandal takes centre stage in political competition, in close interaction with the media system, and with the co-operation of judges and prosecutors, the new stars of our political soap operas. Politics becomes a horse race, and a tragicomedy motivated by greed, backstage manoeuvres, betrayals, and, often, sex and violence—a genre increasingly indistinguishable from TV scripts.

As with all historical transformations, the emergence of a new social structure is linked to a redefinition of the material foundations of our life, of *time and space*, as Giddens (1984), Adam (2000), Lash and Urry (1994), Thrift (1990), and Harvey (1990), among others, have argued. I propose the hypothesis that two emergent social forms of time and space characterize the network society, while coexisting with prior forms of time and space. These are timeless time and the space of flows. In contrast to the rhythm of biological time characteristic of most of human existence, and to clock time characterizing the industrial age, timeless time is defined by the use of new information/communication technologies in a relentless effort to annihilate time. On the one hand, time is compressed (as in split second global financial transactions, or in the attempt to fight 'instant wars'), and on the other hand, time is de-sequenced, including past, present, and future occurring in a random sequence (as in the electronic hypertext or in the blurring of life-cycle patterns, both in work and parenting).

The space of flows refers to the technological and organizational possibility of organizing the simultaneity of social practices without geographical contiguity. Most dominant functions in our societies (financial markets, transnational production networks, media systems, etc.) are organized around the space of flows. And so too are an increasing number of alternative social practices (such as social movements) and personal interaction networks. However, the space of flows does include a territorial dimension, as it requires a technological infrastructure that operates from certain locations, and as it connects functions and people located in specific places. Yet, the meaning and function of the space of flows depend on the flows processed within the networks, by contrast with the space of places, in which meaning, function, and locality are closely interrelated.

The central power-holding institution of human history, *the state*, is also undergoing a process of dramatic transformation. On the one hand, its sovereignty is called into question by global flows of wealth, communication, and information. On the other hand, its legitimacy is undermined by the politics of scandal and its dependence on media politics. The weakening of its power and credibility induce people to build their own systems of defence and representation around their identities, further delegitimizing the state. However, the state does not disappear. It adapts and transforms itself. On the one hand, it builds partnerships between nation-states and shares sovereignty to retain influence. The European Union is the most obvious case, but around the world there is a decisive shift of power toward multinational and transnational institutions, such as NATO, IMF/World Bank, United Nations agencies, World Trade Organization, regional trade associations, and the like. On the other hand, to regain legitimacy, most states have engaged in a process of devolution of power, decentralizing responsibilities and resources to nationalities, regions, and local governments, often extending this decentralization to non-governmental organizations. The international arena is also witnessing a proliferation of influential, resourceful non-governmental organizations that interact with governments, and multinational political institutions. Thus, overall the new state is not any longer a nation-state. The state in the information age is a network state, a state made out of a complex web of power-sharing, and negotiated decision-making between international, multinational, national, regional, local, and non-governmental, political institutions.

There are two common trends in these processes of transformation that, together, signal a new historical landscape. First, none of them could have taken place without new information/communication technologies. Thus, while technology is not the cause of the transformation, it is indeed the indispensable medium. And in fact, it is what constitutes the historical novelty of this multidimensional transformation. Second, all processes are enacted by organizational forms that are built upon networks, or to be more specific, upon information networks. Thus, to analyse the emerging social structure in theoretically meaningful terms, we have to define what information networks are, and elaborate on their strategic role in fostering and shaping current processes of social transformation.

SOCIAL STRUCTURE AND SOCIAL MORPHOLOGY: FROM NETWORKS TO INFORMATION NETWORKS

A network is a set of interconnected nodes. A node is the point where the curve intersects itself. Networks are very old forms of social organization. But they have taken on a new life in the Information Age by becoming information networks, powered by new information technologies. Indeed, networks had traditionally a major advantage and a major problem, in contrast to other configurations of social morphology, such as centralized hierarchies. On the one hand, they are the most flexible, and adaptable forms of organization, able to evolve with their environment and with the evolution of the nodes that compose the network. On the other hand, they have considerable difficulty in co-ordinating functions, in focusing resources on specific goals, in managing the complexity of a given task beyond a certain size of the network. Thus, while they were the natural forms of social expression, they were generally outperformed as tools of instrumentality. For most of human history, and unlike biological evolution, networks were outperformed by organizations able to master resources around centrally defined goals, achieved through the implementation of tasks in rationalized, vertical chains of command and control. But for the first time, the introduction of new information/communication technologies allows networks to keep their flexibility and adaptability, thus asserting their evolutionary nature. While, at the same time, these technologies allow for co-ordination and management of complexity, in an interactive system which features feedback effects, and communication patterns from anywhere to everywhere within the networks. It follows an unprecedented combination of flexibility and task implementation, of co-ordinated decision-making, and decentralized execution, which provide a superior social morphology for all human action.

Networks de-centre performance and share decision-making. By definition, a network has no centre. It works on a binary logic: inclusion/exclusion. All there is in the network is useful and necessary for the existence of the network. What is not in the network does not exist from the network's perspective, and thus must be either ignored (if it is not relevant to the network's task), or eliminated (if it is competing in goals or in performance). If a node in the network ceases to perform a useful function it is phased out from the network, and the network rearranges itself—as cells do in biological processes. Some nodes are more important than others, but they all need each other as long as they are within the network. And no nodal domination is systemic. Nodes increase their importance by absorbing more information and processing it more efficiently. If they decline in their performance, other nodes take over their tasks. Thus, the relevance, and relative weight of nodes does not come from their specific features, but from their ability to be trusted by the network with an extra-share of information. In this sense, the main nodes are not centres, but switchers, following a networking logic rather than a command logic, in their function vis-à-vis the overall structure.

Networks, as social forms, are value-free or neutral. They can equally kill or kiss: nothing personal. They process the goals they are programmed to perform. All goals contradictory to the programmed goals will be fought off by the network components. In this sense, a network is an automaton. But, who programmes the network? Who decides the rules that the automaton will follow? Social actors, naturally. Thus, there is a social struggle to assign goals to the network. But once the network is programmed, it imposes its logic to all its members (actors). Actors will have to play their strategies within the rules of the network. To assign different goals to the programme of the network (in contrast to perfecting the programme within the same set of goals), actors will have to challenge the network from the outside and in fact destroy it by building an alternative network around alternative values. Or else, building a defensive, non-network structure (a commune) which does not allow connections outside its own set of values. Networks may communicate, if they are compatible in their goals. But for this they need actors who possess compatible access codes to operate the switches. They are the switchers or power-holders in our society (as in the connections between media and politics, financial markets and technology, science and the military, and drug traffic and global finance through money laundering).

The speed and shape of structural transformations in our society, ushering in a new form of social organization, come from the widespread introduction of information networks as the predominant organizational form. Why now? The answer lies in the simultaneous availability of new, flexible information technologies and a set of historical events, which came together by accident, around the late 1960s, and 1970s. These events include the restructuring of capitalism with its emphasis on deregulation and liberalization; the failed restructuring of statism unable to adapt itself to informationalism; the influence of libertarian ideology arising from the countercultural social movements of the 1960s; and the development of a new media system, enclosing cultural expressions in a global/local, interactive hypertext. All processes, interacting with each other, favoured the adoption of information networks as a most efficient form of organization. Once introduced, and powered by information technology, information networks, through competition, gradually eliminate other organizational forms, rooted in a different social logic. In this sense, they tend to assert the predominance of social morphology over social action. Let me clarify the meaning of this statement by entering into the heart of the argument, that is, by examining how specifically the introduction of information networks into the social structure accounts for the set of observable transformations as presented in the preceding section. Or, in other words, how and why information networks constitute the backbone of the network society.

THE ROLE OF INFORMATION NETWORKS IN SHAPING RELATIONSHIPS OF PRODUCTION, CONSUMPTION, POWER, EXPERIENCE, AND CULTURE

Information networks, as defined above, contribute, to a large extent, to the transformation of social structure in the information age. To be sure, this multidimensional transformation has other sources that interact with the specific effect of information networks, as mentioned above. Yet, in this analysis, I will focus on the specificity of the interaction between this new social morphology and the evolution of social structure. I will be as parsimonious as possible, trying to avoid repetition of arguments and observations already presented in this text.

A social structure is transformed when there is simultaneous and systemic transformation of relationships of production/consumption, power, and experience, ultimately leading to a transformation of culture. Information networks play a substantial role in the set of transformations I have analysed in my work and summarized here. This is how and why.

Relationships of Production

Although I suppose information networks will shape, eventually, other modes of production, for the time being we can only assess their effect in the capitalist mode of production. Networks change the two terms of the relationship (capital, labour), and their relationship. They transform capital by organizing its circulation in global networks and making it the dominant sphere of capital—the one where value, from whichever origin, increases (or decreases) and is ultimately realized. Global financial markets are information networks. They constitute themselves into a collective 'capitalist', independent from any specific capitalist (but not indifferent to), and activated by rules that are only partly market rules. In this sense, capital in the Information Age has become a human-made automaton, which, through mediations, imposes its structural determination on relationships of production. More specifically, global financial markets and their management networks constitute an automated network, governed by interactions between its multiple nodes, propelled by a combination of market logic, information turbulences, and actors' strategies and bets (see Castells 2000).

Relationships between capital and labour (all kinds of capital, all kinds of labour) are organized around the network enterprise form of production. This network enterprise is also globalized at its core, through telecommunications and transportation networks. Thus, the work process is globally integrated, but labour tends to be locally fragmented. There is simultaneous integration of production and specification of labour's contribution to the production process. Value in the production process depends essentially on the position occupied by each specific labour or each specific firm in the value chain. The rule is individualization of the relationship between capital and labour. In a growing number of cases, self-employment, or payment in stocks, leads to workers becoming holders of their own capital—however, any individual capital is submitted to the movements of the global automaton. As labour comes to be defined by a network of production and individualized in its relationship to capital, the critical cleavage within labour becomes that between networked labour and switched-off labour which ultimately becomes non-labour. Within networked labour, it is the capacity to contribute to the value-producing chain that determines the individual bargaining position. Thus labour's informational capacity, by ensuring the possibility of strategic positioning in the network, leads to a second, fundamental cleavage, between self-programmable labour and generic labour. For self-programmable labour, its individual interest is better served by enhancing its role in performing the goals of the network, thus establishing competition between labour and co-operation between capital (the network enterprise) as the structural rule of the game. Indeed game theory and rational choice theory seem to be adequate intellectual tools to understand socio-economic behaviour in the networked economy. While for generic labour, its strategy is survival: the key issue becomes not to be degraded to the realm of discarded or devalued labour, either by automation or globalization, or both.

In the last analysis, the networking of relationships of production leads to the blurring of class relationships. This does not preclude exploitation, social differentiation and social resistance. But production-based, social classes, as constituted, and enacted in the Industrial Age, cease to exist in the network society.

Relationships of Consumption

Relationships of consumption (that is, the culturally meaningful, differential appropriation of the product) are determined by the interplay between relationships of production and culture. Who does what, in a given value production system, determines who gets what. What is valued as appropriation is framed by culture. The networking of production relationships, and the consequent individualization of labour, leads on the one hand to increasing differentiation and thus inequality in consumption. It also leads to social polarization and social exclusion following the opposition between self-programmable labour and generic labour, and between labour and devalued labour. The ability of networks to connect valuable labour and territories, and to discard dispensable labour and territories, so enhancing their performance through reconfiguration, leads to cumulative growth and cumulative decline. The winner-takes-all system is, in the consumption sphere, the expression of value creation by/in the networks.

On the other hand, the fragmentation of culture, and the individualization of positions in relationships of production, lead jointly to a growing diversification of consumption patterns. Mass consumption was predicated upon standardized production, stable relationships of production, and a mass culture organized around predictable senders and identifiable sets of values. In a world of networks, self-programmable individuals constantly redefine their life styles and thus their consumption patterns; while generic labour just strives for survival.

As culture is similarly fragmented and constantly recombined in the networks of a kaleidoscopic hypertext, consumption patterns follow the variable geometry of symbolic appropriation. Thus, in the interplay between relationships of production and cultural framing, relationships of production define levels of consumption, and culture induces consumption patterns and life styles.

Relationships of Power

The most direct impact of information networks on social structure concerns power relationships. Historically, power was embedded in organizations and institutions, organized around a hierarchy of centres. Networks dissolve centres, they disorganize hierarchy, and make materially impossible the exercise of hierarchical power without processing instructions in the network, according to the network's morphological rules. Thus, contemporary information networks of capital, production, trade, science, communication, human rights, and crime, bypass the nation-state, which, by and large, has stopped being a sovereign entity, as I argued above. A similar process, in different ways, takes place in other hierarchical organizations that used to embody power ('power apparatuses' in the old Marxist terminology), such as churches, schools, hospitals, bureaucracies of all kinds. Just to illustrate this diversity, churches see their privilege as senders of belief called into question by the ubiquitous sending and receiving of messages in the interactive hypertext. While religions are flourishing, churches have to enter the new media world in order to promote their gospel. So doing, they survive, and even prosper, but they open themselves up to constant challenges to their authority. In a sense, they are secularized by their co-existence with profanity in the hypertext, except when/if they anchor themselves in fundamentalism by refusing to bend to the network, thus building self-contained, cultural communes.

The state reacts to its bypassing by information networks, by transforming itself into a network state. So doing, its former centres fade away as centres becoming nodes of power-sharing, and forming institutional networks. Thus, in the war against Yugoslavia, in spite of US military hegemony, decision-making was shared in various degrees by NATO governments, including regular video-conferences between the leaders of the main countries where key decisions were taken. This example goes beyond the former instances of traditional military alliances, by introducing joint war-making in real time. NATO was reinforced by NATO's state members, when these states, including the USA, entered the new world of shared sovereignty. But individual states became weakened in their autonomous decision-making. The network became the unit.

Thus, while there are still power relationships in society, the bypassing of centres by flows of information circulating in networks creates a new, fundamental hierarchy: the power of flows takes precedence over the flows of power.

Relationships of Experience

If power relationships are the ones most directly affected by the prevailing networking logic, the role of networks in the transformation of relationships of experience is more subtle. I will not force the logic of the analysis. I do not believe that we must see networks everywhere for the sake of coherence. Yet, I think it could be intriguing to elaborate tentatively on the links between networking and the transformation of relationships of experience.

This transformation, empirically speaking, revolves around the crisis of patriarchalism, and its far-reaching consequences for family, sexuality and personality. The fundamental source of this crisis is women's cultural revolution, and men's resistance to reverse their millennial privileges. Additional sources are the feminization of labour markets (undermining male domination in the family and in society at large), the revolution in reproductive technology, the self-centring of culture, the individualization of life patterns, and the weakening of the state's authority to enforce patriarchalism. What have networks to do with all this?

There is one direct connection between the networking of work and the individualization of labour, and the mass incorporation of women to paid labour, under
conditions of structural discrimination. Thus, new social relationships of production,
translate into a good fit between the 'flexible woman' (forced to flexibility to cope with
her multiple roles) and the network enterprise. Networks of information, and global
communication are also critical in diffusing alternative life styles, role models, and, more
importantly, critical information, for instance about self-control of biological reproduction. Then, there is an additional, meaningful connection. The disintegration of
the patriarchal family does not leave people, and children, isolated. They reconfigure
life-sharing forms through networking. This is particularly true of women and their
children, relying on a form of sociability and solidarity tested by millennia of living
'underground'. But also men, and men and women after going their own ways, come to
rely on networks (sometimes around children of multiple marriages) to both survive
and reinvent forms of togetherness. This trend shifts the basis of interpersonal relationships from nuclei to networks: networks of individuals and their children—which, by
the way, are also individuals. What is left of families are transformed in partnerships
which are nodes of networks. Sexuality is de-coupled from the family, and transformed
into consumption/images, stimulated and simulated from the electronic hypertext. The
body, as proposed by Giddens some time ago, becomes an expression of identity
(1991). It is individualized and consumed in sexual networks. At the level of personality,
the process of socialization becomes customized, individualized, and made out of
composite models. The autonomous ability to reprogramme one's own personality,
in interaction with an environment of networks, becomes the crucial feature for
psychological balance, replacing the strengthening of a set personality, embedded in
established values. In this 'risk society' (Beck 1992), the management of anxiety is the
most useful personal skill. Two conflicting modes of interpersonal interaction emerge:
on the one hand, self-reliant communes, anchored in their non-negotiable sets of
beliefs; and on the other hand, networks of ever shifting individuals.

These are social networks, not information networks. So, in a way, they are a fundamental part of our societies, but not necessarily a feature of the network society—unless
we extend the meaning of the concept beyond what I propose: information networks-
based social structure. However, as communication technology, biological technology, transgender networking, and networks of individuals, develop in parallel, as key
elements of social practice, they are interacting, and influencing each other. Thus, the
Internet is becoming a very instrumental tool of management of new forms of life,
including the building of on-line communities of support and collective learning.

I see, however, a much stronger connection between networks and relationships of
experience through the cultural transformations induced by communication networks,
as experience becomes practice by its rooting in cultural codes.

Networks and Cultural Transformation

Culture was historically produced by symbolic interaction in a given space/time. With
time being annihilated and space becoming a space of flows, where all symbols co-exist
without reference to experience, culture becomes the culture of real virtuality. It takes
the form of an interactive network in the electronic hypertext, mixing everything, and

voiding the meaning of any specific message out of this context, except that is for fundamental, non-communicable values external to the hypertext. So, culture is unified in the hypertext but interpreted individually (in line with the 'interactive audience' school of thought in media theory). Culture is constructed by the actor, self-produced and self-consumed. Thus, because there are few common codes, there is systemic mis-understanding. It is this structurally induced cacophony that is celebrated as post-modernity. However, there is one common language, the language of the hypertext. Cultural expressions left out of the hypertext are purely individual experiences. The hypertext is the vehicle of communication, thus the provider of shared cultural codes. But these codes are formal, voided of specific meaning. Their only shared meaning is to be a node, or a blip, in the network of communication flows. Their communicative power comes from their capacity to be interpreted and re-arranged in a multi-vocality of meanings, depending on the receiver, and on the interactor. Any assigned meaning becomes instantly obsolete, reprocessed by a myriad of different views and alternative codes. The fragmentation of culture and the recurrent circularity of the hypertext, leads to the individualization of cultural meaning in the communication networks. The networking of production, the differentiation of consumption, the decentring of power, and the individualization of experience, are reflected, amplified, and codified by the fragmentation of meaning in the broken mirror of the electronic hypertext—where the only shared meaning is the meaning of sharing the network.

CONCLUSION: SOCIAL CHANGE IN THE NETWORK SOCIETY

Social structures are sets of organizational regularities historically produced by social actors, and constantly challenged, and ultimately transformed by deliberate social action. The network society is no exception to this sociological law. Yet, the character-istics of specific social structures impose constraints on the characteristics of their transformation process. Thus, the recurrence and flexibility of information networks, their embedded ability to bypass, ignore or eliminate, instructions alien to their pro-grammed goals, make social change in the network society a very tricky task. This is because, apparently, nothing must be changed—any new input can theoretically be added to the network, like free expression in the global media system. Yet, the price for the addition is to accept implicitly the programmed goal of the network, its ancillary language and operating procedures. Thus, my hypothesis is that there is little chance of social change within a given network, or network of networks. Understanding by social change, the transformation of the programme of the network, to assign to the network a new goal, following a different set of values and beliefs. This is in contrast to reprogramming the network by adding instructions compatible with the overarching goal.

Because of the capacity of the network to find new avenues of performance by switching off any non-compatible node, I think social change, under these circum-stances, happens primarily through two mechanisms, both external to dominant networks. The first is the denial of the networking logic through the affirmation of values that cannot be processed in any network, only obeyed and followed. This is what I call cultural communes, that are not necessarily linked to fundamentalism, but which are always centred around their self-contained meaning. The second is alternative networks, that is networks built around alternative projects, which compete, from network to network, to build bridges of communication to other networks in society, in opposition to the codes of the currently dominant networks. Religious, national, territorial, and ethnic communes are examples of the first type of challenge. Ecologism, feminism, human rights movements are examples of alternative networks. All use the Internet and electronic media hypertext, as dominant networks do. This is not what makes them networks or communes. The critical divide lies in the communicability or non-communicability of their codes beyond their specific self-definition. The fundamental dilemma in the network society is that political institutions are not the site of power any longer. The real power is the power of instrumental flows, and cultural codes, embedded in networks. Therefore, the assault on these immaterial power sites, from outside their logic, requires either the anchoring in eternal values, or the projection of alternative, communicative codes that expand through networking of alternative networks. That social change proceeds through one way or another will make the difference between fragmented communalism and new history making.

References

Adam, Barbara 'The temporal gaze: the challenge for social theory in the context of GM food', *British Journal of Sociology* (2000) 51.1:125–42.

Beck, Ulrich (1992) *Risk Society: Towards a New Modernity*. London: Sage.

Carnoy, Martin (2000) *Work, Family and Community in the Information Age*. New York: Russell Sage.

Castells, Manuel (2000) 'Information technology and global capitalism', in A. Giddens and W. Hutton (eds.) *On the Edge*. London: Jonathan Cape.

Giddens, Anthony (1984) *The Constitution of Society: Outline of a Theory of Structuration*. Cambridge: Polity Press.

—— (1991) *Modernity and Self-Identity. Self and Society in the Late Modern Age*. Stanford: Stanford University Press.

Giddens, Anthony, and Hutton, Will (eds.) (2000) *On the Edge*. London: Jonathan Cape.

Harvey, David (1990) *The Condition of Postmodernity*. Oxford: Blackwell.

Hutton, Will (1996) [1995] *The State We're In*. London: Jonathan Cape.

Lash, Scott, and Urry, John (1994) *Economies of Signs and Space*. London: Sage.

Thrift, Nigel J. (1990) 'The making of capitalism in time consciousness', in J. Hassard (ed.) *The Sociology of Time*. London: Macmillan.

United Nations Development Programme (1999) *1999 Human Development Report: Globalization with a Human Face*. New York: UNDP-United Nations.

Epilogue: The Future is Present
American Cultural Studies on the Net

Eva Vieth

Welcome to the New World

In this *Reader*, we have tried to collect and juxtapose texts that can be seen as key positions within the heterogeneous field of *American cultural studies*. Our first major point of reference was the New Journalism. As we have made clear elsewhere, this was not meant to indicate some kind of "beginning" of the special brand of cultural studies that we have presented as *American cultural studies*; but it did show a noticeable shift in perception and representation of social and cultural realities, personal and individual visions that set the tone for the critical rereadings of the 1970s, 1980s, and 1990s. We have tried to show that cultural studies can be "provincial" and that this is not necessarily a bad thing. We concentrated on issues and methods that foreground the uniqueness of America's culture, those aspects and debates which cannot be readily transposed onto any given cultural background, but which are in many ways indigenous to the USA and the notion of "America" as we outlined it in the Introduction.

This epilogue, which focuses on cultural studies on the Internet, will try to tackle this question in a slightly different way. On the one hand, the Internet, a network of many different, regional networks, by now counts as thoroughly global medium, easily at hand from most countries if—admittedly a big if—the access technology is available. On the other hand, and in more than one sense, the Internet is more than ever American. The Internet was born American; some thirty years back, its parent ARPAnet originated from Cold War paranoia, programmers' hunger for communication, and academic necessity to use scarce computer resources as well as possible. Even as initially ancillary academic and private communication grew central to Net traffic, and as other nations developed their own networks and linked up, the American context remained dominant. Today, more than 40 per cent of the input into the Net originates in the USA, most netizens are American, and the texts published on the Net are mainly in American language (and spelling).

But the "Americanness" of the Net goes further: we have spoken of America's role as the "great attractor" since the Second World War, of the visions of Americanness circulated both inside and outside of the States regarding the two poles of imperialism and liberation (cf. Hartley's Introduction to this *Reader*). The "American way of life" embraces both free speech and free enterprise capitalism, modernity through ideology and modernity through technology, and a "manifest destiny" to shape the future. In the past decade, exactly the same polarities—whether or not perceived as "American" issues—have structured debates about the possible function and influence of the Net. From its mythology of a virtual new world (cf. Cresher 1994) that waits for colonization, to its promises of new identities/communities/financial successes, to the growing concerns about surveillance, control, and technological imperialism, the Net has taken a position in public discourse that used to be reserved for the notion of "Americanness" itself. If we named *American cultural studies* a "specific regional project", then *cultural studies on the Net* has to take into account that it straddles the gap between the heritage of a specific regional background and a presence that is negotiated between many regional and meta-regional voices. In this sense, the Net is developing into a "province" of its own, an entirely new locus of "transparency, hybridity, mutual attraction and dialogue", both "creating new forms and possibilities in citizenship, identity, even in personhood" (p. 11, above) and working as a forum to negotiate the existing ones.

Cultural studies has taken up the challenge to move into this new territory, prioritizing its functions and possibilities in everyday life, using it both as a tool for academic (and not so academic) exchange and as an object of study. The first part of this chapter will briefly discuss the different forms official and unofficial cultural studies have taken on the Net, introducing specific sites or journals and describing the changes cultural studies on the Net has undergone in comparison to the traditional academic discourse. The second part will take a closer look at how cultural studies deals with the Net *as a region*, in how far it is engaged in the negotiations about the structure, ideology, practices, and nature of its citizens.

Form follows Function

In this collection, we have mainly concentrated on texts that have developed within (albeit sometimes avant-garde) academia, usually published within academic books or journals, subjected to processes of institutionalized gatekeeping and peer-review. Authors and publications could be located relatively easily within an ethnic and national frame, structures of identification are in place. This article, which relies for a considerable part on Net publications, can make no such claims—the problems of net-quoting, the difficulties of net-evaluation, and the quick degeneration of net-evidence are by now well-known nuisances on the borderline between digital and print communication. The high frequency of net-exchange—quick to appear, quick to disappear—already goes against the grain of academic tradition which prefers its sources and archives to be constantly available, reproducible, properly reviewed, and localized. While in many respects academia still embraces the image of a continuously extended constant "building" of knowledge predicated upon a pre-existing core (originating in the high hopes for rationality of the Enlightenment), the Net, though also continuously expanding, does not necessarily accumulate such a "core". Dead links, sites that have moved to other domains without leaving an address, texts made available without any references to sources, author, or date of origin, do not lend themselves easily to academic practices. Nonetheless: the relationship between cultural studies and the Internet has been described as "*amor fati*" [a love made by fate]:

Cultural Studies, a discipline which has always prided itself on its pioneer spirit . . . meets the Internet, a medium built on metaphors of cyberspace and virtual frontiers . . . For a discipline thriving on the diverse, the radical, the popular and the novel, the Internet's near-infinite archive of subcultures, trivia, fan groups, and homemade artefacts, constantly expanding and updated by the second, was just too rich a prospect to pass up. (Brooker 1998: 415)

The very form of engagement with Net sites, the way to accumulate information or to simply enjoy the richness of the Net resources through "browsing", "surfing", or, probably most appropriate, "drifting" from site to site, resonates with the tendency of cultural studies to adopt an individualized approach; this means an approach that includes the perspective of the author, the shifting networks of subjective/objective meanings on the fringes of a subject, the unacknowledged connections between "accepted" and "marginalized" culture. When closing in on cultural studies sites through search engines or meta-sites, the invitation to wander off into seemingly different areas is always present. Worming your way through pop culture sites, side-stepping to the Barbie home page, somehow clicking your way into an e-journal on White Cultural Supremacy, and ending up on a porn page thinly disguised as "Babe Culture" drives home the message that the virtual world does not employ familiar disciplinary barriers. Though the development of virtual high security zones, red light districts, and the "bad part of town" is in full swing, for most users the accepted and the unaccepted alike are only a mouse click away.

But say you have found your way to the "official" cultural studies sites—Cultural Studies Central (CSC), Sarah Zuphko's Cultural Studies Center, The Voice of the Shuttle, Cultustud-L, or the k.i.s.s. of the Panopticon, just to name a few. Apart from k.i.s.s., which functions as a popular "Who's who" of cultural studies, all sites offer an overwhelming richness of links to other sites, other subjects, events, articles, job openings, etc. In the excited self-definition of CSC:

Cultural Studies today is a simmering stew of the ideas, voices and lives of people all over the world. It's the things we use and the people we talk about. It's life and life only. Cultural Studies Central is a gathering spot and central clearing house where those of us who live and breathe Cultural Studies can go to learn more and do more. (<www.culturalstudies.net/index.html#intro>)

More poignantly, the "intellectual questions" faq list of Cultstud-L (<www.cas.usf.edu/communication/rodman/cultstud/ faq.html#3.1>) answers all questions about what Cultural Studies might be—study of culture, study of popular culture, critical theory, etc.—with a decisive yes and no, ultimately refusing those definitions in favour of an extensive bibliography ranging from Tony Bennett over Sarah Franklin and Richard Johnson to Jon Stratton and Ien Ang. Other sites, like Sarah Zupko's, avoid the problem of definition completely, but whether or not any "mission statement" is explicitly given, the form of the sites makes clear that cultural studies on the Net cannot be squeezed into a two-line definition, that the structure of the day is additive, not exclusive. Most servers feature at least a link to American Studies, Critical Theory, Sociology, or Humanities sites, if they are not sub sites of those. Many articles turn up several times under different headings and subjects; the only halfway-viable sort system—apart from meta-collections according to subjects—seems to be the haphazard, but also universal sorting according to alphabetization. Brooker comments on this erosion of subjects, hierarchies, and categorizations, which is a strong departure from the more or less two-dimensional organization of print media, departmental reading lists, and book stores:

Departments of cultural studies currently devote a great deal of energy to feuds over definition and boundaries, enforcing their own identity by stressing their difference from faculties of sociology, film or media. . . . In the virtual academy . . . these restrictions are lifted and the arbitrary nature of such divisions begins to emerge as texts which straddle two or more fields are allowed to occupy both. By discovering cultural studies alongside media, postmodernism, queer theory, postcolonialism, feminism and even critical legal studies, the visitor to the *English Server* may well discover what her subject has in common with others, rather than how it stands apart. (Brooker 1998: 418)

But this does neither mean complete arbitrariness nor an all-embracing harmony. There are some sites, e.g. the *Black Cultural Studies* (BCS) page, which break the often enough terminally hip tone of the mission statements and the cuteness of little flashing icons. They function not only as archives of subject-bound academic activity, but also as places of passionate cultural difference, positioning of identity and political action:

The signifier "Black" and the "meanings that have condensed onto it", in the words of Stuart Hall, form the conceptual basis of the web site. Because the construction and maintenance of this site is a formidable task, we began by risking what Gina Dent called "the essentialist gesture" in including only scholars of African descent. . . . We hope that this web site will provide some helpful resources for those working to dismantle what bell hooks calls "the white supremacist, homophobic, capitalist patriarchy" we inhabit. (<*BCS*, www.tiac.net/users/thaslett>)

This site, among others, indicates that richness and free combination on the Net goes hand in hand with the redrawing of boundaries and facilitation of distinct representations. Even if the distances between areas are now measured in mouse clicks rather than in footsteps, department floors, and bookshelves, the cultural distances remain.

One of the factors contributing to the sometimes chaotic organization of most cultural studies sites is their attempt to simultaneously function as archive, library, journal, meeting place, pin board, and yellow pages. Though e-journals and zines also usually feature link-and discussion-pages, the metaphorical journal-shape makes their contents easier to handle. Since most journals have kept the off-line tradition of weekly, monthly, or quarterly "publication" and attempt to publish new material rather than digitalize elsewhere published old articles, they tend to be more up to date than many other sites.

The journal to mention here, since it cannot be found by typing "cultural studies" into a search engine, is *Bad Subjects*, a collective originating in the University of California, Berkeley in 1992, but by now also including the work of non-academic writers. Celebrating "Political Education for Everyday Life," the collective manages to combine cultural critique with positive utopianism, acute self-awareness with willing extension to otherness, and pragmatism about usabilities with a healthy distrust against the hype. In recent years, *Bad Subjects* has created a distinct voice in the swirl of Net resources that other e-journals, whether *Cultronix* or *Undercurrent*, *M/C* or *Culture Machine*, have yet to achieve. Nonetheless, all of these journals subscribe to interdisciplinary approaches and try to climb down from the ivory tower of academia (*Undercurrent*: "style [of submissions] should be appropriate for the generally educated outsider" (<darkwing.uoregon.edu/~ucurrent/subscribe.html>)). Like the other sites, the journals adopt an additive, interdisciplinary structure. Though at first glance similar to their printed counterparts, e-journals also offer possibilities that challenge the traditional hierarchies of hard-copy texts. The immediacy of response possibilities, via email or notice-boards, and the direct links to other sources or bibliographical entries more and more blur the barrier between author and reader. Instead of a slow, monological exchange between participants whose ranking and authority are relatively clearly defined, a "multilogue" develops, part-public, part-private, an open invitation to participate. The extremity of this form of debate can be found in organizations like alt.culture or the WELL. These can only be read as multi-authorial textual constructs, branching and recombining in different subjects, positions, and methods. Though structures of authority from traditional academia still function, the community participating in these debates also has its own methods of identification and ranking, usually prioritizing the present behaviour of the participant over known background and/or "Real Life" standing.

As a whole, cultural studies on the Net balances between two extremes: on the one hand are structures inherited from traditional academia, e.g. archiving texts written long before the digital revolution, metasites institutionalizing at least something of a canon, offering readily accessible information and relatively easy publication to the aspiring scholar. On the other hand are decidedly counter-disciplinary and even counter-academic structures that erode the barriers between subjects, levels of authority, practices of academic writing, and writers and readers. It remains to be seen how far these structures will influence cultural studies as a subject taught at universities. However, these formal changes in the practices of an academic subject are themselves part of a much more radical shift in the *object* of cultural studies: the practices and structures of everyday life and culture in the "Information Age."

Life in Cyberspace

The transition to an "Information Age" that more and more perceives reality as a form of constructed, malleable, and marketable information has left deep traces in the narratives that present day culture is forming about itself. As an example, the past decade has seen a general shift of paradigm in the blockbuster visions of the future. Whereas the 1960s and 1970s still boldly went where no one had gone before, the futures of the 1990s stay at home. They want to celebrate their *Independence Day* in peace and quiet, brush off their last threads of imperfection in *Gattaca*, or are on the run inside the *Matrix*. On the borderline of sci-fi films, the world has turned into the *Truman Show*, while the *Enemy of the State* is trying to dodge the omnipresent surveillance nets. Where older sci-fi was in love with aliens, androids, and the other-who-becomes-self, present day narratives prefer the self-that-becomes-other, finding strangeness and fragility in the most familiar of all places, ordinary life. Technology is no longer personified as threatening or benevolent other, but forming the backbone of a new continuum—the integration of the technologized self reaching into the technologized other. Though this transition was marked in the 1980s by *Blade Runner* and the developing genre of cyberpunk, it is only now that these visions are seen as more than possible projections into a relatively far-off future for the select clientele of sci-fi lovers and techno-buffs. Sci-fi has been instrumental in developing a language of "will" and "shall" that by now structures the discourse not only of the future, but also of the present. More than ever, the visions of the future are rooted in technological possibilities already available, reflecting the growing feeling that something at the heart of our perceptions of society and everyday life is in the process of changing.

Space

Central to this general notion of change is the Internet itself. It is focus point, creator, and perpetrator of the new future, virtual frontier approaching the end of the first gold rush, somewhere between express way into things to come, source of the future doom of humanity, and everyday medium for the hyperconnected netizen. But it also still functions within the categories used to analyse other "regions": it can be questioned regarding the space it occupies, the people who inhabit it, and the practices and ideologies that govern it. Regarding the space it occupies, together with other media it is part of

the terrain created by the television, the telephone, the telenetworks crisscrossing the globe. These "vectors" produce in us a new kind of experience, the experience of telestheia—perception at a distance. This is our "virtual geography", the experience of which doubles, troubles, and generally permeates our experience of the space we experience firsthand. (Wark 1994: vii)

Virtualized space is not like real space. It forms bridges between real places, changing their nature and location in the process of transmitting information, but it also offers spaces entirely virtual, completely based on textual exchange. The apparent omnipresence and pre-existence of the Net masks its status as fabricated space, constantly constructed and reconstructed within real space:

what we value about cyberspace resembles what the Left has criticized about capitalism. Like global capitalism, computer networks bring people together in alienation rather than solidarity. People who interact on-line are generally not privy to the way those networks are produced by actual people existing within a concrete economic order. Cyberspace is a commodity in the process of being produced by programmers, paid system operators, and a range of volunteers who parcel out memory to users, generate more complicated interactive data spaces, and maintain order on newsgroups, mailing lists, and FTP sites. The Net is not antithetical to the free market, to consumerism, or to alienated labour. After all, science fiction author William Gibson invented the term cyberspace to describe virtual reality in a future dominated by multinational corporations and wealthy elites who prey on a vast, international underclass. (*Bad Subjects* Collective 1995, <english-www.hss.cmu.edu/bs/18/Manifesto.html>

To see cyberspace *only* as produced commodity would be too reductive—but neither is it the Promised Land "naturally" there to be colonized. Again, the similarity to visions of America is striking: metaphors of immeasurable empty space, freedom, and new beginnings combine with a planned, structured, planted environment usable for the profit and power of the "mother country"—or rather, "real life." The Net cannot be interpreted as one or the other—as space of communication and power negotiation, it is both dependent on the input of real life and functions as "other" space that can form the naturalized environment of its inhabitants.

Identities

But what kind of inhabitants are these? The "nature of the netizen" has been under debate since computer life emancipated itself from the image of the nerdy hacker with greasy hair doing unmentionable things in pizza-littered basements. The *Communities in Cyberspace* (Smith and Kolock 1999) have been regarded with amazement, distrust, or enthusiasm, mainly because of their strong hold upon their participants, but only in the last few years has the concept of Net citizenship been seen as viable influence instead of obsession. Jon Katz's analysis of "The Digital Citizen" (1997), based on a survey by *Wired* and the Merrill Lynch Forum, describes the "connected" minority as the model new American citizen rendered so through their willingness to use the possibilities of cyberspace:

For the Connected, technology is seen not as a cure-all, but as a powerful tool for individual expression, democratization, economic opportunity, and education. Their familiarity with technology has helped create what may be the most optimistic segment of our political culture. . . . technologically savvy Americans feel endemic disenchantment with the way our civic institutions perform. . . . The Digital Citizens' rationalism, knowledge, belief in free exchange of information, and passion for change are all antithetical to the political culture of Washington. (Katz 1997: <www.wired.com/wired/archive/5.12/netizen_pr.html>)

This image of the netizen stands in sharp contrast with the notion of the netizen as subscriber to the "Californian Ideology" that Barbrook and Cameron developed two years before. Portraying the netizens as jaded ex-hippies turned conservative, selling out cultural critique to a "virtual class" believing in nothing but "technological determinism," Barbrook and Cameron declare:

The California Ideology is a mix of cybernetics, free market economics, and counter-culture libertarianism and is promulgated by magazines such as *Wired* and *Mondo 2000* as well as the books of Stewart Brand, Kevin Kelly and many others. The new faith has been embraced by computer nerds, slacker students, thirty-something capitalists, hip academics, futurist bureaucrats and even the President of the USA himself. (Barbrook and Cameron 1995: <www.wmin.ac.uk/media/HRC/ci/califi.html>)

Again, we find ourselves on a borderline of an "either/or" where an "and" is necessary. The crossbreed of Hip Jo/e Public and the Evil Capitalist that Barbrook and Cameron describe stands in contrast to Katz's Bright Netizen, but both cover only part of the possible identities and codes of behavior created by life on the Net. The "netizen" is not reducible to one singular negative or positive phenomenon, most especially not in terms of positions inherited from pre-Net political and economic systems. By 1991, Haraway used the image of the cyborg—since then broadly accepted as descriptive term—to describe a vision of a new type of identity not easily reduced to its conventional parts:

The cyborg is resolutely committed to partiality, irony, intimacy, and perversity. It is oppositional, utopian, and completely without innocence. No longer structured by the polarity of public and private, the cyborg defines a technological polis based partly on a revolution of social relations in the oikos, the household. Nature and culture are reworked; the one can no longer be the resource for appropriation or incorporation by the other. The relationships for forming wholes from parts, including those of polarity and hierarchical domination, are at issue in the cyborg world. Unlike the hope of Frankenstein's monster, the cyborg does not expect its father to save it through a restoration of the garden; that is, through the fabrication of a heterosexual mate, through its completion in a finished whole, a city and cosmos. . . . Cyborgs are not reverent; they do not remember the cosmos. They are wary of holism, but needy for connection—they seem to have a natural feel for united front politics, but without the vanguard party. (Haraway 1991: 151)

This notion of identity through partiality, a departure from the idea of the "unit" citizen relatively easily categorized in social, political and economical terms has to be taken into account in any description of the netizen. To make a comparison with ethnic identity, Afro-Americans, Asian-Americans, Italo-Americans, etc. are not only defined through their country of (removed) origin. They are also "something else," and this "something else" as yet awaits description. As cyberspace itself, the netizen is "dual" in nature, and this duality needs to be taken into account.

Power

While cultural critique and social analysis still struggle for a vocabulary that recognizes this double nature (for a working example, see Jackson 1997), the process of registration and classification not only of the declared netizen, but of the population inside modernity as a whole is under way. The increasingly finer woven nets of surveillance and control—nets of closed-circuit camera systems, magnetic strip-cards carrying more information about the user than a pocket-library, data banks of citizens' conduct and consumer preferences, are combining with the information given in the extremely vulnerable form of digital text on the Net into a joint one-way venture of bureaucracy and economy that lends an entirely new twist to the Panopticon:

Bentham's Panopticon employed punitive sanctions against rule-breakers, but more importantly it exercised preventative control. The administrative state, joined by the corporate sector, goes a step further by establishing the statistical probability of the *risk* that categories of people will break the rules. When risk can be confidently calculated, potential rule-breakers can be excluded from the opportunity of noncompliance. (Whitaker 1999: 44)

It is at this point that the connections between the virtual plains and "real life" emerge at their most threatening. While the Net offers the chance of constructing a new public sphere (cf. Poster 1995, Chapter 36 in this *Reader*) with entirely new democratic practices and sovereignties to be had, these data can also be employed in strategies of stronger control and interference. The power negotiations between the state, conglomerates and individual organizations have just begun. While some Net communities have developed quite sophisticated codes of behavior and hierarchies of power, the Net as a whole is still vastly unregulated. Orwell's Big Brother could still be identified—and rebelled against—as one singular apparatus; today's "Little Brothers" have no such singular structure: what agency collects what data about whom, for what reason, and with what right becomes increasingly more difficult to trace and, even worse, where those data end up in the long run is equally unclear. The formation of privacy organizations—the majority of which also feature the blue ribbon of the free speech campaign—and the growing use of anonymizers, proxies, and remailers on the Net are an indication that more and more people are aware of this development, and that the question of data security is becoming one of the more direct and pressing problems of both virtual and real citizenship.

Conclusion

If Poster declares the Internet to be "more like Germany than like a hammer" (p. 403, above), his choice of country was courteous (his article was originally presented in Berlin), but "America" would have been more to the point. I would like to add a third category to his two categories of "thing-like"-ness and "social-construction-of-country-like"-ness: the "idea-like"-ness that regions have as long as they are under construction. More than just the hype surrounding the advent of a still relatively new technology, the Internet has transformed the issues of "Americanness" which we presented in this reader into issues of "Cyberness." The issues of imperialism and liberation, democracy and capitalism, emancipation and marginalization have partly cut loose from the region they were originally centered on, moving into the new virtual colony that by now is beginning to show first signs of a desire for independence. While, as I tried to show, virtual and real space cannot be but dependent on each other, the project of cultural studies on the Net also indicates that they are still "other"—and that the specific type of otherness, vision, and world construction undertaken in virtual space might well reflect back on the conditions of "real life." The Net is constructed through the language of "will" and "shall" that sci-fi prepared, but this time round the constructions are also invested with the lives, feelings, and aspirations of many, many people, American and non-American, black, white, female, male, young, old. Unlike America, you do not have to climb onto a ship to get there—the virtual world is already part of the continuous present, engagement with it a button touch away (at least for those with access to the technology). Negotiations about what this new world is going to be are continuing, and cultural studies on the Net has decided to vividly take part in those negotiations, offering and adapting its strategies to question, analyse, and project structures of space, identity, and power. It does so in the often explicitly stated hope that

What is Utopian about cyberspace at this point in history is that its structure is obviously not entirely fixed. Perhaps, in deciding how we wish to organize the future of cyberspace, we can teach ourselves that, indeed, the future of human society is not fixed either. We can always choose to be different, and more importantly, we can always choose to be better. (*Bad Subjects* Collective 1995, <english-www.hss.cmu.edu/bs/18/Manifesto.html>)

In many respects—quaint. Naive. Utopian. But—what if they are right?

References

Web Sites, etc.
Cultural Studies
    Central:<www.culturalstudies.net>
Black Cultural Studies:<www.tiac.net/users/
    thaslett/>
Culstud-L:<www.cas.usf.edu/communication/
    rodman/cultstud/index.html>

Sarah Zupko's Cultural Studies
    Center:<www.popcultures.com>
MCS:<www.aber.ac.uk/~dgc/media.html>
Voice of the Shuttle:
k.i.s.s. of the panopticon:

alt.culture:<www.altculture.com/>
The WELL:<www.well.com>

Web Journals
Cultronix:<english-server.hss.cmu.edu/
   cultronix/>
Bad Subjects:<english-www.hss.cmu.-
   edu/bs/>
J Spot:<www.yorku.ca/org/spot/jspot/>
Undercurrent:<darkwing.uoregon.edu/
   ~ucurrent/home.html>
M/C:<english.uq.edu.au/mc/>
Culture Machine:<culturemachine.
   tees.ac.uk>
Wired:<www.wired.com>

Books and Articles
Bad Subjects Production Team (1995). "A
   Manifesto for Bad Subjects in Cyberspace."
   Bad Subjects, 18 (Jan). <english-
   www.hss.cmu.edu/bs/18/Manifesto.html>
Barbrook, Richard, and Cameron, Andy
   (1995). "The Californian Ideology." First
   published in *Mute*, 3, (Aug.).
   <www.wmin.ac.uk/ media/HRC/ci/
   calif1.html>
Brooker, Will (1998). "Under Construction:
   Cultural Studies in Cyberspace."
   International Journal of Cultural Studies, 1.
   (3): 415–24.
Cresher, Chris. (1994). "Colonizing Virtual
   Reality." *Cultronix*, 1(1). <eng.hss.cmu.edu/
   cultronix/cresher>
Falk, Cliff (1999). "Sentencing Learners to
   Life: Retrofitting the Academy for the
   Information Age," in *Ctheory*.
   <www.ctheory.com/a70html>
Giroux, Henry, Shumway, David, Smith, Paul,
   and Sosnoski, James (1984). "The Need for

Cultural Studies: Resisting Intellectuals and
   Oppositional Public Spheres." *Dalhousie
   Review*, 64: 472– 86. <eserver.org/theory/
   need.html>
Haraway, Donna (1991). "A Cyborg Manifesto:
   Science, Technology, and Socialist-
   Feminism in the Late Twentieth Century,"
   in *Simians, Cyborgs and Women: The
   Reinvention of Nature*. New York:
   Routledge, 149–81. <www.stanford.edu/
   dept/HPS/Hara . . . /
   CyborgManifesto.htm>
Jackson, Tim (1997). "Working Cyberspace."
   Bad Subjects, 32 (Apr.). <english-
   www.hss.cmu.edu/bs/jackson.html>
Katz, Jon (1997). "The Digital Citizen." *Wired*,
   55 (Dec.). www.wired.com/wired/archive/
   5.12/netizen_pr.html
Poster, Mark (1995). "CyberDemocracy:
   Internet and the Public Sphere." <hnet.uci.
   edu/mposter/ writings/democ.html>
—— (1996). *The Second Media Age*.
   Cambridge: Polity Press.
Rheingold, Howard (1993). *The Virtual
   Community: Homesteading on the Electronic
   Frontier*. New York: Addison-Wesley.
   <www.rheingold.com/book>
Smith, Mark (1999). "Invisible Crowds in
   Cyberspace," in Smith and Kollock (1999),
   195–219.
—— and Kollock, Peter (eds.). (1999).
   Communities in Cyberspace. London and
   New York: Routledge.
Wark, McKenzie (1994). *Virtual Geography:
   Living with Global Media Events*.
   Bloomington and Indianapolis: Indiana
   University Press.
Whitaker, Reg (1999). *The End of Privacy: How
   Total Surveillance is Becoming a Reality*.
   New York: New Press.

Index of Names

Adam, B. 417
Adorno, T. 259
Agamben, G. 119–20
Ahmad, A. 119
Ali, M. 17, 19, 21, 192
Allen, G. 365
Altman, L. 328
Anderson, B. 191
Anderson, D. J. 334
Ang, I. 210–13
Anzaldúa, G. 116
Appadurai, A. 231–2, 251–8, 285
Aquinas, Saint T. 85
Asante, M. 246
Asher, C. 184
Atkins, C. 276

Bacon, F. 86
Bailey, D. 116
Baker, H. 177, 186–97
Bakhtin, M. 201–3, 355, 356, 359, 382
Baldwin, J. 189
Barbrook, R. 433
Barrett, W. 328
Barthes, R. 1, 67, 96, 99, 103 n., 200, 269, 277–9, 411
Baudrillard, J. 67, 319
Bayer, R. 329
Beaufort, M. de 340–1, 344
Beck, U. 424
Bekesy, G. von 92–3
Belzer, R. 337
Bendix, R. 131
Benjamin, W. 411
Bennett, P. 343, 344
Bennett, T. 289, 292, 294
Berelson, B. 128
Berger, T. 48
Bhabha, H. 10, 115–16, 191
Bigelow, B. 376
Birren, F. 98
Black, D. 331, 333
Blumen, S. 200
Bleuel, H. P. 5
Bordo, S. 212
Borland, H. 48
Bourdieu, P. 355, 359–60
Brantlinger, P. 4

Brooke-Rose, C. 335
Brooker, W. 428–9
Brown, C. B. 179, 183
Burns, G. 365
Burns, K. 343
Burns, T. 130
Bush, G. 345
Byrne, D. 402

Cameron, A. 433
Campos, Y. 340–1
Carelli, V. 380
Carey, J. 125, 126, 130–40, 163
Carmichael, S. 19, 21, 39–43
Carnoy, M. 416
Carothers, J. C. 81–4, 87–9, 91–2
Carpenter, J. 341
Carpenter, S. 369
Cassirer, E. 86–7
Castaneda, C. 184
Castells, M. 12, 351–2, 414–26
Cavell, S. 166
Certeau, M. de 115, 240, 285
Cervantes, M. 80, 90
Chakrabarty, D. 6
Chasing Hawk, A. 51
Check, W. 327
Chen, K-H. 1
Cheney, L. 194–7
Cherry, C. 93
Childs, J. B. 248
Chomsky, N. 29
Chow, R. 209, 210, 215
Churchill, W. 4, 177, 179–85
Cicero 85–6
Clifford, J. 116
Clinton, Bill 404
Cooper, J. F. 179
Cornell, D. 214
Coward, R. 260
Crenshaw, K. 246, 248
Cresher, C. 428
Crèvecoeur, H. de 379–80
Cummings, B. 342
Cushman, D. 48

Davis, M. 245–6, 364
DeGrane, L. 343
Deleuze, G. 117

Deloria, V. 4, 19, 21, 44–52, 177, 185, 381
Dent, G. 430
Derrida, J. 240
Dhareshwar, V. 119
Diaz, V. 221–3
Dick, P. K. 367
Didion, J. 20
Donahue, P. 357–60
Donaldson, L. 209
Donzelot, J. 202
Downing, J. 65, 67, 68
Du Bois, W. E. B. 42, 375
Duncan, C. 289, 290–1
During, S. 2

Eco, U. 67, 68, 106–13
Edsall, M. 245
Edsall T. B. 245
Ellison, R. 302

Fain, N. 327
Fanon, F. 181–2
Farnham, M. 75
Farrakhan, L. 192
Feigen, G. 30
Felski, R. 177, 208–17, 405
Ferguson, J. 223
Fiedler, L. 35–7
Fischer, M. 382
Fisher, H. A. L. 87
Fiske, J. 9, 10, 164, 351, 353–62
Flora, C. B. 263
Flora, J. 263
Foote, N. 365
Fonda, J. 314–15
Foucault, M. 67, 201, 202–3, 240, 285, 342
Franco, J. 231, 232, 259–68
Frankenberg, R. 209
Franklin, B. 8
Fraser, N. 405–6
Fresh, D. E. 191, 192–3
Freud, M. 71
Freud, S. 28, 29–30, 31, 69–77
Frieden, B. 67, 69–78, 367
Friedenberg, E. 36
Frow, J. 1